ASSEMBLY LANGUAGE PROGRAMMING AND THE IBM 360 AND 370 COMPUTERS

Prentice-Hall
Series in Automatic Computation

MARTIN,   *Programming Real-Time Computing Systems*
MARTIN,   *Security, Accuracy, and Privacy in Computer Systems*
MARTIN,   *Systems Analysis for Data Transmission*
MARTIN,   *Telecommunications and the Computer*
MARTIN,   *Teleprocessing Network Organization*
MARTIN AND NORMAN,   *The Computerized Society*
MCKEEMAN, et al.,   *A Compiler Generator*
MYERS,   *Time-Sharing Computation in the Social Sciences*
MINSKY,   *Computation: Finite and Infinite Machines*
NIEVERGELT, et al.,   *Computer Approaches to Mathematical Problems*
PLANE AND MCMILLAN,   *Discrete Optimization: Integer Programming and Network Analysis for Management Decisions*
POLIVKA AND PAKIN,   *APL: The Language and Its Usage*
PRITSKER AND KIVIAT,   *Simulation with GASP II: A FORTRAN-based Simulation Language*
PYLYSHYN, ed.,   *Perspectives on the Computer Revolution*
RICH,   *Internal Sorting Methods Illustrated with PL/I Programs*
RUDD,   *Assembly Language Programming and the IBM 360 and 370 Computers*
SACKMAN AND CITRENBAUM, eds.,   *On-Line Planning: Towards Creative Problem-Solving*
SALTON, ed.,   *The SMART Retrieval System: Experiments in Automatic Document Processing*
SAMMET,   *Programming Languages: History and Fundamentals*
SCHAEFER,   *A Mathematical Theory of Global Program Optimization*
SCHULTZ,   *Spline Analysis*
SCHWARZ, et al.,   *Numerical Analysis of Symmetric Matrices*
SHAH,   *Engineering Simulation Using Small Scientific Computers*
SHAW,   *The Logical Design of Operating Systems*
SHERMAN,   *Techniques in Computer Programming*
SIMON AND SIKLOSSY, eds.,   *Representation and Meaning: Experiments with Information Processing Systems*
STERBENZ,   *Floating-Point Computation*
STOUTEMYER,   *PL/1 Programming for Engineering and Science*
STRANG AND FIX,   *An Analysis of the Finite Element Method*
STROUD,   *Approximate Calculation of Multiple Integrals*
TANENBAUM,   *Structured Computer Organization*
TAVISS, ed.,   *The Computer Impact*
UHR,   *Pattern Recognition, Learning, and Thought: Computer-Programmed Models of Higher Mental Processes*
VAN TASSEL,   *Computer Security Management*
VARGA,   *Matrix Iterative Analysis*
WAITE,   *Implementing Software for Non-Numeric Application*
WILKINSON,   *Rounding Errors in Algebraic Processes*
WIRTH,   *Algorithms + Data Structures = Programs*
WIRTH,   *Systematic Programming: An Introduction*
YEH, ed.,   *Applied Computation Theory: Analysis, Design, Modeling*

ASSEMBLY LANGUAGE

PROGRAMMING

AND

THE IBM 360 AND 370

COMPUTERS

WALTER G. RUDD

Department of Computer Science
Louisiana State University

PRENTICE-HALL, INC.

ENGLEWOOD CLIFFS, NEW JERSEY

Library of Congress Cataloging in Publication Data

RUDD, WALTER G.
  Assembly language programming and the IBM 360
and 370 computers.

  (Automatic computations) (Applied math)
  1. Assembler language (Computer program language)   2. IBM 360 (Computer)—Programming.
3. IBM 370 (Computer)—Programming.   I. Title.
QA76.73.A8R8   001.6'42   75-17826
ISBN 0-13-049536-0

© 1976 by Prentice-Hall, Inc.
Englewood Cliffs, New Jersey

20 19 18 17 16 15 14 13 12 11

Printed in the United States of America

PRENTICE-HALL INTERNATIONAL, INC., *London*
PRENTICE-HALL OF AUSTRALIA, PTY. LTD., *Sydney*
PRENTICE-HALL OF CANADA, LTD., *Toronto*
PRENTICE-HALL OF INDIA PRIVATE LIMITED, *New Delhi*
PRENTICE-HALL OF JAPAN, INC., *Tokyo*
PRENTICE-HALL OF SOUTHEAST ASIA (PTE.) LTD., *Singapore*

to SHUG, TIB, the ID, and LILBIT

CONTENTS

13   SUBROUTINE LINKAGE   *276*

14   BIT MANIPULATION   *305*

15   DATA FORMS AND CONVERSION   *328*

16   DECIMAL ARITHMETIC   *354*

17   INPUT/OUTPUT PROGRAMMING   *381*

PREFACE

This book is primarily an assembly language text for the IBM System 360–370 lines of computers. Because it is designed to be the basis for a low-level language course for students of computer science, the text emphasizes two further aspects of computing—the fundamentals of machine function and language and the principles of computer programming. In addition, the text serves equally well as a reference for more advanced students of assembly language.

The emphasis throughout is on principles rather than specific applications. The beginner in computing has little or no idea of what applications he will encounter in the future. What he needs is a firm background in the fundamentals of machine structure and function and assembly language programming, so that when he does encounter a new instruction or a specific application, he will be in a position to refer to the appropriate manual to obtain and use the required information. In a sense, assembly language and computer science in general resemble mathematics in that the stronger the background the student has in the fundamentals, the better prepared he will be to use his knowledge and to learn new things.

The assembly language treated herein is the IBM System/360–370 Operating System Assembler Language. This choice arose from several considerations: (1) the IBM 360 and 370 lines of computers offer most of the facilities available in any modern large-scale computer; (2) the IBM 360 and 370 computers are very popular and are likely to continue to be so; and (3) because they are so widespread, there is little danger that a knowledge of System/360 assembly language will become obsolete. Thus, there is little doubt that the reader will be able to use his IBM assembly language training.

From the instructor's point of view, assembly language offers an immediate hindrance to attempts to base the order of the material upon its logical order of difficulty. Unlike FORTRAN, for example, wherein two or three weeks spent learning a subset of the language enables the student to begin writing and running his own programs; the assembly language per se contains no such convenient subset. The material involved in the subroutine linkages, input/output instructions, and data conversions necessary to code a simple arithmetic routine is too much for the beginning student to manage, especially if the instructor wishes the student to understand the material as it is being presented. If the instructor feels (as does the author) that it is of utmost importance for students to begin coding their own projects as soon as possible, he may decide to treat DCB statements, etc. as a recipe—"Do this and this, and your program will run." To the student who is still trying to figure out what a register does, this approach is confusing at best, and normally is sufficient grounds to make him give up in disgust.

An alternative is to leave the input/output and data conversions to a routine written in a higher-level language, such as FORTRAN or COBOL, thus removing the I/O stumbling block. The main problem with this approach is that the instructor will encounter students who do not know a higher-level language, or whose installations do not support the language of the instructor's choice, thus forcing him to teach another language, or a recipe, in addition to assembly. Furthermore, the necessity of establishing subroutine linkages still exists, and the beginning student probably doesn't know what a subroutine is.

In this text, the author's primary concern is to present the material in its logical order of complexity and necessity while remaining as much as possible within the framework of assembly language. Based upon a set of simple macros and a subroutine to handle I/O and data conversions, the course of study developed herein circumvents the difficulties discussed above. For example, a pair of macros, INITIAL and EOJ (End Of Job), take care of the register-save and base register establishment responsibilities of reader programs. Input/output is facilitated through the RWD (Read WorD), WWD (Write WorD), RCD (Read CarD), and PLN (Print LiNe) macros, all of which call a single subroutine that carries out the indicated functions. Thus, the subroutine linkage, data manipulation, and input/output segments of the course are left until the reader has the background to understand them.

Because assembly language is so intimately related to the computing machine, it is of primary importance in the training of computer scientists and users. The Association of Computing Machinery recognized this fact when it recommended* machine organization and assembly language programming as the basis for the second course in a computer science curriculum. This text emphasizes machine and assembly language programming and therefore serves as the basis for a major portion of the ACM course B2. But

---

*"Curriculum 68, Recommendations for Academic Programs in Computer Science," *Comm. ACM 11*, 151 (1968).

enough introductory material and detail is included to enable a reader with no prior computing experience to master the material.

The text is sufficiently complete and rigorous to allow the more experienced programmer to use it as a reference book or as a means of learning the particulars of the IBM System/360–370 assembly and machine languages. A look at the table of contents should serve to clarify the preceding remarks. The first chapter discusses the fundamentals of computer structure in general. The second chapter contains an introduction to the 360–370 architecture and binary and hexadecimal arithmetic. This is followed by a chapter on the nature of the assembly language and a summary of suggested procedures in computing.

Chapter 4 introduces the reader to the register-to-register arithmetic instructions and the RWD–WWD I/O macros. By the time he has finished the fifth chapter, which covers some practical considerations necessary to run a program, the reader is prepared to begin writing and debugging his own programs. This point is reached in the third week of the usual course. In Chapter 6, the reader encounters the first detailed look at machine language.

In the next five chapters, the basic pattern established in Chapters 4 and 6 is repeated. The introduction of new instruction types and their use in coding examples and projects is followed by explanations of the corresponding machine function and language. Thus, the machine language and action for a given programming facility is introduced after the reader has become familiar with the concepts involved. The instructor who wishes to emphasize programming techniques at the expense of machine principles may deemphasize the machine-oriented material, and vice versa.

The reader who has mastered the material through Chapter 11 will have a firm background in the fundamentals of assembly language programming. The material in the remainder of the text can be considered as applications of the principles developed previously.

After a chapter on debugging techniques and programming etiquette is a series of chapters covering such topics as bit manipulation, data forms and conversions, decimal arithmetic, and subroutine linkages. Then comes a treatment of data management facilities and sequential input/output for DOS and OS systems.

The usual course in assembly language would be nearly finished at this point. The remainder of the text covers more specialized topics, such as floating-point arithmetic and conversions, macro programming, editing, and so on. The instructor is free to choose between the alternatives offered. The author suggests that the instructor adhere closely to the order of presentation in the first eleven chapters. The order of presentation in the remainder of the text can be varied to suit the wishes of the instructor and his students; every attempt is made to keep these chapters as self-contained as possible.

Programming support for this text is achieved through six macro instructions and a subroutine to handle I/O and data conversions. A complete listing of all necessary software, together with a description of how to use it, is to be found in the Instructor's Manual that accompanies this text. In addition, punched decks of the load module for the subroutine and the source code for the macros can be obtained through the publisher. Similar support is given for use of this text with the Waterloo ASMG in-core assembler in the Batch/Execute mode and with the ASSIST assembler.

The instructor who so chooses can use his own methods for carrying out the input/output and subroutine linkages supplied herein. The sections describing the use of the macro instructions can be omitted or replaced by the instructor's description of local facilities. Also, the sections on input/output through the system and on subroutine linkages should be comprehensible to the student who has covered the material through Chapter 11. Chapter summaries are to be found at the end of each chapter, along with problems and questions for review and suggested programming projects designed to emphasize the material in the chapter. The Appendices include a discussion of flow-charting symbols and techniques, a set of tables, and a glossary of terms.

I must express my appreciation to all the people who have helped transform this book from a nebulous idea to its final form. My family has been a big help. Mrs. Miranda Medica and others did an exceptional job in typing the manuscript. Dr. Cecil L. Smith, Dr. John M. Tyler, and Mr. Ronald Cordez made many helpful suggestions. The editor, Mr. Karl V. Karlstrom, has been a big help, as have the reviewers who proved invaluable in helping to find the minor and major flaws that pop up in a work such as this. Ms. Melanie Rose, Mr. Michael Farmer, and Mr. William Michaels helped considerably with the illustrations and problem solutions.

TO THE READER

The modern digital computer has had a large and growing impact in many of man's activities. In science, the computer has enabled us to explore new areas that were previously closed to us because of the sheer weight of the data reduction and analysis and numerical calculations involved. The computer has facilitated technological advances, such as the recent lunar voyages, and is gaining rapid acceptance as a means for controlling industrial processes. Most of our accounting and banking systems are now computer-based, as are many inventory, stock-management, payroll, shipping, and transportation systems. Governmental agencies from local through national levels make heavy use of computers for record-keeping and accounting purposes. Universities use computers in record-keeping, accounting, and payroll applications, as well as for handling the problems involved in class scheduling and registration. Many library systems are now fully automated, and attempts are being made to catalog vast quantities of information, such as court documents and scientific abstracts for computer storage and retrieval of desired information. In short, computers are or soon will be used in every application wherein high-speed processing of large quantities of information is necessary.

This is a book about computers, computing, and assembly language. Its ultimate purpose is to help you learn more about computers in general by exploring some of the basic principles of computer structure and programming. In particular, it is an assembly language textbook.

Assembly language occupies a unique place among computer languages. Unlike FORTRAN, for example, which is basically the same no matter which kind of machine the programmer is using, assembly language is intimately related to the specific type of computer being used. Thus, to learn assembly language, one must also learn a lot about the characteristics of the particular computer to be used.

Because the assembly language varies from machine to machine, an assembly language text could, in principle, treat only the assembly language for a given machine. Or it could emphasize the principles of assembly language programming and machine operation and exclude reference to any particular machine. This text compromises these two extremes. The book can be considered a text on the principles of computer operation and programming. On the other hand, this text also describes in detail the assembly language for the IBM System 360 and 370 computers. Although you will learn a specific assembly language, the principles will apply to most of the other computers you will encounter. You, the reader, will be involved with computers to some extent for the rest of your life. The material in this text cannot but help you become aware of the real nature of the computing machine.

I suggest you use the accompanying workbook, *Assembly Language Exercises*, as an aid to help you study. You should work back and forth between the workbook and text, answering questions, testing your comprehension of each topic as you go.

WALTER G. RUDD

ASSEMBLY LANGUAGE
PROGRAMMING
AND
THE IBM 360 AND 370
COMPUTERS

1 INTRODUCTION TO COMPUTING

The computer is basically an information-processing machine. What do we mean by information? Webster defines it as "knowledge derived from reading, observation, or instruction. . . ." In computing we must restrict this definition slightly; by information we mean "knowledge that can be represented in a symbolic form." Thus, we would say that text from a book; scientific data and formulas; records of balances, deposits, and withdrawals for a bank account; pay rates and time records; class schedules; and radar reports of the distance from a space satellite to Jupiter are all forms of information.

Figure 1-1 shows how a computer closely resembles a very complex factory. The raw materials are the information input into the computer-factory. The computing machine processes the information according to rules determined by the programmer. The finished product is the modified information output from the computer. Thus, if the examples of information listed in the preceding paragraph were input to our computer-factory, we might expect the corresponding output to be a German translation of the text, "answers" to our scientific problem, a printout of the new current balance for the bank account, a paycheck, a list of hours and rooms from the registrar's office, and a suggested course change for the satellite on the way to Jupiter.

To make a profit, the supervisors of a factory must know how the factory functions. The more they know about the details of the operation of the basic components of the factory, the more effective will be their judgment in the use of the machines they supervise. Similarly, to make effective use of a computer, the user must know some details concerning its components. The more he knows about the way the machine works, the more efficient use he can make of it.

1

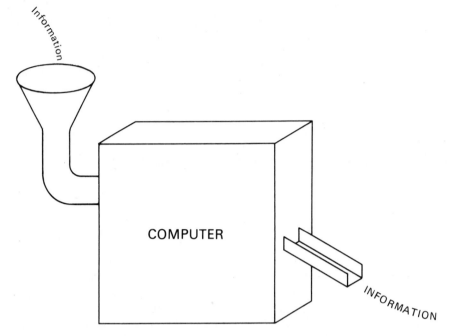

Fig. 1-1. The information machine. Information is fed into the computer and is output in modified form.

We shall now take a first look at the basic computing system and its major components. We shall study the interrelationships between these components and see what it means to "program" a computer.

1.1. THE COMPUTER

The computer consists of four major components, each of which contributes its part toward the operation of the total computing system. Figure 1-2 shows a schematic diagram of the components and how they are linked together. As can be seen, the components are

The Control Unit: the central controller for the entire system.
The Memory: the storage area for programs and information being processed.
The Arithmetic Unit: the component in which arithmetic and logical operations are carried out.
The Input/Output Section: consists of several electromechanical devices for communication between the computer and its users.

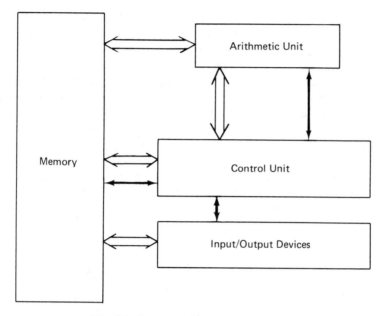

Fig. 1-2. Structure of a computing system.

In Fig. 1-2, the single arrows represent paths through which electronic control signals travel, while the double arrows show the paths of flow of the information being processed.

Let us now consider each of these components in more detail.

1.1.1. The Control Unit

The control unit is the central component, electronically and logically, of the entire system. Its basic function is to supervise the operation of all the other components and to control the flow of information to and from them.

The control unit is told what to do by *instructions* or commands, usually stored in the computer memory. In preparing the computer for a given task, the user ensures that the proper list of instructions, or *program*, has been placed in the memory. The control unit then goes through the program, one instruction at a time, carrying out its commands by sending the appropriate electronic control signals to the other parts of the computer. Thus, programming the computer is really the preparation of a sequence of instructions for the control unit. And that is what this book is all about.

1.1.2. The Memory

As its name suggests, the memory is the component wherein information is stored for later retrieval and use by the system. This information may consist of the programs to be executed by the control unit, data to be manipulated, lists of symbols to be sent to the printer, tables of contents of the memory—in other words, anything the user wishes to have in the memory.

The memory can be considered as a series of slots or locations in which units of information (later we shall call these units *bytes*) can be stored. Each slot has a number associated with it, which is called its *address*. The *contents* of any given slot can be obtained by referring to its address.

Figure 1-3 shows an example of a section of the computer memory and its possible contents at a given instant. To specify the current information stored in a given slot, we refer to the address of the slot. Thus, we would say "the number currently stored at address 101 is the number 15," or, to be more concise, "the contents of location 101 is the number 15." A shorthand notation for this sentence is in common use; we shall use it often. Symbolically, we refer to the contents of a given location by enclosing its address in parentheses. Thus, the following statements all have the same meaning:

1. "The number currently stored at address 103 is 352."
2. "The contents of location 103 is the number 352."
3. "(103) = 352."

Addresses	Contents
100	−3
101	15
102	0
103	352

Fig 1-3. An example of a section of the memory and its possible contents.

The distinction between the address of a memory location and the contents of that location is important. Review this section until you are sure you understand the difference.

The contents of the memory remain unchanged unless the control unit is specifically requested to change them. This changing of the contents of a memory location is called *storing* into the location. We must specify two quantities in a store instruction: what we want stored, which will be the new contents after the instruction is completed, and where we want to store it, or the address at which to store the new contents. For example, we might wish to store the number 0 at address 103. What happens to the previous contents of location 103? They are destroyed.

Using the example in Fig. 1-3, after storing the number 15 at location 103, that section of the memory would look like this:

Address	Contents
100	−3
101	15
102	0
103	15

Notice that none of the contents of the other locations is changed by storing at a given location. Notice also that the previous contents of location 103 are lost in the storage process.

Thus far we have a memory that remembers information we put into it, but, as yet, we have no way to get the information stored therein back out for later use. The retrieval of information is accomplished via *fetches* from the memory. To fetch the contents of a memory location, we must specify its address and request the control unit to obtain the contents of the location given by the address. Referring again to Fig. 1-3, the result of a fetch from location 101 would be the number 15. What happens to the contents of a location when we fetch from that location? *Nothing!* The contents of the location from which we fetch remain unchanged. A memory fetch is equivalent to reading the contents of the specified location as if it were a word printed in this book. Reading a word does not change it.

In summary, the memory consists of a series of slots or locations in which units of information can be kept. Each location has a numerical address associated with it. To refer to a particular location we need only specify its address. The contents of a location remain unchanged unless altered by a store instruction. Memory fetch instructions retrieve contents later when needed.

You will find that some other authors use different terminology when referring to memory operations. For example, another author might write "*Read* the *value of* location 3000 and *assign* the result to location 4000," meaning "*Fetch* the *contents of* location 3000 and *store* the result at location 4000." We prefer to use the term *read* to mean the transfer of information from an external medium into the computer from an external medium in an *input* operation, as discussed in Section 1.1.4.

1.1.3. The Arithmetic Unit

The arithmetic unit contains the circuitry to perform such computations as addition, multiplication, logical operations, and comparisons upon information it receives. Under the supervision of the control unit, information to be operated upon goes to the arithmetic unit, along with control pulses telling the arithmetic unit what to do with the information once it receives it and where to put the result(s) when it has finished. For example, in executing an instruction to add two numbers together, the control unit supervises the fetching of the numbers from their locations and sends them to the arithmetic unit. It then sends the arithmetic unit a control pulse that says "Add!" When the arithmetic unit is through adding the numbers, the control unit supervises the moving of the result to the proper location.

The detailed operation of the arithmetic unit is beyond the scope of this text. All we need to know is that there is a component in the computer that is capable of performing arithmetic and logical operations on units of information and that we control the arithmetic unit indirectly through instructions to the control unit.

This intimate connection between the control and arithmetic units leads to the consideration of two units as a single computer component called the *central processing unit,* or *CPU.* From an overall point of view, the CPU transforms input, programs, and the information upon which programs operate (the *data*), into the desired output or answers.

1.1.4. Input/Output

In principle, the CPU and the memory form a computing machine in the sense that they furnish the computing power to process information. But from where is the information processed to come? How are we to know what the results are, or if the computer did anything at all? What we have developed thus far is the equivalent of a desk calculator with no numeric buttons or visible registers. What is missing is a means of communication between the computing machine and the outside world.

Communication between the computer and the people and/or machines using it is accomplished via the input/output section of the computer. You probably know that although we refer to a single input/output "section" of the computer, we are in reality speaking of several different input/output devices.

Input/output consists of two essential steps. One step is *translation* of information to or from the internal machine representation of the information. This translation is necessary because ultimately all information stored in the memory and processed by the CPU must be in the internal *binary* representation we shall investigate later. On the other hand, people prefer to communicate with the machine through symbols that are more familiar to them. For example, a computer programmer prefers to use the letter "A" in his program, instead of a binary representation for the letter "A," which is, in the EBCDIC binary code, "1100 0001." Once the information has been translated, the second step is the *transmission* of the translated information to the receiving memory locations or external medium.

We shall now introduce two input/output devices of primary importance to the programmer—the card reader and the line printer—and discuss the translation-transmission steps in terms of these devices.

The Card Reader.   The card reader is the device normally used by the programmer for input of information into the computer. In preparing the cards to be read, he punches holes in them using a key-punch machine, which translates the characters he types into a binary code and punches holes representing the coded character through the card.

Figure 1-4 shows an example of a punched card. The character punched is printed at the top of the card. Each of the 80 columns on the card represents one character; the code for a character is punched vertically under the printed version of it.

The card reader contains electromechanical or optical sensors which can determine in which rows and columns holes are punched. The reader reads one card at a time and translates the coded characters punched on the card into their internal binary representations. The control unit then monitors the storing of the information, now in its proper internal form, into the appropriate memory locations.

The Line Printer.   We have seen that character input is encoded and transmitted to the memory by the card reader. An output device which carries out the converse operation is the line printer. The line printer is the most widely used output device, primarily because printed output is cheap and easily interpreted.

Information in the internal binary representation is sent to the line printer by the control unit. The line printer decodes the information, converting it to printable characters, and prints the resulting characters one line at a time. Special codes are used to control the spacing between lines and other carriage

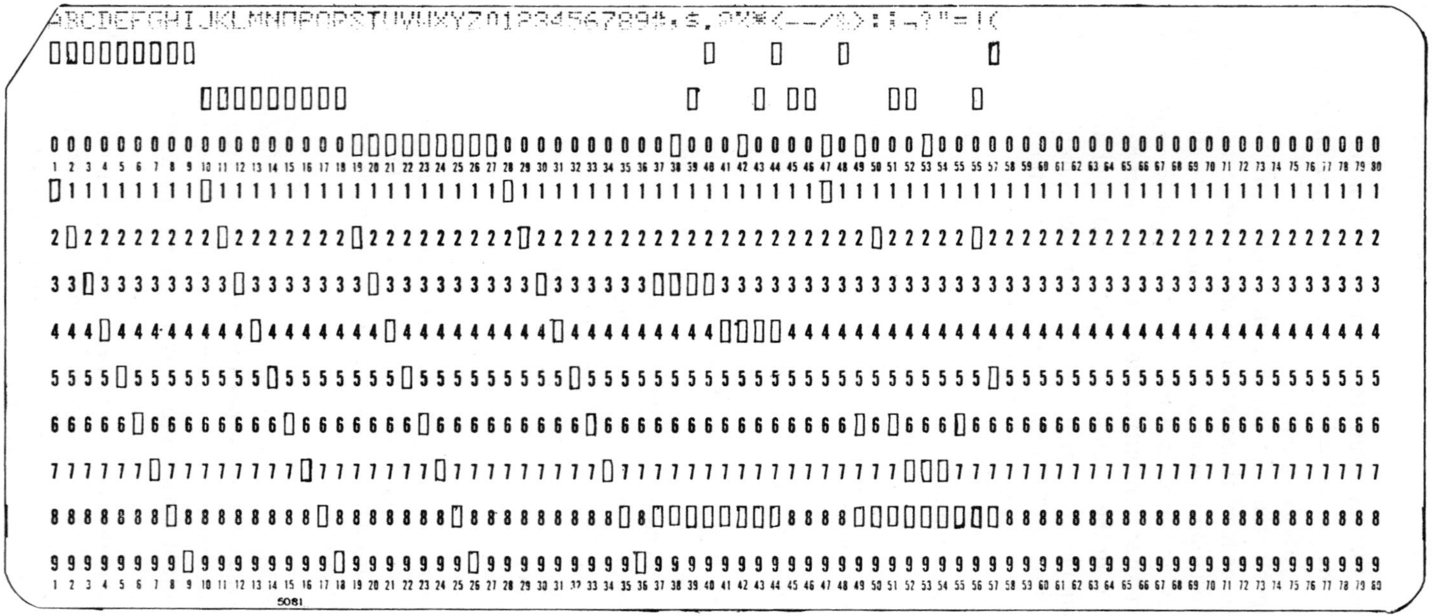

Fig. 1-4. A sample punched card.

8

control functions. The resulting output looks very much like that from a typewriter.

Many other kinds of input/output devices are in constant use in computing. For example, the card punch performs a function complementary to that of the card reader; output is in the form of punched cards similar to those the user punches with the key-punch machine. Magnetic character readers are used heavily in the banking industry in processing personal checks. Magnetic tape and disk units provide a cheap, fast means of input, output and bulk storage of large amounts of information. Typewriter-like remote terminals provide seemingly instantaneous access to the computer. We emphasize the card reader and line printer because they are the devices of primary interest to the programmer. All input/output devices serve the purpose of enabling communication between the computer and the machines and/or people using the computer.

1.2. PROGRAMMING THE COMPUTER

We have seen that the computing system is composed of the CPU, which contains the control and arithmetic units; the memory; and several input/output devices. All operations in the system are carried out under the supervision of the control unit, which is directed by a series of instructions called a program. Programming, then, is the construction of the sequence of instructions to direct the CPU in its operations.

To understand programming, it is first necessary to consider the structure of an instruction to the CPU. Since people design computers, one would expect that the computer machine language in which instructions are written would bear some structural resemblance to the spoken language. Since a machine language instruction is a command to the CPU, we can consider all machine language instructions as codes for imperative English sentences.

For example, we might say

1. "Add the contents of location 50 to the contents of location 7778."
2. "Print the contents of location 1066."
3. "Compare the contents of location 2000 with the contents of location 2001."
4. "Move the contents of location 30 to location 5000."

In the above, we see that each sentence consists of a verb,

    add
    print
    compare
    move

and one or more objects or modifying phrases,

the contents of location 50
the contents of location 7778
with the contents of location 2001
to location 5000

In computing, the verbs in the above sentences are called *operations*, while the objects upon which the verbs operate are called the *operands*.

Mathematics offers a more concise means of writing arithmetic statements, but the fundamentals are the same. When we write the set of symbols

$$x + y$$

we mean "add x to y." The fact that we write the symbol plus ($+$) for the operation between the operands is a matter of convention and has no effect on the meaning of the statement. If we wrote what we mean to do in the order the English language prefers, we would write

$$+xy$$

A machine language instruction is similar in form to that of the English statement we would write to tell the computer to carry out our request. The operation (verb) comes first, followed by the operands (objects). For example, the sentence

"Add   the contents of location 50   to the contents of location 7778."
└──┘   └─────────────────────────┘   └──────────────────────────────┘
verb   object 1   object 2

has the machine language structure

machine language code for "Add"   address or location 50   address 7778
└─────────────────────────────┘   └────────────────────┘   └──────────┘
            operation   operand 1   operand 2

Similarly, the command

"Print   the contents of location 1066."
└───┘   └──────────────────────────────┘
verb   object

has the machine language structure

machine language code for "Print"   address 1066
└───────────────────────────────┘   └──────────┘
            operation   operand

Since most machine language instructions operate on the contents of information storage or memory locations, we usually specify the operands in an instruction by giving their addresses. The fact that the operands are really the contents of the given locations is implied by the operation code. Returning again to our mathematical analogy, we would interpret

$$+xy$$

as meaning add the contents of a location called x to the contents of a location called y. We are safe in using this mathematical analogy provided that we consider algebraic variables as symbolic names for addresses.

A program consists of a sequence of instructions of the form described above. Each instruction contains an operation and one or more operands which we must specify in writing the program. The computer, when carrying out the requests it finds in our program, proceeds step by step, executing each instruction in the order it finds them.

CHAPTER SUMMARY

There are four major components of a modern computing system. The *control unit* supervises the operation of the entire system. The *arithmetic unit* performs arithmetic and logic operations upon the information it receives. The *memory* serves as a medium for storing and returning information as needed. The *input/output* devices permit communication between the machine and its environment.

A *program* is a series of instructions for the control unit to follow. In the machine language, each instruction consists of an *operation*, which describes the action of the instruction, and *operands*, which designate the receivers of the action.

EXERCISES

1. Name the four major components of a computer and describe the function of each component.

2. Write a verbal description of the instructions necessary to interchange the contents of two memory locations.

3. Define the following:
   (a) Address.   (b) Operations.   (c) Operands.
   (d) Program.   (e) Contents of a memory location.

REFERENCES

There are many excellent texts on the material covered in this chapter. A brief, but by no means complete, list of these includes

CHAPIN, NED, *Computers: A Systems Approach*, Van Nostrand Reinhold Company, New York, 1972.

DORF, RICHARD C., *Introduction to Computers and Computer Science*, Boyd & Fraser Publishing Company, San Francisco, 1972.

LEEDS, H. D. and G. M. WEINBERG, *Computer Programming Fundamentals*, Mc-Graw-Hill Book Company, New York, 1966.

MURRILL, P. W., and C. L. SMITH, *An Introduction to Computer Science*, International Textbook Company—College Division, Scranton, Pa., 1973.

SIEGEL, PAUL, *Understanding Digital Computers*, John Wiley & Sons, Inc., New York, 1971.

WALKER, TERRY M., *Introduction to Computer Science: An Interdisciplinary Approach*, Allyn & Bacon, Inc., Boston, 1972.

2 BINARY ARITHMETIC AND THE 360 CONTROL UNIT

Having explored the overall structure of a computing system and the form of the instructions that guide it in its functions we shall now take a closer look at two important facets of the system, the internal form of information representation and the instruction execution sequence of the control unit.

All information in the machine is, in its elemental form, represented as strings of binary digits, which may represent a wide variety of information structures, such as floating-point numbers, codes for the letters of the alphabet, machine operation codes, and integers. We shall examine the properties of arithmetic using binary integers as a first step in exploring the capabilities of the IBM 360 and 370 computing systems.

The control unit is the "boss" of the entire system. To write programs at the machine or assembly language level we must understand the cycle of events that the control unit follows in executing the instructions in our program. We shall then be prepared to begin our attack on assembly language programming.

2.1. BINARY INTEGER ARITHMETIC

The control unit supervises the flow and manipulation of information in the computing system, the memory stores it for later retrieval, the arithmetic unit carries out logical and arithmetic operations upon it, and the input/output devices translate the information from its external form to its internal form and vice versa. In this section we shall study the binary and hexadecimal number systems which form the basis for internal representation of information. We shall then discuss binary integer arithmetic, one of several types of arithmetic available to users of modern digital computers.

13

2.1.1. The Binary and Hexadecimal Number Systems

Binary Number System. Our decimal number system is a *positional* number system in that the value of a number depends on the positions of the digits in it. For example, the number

$$534.686$$

is 10 times larger than the number

$$53.4686$$

because the positions of the digits with respect to the decimal place in the number are different. In fact, when we write the number

$$534.686$$

what we really mean is the number whose value is

$$5 \times 10^2 + 3 \times 10^1 + 4 \times 10^0 + 6 \times 10^{-1} + 8 \times 10^{-2} + 6 \times 10^{-3}$$

The position of a digit with respect to the decimal place determines the power of 10 by which the digit is to be multiplied in the sum.

Note the fundamental role of the number 10 in the decimal number system. The *base* or *radix* of a positional number system is the number which is raised to powers in the expanded, series representation of a number written in that system. Thus, the decimal number system is a base 10 number system.

It is an anthropological accident that we use the decimal number system. Had the human race developed with 8 fingers instead of 10, we would probably use a base 8 number system, which, incidentaly, would have been much easier for us when we got around to inventing and studying computers.

Information in most modern computers is stored and manipulated in base 2, or *binary*, form. There are two permissible digits in the binary number system, the BInary digiTS, or bits, 0 and 1. One reason we use the binary system in computing is that it is convenient to build electronic switches that can be in one of only two states, *off* or *on*. Furthermore, our "logic" is basically a two-valued system; a statement is either "false" or "true." Therefore, we use bits to represent 0 or 1, off or on, or true or false, depending on the application we have in mind.

We use decimal arithmetic in our daily lives. The natural system for use in computing is the binary system. Therefore, in computing we must often *convert* numbers from binary to decimal and vice versa.

Since the base of the binary number system is 2, we can find the decimal value of a binary number by expanding the binary number as a series in powers of 2 and computing the resulting sum using decimal arithmetic. Thus, to convert the binary number

$$11011.1001$$

to its decimal equivalent we write

$$\text{(binary)} \quad 11011.1001 = 1 \times 2^4 + 1 \times 2^3 + 0 \times 2^2 + 1 \times 2^1$$
$$+ 1 \times 2^0 + 1 \times 2^{-1} + 0 \times 2^{-2}$$
$$+ 0 \times 2^{-3} + 1 \times 2^{-4} \quad \text{(decimal)}$$
$$= 1 \times 16 + 1 \times 8 + 0 \times 4 + 1 \times 2 + 1 \times 1$$
$$+ 1 \times \tfrac{1}{2} + 0 \times \tfrac{1}{4} + 0 \times \tfrac{1}{8} + 1 \times \tfrac{1}{16}$$
$$= 27.5625$$

To summarize the above,

$$11011.1001_2 = 27.5625_{10}$$

In other words, we specify the base of the number system in which a given number is written by writing the base as a subscript after the number.

We shall now turn to conversion in the other direction: Given a decimal number, how do we find its binary equivalent? The suggested method closely resembles the algorithm for long division and is best illustrated by an example. We wish to convert the number

$$37.2_{10}$$

to its binary equivalent. We carry out the process in two steps, first treating the whole number part to the left of the decimal place and then computing the binary equivalent of the fractional part.

To convert a decimal integer to binary, we repeatedly divide the decimal number by 2 "upside down," keeping a record of the remainder after each division, for it is the series of remainders which gives us the result. Thus, for our example problem, we calculate

	Remainders
2) 37	1
2) 18	0
2) 9	1
2) 4	0
2) 2	0
2) 1	1
0	

Now to obtain the binary result, we write down the remainders in order starting from the bottom of the list and find

$$37_{10} = 100101_2$$

(Check this result by converting 100101_2 to decimal.)

To convert a decimal fraction to its binary equivalent, we repeatedly multiply the fraction to be converted by 2 and record a 1 each time we carry

1 across the decimal place and 0 when there is no such carry. When there is a carry, we can ignore it in calculating further products. For our example problem we have

$$
\begin{array}{cr}
\text{Carries} & \\
 & .2 \\
 & \times\,2 \\
0 & .4 \\
 & \times\,2 \\
0 & .8 \\
 & \times\,2 \\
1 & .6 \\
 & \times\,2 \\
1 & .2 \\
 & \times\,2 \\
0 & .4 \\
 & \times\,2 \\
0 & .8 \\
 & \times\,2 \\
1 & .6 \\
 & \times\,2 \\
1 & .2 \\
 & \vdots
\end{array}
$$

Evidently we could carry on this process indefinitely; $.2_{10}$ is a repeating fraction when converted to binary. To find the answer for the fractional part we write down the digits in the carries column in order starting at the top. Therefore,

$$.2_{10} = .00110011001100110011\cdots$$

and, to conclude our example,

$$37.2_{10} = 100101.0011001100110011\cdots$$

where the fractional part is continued indefinitely.

A remark concerning this result is in order. We cannot represent most fractions, such as .1, .2, and .06, exactly in a finite number of bits. But computers are necessarily finite machines in that we never have an infinite number of bits to use to specify numbers. This fact leads to insurmountable *truncation* errors which arise when we discard low-order digits from a fraction to make it fit into an information unit of finite length.

The more bits we can use to specify a fraction, the greater the accuracy of the resulting approximation. Thus, the first 4 bits of the binary equivalent for

.2 above yield

$$.0011_2 = \tfrac{1}{8} + \tfrac{1}{16} = .1875_{10}$$

while if we use the first 8 bits we obtain the closer result

$$.00110011_2 = \tfrac{1}{8} + \tfrac{1}{16} + \tfrac{1}{128} + \tfrac{1}{256} = .19841875$$

Hexadecimal Number System. You may have noticed already that specification of quantities in binary is a bit tedious; approximately three times as many digits are required to specify a given binary integer than are needed for its decimal equivalent. Therefore, it is common in computing to use a higher-based number system as a shorthand notation for the binary internal representation of information. The main requirement of such a system is that conversion from binary to the higher-based system and vice versa be easy to do; that is, the binary and higher-based systems should be essentially equivalent.

The hexadecimal, base 16, number system offers this capability and is widely used in systems where binary information is easily represented in groups of 4 bits. Since this system has base 16, there are 16 permissible digits in the hexadecimal number system. We have 10 decimal digits in the decimal system; we borrow these for use as the first 10 digits in the hexadecimal system. For the remaining 6 digits, we arbitrarily choose the 6 letters A, B, C, D, E, and F.

Figure 2-1 shows the first few decimal integers and their binary and

Decimal	Binary	Hexadecimal
0	0000	0
1	0001	1
2	0010	2
3	0011	3
4	0100	4
5	0101	5
6	0110	6
7	0111	7
8	1000	8
9	1001	9
10	1010	A
11	1011	B
12	1100	C
13	1101	D
14	1110	E
15	1111	F
16	10000	10
17	10001	11
18	10010	12
19	10011	13
20	10100	14

Fig. 2-1. Decimal, binary, and hexadecimal integers.

hexadecimal equivalents. Notice that each different four-digit binary number corresponds to a different hexadecimal digit. It is this fact that permits easy conversion from one system to the other. To convert from binary to hexadecimal, we split the binary number into groups of four digits, starting at the decimal place and proceeding to the left and right from there. If necessary, we should add leading and/or trailing zeros to ensure that all groups of binary digits contains 4 bits. Thus, to convert

$$110010110.10101100010101_2$$

to hexadecimal, we write

$$0001, 1001, 0110.1010, 1100, 0101, 0100$$

Then we look up each group of four digits in a table such as that in Fig. 2-1 and write down the hexadecimal digits that correspond to each group of 4 bits (this table look-up becomes unnecessary after a bit of practice). For this example, we have

$$110010110.10101100010101_2 = 196.AC54_{16}$$

To convert numbers from hexadecimal to binary, we carry out the reverse process, replacing each hexadecimal digit with its 4-bit binary equivalent. Thus,

$$6EA.435_{16} = 011011101010.010000110101_2$$

The process of converting from hexadecimal to decimal is done with paper and pencil by expanding the number in powers of its base (16) and computing the resulting sum using decimal arithmetic. Thus,

$$3A8.2_{16} = 3 \times 16^2 + A \times 16^1 + 8 \times 16^0 + 2 \times 16^{-1}$$
$$= 3 \times 256 + 10 \times 16 + 8 \times 1 + 2 \times \tfrac{1}{16}$$
$$= 768 + 160 + 8 + \tfrac{1}{8}$$
$$= 936.125_{10}$$

Finally, conversion from decimal to hexadecimal can be done by a process similar to that used to convert from decimal to binary, the difference being that we divide the decimal number by 16 at each step and record the remainders as the hexadecimal equivalents of their decimal values.

To convert 638.0 to hexadecimal we proceed as follows:

		Remainder
16)	638	E
16)	39	7
16)	2	2
	0	

and find

$$638_{10} = 27E_{16}$$

To convert the fractional part of a decimal number to hexadecimal, we can use the same procedure we used to convert a decimal fraction to binary, except that we multiply by 16 at each step and write the numbers carried across the decimal place in the hexadecimal system.

Multiplication and division by 16 are more difficult processes for most people than multiplication and division by 2. Therefore, conversion from decimal to hexadecimal is more easily done by first converting the decimal number to binary and then converting the result to hexadecimal.

The easiest way to convert from decimal to hexadecimal and vice versa is through the use of a conversion table as in Appendix D or on the IBM *green card** (some are tan, but we shall call them green cards anyway).

2.1.2. 2's Complement Binary Arithmetic

Having seen how to convert numbers from decimal to their binary and hexadecimal equivalents, we shall now turn to a study of arithmetic in the binary and hexadecimal systems. While it is possible to do binary arithmetic with fractions or mixed numbers using *floating-point arithmetic* (see Chapter 19), we shall restrict our attention here to arithmetic with whole numbers, or *fixed-point* arithmetic.

Addition.   Addition in binary is done in much the same way as in the decimal system. We can use the following addition table to decide what the possible sums of individual binary digits will be:

$$
\begin{array}{ccccc}
0 & 1 & 0 & 1 & 1 \\
+0 & +0 & +1 & +1 & 1 \\
\hline
0 & 1 & 1 & 10_2 & +1 \\
& & & & \hline
& & & & 11_2
\end{array}
$$

If it is not clear why this table is correct, convert all the numbers to decimal, carry out the indicated additions and convert the results back to binary (this is always a valid way to do binary arithmetic anyway).

Let us add together the two binary integers

$$11011001_2 \quad (= 217_{10})$$

and

$$1011101_2 \quad (= 93_{10})$$

We find

$$
\begin{array}{r}
① \quad ① ① \quad\; ① \\
1\;1\;0\;1\;1\;0\;0\;1_2 \\
+\;1\;0\;1\;1\;1\;0\;1_2 \\
\hline
1\;0\;0\;1\;1\;0\;1\;1\;0_2
\end{array}
$$

---

where the encircled numbers represent carries. As in decimal arithmetic, we start with the right-most digit and go through the following steps, proceeding one digit to the left with each step:

$$1 + 1 = 0 \quad \text{with carry 1}$$
$$1 + 0 + 0 = 1 \quad \text{with carry 0}$$
$$0 + 1 = 1 \quad \text{with carry 0}$$
$$1 + 1 = 0 \quad \text{with carry 1}$$
$$1 + 1 + 1 = 1 \quad \text{with carry 1}$$
$$1 + 0 + 0 = 1 \quad \text{with carry 0}$$
$$1 + 1 = 0 \quad \text{with carry 1}$$
$$1 + 1 = 0 \quad \text{with carry 1}$$
$$1 + 0 = 1 \quad \text{with carry 0}$$

Check the sum by converting it to decimal.

In testing and debugging assembly language programs, it is often necessary to add pairs of hexadecimal numbers. We use the same algorithm as we use in decimal arithmetic, except that we must remember that $10_{16} = 16_{10}$; that is, when we carry, we carry 16, not 10. Let us first do a simple example and calculate

$$\begin{array}{r} A_{16} \\ + \ 8_{16} \\ \hline 12_{16} \end{array}$$

A perfectly legal way to compute this sum (and the way most experienced programmers do it) is to convert the digits in a column to decimal, add the digits, and convert the result back to hexadecimal, carrying 1 from the result if necessary in order to have the rightmost digit less than (decimal) 16. Thus, we would think, "A_{16} is 10_{10} and 8_{16} is 8_{10}, and the sum is thus 18_{10}. There is no digit in hexadecimal for 18_{10}, so I must subtract 16_{10} to get 2 but then must carry a 1 to add back the 16 I subtracted." Let us do a more complex example to see how this works:

$$\begin{array}{c} ①\,① \quad ① \\ 8\ E\ 3\ 8\ C \\ \underline{5\ D\ 3\ 5} \\ 9\ 4\ 0\ C\ 1 \end{array}$$

Again, the encircled numbers represent carried digits. To compute the sum, we follow the steps

$$C + 5 = 17_{10} = 1_{16} \quad \text{with carry 1}$$
$$1 + 8 + 3 = 12_{10} = C_{16} \quad \text{with carry 0}$$

$$3 + D = 16_{10} = 0_{16} \qquad \text{with carry 1}$$
$$1 + E + 5 = 20_{10} = 4_{16} \qquad \text{with carry 1}$$
$$1 + 8 = 9_{10} = 9_{16} \qquad \text{with carry 0}$$

We could use methods similar to those we use in decimal arithmetic to subtract binary or hexadecimal numbers. We would simply have to remember that when we "borrow" from digits further to the left, we borrow 2 or 16, respectively, instead of 10 as in decimal arithmetic. However, this is not how modern computers, and in particular, the IBM 360 and 370 computers, compute differences between numbers. Since we shall be dealing intimately with computer arithmetic, we shall now describe how the computers do it.

For economic reasons, modern arithmetic units do not contain separate circuitry for addition and subtraction. Both these operations are carried out in the same circuit, the *adder*, which can only add numbers. To subtract a number b from a number a, the computer adds the negative of b to a. In other words, the computer does not calculate

$$a - b$$

but instead

$$a + (-b)$$

where here the minus sign indicates not the subtraction operation but, instead, the negative of the number following it.

In the 360, we usually store and calculate binary numbers in information units called *full words*. Each word consists of 32 binary digits or bits. Thus, if we had the number 5 stored in a word, the actual binary contents of the word would be

0000 0000 0000 0000 0000 0000 0000 0101

Notice that we can also specify the contents of a word by writing it as an eight-digit hexadecimal number, in this case

00000005

The negative of a number is represented by its *2's complement*. We shall show how to calculate the 2's complement of a number and then show how to do addition using 2's complement arithmetic. Finally we shall show how the computer uses these concepts in carrying out operations with signed integers.

To compute the 2's complement of a binary integer, we first compute its logical complement, or 1's complement. The *logical complement* of a number is obtained by changing each 1 in the number to 0 and each 0 to 1. The terminology becomes clearer when we realize that the logical complement of *true* is *false* and vice versa.

Thus, the logical complement of the word

11010101110110100011100001010111

is the word

$$00101010001001011100011110101000$$

The 2's complement of a binary number is obtained by adding 1 to its logical complement, that is,

2's complement = logical complement + 1

Returning to our previous example, the 2's complement of a word containing the number 5 is computed as follows:

$5_{10} = 00000000000000000000000000000101$

logical complement = $11111111111111111111111111111010$

$+1$

2's complement = $11111111111111111111111111111011$

These operations can of course be more conveniently expressed in the hexadecimal number system. But be careful in computing the logical complement of hexadecimal digits. For the example above we could write

$5_{10} = 00000005_{16}$

logical complement = $FFFFFFFA_{16}$

2's complement = $FFFFFFFB_{16}$

We usually represent internal binary information in its hexadecimal form. If you have any doubts about results obtained, convert the hexadecimal values to binary and carry out the indicated operations in the binary system. Remember that it makes no difference whether we represent computer information in binary or in hexadecimal; the binary and hexadecimal systems are really equivalent.

The claim now is that the 2's complement of a number behaves arithmetically as if it were the negative of the number, provided we do the arithmetic correctly. Let us illustrate this fact by computing $13 - 13$ using 2's complement arithmetic. We have

$$13_{10} = 0000000D_{16}$$

as it is stored in a full word in the computer, while the 2's complement of 13 (check this) is

$$-13_{10} = FFFFFFF3_{16}$$

again as it would appear as a 32-bit word.

We now compute the sum

```
? ①  ① ① ① ① ① ① ①    carried digits
    0 0 0 0 0 0 0 D
+   F F F F F F F 3
    0 0 0 0 0 0 0 0
```

We got 0, the right answer, but what about the 1 to carry that will not fit into our 32-bit word? The answer is

In 2's complement arithmetic, a 1 carried out of the leftmost bit of a word is ignored.

We conclude that if we ignore carries out of the topmost bit of a number, the 2's complement of a number behaves arithmetically as if it were the negative of a number.

If we view this process from another angle, we can see why it works. Suppose that we have a binary number A. Actually

$$\text{2's complement of } A = 2^{32} - A$$

Now 2^{32} is represented in binary by a 1 followed by 32 zeros. Thus, if we try to fit 2^{32} into a 32-bit computer word, the result would be the last 32 zeros, which fit, and the 1, which will not fit. If we ignore the 1 which does not fit, then 2^{32} is arithmetically 0. Thus, to calculate $B - A$ we write symbolically

$$B_{10} - A_{10} = B_2 + (\text{2's complement } A)_2 = B_2 + (2^{32} - A)_2$$
$$= \text{(effectively) } B_2 + 0 - A_2 = (B - A)_2$$

The mathematicians would tell us that when we are doing 32-bit 2's complement arithmetic, we are in fact doing arithmetic *modulo* 2^{32}.

Magnitude of Binary Numbers.   For the adder circuit in the arithmetic unit, there is no difference between subtraction and addition operations. The distinction between the operations arises in the numbers which are sent to the adder. If the second operand is actually the 2's complement of the original second operand, the effective result of the addition of the numbers will be the difference between the two numbers. However, it is important in other parts of the machine and to us when we interpret the results of arithmetic operations to be able to distinguish between positive and negative numbers and to be able to determine their *absolute value* or *magnitude*.

To decide whether a number in a computer word will behave arithmetically as a positive or a negative number, we look at the first bit (bit 0) of the word, which is often called the *sign bit*. If the sign bit of the number is 0, the number will behave as if it is positive; that is, if we add it to another number, the result will be larger than the original number. The *magnitude*, or *modulus*, of the number is simply the number itself.

If, on the other hand, the sign bit is 1, the number can be considered to be negative in that when it is added to a positive number, the result will be less than the original number. The magnitude of a negative number is its 2's complement. To summarize these paragraphs, the magnitude of a number A is the same as its absolute value, which we write as $|A|$. In interpreting a binary number we have

$$A \geq 0 \quad \text{if its sign bit is } 0$$
$$A < 0 \quad \text{if its sign bit is } 1$$
$$|A| = \begin{cases} A & \text{if } A \geq 0 \\ 2\text{'s complement of } A & \text{if } A < 0 \end{cases}$$

Overflow. We have seen that a binary integer as represented in a computer word consists of 31 bits and a sign bit. What happens if we add two numbers together that are such that the resulting sum will not fit into a computer word; that is, the resulting sum requires more than 31 digits to specify its magnitude? This situation is normally treated as an error condition which is called an arithmetic *overflow.* Suppose that we were to compute

$$\begin{array}{r} 30000000 \\ +70000000 \\ \hline \end{array}$$

using the rules described above. The resulting sum of these two large positive numbers would be

$$A0000000$$

which is a *negative* number (compute its magnitude). We can have the computer check for this overflow condition and terminate execution of the program if it occurs.

Multiplication and Division. Anyone who has once tried multiplication or division by hand in the hexadecimal number system knows that the easiest way to calculate products or quotients of hexadecimal numbers is to convert the operands to decimal or binary, calculate the answer in that system, and convert the results back to hexadecimal.

Binary integer multiplication and division can be done using the same algorithms we use for decimal multiplication and division, the difference being that all arithmetic is of course in the binary system. Thus, to compute 1101101_2 times 1001001_2 we proceed as follows:

$$\begin{array}{r} 1101101_2 \\ \times 1001001_2 \\ \hline 1101101 \\ 0000000 \\ 0000000 \\ 1101101 \\ 0000000 \\ 0000000 \\ 1101101 \\ \hline 1111100010101_2 \end{array}$$

Notice that multiplying two numbers together produces a product which is as long as the sum of the lengths of the two multiplicands. Therefore, when the machine computes the product of two 32-bit full words, the resulting product may require 64 bits to specify it. As we shall see, the binary integer multiply instructions multiply the contents of one register by the contents of another word, which may be in a register or in the memory. The resulting product occupies two registers which should be considered as containing a single 64-bit binary integer.

Paper-and-pencil integer division is done by the "long division" technique we all learned long ago. To divide 111011101_2 by 11011_2, we write

$$
\begin{array}{r}
10001 \\
11011 \overline{)\ 111011101} \\
11011 \\
\hline
101101 \\
11011 \\
\hline
10010
\end{array}
$$

Thus, the quotient is 10001_2 and the remainder is 10010_2.

The quotient and remainder in full-word arithmetic can each occupy one word. If the divisor is one full word, then we have room to divide two full words considered as a single 64-bit integer by the single word divisor. The integer divide instruction is designed to take this fact into account, as we shall see later.

This concludes our formal discussion of binary integer arithmetic, although we shall be seeing much more of it in examples and exercises throughout the remainder of this text. Facility with binary arithmetic is of great benefit to the programmer in making easier some of the computational chores involved in writing and debugging programs. Be sure you can add and subtract numbers expressed in the hexadecimal notation and that you have a good understanding of 2's complement arithmetic.

2.2. THE 360 CONTROL UNIT

In the preceding chapter we examined the general structure of computing machines.

This text is primarily a text on computer organization and assembly language programming. To really understand the principles involved it is necessary to study in depth the structure of a real computing system. We have chosen the IBM 360 and 370 lines of computers as representative of the current generation of computers to illustrate the principles involved.

While the IBM 360 computers and the IBM 370 computers have different names, they are structurally identical from the point of view of the programmer. All the instructions valid for IBM 360 computers are also valid for the

370 computers. Thus, if we learn to program the 360 computers, we shall be able to use most of the facilities of the 370 machines. Programs written for an IBM 360 computer will run properly on an IBM 370 machine.

The converse is not true, however. The IBM 370 contains some instructions that are not implemented for the 360 machines. In particular, the 370 machines include instructions that permit greater flexibility in the manipulation of character data and a higher degree of accuracy in numerical calculations. Programs that include these instructions will not run on 360 machines.

Since the machines from the two lines of computers are so much alike, we shall use "IBM 360/370," "IBM 360," or simply "computer" to represent any of the computers in the two lines. We shall point out those instructions that are for use only with 370 computers when such instructions are encountered in the text.

There are two basic reasons for the choice of the 360/370 machines as the basis for this text. First, these machines are extremely popular in that more than 50% of all the medium- and large-scale computers in the world are IBM 360/370 machines. This percentage is even higher in educational institutions. Therefore, there is a very good chance that a student who learns the structure and assembly language of a 360 will be able to use this knowledge when he is in school and after he graduates. The second reason for choosing the IBM 360 computers is that, structurally, they are representative of all modern computers of their size. Thus, most of the features incorporated in the 360 machines are to be found, perhaps with differences in name and details of use, in all modern computing systems.

In view of these facts, it is unnecessary to state throughout this text when each concept or hardware facility we encounter is particular to the IBM 360 and when it is applicable to all computers. The reader should not get the idea that the IBM 360 is the *only* kind of computer in the world but should be aware that, while he is indeed learning many details concerning the IBM 360, principles behind what he is doing apply to all modern computing systems.

Let us now begin our study of the IBM 360 computers and assembly language programming. As the central component of the computer, the control unit is of fundamental importance. A knowledge of the basic principles of the function of the CPU is prerequisite to assembly language programming and enables the programmer using other languages to make more effective use of the computing system. In this section, we shall examine the structure and function of the control unit in greater detail.

2.2.1. Machine Language

As is all internal information in the computer, machine language instructions suitable for processing by the control unit are in the form of a series of binary digits. A machine language instruction consists of two sections, or *fields.* The first is the *operation field,* which contains the operation to be carried out in the instruction. The other field in the instruction is the *operands field,* which normally contains the addresses of the operands.

The operation field of the machine language instruction consists of 8 binary bits which form a code, the *operation code.* In part of its cycle of operation, the control unit transforms the operation code into the electronic pulses necessary to carry out the operation. For example, the binary operation code for addition of two binary integers, one contained in a register and the other stored in the memory, is

$$01011010$$

while the operation code to move the contents of a series of memory locations from one place to another is

$$11010010$$

In general, each different machine operation is assigned a unique operation code. Figure 2-2 shows a list of operations and their corresponding operation codes. To facilitate construction of the machine and readability of the machine language, similar operations have similar operation codes. For example, the operation code for addition, 01011010, differs only in the last bit from the operation code for subtraction, 01011011. Look for similar patterns in Fig. 2-2.

add	01011010
subtract	01011011
add register	00011010
subtract register	00011011
multiply	01011100
divide	01011101
and	01010100
or	01010110
shift left	10001011
shift right	10001010

Fig. 2-2. Some representative operations and their operation codes.

As noted in a previous section, operands are usually specified by their memory or register addresses. In the machine language operands field, addresses are given their binary integer values. For example, "the contents of register 5" has the machine language representation 0101, which is the binary representation of the number 5, while "the contents of memory location 105" has the machine language representation 01101001, the binary equivalent for the decimal number 105.

In summary, the machine language instruction contains two fields, the operation field and the operands field. The operation field contains a binary code for the desired machine operation, while the operands field contains the binary values of the numerical addresses of the operands.

2.2.2. The Program Counter

The program is stored in the computer memory. Normally, the control unit executes the instructions in the program in the order in which it finds them stored in the memory. How does it know where to find the next instruction to be executed after it has finished an instruction?

The *program counter* contains the memory address of the next instruction to be executed. Part of the operation cycle of the control unit is to compute the address of the next instruction to be executed. When the current instruction is completed, the next instruction is fetched from the location addressed by the program counter and placed in a special location in the control unit called the *instruction register*. The address of the "new" next instruction then replaces the previous contents of the program counter.

For example, suppose that we have a sequence of instructions stored at the following locations:

$$100$$
$$102$$
$$106$$
$$112$$

While the computer is executing the instruction at location 100, the program counter contains the number 102 (the binary equivalent of 102, to be more precise). Upon completion of this instruction, the instruction stored at 102 is moved into the instruction register, and the binary equivalent of 106 is stored in the program counter.

Under some circumstances we may wish to ignore the usual sequence of instructions as stored in the memory and *branch* to an instruction out of the normal sequence. The effect of a branch operation is to change the contents of the program counter. Thus, in our previous example, if the instruction at location 106 is an instruction to branch to the instruction at location 100, the effect of the operation is to store the binary equivalent of 100 in the program counter.

2.2.3. The General-Purpose Registers

We have already discussed the function of two registers, the program counter and the instruction register. The program counter holds the memory address of the next instruction to be executed, and the instruction register contains the instruction currently being executed. The contents of these registers change with the execution of every instruction, and therefore these registers are used for temporary storage of information of current interest.

In general, a register serves as a location used for temporary storage of information. Registers are distinguished from memory locations in two basic ways. First, the time required to alter or fetch the contents of a register is usually much less than that required to carry out the same operation upon the contents of a memory location. Second, registers are usually electronically wired to serve other purposes than simply to hold information until it is needed, as is the case with the memory. The computer "knows" electronically that the address of the next instruction is in the program counter.

The instruction register and program counter are examples of special-purpose registers. We cannot modify the contents of the instruction register. Nor can we add a number to the contents of the program counter. In other words, these registers are closely linked to the operation of the control unit and are not normally usable by the programmer for purposes other than those for which they were designed.

To provide for greater flexibility and speed in information processing, the IBM System/360 contains 16 *general-purpose registers* numbered 0 through 15. They serve as intermediate links between the control unit, the arithmetic unit, and the memory. At least one of the operands in most arithmetic, logical, and comparison instructions must be in a general-purpose register. After the instruction has been executed, the result is usually left in a register.* Hence, the registers function as *accumulators*, or temporary storage locations for the results of computations.

For example, suppose that general-purpose register 3 initially contains the number 50. We wish to add the number stored at location 1000, whatever it is, to this number. We would then write an instruction as follows,

"Add"	contents of register 3	contents of location 1000
operation	operand 1	operand 2

or, in machine language,

machine language code for "Add"	3	1000
operation	operand 1	operand 2

The result of the addition would end up in register 3. Thus, if location 1000 contained the number 100 before the instruction was executed, the contents of register 3 after execution of the above instruction would be the number 150. The contents of memory location 1000 would remain unchanged.

Let us examine the execution of this instruction in more detail. First the machine language translation of the instruction above is moved to the instruction register, and the program counter is adjusted to point to the next instruction to be executed. The first operand is retrieved from register 3 and sent to the arithmetic unit. The second operand is fetched from memory location 1000 (remember that this does not change the contents of location 1000) and sent to the arithmetic unit. The numbers (50 + 100) are added there. The result (150) is then stored in register 3, destroying its previous contents.

*Because of the importance of the general-purpose registers, we shall simply say "register" from here on to mean "general-purpose register." Other registers will be specified using their full names.

The specification of the actual memory addresses of a series of operands can be tedious, or even impossible, if the number of operands is large. The general-purpose registers can be used for address computations to simplify the manipulation of large quantities of related data.

For example, suppose that we have 10,000 numbers stored in consecutive memory locations and that we wish to compute the sum of all these numbers. Since each of the numbers has a different address, we need to carry out 10,000 addition instructions containing 10,000 different operand addresses. The "brute force" technique to accomplish this task would be to write a separate addition instruction to add each of the numbers to the contents of a register. But, since the numbers are stored consecutively, we could save ourselves a lot of work if we could use the computer to calculate the necessary addresses of the operands. We would put the memory address of the first number in our list into a register. We would then use the contents of that register as the *address* of the next number to be added. We could then simply count the contents of the address register up every time we added another number to our running total until we were through adding the entire list of numbers.

The procedure outlined above is an example of a *loop*, or a sequence of instructions executed repeatedly until the desired computations have been completed. How can we know when the calculations are finished? Usually, we use a general-purpose register as a *loop counter*. We start the contents of the register out at zero, say, and increment its contents every time we go around the loop. When the contents of the loop counter register reach the total number of times we want to go around the loop, we branch out of the loop.

Loops are of primary importance in computing. In fact, if computers could not repeatedly execute series of instructions, we probably would not use them, because in most cases writing the program would be as difficult and time-consuming as doing the problem by hand. We mentioned the example of computing an average. The sum of the numbers can be calculated using a loop that consists of two machine language instructions, one to add the next number in the list, and the other to increment and test the loop counter contents. Once programmed, we can use the program containing the loop, without further modification, to compute the average of any number of numbers.

But without the loop, we would have to write a separate addition instruction for each number in the sum: 10,000 instructions to add 10,000 numbers. Furthermore, we would have to change the program if we changed the number of numbers to be summed. Why not use a desk calculator?

The computation of averages is but one example of the use of the power of the computer to do repetitive calculations. Many scientific and mathematical problems involve iterative computational techniques. Many functions (the *sine* function, for example) are computed by adding a series of numbers together. Most equation-solving techniques involve making an initial guess at a solution and then repeatedly improving upon this estimate until satisfactory accuracy is achieved. Matrix manipulations invariably require repetitive calculations. In Monte Carlo computer simulations, we repeatedly generate data to be used as input to a computer model of the phenomenon being studied. The model itself usually contains several loops. We use more loops in simulation to do statistical analyses of the outputs from the computer model.

Most data-processing applications are repetitive in nature. For example, the periodic updating of account records in a banking system involves cycling through the accounts, making changes in those account records for which there have been deposits or withdrawals since the last updating. Similar operations occur in the updating of inventory records, student records, income tax records, payroll accounts, and so on. The modification of individual records might require loops, as in computing a customer's balance given all his transactions for the past accounting period. Simple processes, such as listing the current inventory or printing payroll checks, involve loops to cycle through all the records.

In short, there are very few computer applications that do not involve the use of repetitive calculations. In these applications, the registers are of prime importance for loop control. We use them to contain addresses of operands, to count how many times we have passed through loop instructions, and to indicate the total number of times the loop should be executed. The more efficient we are in the use of the registers for such purposes, the more efficient the resulting program will be.

In summary, the general-purpose registers serve as a "scratch pad" memory for storage of intermediate results of computations and for information used repeatedly in calculations. Their functions as accumulators and address modifiers make them attractive for use whenever we can to avoid more time-consuming memory manipulations.

2.2.4. The Instruction Execution Sequence

We have seen that the control unit controls the flow of information to and from the other components of the computer and dictates the manipulation of the information within the other components. In so doing, it must also supply the timing controls to determine the sequence of events that occurs within the machine.

The operation of the control unit is an endless cycle of events. Each cycle contains several steps, which we summarize in the following:

1. *Instruction Fetch*: The next instruction to be executed is fetched from the memory location whose address is contained in the program counter.
2. *Program Counter Adjustment:* The contents of the program counter are modified to contain the address of the next instruction to be executed.
3. *Instruction Decode:* The contents of the operation field of the instruc-

tion are decoded to determine the operation to be carried out in the current instruction.

4. *Operand Fetch:* The addresses of operands are computed, if necessary, and the operands are moved to the appropriate computer component (the arithmetic unit, for example).

5. *Operation:* The operation is carried out.

6. *Storage of Results:* The results are sent to their final destination (a register, for example).

7. *Restart:* The sequence is started over again from step 1.

Normally, the program is stored in sequential memory locations. The program counter adjustment is simply an increment to the address of the next instruction. A further modification to the contents of the program counter occurs during the execution of a branch instruction. The operation step of a branch instruction causes the operand to be stored in the program counter.

In reality, the modern computer can carry out some of these steps simultaneously. For example, the operand fetch step can logically occur at the same time as the instruction decode step and does in many computers. Nevertheless, the basic sequence of events is substantially as described above.

CHAPTER SUMMARY

The internal form of information representation in the computer is in the *binary* number system. A more compact means of representing binary numbers is through the use of their *hexadecimal* equivalents. Each hexadecimal digit is equivalent to a string of four binary digits.

Binary integer arithmetic is carried out using *2's complement* conventions, in which the negative of a number is effectively its 2's complement and a digit carried from the most significant bit of a word is ignored. The algebraic sign of a binary integer is determined by its first bit.

A machine language instruction consists of an 8-bit *operation* code and one or more *operand* address fields. The *program counter register* contains the memory address of the next instruction to be executed, the *instruction register* contains the machine language instruction currently being executed, and the *general-purpose registers* are available for use by the programmer for use as temporary storage, loop counters, and accumulators.

The instruction execution sequence is an endless cycle composed of the following steps:

1. Instruction fetch
2. Program counter adjustment
3. Instruction decode
4. Operand fetch

5. Operation
6. Storage of results
7. Restart

EXERCISES

1. Convert the following numbers to decimal:
   (a) 1011010101110.1011_2. (b) $6A7D.3A_{16}$.
   (c) 1201_3.   (d) 10010_2.   (e) FFF_{16}.
   (f) 7777_8.   (g) 111111111111_2.

2. Convert the following decimal numbers to binary and hexadecimal:
   (a) 37.   (b) .76.   (c) 109.
   (d) 33000.   (e) 8192.

3. Calculate the 32-bit binary 2's complement of the following decimal numbers. Express your results in both binary and hexadecimal.
   (a) 53.   (b) -147.   (c) 8192.

4. Compute the following using 32-bit binary 2's complement arithmetic. Express all partial results and answers in both binary and hexadecimal.
   (a) $45_{10} + 33_{10} =$ (b) $45_{10} \times 33_{10} =$
   (c) $76_{10} - 27_{10} =$ (d) $2_{10}^{32} - 113_{10} =$

5. In some computers, signed integer arithmetic is carried out using the *1's complement* scheme, in which the negative of a number is represented by its logical or 1's complement. In 1's complement arithmetic, a bit carried out of the most significant bit of a number is added to the resulting sum at the least significant bit position. For example, to compute $25_{10} - 13_{10}$ in a 32-bit 1's complement machine, we have

$$
\begin{array}{rl}
25_{10} = & 00000000000000000000000000011001 \\
-13_{10} = & 00000000000000000000000000001101 \\
\hline
& 00000000000000000000000000011001 \\
= + & 11111111111111111111111111110010 \\
\hline
\end{array}
$$

The fourth number above is the 1's complement of 13_{10}. We now compute the sum

The 1 carried to the right end of the number is called the *end-around carry*. Compute the following using 1's complement arithmetic, expressing all intermediate and final results in both binary and hexadecimal:

(a) $FFFFFFFF_{16} + 1 =$
(The result from this exercise demonstrates an awkward complication inherent in 1's complement arithmetic. There are two "different" numbers which behave arithmetically as if they were zero.)

(b) $45_{10} - 22_{10} =$ (c) $23_{10} - 27_{10} =$

The first bit of a number can be treated as a sign bit, just as in 2's complement arithmetic. Calculate the magnitudes of the following:

(d) $0000683A_{16}$.   (e) $FFFF97C5_{16}$.

6. The hexadecimal number system is used to represent binary information in the IBM 360 because all information units have lengths that are multiples of 4; e.g., a word consists of 32 bits. Other popular machines have words that are 36 bits long, and all information units have lengths that are multiples of 3. In these machines, the *octal*, base 8, number system is used to describe internal information. Each group of 3 bits corresponds to one octal digit. Convert the following hexadecimal numbers to binary and then to octal:

(a) 6A3.   (b) 7.C5.   (c) 8342.8F.

Compute the following in the octal number system:

(d) $7_8 + 1_8 =$ (e) $65_8 - 37_8 =$ (f) $1000_8 - 1_8 =$

7. Some of the earlier computing machines, such as the IBM 1620, were decimal computers, in that each group of 4 internal bits 0000 through 1001 behaved arithmetically as if they were the decimal digits 0 through 9. The remaining six bit combinations were not used except for representation of algebraic signs and field delimiters. Compare the efficiency of this form of internal representation of information with the binary from we have been discussing from the following points of view:

(a) Efficiency of storage.

(b) Complexity of circuitry necessary for computations.

(c) Ease of conversion from external to internal forms.

8. In some control units, the program counter contains the address of the instruction *currently* being executed while the instruction is being executed, instead of, as in the 360, the address of the *next* instruction. Revise the instruction execution sequence discussed in the text to accommodate this different use of the program counter. In view of the effect of the branch instruction, is this way of treating the program counter more efficient than the way it works in the 360? Suppose that the computer could fetch the next instruction ahead of time while it was executing the current instruction (some models of the 360 can do this). Discuss the necessary function of the program counter in a machine that has this "look-ahead" capability. What happens in the event of a branch instruction in machines that are so equipped?

REFERENCES

DORF, RICHARD C., *Introduction to Computers and Computer Science*, Boyd & Fraser Publishing Company, San Francisco, 1972.

IBM System/360 Principles of Operation, Order No. GA22-6821, IBM, Corp., White Plains, N.Y.

LEEDS, H. D. and G. M. WEINBERG, *Computer Programming Fundamentals*, McGraw-Hill Book Company, New York, 1966.

SIEGEL, PAUL, *Understanding Digital Computers*, John Wiley & Sons, Inc., New York, 1971.

STRUBLE, G., *Assembler Language Programming: The IBM System/360*, Addison-Wesley Publishing Company, Inc., Reading, Mass., 1969.

3 INTRODUCTION TO PROGRAMMING

Having taken a brief look at the major components and operations of the computing system, we are now ready to begin considering the computing system from the programmer's point of view. In this chapter we shall discuss the nature of assembly language and its significance to the computer programmer.

3.1. ASSEMBLY LANGUAGE

3.1.1. The Language Hierarchy

Let us consider the simple problem of computing the sum of two binary numbers stored in the memory and storing the result into a third memory location. In so doing, we shall use the accumulator capability of a register to hold the intermediate results of the calculations. Three instructions are necessary:

1. "Load" the contents of the first memory location into the general-purpose register which we choose to use as an accumulator. The load instruction fetches the contents of the first memory location (leaving them unchanged) and stores that number into our accumulator register (destroying its previous contents).

2. "Add" the contents of the second memory location to the contents of our accumulator register. As we have seen, the contents of the second memory location remain unchanged, while the results of the addition are in the accumulator register after this instruction is executed.

3. "Store" the result now in our accumulator register into the third memory location. The third memory location then contains the sum of the contents of the first two memory locations, as does the accumulator register.

Suppose, in this example, that the first number is at memory location 256 and the second at location 260 and that the result is to be stored at location 264. We choose to use register 6 as our accumulator. The IBM System/360 binary machine language instructions corresponding to those listed above are

Instruction 1: 01011000   0110   00000000000100000000
                └──────┘ └──────┘ └──────────────────┘
                operation operand 1   operand 2

Instruction 2: 01011010   0110   00000000000100000100
                └──────┘ └──────┘ └──────────────────┘
                operation operand 1   operand 2

Instruction 3: 01010000   0110   00000000000100001000
                └──────┘ └──────┘ └──────────────────┘
                operation operand 1   operand 2

Most computer programs contain many more than three instructions. Yet, for the simple example above, to write the necessary instructions in the binary machine language required the exact specification of $3 \times 32 = 96$ — 0s and 1s. Misplacing any of these digits would cause our program to fail. Furthermore, the binary machine language program is very difficult to read or write because of the lack of correspondence between machine language and "people" language.

Some simplification results if we use the hexadecimal number system as a "shorthand" notation for strings of binary digits. The effect is to replace each group of four binary digits with one hexadecimal digit. We saw how to carry out this conversion in the preceding chapter. The resulting machine language program expressed in the hexadecimal number system is

Instruction 1:   58   6   00100
                └──────┘ └──────┘ └──────┘
                operation operand 1 operand 2

Instruction 2:   5A   6   00104
                └──────┘ └──────┘ └──────┘
                operation operand 1 operand 2

Instruction 3:   50   6   00108
                └──────┘ └──────┘ └──────┘
                operation operand 1 operand 2

This is a significant improvement over the binary form of the machine language. Instead of specifying 96 binary digits, we need write only $3 \times 8 = 24$ hexadecimal digits to program the computer to add the two numbers. Indeed, the most convenient way of representing information in binary form is through the hexadecimal number system. But the machine language, no matter how we represent it, still bears little resemblance to our idea of the computations it represents.

What we need is a means of representing machine language operations and addresses in a form more meaningful to the programmer. Assembly language furnishes this means. Symbolic forms, or *mnemonics*, for the operation codes allow us to write, for example, L to mean the operation code for "Load," A to mean "Add," and ST to mean "STore." Use of mnemonics eliminates the need to use the binary machine language operation codes.

Even more important is the fact that, in assembly language, we can use names, or *symbols*, that represent memory addresses, register numbers, and constants. When we use a symbol in a program, the result is the same as if we had written its machine language equivalent. But, since the choice of the symbol we use to represent a given quantity or address is up to us, we can use the symbol to describe the quantity it represents. For example, if a program computes the average of a series of numbers, we can use the symbol AVERAGE to represent the address at which the average is stored. If we do not use symbols for addresses, then we must keep track of the machine addresses at which all the information the program uses is stored. Use of symbols makes programming much easier, since we need not be concerned about actual machine addresses at all.

Returning to our example, let us call the three memory locations NUMBER1, NUMBER2, and NUM, respectively, and let us call register number 6 REGSIX. We can then write our sequence of instructions as

Instruction 1:   L   REGSIX,NUMBER1
                   operation   operand 1 operand 2

Instruction 2:   A   REGSIX,NUMBER2
                   operation   operand 1 operand 2

Instruction 3:   ST   REGSIX,NUM
                   operation   operand 1 operand 2

Although the above may still seem slightly obscure, you have to admit that the assembly language version of our simple program is easier to write and read than either machine language version.

Assembly language is a *symbolic representation of machine language*. For every true assembly language instruction there is a corresponding machine instruction, and for every assembly language instruction we write in a program the final machine language program will contain the corresponding instruction.

Once the program has been translated to machine language, it is then ready for *execution* by the computer. In its execution, the computer carries out the operations dictated by the program, as discussed in the previous chapter. Thus, the translation step and the execution steps are two distinct phases in the computer processing of a program written in a symbolic language.

There are computer languages, such as FORTRAN, in which programs more closely resemble the mathematical or verbal description of the computational tasks they represent. In FORTRAN, we could write our example problem as

$$NUM = NUMBER1 + NUMBER2$$

We know that the ultimate form of every computer program is the machine language. How is a program written in the symbolic assembly language translated into machine language? A program called the *assembler* carries out this task. The information input to the assembler program is a program written in assembly language. The output information from the assembler is the machine language translation of the assembly language program.

FORTRAN, COBOL, ALGOL, PL/I, and many other symbolic computer languages belong to a class of languages called *compiler* languages. In general, a single statement or instruction written in a compiler language leads, upon translation by a program called a *compiler*, to a machine language form of the statement consisting of several machine language instructions. We have already seen that the FORTRAN statement to add two numbers and store the result in a third memory location actually requires three machine instructions. This is the primary difference between compiler and assembly languages. In mathematical terms, the compiler language-to-machine language translation could be called a one-to-many mapping, while the assembly language-to-machine language translation may be considered a one-to-one mapping.

Compiler languages are generally considered to be of a *higher level* than the assembly language or machine language. In computing, we speak of a language *hierarchy*; the level of a language in the hierarchy is determined by its "distance" from the machine language, which occupies the lowest level. Figure 3-1 shows a schematic view of the portion of the language hierarchy of concern to us.

The use of any symbolic computer language consists of two fundamental processing steps: (1) the symbolic version of the program, or *source code*, must be translated to machine language, or *object code;* (2) the resulting object code version of the program is the given control of the computer; that is, the program is executed. During the translation step the compiler or assembler* program has control of the computer and treats the source code as

---

*Most modern assemblers are more correctly called *compilers*, which have capabilities beyond that of simply carrying out a one-to-one translation of assembly language instructions to machine language instructions. Nevertheless, we shall continue to call the IBM System/360 assembly language compiler the *assembler*.

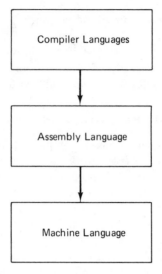

Fig. 3-1. A portion of the computer language hierarchy.

input data. During the execution step the object code version of the user's program has control of the computer and uses as data whatever the programmer told it to use.

3.1.2. Why Learn Assembly Language?

Having decided what assembly language is, we shall now discuss its uses and the benefits derived from a knowledge of it. Before doing so, we must distinguish between two basic types of programs. The first of these are the so-called *problem* programs. From the point of view of the administrator of the computer installation, problem programs are written by *users*, and it is the administrator's primary goal to make the users' task as easy and inexpensive as possible. The administrator has *systems* programmers working for him. The systems programs they write are for the purpose of helping the user to solve his problems.

Most problem programs are written in a compiler or higher-level language because compiler languages are, in a sense, easier to use and require less attention to specific machine-oriented details than does assembly language. On the other hand, because of the possibility of increased efficiency using assembly language and because systems programs *are* concerned with the detailed operation of the machine, most systems programming is done in the assembly language. In the following, we shall see that knowledge of assembly language is essential to systems programmers and is of great help to problem programmers as well. We shall first take a look at assembly language from the user's point of view.

In many cases, writing a computer program to accomplish a given task is easier in a compiler language than in assembly language, because most compiler languages have been developed to facilitate the programming of specific kinds of jobs. The designers of FORTRAN (FORmula TRANslator) were primarily scientists; the FORTRAN language couples numerical computing power with relative simplicity of programming algebraic equations to make it by far the most popular language for use in scientific and numerical computations. COBOL (COmmon Business Oriented Language) was designed for business applications; the processing of large files of information, such as inventory or payroll records, is most easily done in the COBOL language. ALGOL (ALGOrithmic Language) is a formal language used for the description of algorithms, or rules for computation.

Each of these languages serves its purpose reasonably well. But the specialization inherent in a given compiler language implies difficulty for the programmer who attempts to use it for purposes other than those for which it was designed. Business data processing, while possible, is difficult in FORTRAN; the more remote the problem is from numerical computations, the more difficult the use of FORTRAN is for that program. In COBOL, on the other hand, the writing of complex algebraic statements is tedious at best. Furthermore, the COBOL language lacks some facilities essential to scientific programming, such as a large library of mathematical programs, and is too "wordy" for most scientists to use. ALGOL is an international language for description of algorithms; you can find algorithms published in ALGOL in computing journals such as the *Communications of the Association for Computing Machinery*. However, most programmers will agree that the language is more difficult to apply in specific problems. The language, per se, includes no specific input/output statements, and, furthermore, the syntax, or language structure, necessary to enable the description of algorithms seems to hinder computational work. Thus, each of these specialized languages serves its purpose, but the price paid for ease of programming for a given kind of application is a decrease in overall power of the language.

The PL/I language (Programming Language I) offers the generality that the previously mentioned procedural languages lack. Syntactically, this language appears to be a combination of ALGOL, FORTRAN, and COBOL and, in addition, offers some special language elements which make possible the writing of a complete operating system in the PL/I language. The price paid for this flexibility is the apparent complexity of the language to the beginning programmer. It is largely this difficulty which has delayed and will probably prevent the emergence of PL/I as the universal language for use on IBM machines. For the beginning student of computer science, the fact that PL/I is a compiler language means that a knowledge of the language will not furnish him with what assembly language can—a firm understanding of the structure and function of the computing system.

The assembly language programmer has all the capabilities of the computer at his disposal. Assembly language *is* machine language. Specialized compiler languages tend to use only a portion of the total machine capabilities. This is not to suggest that once one learns assembly language he should write all his programs in that language. That would be like suggesting that once one has learned to drive a car he should stop walking. But he can use assembly language to fill in the gaps in the capabilities of the compiler language he is using. In fact, most compiler languages allow the user to write *subroutines* or subprograms in assembly language to carry out those tasks which would be awkward or impossible in the compiler language.

For the compiler language programmer, knowledge of assembly language furnishes further useful side benefits. The more he knows about the basic fundamentals and capabilities of the computer, the better use he is able to make of them, no matter what language he is using. For example, if he knows assembly language, he knows the reasons for the format rules in FORTRAN and the-file definition statements in COBOL. He will know what the = sign in FORTRAN really does and what the difference between REAL and INTEGER variables is. When faced with the question "Can I do this in FORTRAN?" he can refer to his knowledge of machine capabilities to decide whether or not his question makes sense from the machine's point of view. This is often enough to furnish him with at least a partial answer to his question.

Furthermore, knowledge of assembly language can be a significant help in finding mistakes in programs written in a compiler language. Most compilers offer the option of obtaining a printed list of the assembly language translation of the program being compiled. Armed with this and printed listings of the memory and register contents from the time his program went awry, the programmer who knows assembly language has a clear advantage in finding the error in his program.

Finally, we should point out the fact that efficiency of the use of the computing facilities is of importance to all programmers. We shall discuss this point later in more detail. For now we shall simply state that a knowledge of the basic principles of operations of the computer is necessary in order to make efficient use of the computer.

We have seen in the above that knowledge of assembly language and computer principles provides several advantages to the compiler language programmer. We shall now turn to a discussion of assembly language from the systems programmer's point of view. We shall see why almost all systems programs are written in assembly language and what effect this has upon the use of the computing facilities.

Systems programs serve the general purpose of relieving the user of the responsibility for carrying out machine- or system-oriented tasks not of immediate interest to him. For example, the programmer uses compilers or assemblers to translate his program to machine language; the user who had to write a compiler before he could write a FORTRAN program would probably give up on the problem. Such necessities as converting numerical data from character-code form to binary representation suitable for arithmetic manipulation, control of input/output devices, and management of the computing facilities in general are not of immediate concern to the problem programmer and are left to systems routines. In short, systems programs serve as buffers between the programmer and the details of machine operation.

Because systems programs are in an intermediate position between the user and the machine, most systems programming is done in the assembly language. Systems routines need to deal with the details of the machine operation, and details of this sort are not usually accessible from a compiler language. For example, the FORTRAN programmer is not concerned with the exact location of his program in the computer memory, and he does not really care which of several possible card readers was used to read the data for his program. In fact, he is using a compiler language so that he need not worry about details such as these. But certainly some systems programs need to monitor this kind of information in order to ensure that the user's programs run properly and receive the proper data. Assembly language is the language that furnishes the power necessary to accomplish these tasks.

We now return to the matter of efficiency mentioned earlier. Computer time, usually measured in terms of the time a user has control of the CPU, is expensive, normal rates being on the order of $250 to $500 per hour. Some installations also charge rental fees for the use of the storage and input/output equipment. Some problems require a considerable amount of storage space and computer time, to the extent that whether or not it is economically or physically possible to run them on a given machine depends on how efficient the program is.

In writing the assembly language program, the programmer can in principle write the most efficient program possible. Furthermore, he has the facility for assigning priorities for use of computer facilities at his disposal. Thus, he may decide to use more memory space in exchange for increased execution speed in his program and *vice versa*.

Compilers in general do not produce the most efficient machine language programs possible. The designer of a compiler cannot anticipate all the possible statements that will occur in programs translated by the compiler. Therefore, the compiler must be written so as to classify certain types of statements into general categories and treat each statement within a category in the same manner. This generality results in decreased efficiency of the resulting machine language.

Efficiency is of major importance to the systems programmer. The user cannot be expected to pay for inefficiencies in the operating system, and the computer installation, for whom the systems programmer works, is left with the bill. Thus, a measure of the capability of a systems programmer is his ability to make efficient use of the machine's resources.

In summary, computers are like many other machines in that the more we know about them, the more effective use we can make of them. Knowledge of assembly language helps the problem programmer in many ways, including making it possible for him to accomplish tasks that are difficult or impossible to do using a procedural language, helping him to find mistakes, and helping him to make the most efficient use of computer resources. Because of its power and efficiency, assembly language is also indispensable to the systems programmer.

But the main reason to learn assembly language is to learn more about computers. To learn assembly language you must understand the principles of computer structure, function, and information representation. Not only will this knowledge make you a better programmer and computer scientist, but it will also open new doors for you. For example, an area of computing of increasing importance is the use of small *minicomputers* and even *microcomputers* to accomplish specific tasks in data processing, industrial process control, and scientific research. The intelligent use of these relatively primitive systems is much easier if you understand how a computer works.

3.2. "LET'S PUT IT ON THE COMPUTER!"

By now you should have at least a vague idea of what computer programming is all about and of what assembly language is and what it is for. I ask that you restrain your impatience to start writing programs long enough to read this section, which discusses a series of steps that the programmer must follow between the stages when he decides "Let's put it on the computer!" and when he thinks "It works!"

The steps discussed below and outlined in Fig. 3-2 are really a set of guidelines. Follow them closely until they become natural. Experienced programmers follow these steps by instinct, but may also obtain some benefit in an analysis of what they do.

1. Analysis of the Problem
2. The Algorithm
3. Translation to a Flow Chart
4. Translation to a Computer Language
5. Preparation of Program and Data
6. Translation to Machine Language
7. Execution
8. Debugging and Testing   **Fig. 3-2.** Steps in using the computer.

3.2.1. Analysis of the Problem

The first step in the use of the computer to accomplish a given task is a thorough analysis of the problem. This is the most important step of all; a great deal of time and money can be wasted if insufficient thought is given to the nature of the problem and what is required to solve it.

The user must have a firm idea of what he expects the computer to do for him before he can use the computer effectively. He needs to "know what he knows" and "what he doesn't know." In other words, in any given problem, certain information to be processed is available—mathematical formulas and data from experiments, a list of student names and grades, an airline schedule, and police records, to name some examples. The user wants to use the computer to modify the input information to obtain some output. He must decide what that output is to be. He must have a good idea of how the computer is to serve in the processing of his information.

He then must decide whether or not the use of the computer to solve his problem is worth the effort and expense involved. A personal experience of mine may serve to illustrate this point. I came upon a contest for which the prize was a trip to Hawaii. The rules of the contest were simple: The entrant who submitted the longest list of 4-letter words in the English language to be constructed from a given set of 14 letters would win first prize. A quick calculation shows that there are 14^4 or 38,416 possible 4-letter combinations of the 14 given letters. I then wrote and ran a program whose input was the 14 given letters and output was all the possible combinations of the letters, 2744 lines of printed output, each line consisting of 14 4-letter combinations.

What now? It was easy to eliminate "words" such as CCCC. But how about some more questionable ones such as PITH (or is it PYTH?). Do slang or vulgar words count? The next step was to sit down with the dictionary and go through the list of words, deciding which ones were real words and which ones were not. I belatedly realized that this is exactly what I would have had to do even if I had not used the computer to generate the list of words; all the computer did was to supply a list of groups of letters. Had a list of all valid 4-letter words been available for use by the computer, the computer could have completed the entire problem. However, this was not the case.

In other words, the example described above is an example of failure on my part to analyze the problem involved from start to finish. Had I done so, I would have realized that the cost in my and the computer's time would be really wasted. Millions of dollars and thousands of man-hours are wasted every year for exactly the same reason. The user must determine if the use of the computer could help him and, if so, whether or not the benefits he could derive from its use justify the time and expense involved.

Many problems are simply not suited for computer use at all. The computer's main forte is its ability to mindlessly carry out repetitive calculations without human intervention. It is not so well suited to analysis of complex decision-making problems. A case in point is the game of chess. While some progress has been made toward programming the computer to play chess, this has been achieved at great expense in human and computer resources. Unfortunately, it is difficult to calculate if a problem is too complex to make practical usage of the computer. Perhaps it is reasonable to try to have the computer play chess. But to write a program to solve a specific chess problem would be a waste of time—the effort we would have to put into designing and writing the program could have been more efficiently used in solving the problem by hand. The point is that computers cannot do our thinking for us; they do only what we tell them to in our programs. Due account must be taken of this fact when we analyze a problem.

A further necessary consideration in the use of the computer is the availability of the necessary human and mechanical resources. A fact often overlooked is that the cost of development of *software* (programs and systems) for a large computer problem often outweighs hardware expenses. Large programming projects often require a team of programmers and supervisors. The expense of establishing and maintaining such a team for the time necessary to complete the project is often underestimated in the planning stages of the project. Many a large project has had to be abandoned in intermediate stages of its development because the computing and/or human resources were found to be insufficient to support its completion. Sufficient forethought on the part of the people involved in analyzing the problem can eliminate the waste in starting a project for which the necessary facilities are unavailable.

For example, many universities are interested in "computerizing" the registrar's office. It is commonly agreed that, once the registrar system has been implemented, the savings resulting from decreased personnel to run the registrar's office will cover the increased expenses for use of the computer. The net result would be increased speed in serving administration and student requests and augmented services for the student and university.

What resources are necessary to computerize the registrar's office? Thought must be given to the hardware requirements for the job. Additional core memory space, more disk or magnetic tape storage capacities, a faster or more powerful CPU, and increased input/output facilities may be required. But, beyond the hardware expenses, the initial expense of preparing the programs and original data may be the deciding factor in whether or not to go ahead with the project.

Writing the original programs will be a one-time initial expense that can be considerable. But a necessity that should not be overlooked is that of preparing the original files for input into the computer. Suppose, for example, that 20,000 students attend the university, each of which has an average number of 20 courses to his credit. If each course requires 1 punched card for input into the computer records, it will be necessary to have 400,000 cards punched just to establish the records for the students currently attending the university. Note that this does not include the records of students who have left the university for one reason or another.

In short, while in the long run the savings from use of the computer might be considerable, due attention must be paid to the expenses incurred in acquiring the additional human and hardware resources necessary to implement the project.

Let us suppose that, after weighing the costs of using the computer against the benefits he will derive from its use, the user decides to go ahead with his project. He is then ready to begin considering the problem in more depth.

A decision he must make is what portion of the total information input for his problem will be *data* and which will be his program. Since the program and data are both forms of input, the distinction between the program and data is not a natural one. We cannot give definite rules as to which is which; the distinction depends on the problem at hand. We can, however, suggest some guidelines to assist in making the decision.

After the program has been written and translated to machine language, it should be considered to be part of the machine. The program usually requests further input information, or data, which it processes to produce the final output information, which we also consider to be data. Once a program has been written, it can be used over and over again to process different input data.

Changing a program is usually more difficult and expensive than changing the data it processes. To change data we need simply change data cards. To change a program, however, we must first make the changes in the punched cards and then retranslate the program to machine language, and if we make a mistake in the change, we have to repeat the process until the program works again. The expense involved is due to the additional work necessary to eliminate errors and the cost of computer time in retranslating the program. Thus, we tend to use as data those parts of the input information we intend to change frequently. We are more reluctant to make frequent changes in the program itself.

Suppose that we are given a list of 800 numbers and are assigned the problem of using the computer to calculate the average of the numbers. The procedure is obvious; we calculate the sum of the numbers and divide it by 800. We could write the numbers into our program or use them as input data to be processed by the program. In the latter case, we would include in our program instructions in a loop to read the numbers from punched cards. Which is preferable?

Suppose, after some effort, that we wrote the numbers into the program and that it calculated the correct result. Then we are told that one of the numbers is wrong. We then would have to correct the program and retranslate it to machine language just to change one number. On the other hand, if our program treated the list of numbers as data, then we would have to change only one data card and rerun the program.

To change one number presents no particular difficulty, no matter whether we wrote the numbers into the program or treated them as data for the program. But suppose that we were given an entirely different list of 800 numbers. If we wrote the original list into our program, we would have to rewrite the entire program to do the new problem. And if we were given 500 different lists of 800 numbers, we would have to rewrite and retranslate our program at least 500 times to compute the required averages. It appears that it is logically simpler and uses less computer time if we simply write one program that could compute the average of *any* list of 800 numbers and changed the data cards instead of the program whenever we wanted to average a new list of numbers.

Now suppose that we had properly written a program that computes the average of 800 numbers punched on cards and read by the program as input data. Then we are asked to compute the average of 801 numbers. We then have to rewrite our program to take care of this case. Or do we? If we had analyzed the problem sufficiently, we might have foreseen this possibility and designed our program to calculate the average of *any* number of numbers. We would do this by having the program treat the number of numbers to be averaged as input data. The first data card would tell the program how many more data cards it needs to read and how many numbers it will find on those cards. The list of numbers to be averaged would be punched on the following data cards.

We can summarize this discussion by stating the principle that the more a program is designed to treat the general case of the problem it is written for, the more useful the program is. We would probably not write a program to average a single list of 800 numbers; it would be far easier to sit down at an adding machine and compute the average ourselves. On the other hand, a program that will calculate the average of any list of numbers is certainly worth having.

A further important part of the planning phase of a computer project is a consideration of the environment in which the finished product will operate. The programmer should try to anticipate all the uses or special cases his program will be expected to service. He should include in the program the necessary tests and instructions to ensure that these cases are treated properly. He should make every attempt to make the use of his program as easy as possible for users to apply to their own tasks. The program should check for mispunched or misformatted data and for cases that it is not designed to handle and should output appropriate warning or error messages when it encounters such situations. In short, the program must include "fail-safe" facilities to guard against its misuse.

Finally, consideration must be given to the nature and form the data should have. Let us return to the registrar's problem. When designing such a system, we must anticipate the final uses of the program. As we have seen, the preparation of data is a major portion of the implementation of this system. Insufficient attention to what is or will be necessary to include in the data files could mean a costly revision of the entire data bank for the problem.

For example, if we failed to include the student's academic major department as part of the information in his record, then when a request is made by the administration to find out the grade point average of the students by department, the request cannot be honored by the computing system. To alter the files so that they include this information means punching another data card for each student and going through the entire file just to add this information. The fact that the administration would request information by department should have been anticipated and the necessary data should have been included in the records.

However, the more information we put into the files, the more time-consuming and expensive it is to keep the files up-to-date. Therefore, in planning for such a project, one must make some compromises between the amount of information that the system can retrieve and the expense of maintaining the system.

Some thought must also be given to the internal structure of the data files. In some cases, the file need have little or no structure; the data can be treated in random order. In other instances, a complex structure may be necessary to facilitate fast access to relevant information. In the registrar problem the file would probably be sorted alphabetically using the student name as the *key*, or record identifier, because it is easier to find a given record in a sorted file. Cross-indexes may be necessary so that information can be retrieved according to attributes other than the student name, such as the student number. In other problems, the data might be more appropriately represented in structures that provide more information about the interrelationships between the records.

We cannot overemphasize the importance of a thorough analysis of the problem before the details of the computations are tackled. The computer user must know what his use is going to cost in terms of effort and money, whether the necessary resources are or can be made available at not too great an expense, what sort of information his problem requires, and how he plans to handle the information at his disposal before he is prepared to use the computer effectively to solve his problem. The more time he spends in this planning stage, the less grief he will encounter in the later stages of computer utilization.

3.2.2. The Algorithm

Having made a thorough analysis of the problem, the user is now prepared to consider in greater depth the details of the computations. He must design an *algorithm*, which is a verbal description of the methods used in solving the problem, or, in other words, a list of rules and computational steps that will eventually be carried out by the computer.

The amount of detail necessary in an algorithm varies with the complexity of the problem, the thoroughness of the programmer, and the amount of experience the programmer has. Thus, the more complex a program is, the more detailed the algorithm should be. In any case, the algorithm should be sufficiently detailed to permit the person who eventually writes the program to understand exactly what is required of the program and the computational steps necessary to be programmed. It is not sufficient to simply hand the programmer a problem and say "Solve it!"—particularly if the programmer is unfamiliar with the problem.

Let us return to the example in which we wished to compute the average of a list of numbers. We decided when we analyzed the problem that we should write it so that the program would

1. Read a data card stating how many numbers are to be read from the following data cards. We could call the number on this first card N, which is the number of numbers to be averaged.
2. Read N cards.
3. Compute the sum of the numbers that were punched on the N cards.
4. Divide this sum by N.
5. Print the result.

The above list of steps to solve our problem is an algorithm for the problem. We see that many of the details of the calculations are left out. For example, how is the computer to know when it has finished reading all the data cards? Are the numbers to be stored in the memory for later use? In the event that the answer is not a whole number, how many decimal places should be devoted to the fractional part? These are examples of questions that must be answered before we can finish writing the program. The experienced programmer can delay answering many of these until he writes the program, but he will be thinking of them all through his work. The beginner should attempt to answer as many questions of this nature as he can as soon as he can.

3.2.3. Translation to a Flow Chart

A *flow chart* is a pictorial description of the algorithm. It usually consists of various-shaped boxes to represent computer operations. The boxes are connected to each other by arrows whose directions show the flow of the logic or operations in the program as it processes the data. Study Appendix A if you are not familiar with flow-charting techniques.

The flow chart is actually a translation of the algorithm from a verbal description of the method of attack to a pictorial description of it. It is at the flow-charting stage that the real logical structure of the program becomes clear. Here the answers to most of the questions of the sort mentioned above should be depicted. The amount of detail that is necessary in the flow chart is again a matter of the complexity of the problem and the nature of the programmer. Normally, the programmer includes enough detail in the flow chart to enable him to treat the writing of the program as a translation from the "flow chart language" to the computer language he is using.

Figure 3-3 shows a flow chart for our problem. Notice that some of the questions raised above are answered in the flow chart. The program will count the number of cards read by using a *counter variable* called J and will read the numbers and compute their sum in a single loop. All the numbers will not be stored in the memory for later use; the last one read is stored in a location called A, which is erased each time a new number is read.

The more detail we include in the flow chart, the easier it is to write the program for two reasons: (1) We have a good pictorial version of the program to consult for details, and (2) in designing the flow chart we did most of the thinking about the structure of the program. For the beginning programmer, the unfamiliarity with the language is hindrance enough, without the additional burden of having to design the program while he is writing it. Thus, he should pay particular attention to the drawing of flow charts before writing programs.

3.2.4. Translation to a Computer Language

This is the step in which the programmer writes the program in whatever symbolic computer language he is using. By now he must know exactly what his program requires and what the sequence of instructions must be. The computer cannot guess what he intended to do, nor can it fill in the details he failed to supply.

Up to this point, we see that each step has required deeper and deeper analysis of the problem, from a general overview of the nature and requirements of the problem to a verbal and then pictorial description of it, and finally to the most detailed part of the procedure of all the writing of the program. With each step, we get closer to the machine.

3.2.5. Preparation of Program and Data

In this step the program and data are prepared for input into the computer. If punched-card input is used, the symbolic program is punched on cards, hopefully after a last check for mistakes. Necessary preliminary calculations and manipulations with the data are carried out and the data are punched on cards.

3.2.6. Translation to Machine Language

We have seen that, for the program to work, it must first be translated to machine language by the proper assembler or compiler program. This step is often called the *compilation* step.

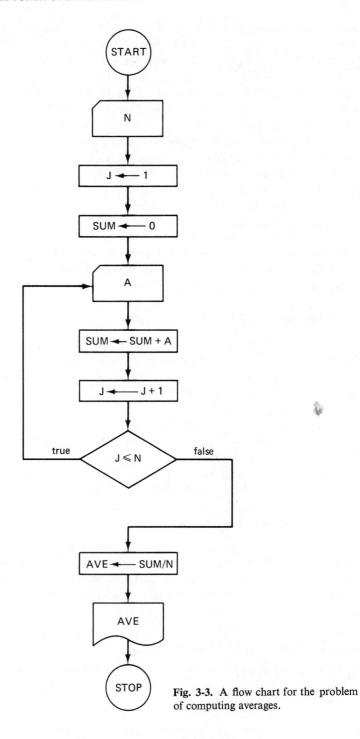

Fig. 3-3. A flow chart for the problem of computing averages.

3.2.7. Execution

The machine language translation of the program is given control of the CPU, which then supervises the input of the data, the calculations, and the output of the answers.

3.2.8. Debugging and Testing

Having gone through the steps above, the programmer now receives some indication of the fruits of his efforts, usually in the form of printed computer output. His primary concern now is whether or not his program worked. Did it accomplish the task it was designed to do?

A large amount of the work involved in using the computer is human effort, and humans do make mistakes. Thus, it often happens that, in the initial stages of computer use for a given problem, something was done incorrectly. The computer does exactly what its programs tell it to do. If there are errors in the input to it, these errors will be reflected in the output it produces.

Debugging.   An error in a computer program is called a *bug*, and the act of finding and removing bugs is called *debugging*. Bugs can be grouped into two general types. The first we might call *mechanical* bugs. These result from improper use of the symbolic language in the program. For example, suppose that we included in our program an instruction that makes no sense in the language we were using. The compiler program expects to find only meaningful instructions; what is it to do with instructions that are not in its vocabulary? Rather than trying to guess what the programmer intended to do, the compiler usually prints an error message indicating the nature of the error and, depending on the severity of the error and the nature of the compiler, may give the compilation up as hopeless.

Thus, the first thing a programmer does when he receives his printed output is to look through it for printed error messages indicating mechanical bugs. If he finds some, he makes the appropriate changes (usually after a bit of head scratching and soul-searching) and resubmits his program and data for retranslation to machine language and execution. He repeats this process until the mechanical bugs are dead.

A mechanical bug usually prevents the normal completion of the task. If the task was completed, the output is nevertheless suspect; we are reluctant to consider the answers printed as correct as long as there are noticeable errors in the program and/or data.

Once the mechanical bugs have been eliminated, the programmer now looks at the output and tries to decide if the program did what he wanted it to do. If the output appears to be in order, then he is in a position to begin a more exhaustive testing of the details of the program. But what if the output is not correct? He then is faced with a more hardy species of bug, the *logical* bug.

Logical bugs are errors in the design of the program. Somewhere in the process of analyzing the problem, designing the algorithm, drawing the flow chart, or writing the program the programmer made a mistake in his reasoning about how to do the problem. Thus, he has to go back several steps and do some further studying of the fundamentals of the problem. Was the algorithm designed to take care of the case under consideration? Do the loop counters perform properly? Are they given the proper initial and final values? Are the data in the form expected by the program? Are the equations upon which the calculations were based correct? These are the kinds of questions he asks at this stage. The appearance of logical bugs forces him to reexamine all or part of the procedure from the beginning.

Depending on the nature of the logical bug, the elimination of it usually entails the rewriting of some or all of the program, after making the necessary changes in the algorithm and flow chart. This procedure is costly in computer time and human effort and can usually be avoided if proper attention is given to the beginning steps *before* using the computer.

Typographical errors, in preparing the program and data, often produce errors which can have symptoms of either kind of bug. Mispunching a register number in a program might look like a logical bug, since there may be no error messages and yet the output appears to be wrong. Typos in punching the data can produce error messages because the input is not in the required format or can lead to incorrect output. Unfortunately, most programmers check the input data only as a last resort, after spending a lot of time looking in the program for nonexistent bugs.

After the mechanical and logical bugs and typographical errors have been removed, the output contains no serious error messages and indicates that the task has been performed correctly. The programmer must then *test* the program.

Testing.   The programmer has responsibilities beyond demonstrating that his program works for just one special case. In most on-the-job situations, the program will be used by others besides the programmer himself. These users will not be familiar with the details of the program; they want only to use the program with *their* data to obtain the correct results.

The process of testing a program is an art in itself. The programmer, who is intimately concerned with the details of his work and knows exactly how to use his own program, must put himself in the place of the users, who know little or nothing about these matters. He must try to anticipate everything the user could do with his program and try his program out in all these situations. In other words, he should try to simulate as best he can the environment in which his program will eventually be used. We shall discuss the problem of testing programs in more detail in Chapter 12.

Thus, "putting it on the computer" requires much more than simply writing a program. The programming part of the job is a minor part of the entire job. Before the program can be written, due consideration must be given to the analysis of the problem and the design of the program which will solve it. After the program is written and run, the programmer must eliminate the mechanical and logical bugs that appear and test the final program.

3.3. USE OF THE REFERENCE MANUALS

No outside references are necessary to use this book. But no book of reasonable length could possibly encompass all the hardware and software features of a system of the size of the 360. In fact, no book of this size could offer a complete treatment of all the many details in assembly language programming. Therefore, as you progress in programming abilities and tackle increasingly complex and specialized projects, you must rely increasingly on the material to be found in reference manuals. We cannot anticipate all the possible reference materials you might need in the future, so we shall discuss here those manuals that will be used most frequently by the readers of this text. The manuals described below are those for systems which use the Operating System (OS). There is a similar set of manuals for each of the other operating systems, such as the Disk Operating System and the Virtual Systems.

Some of the terms used in the following discussion may be unfamiliar. This is intentional—it is hoped that in using this text as a reference (after you have studied everything in it) you will refer back to this section when you need to know which manual to consult to obtain some more specific information.

The Green Card.   The most often-used reference source is probably the IBM *green card.* (As we mentioned, some "green" cards are tan.) This is an inexpensive pocket-sized set of tables containing such information as a table of machine instructions, their operation codes and the forms of their respective operands, a hexadecimal-to-decimal conversion table, a character translation table, and descriptions of various hardware features that are of frequent interest to the programmer. Every assembly language programmer should have a green card for quick access to information that is often used in programming.

Principles of Operation.   The green card shows the programmer how to write assembly or machine language instructions. The *principles of operation* manual offers a detailed description of what each instruction does. It is the primary source of information about those aspects of machine operation that are of importance to the programmer. In addition, it contains descriptions of the input/output facilities at a level which the programmer can understand and use.

Assembly Language. The *assembler language* manual describes those aspects of the assembly language which are not really machine-oriented but, instead, are necessary for the use of the assembly program itself. Thus, this manual discusses the assembly language statements which indicate the beginning and end of assembly language programs, the statements which reserve memory space and assign values to constants in the program, and the writing of assembly macro-instructions. As stated above, the description of hardware-oriented facilities is to be found in principles of operation manual. The assembler language manual, the principles of operation manual, and the green card are the primary sources of information for assembly language programming.

Assembler F Programmer's Guide. In this manual we find the information necessary to assemble, link-edit, and execute an assembly language program. Details concerning the job control language (JCL) necessary for use of the assembler, estimates of memory and disk space requirements, the assembler output, and the options available to the programmer in the use of the assembler are contained in this manual.

Supervisor Services and *Data Management Services.* These two manuals describe the capabilities and facilities available through the operating systems. The *supervisor services* manual examines the aids that the supervisor provides for the user, such as program management, task creation and management, and main storage allocation. The *data management services* manual discusses the input/output facilities of the operating system, including file organization, access methods, and disposition and space allocation for data files.

Supervisor and Data Management Macros. This manual is a "how-to-do-it" book for programmers who use the data management or supervisor facilities at the assembly language level.

Messages and Codes. Errors generated during the execution of a program are indicated to the programmer via printed error messages, which normally consist of an error message number and a cryptic note as to the nature of the error. Further information regarding the error may be found in the *messages and codes* manual by looking up the error number and reading the associated material.

These are but a few of the manuals that the programmer has occasion to use and are the ones he tends to use most often. At this point, it suffices that you know that these sources are available for use when necessary. In this text, every attempt is made to make trips to the manuals unnecessary. However, in a real programming environment, familiarity with the use of these reference sources is essential. The programmer quickly learns which manuals to use for general information. However, he must often resort to the *master index* manual when he needs specific information or when he does not know which manual to try first.

3.4. ASSEMBLY LANGUAGE FORMAT

As is the case with all computer languages, the programmer must follow certain rules in writing the statements that form an assembly language program. The set of rules which describes the physical layout of a statement is called the *format* for that language. In this section we shall discuss the format of assembly language.

Most assembly language programs are input into the computer from punched cards. As we have seen, a punched card is divided vertically into 80 columns, each of which may contain a character or may be left blank. Each card normally contains one assembly language statement, although there is a facility for continuing long statements onto subsequent cards if necessary.

As a guide in preparing programs to be punched on cards, the programmer uses a coding form, an example of which is shown in Fig. 3-4. The coding form is divided into 80 columns which correspond to the columns on computer cards. Each horizontal line on the coding form represents one card. In preparing a program to be punched, the programmer writes the statements on the coding form exactly as he wishes them to appear on the cards, with the characters in the proper columns and the statements in the order in which they are to appear in the finished program.

An assembly language statement consists of four fields, the *name, operation, operands*, and *comments* fields. In a statement, these fields are specified in the order

name   operation   operands   comments

with at least one blank separating the individual fields.

The name field, if present, usually serves the purpose of attaching the symbolic name in this field to the memory location at which the machine language form of that statement will be placed. Once a symbol has been *defined* by placing its name in the name field of a statement, other statements may then use that symbol as an operand, instead of the numerical machine address to which the symbol corresponds.

A symbol consists of from one to eight characters, the first of which must be a letter A–Z or one of the special characters $, #, or @. The remaining characters can be chosen from the letters of the alphabet, the characters $, #, or @, or the digits 0–9 and can be written in any order. Thus, for example, ABCDE, Z10239, $$$@#, and I are all valid symbols, while 1AB,

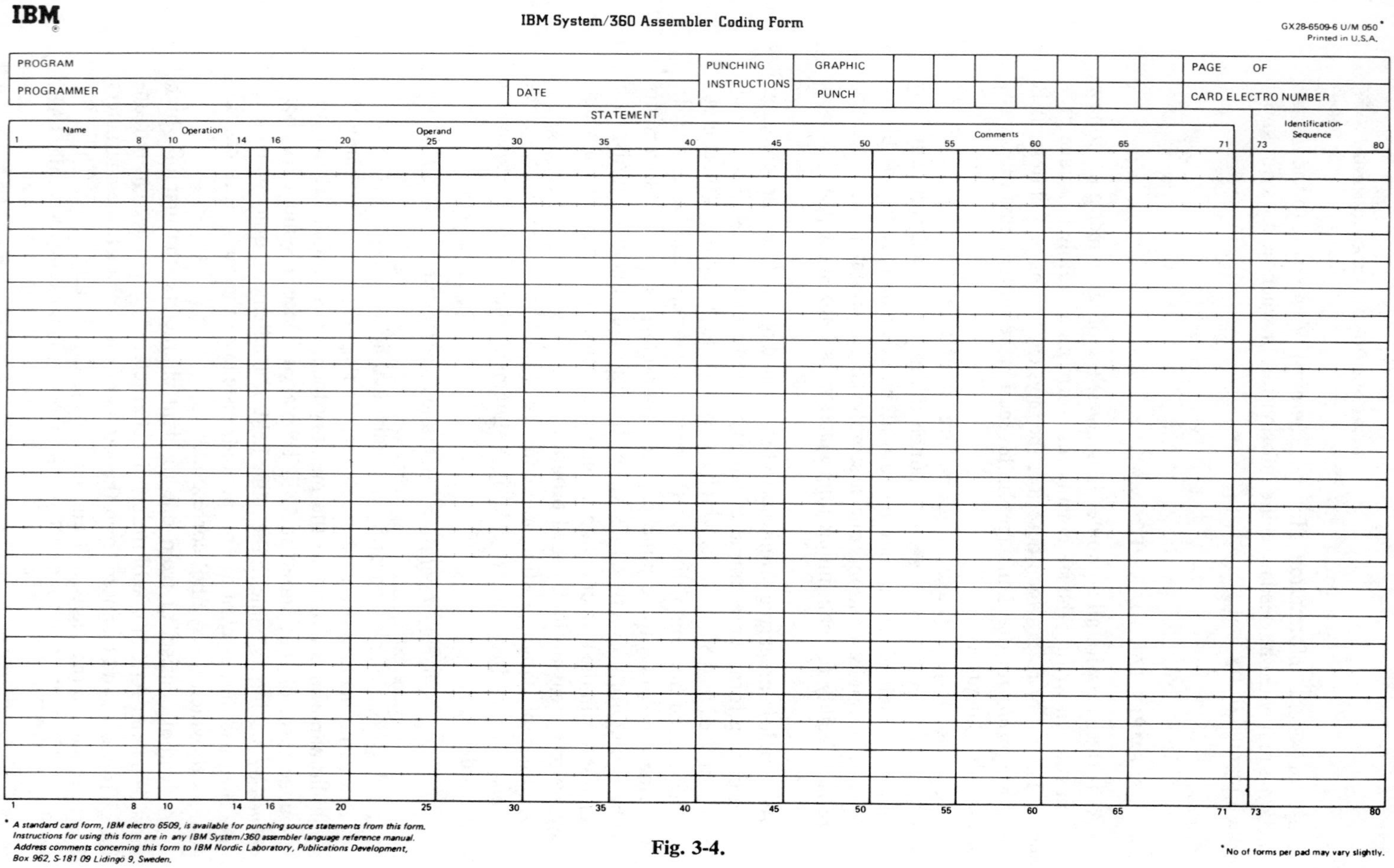

IBM

IBM System/360 Assembler Coding Form

GX28-6509-6 U/M 050 *
Printed in U.S.A.

PROGRAM					PUNCHING	GRAPHIC		PAGE	OF
PROGRAMMER		DATE			INSTRUCTIONS	PUNCH		CARD ELECTRO NUMBER	

STATEMENT

Name	Operation	Operand	Comments	Identification-Sequence
1	8 10 14 16	20 25 30 35 40 45 50 55 60 65	71 73	80

Fig. 3-4.

* A standard card form, IBM electro 6509, is available for punching source statements from this form.
Instructions for using this form are in any IBM System/360 assembler language reference manual.
Address comments concerning this form to IBM Nordic Laboratory, Publications Development,
Box 962, S-181 09 Lidingö 9, Sweden.

* No of forms per pad may vary slightly.

ELEPHANTS, NUMBER 1, and 1 are not. If the name field is used in a given statement, the first character of the symbol must be in column 1. Otherwise, column 1 must be left blank.

There is one exception to this rule. If column 1 contains an asterisk, *, the whole statement is a comment; the assembler does not analyze anything further on the card.

The name field, if used, is followed by at least one blank space. Then comes the operation field, which normally contains an assembler mnemonic for a machine operation code, for example, MVC or A or ST. The mnemonics must be written exactly as prescribed, with no embedded blanks. There must be at least one blank separating the operation field from the next field in the statement, the operands field.

As we have seen, an operand is usually a register or memory address specified either by the numerical address itself or by a symbolic name for the address. If a symbol is used to represent an address, the symbol must, of course, appear in the name field of a statement in the program. If the machine instruction specified in the operation field requires more than one operand, the operands are written in their necessary order and are separated from each other by commas. For example, in the operands field

$$3,12,\text{ADDR1}$$

the number 3 (probably referring to register 3) is the first operand, the number 12 (probably register 12) is the second operand, and the symbol ADDR1 is the third operand. There can be no spaces in the operands field, except under special circumstances.

The operation and operands fields are required in assembly language statements. The name field is optional but has a definite meaning to the assembler when used. The fourth field, the comments, or remarks, field, is not required in a statement and is in fact solely for the aid of the programmer. After at least one blank following the operands field, the programmer can write anything he wishes. There are no restrictions on the characters that can be used, provided they can be punched on a card. The comments field ends at column 71. In other words, the assembler ignores everything it finds from the end of the operands field through column 71.

In analyzing an assembly language statement, the assembler first checks to see if column 1 contains an asterisk. If so, it goes on to the next statement. If column 1 is nonblank and not an asterisk, the assembler considers all the following characters as part of the name field until it finds a blank. The next group of characters it finds are the operation field, which is again separated from the operands field by at least one blank. In other words, the blank character is the divider between the various fields of the instruction.

In some cases, it is impossible to fit an entire statement on one card. To *continue* an assembly language statement onto the next card, simply put any nonblank character in column 72 and continue the statement starting at column 16 of the next card.

Figure 3-5 shows some assembly language statements as they would appear on a coding form.

We see that, as is necessary, each field is separated from the others by a blank. While the statements shown are certainly legal in assembly language, we can make them more easily readable by following a convention that is in almost universal use. We align the fields of the various statements into columns as follows:

Column	Field
1	Name
10	Operation
16	Operands
30	Comments

The results of following this convention are to line up the fields of the statements of a program in columns, thus making the program much easier to read.

CHAPTER SUMMARY

Assembly language is a symbolic representation of *machine language*. Programs written in assembly language are translated to machine language by the *assembler* and then *executed*.

Assembly language is the primary language used by *systems programmers* because of its generality and efficiency. Knowledge of assembly language helps the *user* to make more efficient use of the computer resources and furnishes him with an understanding of the capabilities of computing machines and the principles of computing.

Use of the computer involves several steps, including

1. Analysis of the problem.
2. Designing of an algorithm.
3. Drawing of a flow chart.
4. Writing of the program.
5. Preparation of the program and data.
6. Translation of the program to machine language.
7. Execution of the program.
8. Debugging and testing.

IBM

IBM System/360 Assembler Coding Form

GX28-6509-6 U/M 050
Printed in U.S.A.

| PROGRAM | | PUNCHING | GRAPHIC | | PAGE | OF |
| PROGRAMMER | DATE | INSTRUCTIONS | PUNCH | | CARD ELECTRO NUMBER | |

```
Name      Operation   Operand                                        Comments                        Identification-Sequence
1    8  10      14 16        20      25      30      35      40      45      50    55      60    65      71  73        80

STEPØNE  STM 14,12,12(13)  THIS IS A CØMMENT
         L SIX,NUMBER1   SØ IS THIS
ØUTDCB DCB DDNAME=SYSPRINT,MACRF=GL,RECFM=F  INPVT DCB
GØTIGERS START O PRGRAM BEGINNING
*  THIS STATEMENT IS A COMMENT
*  REWRITE THE STATEMENTS ABOVE ALIGNING THE FIELDS
*  IN COLS. 1, 10, 16, AND 30 AND SEE THE DIFFERENCE
```

Fig. 3-5.

* A standard card form, IBM electro 6509, is available for punching source statements from this form.
Instructions for using this form are in any IBM System/360 assembler language reference manual.
Address comments concerning this form to IBM Nordic Laboratory, Publications Development,
Box 962, S-181 09 Lidingö 9, Sweden.

*No. of forms per pad may vary slightly.

The *assembly language statement* consists of four fields, the *name, operation, operands,* and *comments* field in that order. The various fields are separated by one or more blank characters.

EXERCISES

1. Using only Load and Store instructions, four instructions are necessary to interchange the contents of two words in the memory. Write the necessary instructions to interchange a word stored at NUM1 with a word stored at NUM2.

2. Draw a flow chart for a program that will read a series of cards and find the largest number that was punched on them.

3. Suppose that you just bought a bank and decided to computerize your accounting system. Discuss in as much detail as you can how you would go about doing this, keeping in mind the problem-solving steps in Section 3.2.

4. The valid assembly language mnemonics are listed in Appendix E. Suppose that SPRING, TIME, IN, and PARIS are names used as addresses in a program. Which of the following are valid assembler language statements? For those which are in error, state what is wrong.

STEP1	LA	5,SPRING
2STEP	MVC	IN,TIME
	L	6,TI ME
LOCO	ADD	7,PARIS
RIGHT	MV C	TIME,IN
WRONG	CLC	SPRING,TIME
WHOOPS!	L	10,IN
THE END	A	7,PARIS

REFERENCES

CHAPIN, NED, *Computers: A Systems Approach*, Van Nostrand Reinhold Company, New York, 1972.

DORF, RICHARD C., *Computers and Computer Science*, Boyd & Fraser Publishing Company, San Francisco, 1972.

IBM System/360 Operating System Assembler F Programmer's Guide, Form GC26-3756, IBM Corp., White Plains, N.Y.

IBM System/360 Operating System Assembler Language, Form GC28-6514, IBM Corp., White Plains, N.Y.

IBM System/360 Operating System Data Management Services, Form GC26-3746, IBM Corp., White Plains, N.Y.

IBM System/360 Operating System Supervisor and Data Management Macro Instructions, Form GC28-6647, IBM Corp., White Plains, N.Y.

IBM System/360 Operating System Supervisor Services, Form GC28-6646, IBM Corp., White Plains, N.Y.

IBM System/360 Principles of Operation, Form GA22-6821, IBM Corp., White Plains, N.Y.

IBM System/370 Principles of Operation, Form GA22-7000, IBM Corp., White Plains, N.Y.

IBM System/360 Reference Data, Form GX20-1703, IBM Corp., White Plains, N.Y.

LEEDS, H. D. and G. M. WEINBERG, *Computer Programming Fundamentals*, Mc-Graw-Hill Book Company, New York, 1966.

SIEGEL, PAUL, *Understanding Digital Computers*, John Wiley & Sons, Inc., New York, 1971.

WALKER, TERRY M., *Introduction to Computer Science: An Interdisciplinary Approach*, Allyn & Bacon, Inc., Boston, 1972.

4 USING THE REGISTERS

Now we shall begin our study of the IBM System/360 Assembler Language. Section 4.1 is devoted to some preliminary considerations that will facilitate our study throughout the remainder of the text. We shall investigate two methods for classifying assembly language instructions, develop a notation that will help us to describe individual instructions, and find out what happens when we misuse an instruction.

Many of the computational procedures in a program can be done without reference to the computer memory at all. We use the arithmetic and storage capabilities of the general-purpose registers in such calculations. Because of this and because of the importance of attaining a good understanding of how to use the registers, the rest of this chapter and part of Chapter 5 is devoted to a discussion of register-oriented instructions. You may find the treatment a little tedious at times, but we must develop a basic working vocabulary of instructions before we can begin writing programs. So, with patience the key word, let us begin.

4.1. PRELIMINARY CONSIDERATIONS

4.1.1. Instruction Type

We have seen that a machine instruction consists of two parts, the operation field and the operands field. There are actually three possible operand types in the 360. An operand can be contained in a general-purpose register, the memory, or the actual numerical value of an operand can be included in the instruction itself. The latter operand type is called an *immediate operand*. These operand types may be used in various combinations to yield a total of five *instruction types*. Each different instruction type corresponds to a machine language instruction *format*. The type of an instruction is determined by the types of its operands. Thus, we have the following instruction types, with their standard abbreviations enclosed in parentheses:

Register to Register (RR): Both operands are in general-purpose registers.

Register to IndeXed Storage (RX): The first operand is a general purpose register, the second is a memory location which may be addressed with the aid of an index register.

Register to Storage (RS): The first two operands are in registers, and the third in main storage.

Storage to Storage (SS): Both operands are in main storage.

Storage Immediate (SI): The first operand is in main storage, while the second is an immediate operand.

4.1.2. Instruction Function

The instruction type classifies the instruction from a mechanical point of view; the type of an instruction depends on the type of its operands and informs the programmer as to how to write the instruction and specify its operands. Another useful way to classify instructions is by *instruction function*, which furnishes the programmer with a general description of what the instruction does. We classify instructions by function according to the following five general categories:

Information Move Instructions: Instructions in this category move information from one area in the computer to another. For example, the MVC instruction moves the contents of memory areas from one set of addresses to another, while the LR instruction moves the contents of one register to another.

Arithmetic Instructions: These are the "working" instructions that modify the information being processed. Arithmetic instructions include such operations as "add" and "multiply"; the logical operations, such as "and" and "or"; and some special instructions to convert data from one form to another.

Comparison Instructions: It is often necessary to compare two information units with each other without changing either one. For example, we can determine whether or not the contents of register 3 are less than the contents of register 10 using an RR comparison instruction.

Transfer of Control Instructions: These include the unconditional and conditional branch instructions which allow modification of the order of execution of the instructions in the program. For example, we might use a conditional branch instruction to branch to a desired location if the result of a preceding addition instruction was negative.

Input/Output Instructions: These instructions control the input/output devices and direct the flow of information to and from them.

In deciding which of the instructions from the 360 instruction repertoire to use to accomplish a given task, the programmer narrows down the possible choices by determining the instruction type and function. The nature and locations of the operands determine the instruction type, while the desired operation determines the instruction function. In many cases this classification enables the programmer to choose the exact instruction he needs. In other instances, he may have to make a further decision, such as the kind of arithmetic he wishes to do. In any event, use of the classification schemes outlined above is a big help in programming in assembly language.

In the next several chapters, we shall examine each of the instruction types in turn. We shall demonstrate some of the typical uses of each type of instruction and consider their machine language forms in detail. Once we have covered all five instruction types in this manner, we shall be in a position to apply these basic principles to some of the more specialized aspects of assembly language programming.

4.1.3. Symbolic Description of Instructions

Throughout this text we shall use a symbolic notation to portray the effects of the instructions under investigation. We shall present additional facilities of this notation as we need them. For now, let us agree that all register operands will be represented by the letter R followed by a digit which specifies which operand we are talking about. For example, the symbol R2 represents any of the general-purpose registers numbered 0 through 15, and the chosen register is the second operand in the given instruction. Remember that we designate symbolically the contents of a given register or memory location by placing its address inside parentheses. Thus, (5) means either the contents of register 5 or of memory location 5. Whether the address represents a register number or a memory address will be made clear in the discussion.

Let us use an arrow ($\leftarrow$) to represent the operation *store*. Putting all this together, we would represent symbolically the effect of the AR instruction as

$$R1 \leftarrow (R1) + (R2)$$

which we would state verbally as "The contents of the register operand specified first are added to the contents of the register operand specified second and the results are stored in the first operand register." We draw the arrow pointing to the left because in most cases this is the actual direction of the flow of information. The result of the operation is usually stored at the address given as the first operand, which is written first in the operands field.

4.1.4. Program Exceptions

We naturally emphasize what occurs when instructions are written properly and executed normally. However, times arise in programming when, due to an error on our part, the execution of an instruction is attempted which is impossible to complete or, if completed, leads to meaningless results. For example we have seen that the addition of two large numbers may result in an overflow condition, the result of which is usually a number which is meaningless as a sum of two numbers.

Such errors, which are really requests of the computer to do things it was not designed to do, are called program *exceptions*. An exception usually leads to termination of the program execution together with the output of a code which gives us some indication as to why the system stopped executing our program. We shall cover the use of these codes in Chapter 12; for now we shall simply point out those instances in which they might occur.

4.2. REGISTER-TO-REGISTER INSTRUCTIONS

The registers play an indispensable role in programming. We have seen that the registers function as accumulators in binary integer arithmetic. Because of their relatively high speed in information transfer, they are used for temporary storage of numbers that are frequently used and/or changed in a program. We often use the registers to hold the loop counters necessary for control of repetitive operations. The computer uses the registers to compute memory addresses, as we shall see in Chapter 8. Every useful program uses registers for at least one of these purposes.

In the preceding section we saw that in the register-to-register instructions both operands are in general-purpose registers. Each of the 16 registers contains a *full word*, or 32 binary digits. In most cases, the full word is treated as if it were a single 32-bit binary integer. When the negative of a register's contents is calculated, the result is the 32-bit 2's complement of the original register contents. Similarly, in the register-to-register addition instruction, the addends are the 32-bit numbers contained in the registers specified as operands; the result is a 32-bit binary integer.

We have seen that the hexadecimal number system affords a compact means of specifying long binary numbers. Remember that, unless otherwise stated, all machine-oriented quantities, such as machine language instructions and register and memory contents, will be written in hexadecimal.

On the other hand, the assembler relieves the programmer of the responsibility of translating desired numbers to their hexadecimal equivalents. The assembler assumes that a number in an assembly language statement is a decimal number unless otherwise specified. For example, if we want to use register 14 as an assembly language operand, we write 14. If we wish to specify the same register as an operand in a machine language instruction, we write E. Similarly, if a register contains decimal 50, we designate its contents as its full-word eight-digit hexadecimal equivalent, 00000032.

With these thoughts in mind, let us now investigate the RR information move instructions.

4.2.1. Information Move Instructions

The most important of the RR information move instructions is the Load Register (LR) instruction, which we describe as follows:

Operation	Operands	Name	Effect
LR	R1,R2	Load Register	R1 ⟵ (R2)

The above is an example of how we shall summarize new instructions as we encounter them. The first column gives the mnemonic for the operation and the second shows the operands in the symbolic notation. In the third column we find the name of the instruction, while the last column indicates the effect of execution of the instruction.

The LR instruction simply moves the contents of the second register operand into the first register operand. From a more fundamental point of view, the effect of the LR is to *fetch* the contents of the second register operand, leaving them the same as before execution of the instruction, and to *store* the number thus obtained in the first register, erasing its original contents.

Suppose that we have the register contents

$$(5) = 00000170$$
$$(10) = FFFFFFE0$$

Suppose that we want to move the contents of register 10 into register 5 using the LR instruction. Looking at the symbolic description of the effect of the LR instruction, it is apparent that we should use register 5 as the first operand, R1, and register 10 as the second operand, R2. Thus, we write

$$LR \qquad 5,10$$

to accomplish our purpose. Execution of this instruction produces

$$(5) = FFFFFFE0$$
$$(10) = FFFFFFE0$$

On the other hand, if we write

$$LR \qquad 10,5$$

we would have

$$(5) = 00000170$$
$$(10) = 00000170$$

after execution of the instruction. The LR instruction simply copies the contents of the second operand register into the first operand register.

In addition to the LR instruction, there are several register-to-register information move instructions which modify the second register contents before putting them into the first register. Using these instructions it is possible to move the complement, the absolute value, or the negative of the absolute value of the contents of the second-named register into the first register. We shall now examine each of these instructions in turn.

LCR   R1,R2   Load Complement Register   R1 ◄—— —(R2)

The Load Complement Register instruction computes the binary 2's complement of the contents of the second operand and places the result in the first-named register. The arithmetic effect is to move the negative of the second operand contents into the first operand. Thus, if

$$(5) = 0000000A$$
$$(7) = 36B42975$$

before execution of the instruction

LCR   7,5

then after the execution of this instruction we have (check this)

$$(5) = 0000000A$$
$$(7) = FFFFFFF6$$

In effect, LCR *fetches* the contents of the second register, computes its *2's complement*, and *stores* the result in the first register. To move the negative of the contents of register 13 into register 1, we write

LCR   1,13

LPR   R1,R2   Load Positive Register   R1 ◄— |(R2)|

The Load Positive Register instruction moves the magnitude or absolute value of the contents of the second operand into the first register operand. Thus, if the second register contains a positive number, the LPR instruction moves the number *as is* into the first register. On the other hand, if R2 contains a negative number, the 2's complement of (R2) moves into R1.

Supposing we have

$$(6) = 00011A6C$$
$$(8) = FFFFFFE3$$

then after

LPR   8,6

we have

$$(6) = 00011A6C$$
$$(8) = 00011A6C$$

which is as if we had written

LR   8,6

However, if we write

LPR   6,8

instead, the result is

$$(6) = 0000001D$$
$$(8) = FFFFFFE3$$

which is the result we obtain if we write

LCR   6,8

In other words, LPR has the effect of the LR instruction when the second register contents are positive and that of the LCR instruction when (R2) is negative.

LNR	R1,R2	Load Negative Register	R1 ⟵ − |(R2)|

The Load Negative Register instruction moves the negative of the magnitude of the contents of the second register operand into the first register. If, before execution of the instruction

LNR   5,2

the register contents are

$$(2) = 00000100$$
$$(5) = FFFFFC63$$

then after execution of the instruction

$$(2) = 00000100$$
$$(5) = FFFFFF00$$

The negative of the magnitude of (2) is moved to register 5.

The information move instructions discussed above move words from one register to another. But how did the register contents get there to start with? There are several possible means of loading registers with initial values for later manipulation. One way is through input operations, which we shall study in Section 4.3. Another means is through the use of an information move instruction which can move a word from the memory into a register.

To load a register R1 with the binary equivalent of a decimal number d

we write

L   R1,=F'd'

This is a special case of the use of the Load instruction, which we shall investigate in more detail when we study instructions of the RX type. The effect of the above instruction is to cause the assembler to store the binary equivalent of decimal *d* into a word in the program. When the program is executed, this word will be moved into the register designated as R1 upon execution of the instruction. We call an operand such as =F'1' a *literal*. A literal of this form causes a full word to be stored in the memory ready to be used at execution time. If we write in our program

L   3,=F'1'

the result upon execution of the instruction is

$$(3) = 00000001$$

4.2.2. Binary Integer Arithmetic

Having seen how full words, possibly modified by complementing, can be moved around among the registers, we now turn to the register-to-register arithmetic instructions. There are four of these—AR, SR, MR, and DR—which perform the binary integer arithmetic operations of addition, subtraction, multiplication, and division, respectively.

In each of these instructions, the *first operand register functions as an accumulator*: It indicates where one of the two original arithmetic operands before execution of the instruction is to be found and contains all or part of the answer after the instruction is executed. The second operand contents are not affected by execution of these instructions.

AR	R1,R2	Add Register	R1 $\longleftarrow$ (R1) + (R2)

The Add Register instruction computes the sum of the contents of the two specified registers and places the result in the first register. The contents of R2 are left the same as before execution of the instruction. Suppose that we have

$$(5) = 00000023$$
$$(8) = 00000016$$

and the instruction

AR   5,8

is executed. The result is

$$(8) = 00000016 \quad \text{(unchanged)}$$
$$(5) = 00000023 + 00000016 = 00000039$$

Original Register Contents	Instruction		Final Register Contents
(3) = 00000010 (4) = 00000005	AR	4,3	(3) = 00000010 (4) = 00000015
(10) = 00016032 (12) = FFFFFFE2	AR	10,12	(10) = 00016014 (12) = FFFFFFE2
(0) = FFFFFFF5 (2) = FFFFFFF6	AR	2,0	(0) = FFFFFFF5 (2) = FFFFFFFB

Fig. 4-1. The AR instruction.

Figure 4-1 shows some more examples of the effect of the AR instruction. Thus, to compute the sum of two numbers contained in registers, we use the AR instruction with the desired registers as operands, with the register in which we wish the answer to appear written first.

To double the contents of a register, we simply specify the desired register in both operand positions. The instruction

AR   7,7

in effect multiplies the contents of register 7 by 2.

We have seen that when the addends are so large that their sum does not fit into a full word, an overflow condition is the result. This can lead to a machine exception called a *fixed-point exception*.

SR	R1,R2	Subtract Register	R1 ⟵ (R1) − (R2)

In the Subtract Register instruction, the difference between the contents of the first register operand and the contents of the second register operand replaces the original contents of the first register operand, leaving the contents of the second register unchanged. Notice that the order of specification of the operands determines which number is subtracted from which and that the usual sign rules are obeyed.

For example, if we start with

(5) = 00000006
(7) = 00000020

then the instruction

SR   7,5

leaves as a result

(5) = 00000006
(7) = 0000001A

Original Register Contents	Instruction		Final Register Contents
(5) = FFFFFFF6 (7) = 00000020	SR	5,7	(5) = FFFFFFD6 (7) = 00000020
(4) = 00000030 (6) = 00000007	SR	4,6	(4) = 00000029 (6) = 00000007
(10) = FFFFFF72 (3) = FFFFFF31	SR	10,3	(10) = 00000041 (3) = FFFFFF31

Fig, 4-2. The SR instruction.

Figure 4-2 shows some more examples of the effect of the SR instruction.

When we subtract the contents of a register from itself, the result is 0 in that register, regardless of what the original register contents were. The instruction

$$SR \qquad 8,8$$

results in

$$(8) = 00000000$$

The subtract instruction complements the contents of the second-named register and sends the result to the adder. The contents of the first register are added and the sum moved from the adder back to the first register.

An overflow condition can result in the addition portion of the SR instruction in the same manner as it does in the execution of the AR instruction. The result is again a fixed-point exception.

MR   R1,R2   Multiply Register   R1,R1+1 ←— (R1+1) × (R2)

We have already commented on the fact that in multiplication of two integers the length of the resulting product may be as long as the sum of the lengths of the operands. The computer design must take this fact into account by providing two words to hold the product that results from multiplying the contents of two full words together.

The MR instruction leaves results in two registers, which should be considered as linked together so as to form a single 64-bit binary integer. The registers that contain the final product are R1, the first register operand, and the next register after R1, which we designate by R1+1. Note that R1+1 means one register beyond R1, *not* (R1)+1. If R1 is register 4, then R1+1 is register 5. In the symbolic notation, we indicate that two registers are to be considered connected so as to form a *double word* by writing their register numbers separated by a comma, as in R1,R1+1.

The first operand in the MR instruction must be an *even-numbered regis-*

ter; otherwise a *specification exception* results. The actual multiplicands are contained in registers R1+1 and R2. In the event that the product fits into one register, it is in R1+1 after execution of the instruction, while R1 contains 00000000 if the product is positive or FFFFFFFF if the product is negative. This is what we would expect if we follow the sign convention for 2's complement arithmetic. The MR instruction changes the original contents of R1, even though the use of R1 was not necessary to contain the entire product.

Suppose that we wish to calculate the product of the contents of registers 7 and 10. In view of the above comments, since R1 must be an even-numbered register, one of the multiplicands must be in an odd-numbered register. Since we have register 7 as an operand, we decide that the first register operand should be register 6. We should write

$$\text{MR} \qquad 6,10$$

Now suppose that we have

$$(6) = 0126C349$$
$$(7) = 00000021$$
$$(10) = 00000003$$

before execution of the instruction. Then the MR instruction above produces

$$(6) = 00000000$$
$$(7) = 00000063$$
$$(10) = 00000003$$

Considering registers 6 and 7 as forming a single integer, we see that the double-word representation of the product is

$$00000000 \; 00000063$$

as expected.

Supposing instead that we have originally

$$(6) = 0126C349$$
$$(7) = FFFFFFDF$$
$$(10) = 00000003$$

then after execution of

$$\text{MR} \qquad 6,10$$

we have

$$(6) = FFFFFFFF$$
$$(7) = FFFFFF9D$$
$$(10) = 00000003$$

The product is thus

FFFFFFFF FFFFF9D

which is the double-word 2's complement representation of -63_{16}. Figure 4-3 shows some further examples of the effect of the MR instruction.

Initial Register Contents	Instruction		Final Register Contents
(11) = 0000003A	MR	12,11	(11) = 0000003A
(12) = FFFFF68C			(12) = 00000000
(13) = 00000007			(13) = 00000196
(2) = 0000000C	MR	2,7	(2) = FFFFFFFF
(3) = 000000C0			(3) = FFFFFFD0
(7) = FFFFFFFC			(7) = FFFFFFFC
(5) = 00002000	MR	8,5	(5) = 00002000
(8) = 00300001			(8) = 00000006
(9) = 9FFFFFFF			(9) = 00002000

Fig. 4-3. The MR instruction.

In most applications, use of MR leads to a product which fits entirely in register R1+1. The use of such products in further calculations is easy; R1+1 contains a full-word binary integer which can be treated as though it arose from any other computation. However, if two words are indeed necessary to contain the product, then the ensuing program logic must take this fact into account.

DR	R1,R2	<u>D</u>ivide <u>R</u>egister	(R1,R1+1) ÷ (R2):
			R1 ←— remainder
			R1+1 ←— quotient

Just as the MR instruction provides for a double-length product, the DR instruction allows for the fact that division of a number that requires a double word to contain it may result in a quotient that fits into a single word. The dividend is a 64-bit binary integer contained in registers R1 and R1+1. The divisor is in the second register operand. The quotient appears in R1+1 and the remainder in register R1 after execution of the instruction. R1, the first register operand, must again be an *even-numbered register*. Otherwise, the result is a specification exception upon attempted execution of the instruction.

We should view the operation of the DR instruction as obeying the formula

$$\text{dividend} = \text{divisor} \times \text{quotient} + \text{remainder}$$

Dividing this equation through by the divisor results in the equation we are perhaps more accustomed to using. However, use of the above permits specifying all quantities as integers, as we must do in using integer arithmetic. The sign of the quotient is the algebraic sign resulting from division as usual; the quotient is positive if the dividend and divisor have the same sign; otherwise the quotient is negative. The remainder always has the same sign as the dividend. Let us consider an example:

$$(2) = FFFFFFFF$$
$$(3) = FFFFF100$$
$$(9) = 00000007$$

The instruction we shall consider is

$$DR \qquad 2,9$$

The dividend is the double word

$$FFFFFFFF \ FFFFF100$$

formed by concatenating registers 2 and 3, with the value $-F00_{16} = -3840_{10}$ This number is divided by the divisor, which is 00000007, as contained in register 9. The result is (check this) a quotient of -224_{16} with a remainder of -4. The remainder goes to R1 (register 2) and the quotient to R1+1 (register 3). This means that after execution of the DR instruction we have

$$(2) = 00000004$$
$$(3) = FFFFFDDC$$
$$(9) = 00000007$$

Figure 4-4 shows some further examples of the DR instruction.

A special kind of error condition can arise through misuse of the integer division instructions. When the quotient is too long to fit into a 32-bit full

Initial Register Contents	Instruction		Final Register Contents
(0) = 00000000 (1) = 00000040 (12) = 00000005	DR	0,12	(0) = 00000004 (1) = 0000000C (12) = 00000005
(8) = FFFFFFFF (9) = FFFFFF65 (3) = 0000000C	DR	8,3	(8) = FFFFFFF5 (9) = FFFFFFF4 (3) = 0000000C
(6) = 00369C36 (7) = 000CC935 (11) = 03000000	DR	6,11	(6) = 000CC935 (7) = 12341200 (11) = 03000000

Fig. 4-4. The DR instruction.

word, the result is a *fixed-point divide exception*, which normally causes termination of the execution of the program. Suppose that the register contents are

$$(2) = 00000006$$
$$(3) = 00000000$$
$$(6) = 00000003$$

and the instruction

DR   2,6

is attempted. The quotient

$$200000000$$

requires 34 bits to specify it, too many to fit in the 32 bits permitted in a general-purpose register, in this case register 3. Under usual circumstances, the results of the division would be meaningless for further arithmetic computations. The machine indicates this fact by terminating execution of the program, giving the programmer an indication as to what the error was.

In most programming applications, we rarely need to use two registers to contain the dividend; numbers of the size we usually deal with fit readily into a single full word. However, the DR instruction uses a double-word dividend, whether necessary for our application or not. In such cases it is necessary to prepare for the division by making sure that the first register of the first operand register pair contains a number that will give us the correct result in the division, while the second register of the pair must contain the desired dividend. Suppose that we have

$$(5) = 00000050$$

and we wish to divide this number by (7). The instruction we use is

DR   4,7

provided that we do not need the contents of register 4 for other purposes. Suppose that

$$(4) = 00200000$$

Then the effective dividend is

$$(4,5) = 00200000 \ 00000050$$

The results will certainly not be correct, since the dividend used is a very large positive number, not 50_{16} as desired. Thus, we must move a 0 into register 4 before using the DR instruction.

On the other hand, suppose that

$$(5) = FFFFFFE0$$

a negative number. At first thought, we might move a 0 into register 4 before dividing. This would mean an effective dividend of

$$(4,5) = 00000000 \text{ FFFFFFE0}$$

which, considered as a single 64-bit number, is a large positive number, and we would again get the wrong result. Instead, we should move FFFFFFFF into register 4 before dividing. This gives us

$$(4,5) = \text{FFFFFFFF FFFFFFE0}$$

which behaves properly as the small negative number we wish to use as the dividend.

What we really need to do when the actual dividend fits in a single register is

1. Make sure that the dividend is in an odd numbered register, and
2. Make a copy of the sign bit of the dividend throughout the preceding register.

Step 1 ensures that we shall be able to use an even-numbered register, while step 2 provides for the computer's demand to use a register *pair* for the dividend.

Figure 4-5 shows an example of one way to accomplish these objectives in which we want to divide the number originally in register 4 by the contents of register 9. We first move (4) to an odd-numbered register, arbitrarily chosen as register 7 (in most instances our choice of registers would be restricted by the designation of various registers for other purposes). We then load register 8 with 00000001 to prepare for the next instruction which multiplies (7) by (8). The MR instruction accomplishes step 2 above so that we are finally ready for the division instruction.

The use of MR in this way is not very good programming practice in that it is inefficient and uses an extra register. In preparing for an integer division, we usually test the sign of the dividend and load the preceding even-numbered register with 0 if the dividend is positive and with FFFFFFFF if it is negative. We shall see how to do this in Chapter 5.

```
LR    7,4       MOVE (4) TO AN ODD-NUMBERED REGISTER
L     8,=F'1'   PUT THE NUMBER 1 IN REG. 8
MR    6,8       MULTIPLY (7) BY 1 TO BE SURE (6) WILL
DR    6,9       BE CK FOR THE DIVIDE INSTRUCTION
```

Fig. 4-5. Division of (4) by (9).

4.3. INPUT/OUTPUT; RWD AND WWD

The details of input/output processing and data conversion are too complex for us to tackle now. For the time being, we shall use a pair of special instructions, RWD and WWD, for input/output until we have learned some more about the fundamentals of assembly language programming.

RWD and WWD are examples of *macro-instructions*; they are *not* true assembly language instructions. A macro-instruction, or *macro* for short, is a series of instructions which can be inserted into a program at any desired point simply by using the macro *name* in the operation field of an assembly language statement. The effect is to replace that statement with the series of instructions that the macro represents. We shall see how to write macros in Chapter 18.

The software support that comes with an IBM system includes a large number of macros that help relieve the programmer of much of the responsibility for many bookkeeping chores required of him by the operating system. RWD and WWD are written for the same purpose as are the IBM-supplied macros, but they are not standard IBM macros. Therefore, your instructor has probably taken the proper steps to make it possible for you to use these macros in your programs. However, the odds are that computer installations other than the one you use in this course will not have these macros as part of their system. If such is the case and you wish to continue using RWD, WWD, and the other special macros prepared for this course, your instructor can help you install them in other systems.

RWD	R1	Read WorD	Number from data card $\longrightarrow$ R1

The Read WorD macro-instruction converts a decimal integer that was punched on a data card to a 32-bit binary integer and places the result into the register R1. The number on the data card is in what we might call *free format* in that the number can appear anywhere on the card, may be positive or negative, and may have any value between -2147483648 and 2147483647, which are the smallest and largest integers respectively, that fit into a 32-bit full word. A number to be read by RWD must not contain any embedded commas, blanks, decimal points, or other nondigit characters and may be preceded by a $+$ or $-$ sign. This means that

$$20$$
$$-30$$

and

$$+123456789$$

are valid numbers to be punched on data cards and read using RWD, while

$$1,000$$
$$-33.2$$
$$\$68.32$$

and

$$43\ 896$$

are invalid and result in errors if an attempt is made to read them.

RWD reads one card each time it is executed, which means there must be only one number punched per data card. Once a card has been read, it cannot be read again; a series of five consecutive RWD executions reads five data cards in the order in which they occur.

Thus, if we have

$$-30$$

punched on a data card and execute

$$\text{RWD} \qquad 5$$

the result is

$$(5) = \text{FFFFFFD0}$$

immediately after execution of the RWD macro. If we have data cards with

$$-3$$
$$39$$
$$257$$

punched on them, then execution of

$$\text{RWD} \qquad 6$$
$$\text{RWD} \qquad 10$$
$$\text{RWD} \qquad 12$$

produces register contents

$$(6) = \text{FFFFFFFD}$$
$$(10) = 0000002\,7$$
$$(12) = 000001\,0\,1$$

WWD	R1	Write WorD	Print (R1)

The output macro-instruction complementary to RWD is WWD, which converts the binary integer contained in R1 to decimal and prints the result, including a minus sign if the original number was negative. The contents of R1 are unaffected by the WWD instruction.

If

$$(2) = 00000040$$
$$(6) = \text{FFFFFF6C}$$
$$(7) = 00000100$$

then the instructions

$$\text{WWD} \qquad 2$$
$$\text{WWD} \qquad 7$$
$$\text{WWD} \qquad 6$$

result in the printed output

$$64$$
$$256$$
$$-148$$

appearing in the order shown, one number per line.

CHAPTER SUMMARY

Machine instructions can be classifed by *instruction type*,

RR: Register to register
RX: Register to indexed storage
RS: Register to storage
SS: Storage to storage
SI: Storage immediate

and by *instruction function*,

Information move
Arithmetic
Comparison
Transfer of control
Input/output

Table 4-1 shows the instructions discussed in this chapter.

Table 4-1 INSTRUCTIONS DISCUSSED IN CHAPTER 4

Mneumonic	Operands	Name	Effect
LR	R1,R2	Load Register	R1 ← (R2)
LCR	R1,R2	Load Complement Register	R1 ← −(R2)
LPR	R1,R2	Load Positive Register	R1 ← |(R2)|
LNR	R1,R2	Load Negative Register	R1 ← −|(R2)|
L	R1,=F'd'	Load (literal operand)	R1 ← d
AR	R1,R2	Add Register	R1 ← (R1) + (R2)
SR	R1,R2	Subtract Register	R1 ← (R1) − (R2)
MR	R1,R2	Multiply Register	R1,R1+1 ← (R1+1) × (R2)
DR	R1,R2	Divide Register	(R1,R1+1) ÷ (R2): quotient ⟶ R1+1 remainder ⟶ R1
RWD	R1	Read WorD (macro)	Number from data card ⟶ R1
WWD	R1	Write WorD (macro)	(R1) ⟶ printer

EXERCISES

1. Define the following:
   (a) Instruction type.   (b) Instruction function.   (c) Exception.
   (d) Full word.   (e) Literal.   (f) Macro-instruction.

2. Write the instructions necessary to compute the following:
   (a) The sum of (3), (4), (5), and (6).
   (b) The average of (7), (8), (9), and (10).

   (c) (4) × (5).   (d) (5)².   (e) $\dfrac{(4) + (5)}{(4) + (5)}$.   (f) 7 × (4) − 3 × (2).

3. Write the instructions necessary to read five numbers from data cards, compute their average, and print their result.

4. Write the instructions necessary to read two numbers from data cards, divide the second into the first, and print the quotient and remainder.

REFERENCES

IBM System/360 Principles of Operation, Form GA22-6821, IBM Corp., White Plains, N.Y.

IBM System/370 Principles of Operation, Form GA22-7000, IBM Corp., White Plains, N.Y.

5 PROGRAM AND JOB STRUCTURE

In the preceding chapter we introduced some working instructions—information move and arithmetic instructions and input/output macros—that allow us to compute with information input into the program and output the results. We shall now introduce the transfer of control, or branch, instructions, which make possible the modification of the order of execution of the list of instructions that constitutes a program. We shall see that the branch instructions enable us to make full use of one of the real powers of a computer—the ability to mindlessly carry out repetitive calculations with large amounts of data. Then we shall investigate those statements necessary to direct the assembler in its processing of our symbolic programs.

We shall introduce the operating system and discuss the job control language necessary to have the operating system process our programs as we wish. A discussion of the programmer's responsibilities in program documentation concludes the chapter.

When you have mastered the material in this chapter, you will be able to write complete programs and submit them to your computer center for processing. I shall suggest some programming projects in the exercises, or you may wish to dream up your own.

5.1. PROGRAM STRUCTURE

By program structure, we mean the statements necessary to form a complete program and the statements within the program which control the order of execution of its instructions. Let us consider the second of these types of statements first to answer the question, "How can we control the order of the execution of the instructions in a program?"

5.1.1. Transfer of Control

The normal order of execution of program instructions is the order in which they appear. The programmer must be careful to write the instructions in a program in exactly the order he wishes to have them executed. Misplacement of one instruction in a sequence can have disastrous consequences insofar as the calculations are concerned. For example, the instructions

LR	3,5
LR	5,4
LR	4,3

interchange the contents of registers 4 and 5. These three instructions in any other order will not have the desired effect (try it).

But there are many instances in which we wish to have the instructions executed in some order other than that in which they are written. Suppose, for example, that we wish to compute the sum of a series of five numbers that are punched on data cards. Figure 5-1 shows one way to go about this, in

```
SR     5,5      CLEAR REGISTER 5 TO ZERO
RWD    2        READ FIRST NUMBER FROM DATA CARD
AR     5,2      ADD IT TO (5)
RWD    2        READ SECOND NUMBER
AR     5,2      ADD IT TO (5)
RWD    2        READ THIRD NUMBER
AR     5,2      ADD IT
RWD    2        READ FOURTH NUMBER
AR     5,2      AND ADD IT
RWD    2        READ LAST NUMBER
AR     5,2      ADD IT TO THE SUM AND
WWD    5        PRINT THE FINAL TOTAL
```

Fig. 5-1. One way to compute the sum of five numbers punched on data cards.

which register 5 is used to contain a running sum of numbers read into register 2 via the RWD instruction. There is nothing inherently wrong with this technique, provided we are willing to spend the time to punch the program cards and have computer memory space to spare. But what if we want to compute the sum of 100 numbers?

What we need to do is include an RWD and an AR instruction in a *loop*, so that these instructions are executed repeatedly as the CPU cycles through the instructions in the loop. Figure 5-2 shows a flow chart for a second attempt at this problem. After reading the first number and adding it to SUM we *branch* back to the instruction that reads another card. This is an *unconditional* branch; the transfer of control occurs no matter what the circumstances.

B	S2	Branch (unconditional)	PC ⟵ S2

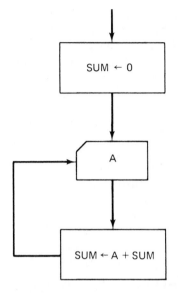

Fig. 5-2. A flowchart for a loop that computes the sum of a series of numbers punched on data cards.

In the description of the Branch instruction above we show the single operand as S (meaning storage) with a 2 following it. We do this because, as we shall soon see, the operand is really the second operand insofar as the machine is concerned. The operand S2 is usually the symbolic name of the instruction to which we want the CPU to branch. Thus, if we wish to branch to the statement named AGAIN, we write

B   AGAIN

The effect of this instruction when executed is to move the memory address corresponding to the name AGAIN into the program counter. After the branch instruction is executed, execution resumes at the statement labeled AGAIN.

Figure 5-3 shows a program segment corresponding to the flow chart of Fig. 5-2. Here we have made the identifications

$$\text{SUM} \longleftrightarrow \text{register 5}$$
$$\text{A} \longleftrightarrow \text{register 2}$$

Notice that we have solved the problem of how to have the computer execute instructions in a loop repeatedly; now we must find out how to stop it.

```
           SR      5,5        START SUM AT 0
NEWNUM     RWD     2          READ NEXT NUMBER
           AR      5,2        ADD IT TO SUM
           B       NEWNUM     GO BACK FOR MORE
```

Fig. 5-3. A loop to compute the sum of a series of numbers punched on data cards.

We can have the machine branch to a given location or not, depending on the results of preceding calculations, by using a *conditional branch* instruction. The conditional branch instructions examine an indicator called the *condition code*, and branch if the condition-code value matches the value designated by the branch instruction.

For example, the result of an AR instruction can be zero, negative, positive, or an overflow (which we shall ignore for now). Execution of an AR instruction sets the condition code to indicate which of these possibilities actually occurred. Thus, if the register contents are

$$(3) = \text{FFFFFFF0}$$
$$(5) = 00000002$$

the instruction

AR 3,5

sets the condition code to indicate that the result of the addition is negative. Of the instructions we have described thus far, SR and RWD also set the condition code depending on whether the computed difference or the number read, respectively, was positive, negative, or zero. LNR, LCR, and LPR set the condition code depending upon the number moved.

The condition code maintains its value throughout execution of the program until another instruction that sets it is executed. Given the register contents above, the condition code would remain as indicating a positive result when the machine began executing the instruction named BOT and also the one named TOP (somewhere else in the program) in the following instruction sequence:

	SR	5,3
	LR	4,6
	MR	4,3
BOT	B	TOP

The conditional branch instructions send the address to which to branch to the program counter only if the condition code matches the condition that is indicated in the branch instruction. Otherwise, the program counter is left unchanged. Since the program counter contains the address of the next instruction in the memory if unaltered by a branch instruction, execution continues with the next instruction in sequence if the condition in a conditional branch instruction is not satisfied.

For now, we shall be content to investigate six conditional branch instructions. Chapter 9 contains a complete discussion of the branching facilities of the system.

BP	S2	Branch on Plus	PC ⟵ S2 if result > 0

In the description of these instructions, the word *result* means the result upon execution of the last instruction that sets the condition code. The Branch on Plus instruction branches to the instruction whose name appears as S2 if this result was strictly greater than zero.

| BZ | S2 | Branch on Zero | PC ←— S2 if result $= 0$ |

The Branch on Zero instruction branches to the instruction whose name appears as S2 if the condition code indicates that the result of the last instruction that can effect the condition code was 0.

| BM | S2 | Branch on Minus | PC ←— S2 if result < 0 |

The Branch on Minus instruction causes a branch to the statement whose name appears as S2 if the result of the last instruction that sets the condition code was strictly less than 0.

Refer now to Fig. 5-4. The register contents shown are the register contents before execution of each of the four groups of instructions shown. The

```
(7) = 00000002
(8) = FFFFFFFE
(9) = 00000010
```

a.	AR	7,9		b.	SR	7,8
	BP	YES			LR	7,9
	B	NO			BZ	NO
					B	YES
c.	MR	8,7		d.	AR	7,8
	AR	8,7			LCR	9,9
	BP	YES			BP	YES
	BM	NO			BM	NO

Fig. 5-4. Use of conditional branch instructions.

question is, which instruction will be executed next after each group is executed, the one whose name is YES or the one whose name is NO? In case (a), the sum is 00000012, which is positive, so that the BP instruction branches to the instruction named YES. Case (b) results in a branch to YES, since the result of the SR instruction is positive and the LR instruction has no effect on the condition code. The MR instruction in group (c) leaves 00000000 in register 8. The ensuing addition leaves a positive result; the next instruction executed will be the one labeled YES. Finally, in group (d) the sum is 00000000; the LCR instruction moves a negative number, and so the machine branches to NO.

Many instances occur in which we wish to execute a branch if the result of an arithmetic instruction is *not* positive, *not* zero, or *not* negative. The conditional branch instructions that do this are

BNP	S2	Branch on Not Plus	PC ←— S2 if result ≤ 0
BNZ	S2	Branch on Not Zero	PC ←— S2 if result ≠ 0
BNM	S2	Branch on Not Minus	PC ←— S2 if result ≥ 0

In these instructions, *plus* means strictly greater than 0 (0 is not positive) and *minus* means strictly less than 0 (0 is not negative). Thus, for example, the BNP instruction causes a branch if the current setting of the condition code indicates a result that was negative *or* zero.

Let us return to our problem of computing the sum of a series of numbers punched on data cards. What we should do is establish a loop counter to which we add 1 every time we process another data card. When the loop counter value has reached the total number of cards to be read, we exit from the loop. The test to see when the loop counter has reached its final value is carried out via a conditional branch instruction.

Figure 5-5 shows a flow chart of a program segment which reads five data cards and computes the sum of the numbers that are punched on them. In Fig. 5-6, we show the corresponding assembly language statements, wherein we have identified

$$\text{SUM} \longleftrightarrow \text{register 5}$$
$$\text{A} \longleftrightarrow \text{register 2}$$
$$\text{K} \longleftrightarrow \text{register 9} \quad \text{(final value of loop counter)}$$
$$\text{I} \longleftrightarrow \text{register 7} \quad \text{(loop counter)}$$

Notice that we have also used register 4 to hold a 1 to be added to the loop counter.

5.1.2. A Comparison Instruction and
Load and Test

In comparing one number with another, using only the instructions considered thus far, we must subtract one from the other and test the resulting condition-code setting. But the SR instruction leaves the result of the subtraction in R1, thus destroying one of the numbers used in the comparison.

In Fig. 5-6 we avoided this problem by keeping a copy of K, the final value of the loop counter, in register 8. Before comparing I, the loop counter in register 7, with the final value, we copied register 8 into register 9 and used the instruction

$$\text{SR} \qquad 9,7$$

to set the condition code for the ensuing conditional branch instruction. This method is inefficient for at least two reasons: It uses an additional register to keep a copy of the final value for the loop counter (and we are always running

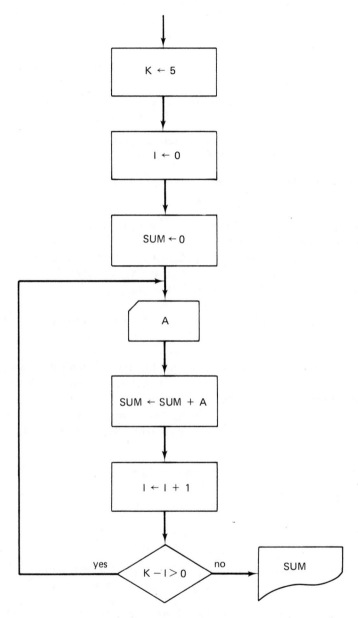

Fig. 5-5. A flowchart of a program segment to compute the sum of five numbers.

```
            L       9,=F'5'      FINAL VALUE OF LCCP COUNTER IN REG. 9
            L       7,=F'J'      STARTING VALUE OF LOOP COUNTER IS 0
            L       4,=F'1'      INCREMENT FOR LOOP COUNTER IS 1
            SR      5,5          START SUM AT 0
NEXTNUM     RWD     2            READ A NUMBER
            AR      5,2          ADD IT TO SUM
            AR      7,4          INCREMENT LOOP COUNTER
            LR      8,9          MAKE A COPY OF FINAL COUNTER VALUE
            SR      8,7          COMPUTE DIFFERENCE K-I
            BM      NEXTNUM      GO BACK FOR MORE IF NOT DCNE
            WWD     5            PRINT RESULTING SUM
```

Fig. 5-6. A program segment that calculates and prints the sum of five numbers that were punched on data cards.

short of registers to use), and the instruction

$$\text{LR} \qquad 9,8$$

used to copy K into register 9 is a wasted instruction in that it does nothing to further the actual calculations.

Both of these problems could be eliminated if we had an instruction that simply compared the contents of two registers without changing the contents of either one. The Compare Register instruction

---

CR	R1,R2	Compare Register	Set CC according to value of
			$(R1) - (R2)$

---

subtracts (R2) from (R1) and sets the condition code to indicate whether the result was zero, positive, or negative. But it does not store the resulting difference anywhere. Thus, (R1) is left unchanged.

We use the CR instruction whenever we want to compare the contents of two registers without changing their contents. Suppose that we have

$$(9) = 00000005$$
$$(7) = 00000004$$

The instruction

$$\text{SR} \qquad 9,7$$

results in

$$(9) = 00000001$$

and a condition code indicating a positive result. The instruction

$$\text{CR} \qquad 9,7$$

computes the same difference, 00000001, and the same condition-code setting but leaves the original register contents

$$(9) = 00000005$$
$$(7) = 00000004$$

as they were before execution of the instruction.

```
        L       9,=F'5'     FINAL VALUE OF LOOP COUNTER IN REG. 9
        L       7,=F'0'     STARTING VALUE OF LOOP COUNTER IS 0
        L       4,=F'1'     INCREMENT FOR LOOP COUNTER IS 1
        SR      5,5         START SUM AT 0
NEXTNUM RWD     2           READ A NUMBER
        AR      5,2         ADD IT TO SUM
        AR      7,4         INCREMENT LOOP COUNTER
        CR      9,7         COMPARE K WITH I
        BM      NEXTNUM     GO BACK FOR MORE IF NOT DONE
        WWD     5           PRINT RESULTING SUM
```

Fig. 5-7. The program of Fig. 5-7 using a CR instruction to compare the loop counter with its final value.

Figure 5-7 shows the program segment of Fig. 5-6 modified to take advantage of the CR instruction. We no longer need to keep a copy of (9) in register (8), and we eliminate the instruction

LR   9,8

by replacing the pair of instructions

LR   9,8
SR   9,7

with the single instruction

CR   9,7

Now we shall return to the division problem discussed in Chapter 4. We found that it is necessary to test the sign of the dividend and move a 0 or FFFFFFFF to the preceding even-numbered register if the dividend is positive or negative, respectively. An instruction that helps with such problems is $\underline{L}$oad and $\underline{T}$est $\underline{R}$egister.

LTR   R1,R2   Load and $\underline{T}$est $\underline{R}$egister   R1 ←— (R2), set CC

LTR moves (R2) to R1 just as does LR. In so doing, it sets the condition code to indicate whether the number moved is positive, negative, or zero. if

(5) = FFFFFFF3
(6) = 00000018

then

LTR   5,6

produces

(5) = 00000018
(6) = 00000018

and the condition code shows that a positive number was moved. Notice that if R1 and R2 are the same register, LTR simply sets the condition code to indicate whether (R1) is positive, negative, or zero.

```
        SR     6,6        ZERO IN FIRST REGISTER
        LTR    7,4        SEE IF DIVIDEND POSITIVE
        BP     DIV        IF SO, OK TO DIVIDE
        L      6,=F'-1'   IF, NOT, ALL ONES IN REGISTER 6
DIV     DR     6,9        AND DIVIDE
```

Fig. 5-8. Division of (4) by (9) using LTR to test the sign of the dividend.

Figure 5-8 illustrates the use of LTR to solve the problems of Fig. 4-5, in which we divide (4) by (9). After placing 0 in register 6 we move (4) to 7 using LTR, which determines the sign of (4) in the process. If this number is negative, we move -1 (FFFFFFFF$_{16}$) into register 6 and do the division.

5.1.3. START, INITIAL, EOJ, and END

Now that we have seen how to program loops, let us investigate the remaining statements necessary to form a complete program. Of these, there are two types: assembly language *pseudo-operations* and *subroutine linkage macros*.

Assembly language *pseudo-operations* are really directives to the assembler telling it how to process the deck of cards we furnish it as input. The qualifier *pseudo* arises from the fact that the actions requested are not machine operations but commands to the assembler. As such, they have at most an indirect effect on the execution of the program and generate no actual machine language instructions. For example, pseudo-operations are used to designate the beginning and end of the program, control the type of printed output from the assembler, reserve memory space, and assign symbolic names to constants and addresses.

The *subroutine linkage macro-instructions* fulfill certain conventions required of all programs run under the auspices of a large computer system.

The first statement of an assembly language program is usually the START statement, written as

name   START   0

The name field contains the name of the program, which can be any valid assembly language name.

The START pseudo-operation orders the assembler to begin the assembly process, treating all the following cards as statements in the same program until an END statement is reached. The END pseudo-operation, written

END   name

marks the end of the program and terminates the assembly process. The name in the operands field is the name of the statement that will be executed first when the program is run. Since we usually have the program executed starting at its beginning, we normally specify the program name as presented on the START statement.

After the START statement we usually insert a statement

PRINT   NOGEN

This statement is not absolutely necessary, but its inclusion makes the assembler output easier to read. The PRINT NOGEN statement requests the assembler not to print the instructions that comprise the macro-instructions in the program. You should run a program once without it to see what happens.

The INITIAL macro signals the beginning of the executable portion of the program and is the first statement which leads to some machine language instructions. We shall soon see that every program has subroutine linkage responsibilities which must be fulfilled in order for the program to execute properly in a large computer system environment. Since the details of these responsibilities are unnecessarily complicated for us at this point, we use the INITIAL macro at the beginning of the program to take care of the problem.

Similarly, the EOJ (end-of-job) macro-instruction fulfills the program responsibilities for terminating the execution of the program. The EOJ statement may be placed anywhere in the program; execution of it stops the execution of the program and returns the use of the CPU back to the system.

Like RWD and WWD, INITIAL and EOJ are *not* standard IBM macros. They cannot be used unless your computer center staff or your instructor has placed them in the local system library.

Figure 5-9 shows a schematic view of the structure of a complete program whose name is CALC. The START, PRINT NOGEN, and INITIAL state-

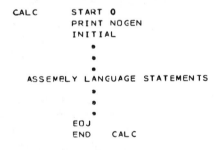

```
CALC        START  0
            PRINT  NOGEN
            INITIAL
               •
               •
               •
ASSEMBLY LANGUAGE STATEMENTS
               •
               •
               •
            EOJ
            END    CALC
```

Fig. 5-9. A schematic diagram of the structure of a program including assembler directives and subroutine linkage macros.

ments are followed by the "working" part of the program, which ends with the EOJ and END statements.

In Fig. 5-10 we return to our example of computing a sum of numbers (see Fig. 5-7). We have added the necessary instructions to compute the average of the numbers and print the result. Figure 5-10 constitutes a complete assembly language program, including assembler directives and subroutine linkage macros, ready for processing by the assembler.

INITIAL, EOJ, RWD, and WWD follow the normal register usage conventions dictated by the operating system. This means that not all of the 16

```
AVERAGE   START  0          START OF PROGRAM
          PRINT  NOGEN      DO NCT PRINT MACRO EXPANSICNS
          INITIAL           BEGIN EXECUTION HERE
          RWD    9          REAC NUMBER OF NUMBERS TO USE
          LR     10,9       KEEP A COPY IN REGISTER 10
          L      6,=F'1'    CECREMENT FCR CCUNTING
          SR     5,5        START SUM AT 0
NEXTNUM   RWD    2          REAC A NUMBER
          AR     5,2        ADD IT TO SUM
          SR     9,6        DECREMENT LOOP CCUNTER
          BNM    NEXTNUM    GO BACK FCR MORE IF NOT CONE
          MR     4,6        PREPARE FOR DIVISICN BY NUMBER OF
          DR     4,10       NUMBERS TO COMPUTE AVERAGE
          WWD    5          QUCTIENT IN REGISTER 5
          WWD    4          ANC REMAINDER IN REGISTER 4
          EOJ               PRCCESSING FINISHED, STOP
          END    AVERAGE    END OF PRCGRAM
```

Fig. 5-10. A complete program to compute the average of a set of numbers and print the result.

registers are available for use by the programmer. In particular, registers 1, 13, 14, and 15 are reserved for special use dictated by the system. In Chapter 13 we shall detail the standard uses for these registers. You should not use these registers in your calculations, as their use for purposes other than those required by the system will produce unpredictable results at best and may cause termination of the execution of the program.

We now have all we need in order to write complete assembly language programs to carry out many useful calculations. Let us consider the additional efforts necessary in order to transform our assembly language program and data cards into a complete job in a form acceptable to the computing system.

5.2. RUNNING THE PROGRAM

A typical IBM System/360 or 370 installation services the computing needs of many, perhaps hundreds, of users per day. Each user may submit several jobs, each of which may require different I/O (input/output) techniques, language processing, and computer resources. In some systems, those which permit *multiprogramming*, several users' jobs may be actively processed by the system at the same time. Because of the complexity of managing such a system, it is impossible for human computer operators to carry out this task. We use a collection of programs called the *operating system* to help the computer system control its own use.

The operating system carries out several important tasks, including the control of I/O devices; the management of queues, or waiting lines, of jobs and steps within jobs waiting to be executed; the allocation of computer resources such as memory, the CPU, and I/O devices to the competing users; the protection of each user's program and data from infringement by other users; the control of input/output operations; and data file management. In so doing, the operating system relieves the user of the burden of these tasks. There are three popular operating systems that are in current use in IBM 360 or 370 systems. These are, in order of increasing sophistication, the Disk Operating System (DOS), the Operating System (OS), and the Virtual Systems (DOS/VS and OS/VS). Which operating system is in use at a given installation depends on the size of the system, the number and variety of input/output devices in the system, and the type of processing normally carried out at the installation. A system that is relatively small in terms of memory size and the number and types of auxiliary storage devices in the system and which is used primarily for business data-processing applications normally uses the Disk Operating System. A larger general-purpose system, such as a university computing center, which is used for administrative accounting jobs, student jobs, and research computing utilizes the more powerful OS. A system equipped with the hardware to permit virtual storage manipulations uses one of the virtual systems.

When we submit requests for computer services in the form of a job to the computing system, we communicate with the operating system via a *job control language*, which is a language especially designed for just this purpose. The job control language statements that accompany our program and data are requests for the use of computer resources. The operating system analyzes these requests and services them in a manner which should ensure that the job is processed correctly while making optimal use of the computer system resources.

5.2.1. Job Steps

For the time being, we shall suppose that our job consists of an assembly language program with its associated input data. We wish to have the system process the program so that it will eventually gain control of the CPU and present us with a printed listing of the results of its execution. When we ask the system to process such a job, we request execution of three job steps, each of which requires the execution of a different program.

The first step is the *assembly* step, in which our assembly language program is translated into machine language. In this step, the assembler is given control of the CPU. Our program, the *source module*, is input data for the assembler, which translates the mnemonics for the operation codes into their machine language equivalents, replaces symbolic names with their numerical or machine address equivalents, and, if the program so requests, reserves space in the machine language version of the program for storage of data that the program will process. The output from the assembler is an *object module*, which is the machine language version of the original assembly language program or source module.

Most programs depend on outside assistance from other programs during their execution. For example, a program that does input/output operations calls upon *subroutines*, or separate programs, to take care of the input/output operations, freeing the programmer from such concerns. In addition, a given program may require data or information that are not actually a part of the program itself. In the second step of program processing, the *link-edit* step, all the subroutines and external data required by the original program are input into the link-editor program and combined to form a *load module*, a machine language program package which, if placed in the memory and executed, requires only the support of the operating system to run.

The final step, the *execution* step, includes the final preparation of the load module for execution and the execution of our program. The load module is stored in the main memory, the necessary links are established between it and the operating system, and the load module, now in executable form, is given control of the CPU.

Figure 5-11 summarizes the three steps in processing an assembly language program. We should point out that the same steps are necessary in processing

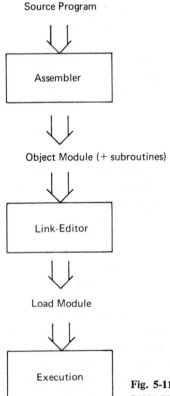

Source Program

Assembler

Object Module (+ subroutines)

Link-Editor

Load Module

Execution

Fig. 5-11. Processing an assembly language program.

programs written in other languages, the only difference being in the program we use to translate the source program into machine language. In processing a FORTRAN program, for example, we would execute the FORTRAN compiler instead of the assembler in the first step; the remaining steps are the same as for an assembly language job.

An alternative to the three-step job discussed above is to use a program called the *loader*. The loader combines the link-edit and execute steps into one step. No separate load module is produced—the object module and supporting subroutines are loaded directly into the memory, linked together, and executed. Use of the loader is similar to the three-step job processing described below.

We shall now investigate the job control language statements necessary to process assembly language programs using systems controlled by the operating systems discussed above. Details in the actual job control statements needed vary from installation to installation depending on local conventions and accounting procedures. Your instructor or computer system staff will inform you of the necessary changes in those cases where your installation's requirements differ from those described below.

5.2.2. OS and OS/VS job control

For our present purposes, there is no difference between OS and the virtual OS operating systems. The job control language described below works in either kind of system.

Job control language statements differ from other statements and data cards in that they begin with two *slash* characters (/ /). The format for a job control statement is the same as that of an assembly language statement, with the exception that it begins in column 3 instead of column 1. Thus, the first field contains a *name*, which must begin in column 3 if a name is present; otherwise column 3 must be left blank. Next comes the *operations* field, then the *operands* field, and an optional *comments* field. Each field is separated from its neighbors by at least one blank, just as in an assembly language statement.

The first statement of every job is the JOB statement, which has the format

//jobname   JOB   accounting information and options

The *jobname* field must contain the name of the job. The job name distinguishes this job from all the others the system is processing. The job name may be any name that is valid in assembly language, but you should check with your instructor to make sure that your local installation does not require a special convention in the naming of jobs. The operation field contains the word JOB, which informs the operating system that this is the first statement of a new JOB with a name as given in the name field and that the accounting and other information to complete the identification of the job is to be found in the following operands field.

The information required in the operands field of the JOB card varies widely from installation to installation. Your instructor or computer system staff will tell you what is required at your computer center. Typically, this field contains billing information, such as department and project numbers to which the computer expenses can be changed; estimates of the amount of memory, time, and output the job will require; and other information that applies to the job as a whole, such as a request to have all the output from the job printed on plain white paper with a new black ribbon.

The next card in a job is an EXEC statement, which has the form

//stepname   EXEC   ASMFCLG

The *stepname* field contains the name of this job step. Your instructor may want you to follow special rules for the step name. If not, you may use this field for a name which helps you remember what the job does.

The operation EXEC is short for EXECute. The operand, ASMFCLG, is the name of a job control language program, or *catalogued procedure*, which is to be executed. A catalogued procedure is a series of job control language statements which are stored in a permanent system library. We request their insertion into our job by writing an EXEC statement as shown above.

The effect of using a catalogued procedure is to make it unnecessary for us to write all the job control statements it contains. The ASMFCLG procedure contains all the job control statements necessary to request the system to execute the assemble, link-edit, and execute job steps discussed in the preceding paragraphs. All we have to do is inform the system as to the source of input data for the assembler and program and the destination of the printed output. The name ASMFCLG can therefore be interpreted as meaning "Using the F assembler, Compile, Link-edit, and GO (execute)!" You may wish to examine the statements in the ASMFCLG procedure. These begin with XX in the first two columns of the printed output you receive after your job has been run.

The remaining job control statements are Data Definition (DD) statements which inform the system as to the source (destination) of the input (output) data for the job. The source program, the input data for the assembler, follows a DD statement that identifies it as such:

//ASM.SYSIN   DD   *

The assembler expects to find the source program defined by a DD statement named ASM.SYSIN. The asterisk (*) means that the program follows on punched cards. The last statement of the assembly language program, usually an END statement, is followed by a data delimiter card,

/*

which marks the end of this input data set.

Next comes a card which tells the system what to do with the output from your program when it is executed. Written

//GO.SYSPRINT   DD   SYSOUT=A

this card instructs the system to route all the printed output from the GO step to the standard system output device, which is usually a line printer.

In the debugging and testing stages of program development, the program might not complete its execution because of a mistake in the program or data. In such cases, the cause of the error can be very difficult to find without the use of some additional information. Inclusion of the statement

//GO.SYSUDUMP   DD   SYSOUT=A

at this point in the job causes a printed *dump* of all register and memory contents and other useful information when an error condition prevents complete execution of the program. The dump may appear incomprehensible for now, but it will be a big help to your instructor or computer staff in helping you find your mistake. We shall find out how to use the dump in Chapter 12.

Finally, we must include the job control cards that define the input data the program reads during its execution. The system is told that the input data are punched on the cards following through the use of the statement

//GO.SYSIN   DD   *

The data cards follow this statement. After the last data card should be a data delimiter card,

/*

followed by a card,

//

that designates the end of the job.

Figure 5-12 shows the organization of the program, data, and job control statements necessary to form a complete job to be run under a typical OS-type operating system. Remember that your own computer center may follow different conventions regarding job names, accounting information, and other details. However, the basic structure shown is universal.

5.2.3. DOS and DOS/VS Job control

Disk Operating System job control statements begin with two *slash* characters (/) in columns 1 and 2, followed by at least one space. Then comes an operation field and an operands field in the same format as in assembly language statements.

```
//CSC52R56  JOB  (100,1105),'10055  W.  RUDD'
//COMPUTE  EXEC  ASMFCLG
//ASM.SYSIN  DD  *
        .
        .
        .

ASSEMBLY  LANGUAGE  SOURCE  PROGRAM  GOES  HERE
        .
        .
        .
            END         PROGRAM     END STATEMENT OF PROGRAM
/*
//GO.SYSPRINT  DD  SYSOUT=A
//GO.SYSUDUMP  DD  SYSOUT=A     (OPTIONAL)
//GO.SYSIN  DD  *
        .
        .
        .

DATA  CARDS  GO  HERE
        .
        .
        .
/*
//
```

Fig. 5-12. Structure of a job ready to submit for processing in a system operating under ØS or ØS/VS.

The first statement in a DOS job is the JOB statement written

//   JOB   jobname

This statement marks the beginning of the job and assigns the name in the operands field to the job. The job name may be any name that is valid in assembly language, but your instructor or computer center staff might ask you to follow some local conventions regarding job names for your programs.

The next statement is an option card, written

//   OPTION   options

The operands field contains a list of options to be in effect while the job is being processed. For example, if we wish to have a symbolic LISTing of the assembly language source program printed, the output from the assembler to be passed to the LINK-editor, and a DUMP, or list of register and memory contents and other information for use in debugging, to be printed in the event that the program cannot continue execution because of an error, we write

//   OPTION   LIST,LINK,DUMP

Your instructor might have different options that he wants you to use and might also ask that you include some ASSGN statements to ASSiGN input/output devices to your job.

Normally, the next card in the job is written

//   EXEC   ASSEMBLY

which requests <u>EXEC</u>ution of the assembler. The assembly language source program follows this statement. After the last statement of the program, usually the END statement, an end-of-file card,

/*

is used to mark the end of the input to the assembler.

Then comes the statement requesting execution of the link-edit step,

//   EXEC   LNKEDT

followed by the statement that orders loading and execution of the program,

//   EXEC

If the program requests data from cards, the data cards follow this EXEC statement. The end of the input data is denoted by an end-of-field card,

/*

and finally, the end-of-job card,

/&

indicates that there is no more input from cards for this job.

Figure 5-13 shows the organization of a job for processing by a DOS system. Local conventions might require minor modifications to the job control language shown, but the overall job structure is universal.

5.2.4. Examples

Figure 5-14 shows our program to compute averages (Fig. 5-10) and some sample data to be used with the program, together with the job control

```
// JCB CSC52R56
// OPTION LIST,LINK,DUMP
// EXEC ASSEMBLY
        .
        .
        .
ASSEMBLY LANGUAGE SOURCE PROGRAM GOES HERE
        .
        .
        .
/*
// EXEC LNKEDT
// EXEC
        .
        .
        .
INPUT CARD DATA GOES HERE
        .
        .
        .
/*
/&
```

Fig. 5-13. Structure of a job ready to submit for processing in a system operating under DØS.

```
//CSCS2R56 JOB (100,1105),'10055 W. RUDD'
//COMPUTE EXEC ASMFCLG
//ASM.SYSIN DD *
AVERAGE   START  0            START OF PROGRAM
          PRINT  NOGEN        DO NOT PRINT MACRO EXPANSIONS
          INITIAL             BEGIN EXECUTION HERE
          RWD    9            READ NUMBER OF NUMBERS TO USE
          LR     10,9         KEEP A COPY IN REGISTER 10
          L      6,=F'1'      DECREMENT FOR COUNTING
          SR     5,5          START SUM AT 0
NEXTNUM   RWD    2            READ A NUMBER
          AR     5,2          ADD IT TO SUM
          SR     9,6          DECREMENT LOOP COUNTER
          BNM    NEXTNUM      GO BACK FOR MORE IF NOT DONE
          MR     4,6          PREPARE FOR DIVISION BY NUMBER OF
          DR     4,10         NUMBERS TO COMPUTE AVERAGE
          WWD    5            QUOTIENT IN REGISTER 5
          WWD    4            AND REMAINDER IN REGISTER 4
          EOJ                 PROCESSING FINISHED, STOP
          END    AVERAGE      END OF PROGRAM
/*
//GO.SYSPRINT DD SYSOUT=A
//GO.SYSUDUMP DD SYSOUT=A
//GO.SYSIN DC *
     5
        -10
 500
           -30
         1
     3
/*
//
```

Fig. 5-14. A complete job with ØS job control language ready for submission to the computer center.

statements necessary to control OS or VS processing of the job. Figure 5-15 shows the same job as it would appear if it were prepared for processing by a DOS-based system.

Some systems may be equipped with the G level assembler created by the Department of Computer Science of the University of Waterloo in Canada or the ASSIST system developed at Pennsylvania State University or one of several other special assembler systems. Your instructor or computer system staff will help you use it if your local installation has one of these.

5.3. PROGRAM DOCUMENTATION

The exercises at the end of this chapter can all be done using only the instructions we have discussed to this point. I urge you to write programs for as many of these exercises or problems of your own choice as you can, and to run, debug, and test at least one of them if possible with local facilities. We now have covered all we need in order to write and run simple assembly language programs.

```
// JCB CSC52R56
// OPTION LIST,LINK,DUMP
// EXEC ASSEMBLY
AVERAGE    START  C            START OF PROGRAM
           PRINT NOGEN         DC NOT PRINT MACRO EXPANSIONS
           INITIAL             BEGIN EXECUTION HERE
           RWD    9            READ NUMBER CF NUMBERS TO USE
           LR     10,9         KEEP A COPY IN REGISTER 10
           L      6,=F'1'      DECREMENT FOR COUNTING
           SR     5,5          START SUM AT 0
NEXTNLM    RWD    2            REAC A NUMBER
           AR     5,2          ADD IT TO SJM
           SR     9,6          DECREMENT LOOP COUNTER
           BNM    NEXTNUM      GC BACK FOR MCRE IF NOT DONE
           MR     4,6          PREPARE FOR CIVISION BY NUMBER CF
           DR     4,10         NLMBERS TO CCMPUTE AVERACE
           WWD    5            QUCTIENT IN REGISTER 5
           WWD    4            AND REMAINDER IN REGISTER 4
           EOJ                 PROCESSING FINISHED, STOP
           END    AVERAGE      END OF PROGRAM
/*
// EXEC LNKEDT
// EXEC
     5
       -10
500
         -30
     1
  3
/*
/&
```

Fig. 5-15. A complete job with DØS job control language ready for submission to the computer center.

But a well-prepared program consists of more than the minimal set of instructions, job control language, and data that produce the correct results when run on the computer. It is important, of course, to have a working program that produces the correct results. However, a complete computing project includes not only the program and data itself, but also sufficient information regarding the workings of the program to ensure its profitable use for the purpose for which it was designed. This additional information is called the program *documentation*. It is not too early to get into the habit of carefully documenting programs as they are written, debugged, tested, and finally put into operational use.

There are many reasons for adequate program documentation, any one of which is sufficient to justify the additional effort involved. In most programming environments, the programs written by any one individual or group will be used, perhaps quite heavily, by people who had nothing to do with the design and implementation of the program. These users must be told how to use the program, what the program expects for input data, what to expect as output, and any additional information they might need regarding the techniques used in the program itself. If the program requires unusual treatment with regard to memory space, input/output devices, and data formats, the user must know about it. It does no good to simply mail someone a deck of cards with a cryptic message to the effect that this program calculates new bank balances given the day's transactions.

Most programming in on-the-job situations is done by teams of programmers. Each member of a given team is assigned a small section of the total project. When all the pieces have been finished they are put together into the final product. A great deal of communication between the team members is needed to be sure that the separate sections will function together to produce the desired result. A major portion of this communication must be achieved through program documentation.

A further instance in which documentation is essential is that in which the user must modify the program itself. Occasions in which users must modify a program occur frequently in practice, either because the user wishes to adapt the program to his own special needs or because the original program contains some errors. Programs, especially those written in assembly language, are difficult enough to read even by the programmer who wrote them. When someone unfamiliar with the details of the program must learn enough about the program to make changes in it, he will waste many hours if the program is poorly documented. It is the programmer's responsibility to make program modification as easy as possible for the user.

In summary, the programmer must put himself in the position of the user of his product. He should include with his program all the documentation needed to permit the user to understand how the program works, what resources the program requires, how to modify the program, if necessary, and what results can be expected of the program.

Program documentation is most effectively done while the program is being designed, written, and tested. The documentation process fits in naturally with the steps in programming we discussed in Section 3.2. At intermediate stages in program development, the documents help the programmer remember what he is doing, help keep the smaller units of the program in perspective, and suggest better techniques to use in solving the problem.

How much documentation is enough depends on the magnitude and complexity of the project, the uses to which the program will be put, and the depth of detail the user must have in order to make effective use of the program. I suggest that a minimum for adequate program documentation, regardless of the nature of the problem, consists of a written description of the program, one or more block diagrams and/or flow charts, and enough comments within the program itself to make it understandable in detail by a reader who knows the language in which it is written and who has access to all the documentation.

The written description of the program consists of a neat presentation of the results of the problem analysis and algorithm design stages of the program development. Here all the names used for variables must be clearly identified. The mathematical and/or information-processing techniques employed must be described as must data formats, job control language requirements, and language-processing requirements for use of the program. The results of the testing phase should also be included. It is as important that the user know in which cases the program will not work, as it is for him to recognize those in which the program operates properly. In other words, the verbal description should tell the user what the program does, how to use it, and when it can be expected to yield the correct results.

The discussion of flow charts in Section 3.2 applies in program documentation as well. If sufficient care is taken in keeping the flow chart for the program up-to-date, then little additional effort is necessary in preparing the flow chart for inclusion in the program documentation. In those instances in which the project is sufficiently complex to warrant subdividing it into separate subprograms, a block diagram showing the interrelationships among the subprograms should be included in the overall documentation, as should the complete documentation for each of the subprograms.

Finally, we come to the program itself. We have seen that, in assembly language, the comments field is available for program description and that a card with an asterisk (*) in column 1 can be used entirely for comments. More than three-quarters of many well-documented programs are comments statements. Space does not permit such extensive use of comments in the examples in this text. However, Fig, 5-16 shows our example program of Fig. 5-10 rewritten to include an adequate set of comments. Make every effort to keep your programs *readable*.

```
******************************************************
*                                                    *
*    THIS PROGRAM COMPUTES THE AVERAGE OF A LIST      *
*    OF NUMBERS PUNCHED ON DATA CARDS.                *
*       REGISTER USAGE IS AS FOLLOWS                  *
*          REG. 2   -   TEMPORARY STORAGE OF NUMBERS  *
*          REG. 4   -   LEFT HALF OF DIVIDEND         *
*          REG. 5   -   RUNNING SUM OF NUMBERS READ   *
*          REG. 9   -   LOOP COUNTER                  *
*          REG. 10  -   NUMBER OF NUMBERS TO AVERAGE  *
*                                                    *
*    TO USE                                           *
*             ASSEMBLE, LINK EDIT, AND EXECUTE USING  *
*             THE ASMFCLG CATALOGUED PROCEDURE        *
*       DATA                                          *
*             ALL DATA CARDS ARE TO BE PUNCHED IN FREE*
*             INTEGER FORMAT                          *
*             CARD 1 - NUMBER OF NUMBERS TO BE AVERAGED*
*             REMAINING CARDS - DATA NUMBERS, ONE PER *
*             CARD                                    *
*                                                    *
******************************************************
```

Fig. 5-16. A program that makes extensive use of comments for documentation.

```
*
*    PROGRAM PRELIMINARIES
*
AVERAGE   START   0               START OF PROGRAM
          PRINT   NOGEN           DO NOT PRINT MACRO EXPANSIONS
          INITIAL                 BEGIN EXECUTION HERE
*
*   FIRST DATA CARD TELLS NUMBER OF NUMBERS TO TREAT
*   THIS NUMBER IS READ INTO REG. 9 AND COPIED IN REG. 10
*    FOR LATER USE IN COMPUTING THE AVERAGE
*
          RWD     9               READ NUMBER OF NUMBERS TO USE
          LR      10,9            KEEP A COPY IN REGISTER 10
*
*   A ONE IS PUT INTO REG. 6 FOR USE IN DECREMENTING THE LOOP
*   COUNTER, REG. 9
*
          L       6,=F'1'         DECREMENT FOR COUNTING
*
*   REGISTER 5 WILL CONTAIN TH RUNNING SUM OF THE NUMBERS AS THEY
*   ARE READ. THE SUM MUST START AT 0
*
          SR      5,5             START SUM AT 0
*
*   THE LOOP STARTS HERE. FIRST READ A NUMBER INTO REGISTER 2
*
NEXTNUM   RWD     2               READ A NUMBER
*
*   THEN ADD IT TO THE RUNNING SUM IN REG. 5
*
          AR      5,2             ADD IT TO SUM
          SR      9,6             DECREMENT LOOP COUNTER
*
*   REG. 9 WILL BE COUNTED DOWN BY ONE EACH TIME A NUMBER IS READ
*   AND ADDED TO THE SUM. WHEN (9) IS NEGATIVE, ALL NUMBERS WILL
*   HAVE BEEN READ
*
          BP      NEXTNUM         GO BACK FOR MORE IF NOT DONE
          BZ      NEXTNUM         ONE MORE TO DO IF LOOP COUNTER IS 0
*
*   NOW PREPARE FOR THE DIVISION BY EXTENDING SIGN BIT OF REG. 5
*   THROUGH REG. 4
*   DO THIS BY MULTIPLYING (5) BY 1
*
          MR      4,6             PREPARE FOR DIVISION BY NUMBER OF
*
*   DIVIDE THE SUM BY THE NUMBER OF NUMBERS
*
          DR      4,10            NUMBERS TO COMPUTE AVERAGE
*
*   PRINT THE QUOTIENT PORTION OF THE AVERAGE
*
          WWD     5               QUOTIENT IN REGISTER 5
*
*   PRINT THE REMAINDER PORTION OF THE AVERAGE
*
          WWD     4               AND REMAINDER IN REGISTER 4
*
*   THE JOB IS OVER
*
          EOJ                     PROCESSING FINISHED, STOP
*
*   END STATEMENT TERMINATES THE ASSEMBLY OF THE PROGRAM
*
          END     AVERAGE         END OF PROGRAM
```

Fig. 5-16 *continued.*

106

As everyone familiar with computer software development or use knows, the importance of adequate program documentation cannot be overemphasized. The most carefully designed and written program is just so much paper if a potential user is not given enough information to enable him to use it. If you do not already have the "documentation habit," start now on the road to a *healthy* addiction.

CHAPTER SUMMARY

The *unconditional* and *conditional branch* instructions provide for execution-time modification of the order of execution of the instructions in a program. The conditional branch instructions test the *condition code* to determine if the branch should be taken:

B	S2	Unconditional Branch	PC ←— S2
BP	S2	Branch on Plus	PC ←— S2 if result > 0
BM	S2	Branch on Minus	PC ←— S2 if result < 0
BZ	S2	Branch on Zero	PC ←— S2 if result $= 0$
BNP	S2	Branch on Not Plus	PC ←— S2 if result ≤ 0
BNM	S2	Branch on Not Minus	PC ←— S2 if result ≥ 0
BNZ	S2	Branch on Not Zero	PC ←— S2 if result $\neq 0$

Assembler directives control the action of the assembler in processing the source program.

The *operating system* is a set of programs that provide for management of the computer system resources. *Job control language* statements are requests for use of system resources.

Adequate *program documentation* includes a complete *written description* of the program and its use, *block diagrams and flow charts*, and *comments* included in the source program.

EXERCISES

1. Define and/or describe:
   (a) Unconditional branch.
   (b) Condition code.
   (c) Conditional branch.
   (d) Pseudo-operation.
   (e) Operating system.
   (f) Job control language.
   (g) OS.
   (h) VS.
   (i) DOS.
   (j) JOB statement.
   (k) EXEC statement.
   (l) DD statement.

2. Modify the program in Fig. 5-10 so that more than one group of numbers can be averaged per execution of the program.

3. It is in fact not necessary for a program to know how many numbers are to be processed before it begins processing them. Suppose that we can assume that all the numbers to be averaged in our example are less than 1 million, say, or or perhaps they are all positive. Then a data card with a number greater than 1 million or a negative number punched on it can be used as a *trailer card* to indicate when the end of the data has been reached. Modify the program of Fig. 5-10 so that, instead of reading the number of numbers to be averaged from a data card, it checks each number it reads to see if it was less than 1 million and stops reading cards as soon as it finds an exception, the trailer card. Is it still necessary to count the number of cards read?

4. Given a set of data cards containing a series of numbers, none of which is greater than 2000 in absolute value, write a program to read the set of cards, printing each number as it is read, and count the number of cards that had negative numbers, numbers that were either positive or zero, and numbers that were exactly zero. Print each of the resulting counts.

5. Write an assembly language program that plays the "party game." The calculations to be made are as follows:
    (a) Read into the machine two numbers. The first number represents the date and month of your birth. For example, if you were born on August 14, this would be 148. The second number is your age at your last birthday.
    (b) Multiply the first number by 2.
    (c) Add 5 to the result.
    (d) Multiply the result by 50.
    (e) Add your age to the result.
    (f) Add 365 to the result.
    (g) Subtract 615 from the result.
    (h) Print the two numbers read and the result from step 7.
    Your program should treat several pairs of cards containing birthdays and ages, and should stop when a trailer card is encountered.

6. Write a program to simulate a change return machine which returns the appropriate change in quarters, dimes, nickels, and pennies from purchases under $1. The machine should return the smallest total number of coins possible. Your program should print the original purchase price, the total amount of change to be returned, and the number of quarters, dimes, nickels, and pennies returned. It should process a series of purchases until a purchase price greater than $1 is entered.

7. The mathematically useful Fibonacci sequence is a series of numbers each of which is the sum of the two preceding numbers in the sequence. The first two numbers are 0 and 1, and the sequence continues

    $$0, 1, 1, 2, 3, 5, 8, 13, 21, 34, \ldots .$$

    Write a program to find out which term in the sequence is the first one larger than a number read from a data card. Your program should print the number read, the number of terms in the sequence it calculated, and the value of the first term greater than the number read.

8. There are many ways to compute the square root of a number, one of the more efficient of which makes use of the fact that the sum of the first N odd integers

is N^2. For example, if $N = 6$, the sum of the first six odd integers $= 1 + 3 + 5 + 7 + 9 + 11 = 36 = 6^2$. Write a program to calculate the integer parts of the square roots of numbers using this technique.

9. Write a program to find all the factors of numbers read from data cards.

10. Write a program to find all the prime factors of numbers read from data cards. (*Note:* If you are not careful to design an efficient algorithm for Exercises 9 and 10, you will waste much computer time).

11. Write a program to convert numbers from decimal to their equivalents in another number system. Your program should read one data card which indicates the base of the desired system. It should then print this number and read and print a number to be converted from the next card. The digits in this number expressed in the system whose base was read should then be printed, one per line in reverse order. For example, suppose that we wish to compute the base 3 (ternary) equivalent of 38_{10}. The input data cards should be

$$3$$
$$38$$

The output should be

$$3$$
$$38$$
$$2$$
$$0$$
$$1$$
$$1$$

indicating that

$$38_{10} = 1102_3$$

REFERENCES

IBM Disk Operating System System Control and System Service Programs, Form GC24-5036, IBM Corp., White Plains, N.Y.

IBM Operating System Job Control Language Reference, Form GC28-6704, IBM Corp., White Plains, N.Y.

IBM Operating System Job Control Language User's Guide, Form GC28-6703, IBM Corp., White Plains, N.Y.

IBM System/360 Assembler F Programmer's Guide, Form GC26-3764, IBM Corp., White Plains, N.Y.

IBM System/360 Disk and Tape Operating System Assembler Language, Form GC24-3414, IBM Corp., White Plains, N.Y.

IBM System/360 Operating System Assembler Language, Form GC28-6514, IBM Corp., White Plains, N.Y.

IBM OS/VS—DOS/VS Assembler Language, Form GC33-4010, IBM Corp., White Plains, N.Y.

6 THE MEMORY

"Two bits, four bits, six bits, a byte!
All for the Tigers, stand up and fight!"—Anon., 1972

The memory plays a central role in computing. In most applications, the information a program processes is stored in the memory, as are the instructions in the programs which do the actual processing. In preparation for study of the instructions that allow us to use the memory, we must determine the ways in which information can be stored and retrieved using the memory.

Because assembly language is so closely related to machine language, it is impossible to become truly proficient at assembly language programming without a detailed background in the details of the machine language. In Section 6.2 we shall find our first discussion of the machine language—in this case, a consideration of the RR instruction format. In Section 6.3 we shall see how the assembler translates assembly language programs into machine language.

Finally, the management of the memory is of primary concern to assembly language programmers. In assembly language, we have direct control over how programs and data use the memory space. In Section 6.4 we shall discuss one aspect of this problem, that of how to reserve memory space and assign symbolic names to the addresses of the reserved space.

6.1. INFORMATION UNITS

Until now, all the information move, arithmetic, and comparison instructions that we have dealt with have required two full-word operands, both of which are in general-purpose registers. In preparation for instructions that have one or more memory operands, let us now discuss more fully the

110

structure of the memory and the addressing of memory operands in the IBM 360. In particular, what are the fundamental units we can use to hold information in the memory?

We have already seen that the basic unit of information in a modern computer is the binary digit, or bit. The register-to-register instructions we studied have 32-bit full-word operands which are treated as signed binary integers in the RR arithmetic and comparison instructions. Another primary quantity of information is the *byte*, which consists of *8 bits.*

The byte is of primary importance in the memory structure of the IBM 360 because it is the fundamental unit upon which the memory addresses are based. The memory is a collection of bytes arranged in numerical order starting with byte number 0:

0	1	2	3	4	5	6	7	8	9	A	B	C	D	...
														...

When we speak of a memory address, we really mean the position of the corresponding byte in the memory; the byte at address 30AC (remember that addresses are given in hexadecimal unless otherwise specified) is actually byte number 30AC in the memory.

This is not to say that every memory operand in the 360 is exactly 1 byte long. But the byte is the *smallest* information unit that can be fetched from or stored in the memory. In addressing larger operands, we give the address of the first byte of the operand; the address of a full word, for example, is the address of the first byte of that full word. The number of bytes in an operand is determined by the operation being carried out or by a portion of the instruction in which we specify the length of the operand.

Since the byte is the smallest addressable unit of storage in the memory, we cannot address specific bits, half-bytes, or other portions of bytes in the memory. To modify information units smaller than bytes we must find some means other than the operand address to designate the actual bits to be changed. We shall discuss this question in more detail in Chapter 14. Let us return to the problem of addressing bytes and larger units.

A 32-bit full word contains 4 8-bit bytes. In using instructions which have full-word memory operands, the effective address is the address of the first byte of the full word. We might think of the memory as consisting of a series of full words, the address of each of which is 4 higher than that of its predecessor. The first full word is at address 0, the next at address 4, then at 8, C, 10, 14, and so on throughout the memory. In using an instruction that requires a full-word memory operand, we must obey the following *boundary rule*:

The memory address of a full word is a multiple of 4.

Boundary rules restrict the addresses which can be used for storing information units larger than bytes. These rules are mechanical, rather than logical. Thus, we can operate on information that has a logical length of 4 bytes for a given application and ignore the boundary rule if we never process that information using an instruction that treats the 4 bytes as a full word. Furthermore, the fact that a given information segment begins at a full-word boundary does not mean that we must use only instructions that treat the information as a full word in order to use that information segment. We often store information as full words and then modify selected bytes in them using byte-oriented instructions. But, to paraphrase the boundary rule above, when we do use an instruction which has a full-word memory operand, the address of that operand must be a multiple of 4. Failure to obey this and the other boundary rules results in a *specification* exception, indicating that an error was made in specifying an operand.

Common terminology applied to boundary rules is to speak of information *alignment*; an information unit is *aligned* on a full-word boundary if its address is a multiple of 4.

In many programming applications, full-word memory space is more than is necessary for the desired calculations. For example, we almost never require the 32-bit precision offered by the full-word binary integer arithmetic instructions for the processing and testing of loop counters. Therefore, a set of instructions is available that does binary integer arithmetic using 16-bit *half-word* memory operands. Each half-word is 2 bytes long and, as with the full words, half-word addresses are designated by the address of the first byte of the operand. We might guess, and correctly so, that half-word addresses must obey the following boundary rule:

The memory address of a half-word is a multiple of 2.

The *double word* is 8 bytes or 64 bits long and is used in double-precision floating-point calculations as well as in some of the data conversion instruc-

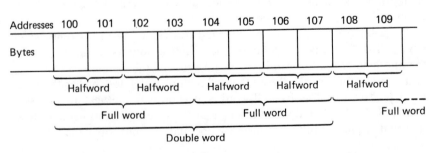

Fig. 6-1. A schematic view of information units and their positions in the memory.

tions (Chapters 19 and 15, respectively). The boundary rule associated with double words is

---

The address of a double word is a multiple of 8.

Figure 6-1 shows a schematic view of a section of memory and its division into the various information units. It is certainly possible to address individual full words, half-words, and/or bytes within a given double word, for example; the boundary rule that applies depends on the instruction chosen. Table 6-1 summarizes the boundary rules discussed above.

Table 6-1

Information - Unit	Length in Bits	Length in Bytes	Address Is Multiple of	Address Ends with Digits
Byte	8	1	1	0, 1, 2, ... , E, F
Half-word	16	2	2	0, 2, 4, 6, 8, A, C, E
Full word	32	4	4	0, 4, 8, C
Double word	64	8	8	0, 8

In summary, the programmer can choose from instructions that require byte, half-word, full-word, or double-word boundary alignment of memory operands. The choice of the appropriate information unit depends on the desired operation and convenience. The programmer often treats a given segment of the memory as composed of different information units at different stages in the calculations. Thus, he might move the information to a full-word address using a byte-oriented instruction, then process the information using full-word binary integer arithmetic and floating-point and logic instructions, manipulate bytes within the area with byte-oriented instructions, and move the final results with byte-oriented move instructions. The boundary rules are nothing more than restrictions on the addresses that can be used with instructions that process information stored in the different quantities available.

6.2. INSTRUCTION FORMAT: THE RR INSTRUCTIONS

The machine language form of a program is stored in the memory just as are the data and other information necessary for the proper operation of the program. To make the design and decoding of machine language instructions easier for the programmer and for the machine, all instructions have the same basic structure.

Machine language instructions are either 2, 4, or 6 bytes long, depending on the instruction type. We know that an assembly language instruction consists of two essential fields, the operation field and the operands field. A machine language instruction contains the same two fields, which appear in the same order as in its assembly language equivalent. In all machine language instructions, the first byte contains the 8-bit operation code. The second (and perhaps additional) byte(s) contain the machine language equivalent of the operands field. The control unit assumes that all instructions are aligned on half-word boundaries; all instruction addresses are multiples of 2.

Let us now consider the register-to-register (RR) machine language instruction format. Schematically, we can represent the machine language format of all the RR instructions as follows:

Byte 0   Byte 1

| OP | R1 | R2 |

Here the symbol OP stands for the 8-bit binary operation code for the instruction, while R1 and R2 have the same meanings as in Chapter 4. The symbolic notation for the general RR instruction shown above would be

MOP   R1,R2

where MOP is the assembly language mnemonic for the desired operation.

The first byte of an RR instruction contains the operation code for the instruction. The second byte contains the binary equivalents for the register numbers R1 and R2. Notice that it takes 4 bits = 1 hexadecimal digit = 1 half-byte = 1 *nibble* to specify one of the registers 0 through 15. In the machine language, the registers 0 through 15 are numbered 0000_2 through 1111_2, so that all the registers can be addressed using 4 bits. For example, register 12_{10} is represented by $1100_2 = C_{16}$, while register 2 is specified in the machine language as $0010_2 = 2_{16}$.

Let us derive the machine language equivalent of the instruction

LR   10,12

Reference to the green card or to Appendix C shows that the operation code for the LR instruction is 18_{16}. The register operands 10 and 12 appear in the machine language as registers A and C, respectively. The operation code goes first and is followed by the two operands in the same order they are in the assembly language. Thus, we have established the fact that

18AC

is the machine language equivalent of the assembly language instruction LR 10,12.

In most programs, the instructions follow one another in the order in which they will be executed with no intervening space between them. The result of translating such a sequence of instructions into machine language is the equivalent series of machine language instructions in sequence, each translated instruction immediately following its predecessor. Thus, the instruction sequence

AR	1,3
DR	0,5
LR	10,1

yields, upon translation to machine language,

$$1A131D0518A1$$

Notice that the second instruction, 1D05, begins 2 bytes after the first, the third 2 bytes after the second, and so on. If the above were stored in the memory starting at an even address and the program counter contained that address, the three instructions would be executed in the order shown.

Thus, we see that translating the RR instructions into machine language is simple. We translate the mnemonic for the operation code into its 8-bit machine language equivalent, placing the result in the first byte of the machine language instruction. We then convert the register operands into their 4-bit hexadecimal equivalents and insert the results into successive nibbles in the second byte of the instruction. In a sequence of instructions, we carry out this process upon each instruction in turn and place the resulting machine language instructions in order as they are generated. We can now begin to envision how the assembler works in translating our programs into machine language.

6.3. THE ASSEMBLER OUTPUT

By now you should be writing and debugging your own programs using the instructions and techniques we have discussed up to this point. In the preceding section, we saw how sequences of RR instructions are translated into machine language. It is of interest now and will be helpful later to examine the function of the assembler in more detail.

6.3.1. The Assembly Listing

The assembler is itself a program whose input is an assembly language program and whose output is a machine language program and the associated assembler *listing*, which shows what the assembler did in processing the program. An analysis of a typical assembler listing will give us some insight into the workings of the assembler in the translation process.

Figure 6-2 shows the assembler listing for the program shown in Fig. 5-10. The listing is divided into six columns labeled LOC, OBJECT CODE, ADDR1, ADDR2, STMT, and SOURCE STATEMENT. The SOURCE

LOC	OBJECT CODE	ADDR1	ADDR2	STMT	SOURCE STATEMENT	
000000				1	AVERAGE START 0	START CF PROGRAM
				2	PRINT NOGEN	DO NOT PRINT MACRO EXPANSIONS
				3	INITIAL	BEGIN EXECUTION HERE
				13	RWD 9	READ NUMBER OF NUMBERS TO USE
00006A	18A9			17	LR 10,9	KEEP A COPY IN REGISTER 10
00006C	5860 D09C	00C84		18	L 6,=F'1'	DECREMENT FOR COUNTING
000070	1B55			19	SR 5,5	START SUM AT 0
				20	NEXTNUM RWD 2	READ A NUMBER
00007C	1A52			24	AR 5,2	ADD IT TO SUM
00007E	1B96			25	SR 9,6	DECREMENT LOOP COUNTER
CC0080	4720 D05A	00072		26	BP NEXTNUM	GO BACK FCR MORE IF NOT CONE
000084	4780 D05A	00072		27	BZ NEXTNUM	ONE MORE TC DO IF LOCP COUNTER IS 0
000088	1C46			28	MR 4,6	PREPARE FOR DIVISION BY NUMBER OF
00008A	1D4A			29	DR 4,10	NUMBERS TO COMPUTE AVERAGE
				30	WWD 5	QUOTIENT IN REGISTER 5
				34	WWD 4	AND REMAINDER IN REGISTER 4
				38	EOJ	PRCCESSING FINISHED, STOP
				44	=V($$IO)	
				45	=F'1'	
0000B0	0C000000			46	END AVERAGE	END OF PRCGRAM
0C00B4	000000001					
000000						

Fig. 6-2. An assembler listing.

116

STATEMENT column contains our symbolic assembly language source program exactly as it appeared on the punched-card input to the assembler.

The assembler assigns *statement numbers* to each statement in the source program. These appear in the column labeled STMT. Notice the gaps in the statement numbers, occurring, for example, after the INITIAL statement. Recall that INITIAL, RWD, WWD, and EOJ are macro-instructions which consist in reality of several assembly language statements. Since we used the PRINT NOGEN assembler directive, the statements in these macros are not printed. But the assembler has included them in the program and has assigned statement numbers to them as well as to the nonmacro statements. The statement numbers are supplied as a matter of convenience. In a later example, we shall see that the assembler refers to errors in the program via the statement numbers of the erroneous statements. We use these numbers to refer to statements within a program.

The column labeled LOC is of special importance to the programmer. LOC stands for *location counter*. Remember that the assembler passes through the program, translating each instruction in turn into machine language. As it does so, it keeps a record of the address of each instruction *relative to* the address of the first byte of the machine language program. Thus, the location counter value associated with a given statement is the number of bytes between the first byte of the machine language form of the program and the first byte of the machine language form of the corresponding statement. We might also view the location counter as measuring the distance, in bytes, between the first byte of the program and the first byte of the instruction to which the location counter value corresponds.

In Fig. 6-2, statement 25 is the statement

    SR   9,6   DECREMENT LOOP COUNTER

It has location counter value 00007E, indicating that the first byte of the machine language form of this SR instruction is $7E_{16}$ bytes beyond the beginning of the program. Since this instruction is an RR instruction, it is 2 bytes long. Therefore, the next instruction, a BP, begins 2 bytes later and has location counter value 000080. The BP instruction is 4 bytes long, and so the location counter jumps by 4 to give the location counter value 000084 for the next instruction.

As is the case with the statement numbers and all other information suppressed by the PRINT NOGEN statement, the location counter values are not shown for statements within macro-instructions. For example, the RWD macro in statement 20 causes a jump of C_{16} bytes in the location counter, indicating that the machine language form of the macro consists of 12 bytes. Notice that assembler directives, such as the END statement, have no effect on the location counter, since these directives lead to the creation of no machine language.

The OBJECT CODE column contains the machine language that results from the corresponding assembly language statement. Thus, in the OBJECT CODE column for statement 25 we find 1B96, the hexadecimal machine language for the instruction

SR   9,6

Similarly, we find the 4 bytes of the machine language equivalent for statement 26,

BP   NEXTNUM

to be 4720D05A.

Recall that, depending on the instruction type, one or two of the operands may be stored in the memory. The ADDR1 and ADDR2 columns show the addresses of memory operands given in terms of the location counter values for the operands. Thus, in statement 26, we see the number 00072 in the ADDR2 column. The location counter value for the statement named NEXTNUM is not shown, since NEXTNUM really refers to the address of the first instruction in the RWD macro. However, since the preceding instruction, statement 19, has location counter value 000070 and is 2 bytes long, we can infer that the location counter value corresponding to the symbol NEXTNUM is 000072, as expected. We shall see that the location counter values, or the numbers in the ADDR columns, are not the actual addresses that are used in the machine language program. The location counter values are used in the calculation of the machine language addresses, however.

6.3.2. The Assembler

The assembler listing shows the original source program, the resulting machine language program, and some other intermediate information. In addition to this output, the assembler produces the object module, which is the machine language program in a form suitable for link-editing, loading, and execution.

Most IBM systems use an assembler called ASSEMBLER F to process assembly language source programs. The F assembler is a *two-pass macro-assembler*. The assembly process consists of two phases, the *macro expansion* phase and the two-pass assembly phase.

In the macro expansion phase, the assembler inserts the statements that form the macros into the program. It obtains these statements either from the source program input or from a library of macro-instructions which is stored on an auxiliary storage device, such as a magnetic disk unit. The output from the macro expansion phase is the original assembly language program with its macro-instructions replaced by their assembly language equivalents.

The first pass of the assembly phase creates the backbone of the machine language form of the program. The assembler assigns location counter values to each statement and constructs a *symbol table*. The symbol table contains one entry for each symbolic name encountered in the program. A symbol table entry consists of the symbol itself, the location counter value of the statement in which it is defined, and the length, in bytes, of the machine language equivalent of the symbol. For example, the symbol table entry for the symbol NEXTNUM in Fig. 6-2 would be

SYMBOL	LEN	VALUE
NEXTNUM	00004	000072

Here LEN stands for length, and VALUE is the location counter value.

The symbol table generated in the first pass is used in the second and final pass to supply the machine addresses and constants that correspond to the symbols used in the program. The assembler proceeds through the expanded source program one statement at a time and inserts the operation codes into their proper positions. It converts constants to their proper machine language equivalents. Whenever a symbol is encountered, it is looked up in the symbol table, and the corresponding VALUE is used to compute the machine address corresponding to the symbol. Thus, the final pass is the one in which all the machine language code is generated.

What happens if, for example, a symbol is used for which there is no entry in the symbol table? That is the topic of the next paragraph.

6.3.3. Error Messages

Try as we do, there are times when we make "mechanical" errors in the preparation of our programs. In the process of writing the program or keypunching it we misspell the names of symbols, specify operands incorrectly, or get the mnemonic for an operation wrong. The assembler usually catches this kind of error and prints a cryptic message indicating the general nature of the error and the statement number in which it appeared.

Figure 6-3 shows the assembler listing of our sample program as it might have been prepared. It includes several key-punching errors and misspellings. Figure 6-4 shows the associated assembler error diagnostic listing.

The assembler listing indicates that three errors were detected. These are indicated by the line

$$*** \text{ ERROR } ***$$

after each of the offending statements. The DIAGNOSTICS page describes the nature of each of the errors. In the table shown, STMT stands for the statement number of the erroneous statement. The MESSAGE is a brief description of the nature of the error. Thus, we see that in statement 26 there is an UNDEFINED symbol in the operand field. A check back to the

```
LOC   OBJECT CODE   ADDR1 ADDR2  STMT   SOURCE STATEMENT

000000                              1 AVERAGE  START   0            START OF PROGRAM
                                    2         PRINT   NOGEN        DO NOT PRINT MACRO EXPANSIONS
                                    3         INITIAL              BEGIN EXECUTION HERE
                                   13         RWD     9            READ NUMBER OF NUMBERS TO USE
00006A 18A9                        17         LR      10,9         KEEP A COPY IN REGISTER 10
00006C 5860 D09C    00084          18         L       6,=F'1'      DECREMENT FOR COUNTING
C00070 1855                        19         SR      5,5          START SUM AT 0
                                   20 NEXTNUM  RWD     2            READ A NUMBER
00007C 1A52                        24         AR      5,2          ADD IT TO SUM
00007E 1E96                        25         SR      9,6          DECREMENT LOOP COUNTER
C00080 0000 0000    C0C00          26         BP      NEXTNMU      GO BACK FOR MORE IF NOT DONE
      *** ERROR ***
                                   27         BN      NEXTNUM      ONE MORE TO DO IF LOOP COUNTER IS 0
      *** ERROR ***
000084 1C46                        28         MR      4,6          PREPARE FOR DIVISION BY NUMBER OF
000086 0C00                        29         DR      5,10         NUMBERS TO COMPUTE AVERAGE
      *** ERROR ***
                                   30         WWD     5            QUOTIENT IN REGISTER 5
                                   34         WWD     4            AND REMAINDER IN REGISTER 4
                                   38         EOJ                  PROCESSING FINISHED. STOP
0000B0 0C000000                    44                 =V($$IO)
0000B4 0C000001                    45                 =F'1'
C00000                             46         END     AVERAGE      END OF PROGRAM
```

Fig. 6-3. An assembler listing of a program with some errors in it.

120

```
                          DIAGNOSTICS


STMT  ERROR CODE   MESSAGE

 26   IEU024    NEAR OPERAND COLUMN   1--UNDEFINED SYMBOL
 27   IEU088    UNDEFINED OPERATION CODE
 29   IEU010    NEAR OPERAND COLUMN   2--INCORRECT SPECIFICATION OF REGISTER CR MASK FIELD


  3 STATEMENTS FLAGGED IN THIS ASSEMBLY
 12 WAS HIGHEST SEVERITY CODE
*STATISTICS*    SOURCE RECORDS (SYSIN) =    18      SOURCE RECORDS (SYSLIB) =   61
*OPTIONS IN EFFECT*  LIST, NODECK, LOAD, NORENT, XREF, NOTEST, ALGN, OS, NOTERM, LINECNT =   55
 49 PRINTED LINES
```

Fig. 6-4. The error diagnostics for the program of Fig. 6-3.

assembler listing shows that NEXTNMU was accidently punched instead of NEXTNUM. Statement 27 contains an UNDEFINED OPERATION CODE. BM should have been punched instead of BN. The ERROR CODE column contains a number for each error. This number can be used to look up a more detailed description of the nature of the error in the assembler language manual.

6.4. SYMBOLIC NAMES IN ASSEMBLY LANGUAGE

In some higher-level languages, such as FORTRAN, the use of a symbolic name (a variable) as an operand instructs the compiler to reserve the required space for the value to which the name corresponds and to associate the name with the address of the space reserved. This is *not* the case in assembly language. When we use a symbol in assembly language, we must *define* that symbol somewhere in the program by putting its name in the name field of an assembly language statement. We have seen, for example, that putting the name LOOP on the instruction

LOOP   AR   10,5

allows us to use the instruction

B   LOOP

to cause the machine to take up execution of the program at the AR instruction labeled LOOP. What happens in fact is that the assembler associates the name LOOP with the address of the first byte of the AR instruction. The memory operand in the machine language equivalent of the branch instruction will be the memory address corresponding to the symbol LOOP.

We reserve memory space and assign symbolic names to the addresses of the associated space via DS and DC statements. We assign names to constants by using the EQU pseudo-operation.

6.4.1. The DS Directive

When we write a program that uses or modifies information stored in the memory we must reserve space for the storage of that information. One way to reserve space in a program is through the use of the DS, or D̲efine S̲torage, directive.

The DS directive is an assembler directive or pseudo-operation which requests that storage be reserved and that the associated name, if present, be assigned to the address of the first byte of the area so reserved. The DS statement itself has no machine language equivalent; it is a message to the assembler. However, it *does* have an effect on the machine language output from the assembler. The DS statement causes the requested space to be reserved in the machine language program. The address fields of those instructions which use the associated name will contain the memory address corresponding to that name.

As an example of the use of the DS directive, consider the statement

WORDS   DS   3F

The DS directive appears in the operation field of the statement. This DS statement requests that three full words (3F) be reserved and that the name WORDS be used to represent the address of the first byte of the 12 bytes of storage so reserved. Since we requested the space to be in full-word units, the space reserved will be aligned on a full-word boundary; the address corresponding to WORDS will be a multiple of 4.

The space will be reserved in the position in the machine language program corresponding to that in the assembly language program in which the DS statement appeared. Suppose that the statements near the DS statement were

	LR	3,8
	AR	4,6
WORDS	DS	3F
	MR	2,6

The assembler will skip some memory space if necessary in order to ensure the proper alignment of the reserved space. After assembling the LR and AR instructions, with the result

18381A46

if the next available byte is on a full-word boundary, the reserved space will be inserted there:

18381A46 ←— 12 bytes —→ 1C26
reserved

If, on the other hand, the next available byte after the AR instruction is not on a full-word boundary, the assembler will skip the necessary 2 bytes to ensure that the first byte of the three-word area starts at a full-word boundary:

18381A46 ←— 2 bytes skipped —→ ←— 12 bytes —→ 1C26
reserved

In this example, we have put the DS statement in among some machine instructions just to illustrate what the assembler does. But notice that the machine would try to execute the information stored in the space we have called WORDS, with unpleasant results. Therefore, in programming, *do not reserve memory space for data storage where it is in danger of being executed.* We shall return to the question of where to put DS and DC statements later.

We write the general form of the DS directive as

name   DS   DupType

The name field contains any valid assembly language name or may be left blank. The abbreviation "Dup" stands for duplication factor and represents an integer which designates the number of units of type "Type" to be reserved. For now, we introduce the following letters and their meanings which can be used in the "Type" position:

F: Full word
H: Half-word
D: Double word
C: byte (Character)

The effect of the DS statement consists of two steps:

1. Reserve "Dup" units of memory space of type "Type," providing for appropriate boundary alignment for the type requested.
2. Assign the symbolic name in the name field, if present, to the address of the first byte of the reserved space.

For example, the statement

HALVES   DS   5H

reserves five half-words and assigns the name HALVES to the address of the first byte of the area. Similarly, the statement

DOUBLE   DS   D

reserves one double word (if "Dup" is 1, it can be omitted) which can then be referred to by the name DOUBLE.

The DS statement has no effect on what is found in the space it reserves when the program is run. When the program begins execution, the area allocated contains whatever was left in the memory by the preceding job that used that section of the memory. Therefore, it is *not* safe to assume that the memory space reserved by the DS statement contains anything of value to the programmer. He must put the information he wants in the reserved space.

6.4.2. The DC Directive

The Define Constant directive has the same effect as the DS directive with the additional feature of allowing the programmer to have initial values stored in the reserved space. Thus, when the program execution begins, the space the programmer requested via the DC statement contains information the programmer wants there, instead of the effectively random data provided by the DS statement.

For now, we shall use the DC directive in the form

name   DC   DupType'Value'

"Dup" and "Type" have the same meanings as for the DS statement. For the time being, we shall use three types with the DC statement:

F: Full word
D: Double word
H: Half-word

Other types are available for use with DC; we shall investigate them as we need them.

For types D, F, and H, the "Value" parameter is a decimal number whose binary equivalent will be stored in the memory at the reserved location when program execution begins. This specification of values in decimal in assembly language is another instance of the following general rule: All numerical constants in an assembly language program are to be treated as decimal numbers unless otherwise specified.

The DC statement has three effects from the point of view of the programmer:

1. "Dup" units of type "Type" are reserved in the machine language program, the resulting space having the boundary alignment appropriate for "Type."

2. The symbolic name in the name field, if present, is assigned to the address of the first byte of the area.

3. The binary equivalent of "Value" is inserted into the reserved space.

Notice that the desired value for the constants is enclosed in *single quotes* or apostrophes.

For example, let us consider the effect of the statement

ONE   DC   1F'1'

Here the name is ONE, "Dup" is 1 (as with the DS statement, we can omit a duplication factor of 1), "Type" is F, and "Value" is 1. The effect is to reserve one properly aligned full word, assign the name ONE to the address of its first byte, and to insert a full word 1, 00000001, into the reserved space.

As another example, consider

HALF   DC   3H'−2'

This statement reserves three half-words, each of which will contain the 16-bit binary equivalent of −2, FFFE. The assembler will consider the name HALVESM2 as synonymous with the memory address of the first byte of the first of the three half-words.

Suppose that the above statement were included in a program segment as follows (remember: do *not* put DS or DC statements in the middle of the program; we do it here for illustration purposes only):

	AR	5,7
	LR	8,5
HALF	DC	3H′−2′
	SR	8,7

Notice that, since instructions are of even length, the area reserved by the DC statement is automatically aligned on a half-word boundary. The machine language that results from the statements above is

$$1A571885FFFEFFFEFFFE1B87$$

Finally, let us suppose that we want to reserve a double word with the name DUB and the initial value 100_{10} stored in it. The statement

DUB   DC   D′100′

has the desired effect.

All instructions which require information from the memory or which put information into the memory must have space reserved for this information. The DS and DC statements are most often used for this purpose. However, the fact that a memory area has been reserved does not mean that it cannot be used for other purposes. For example, we might use a DC statement to reserve a full word 1 ready for use when our program starts executing. When we no longer need this word for its original purpose, we are free to use the same space for storage of other information.

Where do we put DS and DC statements?

Most data that are being processed by a program do not consist of executable instructions. In the example above we put DC statements in the middle of a program segment and asked what would happen if the segment were executed. The answer is that the AR and LR instructions would execute normally. Then we would try to execute the "instruction" labeled HALF. If this number stored there, FFFE, is to be interpreted as an instruction, then its operation code is FF. There is no machine instruction with this operation code, and so the machine will stop with an *operation exception* indicating that an attempt was made to execute a nonexistent instruction.

Therefore, we should not store data where they are in danger of being interpreted as machine instructions. We can, and often do, store data in the middle of a program, but when we do so, we must include branch instructions to preclude execution of the data. Figure 6-5 shows how this might be done with the example mentioned above.

If there is no reason to do otherwise, define all the data storage areas *after the last executable statement in the program*. For now, this means that

```
              AR    5,7
              LR    8,5
              B     AROUND
HALVESM2 DC         3H'-2'
AROUND   SR         8,7
```

Fig. 6-5. Branching around a data storage area.

all DS and DC statements should be placed between the last EOJ statement and the END statement of the program.

6.4.3. The EQU Directive

The EQU assembler directive allows the programmer to EQUate symbolic names to other symbolic names, expressions, or constants. In so doing, it assigns the name in the name field to the quantity that appears in the operands field. Let us consider an example:

REGSIX   EQU   6
R7   EQU   7

The first statement equates the name REGSIX to the numerical constant 6, while the second assigns the name R7 to the number 7. If these two statements appear in a program which also contains the instruction

AR   REGSIX,R7

the result is the same as if the programmer writes

AR   6,7

The values in the operands field are simply substituted for the symbolic names for these values.

As a further example, consider the following statements:

A   DS   3F
B   EQU   A
C   EQU   A+8

The DS statement reserves three full words of storage and assigns the name A to the address of the first byte of the reserved area. The second statement indicates that the name B is equivalent to the name A; the two can be used interchangeably. Use of B in a memory operand field of a memory reference instruction has the same effect as if A is used. The EQU statement has no direct effect on the machine language form of the program. In particular, it does not reserve memory space for B. It simply equates the *name* B to the *name* A.

The third statement introduces a new feature in the use of symbolic names for memory addresses. The symbol A represents the address of the first byte of the storage reserved by the DS statement. A+8 means what it looks like: the *address* represented by A+8, or 8 bytes beyond the byte named A. The EQU statement then means that the symbol C is equivalent to the address of the third full word of the area called A.

While it is possible to write complex expressions to represent addresses or constants, we rarely use expressions more complicated than those of the form

symbolic name $\pm$ constant

For general rules on the writing of expressions, the reader should refer to the appropriate assembler language reference manual.

Finally, let us consider the effect of the statements

NEXTNUM   EQU   *
           RWD   2

When used in the operand field of an assembly language statement, the symbol * represents the value of the location counter at the point where the * appears. In this case, since the EQU statement generates no machine language code, the value of the location counter is that of the first byte of the first instruction in the RWD macro-instruction. The pair of statements above is equivalent to the single statement

NEXTNUM   RWD   2

Experienced programmers often use this method to label statements. It increases the readability of the program and makes program modification and reorganization easier.

```
AVERAGE   START  0           START OF PROGRAM
          PRINT  NOGEN        DO NOT PRINT MACRO EXPANSIONS
          INITIAL            BEGIN EXECUTION HERE
SUM       EQU    5           SUM IS IN REGISTER 5
A         EQU    2           A IS IN REGISTER 2
K         EQU    9           K IS IN REGISTER 9
ONE       EQU    6           REGISTER 6 WILL CONTAIN A 1
KK        EQU    10          REGISTER 10 CONTAINS A COPY OF K
REM       EQU    4           REGISTER 4 WILL CONTAIN THE REMAINDER
          RWD    K           READ NUMBER OF NUMBERS TO USE
          LR     KK,K        KEEP A COPY IN REGISTER 10
          L      ONE,=F'1'   DECREMENT FOR COUNTING
          SR     SUM,SUM     START SUM AT 0
NEXTNUM   EQU    *
          RWD    A           READ A NUMBER
          AR     SUM,A       ADD IT TO SUM
          SR     K,ONE       DECREMENT LOOP COUNTER
          BNM    NEXTNUM     GO BACK FOR MORE IF NOT DONE
          MR     REM,ONE     PREPARE FOR DIVISION BY NUMBER OF
          DR     REM,KK      NUMBERS TO COMPUTE AVERAGE
          WWD    SUM         QUOTIENT IN REGISTER 5
          WWD    REM         AND REMAINDER IN REGISTER 4
          EOJ                PROCESSING FINISHED, STOP
          END    AVERAGE     END OF PROGRAM
```

Fig. 6-6. Use of EQU statements to assign symbolic names to register numbers and memory addresses.

Figure 6-6 shows the program of Fig. 5-10 rewritten to include the use of EQU statements to assign symbolic names to the registers. The names used are those shown in the accompanying flow chart (Fig. 5-5).

The extent to which a programmer uses EQU statements is largely a matter of his personal taste and occupational environment. Some programmers use EQU statements whenever possible, so that register numbers are rarely to be seen in their programs. Others prefer to forego the use of EQU statements when their use might lead to uncertainties in how to specify operands correctly. Still others use them rarely, relying on program documentation to explain register contents and memory addresses. I suggest that you stick with the latter alternative for now.

CHAPTER SUMMARY

The smallest addressable unit of memory space is the *byte*. Other addressable units are the *half-word, full word,* and *double word*. The *boundary rules* must be obeyed in addressing memory operands.

The first byte of a machine language instruction contains the operation code. In the RR instruction format, the remaining byte indicates which registers are to be used as operands.

The *assembler listing* indicates the action taken by the assembler in processing an assembly language program.

The *DS assembler directive* reserves memory space and permits the assignment of a symbolic name to the reserved space. The *DC directive* places initial values in the space it causes to be reserved. The *EQU directive* provides for the assignment of names to constants and addresses.

EXERCISES

1. Because the basic addressable unit in the 360 is the *byte*, the IBM 360 and 370 computers are called *byte-oriented* machines. Some other computers, such as the Xerox Data Systems Model Sigma 5, are *word-oriented* machines, in that the smallest addressable unit is a word, which is 32 bits in the Sigma 5. Answer the following questions concerning a word-oriented computer:
    (a) What boundary rules, if any, could be necessary?
    (b) To what does the address 103 correspond?
    (c) What is the shortest possible instruction length?
    (d) Is a word-oriented machine as efficient as a byte-oriented machine in terms of memory required for storage of programs?
    (e) If the answer to part (d) is no, how can the designer of a word-oriented machine make up for this deficiency.
    (f) In what types of applications would a word-oriented machine be more efficient than a byte-oriented machine?

2. Translate the following program segments into machine language, assuming that each segment begins on a double-word boundary:

(a)   LR   5,12
       AR   5,6
       LR   12,5

(b) EIGHT   EQU   8
    NINE   EQU   9
               LR   EIGHT,NINE
               AR   12,EIGHT
    TEN   DC   F'EIGHT+NINE'

(c)   BALR   12,NIL
    NIL   EQU   0
    ONE   EQU   NIL+1
               DC   H'ONE'
               DC   D'NIL'

(d)   DC   H'2'
               DC   D'5'
               DC   H'3'
               DC   F'0'

3. To ensure proper boundary alignment of the reserved space, the DS and DC directives may cause up to 7 bytes of memory space to be skipped, as is the case when a double word is reserved and the previously used space ends on an address whose last digit is 1 or 9. Formulate a general rule for the ordering of information units of byte, half-word, full-word, and double-word sizes to minimize memory space wasted to provide for proper alignment.

4. Remove the PRINT NOGEN card from one of your programs and have it run as usual. In the SOURCE STATEMENT column of the assembler listing, those statements that arose from expansion of macro-instructions have a plus (+) sign following their statement numbers. Construct a complete symbol table for your program.

5. The cross-reference table is an extension of the symbol table in which an entry for a symbol contains the symbol table entry and, in addition, the number of the statement in which the symbol is defined and the statement numbers of all the statements that use the symbol as an operand. The latter statements are said to *refer* to the symbol. Using the output from Exercise 4, construct a cross-reference table for your program.

REFERENCES

IBM System/360 Disk and Tape Operating System Assembler Language, Form GC24-3414, IBM Corp., White Plains, N.Y.

IBM System/360 Operating System Assembler Language, Form GC28-6514, IBM Corp., White Plains, N.Y.

IBM System/360 Principles of Operation, Form GA22-6821, IBM Corp., White Plains, N.Y.

IBM System/370 Principles of Operation, Form GA22-7000, IBM Corp., White Plains, N.Y.

IBM OS/VS—DOS/VS Assembler Language, Order No. GC33-4010, IBM Corp., White Plains, N.Y.

7 USING THE MEMORY

Most of the instructions we have discussed thus far have been of the register-to-register type; both operands are general-purpose registers, and no reference is made to the memory in their execution. We saw that we can do many useful calculations using only the registers. But we can realize the full power of the computing machine only when we use the facilities it provides to retrieve, modify, and store information in the memory.

We shall introduce memory reference instructions with the RX—Register to indeXed storage—instruction type. First we shall investigate those RX instructions in which the first operand is a register and the second is a full word in the memory. These instructions together with the memory-reserving assembler directives discussed in Chapter 6 will permit us to use the memory for information storage.

The memory address portion of an RX instruction permits modification of the memory address by the contents of an *index register*. This indexing capability provides for increased flexibility in the specification of memory addresses at execution time. Finally, we shall investigate those RX instructions in which memory operands are half-words.

7.1. MEMORY REFERENCE INSTRUCTIONS

We just saw how we can use the DS and DC statements to reserve the space for memory operands. We shall begin our investigation of the instructions that use the memory by considering the use of those RX instructions that use *full-word* memory operands. The first operand in these instructions is a register, and the second is a full word from the memory. The arithmetic and comparison instructions considered herein result in binary integer arithmetic using these full-word operands. Let us begin with the information move RX instructions.

7.1.1. The Load and STore Instructions

The Load instruction moves a full word from the memory into a register. In effect, it *fetches* a word from the memory and *stores* it in the designated register operand. Thus, the word that was fetched from the memory is left unchanged, while the original register contents are destroyed.

The symbolic description of the Load instruction is

$$L \quad R1,S2(X2) \qquad \underline{Load} \qquad R1 \longleftarrow (S2(X2))_F$$

The first operand is any one of the 16 general-purpose registers. S2 represents a symbolic name or an expression whose value is a memory address. The symbolic name usually appears on the DS or DC statement which reserves the space for the memory operand. For example, we might write the instruction

$$L \qquad 3,WORD$$

where WORD is defined elsewhere in the program by the statement

WORD   DS   1F

The Load instruction loads whatever is stored at WORD and the following 3 bytes into register 3.

An example of the use of an expression for the S2 portion is

$$L \qquad 7,ABA+8$$

where ABA is defined by

ABA   DS   10F

The result of executing the Load instruction is to load the contents of the *third* word of the area ABA into register 7 (the first word is at ABA + 0, the second at ABA + 4, and the third at ABA + 8). Thus, S2 represents a memory address involving a symbolic name and, possibly, some modifiers to form an expression.

X2 in the symbolic notation represents an index register. When written as part of a memory operand, the number of the index register is enclosed in parentheses. If no index register is desired, the portion of the operand represented by (X2) is omitted, as has been done in the examples above. We shall study the use of index registers in detail in Section 7.2.

The effect of the Load instruction is shown as

$$R1 \longleftarrow (S2(X2))_F$$

which means that the contents of the full word stored at S2 + (X2) are placed into R1. The subscript F after the parentheses is used to emphasize the fact that a Full word is moved. This means, of course, that the operand address must obey the boundary rule for full words: The address must be a multiple of 4. We saw that if we specify a unit of type F (or D) in a DS or DC statement, the space reserved is automatically aligned on a full-word boundary. Therefore, if our operands are defined in this manner, we need not worry about the boundary alignment. However, when we calculate our own addresses, as we shall shortly, the boundary-alignment problem will reappear.

Let us now consider an example. Suppose that a program contains the following statements:

X	DC	F'−3'
Y	DC	F'15'
Z	DC	F'100'

If we were to look in the memory where the results of these statements were stored, we would find, starting at the memory address corresponding to X,

FFFFFFFD0000000F00000064

The instruction

L   10,X

places the number FFFFFFFD in register 10, while 00000064 is moved to register 3 by

L   3,Z

Notice that we specify the address of the full word to be moved by the address of the first byte of the full word. The machine "knows" that the Load instruction requests a full word from the memory and responds by moving the byte at the specified address and the next three beyond it into the register. This is the case with all the instructions that have operands of length greater than 1 byte; the address used is that of the first byte of the operand. The effective length of the operand is determined by the operation or by other portions of the instruction.

What about

L   5,X+4

The effective address is 4 beyond that of X. Since X is aligned on a full-word boundary, X + 4 must be also. Therefore, this instruction loads register 5 with the number 0000000F, which is the same result we expect from

L   5,Y

The counterpart of the Load instruction is the STore instruction, which moves a full word contained in a register into a full-word position in the memory. The effect is to *fetch* the contents of the register and to *store* the result into the memory, erasing the original contents of the full word stored there.

ST	R1,S2(X2)	STore	$(R1)_F \longrightarrow S2(X2)$

The operands have the same meaning as discussed for the Load instruction. R1 is any of the registers, S2 is a symbolic name or expression, and (X2) denotes an index register, which may or may not be used in a given application of the instruction.

The STore instruction and its relatives, STH, STC, and STM, are different from the other instructions in that the "flow" of information is from left to right as the operands are written. In all other instructions the first operand receives the results, or is the *destination* operand, while the second operand is a *source* operand. For example, in the instruction

$$AR \qquad 5,3$$

the flow of information is from right to left in that the contents of register 3 are added to the contents of register 5, the result being left in register 5. But in the STore instructions, the first operand is the *source* operand, while the *second* operand is the *destination* operand. The instruction

$$ST \qquad 6,B$$

moves the word from the first operand to the second.

Suppose that a program contains the statement

$$SPACE \qquad DS \qquad 2F$$

and that when the program is executed, the storage area corresponding to this area contains

$$4736507658CCA069$$

Further suppose that register contents are

$$(5) = 00000008$$
$$(6) = FFFFFF10$$

when the instruction

$$ST \qquad 6,SPACE$$

is executed. The result is

$$FFFFFF1058CCA069$$

in the memory starting at SPACE. The instruction stores the full-word contents of register 6 into the first word of the area called SPACE.

Similarly, the instruction

$$ST \qquad 5,SPACE$$

yields

$$0000000858CCA069$$

at SPACE and

> ST   6,SPACE+4

results in the memory contents

> 47365076FFFFFF10

starting at SPACE.

We can combine sequences of Load and STore instructions to move full words about in the memory at will. Suppose that we wish to move a full word stored at APPLE to a full-word area called ORANGE. The instructions

> L   6,APPLE
>
> ST   6,ORANGE

accomplish this task.

7.1.2. Arithmetic Instructions

We saw how in the RR arithmetic instructions AR, SR, MR, and DR the first operand is a register or a register pair and functions as an arithmetic accumulator. The second operand is also a register and serves as the source of the second arithmetic operand, which remains unchanged in the execution of the operation.

The RX equivalents of these instructions are A, S, M, and D, respectively. The only difference between these and their RR forms is that the second operand is the address of a full word from the memory, instead of the number of a register. None of these instructions has any effect on memory contents. The A and S instructions set the condition code, while M and D have no effect on it.

The AR instruction adds a full word from the second specified *register* to the contents of the first register operand, leaving the result in the first register. The A instruction adds a full word from the *memory* to the contents of the (first) register operand, leaving the result in this register. Thus, we describe the Add instruction as follows:

A   R1,S2(X2)   Add   R1 ←— (R1) + (S2(X2))$_\mathrm{F}$

The symbols R1 and S2(X2) have the same meaning as for the L and ST instructions discussed previously. The A instruction sets the condition code in the same way as does the AR instruction. Conditional branch instructions can then be used to test for a zero, negative, or positive result or for an overflow.

Suppose that we have

$$(5) = 00000100$$

at a certain time during the execution of a program and that the contents of memory starting at an address whose symbolic name is NUMS are

NUMS: 00000023FFFFFFA0

Then if the instruction

A   5,NUMS

is executed, the result is to replace the contents of register 5 with the sum of its original contents and the contents of the full word stored at NUMS. That is, after execution of the instruction, we have

$$(5) = 00000123$$

The condition code indicates a positive result. If the next instruction is

A   5,NUMS+4

the new contents of register 5 are

$$(5) = 000000C3$$

The Subtract instruction

| S | R1,S2(X2) | Subtract | R1 ⟵ (R1) − (S2(X2))$_F$ |

---

replaces the original contents of R1 with the difference between (R1) and the full word stored at the address corresponding to S2(X2), setting the condition code in the process. If again we have

$$(5) = 00000100$$

and at NUMS we have

NUMS: 00000023FFFFFF50

then the instruction

S   5,NUMS

results in

$$(5) = 00000100 - 00000023 = 00000100 + FFFFFFDD$$
$$= 000000DD$$

The Multiply instruction

| M | R1,S2(X2) | Multiply | R1,R1+1 ⟵ (R1+1) × (S2(X2))$_F$ |

---

works in the same way as does the MR instruction with the exception that the second operand is taken from the memory instead of from a register. The double-length product is left in the register specified as R1 (which must be an *even*-numbered register) and the next register after R1, R1+1. The product computed is that of the contents of the register R1+1 and the full word that the address S2(X2) represents. Like the MR instruction, M has no effect on the condition code.

If
$$(4) = 001286EC$$
$$(5) = 00000100$$
and the memory contents starting at NUMS are again

NUMS: 00000023FFFFFF50

the instruction

M   4,NUM5+4

has the result
$$(4) = FFFFFFFF$$
$$(5) = FFFF5000$$
If instead we execute the instruction

M   4,NUMS

the result is
$$(4) = 00000000$$
$$(5) = 00002300$$

Finally, the RX equivalent of the DR instruction is the D̲ivide instruction:

D R1,S2(X2)	D̲ivide	$(R1,R1+1) \div (S2(X2))_F$:
		R1 ⟵ remainder
		R1+1 ⟵ quotient

Like the DR instruction, the D instruction provides for a double-length quotient, which is obtained from the *even*-numbered register R1 and the following register R1+1. The divisor is the full word stored at the address corresponding to S2(X2). After execution of the instruction, the remainder is to be found in the register R1, while the quotient appears in R1+1.

As a final example, let the register contents be
$$(4) = 00000000$$
$$(5) = 00000100$$
and let the memory contents starting at NUMS be

NUMS: 00000023FFFFFF50

The instruction

D   4,NUMS

produces the remainder
$$(4) = 0000002E$$
and the quotient
$$(5) = 00000006$$

7.1.3. The Compare Instruction

The Compare instruction

C	R1,S2(X2)	Compare	Set CC according to value of $(R1) - (S2(X2))_F$

compares the contents of the register with the contents of the full word whose address is given by S2(X2). The condition code is set depending on whether the difference $(R1) - (S2(X2))_F$ is positive, negative, or zero.

For example, if

$$(11) = 00000010$$

and at P we have stored

$$P: \quad 00000020$$

the instruction

$$C \qquad 11,P$$

sets the condition code indicating that a negative result was obtained. The Compare instruction has no effect upon any register or memory contents.

7.1.4. Use of Literals

We saw in Chapter 5 that we could load numbers into registers through the use of an instruction of the form

$$L \qquad R1,=F'value'$$

where "value" is a decimal number. For example, the instruction

$$L \qquad 7,=F'4'$$

places the full-word binary equivalent of 4 into register 7.

This is an example of the use of a *literal*. The equals sign instructs the assembler to insert the binary equivalent of the following constant into the machine language form of the program. The Load instruction requires that the second operand be in the memory; the assembler places the memory address of the space it allocated into the address portion of the instruction. We might think of the instruction above as equivalent to the pair of statements

	L	7,FOUR
FOUR	DC	F'4'

We leave it up to the assembler to provide the DC statement when we use a literal.

We can use a literal operand with any of the memory reference instructions, provided the operand is a *source* operand. Thus, we can add 10 to the contents of register 2 via the statement

$$A \qquad 2,=F'10'$$

while the statement

$$M \qquad 6,=F'110'$$

multiplies the contents of register 7 by 110.

7.2. INDEXED ADDRESSES

We now have at our disposal the instructions necessary to do arithmetic using operands stored in the computer memory. However, without using index registers, the processing of large amounts of information is often difficult, if not impossible.

Let us illustrate this point with an example. Suppose that we have 10 full words stored in the memory starting at an address called TABLE and that we wish to calculate the sum of the contents of these full words. Figure 7-1

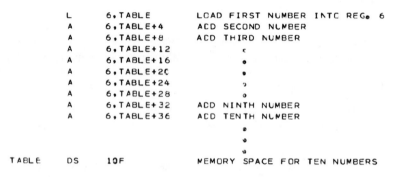

```
    L       6,TABLE          LOAD FIRST NUMBER INTC REG. 6
    A       6,TABLE+4        ACD SECOND NLMBER
    A       6,TABLE+8        ACD THIRD NUMBER
    A       6,TABLE+12          c
    A       6,TABLE+16          •
    A       6,TABLE+2C          •
    A       6,TABLE+24          ͻ
    A       6,TABLE+28          ₒ
    A       6,TABLE+32       ACD NINTH NUMBER
    A       6,TABLE+36       ACD TENTH NLMBER
                                •
                                ₒ
                                ₒ
TABLE   DS    10F            MEMORY SPACE FOR TEN NUMBERS
```

Fig. 7-1. Calculation of the sum of the contents of ten full words stored consecutively starting at TABLE.

shows how this can be done without using an index register. While this task is straightforward but somewhat tedious, suppose that we have to compute the sum of 100 or 1000 such numbers.

In Fig. 7-1 we had to write separate instructions to access each of the different words stored starting at TABLE. This we must do if we have no way to modify memory operand addresses at execution time. Suppose that we *could* modify the memory address used at execution time. Then we could put a single Add instruction in a loop and have the computer do the address modification for us.

The index register provides this facility. In the preceding sections we wrote symbolic representations of memory addresses as S2(X2) and left discussion of the use of the (X2) part of the operand specification until now. X2 represents any of the general-purpose registers 1 through 15 (register 0 is excluded from use as an index register). The *effective address*, the address that will be used at execution time, is the address represented by S2 plus the contents of the index register specified.

Effective address = S2 + (X2)

Suppose that we use register 9 as an index register and that we put an Add instruction inside a loop to compute the sum of the numbers stored at TABLE. We would write the Add instruction as

A   7,TABLE(9)

Each time this instruction is executed, the effective address is that corresponding to the symbol TABLE plus the contents of register 9. We must make sure that register 9 contains the proper values to make the effective addresses those of the desired words in TABLE.

To do this, the first time the instruction is executed the effective address should be that of the first word of the area called TABLE. Thus, register 9 should contain 0 the first time through the loop, for the effective address will then be

TABLE + (9) = TABLE + 0

which is the address of the first word of TABLE.

The second time through the loop we wish to add the second full word from TABLE which is stored 4 bytes beyond the beginning of the first word. Thus, register 9 should contain 4 the second time through the loop, for then the effective address will be

TABLE + (9) = TABLE + 4

In general, to address consecutive words in TABLE, we simply add 4 to the contents of register 9 each time we go around the loop. The effective addresses used will be the same as those in Fig. 7-1. The final contents of register 9, if we are to add 10 numbers together, should thus be 36_{10}. In general, if we wish to process N full words in a loop, then the final value of the index should be $4 \times (N - 1)$.

Figure 7-2 shows the use of an index register in computing the sum of 10 numbers stored in full words starting at TABLE. Register 3 is used as a loop counter which is started at 10 and counted down to 0 as the numbers are processed. Register 9 is the index register; its contents are counted up by 4 from 0 to 36_{10}.

An improvement in efficiency in the use of index registers often results if we observe that an index register can be used as a loop counter as well. Figure 7-3 shows the same calculations using register 9 both as an index register and as a loop counter.

The example of Fig. 5-9 indicates that it is not necessary to store a list of numbers in the memory if we need to use each number only once, as in computing the average of a series of numbers. Each number can be used as it is read from a card, and there is no need to store it in the memory. However, if we need to use data items more than once in a calculation, it is neces-

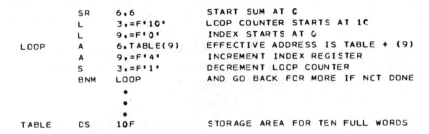

```
        SR    6,6            START SUM AT 0
        L     3,=F'10'       LOOP COUNTER STARTS AT 10
        L     9,=F'0'        INDEX STARTS AT 0
LOOP    A     6,TABLE(9)     EFFECTIVE ADDRESS IS TABLE + (9)
        A     9,=F'4'        INCREMENT INDEX REGISTER
        S     3,=F'1'        DECREMENT LOOP COUNTER
        BNM   LOOP           AND GO BACK FOR MORE IF NOT DONE
              •
              •
              •
TABLE   DS    10F            STORAGE AREA FOR TEN FULL WORDS
```

Fig. 7-2. Calculation of the sum of the contents of ten full words
stored consecutively starting at TABLE. Here we have used register
3 as a loop counter and register 9 as an index register.

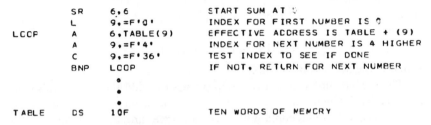

```
        SR    6,6            START SUM AT 0
        L     9,=F'0'        INDEX FOR FIRST NUMBER IS 0
LOOP    A     6,TABLE(9)     EFFECTIVE ADDRESS IS TABLE + (9)
        A     9,=F'4'        INDEX FOR NEXT NUMBER IS 4 HIGHER
        C     9,=F'36'       TEST INDEX TO SEE IF DONE
        BNP   LOOP           IF NOT, RETURN FOR NEXT NUMBER
              •
              •
              •
TABLE   DS    10F            TEN WORDS OF MEMORY
```

Fig. 7-3. Calculation of the sum of the contents of ten full words
starting at TABLE, using register 9 both as an index register and
a loop counter.

sary to store them in the memory, for we cannot reread a data card once it
has been read. An example of such a problem is the computation of the average of a series of numbers followed by the calculation of the difference
between each of the numbers and the computed average.

Figure 7-4 shows a flow chart to carry out these calculations. First, a data
card is read to indicate how many numbers are to be processed; the maximum number of numbers that can be processed is 100, as dictated by the DS
statement in Fig. 7-5 for the storage area called NMBRS. The next statements calculate the final value for the index register/loop counter. The
remainder of the program consists of three loops: The first reads the numbers
from data cards, the second computes their sum to be used to determine the
average, and the third computes and prints the difference between each of the
numbers and the average. Figure 7-5 is a program for this problem.

In this section we have emphasized the use of index registers in the serial
processing of lists of consecutive full words. The use of index registers is
certainly not restricted to just such problems. In the next section we shall
indicate that index registers can be used for serial processing of half-word
data. In general, the use of index registers is beneficial whenever we wish to
modify memory addresses at execution time. This flexibility permits the access
of single desired items from tabular data, as is indicated in the exercises.

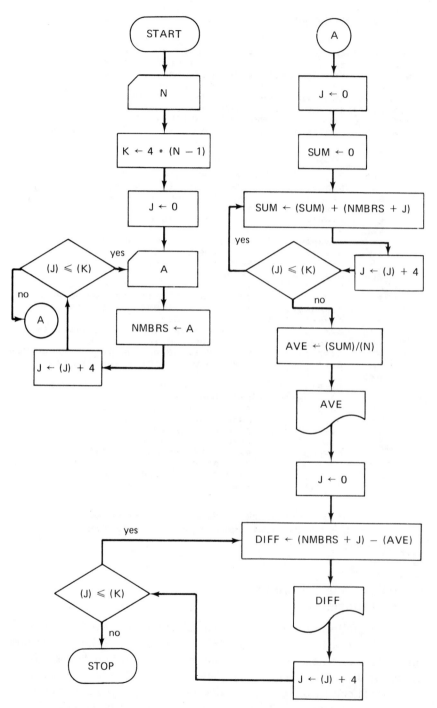

Fig. 7-4. Flowchart of a program to calculate the average of a series of numbers and the difference between each number and the computed average.

```
*     THIS PROGRAM READS A DATA CARD WHICH TELLS HOW MANY
*     NUMBERS ARE TO BE PROCESSED.  THAT NUMBER IS KEPT IN
*     REG.  8.  IT THEN CALCULATES THE UPPER VALUE FOR INDEX
*     REGISTERS AND LEAVES THAT NUMBER IN REG. 3
*     IT READS THE NUMBERS ONE AT A TIME. STORING THEM IN
*     CONSECUTIVE FULL WORDS OF THE AREA CALLED NMBRS.  THE
*     AVERAGE OF ALL THE NUMBERS IS COMPUTED. AS IS THE
*     DIFFERENCE BETWEEN EACH OF THE NUMBERS AND THE AVERAGE.
AVEDIF    START 0
          PRINT NOGEN
          INITIAL
          RWD   3                READ NUMBER OF NUMBERS TO USE
          LR    8,3              KEEP A COPY IN REG. 8
          S     3,=F'1'          COMPUTE FINAL INDEX VALUE,
          M     2,=F'4'          4*((3) - 1)
          L     9,=F'0'          INDEX FOR READ LOOP STARTS AT 0
READLOOP  RWD   4                READ A DATA NUMBER
          ST    4,NMBRS(9)       STORE IT AT EFF. ADDRESS NMBRS + (9)
          A     9,=F'4'          NEXT NUMBER STORED AT ADDRESS 4 HIGHER
          CR    9,3              TEST INDEX AGAINST FINAL VALUE KEPT
          BNP   READLOOP         IN REG. 3
          L     9,=F'0'          INDEX FOR LOOP TO COMPUTE SUM AT 0
          SR    7,7              START SUM AT 0 (IN ODD NMBRD REG.)
ADDLOOP   A     7,NMBRS(9)       ADD NUMBER AT NMBRS + (9) TO SUM
          A     9,=F'4'          ADD 4 TO INDEX
          CR    9,3              COMPARE WITH FINAL VALUE STILL IN 3
          BNP   ADDLOOP          GO TO ADDLOOP IF NOT DONE
          M     6,=F'1'          WHEN HERE. READY FOR DIVIDE TO COMPUTE
          DR    6,8              AVERAGE BY DIVIDING SUM BY (8)
          WWD   7                PRINT THE AVERAGE
          L     9,=F'0'          AND PREPARE TO COMPUTE DIFFERENCES
DIFLOOP   L     10,NMBRS(9)      GET NUMBER FROM NMBRS + (9)
          SR    10,7             SUBTRACT AVERAGE IN REG. 7
          WWD   10               PRINT THE DIFFERENCE
          A     9,=F'4'          INCREMENT INDEX REG.
          CR    9,3              COMPARE WITH FINAL VALUE
          BNP   DIFLOOP          REPEAT IF RESULT NEGATIVE OR 0
          EOJ                    PROCESSING COMPLETED
NMBRS     DS    100F             STORAGE SPACE FOR NUMBERS PROCESSED
          END   AVEDIF           END OF PROGRAM
```

Fig. 7-5. A program to calculate the average of a series of numbers and then calculate the difference between each number and the average.

7.3. HALF-WORD OPERANDS AND INSTRUCTIONS

A 32-bit full word can be used to contain binary integers between -2^{31} and $+2^{31} - 1$ or between $-2,147,483,648$ and $2,147,483,647$. For most numerical applications, integers of such magnitude are rarely used. Index register values, loop counters, and data numbers often fit into half-word units, which consist of 16 binary digits. Integers represented as half-words can have values between -2^{15} and $+2^{15} - 1$, that is, between $-32,768$ and $32,767$.

When dealing with large amounts of numerical data that must be stored in the memory, a considerable savings in memory space can result from the use of half-word representation of the data, if the numbers are small enough. The IBM 360 supports this option by providing a set of half-word information move, arithmetic, and comparison instructions.

These instructions are all RX instructions; the first operand is a general-purpose register, while the second is a half-word from the memory. When a half-word is brought from the memory for use as an operand, it is first converted to a full word by extension of its sign bit through 16 bits to the left. Thus, if the binary half-word

$$1100\ 1001\ 0010\ 1010$$

is used as an operand, it is first converted to its full-word equivalent,

$$1111\ 1111\ 1111\ 1111\ 1100\ 1001\ 0010\ 1010$$

since the half-word value is negative. A positive half-word, such as

$$0000\ 0000\ 1000\ 0000$$

is converted to

$$0000\ 0000\ 0000\ 0000\ 0000\ 0000\ 1000\ 0000$$

before use as an operand. The full-word form of the number thus converted is then ready for use as if it were a full-word operand.

7.3.1. Information Move

LH	R1,S2(X2)	Load Half-word	R1 ⟵ (S2(X2))$_H$
STH	R1,S2(X2)	STore Half-word	(R1)$_H$ ⟶ S2(X2)

The Load Halfword instruction moves the full-word expansion of the half-word stored at S2 + (X2) into the register designated as R1. Suppose that we have the DC statements

HONE	DC	H'1'
HMFOUR	DC	H' − 4'

Then the instruction

LH   3,HONE

places 00000001 in register 3, while

LH   8,HMFOUR

or

LH   8,HONE+2

moves FFFFFFFC into register 8.

STH moves the low-order 16 bits, bits 16 through 31, of (R1) to the memory half-word at effective address S2 + (X2). The instruction

STH   5,HW+6

stores FFF0 at the fourth half-word of the area HW if register 5 contains FFFFFFF0 (or 0186FFF0).

7.3.2. Arithmetic

The half-word arithmetic instructions are

AH	R1,S2(X2)	Add Half-word	$R1 \longleftarrow (R1) + (S2(X2))_H$
SH	R1,S2(X2)	Subtract Half-word	$R1 \longleftarrow (R1) - (S2(X2))_H$
MH	R1,S2(X2)	Multiply Half-word	$R1 \longleftarrow (R1) \times (S2(X2))_H$

The Add Half-word and Subtract Half-word instructions have the same effect as their full-word counterparts, A and S, respectively, with the exception that the memory operand is a half-word which is converted to a full word before the operation is carried out. These instructions set the condition code in the same way as do A and S.

The Multiply Half-word instruction differs from the M and MR instructions in that the resulting product is contained in a single register. The product computed is that of the contents of R1 and the half-word stored at S2 + (X2). R1 may be any of the general-purpose registers; there is no requirement that it be an even-numbered register.

The form for a literal half-word constant is

$$=H'value'$$

where "value" is a decimal number of magnitude within the prescribed bounds for storage in a half-word. Thus, the instruction

MH   3,=H'4'

multiplies the contents of register 3 by the number 4.

The result of an MH instruction might be a number requiring 46 binary digits to specify its magnitude. If a product does not fit into a 32-bit full word, the leftmost bits that do not fit are lost. There is no indication to the programmer when this occurs. Therefore, he must be sure that this truncation either will not occur or that it does not matter when he uses the MH instruction.

7.3.3. Comparison

The half-word comparison instruction is

CH	R1,S2(X2)	Compare Halfword	Set CC according to value of $(R1) - (S2(X2))_H$

Its effect is to subtract the contents of the half-word stored at S2 + (X2) from (R1) and to set the condition code to reflect the nature of the result. Thus, given the following stored at TESTS,

TESTS: 0010FF000004

and the register contents

(6) = 00000004

the instructions

CH	6,TESTS
CH	6,TESTS + 2
CH	6,TESTS + 4

set the condition code to indicate a negative, positive, and zero result, respectively.

As is the case with all the comparison instructions, the CH instruction has no effect on any memory or register contents.

CHAPTER SUMMARY

Table 7-1 shows the *full-word RX instructions* discussed in this chapter.

The *index register* makes possible the processing of lists of related data through address modifications at execution time.

Table 7-2 shows the *RX half-word instructions* discussed in this chapter.

Table 7-1   INFORMATION MOVE, ARITHMETIC, AND COMPARISON RX INSTRUCTIONS WHICH USE FULL WORD MEMORY OPERANDS

L	R1,S2(X2)	Load	$R1 \leftarrow (S2(X2))_F$
ST	R1,S2(X2)	STore	$(R1) \rightarrow S2(X2)_F$
A	R1,S2(X2)	Add	$R1 \leftarrow (R1) + (S2(X2))_F$
S	R1,S2(X2)	Subtract	$R1 \leftarrow (R1) - (S2(X2))_F$
M	R1,S2(X2)	Multiply	$R1,R1+1 \leftarrow (R1+1) \times (S2(X2))_F$
D	R1,S2(X2)	Divide	$(R1,R1+1) \div (S2(X2))_F$
			quotient $\rightarrow R1+1$
			remainder $\rightarrow R1$
C	R1,S2(X2)	Compare	Set CC according to value of $(R1) - (S2(X2))_F$

Table 7-2   INFORMATION MOVE, ARITHMETIC, AND COMPARISON RX INSTRUCTIONS WHICH USE HALF-WORD MEMORY OPERANDS

LH	R1,S2(X2)	Load Half-word	$R1 \leftarrow (S2(X2))_H$
STH	R1,S2(X2)	STore Half-word	$(R1)_H \rightarrow S2(X2)$
AH	R1,S2(X2)	Add Half-word	$R1 \leftarrow (R1) + (S2(X2))_H$
SH	R1,S2(X2)	Subtract Half-word	$R1 \leftarrow (R1) - (S2(X2))_H$
MH	R1,S2(X2)	Multiply Half-word	$R1 \leftarrow (R1) \times (S2(X2))_H$
CH	R1,S2(X2)	Compare Half-word	Set CC according to value of $(R1) - (S2(X2))_H$

EXERCISES

1. Redo the party game in Exercise 5 in Chapter 5 using DC statements to define the numerical constants.

2. Redo the change return problem in Exercise 6 in Chapter 5 using DC statements to define the numerical constants.

3. Redo the party game in Exercise 5 in Chapter 5 using half-word arithmetic.

4. Write a program to read a series of up to 100 data cards and print the numbers punched on them in reverse order from that in which they were read.

5. Write a program to read a series of up to 100 numbers from cards, print the numbers in the order read, sort them into ascending numerical order, and print the results.

6. The standard deviation of a set of numbers is the square root of the average of the squares of the differences between the numbers and the average of the numbers. Let XBAR be the average of the numbers $X_1, X_2, \ldots, X_N$. Then the standard deviation SIGMA of the set of numbers is

$$\text{SIGMA} = \sqrt{\frac{\sum_{i=1}^{n} (X_i - \text{XBAR})^2}{N}}$$

Write a program to calculate the standard deviation of up to 100 numbers, using the technique described in Exercise 8 in Chapter 5 to compute the square root to the nearest integer.

7. A crude bank account routine can be designed as follows:
   (a) The program reads a data card which determines the number M of active accounts.
   (b) M pairs of data cards follow. Each pair consists of an account number and the current balance for that account. The account number is used as an index to use in storing the current balance in a list. The balance is in pennies.
   (c) The remaining data cards consist of pairs of cards indicating banking transactions. The first number of each pair is an account number; the second contains the amount of the transaction, a negative amount for a withdrawal and a positive amount for a deposit. For each transaction pair the account number is used as an index designating to which current balance the transaction amount should be added. Transaction pairs are processed until a trailer card containing a negative account number is encountered.
   Write a program to implement this model bank account procedure for a bank that has at most 100 customers.

8. The use of the account number as an index in Exercise 7 puts unnecessary restrictions on the possible account numbers, since they must be between 0 and 396. Why? An alternative is to use any positive integer as an account number and to use four times the remainder upon division of the account number by 100 as the index for the table of balances. This is a simple example of the use

of information contained in a *key*, the account number in this example, to determine the computer address of information associated with the key. This technique is called *hashing* or *mapping*. The index so calculated is called a *hash code*.

9. Redo the number conversion in Exercise 11 in Chapter 5 so that the digits in the converted number will be printed in the proper order.

REFERENCES

IBM System/360 Disk and Tape Operating System Assembler Language, Form GC24-3414, IBM Corp., White Plains, N.Y.

IBM System/360 Operating System Assembler Language, Form GC28-6514, IBM Corp., White Plains, N.Y.

IBM System/360 Principles of Operation, Form GA22-6821, IBM Corp., White Plains, N.Y.

IBM System/370 Principles of Operation, Form GA22-7000, IBM Corp., White Plains, N.Y.

IBM OS/VS—DOS/VS Assembler Language, Form GC33-4010, IBM Corp., White Plains, N.Y.

8 MACHINE LANGUAGE: MEMORY ADDRESSES

Research is currently going on to develop a *contents-addressable memory* in which symbolic names could be used for actual memory addresses. Unfortunately, the fruits of this research are not yet available to us. Therefore, machine language addresses are numerical, and assemblers and compilers must translate symbols that stand for memory addresses into their numerical machine equivalents. The IBM 360 and all other commercially available machine have *coordinate-addressable memories* in which this numerical addressing is necessary.

Our programming capabilities and understanding of computing principles will improve significantly when we see how addressing is done in the computer. The RX machine language instruction format offers a good basis for discussion of this matter. We shall see that an alternative to using symbolic names to stand for memory addresses is to specify the actual addresses we want. Finally, we shall consider a handy instruction that allows us to use the memory address hardware to do arithmetic.

8.1. MEMORY ADDRESSES

In assembly language we can assign symbolic names to memory addresses, and then use these names as operands. The assembler takes care of the problem of converting these symbols to their equivalent memory addresses. But there are some problems in which it is necessary for the program to compute memory addresses and others in which we must specify addresses in their machine language form. Thus, a study of the machine language equivalent of symbolic addresses will both increase our programming power and help us understand how the machine works.

At first thought, the problem of assigning actual memory addresses to symbolic names has a simple solution. We use a counter, such as the location counter, to supply the addresses at which the information is stored, relative to the beginning of the program. If the instruction corresponding to the symbolic name LOOP has location counter value 70, then we could use 70 as the memory address corresponding to the symbol LOOP. If we had the instruction

B   LOOP

in the program, then the machine language memory address field in the Branch instruction would contain the number 70. This is the way machine language addresses are treated in the smaller computing machines. The numerical memory address, the *absolute* address, corresponding to a symbolic operand is placed in the memory address fields of the instructions that use that symbol as an operand.

The use of absolute addresses creates problems that severely restrict the flexibility of memory use. In the example above, the first byte of the program has to be stored at address 0 in order for the program to work. If the program is stored starting at address 200 instead, the instruction labeled LOOP is stored at address 270. The Branch instruction causes a branch to location 70, which is not even part of the program, much less the desired address. The problem with absolute addressing is that the machine language program must be stored in the memory exactly where the programmer and the assembler assume it will be stored. Otherwise, data and instruction addresses will not be the same as the absolute addresses in the machine language form of the instruction.

This problem becomes even more serious when we wish to have several programs stored in the memory at the same time. We can arrange matters so that the first byte of a program can be stored at an address other than 0. We could have an assembler directive saying, for example, "Add 200 to the value of the location counter to obtain the machine address of an operand." If we used this directive in our example program, then LOOP would correspond to the address 270, and the program would work properly if the program were stored starting at address 200. But now suppose that we have a program which requires the use of several other programs, or *subroutines*, in its execution. We then have to plan ahead to make sure that each program is assembled so that the proper addresses are placed in the machine language versions of the programs. In this planning, we have to know in advance the length of each program to be sure that they do not overlap when we store them in the memory. And we must use the absolute addresses of the subprograms in those instructions which branch to them.

In a modern multiprogramming system, in which several programs for each of several users are stored in the memory at the same time, the operating system decides where each program is to be stored. It is impossible for the programmer to specify where his programs will be stored. Machine language addresses must be such that the programs are *relocatable*. A relocatable program is one that will function properly no matter where it is stored in the computer memory. This means that the effective memory addresses of the operands in the program are calculated not by the assembler or by the programmer but by the computer at program execution time.

If we cannot use absolute addresses, how, then, can we have the machine calculate memory addresses to ensure that the proper final addresses are obtained? Our example above sheds some light on this question. No matter where the instruction named LOOP is stored in the memory, it is always 70_{16} bytes beyond the beginning of the program. Similarly, if the same program also contains the statement

WDS   DS   2F

and the symbol WDS has location counter value 150, then no matter where the program is stored, the first byte of the area called WDS is 150_{16} bytes beyond the beginning of the program (see Fig. 8-1). We would say that the

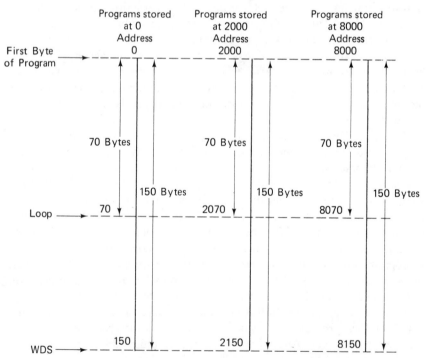

Fig. 8-1. No matter where the program is stored, LOOP and WDS will always be 70_{16} and 150_{16} bytes, respectively, beyond the beginning of the program.

address of WDS is 150 *relative to* the first byte of the program. We might think of the address of memory area A relative to that of memory area B as the *distance*, in bytes, between the machine language equivalents of A and B. Or, we can say,

address of A relative to B = address of A − address of B

In some modern computer systems, location counter values are used to solve the relocatability problem. The assembler places the location counter value of a symbol into the operands fields of those instructions which use it as an operand. When the program is loaded, a record is kept as to where the first byte of the program has been stored. At execution time, this address, the *load address*, is added to the numbers in the operands fields to obtain the effective operand addresses.

If it were done this way in the IBM 360, the machine language address field in the instruction

B   LOOP

would contain the location counter value 70, which is that of LOOP. Suppose that the program is stored in the memory starting at address 50000. Then when the branch instruction is executed, the load address 50000 would be added to the number in the address field of the instruction to form the operand address 50070, which is the address where the instruction labeled LOOP is actually stored.

The IBM System/360–370 software and hardware use a generalization of this technique to ensure the relocatability of machine language programs. Let us see how it is done.

8.1.1. The Displacement

In the examples above, we used the location counter values for the relative addresses to be used in calculating final memory addresses. These final addresses were computed as the sum of the location counter value and the program load address.

However, it is not necessary to use location counter values for the relative addresses. The address of any location in a program relative to any other location in the same program is constant, regardless of where the program is stored. Thus, we can use any position in the program as the *base position*, which is the position in the program relative to which the relative addresses are calculated. The *displacement of a quantity is its address relative to the address of the base position.* The only restriction on base positions is that they must be selected so as to ensure *positive* displacements that are less than 4096_{10}.

Returning to our previous example, wherein the symbols LOOP and WDS had location counter values 70 and 150, respectively, let us suppose that the base position in the program had location counter value 60. The displacement of LOOP would then be 10, while that of WDS would be F0.

The *base address* is the memory address at which the byte corresponding to the base position is stored in the memory at execution time. At execution time, the effective address equivalent to a given symbol is simply the base address plus the displacement of the symbol:

effective address = base address + displacement

Suppose in our example that the base address is 50060. Then the effective address corresponding to LOOP is

address LOOP = 50060 + 10 = 50070

while that of WDS is

address WDS = 50060 + F0 = 50150

Notice that these addresses are the same as those we obtained using the location counter values for relative addresses and the load address for the base address. If we choose the base position to be that of the first byte of the program, then the displacement of a symbol is the same as its location counter value.

Figure 8-2 shows some further examples of base-displacement addressing.

8.1.2. The Base Register

The assembler inserts the displacements corresponding to symbols into their appropriate places in the machine language operands fields. When an instruction that refers to the memory is executed, the displacement is added to the base address to determine the effective memory address. This process is repeated every time the machine encounters a memory operand. How does the machine find the base address?

The logical place in which to keep a number that is used so often is in a register, and indeed that is just what is done. Any of the general-purpose registers except register 0 can be used as a *base register*. The number of the register being used as the base register is part of the machine language address field of a memory operand. When the machine encounters a memory address field, it computes the effective address as the displacement plus the contents of the designated base register:

effective address = displacement + (base register)

Thus, if we have the base address stored in the base register, the operands are addressed as we expected when we wrote the assembly language program.

Until now, we have been designating memory operands by the symbol S2 and saying that S2 represents a symbolic name or expression whose value is a memory address. We can now improve upon that definition by the statement that S2 is any *relocatable* symbol or expression. In general, a

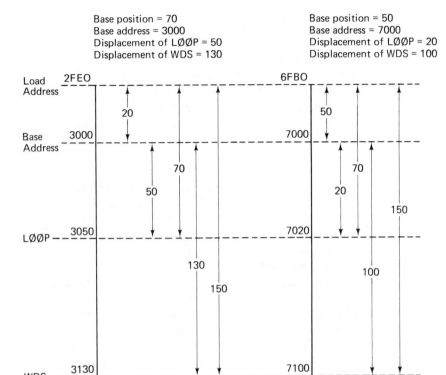

Fig. 8-2. The use of base addresses and displacements in computing memory addresses.

relocatable program is one that can be moved from one portion of storage to another and still be executable. In the IBM 360 and 370, programs are made relocatable by using relocatable symbols, which we represent in the machine language as a base register and a displacement. We again point out that the *assembler* takes care of the machine addresses so that programs are relocatable.

The programmer has some responsibilities in ensuring the proper designation and use of the base register. We must select the base position, specify the base register, and include an instruction to load the base register with the the base address. The INITIAL macro contains the necessary statements to carry out these tasks; INITIAL establishes register 13 as the base register and loads it with the base address. Chapter 13 provides details on how this is done.

The use of the base register and displacement rule for addresses solves the relocatability problem. The program can be stored anywhere in the memory, and, provided that the base register is properly loaded, the correct memory operand addresses will be used when the program is executed.

8.1.3. Relocatable Addresses: Machine Language
Format

We shall now investigate the form a relocatable address consisting of a base register and displacement takes in the machine language. We have described the machine language format as consisting of two fields—the operation field and the operands field. The operands field contains one *subfield* for each operand; in the RR instructions the two subfields contain register numbers. In memory reference instructions, those subfields that correspond to memory operands indicate the displacements and base registers corresponding to the desired memory addresses. We shall call such a subfield an *S-type address field* because it represents a relocatable Storage address.

The displacement in machine language is a 12-bit *unsigned* binary integer. Thus, the minimum hexadecimal value a dispalcement can have is 000, while the maximum is FFF. The decimal equivalents of these numbers are 0 and 4095, respectively, and thus the rule we stated above: The displacement must be between 0 and 4095 inclusive.

The base register is specified by a 4-bit binary integer 0001 through 1111. This can, of course, be represented by the hexadecimal values 1 through F.

An S-type address field is 2 bytes long. The first nibble indicates the base register, and the remaining three nibbles contain the displacement. In the symbolic notation, we represent the base register by B and the displacement by D, with integers afterward describing to which operands the letters correspond. For example, B1 represents the base register for the first operand, while D2 means the displacement for the second operand. In this notation, we write

$$\text{effective address} = D + (B)$$

The machine language structure of an S-type address field is

$$\boxed{\quad B \quad | \quad \longleftarrow \quad | \quad D \quad | \quad \longrightarrow \quad}$$

The solid vertical lines denote byte boundaries. The dashed lines divide each byte into nibbles. The base register number occupies the first nibble, and the displacement fills the remainder of the 2 bytes.

Suppose that we are using register 12 as the base register and that LOOP has displacement 38. Then the S-address field of an instruction that refers to LOOP is

$$\boxed{\quad C \quad | \quad 0 \quad | \quad 3 \quad | \quad 8 \quad}$$

Notice that we must fill in all the displacement area even if three hexadecimal digits are not needed to specify the displacement. There are no "blanks" in the machine language.

Register 0 is not available for use as a base register. Specification of 0 in the base register position of an S-type address means that no base register is to be used; the effective address is just the displacement. Thus, absolute addressing is possible in the 360 machines, although the maximum address that can be used in this manner is FFF.

Recall that step 4 in the machine instruction execution cycle is the *operand fetch* step, in which the addresses of the operands are computed, if necessary, and the operands are fetched and sent to the appropriate computer component. Now we see that, in computing the operand addresses, the machine adds the contents of the base register to the displacement.

The effective addresses are calculated in special arithmetic circuitry dedicated to this purpose. The final form of a machine address is a 24-bit unsigned binary integer that is stored in a *memory address register* (MAR). In the operand fetch step of an instruction, the machine sends the displacement to the memory address register. It then examines then base register segment of the S-address. If this segment contains 0, then no modification of the MAR contents takes place; the effective address is the 24-bit number stored in the MAR. If the base register segment is not 0, the machine adds the contents of the indicated base register to the contents of the MAR. The resulting MAR contents are used for the memory address from which the operand is to be fetched or into which the operand is to be stored.

8.1.4. The Index Register

In the RX instructions, modification of the effective address can be accomplished through the use of an index register. We describe the memory operand in the symbolic notation as

$$S2(X2)$$

where now we realize that S2 represents any relocatable symbol or expression. That is, S2 implies a base register and displacement representing the symbol or expression used in this portion of the operand. X2 is an index register that permits modification of the basic relocatable address that S2 represents.

The effective address corresponding to S2(X2) we saw to be

$$\text{effective address} = S2 + (X2)$$

But we now know that S2 stands for a base register and displacement pair:

$$S2 = D2 + (B2)$$

Putting this together we have, for an indexed address,

$$\text{effective address} = D2 + (B2) + (X2)$$

The contents of the index register is added to the S-type address to provide the desired address modification.

For example, if the displacement of the symbol NMBRS is 200, if register

12 is the base register and contains 00060000 (the base address), and if register 6 contains 00000008, then the instruction

ST   2,NUMBRS(6)

stores (2) into the full word starting at address

$$200 + (12) + (6) = 200 + 00060000 + 00000008 = 060208$$

An indexed address is thus a modification of an S-type address. In an *X-type address field*, the index register is specified before the S-type address it modifies. Thus, an X-type address has the form

X	B	←	D	→

In the instruction

ST   2,NMBRS(6)

discussed above, the memory address field of the equivalent machine language instruction is

6	C	2	0	0

As is the case with the base register, specification of 0 in the X segment of the S-type address means that no index register will be used. In this case the effective address is simply D2 + (B2).

Returning to our discussion of machine address calculation, in computing the effective address corresponding to an X-type address, the S portion of the address is calculated as discussed above. The index register nibble is then examined. If this nibble is 0, the MAR is left unchanged. If it is not 0, the contents of the indicated register are added to the contents of the MAR to produce the effective address.

8.1.5. Memory Address Exceptions

Before reference to the memory is permitted, the system checks the final address contained in the MAR for two possible error conditions. The first arises when the final address is not to be found in the system in which the program is being executed. Very few IBM 360 or 370 systems include the full 16,777,216 bytes possible in the largest memory available for the system. A normal memory size is closer to one million bytes. Therefore, it is possible to compute addresses for which there are not corresponding memory locations, since the 24-bit MAR can, in principle, contain any address up to 16 million-plus. When the final address is one that is not included in the memory of the particular system being used, an *addressing exception* results, which terminates program execution.

The second kind of memory address error arises when we attempt to access a memory location that is available in the machine but is not within our designated area. When a job step is initiated, it is given a section, or *region*, of the memory for use by the program that is executed in the step. In most systems, we are not permitted to store information outside the area allocated to us. In some systems we are not even permitted to fetch from locations beyond the boundaries of our region. The former facility is called *storage protection*, and the latter *fetch protection*. Their purpose is to protect the operating system and other users from accidental or intentional misuse of the memory. When an attempt is made to access memory outside our region, a *protection exception* results, with accompanying termination of program execution.

A protection or addressing exception usually is the result of the misuse of index and/or base registers in a program.

8.2. THE RX INSTRUCTION FORMAT

We now know how memory addresses are specified in machine language. Let us use this information to develop the RX machine language instruction format.

The RX instructions are 4 bytes long. Recall that in all machine language instructions the first byte contains the operation code. Thus, we have so far

OP			

where OP stands for the 8-bit code for the desired operation.

The memory address portion of the instruction is an S-type address field modified by an index register to form an X-type address field. The S-type address goes into the last 2 bytes:

OP		B2	←	D2	→

B2 is the number of the base register, while D2 is the 12-bit displacement. To get the X-type address, we include the index register, X2:

OP		X2	B2	←	D2	→

All we have left is to insert the first register operand, R1, which goes into the remaining nibble to give the complete format for a RX instruction:

OP	R1	X2	B2	←	D2	→

Let us try some examples. Suppose that the symbol CAB has a displacement of 1C8 and that register 3 is the base register. The instruction

A   5,CAB(8)

is translated as the machine language equivalent

5A	5	8	3	1	C	8

How did this arise? The operation code for Add is 5A. Register 5 is the first register operand and goes into the R1 position in the machine language. The base register, register 3, goes into the B2 position. The displacement, 1C8, corresponding to D2 appears in the last 3 nibbles to complete the S-type address field. The index register is register 8, which has been placed in the X2 position in the instruction, completing the translation.

What about the instruction

$$\text{M} \qquad 10,\text{CAB}+4$$

The symbol CAB implies base register 3 and a displacement 1C8. The requested address is 4 bytes higher; the displacement we use is thus 1CC. We did not specify an index register; the nibble in the X2 position must be 0. Since the operation code for M is 5C, the resulting instruction is

5C	A	0	3	1	C	C

8.3. OPERAND SPECIFICATION

The specification of register operands is simple; we give the numbers of the desired registers. The specification of memory addresses is just as easy as long as we use symbolic names for memory addresses. The possibility of using an index register allows greater flexibility in the use of memory operands. Let us now investigate some further means of specifying memory operand addresses.

8.3.1. Implicit Addresses

When we use a symbolic name to represent a relocatable address, that name is a *relocatable symbol*. Similarly, when we use an expression to represent a relocatable address, that expression can be called a *relocatable expression*. A relocatable symbol or expression is replaced by a base register and displacement in its machine language equivalent.

When we use a relocatable symbol or expression, we leave it up to the assembler to insert the appropriate base register number and displacement into the machine language. A relocatable symbol or expression *implies* a base register-displacement pair. The symbol ABC in the instruction

$$\text{L} \qquad 2,\text{ABC}$$

is an implicit specification of a memory address consisting of a base register and displacement. The use of relocatable symbols and expressions is called the *implicit specification* of operand addresses.

8.3.2. Explicit Addresses

In most applications, we let the assembler take care of the busy work involved in supplying displacements and base registers for memory addresses; we specify the base register and displacement implicitly through the use of relocatable symbols and expressions to represent memory addresses. However, many instances occur in which it is necessary for us to designate our own base registers and displacements. We shall soon see that many problems involving character manipulation cannot be done using implicit operand specification. And improvements in efficiency often result when we choose our own base registers and displacements.

Specification of base registers and displacements by the *programmer* is called *explicit specification*, in contrast to implicit specification of these quantities, in which the *assembler* furnishes them. The explicit form of an address consists of a base register, index register, and displacement for an X-type address. In our symbolic notation, the memory address field of an RX instruction written in assembly language has the form

$$D(X,B)$$

where D, X, and B stand for the displacement, index register, and base register, respectively. D is usually written in decimal; the assembler converts the decimal value to its hexadecimal equivalent for insertion into the machine language.

In the symbolic description of the Load instruction, for example, we wrote

$$L \qquad R1,S2(X2)$$

in which the memory address is given in its implicit form. S2 stands for a relocatable symbol or expression. The equivalent of this description in which the memory address given in its explicit form is

$$L \qquad R1,D2(X2,B2)$$

From now on we shall give the explicit forms for the memory operands in the description of new instructions. You should be aware of the fact that whenever an operand includes a base register and displacement, the implicit form is also available for use.

Consider the instruction

$$A \qquad 7,100(5,10)$$

The effective address is of course

$$\text{displacement} + (\text{index register}) + (\text{base register})$$

In this case, the displacement is $100_{10} = 64_{16}$, Register 5 is the index register, and register 10 is the base register. The effective address in this case is

$$64 + (5) + (10)$$

If

$$(5) = 00000008$$

and

$$(10) = 00020000$$

then execution of the instruction causes the full word at address 02006C to be added to the contents of register 7. Figure 8-3 illustrates the, use of an explicit address in an Add instruction.

```
        SR    6,6           START SUM AT 0
        L     9,=F'0'       INCEX FOR FIRST NUMBER IS 0
        LA    10,NMBRS      LOAD REGISTER 1C WITH ADDRESS CF NMBRS
LOOP    A     6,0(9,10)     EFFECTIVE ADDRESS IS (9) + (10)
        A     9,=F'4'       INDEX FOR NEXT NLMBER IS 4 HIGHER
        C     9,=F'36'      TEST INDEX TO SEE IF DONE
        BNP   LOOP          IF NOT, RETURN FCR NEXT NUMBER
              •
              •
              •
NMBRS   CS    10F           TEN WORDS OF MEMCRY
```

Fig. 8-3. The use of an explicit address. In the instruction labeled LOOP, register 9 is used as an index register and register 10 as a base register.

The machine language form of the above instruction is easy to derive, since we have all the components displayed explicitly. It is

$$5A75A064$$

Suppose that we want to store the contents of register 3 at 4 bytes beyond an address contained in register 6 and use register 2 to modify the address. We choose register 6 as the base register and register 2 as the index register and use a displacement of 4. Thus, we write

$$ST \qquad 3,4(2,6)$$

to accomplish our objective.

Notice that, insofar as the machine is concerned, there is no real difference between an index register and a base register in the calculation of memory addresses. We could just as well have written

$$ST \qquad 3,4(6,2)$$

interchanging the roles of registers 2 and 6. However, there *is* a difference between the base register and the index register to the assembler. The assembler supplies an implied base register when filling in the address portion of a memory reference instruction. There is no such thing as an implied index register. While the order in which we specify the index and base registers in an explicit operand is immaterial, it helps the programmer and others who read his programs to keep the two distinct by writing them in their proper order.

Suppose that we do not want to use an index register. Say that we want to subtract the contents of the half-word stored 10 bytes beyond the address contained in register 12 from the contents of register 11. In this case we should specify 0 as the index register, meaning that no indexing is to be done. We should write

> SH   11,10(0,12)

The assembler is fairly liberal in allowing shorthand ways to specify explicit addresses when no index register and/or no base register is being used. We could have written the above as

> SH   11,10(,12)

where we have omitted the 0, leaving in the comma, or even as

> SH   11,10(12)

where we have omitted both the 0 and the comma. You should refrain from using either of these abbreviations until you are sure you have mastered the principles of explicit address specification and addressing memory operands in general.

Suppose that we want to store the contents of register 5 at the address contained in register 8. Since we do not want to use an index register and the exact address is already in register 8, then 0 should be specified for both the index register and the displacement. The instruction

> ST   5,0(0,8)

is the proper answer.

In Section 8.1 we saw that the base register and displacement technique allows us to forego absolute addressing. But in some systems programming applications and in using the LA instruction described in the next section, absolute addressing is necessary. If we specify an address in which there is no base register or index register, the effective address is simply a number, the displacement portion of the address field. Suppose that we wish to store the contents of register 5 at address 8. We eliminate the index register and base register address modifications by placing 0 in the corresponding positions in the explicit form of the address field. Thus, we write

> ST   5,8(0,0)

Here the displacement has been given as 8. Since no base or index register contents will be added to the displacement, the effective address is simply the displacement, 8.

Shorthand versions for absolute addresses are also possible. Thus, we could write

ST   5,8(,0)

or

ST   5,8(,)

or even

ST   5,8

Again, I suggest that you not use these shortened forms for a while.

Thus, the assembler permits two means of specifying memory addresses. We can use the explicit form, in which we ourselves specify the displacement and base register, or we can use the implicit form in which we leave it up to the assembler to supply the displacement and base register. When we use relocatable symbols or expressions for memory addresses, we in effect choose the implicit form.

We use the implicit form whenever possible because programming is easier when we use symbolic names for memory addresses. Indeed, that is one of the main reasons we program in assembly language instead of machine language. Circumstances arise when we must write the addresses in their machine language form. In those cases, we use the explicit form for memory addresses.

8.4. THE LA INSTRUCTION

By now, the distinction between memory addresses and the contents at those addresses should be clear to you. If not, I suggest that you go back and review before proceeding with this section.

It is often necessary to place a memory address in a register. As discussed in the proceding section, a register that contains an address can be used as a base register in the explicit designation of a memory address. It is also often necessary to load small numbers, constants, into registers for use as loop counters, increments, or indexes, for example. Loop counters and indexes must often be incremented or decremented in a loop. We can use the powerful Load Address instruction to accomplish all these tasks, often with a significant savings in time and memory space.

LA   R1,D2(X2,B2)   Load Address   R1 ←— D2 + (X2) + (B2)

The LA instruction is an RX instruction that loads the effective address into the register operand. It makes no reference whatsover to the memory; the final contents of the memory address register are moved into R1.

Consider the instruction

LA   9,NMBR

NMBR is a relocatable symbol representing an implied base register and displacement. In the execution of this instruction, the machine computes the sum of the displacement and the base register contents in the MAR and moves the result into register 9. The effect is to load the memory address NMBR stands for into register 9.

But memory addresses are 24 bits long, while the registers consist of 32-bit full words. The 24-bit contents of the MAR go to the low-order 24 bits of the register, bits 8 through 31 (we start counting bits at 0, remember). LA always resets the first 8 bits of the register to 0.

Suppose that the implied base register is register 12, with contents

$$(12) = 0060480C$$

and that the displacement of NMBR is 200. Then the effective 24-bit address of NMBR is 604A0C. No matter what the previous contents of register 9 were, execution of the instruction above results in

$$(9) = 00604A0C$$

If we had written

    LA   9,NMBR(6)

and

$$(6) = 00000008$$

then the result is (check this)

$$(9) = 00604A14$$

Notice this is not the same result we would have had had we written

    L   9,NMBR(6)

which loads the *contents* of the full word stored at address 604A14 into register 9.

Once we have loaded an address into a register using the LA instruction, we can then use the register as a base register in subsequent explicit operand specification. Figure 8-4 shows a program segment to compute the sum of 10 numbers stored in consecutive full words starting at NMBRS. We have used the LA instruction to load the address corresponding to NMBRS into register 10, which we then use as a base register in the address field of the Add instruction. Compare Fig. 8-4 with Figs. 7-3 and 8-3.

Use of the LA instruction with an explicit operand address furnishes an efficient way to do some arithmetic with register contents. The effect is the following: Compute the sum of a constant (the displacement) and the contents of two registers (the base and index registers) and place the result into a register. Insofar as arithmetic is concerned, there is no busier instruction.

We must remember, however, that we are restricted in the possible final outcomes of the arithmetic so done by the fact that memory addresses are 24 bits long. Thus, if the result of the arithmetic done by LA is a negative

```
        SR      6,6             START SUM AT 0
        L       9,=F'0'         INDEX FOR FIRST NUMBER IS 0
        LA      10,NMBRS        LOAD REGISTER 10 WITH ADDRESS OF NMBRS
LOOP    A       6,0(9,10)       EFFECTIVE ADDRESS IS (9) + (10)
        LA      9,4(0,9)        INDEX FOR NEXT NUMBER IS 4 HIGHER
        C       9,=F'36'        TEST INDEX TO SEE IF DONE
        BNP     LOOP            IF NOT, RETURN FOR NEXT NUMBER
                 •
                 •
                 •
NMBRS   DS      10F             TEN WORDS OF MEMORY
```

Fig. 8-4. Use of the LA instruction to increment register 9 being used as an index register.

number, FFFFFFFE, for example, the result that appears in the first operand register is 00FFFFFFE, which is a large positive number. We must also be sure that none of our results will be greater than $2^{24} - 1 = 16,777,215$. Otherwise, significant bits to the left of bit 8 in the answer will be discarded, producing the wrong result.

With these cautions in mind, let us explore the use of the LA instruction. Suppose that we write the instruction

$$LA \qquad 5,6(8,10)$$

The effective address is

$$6 + (8) + (10)$$

This sum is computed and placed into register 5. Consider

$$LA \qquad 6,0(6,6)$$

Here the effective address is

$$0 + (6) + (6) = 2 \times (6)$$

Thus, the above instruction has the effect of multiplying the contents of register 6 by 2 and returning the result to register 6.

To use the LA instruction to increment the contents of a register, we use the amount of the increment as the displacement and the register to be incremented as the register operand and as the base register. Thus, the instruction

$$LA \qquad 10,4(0,10)$$

adds 4 to the contents of register 10. We can use this trick to make the programming of loops more efficient. Figure 8-5 shows the program segment of Fig. 8-3 rewritten to use the instruction

$$LA \qquad 9,4(0,9)$$

to increment the index register/loop counter register 9 instead of the instruction

$$A \qquad 9,=F'4'$$

```
        LA      6,0         START SUM AT 0
        LA      10,NMBRS    REG. 10 STARTS WITH ADDR. OF FIRST NUMBER
        LA      11,NMBRS+36 FINAL VALUE OF ADDRESS IN REG. 11
LOOP    A       6,0(0,10)   ADD NEXT NUMBER (ADDR. IN REG. 10)
        LA      10,4(0,10)  NEXT NUMBER AT ADDRESS 4 HIGHER
        CR      10,11       CHECK FOR FINAL ADDRESS
        BNP     LOOP        TREAT NEXT NUMBER IF NOT DONE
                  .
                  .
                  .
NMBRS   DS      10F
```

Fig. 8-5. Use of the LA instruction to load constants into registers. Register 10 is used as a base register and loop counter.

The use of the LA instruction in a case such as this results in increased efficiency for three reasons. First, the use of the literal $=F'4'$ means that a full word of memory must be devoted to the increment, 4. Second, the Add instruction takes more time than does the LA instruction because the increment must be fetched from the memory before the addition can be performed. Finally, the LA instruction is essentially finished when the memory address has been calculated. The Add instruction requires that the operands be sent to the arithmetic unit and added after the memory address of the literal has been calculated.

Since we cannot specify negative displacements, to decrement a register we must have the decrement stored in a register to be used as an index register. If register 7 contains FFFFFFFC, the instruction

$$LA \qquad 2,0(7,2)$$

subtracts 4 from the contents of register 2.

Finally, if we specify 0 in the base and index register positions, the effective address is simply the displacement. Thus, to load register 3 with 0, we can write

$$LA \qquad 3,0(0,0)$$

while

$$LA \qquad 7,100(0,0)$$

loads register 7 with 00000064, the hexadecimal equivalent of 100_{10}. Since the displacement must be between 0 and 4095, inclusive, these are the values that can be loaded into a register using the LA instruction.

It is common practice to omit the index register and/or base register designation when no index register and/or base register is to be used. The instructions

$$LA \qquad 3,0$$

and

$$LA \qquad 7,100$$

perform the same tasks as those in the last two examples above.

```
*       THIS PROGRAM READS A DATA CARD WHICH TELLS HOW MANY
*       NUMBERS ARE TO BE PROCESSED.  THAT NUMBER IS KEPT IN
*       REG.  8.   IT THEN CALCULATES THE UPPER VALUE FOR ADDRESSES
*        AND LEAVES THAT NUMBER IN REG. 11
*       IT READS THE NUMBERS ONE AT A TIME, STORING THEM IN
*       CONSECUTIVE FULL WORDS OF THE AREA CALLED NMBRS.  THE
*       AVERAGE OF ALL THE NUMBERS IS COMPUTED, AS IS THE
*       DIFFERENCE BETWEEN EACH OF THE NUMBERS AND THE AVERAGE.
AVEDIF     START  0
           PRINT  NOGEN
           INITIAL
           RWD    3              READ NUMBER OF NUMBERS TO USE
           LR     8,3            KEEP A COPY IN REG. 8
           S      3,=F'1'        COMPUTE FINAL INDEX VALUE,
           M      2,=F'4'        4*((3) - 1)
           LA     9,NMBRS        ADDRESS OF FIRST WORD IN REG. 9
           LA     11,0(3,9)      ADDRESS OF LAST WORD IN REG. 11
READLOOP   RWD    4              READ A DATA NUMBER
           ST     4,0(0,9)       STORE IT AT  ADDRESS  IN REG. 9
           LA     9,4(0,9)       NEXT NUMBER STORED AT ADDRESS 4 HIGHER
           CR     9,11           TEST ADDRESS IN REG. 9 AGAINST FINAL VALUE
           BNP    READLOOP       IN REG. 11
           LA     9,NMBRS        START AT FIRST WORD AGAIN
           LA     7,0            START SUM AT 0 (IN ODD NMBRD REG.)
ADDLOOP    A      7,0(0,9)       ADD NUMBER AT (9) TO SUM
           LA     9,4(0,9)       ADD 4 TO ADDRESS IN REG. 9
           CR     9,11           COMPARE WITH FINAL VALUE STILL IN 11
           BNP    ADDLOCP        GO TO ADDLOOP IF NOT DONE
           M      6,=F'1'        WHEN HERE, READY FOR DIVIDE TO COMPUTE
           DR     6,8            AVERAGE BY DIVIDING SUM BY (8)
           WWD    7              PRINT THE AVERAGE
           LA     9,NMBRS        AND PREPARE TO COMPUTE DIFFERENCES
DIFLOOP    L      10,0(0,9)      GET NUMBER FROM ADDRESS IN REG. 9
           SR     10,7           SUBTRACT AVERAGE IN REG. 7
           WWD    10             PRINT THE DIFFERENCE
           LA     9,4(0,9)       INCREMENT REG. 9 TO NEXT ADDRESS
           CR     9,11           COMPARE WITH FINAL VALUE
           BNP    DIFLOOP        REPEAT IF RESULT NEGATIVE OR 0
           EOJ                   PROCESSING COMPLETED
NMBRS      DS     100F           STORAGE SPACE FOR NUMBERS PROCESSED
           END    AVEDIF         END OF PROGRAM
```

Fig. 8-6. A revision of Fig. 7-5 making full use of the LA instruction and explicit memory addresses.

Figure 8-6 shows the program of Fig. 7-5 rewritten to make full use of the LA instruction. While but a minor gain in efficiency and memory space saved results from such a modification in this case, in many situations the LA instruction can replace two or even three other instructions.

CHAPTER SUMMARY

To provide *relocatability* of memory addresses, the effective address of a memory operand is the sum of a *displacement* and the contents of a *base register*. If further modification of the address in required, the contents of an *index register* can be added to the resulting sum.

RX instructions have the machine language format

OP	R1	X2	B2	←	D2	→

In the *implicit* designation of memory addresses, we use a symbol or expression to represent the address. The assembler places the *implied* base register and displacement into the machine language equivalent of the address field. In *explicit* operand specification, the programmer selects the base register and displacement that will be used in the memory address field.

The LA instruction

LA   R1,D2(X2,B2)   Load Address   R1 ← D2 + (X2) + (B2)

---

loads the effective memory address into R1.

EXERCISES

1. In some systems other than the IBM 360 and 370 machines, *indirect addressing* is possible. In indirect addressing, the machine language instruction contains the address of a memory location. The contents of that location are not used as the operand but, instead, are the address of the actual operand. Let us use the symbol * to designate indirect addressing. Then, borrowing IBM mnemonics and assembly language format, the instruction

L   5,*ADDR

would load register 5 with the word stored at the *address* contained at ADDR. If we had 00002000 stored at ADDR, then the instruction above would load register 5 with the full word stored at address 2000. Write the two IBM assembly language instructions equivalent to the instruction

ST   7,*B

from a machine which permits indirect addressing.

2. In the IBM machines under consideration, all the general-purpose registers with the exception of register 0 are available for use as index registers and/or base registers. Some other computer systems contain special-purpose registers which can be used only as index registers and may also have a single special register for use as a base register. What effect does such a structure have upon the instruction set necessary for such a machine? In some systems, addressing is done relative to the program counter contents. Design a possible memory address field for such a machine. Add to your design the capability of indirect addressing and indexing by one of two special index registers.

3. Suppose that a given computing system has a memory consisting of 256K bytes (1K $= 2^{10} = 1024$ in computing) and that the memory region allocated to a program executing in this system was the space between addresses 10000

and 20000. Suppose that register 11 is the implied base register and that the register contents are

$$(6) = \text{FFFFFFF4}$$
$$(10) = 00000010$$
$$(11) = 00015030$$

Translate each of the following groups of instructions to machine language, assuming that the base position of the program has location counter value 30 and that each group of instructions begins at location counter value 60. Then describe in detail the result of executing each group of instructions, indicating when a memory addressing exception occurs.

(a)   LA   6,WORDS   (b)   LA   6,4
            L   7,WORDS(6)   L   7,WORDS(6)
WORDS   DC   F'5'   WORDS   DC   F'5'
            DC   F'6'   DC   F'6'.
(c)   LA   4,0(6)   (d)   LA   7,4(6,10)
            ST   10,0(4)   WORDS   DS   20F.

4.   Many computer instruction sets include a *load immediate* instruction which can be used to load a register with any possible full-word contents, thus avoiding the restriction the LA instruction imposes upon the sizes of the numbers that can be loaded. If the IBM 360 and 370 computers had such an instruction (they do *not*), then the instruction

$$\text{LI} \qquad 6, -10$$

would place FFFFFFF6 into register 6. How long would such an instruction have to be if it were implemented in the IBM machines? Design a possible machine language format for it. How does the IBM 360 Assembler F make up for the lack of instructions with full-word immediate operands?

5.   Write the program of Exercise 6 in Chapter 7 using explicit addresses wherever possible and using the LA instruction to increment and decrement register contents whenever such action is necessary.

REFERENCES

IBM System/360 Disk and Tape Operating System Assembler Language, Order No. GC24-3414, IBM Corp., White Plains, N.Y.

IBM System/360 Operating System Assembler Language, Form GC28-6514, IBM Corp., White Plains, N.Y.

IBM System/360 Principles of Operation, Form GA22-6821, IBM Corp., White Plains, N.Y.

IBM System/370 Principles of Operation, Form GA22-7000, IBM Corp., White Plains, N.Y.

IBM OS/VS—DOS/VS Assembler Language, Order No. GC33-4010, IBM Corp., White Plains, N.Y.

9 BRANCHING AND LOOP CONTROL

The conditional branch instructions allow the modification of the order of execution of the program instructions depending on the information being processed. The condition code plays a central role in this facility. We now have the background to explore the relationship between the condition code and the branch instructions from the machine's point of view.

Since so much of computing involves repetitive calculations, it is only natural that the computer designers would include instructions to make the programming and execution of loops easier and more efficient. We shall introduce the special loop control instructions now, and in so doing, we shall encounter the RS instruction type.

9.1. THE CONDITION CODE

We have seen that a step in the execution of some of the arithmetic and the comparison instructions is the setting of an indicator called the condition code. After an instruction that sets the condition code has been executed, a conditional branch instruction can be executed to test the current condition-code setting. The conditional branch instruction asks if the condition code has been set to indicate certain results. If so, the contents of the program counter are altered to contain the address of the desired instruction. If the condition code does not meet the requirements designated in the conditional branch instruction, the PC contents are not altered, and the next instruction in the program sequence is the next instruction executed.

The comparison and arithmetic instructions we have considered thus far set the condition code depending on the arithmetic results of the comparison or operation. There are four possible condition-code settings upon

171

execution of an arithmetic calculation: The result can be zero, negative, or positive or an overflow can occur. Thus, if we were to assign numerical values to the condition code, we would need four different possible values. A binary machine requires two binary digits for this purpose, since, using 2 bits, we can represent the four values as binary 00, 01, 10, and 11.

This is how it is done in the IBM 360. The condition code consists of 2 bits reserved in a special register called the Program Status Word, which we shall discuss in detail in Chapter 11. To each of the four possible values of the condition code we assign the following meanings:

Condition Code Setting		Meaning
Binary	Decimal	
00	0	Zero result
01	1	Negative result
10	2	Positive result
11	3	Overflow

An instruction which sets the condition code sets it to one of these values depending on the result of the operation. The branch instructions test the current contents of the condition code and respond in a manner appropriate to this value.

Suppose that

$$(5) = 00000100$$

$$(6) = 00000050$$

The instruction

$$AR \qquad 5,6$$

results in

$$(5) = 00000150$$

and sets the condition to 10_2, indicating a positive result.

Similarly, given the above register contents, the instruction

$$CR \qquad 6,5$$

indicates a negative result by setting the condition code to 01_2.

Suppose that the condition code is 00_2, indicating that the previous instruction that set the condition code had a zero result. The instruction

$$BP \qquad LOOP$$

asks if the condition code is currently 10_2 and the branch will not occur. The instruction

$$B \qquad LOOP$$

really means "Branch to LOOP no matter what the current value of the condition code."

In summary, use of conditional branching facilities really consists of two steps. First an instruction sets the condition code to one of four possible values depending on the results of the instruction. The branch instructions then test the condition-code setting and branch if this value matches those indicated in the branch instruction. Let us now see how this is related to the machine language and function.

9.2. BRANCH INSTRUCTIONS

Although we have dealt with branching as if there are several different conditional branch instructions, this is not in fact the case. The various instructions we have used are actually examples of the use of the only RX conditional branch instruction there is: the B̲ranch on C̲ondition (BC) instruction. The assembler translates an *extended mnemonic*, such as B, BZ, or BNM, into the machine language form of the BC instruction, with the appropriate information required to specify which values of the condition code will cause a branch.

9.2.1. The Mask

The condition code values which should lead to a branch must be indicated to the CPU when the conditional branch instruction is executed. This information is presented to the processor in the form of a *mask*. In general, a mask is a binary number which specifies which of several logical decisions are to be made. We might think of a mask as a series of switches. If a switch is on—a given bit of a mask is 1—the decision corresponding to that bit should be made. If the switch is off—the mask bit is 0—no action is taken with regard to the corresponding decision.

One of the operands in a BC instruction is a 4-bit mask. We should think of the mask bits as being numbered 0 through 3. Each bit of the mask corresponds to one of the four possible values of the condition code:

Mask Bit Number: 0   1   2   3

Condition Code Value: 0   1   2   3

The mask determines which condition code values cause a branch. For example, if mask bit 2 is on in a BC instruction, the branch is taken if the current value of the condition code is 2. If a given mask bit is off, a condition-code value corresponding to that bit does not cause a branch.

Let us consider a BC instruction in which the mask is 0100_2. Since bit 1 is on, the branch occurs if the condition code contains 01_2. Bits 0, 2, and 3 are off; no branch occurs if the condition code is 0, 2, or 3. Since condition-code value 1 corresponds to a negative result, a BC instruction with this mask is equivalent to what we have been calling the BM instruction.

When more than 1 bit of the BC mask is on, the machine branches if the condition code has *any* of the values indicated by the mask. If the mask is 1011_2, the branch occurs if the condition code contains 0, 2, *or* 3 but not if the condition code is 1. Thus, the result of using a BNM extended mnemonic is a BC instruction with mask 1011_2. Similarly, a BC instruction with a mask of 1111_2 branches no matter what value the condition code has. Such an instruction has the extended mnemonic B, which we called an unconditional branch.

In the execution of a BC instruction, the condition code value is used as an index which designates which mask bit the machine should check. If that mask bit is 1, the branch is taken.

Thus, the mask serves as a link between the programmer and the machine. The programmer indicates his choice of conditions he wishes to cause a branch. This he can do by using an extended mnemonic, which the assembler translates into the BC instruction with the proper mask. Or he can specify the mask explicitly, as we shall see in the next section.

9.2.2. The BC Instruction

The BC instruction is a modified RX instruction. We just saw that we must supply a 4-bit mask as an operand to specify which condition-code values should permit a branch. This mask, designated M1 in the symbolic notation, replaces the R1 operand in the usual RX instruction format. Thus, we describe the BC instruction as follows:

BC   M1,D2(X2,B2)   <u>B</u>ranch on <u>C</u>ondition   PC ⟵ D2 + (X2) + (B2)
                                                if CC is
                                                as specified by M1

Notice that we have specified the memory address to which to branch in its explicit form, giving the displacement, D2, the index register, X2, and the base register, B2. From now on in describing memory operand addresses, we shall give their explicit form. Remember that whenever a displacement-base register pair occurs, a symbol or expression can be used to form an implicit operand address. For example, an alternative form for the BC instruction is

BC   M1,S2(X2)

Since the assembler assumes that numbers are decimal unless otherwise specified, we can set the mask in the BC instruction by writing a number between 0 and 15, inclusive. To decide what the mask should be, we usually convert the desired binary mask to decimal. If the mask we want is 1000_2, indicating that the branch should occur if the condition code is 0, we could write

> BC   8,LOOP

if we wish the instruction to branch to LOOP if the condition is satisfied. If we want to branch to LOOP no matter what the condition code, we should use the mask $1111_2 = 15_{10}$ and write

> BC   15,LOOP

This conversion of the mask to decimal, while simple enough, is a potential source of programming error and can be a nuisance in programming. The assembler permits the specification of numerical quantities in other number systems. We use the other bases whenever convenient, as in this case.

To specify a *binary* constant, we write

> B'value'

"Value" is a binary number enclosed in single quotes. The B tells the assembler that this number is to be interpreted as a binary number.

Hexadecimal constants are written

> X'value'

the X meaning heXadecimal.

We can use these alternative forms whenever we need to designate a numerical constant. In connection with the BC instruction, all the following represent the same machine language instruction:

> BC   13,LOOP
> BC   B'1101',LOOP
> BC   X'D',LOOP
> BNP   LOOP

The machine language format of the BC instruction is that of the RX instruction, with the first register operand replaced by the mask. Since there is only one BC instruction, we give its operation code, 47, in the following diagram for the machine language equivalent of the instruction

> BC   M1,D2(X2,B2)

47	M1	X2	B2	←	D2	→

We should recognize the last 2 bytes as an S-type address, with the preceding nibble the index register modifier to form an X-type address. The 4 bits normally occupied by the number of the first register operand contain the 4-bit mask instead.

Let us translate the instruction

> BNP   32(3,11)

to machine language. Here the displacement is 32_{10}, register 3 is the index register, and register 11 is the base register. The BNP extended mnemonic leads to the equivalent instruction

BC   13,32(3,11)

or

BC   X'D',32(3,11)

The result is, remembering to convert the displacement to hexadecimal,

47D3B020

As another example, consider the instruction

BZ   TOP

where TOP has displacement 150_{16} and register 9 is the base register. The mask is $1000_2 = 8_{16}$. Thus, the machine language equivalent is

47809150

In processing branch instructions, the assembler carries out the same conversions as we did in the preceding examples. If the BC instruction is used, the translation to machine language is straightforward. When an extended mnemonic is used, the assembler looks up the mnemonic in a table which indicates the correct mask for the BC instruction. It then inserts the operation code 47 and the mask thus obtained into the machine language instruction.

Table 9-1 shows the extended mnemonics recognized by the OS/360 Assembler F. Until now, we have emphasized the arithmetic determination of the condition code. In the following chapters we shall see that an alternative means of setting the condition code is through the use of instructions which manipulate *logical* data. Extended mnemonics appropriate for logically set condition codes are also shown in Table 9-1. Notice that these are often duplicates of the ones we have already studied. For example, the BE mnemonic is interchangeable with the BZ mnemonic, since both lead to the BC instruction with mask 1000_2. Notice also that the extended mnemonic NOP, for No Operation, corresponds to a BC instruction with mask 0000_2, which means that the branch occurs under *no* conditions. What use could we have for an instruction that does absolutely nothing? NOP is used to reserve space in a program in the anticipation that an instruction that *does* do something will be stored there when the program is executed. It can also be used in connection with the EXecute instruction discussed in Chapter 13.

There are 16 different possible masks, not all of which have associated extended mnemonics. Thus, if we wish to branch to LOCO if either a result was 0 or an overflow occurred, we write

BC   9,LOCO

Table 9-1 EXTENDED MNEMONICS, THEIR MASKS, AND THEIR EQUIVALENT BC
INSTRUCTIONS WITH MASKS

Extended Mnemonic	Meaning	Mask (Binary)	Mask (Decimal)	Equivalent BC Instruction and Mask	
B	Branch (unconditional)	1111	15	BC	15
NOP	No Operation	0000	0	BC	0
BZ	Branch on Zero	1000	8	BC	8
BE	Branch on Equal	1000	8	BC	8
BM	Branch on Minus	0100	4	BC	4
BL	Branch on Low	0100	4	BC	4
BP	Branch on Plus	0010	2	BC	2
BH	Branch on High	0010	2	BC	2
BO	Branch on Overflow	0001	1	BC	1
BNZ	Branch on Not Zero	0111	7	BC	7
BNE	Branch on Not Equal	0111	7	BC	7
BNM	Branch on Not Minus	1011	11	BC	11
BNL	Branch on Not Low	1011	11	BC	11
BNP	Branch on Not Plus	1101	13	BC	13
BNH	Branch on Not High	1101	13	BC	13
BNO	Branch on Not Overflow	1110	14	BC	14

While we do not often use an index register with the branch instruction, the capability of modifying the branch address at execution time is sometimes useful. An example of such usage is the use of a branch table. Suppose, for example, that there are four sections of a program, the first instruction of each of which is labeled SEC1, SEC2, SEC3, and SEC4, respectively. We wish to branch to one of these sections depending on the outcome of some logical manipulations in a preceding part of the program. One way to do this is to write the following sequence of instructions:

```
            BC        15,BTAB(9)
BTAB        BC        15,SEC1
            BC        15,SEC2
            BC        15,SEC3
            BC        15,SEC4
```

Here we have used register 9 as an index register in the first branch instruction. We assume that the contents of 9 were determined in the logic of the earlier part of the program. If, in a previous part of the program, it was decided that a branch to SEC3 should occur, then register 9 would contain the number 8 when the instructions above were executed. Those readers familiar with FORTRAN might correctly suppose that the use of a computed GO TO leads to a similar set of machine language instructions.

Another example of the use of a branch table is furnished by the operating system. Many programs, such as assemblers, compilers, linkeditors, and other systems programs indicate whether or not they executed successfully by returning a number called a *completion code* to the operating system. This completion code is always a multiple of 4 and is used by the operating system as a branch table increment. For example, a completion code of 0 means that the program ran correctly and that the next job step should be executed. A code of 4 means that there was an error, but the error was probably not serious enough to keep the next step from executing properly. The operating system prints a warning message and then begins processing of the next step. A completion code of 8 usually means that the error was so severe that successful continuation of execution of the job is unlikely. The operating system discontinues processing of the job. Which course the operating system takes is determined by the value of the completion code, which is used as an index into a branch table, as in the preceding example.

9.2.3. The BCR Instruction

The Branch on Condition to Register instruction is the Register-to-Register form of the BC instruction. It works in exactly the same way as the BC instruction, with the exception that the branch address is obtained from a register, instead of from the memory operand field of the instruction.

BCR   M1,R2   Branch on Condition to Register   PC ◄── (R2) if CC is
                                                   as specified by M1

To use the BCR instruction we first load the branch address into a register. The BCR instruction mask is determined just as for the BC instruction. Instead of specifying a memory address to which to branch, we denote the register which contains the branch address in the R2 field of the instruction. Suppose that we wish to branch to SITU if the condition code is not zero using the BCR instruction. Somewhere in the program before the BCR instruction we might have the instruction

LA   5,SITU

which loads the memory address of the instruction named SITU into register 5. The BCR instruction is then written

BCR   7,5

or

BCR   B'0111',5

which causes a branch to the address contained in register 5 if the condition code is not zero.

Figure 9-1 shows a flow chart of a program segment that finds the maxi-

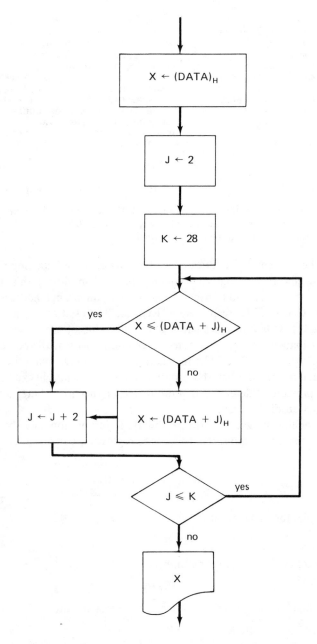

Fig. 9-1. A flow chart of a program segment that finds and prints the maximum of a series of 15 numbers stored in consecutive half-words starting at DATA.

179

```
              LA    9,LESS         PUT ADDRESS OF LESS INTO REG. 9
              LA    10,CHECKER     ADDRESS OF CHECKER GOES INTO REG. 10
              LA    3,2            INDEX/LOOP CCUNTER IN REG. 3
              LA    5,28           FINAL VALUE IN REG. 5
              LH    6,CATA         FIRST NUMBER IN REG. 6
CHECKER       CH    6,CATA(3)      COMPARE NEXT NUMBER WITH (6)
              BCR   B'0100',9      BRANCH TO LESS IF RESULT NEGATIVE
              LH    6,DATA(3)      REPLACE (6) WITH LARGER NUMBER
LESS          LA    3,2(3)         INCREMENT INDEX/LCOP COUNTER
              CR    3,5            COMPARE WITH FINAL VALUE
              BCR   B'1011',10     BRANCH TO CHECKER IF RESULT NCT POS.
              WWD   6              PRINT RESULT
                                     •
                                     •
                                     •
DATA          DS    15H            FIFTEEN HALFWORDS OF MEMCRY
```

Fig. 9-2. A program segment that finds the largest of fifteen numbers stored in consecutive halfwords starting at DATA. The BCR instruction is used for the conditional branches.

mum of the contents of a series of 15 half-words stored starting at DATA. Figure 9-2 shows a program segment that accomplishes this task. The first two instructions load registers 9 and 10 with the branch addresses named LESS and CHECKER, respectively. Register 3 is used as an index register and is loaded with 2 to start with. The final value of the index is 28; this number is loaded into register 5 for later comparison with the contents of register 3 in the loop. The BCR instruction is used in checking the condition code to determine whether the number currently being checked is smaller than the previously determined minium (X in the flow chart) and to test for completion of the loop.

The machine language form of the BCR instruction has the standard RR instruction format, but the 4-bit mask replaces the first register operand:

07	M1	R2

For example, the instruction

$$\text{BCR} \qquad 13,10$$

has the machine language representation

$$\text{07DA}$$

while the machine language equivalent of the instruction

$$\text{BCR} \qquad 15,8$$

is

$$\text{07F8.}$$

The assembler recognizes two extended mnemonics for the BCR instruction. The BR, Branch-to-Register, mnemonic causes an unconditional branch to the address contained in the single register operand. Its general form is

    BR   R2

and is equivalent to

    BCR   15,R2

For example, the instruction

    BR   14

causes a branch to the address contained in register 14, no matter what value the condition code has. The assembler replaces the instruction above with the instruction

    BCR   B'1111',14

The other extended mnemonic for the BCR instruction is NOPR, which results in the instruction

    BCR   0,R2

The result of the use of the NOPR extended mnemonic is to reserve 2 bytes of memory in the program the first byte of which contains 07, the operation code for the BCR instruction. The second byte contains OR2. The result is that an executable 2 bytes of memory are reserved for later occupation by an instruction that does something. The NOPR extended mnemonic can also be used in conjunction with the EX instruction.

In some models of the System 360/370 computers, the time required to retrieve an instruction from the memory depends on the length of the instruction. In these machines, the use of RR instructions instead of RX instructions when possible can result in faster-running programs. However, the use of RR instructions generally requires more preparation. In Fig. 9-2 we see that in order to use the BCR instruction in place of a BC instruction, we must first load the branch address into the register operand. The time required to execute the LA instructions to do this may be longer than the time saved through the use of the BCR instruction. Furthermore, the BCR instruction requires a register that might be used for other purposes if a BC instruction were used instead. Thus, the decision of when to use the BCR instruction in place of the BC instruction depends on several factors including the model of the computer and the number of times the instruction will be executed relative to the number of times the preparatory instructions must be executed.

The BCR instruction is most often used when we do not know the name of the instruction to which we wish to branch. In fact, this instruction may be in a separate program, as is the case at the end of the execution of a subroutine. As we shall see in Chapter 13, one of a subroutine's responsibilities is to return control to the calling program at the proper location. The address of this location is normally passed to the subroutine in register 14. Therefore, the last instruction of a subroutine that follows this convention is

BR   14

Another instance in which the BCR instruction is useful arises from the same considerations discussed in connection with branch tables in the previous section. An earlier segment of the program computes the branch address and places it in a register. When the time comes to branch to the computed address, the BCR instruction is used.

9.3. LOOP CONTROL; THE BCT INSTRUCTION

The use of loops in computing is so important that few machines are developed without some special instructions to make the programming of loops easier and their execution more efficient. The IBM 360 and 370 computers are no exception. Before we investigate these special instructions, let us think about the general structure of a loop.

9.3.1. Loop Structure

Figure 9-3 shows a schematic flow chart of the general structure of a loop. While the elements of the loop may occur in different orders most loops contain all the essential steps shown.

The *initialization* step contains the statements necessary to start the loop counters and address registers at the proper values. Index registers are loaded with their initial contents, and, if necessary, the final values for the loop counter and/or index registers are computed and placed in the memory or registers.

The *calculation* or *function* step is the body of the loop; it contains the statements that carry out the computations for which the loop is designed. In Fig. 9-3, we have drawn arrows leaving the calculation area, indicating that, under circumstances dictated by the data, the loop may be left through means other than normal completion. The calculation step can itself contain one or more loops, each of which has the general structure shown in Fig. 9-3.

In the *increment* step the loop counter is adjusted to reflect the fact that the calculations have been executed one more time. This usually means that an increment is added to the contents of a loop counter, index register, or register being used as a base register. We do not exclude the possibility that the increment might be negative. In some cases we might wish to start a loop counter out at the number of times we wish to go through the loop and count it down by one each time the calculations are executed. In other cases, the increment step might be absent, such as when the calculation step is used to terminate execution of the loop.

The *completion test* determines whether or not a branch to the beginning

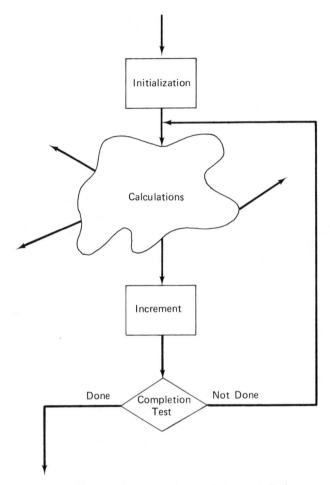

Fig. 9-3. The essential components and structure of a loop.

of the function step should occur. In most instances, the completion test consists of a comparison of the current loop counter value with the final value it should attain. If the loop counter has not yet reached its final value, the calculation step is executed again and looping continues. In those instances in which the calculation step tests for termination of the loop, the completion test becomes a simple branch back to the beginning of the loop calculations.

In the loop structure shown in Fig. 9-3, we have assumed that prior calculations have determined that it is necessary to go through the loop at least once. Otherwise, we should include in the initialization step a test to determine if the loop is to be executed. An alternative is to put the completion test before the calculations.

The loop control instructions facilitiate the programming of loops with structures as discussed above. Their use often leads to an increased efficiency of the program by making it possible to reduce the number of instructions executed in the loop itself. As a rule, the smaller the number of instructions inside a loop, the faster the loop and the program that contains it will be. This increase in speed may cost some additional programming in the initialization step and may also require the use of more registers than would normal programming.

9.3.2. The BCT Instruction

The Branch on CounT instruction is designed for those loops in which a loop counter is to be counted down by one each time the calculation step has been executed until the loop counter has reached 0. In other words, to use the BCT instruction, we place the number of times the calculations are to be executed in a register. BCT does both the increment (in this case decrement) and completion test steps.

BCT   R1,D2(X2,B2)   Branch on CounT   R1 ⟵ (R1) − 1;
                                           PC ⟵ D2 + (X2) + (B2)
                                           if (R1) ≠ 0

Execution of the BCT instruction takes place in two steps. First, the contents of the first register operand are decreased by 1. Then, if the result of this subtraction is *not* 0, a branch to the memory address specified as the second operand occurs. If the result of the subtraction *is* 0, the machine proceeds to the next instruction in the program. It is important to notice that the subtraction occurs *before* the test and branch. The BCT instruction has no effect on the condition code.

The BCT instruction is a standard RX instruction and has the RX machine language instruction format.

In effect, then, Branch on CounT decrements a loop counter by 1 and branches if the result is not 0. This means that, for example, the instruction

        BCT   5,REPEAT

has the same effect as the pair of instructions

        S   5,=F′1′
        BNZ   REPEAT

with the exception that the BCT instruction does not change the condition code.

Figure 9-4 shows a program segment that computes the sum of 10 numbers punched on data cards. The final sum is left in register 7. Figure 9-5 shows a program segment to do the same problem, but we have used the

```
          LA    3,10      NUMBER OF TIMES TO DO LOOP IN REG. 3
          LA    7,0       START SUM AT 0
NEXTNUM   RWD   2         FIRST INSTRUCTION OF CALCULATIONS
          AR    7,2       COMPUTE RUNNING SUM
          S     10,=F'1'  INCREMENT STEP
          BNZ   NEXTNUM   COMPLETION TEST
```

Fig. 9-4. A program segment that computes the sum of ten numbers punched on data cards.

```
MEMBER NAME   IX5
          LA    3,10      NUMBER OF TIMES TO DO LOOP IN REG. 3
          LA    7,0       START SUM AT 0
NEXTNUM   RWD   2         FIRST INSTRUCTION OF CALCULATIONS
          AR    7,2       COMPUTE RUNNING SUM
          BCT   3,NEXTNUM INCREMENT AND COMPLETION TEST
```

Fig. 9-5. Using the BCT instruction to control a loop.

BCT instruction to decrement the loop counter and branch to the RWD statement if all 10 numbers have not yet been added. The initialization step is the same in both figures; we place the number of times the loop is to be executed in register 3. In Fig. 9-5, however, the increment step and the completion test are combined in the single BCT instruction.

The BCT instruction sometimes has uses other than loop control. It can be used whenever we want to subtract 1 from a register and branch, unless the result of the subtraction is 0. In using BCT for loop control, care must be taken not to load the register to be counted down with 0 or a negative number. Otherwise, the loop will never be left.

The BCTR instruction is the Register-to-Register form of the $\underline{B}$ranch on $\underline{C}$oun$\underline{T}$ instruction. As with the BCT instruction, the instruction subtracts 1 from the first register operand. If the result is not zero, the contents of the second register operand are placed in the program counter. If the result of the subtraction is 0, no branch occurs.

BCTR	R1,R2	Branch on $\underline{C}$oun$\underline{T}$ to Register	$(R1) \longleftarrow (R1)-1;$
			$(R2) \longrightarrow PC$ if
			$(R1) \neq 0$

BCTR has the standard RR machine language format and has no effect on the condition code.

Figure 9-6 illustrates the use of the BCTR instruction to control a loop. We use the BCTR instruction more often to subtract 1 from the contents of a register than for loop control, because of a special case: If 0 is given as the second register operand, R2, no branch occurs no matter what the final contents of R1. For example, the instruction

$$\text{BCTR} \qquad 11,0$$

```
        LA      5,NEXTNUM       LOAD BRANCH ADDRESS INTC REG, 5
        LA      3,10            NUMBER OF TIMES TO DC LOOP IN REG, 3
        LA      7,0             START SUM AT C
NEXTNUM RWD     2               FIRST INSTRUCTION OF CALCULATIONS
        AR      7,2             COMPUTE RUNNING SUM
        BCTR    3,5             INCREMENT AND COMPLETION TEST
```

Fig. 9-6. Use of the BCTR instruction to control a loop.

subtracts 1 from the contents of register 11 and does not branch. It does so in about two-thirds of the time required for the instruction

$$S \qquad 11, =F'1'$$

requires less memory space, and does not require a 1 stored somewhere.

9.4. LOOP CONTROL: BXLE AND BXH

While the BCT and BCTR instructions help in programming some loops, we have seen several examples in which the loop counter was not counted down by 1 each pass through the loop. Instead, the loop counter serves double duty in that it is also used as an index register or a base register in addresses in the calculation step of the loop. In such cases, the register used as a loop counter is counted by steps appropriate for the information units being processed. When dealing with full words, for example, we increment the index register by 4 each time through the loop in order to access the next word. Furthermore, the final value for such loop counters is not 0, but the index or address of the last word to be processed.

The BXLE (pronounced BIX-LEE or BIXIL) and BXH instructions are used in these more general loop control problems.

9.4.1. The BXLE Instruction

The BXLE instruction is our first encounter with an instruction of the RS type. Before we delve into the details of this instruction, let us recall that the RS instructions have three operands. Two of these are registers, and the third is in the memory.

BXLE stands for Branch on indeX Low or Equal, indicating that the instruction controls loops by modifying and testing contents of registers used for indexing. We represent the general form of the BXLE instruction as

$$\text{BXLE} \qquad \text{R1,R3,D2(B2)}$$

For reasons I have been unable to determine, the operand specified second as the instruction is written is designated by R3, meaning that it is the *third* operand. As written, the first two operands are general-purpose registers. The third is an S-type memory address, for which we can substitute a relocatable expression or symbol. The memory address field specifies the address to which the machine branches if warranted by the comparison part of the execution of the instruction.

BXLE is most often used for the increment and completion test steps in a loop. To illustrate the use of the instruction, let us consider an example. Suppose that we have

$$(8) = 00000020$$

$$(6) = 00000004$$

$$(7) = 00000028$$

and that the instruction

BXLE   8,6,REPEAT

is executed.

The instruction execution consists of three steps. First, the contents of the second register operand, register 6 in this case, are added to the contents of register 8, the first register operand, with the result

$$(8) = 00000024$$

Then the new contents of register 8 are compared with the contents of the next register past register 6, the second register operand. Thus, the comparison is made between the contents of register 8 and register 7. The result is that (8) is less than (7). Finally, since we got a "less-than" result from the comparison, the memory address corresponding to REPEAT will be placed in the program counter, causing a branch to that address.

Thus, in this example, the BXLE instruction is equivalent to the three instructions

```
A       8,=F'4'    (or LA 8,4(8) or AH 8,=H'4')
CR      8,7
BNP     REPEAT
```

Another execution of the same BXLE instruction results in

$$(8) = 00000028$$

(8) now equals (7), and the branch to REPEAT again occurs. However, execution of the BXLE instruction one more time produces

$$(8) = 0000002C$$

which is greater than (7), and so the branch does not take place, and execution continues with the next instruction in the program sequence.

The BCT instruction is effective only for loops in which a loop counter is counted down by 1 each time through the loop. The BXLE instruction allows complete generality in the choice of loop counter, increment, and final value.

In giving a general description of the BXLE instruction, we must provide for two cases. In the example just considered, R3 was an even-numbered register, register 6. In the case of an *even*-numbered register in the R3 position, the BXLE instruction can be summarized as follows:

BXLE	R1,R3,D2(B2)	Branch on	R1 ← (R3) + (R1);
(R3 even-numbered)		inde**X** Low	D2 + (B2) ⟶ PC
		or **E**qual	if (R1) ≤ (R3+1)

In words, the machine adds contents of the second register operand, R3, to the contents of the first register operand, R1. If the resulting sum is less than or equal to the contents of register R3+1, a branch to the address D2 + (B2) occurs. If the resulting sum is greater than (R3+1), the branch does not occur, and execution proceeds as usual. BXLE has no effect on the condition code.

If we choose to use an *odd*-numbered register for R3, the result is slightly different. In this case, (R3) is added to (R1) as before. But the sum is compared with (R3) instead of with (R3+1).

BXLE	R1,R3,D2(B2)	Branch on	R1 ← (R1) + (R3);
(R3 *odd*-numbered)		inde**X** Low	D2 + (B2) ⟶ PC
		or **E**qual	if (R1) ≤ (R3)

Use of the BXLE instruction takes some preparation in the initialization step. We must load the initial value of the index or loop counter into a register. If we use an even-numbered register for R3, then we must load the increment into R3 and the final value of the index or loop counter into R3+1. If we use an odd-numbered register for R3, the increment and the final value are the same; this number must be loaded into R3.

Figure 9-7 shows a program segment to find the maximum of a series of

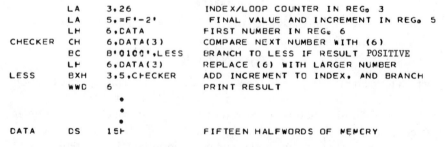

```
         LA    3,26           INDEX/LOOP COUNTER IN REG. 3
         LA    5,=F'-2'       FINAL VALUE AND INCREMENT IN REG. 5
         LH    6,CATA         FIRST NUMBER IN REG. 6
CHECKER  CH    6,DATA(3)      COMPARE NEXT NUMBER WITH (6)
         BC    B'0100',LESS   BRANCH TO LESS IF RESULT POSITIVE
         LH    6,DATA(3)      REPLACE (6) WITH LARGER NUMBER
LESS     BXH   3,5,CHECKER    ADD INCREMENT TO INDEX, AND BRANCH
         WWD   6              PRINT RESULT
                   .
                   .
                   .
DATA     CS    15H            FIFTEEN HALFWORDS OF MEMCRY
```

Fig. 9-7. Use of the BXLE instruction to control a loop. The program segment finds the maximum of 15 numbers stored in consecutive halfwords starting at DATA.

numbers, a flow chart for which appears in Fig. 9-1. In the initialization step, we load register 3, which will be used as an index register, with its initial value, 2. We load register 4, the increment register, with the number 2, since we are processing half-word data. Finally, we load register 5, the next register past register 4, with the final value of the index, 28 in this case. The instruction

BXLE   3,4,CHECKER

carries out the increment and completion test steps. Figure 9-7 should be compared with Fig. 9-2 with regard to efficiency. The BXLE instruction replaces the three instructions

LA	3,2(3)
CR	3,5
BCR	B'1011',10

at the expense of an additional LA instruction outside the loop and loss of register 4 for use in other calculations.

We use BXLE with odd R3 when we want the final value of the index to be the same as the increment. This is appropriate when we place the increment and test steps *before* the calculation is in the loop. In Fig. 9-8 we see

```
        LH      5,=H'-2'    AMOUNT OF INCREMENT IN REG. 5
        LA      3,28        FIRST INDEX+2 IN REG. 3
        LH      6,DATA(3)   LAST DATA NUMBER IN R6
NEXT    BXLE    3,5,DONE    DECREMENT INDEX REG., SEE IF DONE
        CH      6,DATA(3)   IS THIS DATA NUMBER BIGGER
        BC      B'0100',NEXT   IF NOT, GO LOOK AT NEXT NUMBER
        LH      6,DATA(3)   IF SO, KEEP IT
        B       NEXT        AND GO BACK FOR MORE
DONE    WWD     6           PRINT LARGEST FOUND
                .
                .
                .
DATA    DS      15H
```

Fig. 9-8. Use of BXLE with odd R3.

how this can be done in our program segment that finds the maximum of a series of 15 numbers. We start the index so that the second-to-last half-word will be addressed the first time through the loop. The BXLE instruction does not cause a branch until the index has the value -2, the same as the increment.

9.4.2. The BXH Instruction

The Branch on indeX High instruction works in the same way as the BXLE instruction, with the exception that the branch to S2 occurs if the modified index value in R1 is *high* in comparison with its final value given in R3+1, if R3 is an even-numbered register, or in R3 if R3 is an odd-numbered register. This is in contrast with the BXLE instruction in which the branch occurs when the modified index contained in R1 is low or equal in comparison with the final value contained in R3+1 or R3.

BXH (R3 *even*-numbered)	R1,R3,D2(B2)	Branch on inde$\underline{X}$ $\underline{H}$igh	R1 $\leftarrow$ (R1) + (R3); D2 + (B2) $\longrightarrow$ PC if (R1) > (R3+1)
BXH (R3 *odd*-numbered)	R1,R3,D2(B2)	Branch on inde$\underline{X}$ $\underline{H}$igh	R1 $\leftarrow$ (R1) + (R3); D2 + (B2) $\longrightarrow$ PC if (R1) > (R3)

We use the BXLE instruction when the index value is to increase each time through the loop until it reaches a final value. We use the BXH instruction when we wish to count the index down each time through the loop until it has decreased to a value less than or equal to its final value.

For example, in Fig. 9-7 we start at the beginning of the list of numbers stored starting at DATA and count the index register, register 3, up by 2 each time through the loop until it reaches the final value 28. We could just as well start the index out at 28 and count it *down* by 2 each time through the loop until it reaches the final value 0, Figure 9-9 shows a program segment to do this using the BXH instruction to control the loop.

```
          LA      3,26             INDEX/LOOP CCUNTER IN REG. 3
          L       5,=F'-2'         FINAL VALUE AND INCREMENT IN REG. 5
          LH      6,CATA+28        FIRST NUMBER IN REG. 6
CHECKER   CH      6,CATA(3)        COMPARE NEXT NUMBER WITH (6)
          BC      8'010)',LESS     BRANCH TO LESS IF RESLLT NEGATIVE
          LH      6,DATA(3)        REPLACE (6) WITH LARGER NUMBER
LESS      BXH     3,5,CHECKER      ADD INCREMENT TO INDEX, AND BRANCH
          WWD     6                PRINT RESLLT
                          •
                          •
                          •
DATA      DS      15H              FIFTEEN HALFWORDS OF MEMORY
```

Fig. 9-9. Use of the BXH instruction to control a loop. The program segment finds the maximum of a series of numbers stored in consecutive halfwords starting at DATA.

9.5. THE RS INSTRUCTION FORMAT

We have put off consideration of the RS machine instruction format until we encountered some RS instructions. RS instructions are 4 bytes long.

The first byte, as always, contains the operation code. The next byte contains the 4-bit numbers of registers R1 and R3 in that order. The last 2 bytes consist of the S-type address in base register-displacement form. Thus, the machine language form of the general RS instruction

RSOP   R1,R3,D2(B2)

where RSOP is the assembler mnemonic for the operation code OP, is displayed as follows:

OP	R1	R3	B2 ←	D2 →

Of course, the assembler permits writing RS instructions in the form

RSOP   R1,R3,S2

If we do this, the assembler places the S-type address field equivalent to the relocatable symbol or expression S2 into the machine language.

Notice that the RS format is the same as the RX format with the exception that the register operand R3 replaces the index register X2.

Thus, the instruction

BXLE   5,10,32(8)

has the machine language equivalent

875A8020

If the symbol COUNT has displacement 100_{16} and register 13 is being used as the base register, the instruction

BXH   2,4,COUNT+8

has the machine language form

8624D108

CHAPTER SUMMARY

The *condition code* is a 2-bit binary indicator that is set to one of its four possible values upon execution of an instruction which affects the condition-code. A *mask* specifies those values which result in a branch upon execution of a BC or BCR instruction. This mask replaces R1 in the RX and RR instruction formats in BC and BCR instructions, respectively.

The BCT, BCTR, BXLE, and BXH instructions facilitate *loop control*. Table 9-2 summarizes the instructions covered in this chapter.

Table 9-2 INSTRUCTIONS DISCUSSED IN CHAPTER 9

BC	M1,D2(X2,B2)	Branch on Condition	D2 + (X2) + (B2) $\longrightarrow$ PC if CC value is as specified by M1
BCR	M1,R2	Branch on Condition to Register	(R2) $\longrightarrow$ PC if CC values is as specified by M1
BCT	R1,D2(X2,B2)	Branch on Count	(R1) − 1 $\longrightarrow$ R1; D2 + (X2) + (B2) $\longrightarrow$ PC if (R1) $\neq$ 0
BCTR	R1,R2	Branch Count to Register	(R1) − 1 $\longrightarrow$ R1; (R2) $\longrightarrow$ PC if (R1) $\neq$ 0
BXLE	R1,R3,D2(B2)	Branch on indeX Low or Equal	R1 $\longleftarrow$ (R1) + (R3): 1. D2 + (B2) $\longrightarrow$ PC if (R1) $\leq$ (R3+1) and R3 even-numbered 2. D2 + (B2) $\longrightarrow$ PC if (R1) $\leq$ (R3) and R3 odd-numbered
BXH	R1,R3,D2(B2)	Branch on indeX High	R1 $\longleftarrow$ (R1) + (R3): 1. D2 + (B2) if (R1) > (R3+1) and R3 even-numbered 2. D2 + (B2) $\longrightarrow$ PC if (R1) > (R3) and R3 odd-numbered

EXERCISES

1. In some machines, the conditional branch instructions include an actual test of an operand to determine whether or not a branch should occur. Such a machine might include an instruction of the form

    BZR   3,LOCUS

    which would mean "Branch to LOCUS if the contents of register 3 are zero." Another example might be

    BNZ   AT,PLACE

    meaning "Branch to PLACE if the contents of the word stored at AT is not zero." Discuss the relative merits of such a branching structure versus that of the IBM 360 and 370 computers. Consider such factors as the size of the instruction set (a larger instruction set usually means a more expensive processor), the amount of work that must be done to prepare for a conditional branch in terms of machine and programmer effort, and the ability of the IBM 360 and 370 to "remember" a condition code after several intervening instructions have been executed.

2. In a typical 360 processor, the BXLE and BXH instructions require about twice as much execution time as do the BC, LA, and CR instructions. Taking into account the additional instructions necessary to prepare for the use of BXLE or BXH, when is it more efficient to use these loop control instructions instead of the LA, CR, BC sequence of loop control instructions?

3. Describe the use of the BXLE instruction for purposes other than the control of a loop.

4. Exercise 8 in Chapter 5 describes a method for the calculation of the square roots of integers. All the arithmetic and comparison instructions in that problem can be done using BXLE instructions. Try it.

5. Write a program to calculate and print the terms in the Fibonacci sequence (see Exercise 7 in Chapter 5) using the BXLE instruction to compute the terms in the sequence.

6. A program was stopped in the middle of execution because it was using too much time. Examination of the dump accompanying the output from the program showed that the program stopped in a loop controlled by the instruction

    BXLE   2,8,LOOPTOP

The register contents were

$$(2) = F1000000$$
$$(8) = FFFFFFFE$$
$$(9) = 00000100$$

when the program stopped. What is wrong?

REFERENCES

IBM System/360 Disk and Tape Operating System Assembler Language, Form GC24-3414, IBM Corp., White Plains, N.Y.

IBM System/360 Operating System Assembler Language, Form GC28-6514, IBM Corp., White Plains, N.Y.

IBM System/360 Principles of Operation, Form GA22-6821, IBM Corp., White Plains, N.Y.

IBM System/370 Principles of Operation, Form GA22-7000, IBM Corp., White Plains, N.Y.

IBM OS/VS—DOS/VS Assembler Language, Order No. GC33-4010, IBM Corp., White Plains, N.Y.

10 CHARACTER MANIPULATION

We have emphasized the binary integer arithmetic instructions because they furnish a natural starting point for the study of assembly language. But, in many important computer applications, arithmetic plays a secondary role to what we introduce in this chapter as character manipulation. In such problems, the binary arithmetic instructions are used for loop control and address caculations to control the program execution and select the data upon which the program operates.

Character manipulation programs operate upon information presented as character data, changing it to numeric form, translating it, or modifying it in other ways. The assembler is one example of such a program. Its input is the character data that form an assembly language program; its output is the equivalent machine language program. Other character-oriented computer applications include accounting problems, inventory management, the registrar's problem, language translation, compilation, and information retrieval systems. While definite statistics are not available on this subject, it is certainly safe to say that at least 75 % of all computing is basically what we are calling character manipulation.

This chapter could just as well have been called "Byte Manipulation." As we shall see, the internal form of character representation is the EBCDIC code, in which each character has a corresponding code that is 1 byte long. The DS and DC assembler directives offer the capability to reserve space in byte units for use in character-handling problems. The 360 instruction set includes information move and comparison instructions designed for character-oriented operations.

The IBM 370 machines offer extended character manipulation instructions. You might wish to refer to Chapter 20, Section 20.1, for the details of these instructions after reading this chapter.

10.1. CHARACTER DATA

Characters punched on cards for computer input are represented in the *Hollerith code*, of which more will be said in Chapter 15. Printed output consists of printed characters. Other I/O devices have different forms of external character representation. We saw that one of the steps in an input/output operation is the automatic conversion of the *external* form of data representation to/from its equivalent *internal* form.

Once the external characters have been converted to their internal form, they are ready for processing by the computer. For example, the assembler might translate the character information thus represented to machine language. Or a program might convert numerical characters or data to a form suitable for computer arithmetic. Or the characters might represent a social security number to be used to identify a record stored on an auxiliary storage device. The information processed by a computer is normally presented first in character form. The computer and its programs determine how the character data are used.

10.1.1. The EBCDIC Code

In the IBM 360 and 370 computers, the EBCDIC code is used for internal representation of character data. EBCDIC (pronounced IB′-SEA-DICK or IB′-EE-DICK) stands for *Extended Binary Coded Decimal Interchange Code*. In the EBCDIC code, each character is represented by an 8-bit binary code; each character occupies 1 byte.

It is possible to represent 256 different characters using an 8-bit code, since 8 bits can contain 256 different combinations of 0s and 1s. Not all these 256 binary numbers have corresponding characters. Table 10-1 shows some of the commonly used characters and their EBCDIC equivalents. In discussing the code for a given character, we normally portray the 8 bits by two hexadecimal digits. The EBCDIC code for the character A is shown as hexadecimal C1, while that for the + sign is hexadecimal 4E.

The EBCDIC codes for the letters A–Z and the numerals 0–9 are fairly easy to remember, with the help of some finger counting. The first hexadecimal digit, the *zone digit*, of the letters A through I is C. The second digit counts from 1 through 9 to give the codes C1 through C9. The zone digit in the code for the letters J through R is D. Thus, these letters have codes D1 through D9. The remaining letters S through Z have an E as the first digit in their codes. But we skip one in the second digit to obtain the code for S. Thus, the EBCDIC codes for letters S through Z are E2 through E9. The zone digit of the EBCDIC code for the numerals is F, while the second contains the binary code for the numeric digit. This means that the decimal digits 0 through 9 have the EBCDIC codes F0 through F9.

There is no simple relationship between the characters for punctuation

Table 10-1 HEXADECIMAL VALUES OF THE EBCDIC CODES FOR COMMONLY USED
CHARACTERS

Character	EBCDIC Code	Binary	Character	EBCDIC Code	Binary
A	C1	1100 0001	0	F0	1111 0000
B	C2	1100 0010	1	F1	1111 0001
C	C3	1100 0011	2	F2	1111 0010
D	C4	1100 0100	3	F3	1111 0011
E	C5	1100 0101	4	F4	1111 0100
F	C6	1100 0110	5	F5	1111 0101
G	C7	1100 0111	6	F6	1111 0110
H	C8	1100 1000	7	F7	1111 0110
I	C9	1100 1001	8	F8	1111 1000
J	D1	1101 0001	9	F9	1111 1001
K	D2	1101 0010	Blank	40	0100 0000
L	D3	1101 0011	+	4E	0100 1110
M	D4	1101 0100	−	60	0110 0000
N	D5	1101 0101	.	4B	0100 1011
O	D6	1101 0110	,	6B	0110 1011
P	D7	1101 0111	(	4D	0100 1101
Q	D8	1101 1000	)	5D	0101 1101
R	D9	1101 1001	$	5B	0101 1011
S	E2	1110 0010	=	7E	0111 1110
T	E3	1110 0011	;	5E	0101 1110
U	E4	1110 0100	:	7A	0111 1010
V	E5	1110 0101			
W	E6	1110 0110			
X	E7	1110 0111			
Y	E8	1110 1000			
Z	E9	1110 1001			

and algebraic signs and their EBCDIC codes. But one character in particular needs to be pointed out and that is the *blank* character. In typing, punching a card, or reading a print line we tend to consider the blank as being nothing. However, the blank is a *character* in its own right; it has EBCDIC code 40_{16}.

A series of adjacent characters is called a character *string*. The 80 characters punched on a data card (including blanks as characters) are an example of a character string. The reading of the card by the card reader results in the card *image* being stored in the memory. This card image is 80 consecutive bytes containing the EBCDIC character-code equivalents of the 80 characters that were punched on a data card.

Suppose that we cause a data card to be read and its card image to be stored in the memory starting at an address named CARDIN. Suppose that this card has the statement

NEXTNUMbbRWDbbb2bbb ...

punched on it, where we have used lower case b's to represent blanks. The resulting card image, the memory contents starting at CARDIN, are

CARDIN: $+0 +1 +2 +3 +4 +5 +6 \cdots$ $+18 +19$

| D5 | C5 | E7 | E3 | D5 | E4 | D4 | 40 | 40 | D9 | E6 | C4 | 40 | 40 | 40 | F2 | 40 | 40 | 40 | $\cdots$ |

where the vertical lines represent boundaries between bytes and each of the 60 bytes not shown contains 40_{16}. Each character that was punched on the card has been translated to EBCDIC and the resulting 8-bit character codes stored in consecutive bytes starting at CARDIN.

As another example, the internal EBCDIC form of the characters

$$-100$$

is the 4 bytes containing

$$60F1F0F0$$

which bears little resemblance to its binary equivalent

$$FFFFFF9C$$

We conclude that arithmetic with numerical data still in character form is essentially meaningless. We shall discuss the conversion of character data to internal numeric form in Chapter 15.

10.1.2. Character Constants

In Chapter 6 we described the use of the DS and DC assembler directives to reserve memory space and assign names to the reserved space. The DC statement also causes initial values to be stored in the space it reserves. We used the types H, F, and D in connection with these directives, and we delayed discussion of the reservation of byte units and character constants until now.

The assembler recognizes the letter C as indicator to denote information of Character type. Since a character code is 1 byte long, use of type C with a DS̄ statement causes the assembler to reserve the requested number of bytes in the memory for use at execution time. For example, the statement

BYTES   DS   33C

makes 33 bytes of storage available for use when the program is executed. The name BYTES designates the address of the first byte of the reserved space. As is always the case with the DS statement, the reserved space contains whatever was left there by the previous programs when the program execution is begun.

We use the DC statement to cause initial values to be stored in the space reserved. The statement

NONSENSE   DC   C'THE MOON IS PURPLE'

reserves 18 bytes of memory and assigns the name NONSENSE to the memory address of the first byte of the reserved space. The memory contents starting at NONSENSE are

$$\text{E3C8C540D4D6D6D540C9E240D7E4D9D7D3C5}$$

The general form of a character constant is

$$\text{DupCLn'string'}$$

Here "Dup" is an integer duplication factor that indicates the number of areas described by CLn'string' to reserve. "String" is a character string. "Ln" means a "length of n bytes," where n is an integer. If we omit this parameter, the assembler reserves the number of bytes necessary for the given character string. In the example above, we did omit the Ln parameter and saw that the assembler reserves 18 bytes of memory to hold the 18-byte character string

$$\text{THE MOON IS PURPLE}$$

If n is larger than the number of bytes required to store the given character string, the assembler inserts blank characters to make up the difference at the right-hand end of the string. We call these extra blanks *padding* characters. If n is less than the number of bytes required for the given string, the assembler truncates the right-hand end of the string to make it fit into n bytes.

For example, the statement

```
EMPNO          DC          CL15'EMPLOYEE NO.'
```

cause 15 bytes to be reserved starting at EMPNO. These 15 bytes contain the EBCDIC code for the character string

$$\text{EMPLOYEEbNO.bbb}$$

when program execution begins. Since the statement requests 15 bytes for the 12-byte string, the assembler inserts three blank characters at the end. On the other hand, the statement

```
EMPNO          DC          CL8'EMPLOYEE NO.'
```

produces the character string

$$\text{EMPLOYEE}$$

starting at EMPNO. The assembler truncates the last four characters so that the result will fit into the requested 8 bytes.

We use the duplication factor to reserve copies of the same string. For example, the statement

```
REF            DC          3CL8'REFUND'
```

leaves the character codes for the string

$$\text{REFUNDbbREFUNDbbREFUNDbb}$$

stored in the memory starting at REF.

In arranging a character string for output, it is often convenient to have an area filled with blanks reserved by the assembler. If our printed line is to be 133 characters in length, the statement

LINE   DC   CL133' '

reserves such a space. We specify just one character in the string. But since we request 133 bytes for the string, the assembler pads the remaining 132 bytes with the code for the blank character.

In summary, we use the DC statement to define character constants. The assembler responds by reserving the space requested in the length parameter and placing the EBCDIC equivalent of the character string into the reserved space. If no length is specified, the assembler reserves the amount of space required to store the character string given.

10.2. MOVING CHARACTER INFORMATION

Having seen how characters are represented in the machine and how to reserve space for character data, let us now begin our study of the byte-manipulation instructions. In so doing, we shall encounter the remaining instruction types that we have neglected so far, the SS and SI instructions. First we have the MVC and MVI instructions, respectively.

10.2.1. The MVC Instruction

The MVC instruction is of the SS type. From this we infer that both operands are in the memory and that their addresses are of the S-type. Thus, in the explicit forms of the operand addresses, we specify a base register and displacement. In their implicit forms, we can use symbolic names or expressions to designate these addresses. The assembler converts such symbols to base-displacement form.

MVC D1(L1,B1),D2(B2)   MoVe Character $D1 + (B1) \longleftarrow (D2 + (B2))_{L1}$

The MoVe Character instruction moves from 1 to 256 consecutive bytes starting at the second operand address, $D2 + (B2)$ to the area of the same length starting at the first operand address. The number of bytes moves is given by the number L1, which, in our descriptive notation, represents the Length of the first operand. We have indicated that L1 bytes are moved by writing L1 as a subscript in the symbolic description of the effect of the instruction. The MVC instruction has no effect upon the condition code.

If the L1 bytes starting at the address $D1 + (B2)$ do not overlap with the L1 bytes starting at the address $D2 + (B2)$, the MVC instruction simply copies the L1 bytes starting at $D2 + (B2)$ into the L1 bytes starting at $D1 + (B1)$. This destroys the original contents of the L1 bytes starting at D1 +

(B1). To use the implicit forms of the operand addresses, we write

MVC   S1(L1),S2

where S1 and S2 are relocatable symbols or expressions. We can also mix the operand forms, writing an explicit address for the first operand and an implicit address for the second and vice versa.

The assembler directive

DIGITS   DC   CL10'0123456789'

results in the EBCDIC character codes for the string

0123456789

stored in the memory starting at DIGITS, while the statement

LETTERS   DC   CL10'ABCDEFGHIJ'

produces the EBCDIC equivalent of the string

ABCDEFGHIJ

at LETTERS.

Suppose that we wish to move contents of the first 5 bytes starting at LETTERS to the first 5 bytes starting at DIGITS. The length, L1, is 5; DIGITS is the first operand address and LETTERS the second. Thus, we write

MVC   DIGITS(5),LETTERS

Execution of this instruction produces a copy of the first 5 bytes of LETTERS starting at DIGITS. The result is the EBCDIC code for the string

ABCDE56789

at DIGITS.

Given the same intial contents of DIGITS and LETTERS, the instruction

MVC   DIGITS+4(3),LETTERS

produces the string

0123ABC789

at DIGITS, while the instruction

MVC   DIGITS+2(6), LETTERS+3

results in the EBCDIC form of the string

01DEFGHI89

at DIGITS.

To illustrate the use of the explicit means of operand designation, suppose that the hexadecimal memory contents starting at address 20000_{16} are

F301406872816081

while the memory contents starting at address 20500 are

0123456789ABCDEF0123

Suppose further that

(3) = 00020000

and that

(6) = 00020500

at the time of the execution of the instruction

MVC   2(4,3),4(6)

The instruction moves the 4 bytes starting at the address 4 + (6) = 4 + 20500 = 20504 to the 4-byte area starting at address 2 + (3) = 2 + 20000 = 20002. The resulting memory contents starting at address 20000 are

F30189ABCDEF6081

In its execution, we can suppose that the MVC instruction starts at the left-hand ends of both memory areas (the bytes with the lowest addresses) and moves 1 byte at a time until it has moved the required number of bytes. Thus, we can picture the effect of the MVC instruction just discussed as follows:

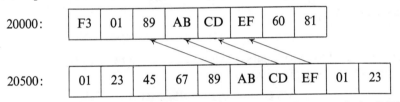

20000:

| F3 | 01 | 89 | AB | CD | EF | 60 | 81 |

20500:

| 01 | 23 | 45 | 67 | 89 | AB | CD | EF | 01 | 23 |

This fact becomes important when we consider the use of the MVC instruction in situations where the source and destination memory areas overlap. Suppose that we have the following stored at an area called A:

A: F0683479428C3

Execution of the instruction

MVC   A+1(5),A

results in

A: F0F0F0F0F0F0C3

In words, the instruction copies the contents of the first byte into the following 5 bytes. To see how this happens, let us suppose that we could watch the MVC instruction as it moves each byte. The first byte is moved from A to A + 1 with the result

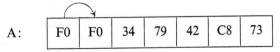

A:

| F0 | F0 | 34 | 79 | 42 | C8 | 73 |

The next byte goes from A+1 to A+2;

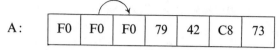

A:

the next from A+2 to A+3;

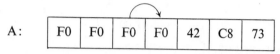

A:

and so on, until a total of 5 bytes have been moved. We often use this trick to store a character code throughout a memory area.

In those cases in which the number of bytes to be moved is the same as the length of the area as specified in a DS or DC statement, we can omit the length parameter, L1. In such use of an *implied length*, the assembler inserts the length of the *first* operand into the machine language form of the MVC instruction (actually, the assembler uses one less than the length, as discussed in the next chapter). Suppose that a program contains the statements

```
AREA1        DS          CL5
AREA2        DC          CL8'KITTYCAT'
```

The instruction

```
        MVC         AREA1,AREA2
```

moves the first five characters of AREA2 into the 5 bytes starting at AREA1 and thus has the same effect as the instruction

```
        MVC         AREA1(5),AREA2
```

In other words, if a length is not specified, the assembler uses the length supplied in the statement that defines the first operand. It is sometimes convenient to make use of the fact that half-words, full words, and double words have lengths 2, 4, and 8, respectively, in using the implied length feature.

Finally, while MVC stands for MoVe Character, it should perhaps be called MoVe Byte, or MVB, because that is actually what it does. The MVC instruction moves whatever is stored at the second operand address and the bytes following, regardless of whether the data moved are EBCDIC codes for characters. Thus, for example, suppose that we want to move the contents of a full word stored at APPLES to a full-word area called ORANGES. The instruction

```
        MVC         ORANGES(4),APPLES
```

is the most efficient way to do this, regardless of the contents of the word stored at APPLES.

The MVCL instruction contained in the instruction set of the IBM 370 machines is an extension of the MVC instruction. It permits the movement of up to 16,777,216 bytes of information from one memory area to another and provides for automatic "padding" of memory space with a designated byte. Now is the time to study the pertinent material in Chapter 20, Section 20.1, if you are interested in learning about this facility.

10.2.2. The MVI Instruction

In character manipulation, it is often necessary to ensure that a single byte in the memory contains a specific number. For example, we saw that the MVC instruction can be used to duplicate a given byte throughout an area in the memory. We often use the MVI instruction to place the desired byte into the first byte of the memory area into which this byte is to be copied.

The MVI instruction is our first encounter with an instruction of the SI type. In assembly language, the first operand is an S-type memory address, given in either the explicit base register-displacement form or as a relocatable symbol or expression. The second operand, the Immediate operand, is exactly 1 byte of information. This byte cannot, of course, be used as an address. The byte given is the actual operand. The MoVe Immediate instruction moves (stores) the byte specified as the immediate operand to the address specified in the first operand and has no effect on the condition code.

MVI	D1(B1),I2	MoVe Immediate	D2 + (B1) ← I2

In the description above I2 represents the 1-byte immediate operand. We can specify this byte in any of a number of ways. We commonly use the MVI instructions to store a character constant in the memory. For example, the instruction

$$\text{MVI} \qquad \text{A1,C'T'}$$

moves the EBCDIC code for the letter T to the memory location called A1. This code can also be written as the hexadecimal constant, X'E3', the binary constant, B'11100011', or the decimal constant, 227. Hence, the following instructions all have the same effect as the one written above:

$$\text{MVI} \qquad \text{A1,X'E3'}$$
$$\text{MVI} \qquad \text{A1,B'11100011'}$$
$$\text{MVI} \qquad \text{A1,227}$$

If at A1 we have

$$\text{A1:} \qquad \text{C2C1D9}$$

Then executing any of the MVI instructions yields

$$\text{A1:} \qquad \text{E3C1D9}$$

Explicit operand specification is the same as with all S-type addresses. Suppose that we have an address in register 5 and want to fill the 150 bytes starting at this address with the character code for blank. The instruction

MVI   0(5),C' '

stores 40_{16} at the address $0+(5)$. The instruction

MVC   1(149,5),0(5)

copies the blank into the remaining 149 bytes.

10.2.3. The IC and STC Instructions

In some cases, it is convenient to use the registers for temporary storage and manipulation of byte-sized information. The Insert Character instruction is an RX instruction which loads the contents of the byte stored at the specified address into the last 8 bits, bits 24 through 31, of the designated register operand.

IC   R1,D2(X2,B2)   Insert Character $R1_{24\text{-}31} \longleftarrow (D2 + (X2) + (B2))_c$

In the description above, the subscript C means 1 byte, while the subscript 24–31 indicates those bits of R1 into which the byte is moved. The remaining bits 0–23 of R1 are unchanged by the IC instruction.

The STore Character instruction stores the contents of the last 8 bits of the register operand into the byte at the specified memory address.

STC   R1,D2(X2,B2)   STore Character $(R1)_{24\text{-}31} \longrightarrow D2 + (X2) + (B2)$

There are no boundary rules associated with byte information units.

We use the IC and STC instructions to carry out arithmetic operations upon the contents of single bytes. To add 1 to the contents of the byte at BYTE we write

IC   3,BYTE
AH   3,=H'1'
STC   3,BYTE

As discussed in Chapter 20, the IBM 370 computers offer extensions ICM and STCM of the IC and STC instructions.

10.3. COMPARING CHARACTER INFORMATION

A great deal of character manipulation involves such applications as the sorting of character data into some prescribed order and the searching of character strings for specific substrings. Thus, we need to look at some character-oriented comparison instructions.

10.3.1. The CLC Instruction

In using the CLC instruction, we specify the operands in exactly the same way as we do for the MVC instruction. The two operands are both in the memory, as is the case with all SS instructions, and we must supply a length, which determines the number of bytes in the two memory areas which are being compared.

CLC   D1(L1,B1),D2(B2)   Compare Logical   Compare $(D1 + (B1))_{L1}$
                             Character   with $(D2 + (B2))_{L1}$
                                                      and set CC

The Compare Logical Character instruction compares the contents of the L1 bytes starting at address $D1 + (B1)$ with the contents of the L1 bytes starting at address $D2 + (B2)$. In this *logical* comparison, the memory operands, which may be up to 256 bytes long, are treated as *unsigned* integers. This means that the first bit of the areas has no special significance as a sign bit; in effect, unsigned integers are always positive. Thus, the largest unsigned integer that fits into one byte is 11111111_2, while the smallest is 00000000_2 (if we were to treat these numbers as signed integers instead, the former would have the value -1, while the latter is 0). In a logical comparison, the half-word $C863_{16}$ is *greater than* the half-word 4632, while the reverse is true if we compare these two numbers using an *arithmetic* comparison.

Using unsigned arithmetic the sorting of character data into ascending numerical order sorts the data into alphabetical order. The blank character, X'40', is less than any of the letters, so that it and punctuation marks are treated properly in sorting applications.

The CLC instruction sets the condition code to indicate whether the first operand is Equal, Low (less than), or High (greater than) in comparison with the second operand. CLC subtracts the second operand from the first using unsigned arithmetic and sets the condition code to indicate the result. Of course, neither of the memory operands is changed as a result of this operation.

CLC sets the condition code to the following values:

Condition Code	Result
0	Operands equal
1	First operand < second operand
2	First operand > second operand
3	Cannot occur

After the condition code has been set, we can use any of the conditional branch instructions to test the result.

Suppose that the following is stored in the memory:

A: C3C1E34040
B: D9C1E34040

The following instructions have the indicated effects upon the condition code:

Instruction		Condition Code
CLC	A(5),B	1
CLC	A+1(3),B+1	0
CLC	A(4),B+1	2
CLC	B(4),A	2

As an illustration of a programming application of the CLC instruction, Fig. 10-1 shows a program segment that might be a portion of a program

```
          LA     9,GERMAN       REG, 9 GETS ADDRESS OF FIRST GER, CHAR.
          LA     6,1            INCREMENT FOR LOOP CONTROL
          LA     7,GERMAN       COMPUTE
          A      7,=F'3995'     FINAL VALUE FOR LOOP COUNTER
NEXTWC    CLC    0(5,9),DIEWD   CHECK FOR ' DIE '
          BE     TRANS          IF FOUND, GO REPLACE IT
          CLC    0(5,9),DERWD   CHECK FOR ' DER '
          BE     TRANS          IF FOUND,GO REPLACE IT
          CLC    0(5,9),DENWD   CHECK FOR ' DEN '
          BNE    FINCHK         TRANSLATE IF FOUND
TRANS     MVC    0(5,9),=C' THE '  REPLACE GER. WORD WITH ' THE '
          LA     9,4(9)         WON'T BE ANOTHER FOR 5 MORE BYTES
FINCHK    BXLE   9,6,NEXTWC     ADD 1 TO ADDRESS, GO TEST NEXT STRING
                    .
                    .
                    .
DIEWD     DC     C' DIE '
DERWD     DC     C' DER '
DENWD     DC     C' DEN '
GERMAN    DS     20CL20C
```

Fig. 10-1. A program segment that translates the German words "die," "der," and "den" to English "the."

that translates German language text to English. A character string 4000 bytes long stored starting at GERMAN is searched for the character strings bDIEb, bDERb, and bDENb. When a match is found with one of these strings, the string bTHEb is moved into its place. The three CLC instructions test for the German words. The MVC instruction makes the replacement. Notice the use of the literal character constant

$$=C'THE '$$

as an operand of the MVC statement. We could just as well have written

MVC   0(5,9),THEWD

with the DC statement

THEWD   DC   C' THE '

included in the data storage section of the program.

The 370 instruction CLCL, Compare Logical Characters Long, is discussed in Chapter 20.

10.3.2. The CLI Instruction

The Compare Logical Immediate instruction is the SI logical comparison instruction. It compares contents of the byte stored at the address given as the first operand with the byte supplied as the immediate operand.

CLI   D1(B1),I2   Compare Logical Immediate   Compare $(D1 + (B1))_c$
                                              with I2 and set CC

The comparison is again an unsigned integer comparison. When the memory operand is equal, low, or high in comparison with the immediate byte, the condition code is set to 0, 1, or 2, respectively. For example, the instruction

CLI   5(3),C'T'

compares the byte stored 5 bytes beyond an address contained in register 3 with the character code for T, which is $X'E3'$. If the resulting condition code is 1, the tested character comes before T in the alphabet, since its EBCDIC code is less than that of T. Condition code 0 indicates that the byte at that address contains $X'E3'$, while a condition code of 2 indicates that the contents of the memory operand is greater than $X'E3'$.

Suppose that we have the following stored at LETTERS:

C5D5E640

The following instructions set the condition code to the indicated values:

	Instruction	Condition Code
CLI	LETTERS,C'E'	0
CLI	LETTERS+2,B'11100101'	2
CLI	LETTERS+3,X'40'	0
CLI	LETTERS,C' '	2
CLI	LETTERS+1,C'N'	0
CLI	LETTERS+3,X'00'	1

Figure 10-2 shows a program segment that counts the number of times the character code for the letter M appears in a 200-byte string stored starting at TEXT. There is no index register in an S-type address. Therefore, when we

```
             LA    7,0              CCUNTER OF 'M''S
             LA    9,TEXT           ACDRESS OF FIRST CHARACTER
             LA    4,1              INCREMENT FOR LOOP
             LA    5,TEXT+199       FINAL ADDRESS OF TEXT
CHECKEM      CLI   0(9),C'M'        TFST FOR LETTER M
             BNE   NOTEM            IF EQUAL, M WAS FOUND
             LA    7,1(7)           ACD ONE TO M COUNTER
NOTEM        BXLE  9,4,CHECKEM      ADD ONE TO ACDRESS, GC CHECK NEXT BYTE
                    •
                    •
                    •
TEXT         CS    200C             2C0 BYTES RESERVED, NAME IS TEXT
```

Fig. 10-2. A program segment that counts the number of times the character code for M occurs in a 200-byte area that starts at TEXT.

process character data in a loop, we must use explicit forms for S-type addresses, since this is the only way we can achieve variable addresses at execution time.

10.4.   CHARACTER INPUT/OUTPUT:
RCD AND PLN

RWD and WWD were designed for numerical input/output and are special macro-instructions to help with input/output for the portions of this text. In all standard programming applications, the primary form of data input or output to or from the machine is in the form of character strings— the 80 characters read from a data card or the characters that form a printed line, for example. For use with this text, we have supplied two more special macro-instructions, RCD and PLN, to assist temporarily with character input/output. In Chapter 17 we shall see how to use the operating system facilities for input/output. Like RWD and WWD, RCD and PLN are special macros that are not to be found in all systems.

RCD   D2(X2,B2)   <u>R</u>ead <u>CarD</u>   80 bytes from data card $\longrightarrow$
D2 + (X2) + (B2)

The RCD macro causes an 80-byte EBCDIC-coded card image to be stored at the address specified as the operand. The memory address can be indexed, as can be seen from the above description. For example, the statement

RCD   INPUT(5)

with

$$(5) = 000000A0$$

will causes the 80-byte image of the next input data card to be stored starting 160_{10} bytes beyond the beginning of the memory area called INPUT. A suitable DS statement to reserve the space INPUT could be

INPUT   DS   400C

The space so reserved has enough room for five card images.

Line printers for IBM systems print either 120 or 132 characters per line. In this text, we shall assume that the line printer you use prints 132 characters per line. Your instructor will tell you which length is appropriate for your local system.

The PLN macro causes the string of 133 (or 121) coded EBCDIC characters starting at the address specified in the operand field to be sent to the printer as part of the printed output resulting from execution of the program.

PLN   D2(X2,B2)   Print LiNe
                      133 (or 121) bytes from D2 + (X2) + (B2) $\longrightarrow$ printer

---

The first byte of the string is used for control of the printer carriage and is not printed. The following carriage control characters cause the carriage spacing shown:

Character	Hexadecimal Equivalent	Carriage Control
Blank	40	Single space
0	F0	Skip one line
1	F1	Top of page
+	4E	No carriage movement

Use of other characters for carriage control when using the PLN macro is not permitted. Suppose that we have the following 133-byte character string stored at OUTPUT,

1THISbWILLbBEbPRINTEDbATbTHEbTOPbOFbTHEbNEXTbPAGF

followed by 84 blanks.

The statement

                PLN   OUTPUT

causes

THIS WILL BE PRINTED AT THE TOP OF THE NEXT PAGE

to be printed as the first printed line on the next page. If the first character had been blank instead of 1, the same line would be printed, but on the next line available for output, instead of at the top of the next page.

Figure 10-3 illustrates the use of RCD and PLN in a program that lists a deck of data cards, stopping when a card is encountered with the characters STOP in the first four columns. In this application, the same memory area, INOUT, is used for input and output. The card image is read starting at

```
LISTER      START  0
            PRINT  NOGEN
            INITIAL
NEXTCARD    RCD    INOUT+1        READ CARD
            CLC    INOUT+1(4),STOPPER  TEST FOR LAST CARD
            BE     DONE           STOP IF LAST CARD
            PLN    INOUT          PRINT
            B      NEXTCARD       GO TO GET NEXT CARD
DONE        EOJ                   STOP EXECUTION
STOPPER     DC     C'STOP'        LAST CARD WILL SAY 'STOP'
INOUT       DC     CL133' '       MEMORY AREA FOR INPUT/OUTPUT
            END    LISTER
```

Fig. 10-3. A program that lists a deck of cards until a card with "STOP" punched in the first four columns is encountered.

INOUT+1, so that the carriage control character, a blank, is not changed by reading the card.

10.5. PROGRAMMING EXAMPLES

We have discussed the most commonly used character manipulation instructions. Because character manipulation is virtually ubiquitous in computing, we shall end this chapter with a detailed consideration of two examples of character manipulation programs. The exercises include some problems you should try.

We shall first consider a program to print mailing lists. These are usually printed on pregummed labels which are then peeled off the backing upon which they come and stuck to envelopes for mailing. We suppose that the labels are designed as shown in Fig. 10-4. The labels come on a long backing sheet containing four columns of labels with four character spaces between each column. Each label is 30 character spaces wide and is separated from the one below it by one line. Three lines can be printed on each label. Thus, we wish to print four mailing addresses on each row of labels, one address per label, skip to the next row, print four more addresses, and so on.

The problem is that a punched-card-based mailing list is most easily handled, sorted, and updated when each card contains a single address. We suppose that the address cards have the following format:

columns 1–30:   name
columns 31–55:   street address
columns 56–80:   city, state, and zip code

The program must read each card and move each of the three fields from the card image into position so that the address is printed on three lines on the appropriate label. It must treat the address cards in groups of four, since four labels are to be printed in each row of labels. We assume that the number of address cards is a multiple of 4. If not, blank cards can be added at the end

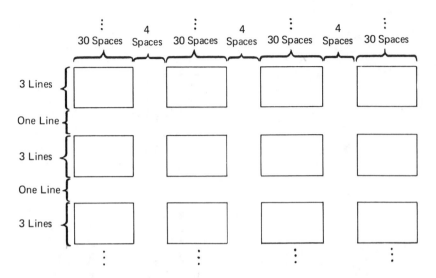

Fig. 10-4. Label design for a computer-printed mailing list.

of the deck to make this true. To stop the program, we add one additional trailer card at the end of the data deck. This card has the string ***** punched in the first five columns of the card.

Figure 10-5 shows an example of an input deck and the output from the program when run with this deck. Figure 10-6 shows a flow chart for the program, and Fig. 10-7 shows the program itself. In the flow chart we indicate the movement of character data by writing the indexes of the bytes to be moved as subscripts of the names of the areas being moved. For example, we show that bytes 0 through 29 of the area called NAME are to be moved to bytes J through J+29 of the area LINE1 by writing

$$\text{LINE1}_{J-J+29} \longleftarrow \text{NAME}_{0-29}$$

In designing a program such as this, it is advisable to begin by considering the memory space that will be needed and the formats of the input and output records. The input records are in the format described above. To make the program easier to read and write, we split the 80-byte area required for the input data cards into three areas of the proper lengths, NAME, STADDR, and CITSTATE. The output consists of three lines per row of labels, each line containing 132 bytes and a leading carriage control character. The extra line skipped between rows of labels can be inserted by using the carriage control character C'0' for the first output line. Notice that we have kept the carriage control character separate from each line to make the addressing of the operands easier.

Next we write the instructions that do the "work" of the program, in this case, the three MVC instructions. Anticipating the fact that the first operand

```
SANTA CLAUSE      19 REINDEER ROW       FRIGID, NORTH POLE 11201
ROY G. BIV        243 GREEN ST.         RED CITY, ARK. 56234
MICKEY MOUSE      704 MINNIE WAY        DISNEYLAND, CALIF. 82301
LASSIE            764 ALPO AVENUE       PURINA PARK, OKLA. 21101
IRVING WASHINGTON 2110 SLEEPY HOLLOW    DUTCHTOWN, PA. 64489
JIMMIN E. CRICKET 222 PINNOCHIO PLACE   PUPPET CITY, FLA. 72245
EDGAR ALLEN POE   47 OLD CROW DRIVE     SECAUCUS, N.J. 07090
CONNIE C. COMPUTER 906 DUMP DRIVE       BIT BUCKET, KANSAS 41109
UNC L. SAM        999 IRS ST.           MUNY, MINN. 11456

*****

SANTA CLAUSE                ROY G. BIV
19 REINDEER ROW             243 GREEN ST.
FRIGID, NORTH POLE 11201    RED CITY, ARK. 56234

MICKEY MOUSE                JIMMIN E. CRICKET
704 MINNIE WAY              222 PINNOCHIO PLACE
DISNEYLAND, CALIF. 82301    PUPPET CITY, FLA. 72245

LASSIE                      IRVING WASHINGTON
764 ALPO AVENUE             2110 SLEEPY HOLLOW
PURINA PARK, OKLA. 21101    DUTCHTOWN, PA. 64489

CONNIE C. COMPUTER          EDGAR ALLEN POE
906 DUMP DRIVE              47 OLD CROW DRIVE
BIT BUCKET, KANSAS 41109    SECAUCUS, N.J. 07090

                            UNC L. SAM
                            999 IRS ST.
                            MUNY, MINN. 11456
```

Fig. 10-5. Input and output for the mailing list program.

212

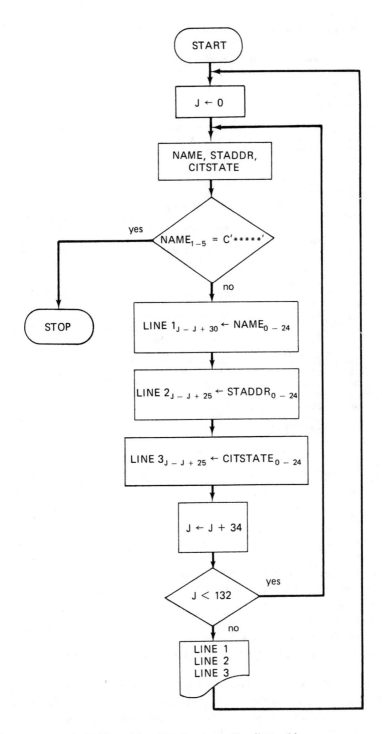

Fig. 10-6. Flowchart for the mailing list problem.

```
*              PROGRAM TO PRINT MAILING LIST ON LABLES, FOUR LABELS PER ROW
*              ADDRESSSES ARE INPUT ONE ADDRESS PER CARD
MAILLIST  START  0
          PRINT  NOGEN
          INITIAL
          LA     4,34            34  COLUMNS PER LABLE
          LA     3,132           132 COLUMNS PER PRINTED LINE
RESTART   LA     2,0             REG. 2 WILL INDICATE WHICH LABEL IS BEING
NXTCARD   RCD    NAME            DONE.  READ ADDRESS CARD.
          CLC    NAME(5),STOPPER    CHECK FOR TRAILER CARD
          BE     DONE            IF FOUND, PROCESSING COMPLETE
          LA     6,LINE1(2)      ADDRESS FOR NAME IN REG. 6
          MVC    0(30,6),NAME    MOVE NAME FIELD TO FIRST OUTPUT LINE
          LA     6,LINE2(2)      ADDRESS FOR STREET ADDRESS
          MVC    0(25,6),STADDR    MOVE STREET ADDRESS TO OUTPUT LINE 2
          LA     6,LINE3(2)      ADDRESS FOR CITY, STAE OUTPUT FIELD
          MVC    0(25,6),CITSTATE    MOVE CITY-STAE FIELD TO OUTPUT LIN 3
          BXLE   2,4,NXTCARD        GO TO PROCESS NEXT ADDRESS INPUT CARD
          PRT    CCNTL1          PRINT RESULTING FOUR LABLES
          PRT    CCNTL2
          PRT    CCNTL3
          B      RESTART         START PROCESSING NEXT ROW OF LABLES
DONE      EOJ
NAME      DS     CL30            SPACE FOR INPUT NAME FIELD
STADDR    DS     CL25            SPACE FOR INPUT STREET ADDRESS FIELD
CITSTATE  DS     CL25            SPACE FOR INPUT CITY-STAE-ZIP FIELD
CCNTL1    DC     C'0'            CARRIAGE CONTROL 1ST LINE - DOUBLE SPACE
LINE1     DC     CL132' '        SPACE FOR 1ST OUTPUT LINE
CCNTL2    DC     C' '            CARRIAGE CONTROL FOR 2OND LINE - SINGLE SP
LINE2     DC     CL132' '        SPACE FOR 2OND OUTPUT LINE
CCNTL3    DC     C' '            CARRIAGE CONTROL FOR 3RD LINE - SINGLE SP
LINE3     DC     CL132' '        SPACE FOR 3RD OUTPUT LINE
STOPPER   DC     CL5'*****'      FIVE STARS WILL MEAN TRAILER CARD
          END    MAILLIST
```

Fig. 10-7.

addresses will vary, depending on which label we are constructing, we use register 6 to contain the addresses of the first operands. The loop control, the test for the trailer card, instructions to calculate addresses, and the remaining statements can then be tailored to fit the basic computational instructions and memory space definition statements.

As our second character manipulation example, we shall consider the construction of a *linked list*. A linked list is a means of storing ordered data in which the logical order of the data is in general not the same as the physical order in which the data items are stored. Instead, to find the item after a given item in the list, we refer to a *pointer* contained in the item currently being considered. This pointer is usually the address of the next item in the list.

Consider the structure shown in Fig. 10-8, which represents a linked list. Each item, or *record*, in the list consists of three portions. The first is the *key* field, which contains an identifier for the record and is the field which determines the record's logical position in the list. For example, the key field

Name

500 | 2000

Address	Key	Data	Pointer
1000	C		4000
2000	A		1000
3000	R		500
4000	F		3000

Fig. 10-8. A linked list.

might contain the number of the student whose grades are given in the data portion of the record. We would sort the file by placing the records such that their keys appear in numerical order. The data field of a record contains the information associated with the given key. The pointer field contains the *address* of the next record in the list.

In Fig. 10-8, four records with keys C, A, R, and F are shown as elements of the linked list. Suppose that we have located the record with key C in our list and that we wish to find the next record. To do this we simply refer to the pointer field in the record C, where we find the address of the next record, 4000. At 4000 we find the key of the next record, F, which points to the record at address 3000, and so on.

To find the first item in the list, we establish a *name* (or rock or head) for the list which contains the address of the first record. This pointer to the beginning of the list must be kept separate from the list itself. In an empty list, the head points to itself; the contents of the name is its address:

Name

500 | 500

The last record in the list points back to the name. Thus, we know we are at the end of the list when we find a record whose pointer points to the name of the list.

A new record to be entered into the list can be stored anywhere in the memory. Suppose that we wish to insert a record with key D into the list of Fig. 10-8 and that this record is stored at address 7000. We start with the head of the list and examine the keys until one is found that is greater than D. We

Name

500	2000

Address	Key	Data	Pointer
1000	C		7000
2000	A		1000
3000	R		500
4000	F		3000
7000	D		4000

Fig. 10-9. The linked list of Fig. 10-8 with a new record with key D inserted.

then place a pointer to that record into the pointer field of D and change the pointer field of the preceding record (C in this example) so that it points to D. Figure 10-9 shows our linked list with record D added to it.

The primary advantage that accrues through the use of the linked list structure instead of sequential storage is that once a record has been entered into the file, it never has to be moved again. The insertion of a record into a sequential file requires the movement of all the following records in order to make space for it. To add a record to a linked list, all we have to do is to change two pointer fields, as discussed above. This means that linked lists are often used for the storage of ordered files in which the records are too long to make frequent movement of them attractive from the point of view of efficiency. Since insertion and deletion of records in a linked list is relatively easy, we tend to use linked lists when records are frequently inserted into and deleted from the file.

Figure 10-10 shows a flow chart for a program that reads a series of 80-byte records from cards and stores them as a linked list in alphabetical order by a key in the first 10 bytes of each record. At the end of each record we add a pointer 4 bytes long. After the record is inserted into the list, the pointer contains the address of the next record in the list. In the flow chart, we have used the abbreviation A(NAME) to stand for the address of the area called NAME. REC(J) means the 80 bytes starting at address J. KEY(J) represents the first 10 bytes of the record at address J, while POINT(REC(J)) means the pointer field in the last 4 bytes of the 84-byte area starting at address J.

In the flow chart, box 1 starts the list out as an empty list. J represents the address of the new record to be inserted in the list. This record is read in box

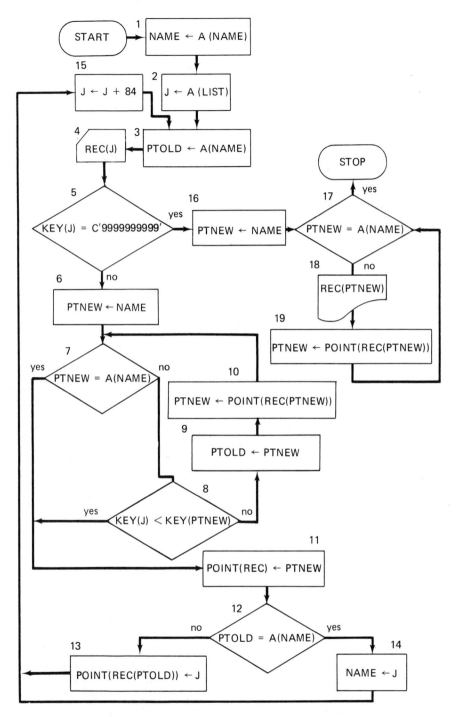

Fig. 10-10. Flowchart of a program that sorts a series of records by insertion into a linked list and prints the records in order.

217

218   CHARACTER MANIPULATION

4, and its key field is compared with a key of 10 9s, which indicates the end of the input card file. When the end of the file is encountered, boxes 16 through 19 go through the list, printing each record in its proper position. Box 6 starts the search at the beginning of the list for the position of the new record. The end of the list is indicated by a pointer field that contains the address of the name; the test for this condition appears in box 7. We then test the key of the new record against the key of the next record in the list, which is at address PTNEW. Boxes 9 and 10 change the pointers PTOLD, the address of the preceding record, and PTNEW to locate the next record.

```
*      PROGRAM TO SORT CARDS BY 10-BYTE KEY BY INSERTION INTO LINKED
*         LIST.
LINKSORT START  0
          PRINT NOGEN
          INITIAL
PTOLD     EQU   10              REG. 10 KEEPS ADDR. OF PRECEDING REC.
PTNEW     EQU   11              REG. 11 KEEPS ADDRESS OF NEXT RECORD
REC       EQU   6               REG. 6 KEEPS ADDR. IF NEW RECORD
          LA    REC,LIST        1ST REC. AT BEGINNING OF LIST AREA
NEWREC    LA    PTOLD,NAME      START  SEARCH AT NAME OF LIST
          RCD   0(REC)          INPUT NEW RECORD
          CLC   0(10,REC),LAST  SEE IF WE SHOULD STOP
          BE    PRINT           IF SO, PRINT THE LIST
          L     PTNEW,NAME      ADDRESS OF NEXT RECORD IN PTNEW
SEARCH    C     PTNEW,ADDNAME   SEE IF NEXT REC. IS LAST IN LIST
          BE    FOUND           IF SO, INSERT NEW RECORD LAST IN LIST
          CLC   0(10,REC),0(PTNEW) COMPARE KEYS OF NEW AND NEXT RECS.
          BL    FOUND           IF LESS, INSERT INTO LIST HERE
          LR    PTOLD,PTNEW     PREPARE TO CHECK NEXT RECORD IN LIST
          L     PTNEW,80(PTNEW)  PUT ADDR. OF NEXT REC. INTO PTNEW
          B     SEARCH          CHECK  NEW  NEXT RECORD
FOUND     ST    PTNEW,80(REC)   PTR. TO POINTER FIELD OF NEW RECORD
          C     PTOLD,ADDNAME   SEE IF IT IS FIRST IN LIST
          BE    FIRSTLST        IF SO, GO CHANGE (NAME)
          ST    REC,80(PTOLD)   ADDR OF NEW REC. TO PRECEDING POINTER
          LA    REC,84(REC)     ADDRESS OF NEXT NEW RECORD FOR INSERTION
          B     NEWREC          GO TO READ IT FORM CARD
FIRSTLST  ST    REC,NAME        ADDR. OF NEW REC. STORED AT NAME
          LA    REC,84(REC)     ADDRESS OF NEXT NEW RECORD
          B     NEWREC          GO READ IT
PRINT     L     REC,NAME        START AT BEGINNING OF LIST
NEXTLINE  MVC   OUTLINE+1,0(REC) MOVE RECORD TO OUTPUT AREA
          PRT   OUTLINE         PRINT IT
          CLC   80(4,REC),ADDNAME SEE IF IT WAS THE LAST ONE
          BE    DONE            STOP IF IT WAS
          L     REC,80(REC)     POINTER TO NEXT RECORD IN REG. 6
          B     NEXTLINE        GO TO OUTPUT NEXT RECORD
DONE      EOJ
OUTLINE   DC    CL133' '        MEMORY SPACE FOR OUTPUT AREA
ADDNAME   DC    A(NAME)         CONSTANT WITH VALUE=ADDR. OF NAME
NAME      DC    A(NAME)         NAME STARTS OUT POINTING TO ITSELF
LAST      DC    CL10'9999999999' LAST CARD WILL HAVE THIS KEY
          DS    0F              ENSURE FULL WORD ALIGNMENT OF LIST
LIST      DS    100CL84         MEMORY SPACE FOR LIST
          END   LINKSORT
```

Fig. 10-11.

When the first key is found that is greater than that of the new record, boxes 11 through 14 modify the pointers so that the new record will appear in its proper position in the list. We then go back for another record to be inserted, which is read into the 80-byte area 84 bytes beyond the preceding record. Notice that in this entire sorting procedure, we move no records except in the process of their original input.

Figure 10-11 shows the program corresponding to the flow chart of Fig. 10-10. The translation from the flow chart to the program is straightforward. Notice that box 1 of the flow chart is accomplished via the statement

NAME   DC   A(NAME)

Here we have used a feature of the assembly language which allows us to specify addresses as constants. The constant

A(PLACE)

has as its value a full word containing the address corresponding to the symbol PLACE. The effect of the statement above is to initialize the full word stored at NAME with its own address.

CHAPTER SUMMARY

The internal form of character representation is the *EBCDIC* code, in which each character has an equivalent 8-bit binary code. The DS statement can be used to reserve memory space in units 1 byte long, while the DC statement permits specification of character constants.

Table 10-2 shows the instructions covered in this chapter.

Table 10-2   CHARACTER MANIPULATION INSTRUCTIONS DISCUSSED IN CHAPTER 10

MVC	D1(L1,B1),D2(B2)	MoVe Character	$D1 + (B1) \leftarrow (D2 + (B2))_{L1}$
MVI	D1(B1),I2	MoVe Immediate	$D1 + (B1) \leftarrow I2$
IC	R1,D2(X2,B2)	Insert Character	$R1_{24-31} \leftarrow (D + (X2) + (B2))_C$
STC	R1,D2(X2,B2)	STore Character	$(R1)_{24-31} \rightarrow D2 + (X2) + (B2)$
CLC	D1(L1,B1),D2(B2)	Compare Logical Character	Compare $(D1 + (B1))_{L1}$ with $(D2 + (B2))_{L1}$ and set CC
CLI	D1(B1),I2	Compare Logical Immediate	Compare $(D1 + (B1))_C$ with I2 and set CC
RCD (special macro)	D2(X2,B2)	Read CarD	80-Byte card image $\rightarrow D2 + (X2) + (B2)$
PLN (special macro)	D2(X2,B2)	Print LiNe	$(D2 + (X2) + (B2))_{133}$ $\rightarrow$ printed output

E X E R C I S E S

1. Write the instructions necessary to move the area 5000 bytes long starting at IN to an area of the same length starting at OUT. This involves placing an MVC instruction in a loop. Refer to Chapter 20, Section 20.1, and redo this problem using the MVCL instruction.

2. Write a program to read and print up to 50 data cards, each of which contains a key in the first 15 bytes. Sort the card images into alphabetical order using this key, and print the resulting sorted file. (Use any sorting technique you wish except the use of linked list.) Compare the number of times your method has to move 80-byte records with the number of moves necessary in sorting by insertion into a linked list.

3. In a card-based inventory system, suppose that the inventory information for each item is punched on a data card in the following format:

Columns	Data
1–10	Part number
11–30	Description
31–40	Price
41–50	Number in stock
51–60	Reorder number—the minimum number of this item that will be in stock without reordering

Write a program to list the inventory records in tabular form. The printed output should consist of a heading which has the form

INVENTORY FOR
THE WHIZZER COMPUTER CO., INC.

The next line should indicate the data as punched on the first data card. The next line should contain column headings as follows,

col. 1	col. 25	col. 50	col. 70	col. 90
PART NUMBER	DESCRIPTION	PRICE	IN STOCK	REORDER NO.

followed by a line of hyphens:

Then comes the inventory list in the format

cols 1–10: part number
cols 25–44: description
cols 50–69: price
cols 70–79: number in stock
cols 90–99: reorder number

4. Exercise 3 is an example of the way in which an inventory system can be managed using punched cards. An alternative is to use an auxiliary memory device to store the records. This file is periodically updated from punched cards. We can simulate such a system by using a portion of the memory for storage of the inventory records. Write a program to do this. The first segment of the program should read up to 100 inventory cards in the same format as in the preceding exercise. These card images are to be stored in consecutive 80-byte areas in the memory. The remaining data cards indicate what changes are necessary in order to bring the file up to date. These control cards have the format

col. 1: control character
cols 2–11: part number
cols 15 on: new data to replace that already in the record with the given part number

The control character in column 1 tells what is to be done to the record with the part number in columns 2–11. The control characters are

P: Part number
D: Description
C: Cost (price)
N: Number in stock
R: Reorder number
E: End

The second segment of the program should read the control cards one at a time, locate the record which has the same part number as that on the control card, and replaced the field indicated by the control character with the character string starting at column 15 of the control card. It should continue this process until a control card with an E in the first column is read, at which time the program should print the inventory file in the format of Exercise 3.

5. Notice that if the EBCDIC forms of two positive numbers with no leading zeros or other characters are compared using a CLC instruction, the resulting condition code indicates the relative sizes of the two numbers. Using this fact, modify your program for Exercise 4 so that every time the reorder number or the number in stock is changed, it compares these two numbers and prints the message

STOCK OF PART NUMBER XXXXXXXXXX TOO LOW, REORDER

whenever the number in stock is less than the reorder number.

6. Modify your program for Exercise 4 to sort the records into numerical order, using the part number for a key. This is to be done by sorting the records into a linked list.

7. To delete a record from a linked list, all we need to do is to change the pointer field of the record before the one to be deleted. The modified pointer contains

the address of the record that was after the record that was deleted. Thus, in a linked list, records can be added or deleted without disturbing the remainder of the list. Add the necessary statements to your program of Exercise 6 so that a control card with an A in column 1 causes the record on the following card to be Added into the list in its proper place and so that a control character X causes the record with the part number from columns 2–11 of the control card to be removed from the list.

8. One of the first actions of a high-level language compiler is to remove the blanks from the input source statements. Write an assembly language program that removes the blanks from each statement in a FORTRAN program (cols. 1–72) and prints the results, one line per statement. Your program should continue to process statements until a statement with the characters END in columns 7–9 is encountered.

9. Modify your program of Exercise 8 so that it checks each statement for equal numbers of left and right parentheses. Your program should print an error message of the form

TOO MANY LEFT PARENTHESES

or

TOO MANY RIGHT PARENTHESES

when a statement with unmatched parentheses is found.

10. In FORTRAN, a C in column 1 indicates that the statement is a comment and should be ignored. Statements are continued by placing any nonblank character in column 6 of the continuation card. Modify your program of Exercise 9 (or 8) to take these factors into account.

11. Write a program to analyze textual data by word length. Your program should read a set of data cards on which some sentences, for example, the statement of this problem, have been punched. It should count the number of one-letter, two-letter, three-letter, etc., words that were used until a card with two periods in a row is found, which designates the end of the text. Your program should then compute and print the average number of letters per word that were in the text. Assume that the only punctuation marks used are commas and periods.

12. One problem the registrar of a university has is to assemble all of a student's individual grade reports at the end of a semester into one record for the student. He receives the grade reports punched on cards in the following format:

cols 1–9:   student number
cols 12–23:   course name
col. 25:   grade

These cards are not in any kind of order. Write an assembly language program that reads the grade report cards, collects all the grades for each student into one record, and prints the results using the following as an example of the output format:

STUDENT NUMBER	COURSE	GRADE
903687260	MATH 1	D
	BASKETRY 2	A
	COMPSCI 50	A
	FRENCH 1	F
602543283		
	BOWLING 3	A
	CANOING 2	A
	COMPSCI 1	D

and so on.

13. A bank accounting system can be set up in a manner similar to that for the inventory system of Exercises 3-7. Design a card-based system that produces up-to-date records for a bank. Each record should include the customer's name, account number, and current balance.

REFERENCES

IBM System 360/Disk and Tape Operating System Assembler Language, Form GC24-3414, IBM Corp., White Plains, N.Y.

IBM System/360 Operating System Assembler Language, Form GC28-6514, IBM Corp., White Plains, N.Y.

IBM System/360 Principles of Operation, Form GA22-6821, IBM Corp., White Plains, N.Y.

IBM System/370 Principles of Operation, Form GA22-7000, IBM Corp., White Plains, N.Y.

IBM OS/VS—DOS/VS Assembler Language, Form GC33-4010, IBM, Corp., White Plains, N.Y.

11 MACHINE LANGUAGE AND THE PROGRAM STATUS WORD

We have introduced the SI and SS instruction types in connection with the character manipulation instructions. A study of the machine language for these types will complete our description of the basic machine language structure. The writing of addresses and operands in SI and SS instructions is often a stumbling block for beginning assembly language programmers. A good understanding of the machine language structure of these instruction types can do a lot to remove this hurdle.

A special register called the Program Status Word plays a central role in the functioning of the IBM 360 and 370 computers. It is essential that we understand the basic components of it, particularly in preparation for the following chapter on debugging techniques.

11.1. MACHINE LANGUAGE: FINISHING UP

We presented the machine language formats for the RR, RX, and RS instruction types in earlier chapters. In this section we shall conclude our formal discussion of the machine language with a description of the SI and SS instruction formats.

11.1.1. The SI Instruction Format

The SI instructions have one memory operand, which is an S-type address, and one immediate operand which we specify in the second operand position in assembly language. In the machine language, the memory address comes *after* the immediate operand.

Recall that an S-type address occupies in 2 bytes in the machine language. The first nibble of the address designates the base register. The remain-

224

ing 3 nibbles contain the 12-bit displacement. We represent S-type addresses pictorially as

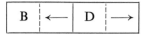

where B is the number of the base register and D is the displacement. In the SI instructions, which are 4 bytes long, the address occupies the last 2 bytes. After the operation code comes the immediate operand, in the second byte. Thus, the machine language for the general SI instruction

MOP   D1(B1),I2

where MOP is the assembly language mnemonic for the instruction, has the form

OP	I2	B1	←	D1	→

I2 is actually part of the machine language instruction. This is why it is called an immediate operand. Its value is immediately available for use and does not have to be fetched from a register or from the memory.

All machine language is in binary. If the immediate operand is not given as a binary number, the assembler converts it to binary before inserting it into its position in the machine language instruction. If, for example, we write an immediate operand byte as $C'A'$, meaning the EBCDIC code for the letter A, the assembler places its binary equivalent, $C1_{16}$ ($= 11000001_2$) into the machine language. Similarly, when we use a decimal number for the operand, the assembler converts it to its binary equivalent.

For example, the instruction

MVI   12(7),C'H'

has the machine language equivalent

92C8700C

while the instruction

CLI   100(10),64

produces

9540A064

in the machine language.

Of course when we use a relocatable expression for the memory address, the assembler fills in the implied base register and displacement. Supposing that register 13 is the base register and that the symbol BEE has displacement 150_{16}, the instruction

MVI   BEE+14,C'B'

translates to
$$92C2D15E$$
in the machine language.

11.1.2. The SS Instruction Format

To designate the operands in an MVC or CLC instruction we must specify three quantities: two memory addresses and the length of the memory operands. Both memory addresses are S-type addresses and thus require 2 bytes apiece. The length is an unsigned binary integer which occupies 1 byte of the instruction. Including the operation code, SS instructions are 6 bytes long.

The two S-type addresses occupy, in order, the last 4 bytes of the instruction. This leaves the second byte for the length. Therefore, the instruction format for the general SS instruction

$$MOP \qquad D1(L1,B1),D2(B2)$$

is

| OP | L1-1 | B1 | $\longleftarrow$ | D1 | $\longrightarrow$ | B2 | $\longleftarrow$ | D2 | $\longrightarrow$ |

In Chapter 10 we stated that we can move or compare at most 256 bytes using the MVC or CLC instructions. The reason for this restriction is that we have just 8 bits to use to indicate the length of the operands. The largest unsigned integer that we can put in 1 byte is $1111\ 1111_2 = FF_{16} = 255_{10}$. We can move or compare 256 bytes because the machine uses a length *one greater* than that given in the L1 field of the instruction. In other words, the number in the length field of the machine language instruction is actually one less than the number of bytes that are used as operands.

The assembler "knows" this fact and therefore permits us to write the lengths we really want in assembly language instructions. In processing a length given as a decimal number in an SS instruction, the assembler converts the number to binary, subtracts 1 from the result, and places it into the second byte of the instruction.

In the instruction

$$MVC \qquad 6(20,3),5(12)$$

we are asking to move the 20 bytes stored starting 5 bytes past an address in register 12 to the 20-byte area starting 6 bytes past the address contained in register 3. Thus, we have

$$D1 = 6$$
$$B1 = 3$$
$$L1 - 1 = 13_{16}$$
$$D2 = 5$$
$$B2 = C_{16}$$

The operation code for MVC is $D2_{16}$. Thus, filling in the blanks, we have

D2133006C005

as the machine language equivalent of the instruction above.

Relocatable expressions result in the same address translation techniques as those we have already discussed. If the symbol BLKS has displacement 200_{16} and register 10 is the implied base register, the instruction

MVC   BLKS(50),40(6)

has the machine language equivalent

D231A2006028

while the instruction

CLC   BLKS+100(30),BLKS+2

results in the machine language

D51DA264A202

11.1.3. Machine Language: Summary

We have now investigated all five instruction formats and the modified RR and RX formats for the BCR and BC instructions. Table 11-1 summarizes the machine language discussions of Chapters 6, 8, 9, and 11. Table 11-2 contains a review of the abbreviations used in Table 11-1. In Table 11-1 we have included an alternative form for those SS instructions which require two lengths. We shall encounter some of these instructions in Chapter 15.

It is important that you be familiar with the material in Tables 11-1 and 11-2. The instruction sets and facilities of the machines under consideration are too complex to make the learning of the assembly language one instruction at a time possible. Tables 11-1 and 11-2 show that there is a definite structure to all the instructions. When we need to use an instruction that we have never used before, the type of the instruction dictates how we must write the instruction in the machine language and in assembly language.

For example, the LM instruction is an RS instruction. Therefore, it has two register operands and a memory operand. Is the following use of the LM instruction correct, given that PLACE is a relocatable symbol?

LM   5,10,PLACE(3)

The answer is *no*. The memory address in an RS instruction must be an S-type address. We have indicated above that register 3 is to be used as an index register, which is impossible with an S-type address. Reference to Table 11-1 shows why this is so; the specification of two register operands and an S-type address in the machine language leaves no room in the instruction for an index register.

As another example, the TM instruction is of the SI type. Thus, the fol-

Table 11-1 SUMMARY OF MACHINE LANGUAGE FORMATS*

Instruction Type	Assembly Language Format		Machine Language Format	Examples
RR	MOP	R1,R2	OP | R1 | R2	AR, SR, LCR
	BCR	M1,R2	07 | M1 | R2	BCR
RX	MOP	R1,D2(X2,B2)	OP | R1 | X2 | B2 | ←D2→	L, ST, A, IC
	BC	M1,D2(X2,B2)	OP | M1 | X2 | B2 | ←D2→	BC
RS	MOP	R1,R3,D2(B2)	OP | R1 | R3 | B2 | ←D2→	BXLE, BXH
SI	MOP	D1(B1),I2	OP | I2 | B1 | ←D1→	MVI, CLI
SS	MOP	D1(L1,B1),D2(B2)	OP | L1−1 | B1 | ←D1→ | B2 | ←D2→	MVC, CLC
SS (with two lengths)	MOP	D1(L1,B1),D2(L2,B2)	OP | L1−1 | L2−1 | B1 | ←D1→ | B2 | ←D2→	PACK, AP

*MOP stands for the assembly language mnemonic for an instruction of the indicated type. OP represents the associated machine language operation code.

Table 11-2 SUMMARY OF SYMBOLS USED TO DESCRIBE INSTRUCTIONS

Symbol	Meaning
MOP	Assembly language mnemonic for operation
OP	8-Bit machine language operation code corresponding to MOP
Rn	nth Register operand
Mn	nth Mask operand
Bn	Base register for nth memory operand address
Dn	Displacement for nth memory operand address
Xn	IndeX register for nth memory operand address
Ln	Length (in bytes) of nth memory operand
Sn	Relocatable Symbol or expression for nth memory operand address; implies base register Bn and displacement Dn

Table 11-3 SOME OPERATION CODES

Assembly Language Mnemonic	Name	Operation Code Binary	Hexa-decimal	Instruction Type	Instruction Length (Bytes)
A	Add	01011010	5A	RX	4
AR	Add Register	00011010	1A	RR	2
AP	Add Decimal	11111010	FA	SS	6
L	Load	01011000	58	RX	4
LR	Load Register	00011000	18	RR	2
LM	Load Multiple	10011000	98	RS	4
BXH	Branch on indeX High	10000110	86	RS	4
MVC	MoVe Character	11010010	D2	SS	6
MVI	MoVe Immediate	10010010	92	SI	4
CLC	Compare Logical Character	11010101	D5	SS	6
CLI	Compare Logical Immediate	10010101	95	SI	4
S	Subtract	01011011	5B	RX	4
SR	Subtract Register	00011011	1B	RR	2
SP	Subtract Packed	11111011	FB	SS	6
LH	Load Half-word	01001000	48	RX	4
AH	Add Half-word	01001010	4A	RX	4
SH	Subtract Half-word	01001011	4B	RX	4
ST	STore	01010000	50	RX	4
STC	STore Character	01010010	52	RX	4

lowing uses of it are both incorrect,

TM	PLACE(5),B'10101010'
TM	PLACE,PLACE+3

the former because we have again tried to index an address that must be of the S-type, and the latter because we have used a memory address in a position where only an immediate operand byte can be used.

Let us try to make some sense out of the operation codes for the instructions. Table 11-3 shows some representative operation codes and their associated assembly language mnemonics. You should look at this table to see if you can find some general rules relating operations and operation codes. In the operation decode step of instruction execution, the processor must analyze the operation code to find out what is to be done. The operation code must indicate (1) the length of the instruction so that the program counter can be updated and (2) the type of the instruction so that the operands will be obtained from the proper places in the computer. Finally, of course, the operation code must indicate what is to be done to the operands.

The first 2 bits of the operation code indicate the length of the instruction and narrow down the possible choices for the instruction type. Notice, in Table 11-3, that the first 2 bits of the RR instructions are 00. Further study shows that we can attach the following meanings to the first 2 bits of the operation codes:

Bits 0–1	Instruction Type	Instruction Length (Bytes)
00	RR	2
01	RX	4
10	RS or SI	4
11	SS	6

There are a few exceptions to this rule in the 370 systems, but the instructions involved are not used in normal programming applications.

You should try to discover further systematic meanings attached to bits in the operation codes. For example, all instructions with $1010_2 = A_{16}$ in the last four digits of their operation codes are addition instructions, while the difference between the operation codes for RX instructions that use half-word memory operands and those that require full-word operands is that the former have a 0 in bit 3 while the latter have a 1 in this position.

Further information about an instruction can often be gained from its assembly language mnemonic. In particular, the last letter of the mnemonic often indicates the type of an instruction. *If* the mnemonic ends with the following letters, *then* it is of the type shown:

Last Letter of Mnemonic	Instruction Type	Exceptions
R	RR	
I	SI	
C	SS	IC, STC

Notice that this is not an "if and only if" situation. The TM instruction is of SI type, but the mnemonic does not end with I. The rule for instructions ending with C is perhaps better stated as "The instruction is either of SS type, or it is an RX instruction with a byte-aligned memory operand." *Usually*, but not always, if an instruction does not end with one of the letters above, it is an RX instruction. Life would be much simpler if the designers of the assembly language had been more careful in the assignment of mnemonics to the operation codes.

11.2. THE PROGRAM STATUS WORD

At any given instant, the computer is in a single *state*, determined by the memory and register contents and some further pieces of information, such as the program counter contents, the condition-code value, and the current action of input/output devices. In addition to the register and memory contents, the information of most interest to the programmer concerning the state of the system is contained in the Program Status Word (PSW). As we shall see, the PSW plays a vital role in program execution. In Chapter 12, we shall make extensive use of knowledge of its contents in helping us to debug programs. We shall examine the PSW in three segments. The first investigates the sections of the PSW that are of most interest to us now. Then we shall examine the role that the PSW plays in interruptions, and finally we shall look into those portions of the PSW that are not of immediate interest to us but that will help us in some of the more advanced material later in the text.

11.2.1. The Central Components of the PSW

The Program Status Word should perhaps be called (as it is in some other systems similar to the IBM 360) the Program Status Double Word. It is in fact a special register 64 bits in length and is split into several sections, as is shown in Fig. 11-1. The problem programmer is most interested in the second word of the program status word; it contains that information which most directly affects his program execution. The first word is of importance to the operating system inasmuch as it contains information which controls the overall action of the system as it affects the executing program.

We shall begin with a discussion of the PSW for the IBM 360 systems. The IBM 370 systems have two modes of operation, the Basic Control Mode and the Extended Control Mode, which is used when the virtual storage feature of the system is in operation. The Basic Control Mode Program Status Word in the 370 systems is in practice identical to the Program Status Word in the 360 systems. In debugging, the different format of the Extended Control Mode PSW of the 370 means we must look in different places for the necessary information. But in most programming applications, the two control modes are indistinguishable.

Word 1

Bits   0   –   5 6   7   8   – 11 12* – 15 16   31

Channel Masks	I/Ø Mask	E Mask	Key	AMWP	Interruption Code

Word 2

32 – 33 34 – 35 36   –   39 40   63

ILC	CC	Program Mask	Program Counter

*In the 370 systems, bit 12 is 0 to indicate Basic Control Mode.

Fig. 11-1. Format of the Program Status Word in the 360 systems and in the 370 systems in the Basic Control Mode.

Until now we have treated the program counter and condition code as if they were separate special-purpose registers. Figure 11-1 shows that the PC and CC are actually parts of the PSW. The program counter contains the 24-bit memory address of the next instruction to be executed and is situated in bits 40–63 of the PSW. The condition code, the 2-bit indicator of the sign of the result of the last arithmetic or comparison instruction that sets it, occupies bits 34 and 35 of the PSW.

The second step in the instruction execution sequence is the adjustment of the program counter so that is contains the address of the next instruction to be executed. This means, in effect, that the length, in bytes, of the instruction currently being executed must be added to the program counter contents. If, for example, the instruction just obtained from the memory at address 2000 is 6 bytes long, then the next instruction has to be at address 2006. Therefore, to increment the program counter, the machine must know the length of the instruction being executed. We saw that the first 2 bits of the operation code indicate the instruction length. When the instruction is brought from the memory, this information is moved, in a modified format, to bits 32 and 33 of the PSW. These 2 bits are called the *Instruction Length Code* (ILC).

The ILC contains a 2-bit binary number which indicates the instruction length in *half-words*. Instructions of the following lengths set the ILC to the values shown:

Instruction Length (Bytes)	Instruction Length (Half-words)	ILC Contents (Binary)
2	1	01
4	2	10
6	3	11

An ILC value of 00_2 is impossible in normal operation but can result from the erroneous use of some instructions.

We have left bits 36–39 of the second word to discuss. Let us leave this *Program Mask* section for later, after we have considered interruptions.

Figure 11-2 shows the format of 370 PSW in Extended Control Mode. In this mode, the program counter is in bits 40–63, just as in the basic mode. The 6 bits that are the condition code and program mask occupy bit positions 18–23. The ILC and other sections usually found in the basic mode PSW are contained in special *control registers*, a discussion of which is beyond the scope of this text.

First Word

0	1					7	8 – 11	12	13–15	16–17	18–19	20 – 23	24	31
O	R	D	O	O	T	T O	E	Key	1	MWP	00	GG	Program Mask	0 0 0 0 0 0 0 0

32	40	63
00000000	Program Counter	

*In the 370 systems, bit 12 is 1 to indicate Extended Control Mode.

Fig. 11-2. PSW format for a System/370 machine in Extended Control Mode.

11.2.2. Interruptions

To the problem programmer, the computer system appears to be dedicated to him in the sense that he is unaware that other users' programs are being processed at the same time as is his. But to the system, your job is one of many that may be active in the system at any given time. One of the outcomes of this fact is that the system must be able to temporarily *interrupt* the execution of one program in order to service more important requests for computer resources. It must then be able to return use of the CPU to the program that was interrupted in such a way that this program is unaffected by the interruption.

Let us consider input/output processing as an example. In the 360 and 370 computers, input/output is handled by special devices called *channels*. A channel is responsible for transferring data to/from the I/O devices from/to the memory and does it in such a way that the processor does not have to participate directly in the data transfer. In other words, the CPU issues a command to the channel and then resumes its normal operation, leaving the data transfer operations to the channel. We say that input/output processing *overlaps* CPU instruction execution. When the channel has finished the operations it was ordered to perform, it must inform the system that it has done so. But to do this, it must stop, or interrupt, the CPU so that another program can be executed. This program, usually part of the operating system, is executed, and then control is returned to the interrupted program.

You have probably already seen the effects of another kind of interruption—the *program interruption*. This is what happens when your program contains a bug that results in a *program exception* or a request of the computer to do something it was not designed to do. Attempted execution of an instruction with an invalid operation code is an example of such a request. What happens is that the execution of your program is interrupted and control is returned to the operating system. If you have requested a dump with the output, and if your program reaches such an AB normal ENDing, or ABEND, the system places the dump data with the rest of the printed output from your program.

The efficient handling of interrupts requires that the status of the system be easily changeable. An interruption really means that one program is stopped, another executed, and the former resumed, without any effect, except for a time delay, upon the executing program. The PSW contains the information necessary to accomplish this status switching. One way to change the sequence of execution of the instructions in a program is through execution of a branch instruction, which changes the PC contents. Another way is to replace the entire PSW. Since the PSW contains the PC, if the new PSW contains a PC value different from that of the executing program, the next instruction executed will be that at the address given in the new PSW. But replacing an entire PSW does much more than a simple branch in that other portions of the new PSW may cause significant changes in the status of the CPU.

An interruption causes a new PSW to be loaded into the PSW register from a fixed address in the memory that depends on the nature of the interruption. In so doing the old PSW contents are lost. But to return to execution of the interrupted program, the old PSW must be saved. Therefore, *before* the new PSW is loaded into the PSW register, the old PSW contents are stored at a fixed address in the memory, which also depends on the nature of the interruption. Figure 11-3 illustrates this PSW "swap" that occurs when an interrupt condition arises.

All of this is completely automatic. The operating system programs have the responsibility for maintaining the new PSWs and ensuring that the interrupted program will be reentered properly. When the interrupt service routine has finished its processing, the old PSW can be loaded into the PSW register via a Load PSW instruction.

We have mentioned two sources of interruptions, those caused by *input/output* operations and those resulting from *program* errors. The following are some further classes of interruptions.

Machine Check: Certain hardware malfunctions are detectable by the

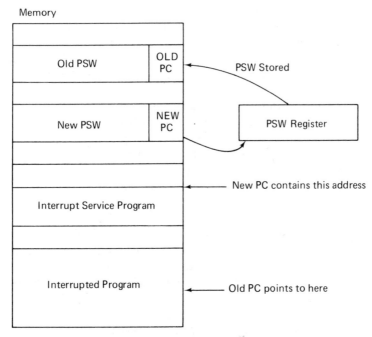

Memory

Fig. 11-3. The exchange of Program Status Words in an interruption.

machine and cause an interruption. The interrupt service routine can analyze the problem, attempt a recovery from the resulting errors, and output appropriate messages.

Supervisor Call: In some instances, the programmer wishes to ask the operating system to do things he cannot do as a problem programmer. He requests an interruption via the SuperVisor Call instruction (SVC), which results in the execution of a supervisor routine to grant his wishes.

External: The operator at the system console and the system timer generate interruptions of the external class.

Interruptions permit the temporary suspension of the execution of a program so that time-sensitive tasks of higher priority can be accomplished. The PSW is exchanged when an interruption occurs, providing an efficient means of responding to interrupt requests. The PSW also determines the status of the executing program with regard to interruptions, as we shall see in the next section.

11.2.3. Additional PSW Components*

Many portions of the PSW indicate those cases in which interruptions are permitted to suspend the execution of the current program. For example,

*This section can be skipped without loss of continuity.

bit 6 of the Basic Control Mode PSW (see Fig. 11-1) is the input/output interruption mask. When this bit is 0, interruptions of the input/output class will not be recognized; such interrupts are said to be *disabled*. When the I/O mask bit is 1, I/O interruptions *are* permitted to interrupt the program; the interrupt is said to be *enabled*. We have seen that the channels are responsible for input/output device control and data transfer and indicate the completion of an I/O operation by requesting an interruption. Each channel has a number. Bits 0–5 of the PSW indicate which channels will be permitted to interrupt the program. A 1 in bit position 3, for example, enables channel 3 to interrupt the program (provided bit 6 is also 1).

The other mask bits have the same function. A mask bit value of 1 indicates that interrupt is enabled, while a mask bit value of 0 means the interrupt is disabled. Thus, bit 8 is a mask for external interruptions, while bit 13 (called M) is the mask for machine check interruptions.

The program mask section is often of interest to the problem programmer because the programmer can use this mask to determine whether or not certain arithmetic conditions, which are usually considered to be errors, are permitted to generate a program interruption. These bits have the following interpretations:

Bit 36: Fixed-Point Overflow Exception. We have seen that when a binary integer arithmetic instruction results in an overflow, the result is usually a fixed-point overflow exception, which results in termination of the execution of the program. If bit 36 is 0, however, an overflow does not cause an interruption.

Bit 37: Fixed-Point Divide Exception. When the quotient resulting from execution of an integer divide instruction (DR or D) does not fit into the register provided for it, a fixed-point divide exception normally results, except when bit 37 of the PSW is 0.

Bits 38 and 39. These are for interruptions due to special circumstances in the use of floating-point arithmetic instructions. We shall discuss their meanings in Chapter 19.

The programmer can select those bits he wishes to have on in the program mask through the use of the SPM (Set Program Mask) instruction. Thus, he can determine whether or not these interruptions will be enabled.

Bits 16–31 of the PSW contain an interruption code which indicates the source of the interruption. For example, an I/O interruption places the channel number and device address in these 16 bits so that the program that is executed as a result of the interruption can determine which device caused the interruption. In the case of a program interruption, the last 4 bits of this section, bits 28–31, contain a code which indicates the nature of the error. We shall discuss this code in the next chapter.

Bits 8–11 contain a storage protection *key*, which limits the executing program's access to the memory. If bit 14 is on, the computer is idle, or in the *Wait* state. Bit 15 determines whether the executing program is in the Problem state or the supervisor state, as discussed in Chapter 12. Bit 12 has different meanings in the 360 and 370 machines. In the 360 systems, a 1 in this bit position indicates that the result of converting binary numbers to decimal will produce sign codes proper for the ASCII code, an alternative to EBCDIC. In the 370 machines, bit 12 determines whether the machine is in the basic or the extended control mode.

Thus, the program status word indicates the current status of the execution of the program in two ways. First, the condition code and program counter have a direct effect upon the executing program. Second, the mask bits indicate the importance, or priority, of the executing program in comparison with other programs or events in the system. For example, a really crucial system program that must be run uninterrupted no matter what happens would have all interrupts disabled. On the other hand, our programs are usually insensitive to the other events in the system and, therefore, can be freely interrupted, as indicated by the masks, without affecting their proper execution. Most systems programs fall between these two extremes in their priority and in the interrupts which are enabled during their execution.

11.3. AN OVERVIEW

You have now completed what might be called an "Introduction to Assembly Language Programming." We have studied the basic principles of assembly language programming, including assembly and machine language formats, assembler directives, memory addresses, program and job structure, and some typical applications and related instructions, including binary arithmetic and character manipulation, loop control, the PSW, and interruptions.

Where do we go from here?

To be best prepared for the topic, we have put off questions concerning debugging techniques until the following chapter so that we can give it the complete treatment the topic deserves. If you have already made use of some of the material therein, so much the better.

Our next task will be to eliminate the need for the special macros INITIAL, RWD, WWD RCD, and PLN that we have supplied for use with this text. That chore will require five chapters, 13–17. Why so many? Because in learning to do without these learning aids we shall, in the process, be finding out about many basic facets of computing that are important to all computer programmers. Included with these are some additional ways in which data are represented in the machine, decimal arithmetic, the operating system, and subroutine linkage.

The remainder of the text is devoted to some advanced topics including floating-point arithmetic, macro programming, and special-purpose and 370 instructions. You and your instructor should pick and choose from these topics as your interests dictate.

CHAPTER SUMMARY

The *SI instruction format* is

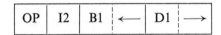

for the instruction

MOP   D1(B1),I2

The *SS instruction format* is

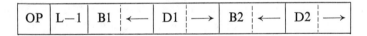

for the instruction

MOP   D1(L,B1),D2(B2).

Table 11-1 summarizes the five instruction formats.

The Program Status Word contains the program counter and condition code and determines the program's status with respect to the entire computing systems. A program's execution can be terminated or temporarily suspended via an *interruption*.

EXERCISES

1. Translate the following program segment to machine language, given that the symbols NEXTCHK, LOOPTST, ADD, and MESS have displacements 100_{16}, 110_{16}, 300_{16}, and 310_{16}, respectively, and that register 10 is being used as the implied base register:

```
           L        2,ADD
           LA       4,1
           LA       5,127(2)
NEXTCHK    CLI      10(2),C'Q'
           BNE      LOOPTST
           MVC      17(13,8),MESS
           LR       3,2
LOOPTST    BXLE     2,4,NEXTCHK
```

2. Write an example of the use of each of the following instructions. Where a memory operand is required, give an example of the use of both its implicit and explicit form. (Don't worry about what the instructions do!)

> NR
> STM
> CVB
> TRT
> XI
> AP

3. Translate the program segment of Fig. 10-1 to machine language given that register 12 is the implied base register and that the symbols have the following hexadecimal displacements:

Symbol	Displacement
NEXTWD	200
TRANS	21E
FINCHK	228
DIEWD	300
DERWD	305
DENWD	30A
GERMAN	30F

4. One source of an external interrupt is the "interrupt" key (or "panic button") on the operator's console. When this button is pressed, an external interrupt results, if enabled. Why is it desirable to have such a capability?

5. An interruption automatically preserves the PSW of the interrupted program by storing it at a dedicated address in the memory. After the interrupt service subroutine has been executed, control is returned to the interrupted program, hopefully with nothing changed insofar as the latter is concerned. What must the interrupt service program do in order to make sure that this is indeed the case?

6. An interruption of a given class stores the old PSW at a location designated for that class. This same location is used every time an interruption of that class

occurs. This means that the previous (old) PSW location contents are destroyed by a new interruption of that class. If this occurs while the interrupt service program for a prior interrupt of that class is executing, the PSW for the program that was interrupted first is lost, thus making it impossible to return control to that program. How can this be avoided? (*Hint*: Consider the function of the interruption masks.)

7. How does overlapping of CPU instruction processing with input/output processing improve the performance of the system?

REFERENCES

IBM System/360 Principles of Operation, Form GA22-6821, IBM Corp., White Plains, N.Y.

IBM System/370 Principles of Operation, Form GA22-7000, IBM Corp., White Plains, N.Y.

12 PROGRAM DEBUGGING AND TESTING

"bug (bŭg) *n.* 1. Any of various wingless or four-winged insects of order *Hemiptera,* . . . 4. A mechanical, electrical, or other systematic defect or difficulty, . . . *v.* . . . *slang,* 1. To annoy; pester."
The American Heritage Dictionary of the English Language, 1971

This chapter is as important as any in this text if your goal is to learn to write assembly language programs that run properly and produce the correct results. The diagnostic messages output by the assembler help us to find errors in use of the language. But when a program is executed and an error occurs, either because of the misuse of an instruction or an error in logic, we must depend on the dump and other information to help us find the bug.

Some very extensive execution-time diagnostic facilities are available for use with higher-level languages. For example, the Waterloo FORTRAN processor (WATFIV) produces error messages such as

ERROR SUBSCRIPT NUMBER 3 OF ARRAY MATR
HAS VALUE 0
STATEMENT NUMBER 10 OF PROGRAM TPROG

indicating that the program tried to store data outside space reserved for an array. Such complete diagnostic facilities have yet to be developed for use with assembly language programs, primarily because of the freedom and generality of the language. In FORTRAN, it *is* an error to store beyond the boundaries of an array. In assembly language, the programmer is in control of memory use, and therefore it is difficult to check for errors of this type during the execution of the program.

This certainly does not mean that we must give up in despair when our

241

program stops or produces the wrong answers during execution. When this occurs, we use the dump to find the source of the error.

A program that runs successfully to completion without producing a dump is still not necessarily correct. The actions a program takes and the answers it produces are always subject to suspicion; the rule of thumb is "GIGO—Garbage In, Garbage Out." How do we find errors that produce the wrong results without any indication of a program error? How do we know whether or not the results are correct? In the second half of this chapter we shall discuss some techniques that help answer these questions.

12.1. THE ART OF DEBUGGING

The first thing you, the programmer, must do in order to find a bug is to adopt the proper frame of mind. The fact that the program does not run properly is proof that something is wrong. What could it be? Very rarely a computer hardware malfunction causes an error in program execution. The operating system, a collection of programs, has bugs in it which can lead to erroneous results. But this kind of error appears so rarely that you are better off to forget it can happen. Many beginning programmers receive their output, see an error message, and send it back to the computer center unchanged to have it run again, thinking that it is the machine's or system's fault. This is a waste of time, effort, and money, and it accomplishes nothing. Do not blame errors on the machine or the operating system until you can eliminate the possibility that *you* made a mistake.

The computer is a complex machine, and programming is a complex process. We *do* make mistakes.

As soon as the output for your program comes back, you can begin debugging without even looking at it. The thickness of the stack of printed output is a broad indication of what happened when your job was run. A very thin output, one or two pages long, indicates a job control language error; your program did not even get off the ground. JCL is very finicky; every space, comma, and character must be exactly right, or the system will not consider your job. On the other hand, if you requested a dump via a DUMP option in DOS JCL or a SYSUDUMP DD card in OS JCL, a thick output listing implies that your output contains a dump; an error occurred during execution of your program. Finally, output of medium thickness usually indicates at least partial success; your program may have run properly and produced the correct results. In the first part of this chapter, we shall emphasize the second case, that in which your output includes a dump. We shall see that the dump is an invaluable aid in finding bugs.

Debugging is partly an art. We can give no hard and fast rules that will find the bug every time. We can, however, indicate some initial bug-hunting steps and some general guidelines concerning what to look for. As with programming, only through practice can one become proficient at debugging.

12.2. THE COMPLETION CODE

We have seen that the response of the computer to the improper use of an instruction, an *exception*, is a *program interruption*. The computer automatically stores a code into PSW bits 28–31, the last 4 bits of the interruption code. This code indicates which exception occurred that caused the interruption. The new PSW loaded as a result of the program interruption returns control to the operating system, which then outputs the appropriate diagnostic information and ends the job.

The system passes the interruption code describing the exception to us in the form of system completion code. In OS systems, the completion code is printed with the JCL output from the job step in which the exception occurred. The system completion code is a three-digit hexadecimal number. All those that correspond to *program* exceptions have 0C as the first two digits. The third is the digit from the last 4 bits of the interruption code. For example. in the completion code 0C4, the first two digits indicate that the error was a program exception, while 4 is the interruption code indicating a protection exception.

A program exception is the result of misuse of the hardware system. Other abnormal endings occur through mistakes in the use of or in communication with the operating system. The place to look for the meaning of a completion code in the event of such an error is the *messages and codes* reference manual.

Let us now investigate the meanings of the completion codes that arise from program exceptions. This study will help us not only with debugging but also in furthering our understanding of the computing machine.

Completion Code 0C1—Operation Exception. An operation exception occurs when the machine tries to execute an instruction with an illegal operation code. Here *illegal* is used in the sense that the operation code has no meaning whatsoever to the processor. An 0C1 is an indication that we have accidentally branched to a nonsensical address or that we have stored some data in the middle of our program or in a subroutine that our program calls. This can occur if the base register or an index register is not properly loaded.

Completion Code 0C2—Privileged Operation Exception. Here again the execution of an illegal instruction results in an exception. But in this case, the operation code is valid in the sense that it corresponds to an instruction that the processor can execute. The instruction is not available for *us* to use, however; it is a *privileged* instruction.

The machine operates in two basic states, the *supervisor* state and the *problem* state. Bit 15 of the PSW indicates which state the processor is in. In the supervisor state, any of the instructions in the machine's repertoire can be executed. In the problem state, privileged instructions cannot be executed.

The privileged instructions are those that are potentially dangerous if they are misused. For example, the LPSW instruction loads the PSW register from the memory. If the problem programmer were permitted to use this instruction, the errors he could make could destroy the operating system, thus making it impossible, at least temporarily, for anyone else to run his programs. Our user programs run in the problem state. When it is necessary to have something done that is not possible in the problem state, we ask that the operating system, or supervisor, do it for us. The programs that service such requests run in the supervisor state and can execute priveleged instructions.

Completion Code 0C3—Execute Exception. In Chapter 15 we shall see that the EXecute instruction permits the execution of a single instruction stored out of the normal program sequence. An attempt to EXecute another EXecute instruction results in an execute exception. (This happens very rarely.)

Completion Code 0C4—Protection Exception. The operating system gives each user an area of memory for use by his programs. To prevent the various users' programs from interfering with each other, a 4-bit *protection key* is also assigned to each user program in such a manner that each user has a different key. The PSW contains a 4-bit key section. When a program attempts to use the memory, the processor first checks the key of the memory area addressed against the key in the PSW. If these keys are not identical, the user must be trying to access memory outside his area, and a protection exception results.

This protection system is optional. Most IBM machines include the *storage protect* feature, which prevents the user from storing outside his region. The storage protect option prevents injury to the operating system and other user programs and data through accidental miscalculation of an address. Those systems in which espionage might be a problem include the *fetch protect* option, which prevents the user from reading from memory addresses outside his area.

A protection exception usually implies that a base register or index register has been misused, so that the effective address of a memory operand is outside the memory area assigned to the user.

Completion Code 0C5—Addressing Exception. This is another exception that occurs because of an illegal memory address. In this case, however, the effective address of a memory operand is larger than the highest memory address at the local system.

Because addresses in the IBM 360 and 370 computers are 24 bits long, the highest possible memory address in these machines is 16,777,215. Memory is expensive; most IBM systems have memories that are considerably smaller than the largest possible, a million bytes being a more normal size. In a million-byte machine, it is still possible to calculate addresses up to 16,777,215. Therefore, it is possible to try to use a memory address that is larger than the highest address for which there is a corresponding byte in a given system. Addressing a memory area for which there is no corresponding byte results in an addressing exception.

An addressing exception usually results from misuse of an index register. A very common mistake is to load an address into a register to be used as an index register, viz.,

```
          LA        3,DATA
LOOP      A         6,DATA(3)
                    .
                    .
                    .
DATA      DS        100F
```

The effective address that will be used will be twice the address of DATA. This is certainly wrong, and chances are that the result will be either an addressing exception (0C5) or a protection exception (0C4). (What should we put in register 3 to address the first word of DATA in the Add instruction above?)

Completion Code 0C6—Specification Exception. A specification exception means that something is wrong in the way we specified an operand. Failure to obey a boundary rule is the most common cause of this error condition. Use of an odd-numbered register as an operand in an instruction which requires an even-numbered register in that position and a branch to an odd-numbered address also produce a specification exception.

Completion Code 0C7—Data Exception. A data exception is the result of the attempted use of an invalid number as an operand in a decimal arithmetic instruction, as we shall see in Chapter 16.

The exceptions described above account for a large portion of assembly language programming errors. We shall present the following for reference purposes.

Completion Code 0C8—Fixed-Point Overflow Exception. This occurs when the sum (or difference) of two binary numbers does not fit into a 32-bit word.

Completion Code 0C9—Fixed-Point Divide Exception. Using a Divide or Divide Register instruction, it is possible to produce a quotient too large to fit into a single register. When this happens, a fixed-point divide exception is the result.

Completion Code 0CA—Decimal Overflow Exception. A decimal overflow exception occurs when the result of a decimal arithmetic instruction is too large to fit into the space provided for it.

Completion Code 0CB—Decimal Divide Exception. When the quotient resulting from decimal division is too large to fit into the area provided for it, a decimal divide exception occurs.

The remaining exceptions occur as results of floating-point calculations, as discussed in Chapter 19.

Completion Code 0CC—Exponent Overflow Exception. In floating-point calculations, an answer was obtained that was too large for accurate representation in the machine.

Completion Code 0CD—Exponent Underflow Exception. In floating-point calculations, an answer was obtained that was too small for accurate representation in the machine.

Completion Code 0CE—Significance Exception. The significance exception is an indication that a floating-point addition or subtraction operation

Table 12-1 COMPLETION CODES FOR PROGRAM EXCEPTIONS AND THEIR MEANINGS

System Completion Code	Exception	Meaning
0C1	Operation	Nonexistent instruction attempted
0C2	Privileged operation	Execution of privileged instruction attempted
0C3	Execute	Subject instruction of EX is another EX
0C4	Protection	Memory reference outside allocated space
0C5	Addressing	Memory reference outside memory
0C6	Specification	Improper specification of operand
0C7	Data	Invalid decimal number as operand
0C8	Fixed-point overflow	Overflow in integer arithmetic
0C9	Fixed-point divide	Overflow in integer division
0CA	Decimal overflow	Overflow in decimal arithmetic
0CB	Decimal divide	Overflow in decimal division
0CC	Exponent overflow	Overflow in floating-point arithmetic
0CD	Exponent underflow	Underflow in floating-point arithmetic
0CE	Significance	Loss of significance in floating-point arithmetic
0CF	Floating-point divide	Floating-point division by zero

produced a zero result. This means that all significant digits of the result were lost.

Completion Code 0CF—Floating-Point Divide Exception. This happens when a floating-point division by zero is attempted.

The 370 computers, if equipped with the virtual storage option, have additional exceptions that arise from errors in the use of this option. These are beyond the scope of this text.

Table 12-1 summarizes the program exceptions for quick reference.

12.3. THE DUMP

The completion code gives a clue as to what happened to stop our program. Sometimes this is enough information to enable us to find the bug, particularly if we are already suspicious of the use of a given instruction. More often, determining the completion code is just a beginning to finding the real source of the error.

It is a good idea to start at the beginning of the output and go through it page by page. The completion code is found on a cover page or in the JCL output. Next comes the output from the assembler. Glance at the assembler output to see if there are errors in the assembly or if something there rings a bell. The link-editor output follows. Then comes the printed output, if any, from the program. In some cases, the output can help in locating the error, particularly if it looks strange. But do *not* depend on the output to locate the position in the program where the abend occurred. Because of the way in which output is stored in preparation for printing, it may be the case that not all the output that the program requested was printed. Finally we find the dump. Figures 12-1 through 12-4 serve as examples of a program to be debugged.

We must remember that details in output formats for JCL listings, assembler and linkage-editor outputs, and dumps may differ considerably from installation to installation. But the problem is not so much *where* to look for indications of sources of error as it is *what* to look for. In most cases, the required information, though it may be buried in a lot of other unnecessary output, is clearly labeled. Your instructor and computer system staff will gladly help you learn about the particulars of the local debugging facilities.

12.3.1. The Preliminary Investigation

The program used for the example for this discussion is our old friend we developed in Chapter 6. The program AVEDIF is supposed to compute the average of a series of numbers and then compute the difference between each of the numbers and the average. But, as shown in Fig. 12-1, the JCL output

```
//DUMPEZ JOB (80.1105,,,,1001,2),'70292 RUDD',CLASS=C,TIME=0000
***ROUTE PRINT LOCAL
// EXEC TIGER1
XXTIGER1 PROC   OUT=A                                                   00000010
XXTIG    EXEC   PGM=IEUASM,PARM='LOAD,NODECK',REGION=50K                00C00020
XXSYSLIB DD DSN=CSCLIB.X73365.MACLIB1,DISP=SHR,UNIT=2314,VOL=SER=LSU007 00000030
XX       DD     DSNAME=SYS1.MACLIB,DISP=SHR                             00000040
***                                                                     00000050
***                                                                     00000060
XXSYSUT1 DD     DSNAME=&SYSUT1,UNIT=SYSSQ,SPACE=(1700,(400,50))         00000070
IEF653I SUBSTITUTION JCL - DSNAME=&SYSUT1,UNIT=SYSSQ,SPACE=(1700,(400,50))
XXSYSUT2 DD     DSNAME=&SYSUT2,UNIT=SYSSQ,SPACE=(1700,(400,50))         00000080
IEF653I SUBSTITUTION JCL - DSNAME=&SYSUT2,UNIT=SYSSQ,SPACE=(1700,(400,50))
XXSYSUT3 DD     DSNAME=&SYSUT3,UNIT=SYSSQ,SPACE=(1700,(400,50))         00000090
IEF653I SUBSTITUTION JCL - DSNAME=&SYSUT3,UNIT=SYSSQ,SPACE=(1700,(400,50))
XXSYSPRINT DD SYSOUT=&OUT                                               00000100
IEF653I SUBSTITUTION JCL - SYSOUT=A
XXSYSPUNCH DD  SYSOUT=B                                                 00000110
XXSYSGO DD DSN=&LOADSET,UNIT=SYSSQ,SPACE=(800,(100,50)),DISP=(MOD,PASS) 00000120
IEF653I SUBSTITUTION JCL - DSN=&LOADSET,UNIT=SYSSQ,SPACE=(800,(100,50)),DISP=(MOD,PASS)
//TIG.SYSIN DD *
IEF236I ALLOC. FOR DUMPEZ    TIG
IEF237I 241   ALLOCATED TO SYSLIB
IEF237I 130   ALLOCATED TO
IEF237I 133   ALLOCATED TO SYSUT1
IEF237I 241   ALLOCATED TO SYSUT2
IEF237I 134   ALLOCATED TO SYSUT3
IEF237I 40E   ALLOCATED TO SYSPRINT
IEF237I 42D   ALLOCATED TO SYSPUNCH
IEF237I 241   ALLOCATED TO SYSGO
IEF237I 40C   ALLOCATED TO SYSIN
IEF142I - STEP WAS EXECUTED - COND CODE 0000
IEF285I    CSCLI3.X73365.MACLIB1                KEPT
IEF285I    VOL SER NOS= LSU007.
IEF285I    SYS1.MACLIB                          KEPT
IEF285I    VOL SER NOS= LSU001.
IEF285I    SYS73282.T075008.RV0C0.DUMPEZ.SYSUT1  DELETED
IEF285I    VOL SER NOS= LSU003.
IEF285I    SYS73282.T075008.RV000.DUMPEZ.SYSUT2  DELETED
IEF285I    VOL SER NOS= LSU007.
IEF285I    SYS73282.T075008.RV0C0.DUMPEZ.SYSUT3  DELETED
IEF285I    VOL SER NOS= LSU004.
IEF285I    SYS73282.T075008.RV000.DUMPEZ.LOADSET  PASSED
IEF285I    VOL SER NOS= LSU007.
IEF373I STEP /TIG    / START 73282.1047
IEF374I STEP /TIG    / STOP  73282.1048 CPU    0MIN 01.84SEC MAIN   50K LCS   OK
(050K,C00K) CORE REQUESTED,      207 EXCP'S, APPROXIMATE COST $    0.11
XXGO     EXEC   PGM=LOADER,PARM=LET,REGION=80K,COND=(4,LT,TIG)          00000130
XXSYSLIB DD DSN=CSCLIB.X73365.CSLIB,DISP=SHR                            00000140
XXSYSLIN DD    DSNAME=&LOADSET,DISP=(OLD,DELETE)                        00000150
IEF653I SUBSTITUTION JCL - DSNAME=&LOADSET,DISP=(OLD,DELETE)
XX       DD    DDNAME=LOADIN                                            00000160
XXSYSLOUT DD   SYSOUT=&OUT                                              00000170
IEF653I SUBSTITUTION JCL - SYSOUT=A
XXSYSPRINT DD  SYSOUT=&OUT                                              00000180
IEF653I SUBSTITUTION JCL - SYSOUT=A
//GO.SYSUDUMP DD SYSOUT=A
//GO.SYSIN DD *
//
IEF236I ALLOC. FOR DUMPEZ    GO
IEF237I 241   ALLOCATED TO SYSLIB
IEF237I 241   ALLOCATED TO SYSLIN
IEF237I 40E   ALLOCATED TO SYSLOUT
IEF237I 41E   ALLOCATED TO SYSPRINT
IEF237I 52E   ALLOCATED TO SYSUDUMP
IEF237I 41C   ALLOCATED TO SYSIN             AN ERROR HAS OCCURRED!
IEW1991 ERROR - USER PROGRAM HAS ABNORMALLY TERMINATED
COMPLETION CODE - SYSTEM=0C6  USER=0000            COMPLETION CODE 0C6
IEF285I    CSCLIB.X73365.CSLIB                KEPT
IEF285I    VOL SER NOS= LSU007.
IEF285I    SYS73282.T075008.RV000.DUMPEZ.LOADSET  DELETED
IEF285I    VOL SER NOS= LSU007.
IEF373I STEP /GO    / START 73282.1048
IEF374I STEP /GO    / STOP  73282.1049 CPU    0MIN 03.75SEC MAIN   80K LCS   OK
(080K,C00K) CORE REQUESTED,      527 EXCP'S, APPROXIMATE COST $    0.27
IEF375I JOB /DUMPEZ  / START 73282.1047
IEF376I JOB /DUMPEZ  / STOP  73282.1049 CPU    0MIN 05.59SEC
```

Fig. 12-1. The job control listing for the program to be debugged.

```
LOC     OBJECT CODE  ADDR1  ADDR2  STMT  SOURCE STATEMENT                                          

                                     1  *   THIS PROGRAM READS A DATA CARD WHICH TELLS HOW MANY    00000100
                                     2  *   NUMBERS ARE TO BE PROCESSED.  THAT NUMBER IS KEPT IN   00000200
                                     3  *   REG. 8.  IT THEN CALCULATES THE UPPER VALUE FOR INDEX  00000300
                                     4  *   REGISTERS AND LEAVES THAT NUMBER IN REG. 3             00000400
                                     5  *   IT READS THE NUMBERS ONE AT A TIME, STORING THEM IN    00000500
                                     6  *   CONSECUTIVE FULL WORDS OF THE AREA CALLED NMBRS.  THE  00000600
                                     7  *   AVERAGE OF ALL THE NUMBERS IS COMPUTED, AS IS THE      00000700
                                     8  *   DIFFERENCE BETWEEN EACH OF THE NUMBERS AND THE AVERAGE.00000800
000000                               9  AVEDIF  START 0                                            00000900
                                    10          PRINT NOGEN                                        00001100
                                    11          INITIAL                                            00001200
                                    21          RWD   3           READ NUMBER OF NUMBERS TO USE    00001300
00006A 1883                         25          LR    8,3         KEEP A COPY IN REG. 8            00001500
00006C 5B30 D0CC           000E4    26          S     3,=F'1'     COMPUTE FINAL INDEX VALUEY       00001600
000070 5C20 D0D0           000E8    27          M     2,=F'4'     4*(3) -1                         00001700
000074 5890 D0D4           000EC    28          L     9,=F'0'     INDEX FOR READ LOOP STARTS AT 0  00001800
                                    29  READLOOP RWD   4          READ A DATA NUMBER
000082 5049 D0D8           000F0    33          ST    4,NMBRS(9)  STORE IT AT EFF. ADDRESS NMBRS + (9)  00002000
000086 5A90 D0D0           000E8    34          A     9,=F'4'     INCREMENT INDEX REGISTER         00002100
00008A 1993                         35          CR    9,3         TEST INDEX AGAINST FINAL VALUE KEPT  00002300
00008C 47D0 D060           000078   36          BNP   READLOOP    IN REG. 3
000090 5890 D0D4           000EC    37          L     9,=F'0'     START SUM AT 0 (IN ODD NMBRD REG.)  00002300
000094 1B77                         38          SR    7,7         ADD NUMBER AT NMBRS + (9) TO SUM 00002400
000096 5A79 D0D8           000F0    39  ADDLOOP  A     7,NMBRS(9)  ADD 4 TO INDEX                   00002500
00009A 5A90 D0D0           000E8    40          A     9,=F'4'     COMPARE WITH FINAL VALUE STILL IN 3  00002600
00009E 1993                         41          CR    9,3         GO TO ADDLOOP IF NOT DONE        00002700
0000A0 47D0 D07E           000095   42          BNP   ADDLOOP     WHEN HERE, READY FOR DIVIDE TO COMPUTE  00002800
0000A4 5C60 D0CC           000E4    43          M     6,=F'1'     AVERAGE BY DIVIDING SUM BY (8)   00002900
0000A8 1D68                         44          DR    6,8         PRINT THE AVERAGE
                                    45          WWD   7
0000B4 5890 D0D4           000EC    49          L     9,=F'0'     AND PREPARE TO COMPUTE DIFFERENCES  00003100
0000B8 58A9 D0D8           000F0    50  DIFLOOP  L     10,NMBRS(9)  GET NUMBER FROM NMBRS + ( )    00003300
0000BC 1BA7                         51          SR    10,7        SUBTRACT AVERAGE IN REG. 7
                                    52          WWD   10          PRINT THE DIFFERENCE
0000C8 5A90 D0CC           000E4    56          A     9,=F'1'     INCREMENO INDEX REGH             00003600
0000CC 1993                         57          CR    9,3         COMPARE WITH FINAL VALUE         00003700
0000CE 47D0 D0A0           0000B8   58          BNP   DIFLOOP     REPEAT IF RESULT NEGATIVE OR 0
                                    59          EOJ   =V($$IO)    PROCESSING COMPLETED
0000E0 00000000                     65          =F'1'
0000E4 00000001                     65          =F'4'
0000E8 00000004                     67          =F'0'
0000EC 00000000                     68
0000F0                              69  NMBRS    DS    100F        STORAGE SPACE FOR NUMBERS PROCESSED  00004000
000000                              70          END   AVEDIF      END OF PROGRAM
```

Fig. 12-2. The assembler listing of the program to be debugged.

₂ ₃   **Fig. 12-3.** The output from the program
- ₁ ₃   to be debugged.

indicates that the program did not work. The underlined message

COMPLETION CODE — SYSTEM=0C6   USER=0000

says that somewhere in the program we failed to specify an operand properly.

Figure 12-2 shows the assembler output for the program. We find no error messages, and a quick check of the Multiply and Divide instructions shows that they all have even register operands. We conclude that we used an improper address in one of the memory-reference instructions. Since we are using index registers, we probably failed to load one properly.

Have you already found the bug? If you have, pretend that you haven't so that we can use the dump to locate it for us.

Figure 12-3 is the little bit of output we got before the program stopped. In Fig. 12-4 we find two pages of the dump. In the interest of conserving space, we have not shown the entire dump but only those segments of it that we normally use. Those portions not shown include tables of interest to systems programmers and several more pages of the listing of the memory contents. Again we point out that the dump format varies from installation to installation. We use here only those portions that appear in all dumps.

Our goal is to use the dump to find out where the program stopped and what caused the error. The obvious place to start looking for this information is in the Program Status Word.

12.3.2. The Program Status Word

In Fig. 12-4(a), the first page of the dump, we find a line that identifies the program and a line that repeats the completion code. The next line says

PSW AT ENTRY TO ABEND   FFA5000D   9006A8CC

The 16 hexadecimal digits shown are the contents of the program status word register when the program stopped.

What information can we get from this? Let us concentrate upon the second word. The first nibble contains the instruction length counter and the condition code. (Refer to Fig. 11-1.) Expressing this nibble in binary,

$$9_{16} = \underbrace{10}_{\text{ILC}} \quad \underbrace{01}_{\text{CC}}$$

we find that ILC=2, meaning that the instruction being executed was 4 bytes long and that the condition code was 1, which indicates that the last instruction executed that sets the condition code produced a negative result.

The program counter contains the address of the *next* instruction that would have been executed if the program had not stopped. Since the program counter occupies the last 3 bytes of the PSW, we see that

$$(PC) = 06A8CC = \text{address of next instruction}$$

Since the instruction that was being executed when the program stopped is 4 bytes long, we can find its address by subtracting 4 from (PC):

$$(PC) = 6A8CC = \text{address of next instruction}$$
$$\underline{-4}$$
$$\overline{6A8C8} = \text{address of current instruction}$$

Thus, the PSW contains all we need in order to find the memory address of the instruction that was being executed when the program exception occurred.

The register and memory dump is a listing of the register and memory contents exactly as they were when the program stopped. We show the first page of the memory dump from this program in Fig. 12-4(b). The first four lines show the register contents. The memory dump follows and is a hexadecimal listing of the memory contents. The entries in the first column are the memory addresses of the first bytes of the corresponding rows. These numbers increase by 20_{16} for each row, indicating that $20_{16} = 32_{10}$ bytes are listed in a row. For example, the address of the first byte of the third row is 6A840. The *word* stored at this address contains FFFFFFF3. Each row is divided in the middle into two sections. The address of the first byte of the second section is 10_{16} higher than that of the first section. The word at adress 6A910 contains 00000009. Each section is divided into four full words.

The listing to the right of the hexadecimal memory contents is the output we receive if we print the contents of the row, assuming that the contents are EBCDIC character codes. Notice that a dot is printed for each byte that does not contain the EBCDIC code for a printable character.

We can now use the address we computed from the PC and ILC contents to find the machine language form of the instruction that caused the program to stop. Looking in the memory dump at location 6A8C8 and recalling that the offending instruction is 4 bytes long, we find that the machine language form of the instruction is

$$58A9D0D8$$

The assembly language equivalent of this instruction is

$$L \qquad 10,X'D8'(9,13)$$

Because the program we are debugging is short and simple, using the assembler listing and register contents we could probably locate the faulty instruction in the program and find the bug. But for more complex problems and bugs, it is easier to follow the procedure presented below to find out where the problem lies.

```
JOB DUMPEZ          STEP GO          TIME 104903    DATE 73282

COMPLETION CODE    SYSTEM = 0C6

PSW AT ENTRY TO ABEND    FFA5000D 9006A8CC

TCB  0152D0  RBP   00014D30  PIE    00000000  DEB  000151A4  TIO 0015A50  CMP 80C6000  TRN 00000000
             MSS   0002215F0 PK-FLG A0850000  FLG  00007F7B  LLS 0001CDD8 JLB 00000000 JPQ 00000000
             FSA   0107DE60  TCB    0011580   THE  00000000  JST 0015580  NTC 00000000 OTC 0015580
             LTC   00000000  IQE    00000000  ECB  0007DF24  STA 20000000 D-PQE 00021F58 SQS 0014868
             NSTAE 00000000  TCT    80016388  USER 00000000  DAR 00000000 RESV 00000000 JSCB 87017570

ACTIVE RBS

PRB  017618  RESV  00000000  APSW   9006A8CC  WC-SZ-STAB 00040082  FL-CDE 00016D30  PSW FFA5000D 9006A8CC
             Q/TTR 00000000  WT-LNK 000152D0

SVRB 015918  TAB-LN 00380220 APSW   F9F0F1C3  WC-SZ-STAB 0012D002  TQN 00000000  PSW 00040033 5000D10A
             Q/TTR  00006108  WT-LNK 00017618
             RG 0-7  FF000018  FFFFFFF3  00000010  00000009  FFFFFFFF  00000002  00000017
             RG 8-15 00000005  00000001  0006A800  4007ED4C  00064828  9006ABD8  0006AA90
             EXTSA   000021BE  8F07D878  00000000  00000000  0001599C  0001599C  E2E8E2C9
                     C5C1F0F1  C9C5C1D0  C1C2C5D5  C4F90C60

SVRB 014D30  TAB-LN 02803C8  APSW   F1F0F5C1  WC-SZ-STAB 0012D002  TQN 00000000  PSW FF04000C 4007D7A6
             Q/TTR  00004F0C  WT-LNK 00015918
             RG 0-7  00000007  00015978  0000E080  000E8000  000152D0  04015580  0001591B
             RG 8-15 00015580  4000CF6A  C5C1F0F1  8F070878  0001SAD0  40000174  00000000
             EXTSA   E2E8E2C9  00000000  00000000  00000000  00000000  00000000  00000000

LOAD LIST

NE 0001E3D8  RSP-CDE 02017478  NE 0001F7D8  RSP-CDE 01020908  NE 0001F9B0  RSP-CDE 010208C8
NE 000210A0  RSP-CDE 01020898  NE 00021ZE8  RSP-CDE 01020B38  NE 00021320  RSP-CDE 01020AC8
NE 00021AB0  RSP-CDE 010208F8  NE 00000000  RSP-CDE 01020868

CDE
016D30  ATR1 09  NCDE 0214C8  ROC-RB 00017618  NM **GO      USE 01  EPA 06A810  ATR2 A0  XL/MJ 016D48
017478  ATR1 30  NCDE 016D30  ROC-RB 00000000  NM IGC0A05A  USE 02  EPA 07D058  ATR2 28  XL/MJ 017C58
020908  ATR1 B0  NCDE 020938  ROC-RB 00000000  NM IGG019CF  USE 02  EPA 0E3090  ATR2 20  XL/MJ 0208F8
0208C8  ATR1 B0  NCDE 020908  ROC-RB 00000000  NM IGG019CL  USE 02  EPA 0E41D8  ATR2 20  XL/MJ 020888
020838  ATR1 B0  NCDE 020BC8  ROC-RB 00000000  NM IGG019AK  USE 02  EPA 0E5310  ATR2 20  XL/MJ 020888
020838  ATR1 B0  NCDE 020868  ROC-RB 00000000  NM IGG019AR  USE 02  EPA 0E5090  ATR2 20  XL/MJ 020828
020AC8  ATR1 B0  NCDE 020808  ROC-RB 00000000  NM IGG019CC  USE 02  EPA 0E4A98  ATR2 20  XL/MJ 020A88
020BF8  ATR1 B0  NCDE 020C28  ROC-RB 00000000  NM IGG019AA  USE 02  EPA 0E5810  ATR2 20  XL/MJ 020BE8
020868  ATR1 B0  NCDE 020898  ROC-RB 00000000  NM IGG019AQ  USE 02  EPA 0E5198  ATR2 20  XL/MJ 020B58

XL          ADR        LN        ADR        LN        ADR        LN        ADR
```

Fig. 12-4a. The first page of the dump.

Fig, 12-4b. First page of the register and memory contents portion of the dump.

253

12.3.3. The Bug in His Natural Habitat

Unless we are very good at translating programs from machine language to assembly language, the information we have gathered so far is not much help in finding and fixing the bug. We know what the instruction was that caused the program to stop. To find out the conditions that made this apparently harmless instruction cause an abend, we need to locate the instruction in the assembly language program itself. Once we have done this, our knowledge of assembly language and the logic of the program should suffice to show us how to correct the error.

We know the memory address of the guilty instruction. What we do not know is where that instruction is in the program. Recall that the location counter provides the address of each instruction of an assembly language program relative to the first byte of the program. If we could find out where the first byte of the program was stored when it was loaded into the memory for execution, we could then determine the location counter value of the instruction that the machine was executing when it stopped.

The *entry point address* (EPA) for a load module is the address of the first instruction executed in the load module. For our present purposes, the entry point address is the same as the *load address*, at which the first byte of the program is stored. In more complex situations in which the entry point address is not the same as the load address, the technique described below must be modified slightly, but the principles remain the same.

Where to look for the entry point address depends on the operating system and the type of dump on hand. In the example shown in Fig. 12-4, a SYStem Utility DUMP from an OS/360 system, the EPA is hidden in the first line of the section labeled CDE, Contents Directory Entries. The contents directory is a table of memory contents for all the memory that the job step requires. The system assigns the name **GO to our load module, and its directory entry is always in the first line of the CDE, which is at the bottom of the first page of the dump. Toward the end of the first line of the CDE we see the statement

$$\text{EPA} \qquad \text{06A810}$$

This is the entry point address that we want.

The situation is sketched in Fig. 12-5. The address of the instruction that failed is the program counter contents minus the length of the instruction. The entry point address is that of the first byte of our load module. If we interpret these addresses as distances from byte 0 of the memory, then evidently

$$(PC) - 2(ILC) = EPA + LOC$$

Hence, the location counter value, LOC, of the instruction that caused the program halt is

$$LOC = (PC) - 2(ILC) - EPA$$

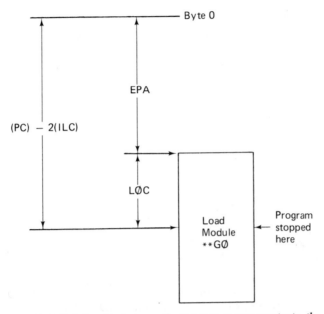

Fig. 12-5. Relationship between the program counter contents, the entry point address, and the location counter, LØC.

Returning to our example, we have

$$6A8C8 = (PC) - 2(ILC)$$
$$-6A810 = EPA$$
$$\overline{\ B8 = LOC}$$

In the assembler output, Fig. 12-2, the statement with location counter value B8 is

DIFLOOP   L   10,NMBRS(9)

This Load instruction is the instruction that caused the program exception.

Notice that we could have found the offending instruction just as well by using the program counter contents unmodified to find the location counter value of the instruction *after* the one that caused the abend. In this example, we calculate

$$6A8CC = (PC)$$
$$-6A810 = EPA$$
$$\overline{\ BC = LOC\ of\ next\ instruction}$$

We then find the instruction with location counter value BC in the assembly listing. The preceding instruction is the one we are looking for.

The technique described above for finding the erroenous instruction works in all cases *except* when the instruction causing the abend is a branch instruction. For example, a branch to an odd-numbered address results in a specification exception, 0C6. If this occurs, the PC contains the address to which we tried to branch, and there is no evidence in the PSW to indicate where the bad branch instruction is. A similar circumstance arises when we branch to an address in protected memory or to an instruction with an illegal operation code. In both cases, the question to be answered is how could we have branched to such a ridiculous address? The cause of such an error is almost always incautious tampering with or misloading of a base register. Analysis of the register contents and inspection of those instructions that load the base register suffice to locate the problem, usually after a lot of effort.

12.3.4. Symptoms of the Bug

Once we have found the instruction that failed to execute, we try to find out what kept the instruction from executing properly. We can give no general rules for doing this, but we can offer some suggestions. An 0C1 indicates that we tried to execute an instruction with an invalid operation code. This can happen if we stored some data in the middle of the program, either through the use of space-reserving statements in the assembly language program or during execution of the program. If the former is true, either move the DS and DC statements somewhere where they will not be executed, or branch around the storage area. The cause of storing data in the program during execution is an error in addressing. Another cause of an 0C1 is simply running off the end of a program into the data storage area. (Did you forget to include an EOJ statement or the equivalent?) Finally, as we mentioned above, we can branch to an invalid instruction. In this case, we again have an error in an address.

Address errors are by far the most common and usually produce one of the system completion codes 0C4, 0C5, or 0C6 (or 0C1, as we just saw). Finding the symptoms of the bug amounts to examining the register contents and displacements used in computing the addresses of the memory operands. This means checking the contents of the base register and the index register if one is used and examining the displacement(s) in the instruction.

Returning to our example, we got an 0C6, indicating an address error. The machine language for the instruction we found to cause the abend shows that for the memory operand the displacement is D8, register 13 is the base register, and register 9 is the index register. To determine the address the instruction actually tried to use, we must calculate

$$D8 + (9) + (13)$$

To find the contents of the regisers, we refer to the section labeled

REGS AT ENTRY TO ABEND

in Fig. 12-4(b). We find that when the program stopped

$$(9) = 00000001$$

$$(13) = 0006A828$$

The effective address of the memory operand was

$$D8 = \text{displacement}$$

$$+1 = (9)$$

$$\underline{+6A828 = (13)}$$

$$6A901 = \text{effective address}$$

"So what?," you say. Let's think a moment. We got an 0C6, saying that something is wrong with an operand we chose to use. We found out that the instruction that crashed is a Load instruction and that the address of the memory operand is 6A901. What does a Load instruction do? It loads the contents of a full word from the memory into a register. The memory address must be a multiple of 4. . . . Aha! We got an 0C6 because we tried to use an instruction that requires a full word from the memory, but the effective address we supplied is not a multiple of 4.

How did this happen? The displacement is a multiple of 4, as are the contents of the base register. The index register contains 1. The index register contents were improperly calculated.

We have traced through the essentially mechanical procedure of finding the direct cause of the abend—what caused the instruction that failed to actually produce an abend. In more complex examples than the one discussed herein, it may be necessary to examine the memory contents in detail before arriving at this stage.

To find something stored in the memory, we must determine its actual address. We know the EPA of the program, and, using the program listing, we can find the location counter value and the EPA:

$$\text{address} = \text{EPA} + \text{LOC}$$

For example, let us find out what was stored at NMBRS when the program of Fig. 12-2 stopped. The EPA is 6B810, while the location counter value for NMBRS is F0. We should examine location

$$6A810 + F0 = 6A900$$

Referring to the memory dump in Fig. 12-4(b), we find that the full word stored at 6A900 contains

$$(6A900) = 0000000A$$

In debugging a program, we often use this procedure to determine the results the program produced before it stopped. The information thus gained helps to tell us how the situation that caused the abend developed.

Do not forget to check the input data. Every programmer wastes a significant amount of time searching a dump for errors when the fault lies in input data for the program.

12.3.5. Killing the Bug

Once we determine why the instruction that failed did so, to find the bug we must find the error in the program logic that generated the conditions under which the instruction failed. In our example, we know that register 9, which we were using as an index register, contained an odd number, causing a specification exception when we tried to Load a full word from the memory. How did register 9 come to contain 1 ? The answer to such a question is often difficult to determine. We must put together the information at hand—the program listing, the output, the dump, and our knowledge of the program logic—and come up with an answer.

In the example, our problem boils down to a study of what is done with register 9 in the vicinity of the Load instruction that failed. We see that register 9 is being used to index a series of full words stored at NMBRS in a loop that starts at DIFLOOP. The instruction before DIFLOOP starts (9) at 0. We load the first number, subtract the average contained in register 7, print the result, increment register 9 for the next word, test (9) for completion, and branch back to DIFLOOP. Hey! What about that increment step? Shouldn't we increment by 4 if we are processing full words? That's the bug! Evidently we forgot that full words are 4 bytes apart. (Don't always trust what comments say; the *instructions* do the computing.). To kill the bug we should change statement 56 to

$$A \qquad 9,=F'4'$$

Because of the infinite number of possible bugs and combinations of bugs, there is no exhaustive series of steps to follow in debugging. However, it *is* possible to give a broad outline of the procedure:

1. Determine the completion code.
2. Examine the assembler and linkage editor outputs for error messages.
3. Using the PSW and EPA, locate the instruction which caused execution to stop.
4. Using the register and memory dump, find out exactly why this particular instruction caused the exception.
5. Using the register and memory dump and any other available information, find out how the conditions arose that caused the instruction to fail.

We have until now concentrated exclusively upon bugs which cause program exceptions. There are many other bugs which can stop execution of a program without an illegal use of an instruction. These bugs arise when we misuse the system. For example, if our program gets stuck in a loop, the system does not let it run on forever. The system stops the program execution after a fixed length of time and presents us with a dump if one was requested (completion code 322 in OS systems). Similarly, our program can attempt to print too many lines, read more data cards than were supplied, or use more memory space than is available. When a program stops with this kind of error, the first step is to find out what the completion code means. This information is to be found in the messages and codes manual. In most cases, the procedure outlined above helps to find out where the program stopped when a system error occurred.

12.4. PROGRAM TESTING

Rumor has it that one of our early attempts to launch a space satellite failed because a programmer misplaced a decimal point. Few programming errors have such spectacular consequences. But errors in program logic cost millions in dollars and man-hours spent in recovering from them. Bugs in systems programs stop multimillion-dollar computing systems for days. The telephone company's billing system gives a customer $7000 credit instead of billing him for $7.00. And who has not been through a hassle with a computerized credit card system?

In the material above we have outlined the procedure we use when the computer hardware or the operating system detects a bug and we get a dump. When we have removed all the errors that can stop the program, the tendency is to say "I didn't get a dump, so the program must be correct," particularly if our supervisor, thesis advisor, or instructor is pushing for the finished product. But we must resist the tendency to assume that a program is finished before we have tested it adequately.

12.4.1. Modular Programming

In many computing problems we are on shaky ground if we conclude that the program is working correctly if it supplies the correct actions or answers for just a single test case. And many problems are so complex that testing by running simple cases is impossible. Thus, the problem is how to detect when a program or system of programs contains errors. If there are errors in logic (we are excluding now those errors which the machine or operating system can diagnose for us), how do we locate them in a complex system?

We should design the program or system of programs anticipating that such problems do arise. We split the program or system up into smaller units, or *modules*, each of which has a distinct and specific purpose.

Ideally, each module is independent of all the others in the sense that making a change in one module has no effect on the performance of the other modules. This means that, ideally, we can change one module without having to make corrections in other modules to compensate for the change. While total module independence is rarely attained in actual practice, the attempt to achieve the ideal results in program packages that are easier to write, test, and debug than if the modular approach is not followed.

In many real-life situations, the problem is so large that many programmers are needed to produce the final system. Typically, a small group of programmers has the responsibility for writing, debugging, and testing a single module. Each group must know exactly what is expected of this module, the format and nature of the data available to it, and the format and nature of the output expected from the module. This team approach to programming requires considerable preparation, planning, and strong supervision, so that each group knows exactly what to do.

Division of a problem into modules is usually straightforward, since most problems consist of several major computational steps. We usually group modules that have related functions together into *subroutines*, which are separate programs each of which consists of at least one module.

Now look at Fig. 12-6. Here we show in a block diagram a possible structure for a simple inventory management system in which the inventory records are maintained on a magnetic disk storage facility. We have four subroutines which deal with card reader input, line printer output, record modification, and disk input/output, respectively. The subroutines and their modules are

Subroutine	Modules
Card reader	1. Card input
	2. Data conversion
Line printer	1. Data conversion
	2. Printed output
Record modifier	1. Number in stock modifier
	2. Recorder number modifier
	3. Price modifier
	4. Others
Disk input/output	1. Input of existing records
	2. Update of existing records
	3. Output of new records

The center block of the diagram is a main control program which controls the flow of data among the subroutines and the sequence of execution of subroutines and modules. Thus, the control program consists mainly of logic to interpret input commands and carry them out through requests for execution of subroutines, subroutine *calls* (see Chapter 13 for details on subroutines).

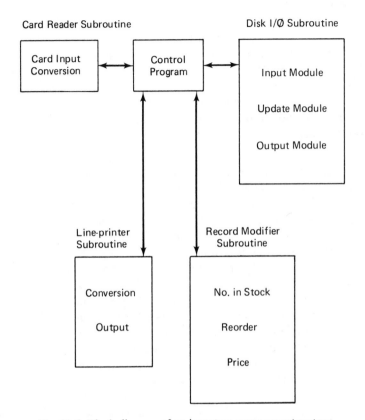

Fig. 12-6. Block diagram of an inventory management system.

A typical transaction is the modification of the current number in stock of a given part because some of those parts were sold. The process of updating the record for that part consists of the following steps:

1. The contral program calls the card reader subroutine requesting that a control card be read. This card contains the part number, a code for the desired transaction, and numeric data indicating the amounts in the transaction.

2. The card input module reads a card.

3. The data conversion module checks the input and converts numeric information from the card to a form appropriate for arithmetic use.

4. The control program examines the control information from the card, determines that an update is to be done, and calls the disk I/O subroutine.

5. The input module of the disk I/O subroutine reads the record from the disk.

6. The control program calls the record modifier subroutine.

7. The number-in-stock module of the record modifier program changes the number-in-stock field of the record.

8. The control program calls the disk I/O subroutine.

9. The update module of the I/O program writes the record (now altered) back onto the disk.

10. The control program calls the line printer subroutine, which converts the numeric information to printable characters and outputs a printed record of the transaction.

Notice that in this scheme each module has its own unique function. If this system were written as one large program with no separation of functions as we described above, testing and debugging the system would be a formidable, if not impossible, task. After the bugs that the machine and operating system can detect are removed, the next run of the program might do something, but what it does would be wrong.

For example, suppose that the number in stock appears to be wrong as shown in the printed output. Is the error in the data card? The data conversion statements? The statements that modify the number in stock?

The modular approach can help us to avoid getting into this situation. What we do is write, test, and debug each module separately. We then combine the modules into subroutines and test the subroutines separately. Only when we are convinced that each module and each subroutine performs correctly do we put the system together and try it with the control program in control. Assuming that the pieces all work, any errors remaining must be in the control program or in the passing of data back and forth among the subroutines.

Before we look into the details of debugging and testing modules, we should point out another important advantage of the modular approach to programming. This is the increase in flexibility we gain by writing the programs in small units, making what would seem to be major changes in the system relatively easy. Suppose that we want to use a teletype terminal for input and output of control data and the printed output, respectively. If the modules for conversion are designed properly, all we need to do is replace the card input and line printer output modules with modules that deal with a teletype. To maintain the inventory file on magnetic tape instead of disk storage, we replace the disk I/O modules. To add a new function to the record modification segment we simply insert a new module and add the logic statements to the modification subroutine that decide when to use the new module.

To achieve the degree of independence needed for such flexibility, each module must be tested and debugged separately. We shall now turn to the question of how to test and debug modules.

12.4.2. Module Debugging and Testing

Whether the module is part of a new system or is to be incorporated into an existing system, start debugging and testing a module before the first card is punched. Play computer with the code you have written, trying various sets of input data and assuming that the data will not always be in the proper form. Put in statements that check for bad data. Such tests help not only in debugging and testing the module but also later when the module is incorporated into the system and out into production. Check loops carefully. What does the code do if a loop is to be traversed 0 times? Is there some maximum number of times a loop should be traversed? See what each branch in the module does. This initial program *walk-through*, while sometimes tedious and seemingly unproductive, can result in significant savings in effort later.

Many of the exercises and examples in this text are short and simple enough to be written as a single-module program containing all the input and output facilities to make them usable as "stand-alone" programs. But in more complex situations, a module might have no input/output facilities of its own and might not be a complete subroutine itself. An example is the number-in-stock modifier module in Fig. 12-6. In such cases, additional programming is necessary to debug and test the module.

The object is to simulate as closely as possible the environment in which the module is used. If the module is not a complete subroutine, we must add temporary necessary subroutine linkage statements to make it usable in the operating system, but in a way that has no effect upon the input, output, or calculations of the module. Otherwise, when we remove the temporary statements and put the module into a larger program it will not work.

If the module itself does not supply its own input, we must write a *driver* program, or a test data generator, that provides input for the module and passes the data to the module in the form that the module is designed to handle. For example, the number-in-stock module expects to receive a record image from the disk and an amount by which to change the number in stock. These data must be supplied by a test data generator.

The design of a driver program and the choice of the data it produces can be nontrivial problems. We want to give the module a good workout. The test data generator should produce sets of data so that every branch in the module is tested. It is not enough to test the module for data in the proper range and in the proper format. The module should be tried with data with errors in it and with data outside the usual range.

In the normal case, the number-in-stock module simply adds or subtracts a number to the number in stock field of an inventory record. But the module should also be written and tested anticipating abnormal situations. If the resulting number in stock is negative, indicating an error in input data, an error in the record to be modified, or a real overselling of the part, the number-in-stock module would indicate an error condition (by passing an error code back to the driver program) to call attention to the problem. The module should check to make sure that the record it is modifying is the right one by comparing the part-number on the disk record with the part number from the control card. If these numbers do not match, the module must warn the user that something is amiss. These details should be considered while the module is being designed, written, and tested, *not* in the later stages of system implementation when the module is incorporated into a larger program package.

Programs for mathematical applications require similar attention to the abnormal as well as the normal cases. For example, consider the problem of testing a matrix inversion subroutine. Perhaps we have worked out a 3 by 3 example by hand. We try it with our subroutine and get the right answer. But this is just the beginning of the testing procedure, although, unfortunately, some programmers would assume that the module is correct and go on to other problems at this point. There are several other aspects that still need testing. We are three-dimensional and it is likely that our thinking in three-dimensional terms would produce programs that work better for three dimensions than for other dimensions. Thus, we must test the program for both lower- and higher-dimensional problems. The program should not "crash" in special cases such as 0 by 0, 1 by 1, or 2 by 2 matrices. It should produce the proper results for higher-dimensional matrices.

What about singular (noninvertable) matrices? The module should include tests for singularity and print a warning message, pass an error indicator to the calling program, and return when a singular matrix is encountered, instead of trying to divide a number by 0, which is what happens if such tests are not included. The module should also be tried with near-singular matrices which can produce large errors. Its response to such tests, restrictions on the size of the matrix the module can invert, and typical errors due to roundoff and truncation for various matrices should be included in the documentation for the module.

In short, whatever the application, the module should be tested when the data are at extreme values or contain errors as well as for data in the correct form and within normal limits.

If the module itself produces no printed output, we must add statements that do produce output so that we can check the action of the module. Earlier in this chapter we discussed the use of the dump that the system produces when an error detectable by the machine or the operating system occurs. In assembly language programming, one way to get printed output from a module that normally produces none is to request such a dump. This can be done through the use of the ABEND macro, written

ABEND   n,DUMP

The result is a dump in the same format as that we discussed above. n is a user completion code which appears in place of the system completion code in the output.

The ABEND macro terminates execution of the program and therefore precludes further testing of the module in the same job. Many programmers or local installations have their own set of debugging aid subroutines that print memory and register contents on demand without stopping execution. You might want to write your own. An alternative is to use the PDUMP subroutine supplied with the standard FORTRAN library. PDUMP prints the contents of selected memory areas in any of several formats and is called via standard subroutine linkage conventions. For further details, see the Manual *OS FORTRAN IV Library: Mathematical and Service Subprograms* (GC28—6818).

Do not be afraid to print a lot of intermediate information when debugging and testing. We can make good use of the computer's power to help us find our own mistakes. A little thought about what output we shall need to locate errors can save a lot of human and computer resources.

12.4.3. Putting the Pieces Together

Once the modules have been tested, the problem is to join the modules together into a single program package.

If several modules are to be in a single subroutine, we must write statements at the beginning of the subroutine to determine which module or modules are to be executed. For example, the record modification subroutine of Fig. 12-6 includes several modules. When the subroutine is called, it must determine which module is to be used. This is usually done by statements in the subroutine which examine a control code passed to it from the calling program as part of the input to the subroutine.

We should test each subroutine using the same procedures outlined above to test modules. This often requires the development of test data generators and output routines, and again we should try to test every branch and every section of code in the subroutine and include error detection capabilities.

Finally, we come to the control program. As a rule, the control program should itself do no calculations other than to determine which subroutines to execute in what order and to provide the proper data and control information for the subroutines. Given a verbal description of what the subroutines and modules do, it should be possible to read the control program and get a good idea of how the whole system works.

Figure 12-7 is a flow chart for the driver program of Fig. 12-6. Notice that all I/O, calculations, and error checking are done in the subroutines; the driver decides which subroutines to execute.

In testing the complete system, we again have the same responsibility to

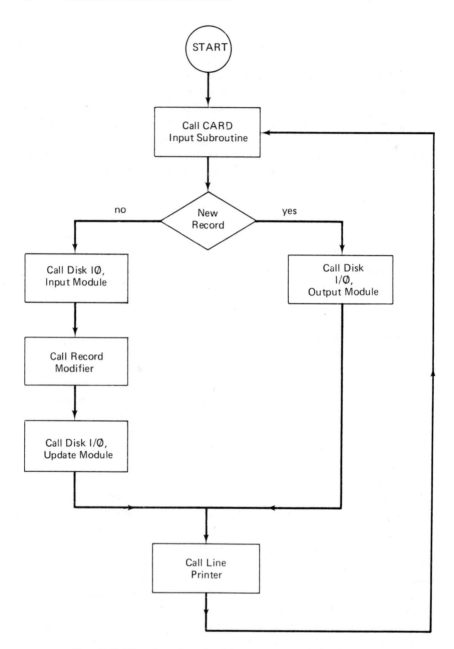

Fig. 12-7. Flowchart for the driver program of the inventory system.

demonstrate that the system responds correctly when the inputs are correct and provides appropriate error information when the inputs are not correct. Perhaps the worst thing we can do is permit the system to appear to behave properly when in fact the data are wrong. It is far better to have the system react when it suspects errors than to lead the user to believe that everything is OK.

12.4.4. Support and Upgrade

Rarely is a system completely free of bugs, no matter how throughly we test it and no matter how much self-checking capabilities we put into it. This means that after the system is put into production use, someone will have to find and fix occasional bugs. Changes in the hardware or software environment in which the system operates often require corresponding modification to systems already in operation. We often add new capabilities to systems that already work. By concentrating related tasks into small packages, modular construction helps in all these software maintenance activities. Adding new capabilities ideally requires simply adding new modules to the system (*after* testing them).

At the risk of seeming repetitious, we again stress the need for adequate documentation of all software. Keeping up the documentation while debugging and testing programs and systems is often a disagreeable task, but it is a very important one. If we do not keep up the documentation, we shall leave out changes that we made during the debugging and testing process. The documentation must convey to users and programmers all the current information they need to maintain the system and add new capabilities to it.

CHAPTER SUMMARY

The *completion code* indicates the reason for program failure. The *program status word* and the *entry point address* are used to locate the instruction that failed in the program. The *memory* and *register dump* help to determine the conditions that led to the abnormal ending.

A well-tested program produces the correct output under normal circumstances and supplies diagnostic information when misused. *Modular programming* helps in debugging and testing program systems and makes future maintenance and upgrading of systems easier.

EXERCISES

1. Find the bug in Fig. 12-8.
2. Find the bug in Fig. 12-9.

```
LOC    OBJECT CODE      ADDR1 ADDR2  STMT  SOURCE STATEMENT

                                       1  *        PROGRAM TO PRINT MAILING LIST ON LABLES, FOUR LABELS PER ROW
                                       2  *        ADDRESSSES ARE INPUT ONE ADDRESS PER CARD
000000                                 3  MAILLIST START 0
                                       4           PRINT NOGEN
                                       5           INITIAL
000060 4140 0022        00022         15           LA   4,34          34  COLUMNS PER LABLE
000064 4150 0084        00084         16           LA   5,132         132 COLUMNS PER PRINTED LINE
000068 4120 D11D        00135         17  RESTART  LA   2,LINE1       REG. 2 WILL INDICATE WHICH LABEL IS BEING
                                      18  NXTCARD  RCD  NAME          DONE. READ ADDRESS CARD.
000078 D504 DOCC D2AB   000E4 002C3   22           CLC  NAME(5),STOPPER   CHECK FOR TRAILER CARD
00007E 4780 D084        00084         23           BE   DONE          IF FOUND, PROCESSING COMPLETE
000082 4162 D11D        00135         24           MVC  6,LINE1(2)    ADDRESS FOR NAME IN REG. 6
000086 021D 6000 DOCC   00000 000E4   25           MVC  0(30,6),NAME  MOVE NAME FIELD TO FIRST OUTPUT LINE
00008C 4162 D1A2        001BA         26           LA   6,LINE2(2)    ADDRESS FOR STREET ADDRESS
000090 0218 6000 DOEA   00000 00102   27           MVC  0(25,6),STADR MOVE STREET ADDRESS TO OUTPUT LINE 2
000096 4162 D227        0023F         28           LA   6,LINE3(2)    ADDRESS FOR CITY, STATE OUTPUT FIELD
00009A 0218 6000 D103   00000 0011B   29           MVC  0(25,6),CITSTATE  MOVE CITY-STAE FIELD TO OUTPUT LIN 3
0000A0 8724 D054        0006C         30           BXLE 2,4,NXTCARD   GO TO PROCESS NEXT ADDRESS INPUT CARD
                                      31           PLN  CCNTL1        PRINT RESULTING FOUR LABLES
                                      35           PLN  CCNTL2
                                      39           PLN  CCNTL3
0000C8 47F0 D050        00068         43           B    RESTART       START PROCESSING NEXT ROW OF LABLES
0000E0 00000000                       44  DONE     EOJ
                                                        =V(SSID)
0000E4                                50  NAME     DS   CL30          SPACE FOR INPUT NAME FIELD
000102                                52  STADDR   DS   CL25          SPACE FOR INPUT STREET ADDRESS FIELD
00011B                                53  CITSTATE DS   CL25          SPACE FOR INPUT CITY-STATE-ZIP FIELD
000134 F0                             54  CCNTL1   DC   C'0'          SPACE FOR 1ST OUTPUT LINE
000135 40404040404040404040           55  LINE1    DC   CL132' '      SPACE FOR 1ST OUTPUT LINE
000189 40                             56  CCNTL2   DC   C' '          CARRIAGE CONTROL FOR 20ND LINE - SINGLE SP
00018A 40404040404040404040           57  LINE2    DC   CL132' '      SPACE FOR 20ND OUTPUT LINE
00023E 40                             58  CCNTL3   DC   C' '          CARRIAGE CONTROL FOR 3RD LINE - SINGLE SP
00023F 40404040404040404040           59  LINE3    DC   CL132' '      SPACE FOR 3RD OUTPUT LINE
0002C3 5C5C5C5C5C                     60  STOPPER  DC   CL5'*****'    FIVE STARS WILL MEAN TRAILER CARD
000000                                61           END  MAILLIST
```

Fig. 12-8a. Find the bug and fix it.

```
JOB DUMPEE              STEP GO              TIME 105053    DATE 73282

COMPLETION CODE         SYSTEM = 0C4

PSW AT ENTRY TO ABEND FFA5000D E006C83C

TCB 015550  RBP 00015278  PIE 00000000  DEB 00015334  TIO 00015A50  CMP 80C4000   TRN 00000000
            MSS 00021320  PK-FLG A0850000 FLG 0007F7B  LLS 00021 0A0 JLB 00000000  JPQ 00000000
            FSA 0107DE60  TCB 00015780   TME 00000000  JST 00015630  NTC 00000000  OTC 00015530
            LTC 00000000  IQE 00000000   ECB 0007DF24  STA 20000000  D-PQE 00021F38 SQS 0001AC78
            NSTAE 00000000 TCT 80016388  USER 00000000 DAR 00000000  RESV 00000000 JSCB 87017570

ACTIVE RBS

PRB 017A28  RESV 00000000  APSW E006C89C  WT-LNK 00015550  WC-SZ-STAB 00040082  FL-CDE 00016C40  PSW FFA5000D E006C89C
            Q/TTR 00000000

SVRB 015878 TAB-LN 00580220 APSW F9F0F1C3  WT-LNK 00017A28  WC-SZ-STAB 0012D002  TQN CC000000  PSW 00040033 5000D99A
            Q/TTR 0006610B
            RG 0-7  FF000018  0006CBF4  0006C810  00000022  00000084  000D928A  000000FF
            RG 8-15 00000000  0007DEA8  0006C800  4007E04C  0006C828  8006C888  0006CAD8
            EXTSA   000021BE  8F07D000  00000000  FF030000  00015 8F4 000158FC  E2E8E2C9
                    C5C1F0F1  C9C5C150  C4F90C40

SVRB 015278 TAB-LN 004803C8 APSW F1F0F5C1  WT-LNK 00015878  WC-SZ-STAB 0012D002  TQN 00000000  PSW FF04000C 4007D7A6
            Q/TTR 00004F0C
            RG 0-7  00000007  00015 8D8 8000D8B2  0000E080  00015550  00015878  04015630  00015878
            RG 8-15 00015630  4000D7FA  8F07D000  8F07D000  00015AD0  000158FC  4000C49C  00000000
            EXTSA   E2E8E2C9  C5C1F0F1  00000000  00000000  00000000  A0400000  00807F7B  00000000
                    00000000  00012C002 00000000

LOAD LIST

NE 00021408  RSP-CDE 02018830  NE 00021900  RSP-CDE 01020AC8  NE 00021908  RSP-CDE 01020BF8
NE 00000000  RSP-CDE 01020868

CDE

016C40  NCDE 0214B0  ATR1 09  NM **GO      USE 01  EPA 06C810  ATR2 A0  XL/MJ 016C58
018830  NCDE 016C43  ATR1 30  NM IGC0A05A  USE 02  EPA 07D058  ATR2 28  XL/MJ 0211D8
020AC8  NCDE 020B03  ATR1 B0  NM IGG019CC  USE 02  EPA 0E4A98  ATR2 20  XL/MJ 020AB8
020BF8  NCDE 020C28  ATR1 B0  NM IGG019AA  USE 02  EPA 0E5810  ATR2 20  XL/MJ 020BE8
020B68  NCDE 020B98  ATR1 B0  NM IGG019AQ  USE 02  EPA 0E5198  ATR2 20  XL/MJ 020858
                                           LN      ADR                 LN      ADR

XL

016C58  SZ 00000010  NO 00000001  80000B08  0006C800
0211D8  SZ 00000010  NO 00000001  30007A8   0007D058
020AB8  SZ 00000010  NO 00000001  800002C8  000E4A98
020BE8  SZ 00000010  NO 00000001  800000A0  000E5810
```

Fig. 12-8b.

269

MIN 017F20   FQEL 00018560   PMIN 00018OCO   NMIN 00000000   NM AO IEA

NQEL 00000000   PQEL 000 17F20   TCB 00015550   SVRB 00015278

SAVE AREA TRACE

**GO   WAS ENTERED VIA LINK

SA   07DE60   WD1 00000000   HSA 00000000   LSA 0006C828   RET 00006 9AA   EPA 0106C810   RO FF000018
             R1 0007DF50   R2 8007DF54   R3 0006C810   R4 0007DFF9   R5 FFFFFFFF   R6 0007DF60
             R7 000000FF   R8 00000000   R9 0007DEA8   R10 0007DFF0   R11 0006C800   R12 4007E04C

                                                                                                                    B8H

**GO   WAS ENTERED VIA CALL   AT EP 01   01Q 01S   5 B   B J B4   J GB   K   G   0

SA   06C828   WD1 50101008   HSA 0007DE60   LSA 43F01018   RET 0006C888   EPA 0006CAD8   RO FF000018
             R1 0006C8F4   R2 0006C945   R3 0006C810   R4 C0000022   R5 00000084   R6 0007DF60
             R7 000000FF   R8 00000000   R9 0007DEA8   R10 0007DFF0   R11 0006C800   R12 4007E04C

INTERRUPT AT 06C89C

PROCEEDING BACK VIA REG 13

**GO   WAS ENTERED VIA CALL   AT EP 01   01Q 01S   & B   B J B4   J GB   K   G   0

SA   06C828   WD1 50101008   HSA 0007DE60   LSA 43F01018   RET 8006C888   EPA 0006CAD8   RO FF000018
             R1 0006C8F4   R2 0006C945   R3 0006C810   R4 00000022   R5 00000084   R6 0007DF60
             R7 000000FF   R8 00000000   R9 0007DEA8   R10 0007DFF0   R11 0006C800   R12 4007E04C

**GO   WAS ENTERED VIA LINK

SA   07DE60   WD1 00000000   HSA 00000000   LSA 0006C828   RET 000069AA   EPA 0106C810   RO FF000018
             R1 0007DF50   R2 8007DF54   R3 0006C810   R4 0007DFF0   R5 FFFFFFFF   R6 0007DF60
             R7 000000FF   R8 00000030   R9 0007DEA8   R10 0007DFF0   R11 0006C800   R12 4007E04C

REGS AT ENTRY TO ABEND

FLTR 0-6   0012C0020000000   0000000000000000   00000004000540001

REGS 0-7   FF000018   0006C8F4   0006C945   0006C810   000161F800000048
REGS 8-15   00000000   0007DEA8   0007DFF0   0006C800   00000022   00000084   000000FF
                                                                 4007E04C   0006C828   0006CAD8

LOAD MODULE   **GO

06C800   5C5CC7D6 4040404D 00000000 00000000   90ECD00C 18AD41D0 F0185040 D0045000   *..GO........................0....*
06C820   40084 7F0 F0601008 50101008 00000022   43F01018 8006C888 0006CAD8 FF000018   *...00.......0....H....Q....*
06C840   0006C8F4 0006C945 0006C810 00000030   00000084 0007DF60 00000000 00000000   *.H4..I....H...............*
06C860   0007DEA8 0007DFF0 0006C800 4007E04C   41400022 41500084 4120D11D 411 0D0CC   *........0..H.........J.....*
06C880   58F0D0C8 45EF0008 D504D0CC D2ABA780   D0644162 D1DD21D 6000D0CC 4162D1A2   *.0.H....N..K.......JK......J.*
06C8A0   D2186000 D0EA4162 D2270218 6000D1 03   8724D054 4110D11C 58F0D0C8 45EF000C   *K.....K.K....J...0.H......*
06C8C0   4110D1A1 58F0D0C8 45EF000C 4110D226   58F0D050 47F0D050 58D0D004   *...J..:0.H......K..0.H.......0....*

Fig. 12-8c.

```
LOC    OBJECT CODE   ADDR1  ADDR2   STMT  SOURCE STATEMENT

                              1  *      THIS PROGRAM READS A DATA CARD WHICH TELLS HOW MANY        00000100
                              2  *      NUMBERS ARE TO BE PROCESSED. THAT NUMBER IS KEPT IN        00000200
                              3  *      REG. 8. IT THEN CALCULATES THE UPPER VALUE FOR INDEX      00000300
                              4  *      REGISTERS AND LEAVES THAT NUMBER IN REG. 3                00000400
                              5  *      IT READS THE NUMBERS ONE AT A TIME, STORING THEM IN       00000500
                              6  *      CONSECUTIVE FULL WORDS OF THE AREA CALLED NMBRS. THE      00000600
                              7  *      AVERAGE OF ALL THE NUMBERS IS COMPUTED, AS IS THE         00000700
                              8  *      DIFFERENCE BETWEEN EACH OF THE NUMBERS AND THE AVERAGE.   00000800
000000                        9  AVEDIF START 0                                                   00000900
                             10         PRINT NOGEN                                                00001000
                             11         INITIAL                                                    00001100
00006A 1883                  21         RWD   3            READ NUMBER OF NUMBERS TO USE           00001200
00006C 5830 DDCC      000E4  25         LR    8,3          KEEP A COPY IN REG. 8                   00001300
000070 5C20 DDD0      000E8  26         S     3,=F'1'      COMPUTE FINAL INDEX VALUE.              00001400
000074 5890 DDC4      000EC  27         M     2,=F'4'      4*((3)-1)                               00001500
                             28         L     9,=F'0'      INDEX FOR READ LOOP STARTS AT 0         00001600
                             29  READLOOP RWD  4            READ A DATA NUMBER                      00001700
000082 5049 D07E      00096  33         ST    4,NMBRS(9)   STORE IT AT EFF. ADDRESS NMBRS + (9)    00002000
000086 5A90 DDD0      000E8  34         A     9,=F'4'      INCREMENT INDEX REGISTER                00002100
00008A 1993                  35         CR    9,3          TEST INDEX AGAINST FINAL VALUE KEPT     00002200
00008C 47D0 D060      00078  36         BNP   READLOOP     IN REG. 3                               00002300
000090 5890 DDD4      000EC  37         L     9,=F'0'      INDEX FOR LOOP TO COMPUTE SUM AT 0      00
000094 1877                  38         SR    7,7          START SUM AT 0 (IN OCC NMBRO REG.)      00002500
000096 5A79 DDC8      000F0  39  NUMBRS A     7,NMBRS(9)   ADD NUMBER AT NMBRS + (9) TO SUM        00002600
00009A 5A90 DDD0      000E8  40         A     9,=F'4'      ADD 4 TO INDEX                          00
00009E 1993                  41         CR    9,3          COMPARE WITH FINAL VALUE STILL IN 3     00002800
0000A0 47D0 D07E      00096  42         BNP   NUMBRS       GO TO NUMBRS IF NOT DONE                00002900
0000A4 5C60 DDCC      000E4  43         M     6,=F'1'      WHEN HERE, READY FOR DIVIDE TO COMPUTE  00003100
0000A8 1C68                  44         DR    6,8          AVERAGE BY DIVIDING SUM BY (8)          00003200
                             45         WWD   7            PRINT THE AVERAGE                       00003300
0000B4 5890 DDD4      000EC  49         L     9,=F'0'      AND PREPARE TO COMPUTE DIFFERENCES      00003400
0000B8 58A9 C0C8      000F0  50  DIFLOOP L    10,NMBRS(9)  GET NUMBER FROM NMBRS + (9)
0000BC 1EA7                  51         SR    10,7         SUBTRACT AVERAGE IN REG. 7
                             52         WWD   10           PRINT THE DIFFERENCE
0000C8 5A90 DDD0      000E8  56         A     9,=F'4'      INCREMENT INDEX REG.
0000CC 1993                  57         CR    9,3          COMPARE WITH FINAL VALUE
0000CE 47D0 D0A0      000B8  58         BNP   DIFLOOP      REPEAT IF RESULT NEGATIVE OR 0          00003600
                             59         EOJ                PROCESSING COMPLETED                    00003700
0000E0 00000000              65               =V($$IO)
0000E4 00000001              66               =F'1'
0000E8 00000004              67               =F'4'
0000EC 00000000              68               =F'0'
0000F0                       69  NMBRS DS     100F         STORAGE SPACE FOR NUMBERS PROCESSED     00003900
000000                       70         END   AVEDIF       END OF PROGRAM                          00004000
```

Fig. 12-9a. Find the bug and fix it.

271

```
JOB DUMPER          STEP GO          TIME 114439   DATE 75217

COMPLETION CODE     SYSTEM = 0C6

PSW AT ENTRY TO ABEND FF95000C A006C096

TCB 088030   RBP   0008A460   PIE    C0000000   DEB  008990A4   TIO  00089D18   CMP   800C6000   TRN  00000000
             MSS   0008FD98   PK-FLG 9B850000   FLG  00007F78   LLS  0008ED38   JLB   00000000   JPQ  00000000
             FSA   0107F660   TCB    00000000   TME  0000CC00   JST  008893A0   NTC   00000000   OTC  000893A0
             LTC   00000000   IQE    00000000   ECB  0007F724   TSF  20000000   D-PQE 0009401B   SQS  0008F768
             NSTAE 00000000   TCT    800891C8   USER 00000000   DAR  00000000   RESV  00000000   JSCB 87088140
             RESV  00000000   IOB    00000000

ACTIVE RBS

PRB 08BA98   RESV  00000000   APSW   A006C096   WC-SZ-STAB 00040082   FL-CDE 0008AD80   PSW FF95000D A006C096
             Q/TTR 00000000   WT-LNK 00088030

SVRB 089460  TAB-LN 00180220  APSW   F9F0F1C3   WC-SZ-STAB C012D002   TQN 00000000   PSW 00040033 5000D5C2
             Q/TTR  0008870E   WT-LNK 0008BA98
             RG 0-7  FF000018  0000000A  0000000A  00000010  FFFFFFFF  0007F760   00CC0FF
             RG 8-15 00000005  0007F7F0  4007F84C  0006C000  0006C028  A006C090   0006C290
             EXTSA   000021BE  8F07F500  FF030000  00000000  000894DC  000894E4   E2E8E2C9
                     C5C1F0F1  C9C5C130            C1C2C5D5            C4F90C60

SVRB 08A460  TAB-LN 00580308  APSW   F1F0F5C1   WC-SZ-STAB 00120002   TQN 00000000   PSW FF04000C 4007EFA6
             Q/TTR  0008BA07   WT-LNK 00089460
             RG 0-7  00000007  8000D4DA  0000F658  00088030  04D893A0  00089460
             RG 8-15 000893A0  40000422  8F07F500  00089D98  000894E4  00000000
             EXTSA   E2E8E2C9  C5C1F0F1  00000000  00000000  000081A   00000000
                     00000200  0C000001  C4C00001

LOAD LIST
   NE 0008F2A8   RSP-CDE 0208B688   NE 0008F338   RSP-CDE 01095A88   NE 0008F88B   RSP-CDE 01095B88
   NE 00000000   RSP-CDE 01095B28

CDE
   08AD80   ATR1 09   NCDE 08E698   ROC-RB 0008BA98   NM **GO       USE 01   EPA 06C010   ATR2 A0   XL/MJ 08AD98
   08B688   ATR1 30   NCDE 08AD80   ROC-RB 0CCC0000   NM IGC0A05A   USE 02   EPA 07E858   ATR2 28   XL/MJ 08B6A8
   095A88   ATR1 B0   NCDE 095AC8   ROC-RB 0CCC0000   NM IGG019CC   USE 02   EPA 0A8228   ATR2 20   XL/MJ 095A78
   095B88   ATR1 B0   NCDE 095BE8   ROC-RB 00000000   NM IGG019AA   USE 02   EPA 0A8CB8   ATR2 20   XL/MJ 095BA8
   095B28   ATR1 B0   NCDE 095B58   ROC-RB 00000000   NM IGG019AQ   USE 02   EPA 0A89C8   ATR2 20   XL/MJ 095B18

                            LN          ADR                 LN            ADR         LN      ADR

XL
   08AC98   SZ 00000010   NO 00000001   0C06C000
   08B6A8   SZ 00000010   NO 00000001   007E858
   095A78   SZ 00000010   NO 00000001   00A8228
```

Fig. 12-9b.

```
MIN 08AA78    FGEL 0008AC90    PMIN 0008AA90    NMIN 00000000    NM 90   IEA
              NGEL 00000000    POEL 0008AA78    TCB  00088030    SVRB 0008A460

SAVE AREA TRACE

**GO    WAS ENTERED VIA LINK

SA  07F660  WD1 00000000  HSA 00000000  LSA 0006C028  RET 00007098  EPA 0106C010  R0  FF000018
            R1  0007F750  R2  8007F754  R3  0006C010  R4  0007F7F9  R5  FFFFFFFF  R6  0007F760
            R7  000000FF  R8  00000000  R9  0007F6A8  R10 0007F7F0  R11 0006C000  R12 4007F84C

**GO    WAS ENTERED VIA CALL        AT EP 01   010 01S      & B.  B J B4    J GB      18   G   0      B8H

SA  06C028  WD1 10000801  HSA 0007F660  LSA 0006C000  RET A006C090  EPA 0006C290  R0  FF000018
            R1  00000005  R2  00000000  R3  0C000010  R4  0007F660  R5  FFFFFFFF  R6  0007F760
            R7  000000FF  R8  00000005  R9  0C000000  R10 0007F7F0  R11 0006C000  R12 4007F84C

INTERRUPT AT 06C096

PROCEEDING BACK VIA REG 13

**GC    WAS ENTERED VIA CALL        AT EP 01   010 01S      & B.  B J B4    J GB      18   G   0      B8H

SA  06C028  WD1 10000801  HSA 0007F660  LSA 00000000  RET A006C090  EPA 0006C290  R0  FF000018
            R1  00000005  R2  00000000  R3  0C000010  R4  0007F660  R5  FFFFFFFF  R6  0007F760
            R7  000000FF  R8  00000005  R9  00000000  R10 0007FFF0  R11 0006C000  R12 4007F84C

**GC    WAS ENTERED VIA LINK

SA  07F660  WD1 00000000  HSA 00000000  LSA 0006C028  RET 00007098  EPA 0106C010  R0  FF000018
            R1  0007F750  R2  8007F754  R3  0006C010  R4  0007F7F9  R5  FFFFFFFF  R6  0007F760
            R7  000000FF  R8  00000000  R9  0007F6A8  R10 0007F7F0  R11 0006C000  R12 4007F84C
```

Fig. 12-9c.

REGS AT ENTRY TO ABEND

FLTR 0-6   0C000004087FC0   0F087F380007D460   0000000000000000   000001012E8E2C3

REGS 0-7   FF000018   0000000A   00000000   00000010   0000000A   FFFFFFF   0007F760   000000FF
REGS 8-15   00000005   00000000   0007F7F0   0006C000   4007F84C   0006C028   A006C090   0006C290

LOAD MODULE   **GO

06C000   5C5CC7D6   40404040   00000000   00000000   90ECD00C   184D41D0   F0185040   D0045OD0   *...GO   ....0... ....*
06C020   400847F0   F0600001   10000801   0007F660   00000000   A006C090   0006C290   FF000018   * ...00.........6........B... ..*
06C040   00000005   00000000   00000010   0007F660   FFFFFFFF   0007F760   000000FF   00000005   *.............6......6....7..... ..*
06C060   00000000   0007F7F0   0006C000   4007F84C   58F0D0C8   45EF0000   12311883   58300DCC   *.....70.... .8..0.H..........*
06C080   5C20D0D0   5890D0D4   58F0D0C8   45EFC000   1241504 9   D07E5A90   D0D01993   47D00060   *....70....M.0.H...............*
06C0A0   5890D0D4   1B775A79   D0D85A90   D0D01993   47D0D07E   5C60D0CC   1D681817   58F0D0C8   *....M...0......0...........0.H*
06C0C0   45EF0004   5890D0D4   58A9D0D8   1BA7181A   58F0D0C8   45EF0004   5A9OD0D0   19934700   *....M...Q.....0.H...........*

Fig. 12-9c. *(continued).*

3. The key to becoming a good debugger is *practice*. Go back over your old dumps and apply the techniques we have described to determine exactly what happened when the programs failed. Practice locating the machine language equivalents of assembly language statements in the memory dump.

REFERENCES

IBM System/360 Operating System Messages and Codes, Form GC28-6631, IBM Corp., White Plains, N.Y.

IBM System/360 Operating System: Programmer's Guide to Debugging, Form GC28-6670, IBM Corp., White Plains, N.Y.

OS FORTRAN IV Library: Mathematical and Service Subprograms, Form GC28-6818, IBM Corp., White Plains, N.Y.

13 SUBROUTINE LINKAGE

"Saving the registers is like hiding a treasure. Saving the save area address is like hiding the treasure map."—Ms. Marsha McGee, answer on exam, 1972

In this chapter we shall treat a rather specialized topic of major significance to all programmers. A *subroutine* is a program that is executed in response to a request by another program, the *calling* program. The problem we shall now consider is the construction of the *linkages*, or communications, between subroutines and calling programs. Our objective is to develop a consistent set of rules so that subroutines do the calculations we request upon the data we wish to use and return properly to the calling program. In the process, we shall find out exactly what the subroutine linkage macros INITIAL and EOJ do.

The entire system of subroutine linkage structure and implementation is a set of conventions that have been developed through the years, aided by special instructions in the IBM machines. While it is possible and sometimes necessary to disobey the conventions, the programmer who does so runs the risk of producing a program that is incompatible with the operating system and/or other programs with which his nonstandard program interacts. Programs written in FORTRAN and COBOL and many other languages follow these conventions, as do most programs supplied by IBM. After you have mastered this material, you will be able to write programs that interface properly with others written in other languages and with the IBM-supplied programs.

13.1. SUBROUTINES

Suppose that we are to write a program which requires the calculation of the square root of a number in several portions of the program. Calculation of the square root of a number is not difficult (see Exercise 8 in Chapter 5), and we could write the necessary sequence of instructions into our program wherever the square root is needed. But this practice can become tedious in a hurry and is certainly one more potential source of error, which we do not need.

Suppose that, instead, we could write a program to calculate square roots and have our original program use this single program every time it needs to calculate a square root. We would call the program that calculates the square roots a *subroutine* and a program which uses it the *calling* routine. We say we *call* the subroutine when we use it to calculate a square root. Through the use of a subroutine, we need write only once instructions to calculate square roots. Whenever we need a square root, we call the subroutine, which calculates it for us.

We usually call a subroutine through the use of a special branch instruction, the Branch And Link instruction, described in the next section. In other words, we simply transfer control to the subroutine. When the subroutine has completed its calculations, we expect it to *return* control to the calling program so that the latter can resume its calculations from where it left off. Figure 13-1 illustrates the use of a subroutine.

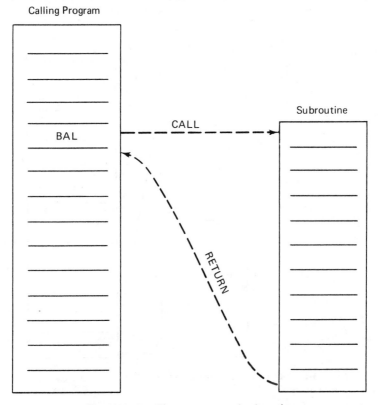

Fig. 13-1. A calling program and subroutine.

In calling a subroutine, we give it control of the computer. We also must tell it what to work on. In our square root example, we must send to the subroutine the number whose square root we want. The subroutine, when it returns control to the calling program, gives the result of its calculations to the calling program. Each of these numbers, the number sent to the subroutine and the result returned, is called an *argument* of the subroutine. An argument is a unit of information passed to or from a subroutine in the call and return process. An argument need not be a data number. For example, if we use a subroutine to sort a series of numbers into numerical order, the arguments might be a word containing the number of numbers to be sorted and another word containing the address of the first number in the list.

Now we shall get a bit more complicated. There is nothing to prevent a subroutine from calling another subroutine. To illustrate this, let us probe deeper into what happens when we use the macro RWD. The instructions

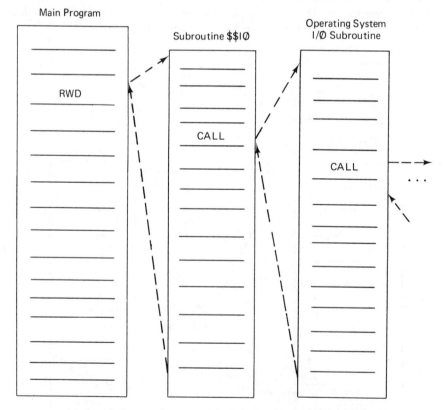

Fig. 13-2. The nested subroutine calls resulting from the use of RWD.

in RWD call a subroutine, $$IO, which asks an input/output subroutine in the operating system to provide the next input card image. This request for data is itself a subroutine call; $$IO calls a system subroutine that makes a request for data. (The system subroutine actually calls another subroutine.) When the system program is finished, the address of the new card image is presented to the calling routine, $$IO, the program RWD called. $$IO then converts the number on the card to binary (as in Chapter 15) and passes this number back to our main program. Figure 13-2 summarizes this series of subroutine calls.

There is a tremendous saving in effort in this process. You, the programmer, do not have to worry about the data conversions or communicating with the operating system. Instead, you make your request through a simple subroutine call. The authors of the subroutine $$IO had similar help in that they were not required to write the actual I/O programs and supporting routines; they simply used the GET macro described in Chapter 17, which calls a subroutine written by IBM systems programmers. In short, use of subroutines in this manner allows the programmer to concentrate on the problem at hand, leaving many of the bothersome details to subroutines.

Another advantage of the use of subroutines is that modifications to a complex program package are easier to make without errors. Returning to our square root example, suppose that we found a faster way to compute square roots or that we found that we really wanted the cube root instead. Without the use of a subroutine, we would have to go through our entire program, modifying it everywhere the square root calculation took place. There is no better way to put new bugs into a program. Had we written a square root subroutine, we would have to change only one program, and at least all the new bugs would be in one spot.

13.2. SUBROUTINE ENTRY AND EXIT

Let us first tackle the problem of how to get to and from a subroutine.

13.2.1. Subroutine and Calling Program Responsibilities

The first instruction to be executed in a subroutine is called the *entry point*; its address is the *entry point address*. The entry point is usually the first byte of the subroutine. The address of the instruction in the calling program that is executed after the subroutine has been executed is the *return address*. The return address is usually the address of the next instruction after the one that branched to the subroutine.

Throughout the remainder of this chapter, we shall be concerned with the responsibilities of programs with regard to subroutine linkages. We shall distinguish between the responsibilities of the calling program and the program it calls as a subroutine. One of the responsibilities of the calling routine is to determine the entry point address of the subroutine and branch to that address when the subroutine is to be executed. The subroutine must know how to get back to the proper instruction in the calling program; evidently, the calling program must supply the return address to the subroutine. Finally, the subroutine must transfer control back to the main program by branching to the return address.

The series of conventions we mentioned above includes the dedication of some of the registers for use in subroutine linkage. (This is why we made the rule that registers 13, 14, 15, 0, and 1 are unavailable for use in our programs.) To begin, *on entry to a subroutine, register 15 contains the address of the first byte of the subroutine, and register 14 contains the return address.* We can now be more specific in our statement of the calling program and subroutine responsibilities:

1. Calling program responsibilities:
   C5: Load address of first byte of subroutine into register 15.
   C6: Load return address into register 14.
   C7: Branch to entry point address.
2. Subroutine responsibilities:
   S5: Branch to address contained in register 14 (return to calling program).

We have not started numbering these requirements at C1 or S1 because we shall be adding to the beginnings of the lists as we proceed.

13.2.2. External Addresses

Let us consider each step in turn. At first glance, we could accomplish step C5 by an instruction such as

$$\text{LA} \qquad \text{15,SUB}$$

or

$$\text{L} \qquad \text{15,} = \text{A(SUB)}$$

if SUB is the name of the subroutine we want executed. But how can the calling program know the address of the subroutine? The use of an LA instruction or the use of an A-type address constant presupposes that the address of SUB is an *internal address* as if SUB were defined by a statement in the program in which the above instruction appears. By definition, however, the first byte of a subroutine cannot be part of the calling program. A symbol that represents the address of the first byte of a subroutine is an example of an *external* symbol; an external symbol is one that is defined outside the program that is using it.

The name of a subroutine automatically becomes an external symbol when we put the name in the name field of the START statement. Thus, to define a subroutine named **SORT** we write

SORT   START   0

If the symbol SORT has been defined as above, we refer to it through the use of a *V-type* address constant. For example, the statement

SORTADDR DS   V(SORT)

reserves a full word called SORTADDR whose contents are the address of the subroutine SORT. We can then load the subroutine address into register 15 via

L   15,SORTADDR

A shortcut which eliminates the need for the DC statement is the equivalent

L   15,=V(SORT)

in which the external address is given as a literal constant.

The assembler does not know the value of a V-type address, since this depends on where the subroutine is stored in the memory when the programs are executed. The assembler reserves a word for the address and marks it as an external reference. When the programs are loaded into memory for execution, the loader determines the address of the external symbol and stores that number in the reserved space.

13.2.3. BAL and BALR

Having loaded the subroutine address into register 15, we are now in a position to load the return address into register 14. Assuming that we wish to have the next instruction after the branch to the subroutine executed when the subroutine is finished, we could write

LA   14,RET
BR   15

RET   --------------------------

to satisfy steps C5 and C6. But the Branch And Link and Branch And Link Register instructions eliminate the need for the LA instruction in this sequence.

BAL	R1,D2(X2,B2)	Branch And Link	R1 ⟵ (PC); PC ⟵ D2 + (X2) + (B2)
BALR	R1,R2	Branch And Link Register	R1 ⟵ (PC); PC ⟵ (R2)

The execution of these instructions takes place in two steps. First, the machine moves the contents of the program counter into the (first) register operand. Noting the function of the program counter, this step actually puts the address of the next instruction into R1. Then, in the RX form, the second operand address is put into the program counter, which causes a branch to that address. In the RR form, the program counter receives the contents of the second register operand. The reason for the name Branch And Link is now apparent; this is a branch instruction which establishes an address link back to the point from which the branch occurred.

A fact that will prove useful to us later is that, if R2 is 0 in the BALR instruction, no branch occurs but (PC) → R1 anyhow.

$$\text{BALR} \qquad 3,0$$

loads the address of the next instruction into register 3, but does not branch.

Since we want the return address to be in register 14, we use it as the first register operand. Returning to our example, if we want to begin execution of SORT at the first byte, we write

$$\text{BALR} \qquad 14,15$$

to accomplish the branch. If we wish to have SORT executed starting at the fortieth byte, we use

$$\text{BAL} \qquad 14,40(15)$$

Having properly loaded registers 14 and 15 and branched to the sub-routine, we can turn our attention to the return to the calling program from the subroutine. Since the address to which to return is in register 14, the last instruction executed in the subroutine is simply

$$\text{BR} \qquad 14$$

To summarize, suppose that we wish to execute a subroutine called PCALC starting at its hundredth byte. The statements

$$\text{L} \qquad 15,=\text{V(PCALC)}$$
$$\text{BAL} \qquad 14,100(15)$$

establish the proper links and get us to the subroutine. The last instruction of PCALC should be

$$\text{BR} \qquad 14$$

13.3. SAVING THE REGISTERS

Now that we have established the conventions for entering and returning from subroutines, let us look into some further subroutine linkage neces-sities. Most programs make rather heavy use of the registers for loop control, address calculations, and other purposes. If a program in an intermediate stage of its execution calls a subroutine, that subroutine is also likely to make some use of the registers. If we do not make some provision for preserving the register contents during the execution of the subroutine, then when control is returned from the subroutine the calling program can no longer assume that the registers have the same contents as when the subroutine was called. In effect, the subroutine destroys the results of some of the calculations done by calling the routine.

To avoid this problem, we *save* the register contents upon entering the subroutine. The natural way to do this is to store them in the memory somewhere the subroutine will not erase them. Just before the subroutine returns control to the calling program, the subroutine *restores*, or *unsaves*, the original register contents by loading them from the places in the memory at which they were originally stored.

We must add two new responsibilities to our list for subroutines. The register save must be done first. The unsave should be done immediately before the return to the calling program. Thus, our subroutine responsibility list now includes the following steps:

S1: Save the registers.
S3: Restore the registers.
S4: Branch to address contained in register 14 (return to calling program).

Before going into the details of steps S1 and S3, we shall consider two new helpful instructions.

13.3.1. Load Multiple and STore Multiple

The Load Multiple and STore Multiple instructions make possible the loading/storing of the contents of several registers from/into the memory in a single instruction. These are RS instructions which require that the memory address be that of a full word.

| LM | R1,R3,D2(B2) | Load Multiple | Load registers R1 through R3 from consecutive full words starting at D2 + (B2) |
| STM | R1,R3,D2(B2) | STore Multiple | Store (R1) through (R3) into consecutive full words starting at D2 + (B2) |

As the description above states, they operate upon consecutive registers, starting with R1 and ending with R3. For example, the instruction

STM   2,5,STOR

stores (2) at STOR, (3) at STOR + 4, (4) at STOR + 8, and the contents of register 5 at STOR + 12. We might visualize this process as shown in Fig. 13-3. If, at a later point in the program, we wish to recover the register

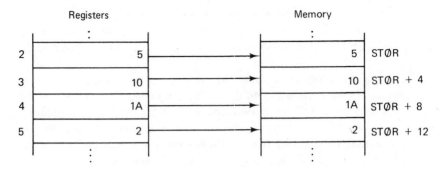

Fig. 13-3. Illustrating the effect of the STM instruction.

contents as they were at the time of execution of the STM instruction, we write

LM   2,5,STOR

This reloads the register contents from the same address at which they were previously stored, as is shown in Fig. 13-4.

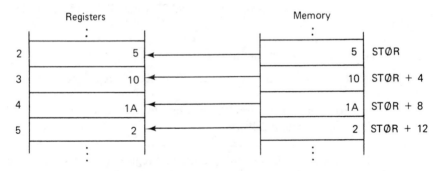

Fig. 13-4. Restoring register contents using LM.

If R1 is greater than R3, the register count goes from R1 to 15 and then "wraps around" from 0 up to R3.

LM   14,3,SA

loads registers 14 from SA, 15 from SA + 4, 0 from SA + 8, 1 from SA + 12, 2 from SA + 16, and 3 from SA + 20. And finally, if R1 = R3, then the only effective register operand is R1. This means that

STM   5,5,32(6)

has the same effect as

ST   5,32(6)

13.3.2. The Save Area

To save the register contents upon entry to a subroutine we use the STM instruction to store the register contents into consecutive full words in a *register save area*. By convention the register save area is 18 full words long, and, *on entry to a subroutine, register 13 contains the address of the save area.*

Convention dictates that we save the register contents starting at the *fourth* word of the save area. And we store the register contents in the order 14, 15, 0, 1, . . . , 11, 12. We shall soon see that register 13 requires special handling in the register save process, and so it is not stored with the rest of the registers.

We want to store the contents of registers 14 through 12 starting at the fourth word of an area whose address is in register 13. The instruction

$$\text{STM} \qquad 14,12,12(13)$$

does this; see Fig. 13-5. To unsave the registers at the end of the subroutine,

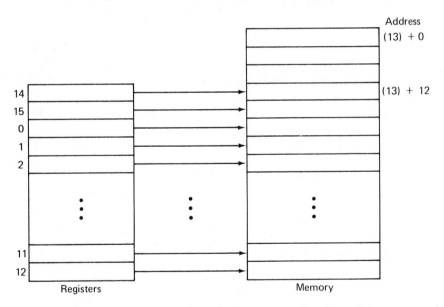

Fig. 13-5. Saving the registers in the save area. Its address is in register 13.

we load the register contents from where we stored them using

$$\text{LM} \qquad 14,12,12(13)$$

This must be done immediately before returning to the calling program.

To summarize our progress toward establishing the conventions with regard to subroutine responsibilities, we have the following basic subroutine structure for a subroutine named **SUBR**:

```
SUBR          START   0
              STM     14,12,12(13)    SAVE REGISTERS
              .
              .
              .
              Calculations
              .
              .
              .
              LM      14,12,12(13)    RESTORE REGISTERS
              BR      14              RETURN
              .
              .
              .
              Data and constants
              .
              .
              .
              END
```

A standard facility offered by the operating system is a macro library containing macros of possible utility to all programmers. Included in this library are the macros SAVE and RETURN. To save the registers we write

```
              SAVE    (14,12)
```

which inserts the instruction

```
              STM     14,12,12(13)
```

in the program. To restore the registers and return to the calling program, we write

```
              RETURN  (14,12)
```

This produces the instructions

```
              LM      14,12,12(13)
              BR      14
```

Whether to use these macros or to write the equivalent instructions is simply a matter of taste.

13.4. THE BASE REGISTER

In Chapter 9 we saw that memory addresses consist of a base register-displacement pair; the effective address is the sum of the displacement and the contents of a register. When we use symbolic names for memory addresses, the assembler automatically supplies a base register and calculates the symbol's displacement relative to the base position of the program. The assembler assumes that the base address will be in the base register when addresses corresponding to symbolic names are used.

How does the assembler know which register to use as a base register and where the base position is? There is no magic involved: Every program that uses symbolic names for addresses must supply this information to the assembler. We shall call this process *establishing a base register* and include it as step S2 of the subroutine responsibilities.

We tell the assembler which register to use for a base register and where the base position is through the use of the USING pseudooperation. In its simplest form, USING is written

USING   address,register

in which *address* is a relocatable symbol, such as a symbolic name defined in the program, and *register* is a general-purpose register other than register 0. The USING pseudooperation tells the assembler, "From this point on in the program, until you are told to do otherwise, use the location given in the first operand as the base position and the register designated in the second operand as the base register."

We are free to use any register, except 0, as the base register. Most programmers prefer register 12 for this purpose. For example,

USING   BASEPOS,12

means that BASEPOS, a symbol defined in the program, is the base position and that register 12 is the base register. BASEPOS will have 0 displacement, and the displacements of all symbols after BASEPOS will be calculated relative to BASEPOS. In these addresses, register 12 will be used as the base register. To load the address of the base position into the base register, we could try (there is something wrong here!)

LA   12,BASEPOS

Suppose that we tried this at the beginning of the program. We might have something like this:

```
SUBR      START  0
          STM    14,12,12(13)
          USING  BASEPOS,3
          LA     12,BASEPOS
BASEPOS
          .
          .
          .
```

But wait! The LA instruction requires the address of the symbol BASEPOS. This relocatable address consists of a base register and a displacement.

What is the assembler to use for the base position and base register? We cannot use symbolic names until we have told the assembler how to calculate their address. In the above we are in the awkward position of trying to use a symbolic name in order to be able to use symbolic names.

The standard way out of this predicament is to use the following instruction pair:

```
BALR    12,0
USING   *,12
```

Recall that the symbol * as part of an operand means the current value of the location counter. Since the USING statement is a pseudooperation, it generates no machine language as such; the * in the USING statement is equivalent to the address of the instruction after the USING statement. Remember that the BALR instruction loads the address of the next instruction into the first register operand and that no branch occurs if the second operand is register 0. Thus, the BALR instruction loads the address of the next instruction into register 12. The USING statement says that the next instruction is the base position and that register 12 will be the base register. In this way, we succeed in establishing a base register without using a symbolic name in an instruction before we have established a base register.

The order of the statements BALR-USING is important. Before reading further, spend a moment to see if you can figure out what happens if the USING statement comes before the BALR instruction. If we write (incorrectly)

```
USING   *,12
BALR    12,0
```

the USING statement says to use the next instruction, the BALR, as the base position and register 12 as the base register. The BALR instruction loads the address of the instruction after it into register 12. But this address is 2 higher than the base address as defined by the USING statement. All effective addresses will be 2 higher than expected, and we can expect that the program will not run very well.

We have now considered all the fundamental subroutine responsibilities, unless the subroutine also happens to be a calling routine, as we shall see in the next section. Figure 13-6 illustrates the structure of a subroutine including the establishment of a base register.

In some programs it is necessary or desirable to have more than one base register. The maximum value a displacement can have is 4095. If a program including its data and constant storage areas is longer than this, then there may be symbols toward the end of the program that cannot be addressed using a base register defined near the beginning of the program.

The general form of the USING pseudooperation is

```
USING   address, R1,R2,R3,...
```

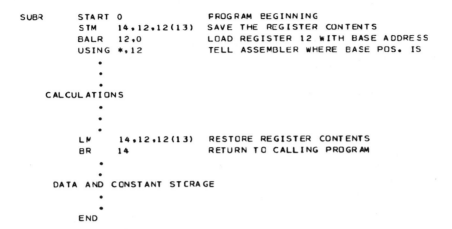

```
SUBR      START  0               PROGRAM BEGINNING
          STM    14,12,12(13)    SAVE THE REGISTER CONTENTS
          BALR   12,0            LOAD REGISTER 12 WITH BASE ADDRESS
          USING  *,12            TELL ASSEMBLER WHERE BASE POS. IS
                 •
                 •
                 •
   CALCULATIONS
                 •
                 •
                 •
          LM     14,12,12(13)    RESTORE REGISTER CONTENTS
          BR     14              RETURN TO CALLING PROGRAM
                 •
                 •
   DATA AND CONSTANT STORAGE
                 •
                 •
          END
```

Fig. 13-6. Outline of subroutine structure.

where R1, R2, R3, . . . is a list of registers, each of which will be used as a base register. For example, we might write

$$\text{USING   HERE,5,6,7}$$

The first register in the list will be the base register for displacements relative to the given address. The remaining registers will be the base registers for base positions at successive intervals of 4096 from the given address. In the example, register 5 will be the base register used when the symbols referred to have displacements less than 4096 relative to HERE. Register 6 will be used when the symbols have displacements less than 4096 relative to the address of HERE + 4096, and the base position corresponding to register 7 will be HERE + 8192.

The use of more than one base register means that the assembler might have to choose between one of several base registers and corresponding base positions in computing an address. The assembler always uses the base register that yields the smallest displacement when faced with such a choice.

Just as is the case when we are using a single base register, we must load the base addresses into the base registers before using symbols that use the registers as base registers. Suppose in our example that we already have one base register established, perhaps via

$$\text{BALR   12,0}$$
$$\text{USING   *,12}$$

so that we can use relocatable symbols that have displacements less than 4086 relative to * for the USING statement above. Registers 5, 6, and 7 can then be loaded using the statement

$$\text{LM   5,7,HEREADDR}$$

with HEREADDR defined via

HEREADDR   DC   A(HERE,HERE+4096,HERE+8192)

In this DC statement, we have illustrated the use of a multiple address constant. It has the same effect as the three statements

HEREADDR   DC   A(HERE)
           DC   A(HERE+4096)
           DC   A(HERE+8192)

There are sneakier (some would say more sophisticated) ways of establishing multiple base registers. We prefer the method given because it is the easiest to write and read and because it always works, provided that the equivalent of HEREADDR is addressable (displacement less than 4096 relative to the base position established previously). Figure 13-7 illustrates the technique.

```
SUBR        START  0
            STM    14,12,12(13)     SAVE REGISTER CONTENTS
            BALR   12,0
            USING  *,12             ESTABLISH BASE REGISTER
            USING  HERE,5,6,7       5,6, AND 7 ARE BASE REGS FOR LATER IN PROG.
            LM     5,7,HEREADDR     LOAD THEM WITH BASE ADDRESSES
              .
              .
              .
        CALCULATIONS
              .
              .
            LM     14,12,12(13)     RESTORE REGISTER CONTENTS
            BR     14               RETURN TO CALLING PROGRAM
HEREADDR    DC     A(HERE,HERE+4096,,HERE+8192)    BASE ADDRESSES FOR 5,6,7
              .
              .
HERE        DS     .  .  .  .
              .
              .
        LARGE DATA AND CONSTANT STORAGE AREA
              .
              .
            END
```

Fig. 13-7. Establishing multiple base registers.

13.5. THE CALLING PROGRAM

We have developed the following list of subroutine responsibilities:

S1: Save the registers.
S2: Establish base register.
S3: Restore the registers.
S4: Branch to address contained in register 14 (return to calling program).

If the subroutine also calls a subroutine, the subroutine also has the responsibilities of a calling program. The responsibility,

S5: Calling program responsibilities if the subroutine is also a calling program,

must be added to the list.

Before launching into calling routine responsibilities in more detail, we must consider the question of when a program has subroutine responsibilities. It is clear that if the program is actually a subroutine, it has the responsibilities of a subroutine. But, if the program is run under the Operating System, OS, or one of its VS descendants, it is a subroutine even if it is what we would consider to be the main program, or the first program executed, in our set of programs and subroutines. In other words, *all programs run in OS or OS/VS systems are subroutines* and thus have all the subroutine responsibilities.

The Disk Operating System, DOS, and its VS descendants, treat the main program differently from those called by the main program. We shall investigate the differences in Section 13.6.

Returning to the list of calling program responsibilities, we can now write the following list:

C1: Subroutine responsibilities.
C4: Load address of first byte of subroutine into register 15.
C5: Load return address into register 14.
C6: Branch to entry point address.

We still have some blanks to fill in this list. When we were discussing saving the registers, we said that, on entry to a subroutine register 13 contains the address of an 18-word register save area. Have you been wondering where this save area is and how its address got into register 13? The answer is that it is the calling program's responsibility to reserve space for a save area and to put its address into register 13 before the program calls subroutines.

The subroutine uses the save area whose address is in register 13 to save the registers. The register contents are stored in the save area section of the main program. If the subroutine calls another subroutine in turn, the called subroutine saves the register contents in the save area supplied by the calling subroutine. This process can be continued indefinitely, each lower-level program storing the register contents in a save area supplied by the program that called it.

Figure 13-8 illustrates the chain of save areas that results from this technique. The program MAIN saves the registers in a special area provided by the operating system. MAIN calls a subroutine SUB1, which saves the

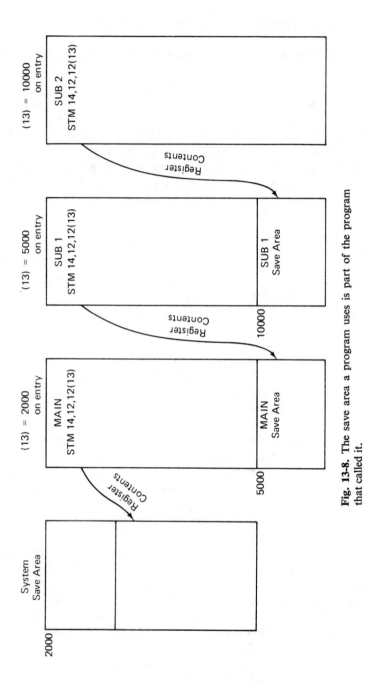

Fig. 13-8. The save area a program uses is part of the program that called it.

292

registers in an area in the main program. SUB1 calls SUB2, which saves the registers in an area in SUB1.

The save area can be established by a statement such as

SAVEAREA DS   18F

and its address can be loaded into register 13 via

LA   13,SAVEAREA

once we have established a base register. We might try the following struc-ture for the calling program (*warning*: There is something wrong here!):

```
CALLER      START   0
            STM     14,12,12(13)
            BALR    12,0
            USING   *,12
            LA      13,SAVEAREA
              .
              .
              .

   subroutine calls and calculations
              .
              .
              .

            LM      14,12,12(13)
            BR      14
SAVEAREA    DS      18F
              .
              .
              .

   other data and constants
            END
```

Let us see how this might work. The STM instruction saves registers 14 through 12 in a save area supplied by the program that called this one. The next two instructions establish a base register, after which we load the save area address into register 13. After the calculations in the program we unsave the registers and return to the calling program. But wait! From where are the registers contents recovered before the return? The LA instruction puts the address of this program's save area in register 13. The LM instruction, assuming that nothing has changed (13) in the meantime, recovers the register contents from SAVEAREA. But this is *not* where the STM instruction put them, which is at a now-unknown address supplied by the calling program.

The problem is that we did not save the contents of register 13 prior to the LA instruction. Once the LA instruction is executed, we have no way to determine where the save area is from which we are to restore the register contents. We have thrown away the treasure map.

Why not save register 13 along with all the other registers, using something like

STM   13,12,8(13)

A moment's reflection shows that this does not help at all, since the LA instruction still wipes out the connection between the program and the save area given to it by the calling program.

What we must do is save (13) somewhere where we can get to it. The convention is to store (13) in the second word of the save area defined by the program. This must be done before changing register 13's contents. Then, before unsaving the registers with the LM instruction, we simply load 13 from where we put its original contents.

The net effect is that each program's save area contains a pointer in its second word. This pointer points to the save area in the calling program. When subroutine calls are nested, the save areas form a linked list, in which each save area points to the save area of the next higher program. A subroutine call adds a save area to the list; return from a subroutine removes a save area from the list.

This fact is often useful in debugging programs in which there are several subroutine calls, some of which are nested. Using the save area pointers we can determine where the calling program's save area is. We can then look into the save area to find out what the register contents were when the subroutine was called. In particular, the old contents of register 14 show us from where in the calling program the subroutine was called. We can also look in word 2 of the calling program's save area to find the address of the save area in the program that called the subroutine and continue this process all the way back to the main program if necessary.

Figure 13-9 shows the structure of a calling program CALLER which calls subroutine SUBR. We have included the necessary statements to provide a save area and preserve (13). Our almost-completed list of calling program responsibilities now reads

C:1 Subroutine responsibilities if not the main program in a DOS system.
C2: Save (13).
C3: Reserve 18-word save area and load its address into register 13.
C4:
C5: Load address of first byte of subroutine into register 15.
C6: Load return address into register 14.
C7: Branch to entry point address.

We have found out how to do everything in subroutine linkage except get the answers out. In the next section we shall show how to do this.

```
CALLER    START  0
          STM    14,12,12(13)     SAVE REGISTER CONTENTS
          BALR   12,0             LCAD BASE REGISTER
          USING  *,12             TELL ASSEMBLER
          ST     13,SAVEAREA+4    SAVE (13)
          LA     13,SAVEAREA      R13 NOW POINTS TO SAVE AREA SUBR WILL USE
                 •
                 •
                 •
          L      15,=V(SUBR)      LOAD SUBROUTINE ADDR. INTC R15
          BALR   14,15            LINK TC SUBROUTINE
                 •
                 •
                 •
          L      13,SAVEAREA+4    RECCVER ADDR. OF SAVE AREA THIS PROGRAM USED
          LM     14,12,12(13)     RESTORE REGISTER CONTENTS
          BR     14               RETJRN TO CALLING PROGRAM
                 •
                 •
                 •
SAVEAREA  DS     18F              DEFINES THE SAVE AREA
                 •
                 •
                 •
          END
```

Fig. 13-9. Calling program structure.

13.6. ARGUMENTS AND DOS CONVENTIONS

Our program responsibilities lists are almost complete. All we have left to do is to find out how to pass the arguments back and forth between the calling program and the subroutine.

13.6.1. Subroutine Arguments

We have defined the arguments of a subroutine as that information passed to a subroutine when it is called and sent back from the subroutine upon return from it. Those arguments we send *to* the subroutine we shall call *input* arguments, while those that are returned *from* the subroutine are *output* arguments.

Suppose, for example, that we have a subroutine ISQRT that calculates square roots of integers. When we call the subroutine, the input argument is a full word containing the number whose square root we desire, while the output argument is the square root of this number to the nearest integer. In such cases, where we have a single-integer input argument and a single-integer output argument, we pass the input argument to the subroutine in register 0. The output argument is returned in register 1.

Suppose that in the calling program we have an integer stored in a full word N and a full word SQN where we want to store the square root of N. Provided that the calling program has satisfied its other responsibilities, we write the following:

L	0,N	INPUT ARGUMENT
		IN REGISTER 0
L	15,=V(ISQRT)	LOAD SUBROUTINE
		ADDRESS
BALR	14,15	LINK TO ISQRT
ST	1,SQN	STORE ANSWER

In the case of single arguments, the subroutine must be careful when unsaving the registers. Use of the usual

> LM   14,12,12(13)

wipes out the answer the subroutine has calculated and put into register 1. What we must do is restore all the register contents except that of register 1, using

> LM   14,0,12(13)
> LM   2,12,24(13)

The same procedure applies when linking to a subroutine whose arguments are single-precision floating-point numbers. We send the input argument to the subroutine in floating-point register 0 and receive the result in floating-point register 1.

A more general situation is that in which we have several input and/or output arguments. If we had enough registers, we could load them with all the input arguments and call the subroutine, which returns the results in registers. But this idea suffers from two defects. It is not always possible to put the arguments into registers, as, for example, when one of the arguments is a list of 100 full words to be sorted or an 80-byte card image. And the use of so many registers to hold arguments makes the writing of the subroutines difficult.

Using the established conventions, it is possible to deal with an arbitrary number of arguments of any length (provided they all fit in the machine) using only one register. The convention is that, with the exception of the single-input, single-output case discussed above, *on entry to a subroutine, register 1 contains the address of a list of the addresses of the subroutine's arguments.*

As an example, suppose that we have a series of full words stored at NUMS. The number of words in this list is stored at N. We wish to call a subroutine SORT which will sort the list of numbers, storing the sorted list at SORTED, and store the largest number in the list at MAX. We have four arguments: N, NUMBS, SORTED, and MAX. The convention says in effect that we must establish a list of the addresses of these arguments and put the address of the list in register 1 before calling the subroutine. To do the former, we could insert the following into the data and constant storage area of the calling program,

```
ADDRLIST    DC        A(N)
            DC        A(NUMS)
            DC        A(SORTED)
            DC        A(MAX)
```

or the equivalent

```
ADDRLIST   DC         A(N,NUMS,SORTED,MAX)
```

When we call the subroutine, we put the address of this list in register 1
before linking to the subroutine:

```
           LA        1,ADDRLIST    ADDR  OF
                                   ARGUMENT LIST IN
                                   REG. 1
           L         15,=V(SORT)
           BALR      14,15
```

Figure 13-10 illustrates the structure of the address table. The DC statements
defining the address list are unnecessary if we write

```
           LA        1,=A(N,NUMS,SORTED,MAX)
           L         15,=V(SORT)
           BALR      14,15
```

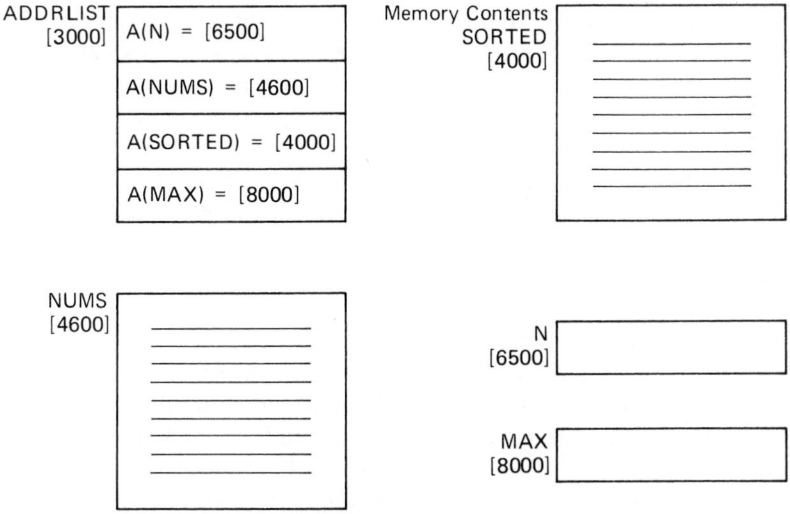

ADDRLIST [3000]

| A(N) = [6500] |
| A(NUMS) = [4600] |
| A(SORTED) = [4000] |
| A(MAX) = [8000] |

Memory Contents
SORTED [4000]

NUMS [4600]

N [6500]

MAX [8000]

Fig. 13-10. On entry to a subroutine, register 1 contains the address
of a table of addresses of the subroutine arguments. The numbers
in square brackets are the memory addresses at which the corresponding data are stored. On entry to SØRT, (1) = 3000.

Here the use of the literal address constant causes the assembler to reserve the space necessary for the address list. At execution time, the LA instruction places the address of that area into register 1, as required.

If the subroutine is working properly, on return from the subroutine, the first N words of the area SORTED will contain the sorted list of numbers and MAX will contain the largest of the numbers.

Let us now look into what the subroutine must do in order to locate the arguments. We first note that it is impossible to write the subroutine without knowing the form of the arguments or the order in which their addresses are supplied. One of the hardiest species of bugs results from improper communication of arguments between programs. This problem is especially severe in situations where a group of people is working on a large programming project. When a member of such a group writes a subroutine, he must know and make sure the others know how the arguments for his subroutine will be supplied.

The subroutine has access to the addresses of the arguments through the address supplied in register 1. In our example SORT subroutine, the address of NUMS, the list of numbers to be sorted, is in the second word of the list of addresses, the address of which is in register 1. Suppose that we want to put the address of NUMS into register 3. The instruction

    L   3,4(1)

loads the contents of the second word of the area addressed by register 1 into register 3. The calling routine puts the address of NUMS into this word, and so we have accomplished our task. If the addresses are as shown in Fig. 13-10, the instruction above yields (3) = 4600. Similarly, the instruction

    L   8,12(1)

puts the address of MAX (8000 in Fig. 13-10) into register 8. Assuming that we have found the largest of the list of numbers and put this number into register 5, the instruction

    ST   5,0(8)

stores this number at MAX.

One final point about subroutine arguments is the case when the number of arguments is itself variable. We might think of a subroutine MAX that returns the maximum of a small number of numbers. Sometimes we might want to find the largest of two numbers, and other times, the largest of five. The procedure here is simple; we simply supply the *number* of arguments as an additional argument. The address of a location that contains the number of arguments is first in the subroutine argument address list, followed by the addresses of the actual arguments.

13.6.2. DOS Subroutine Linkage

In DOS systems, the conventions we have discussed above are not followed as rigorously as in OS and VS systems, although most programmers working in DOS systems try to adhere to the conventions as closely as possible. When you encounter a DOS system, you should make all reasonable attempts to follow the conventions because a fixed set of rules to follow helps to avoid errors and because your programs will be compatible with programs written for OS systems, at least with regard to subroutine linkages.

There is one major difference between the two types of operating systems in subroutine treatment. As we mentioned above, the OS and VS operating systems treat what we would consider to be our main program as just another subroutine. Therefore, in these systems our main program follows the normal conventions regarding saving and restoring registers and returning control to the operating system via a BR 14 instruction.

In DOS systems, the main program is treated differently. In particular the operating system does not expect the main program to preserve the register contents. The STM instruction or SAVE macro at the beginning and the LM instruction or RETURN macro at the end of the main program are unneeded, and, in fact, will not work in some DOS systems. Figure 13-11 shows the structure of a main program for a DOS system.

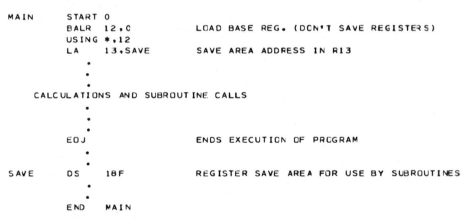

```
MAIN        START  0
            BALR   12,0            LOAD BASE REG. (DON'T SAVE REGISTERS)
            USING  *,12
            LA     13,SAVE         SAVE AREA ADDRESS IN R13
              .
              .
              .
       CALCULATIONS AND SUBROUTINE CALLS
              .
              .
              .
            EOJ                    ENDS EXECUTION OF PROGRAM
              .
              .
SAVE        DS     18F             REGISTER SAVE AREA FOR USE BY SUBROUTINES
              .
              .
            END    MAIN
```

Fig. 13-11. Structure of a main program for a DOS system. The registers are *not* saved and restored by the main program. Control is returned to the operating system with the EOJ macro instruction.

In DOS, we stop execution of the main program through the use of the EOJ macro instruction. EOJ is a special macro prepared for use with this text for those who will be using OS systems. In DOS systems, EOJ is a real macro to be found in system macro libraries.

13.6.3. Wrap-up

We have considered in detail the problems involved in subroutine linkage and their solutions through a series of well-established conventions. Table 13-1 summarizes our findings for future reference. Table 13-2 lists the conventional register uses.

We can now dispense with the use of INITIAL and, with the exception of DOS main programs, EOJ. Take one of your old programs and run it without the PRINT NOGEN card. The statements printed with a + sign immediately after the statement number in the STMT column are the instructions in the macros. Notice that all INITIAL and EOJ do is handle subroutine linkage responsibilities, while RWD, WWD, PLN, and RCD are simply subroutine calls.

Table 13-1 SUBROUTINE AND CALLING PROGRAM RESPONSIBILITIES*

Responsibilities	Conventional Action
Subroutine:	
S1: Save register contents (if not DOS main program)	STM 14,12,12(13)
S2: Establish base register	BALR 12,0 USING *,12
S3: Restore the registers before return (if not DOS main program)	LM 14,12,12(13)
S4: Branch to address in register 14 (EOJ macro if DOS main program)	BR 14
S5: Calling program responsibilities if the subroutine is also a calling program	
Calling program:	
C1: Subroutine responsibilities	
C2: Save (13)	ST 13,SAVEAREA+4
C3: Reserve 18-word save area and load its address into register 13	SAVEAREA DS 18F (in data and constant storage area) LA 13,SAVEAREA
C4: Load address of list of argument addresses into register 1	LA 1,=A(argument list)
C5: Load address of first byte of subroutine into register 15	L 15,=V(SUBR)
C6: Load return address into register 14	BALR 14,15 or BAL 14,n(15) where n = displacement of entry point
C7: Branch to entry point address	

*The examples refer to a subroutine called SUBR.

Table 13-2 REGISTERS 13–15, 0, AND 1 ARE USED FOR SUBROUTINE LINKAGE

Register	Contents
13	Register save area address
14	Return address
15	Subroutine address
0	Integer input argument
1	Pointer to address list or integer output argument

Figure 13-12 shows the statements in the INITIAL macro. Notice that INITIAL establishes register 13 as both the base register and the save area pointer.

```
        INITIAL
        USING  *,15
        STM    14,12,12(13)
        LR     4,13
        LA     13,$AREA
        ST     4,4(,13)
        ST     13,8(,4)
        B      $AREA+72
        USING  $AREA,13
$AREA   DS     18F
```

Fig. 13-12. The INITIAL macro.

```
//      JOB        MULTPRG
//      OPTION  LIST,NODECK,ERRS,DUMP
//      EXEC    ASSEMBLY
          •
          •
          •
        FIRST ASSEMBLY LANGUAGE PROGRAM
          •
          •
          •
/*
//      EXEC ASSEMBLY
          •
          •
          •
        SECOND ASSEMBLY LANGUAGE PROGRAM
          •
          •
          •
/*
//      EXEC    LNKEDT
//      EXEC
          •
          •
          •
        CARD INPUT DATA
          •
          •
          •
/*
/&
```

Fig. 13-13. DØS job control language to assemble two programs, link them together, and execute them.

13.7. JOB CONTROL LANGUAGE FOR MULTIPLE ASSEMBLIES

When we need to assemble a main program and one or more subroutines, we simply execute the assembler once for each separate program. The operating system collects the separate object modules and links them together in the link-edit job step.

Figure 13-13 shows the DOS JCL to assemble, link-edit, and execute two

```
//THREEPRG JOB (100,1105),'50010 RUDD',MSGLEVEL=1,CLASS=C
//ASMBLY1 EXEC ASMFC    ASSEMBLE FIRST PROGRAM
//ASM.SYSIN DD *
PROG1     START   0     BEGINNING OF FIRST PROGRAM
                  .
                  .
                  .
          FIRST PROGRAM
                  .
                  .
                  .
                 END
/*
//ASMBLY2 EXEC ASMFC    ASSEMBLE SECOND PROGRAM
//ASM.SYSIN DD *
PROG2     START   0     BEGINNING OF SECOND PROGRAM
                  .
                  .
                  .
          SECOND PROGRAM
                  .
                  .
                  .
                 END
/*
//ASMBLY3 EXEC ASMFCLG  ASSEMBLE,LINK-EDIT,EXECUTE
//ASM.SYSIN DD *
PROG3     START   0     BEGINNING OF THIRD PROGRAM
                  .
                  .
                  .
          THIRD PROGRAM
                  .
                  .
                  .
                 END     PROG2 EXECUTE STARTING AT PROG2
/*
//GO.SYSPRINT DD SYSOUT=A
//GO.SYSIN DD *
                  .
                  .
          CARD INPUT DATA
                  .
                  .
/*
//
```

Fig. 13-14. ØS job control language to assemble three programs, link them together, and execute the resulting load module.

assembly language programs, while Fig. 13-14 illustrates the assembly and execution of three programs using OS Job Control Language.

CHAPTER SUMMARY

Tables 13-1 and 13-2 show the subroutine linkage and register conventions in common use. Table 13-3 shows the instructions introduced in this chapter.

Table 13-3 SUBROUTINE LINKAGE INSTRUCTIONS

BAL	R1,D2(X2,B2)	Branch And Link	R1 → (PC); PC ← D2 + (X2) + (B2)
BALR	R1,R2	Branch And Link Register	R1 ← (PC); PC → (R2)
LM	R1,R3,D2(B2)	Load Multiple	Load registers R1 through R3 from consecutive full words starting at D2 + (B2)
STM	R1,R3,D2(B2)	STore Multiple	Store (R1) through (R3) into consecutive full words starting at D2 + (B2)

EXERCISES

1. Rewrite your square root program for Exercise 8 in Chapter 5 as a subroutine called ISQRT. Write a main program to read three integers A, B, and C and find the integer parts of the solution of the quadratic equation

$$Ax^2 + Bx + C = 0$$

using your ISQRT routine to calculate the square roots. Watch out for complex roots.

2. The inventory problem described in Exercises 3 through 7 in Chapter 10 is an example of the kind of problem that is most easily done by splitting it up into smaller pieces and writing a subroutine to carry out the calculations required of each piece. Do this problem, writing a main program which contains all the data storage areas and calls subroutines each of which does one of the following:

Sort the records into a linked list.
Carry out the updates.
Delete records.
Add records.
Check for necessary reorders.
Output the entire list in order.

If time does not permit the programming, write at least the main program and one subroutine.

REFERENCES

IBM System/360 Disk and Tape Operating System Assembler Language, Form GC24-3414, IBM Corp., White Plains, N.Y.

IBM System/360 Operating System Assembler F Programmer's Guide, Form GC26-3756, IBM Corp., White Plains, N.Y.

IBM System/360 Operating System Assembler Language, Form GC28-6514, IBM Corp., White Plains, N.Y.

IBM System/360 Principles of Operation, Form GA22-6821, IBM Corp., White Plains, N.Y.

IBM System/370 Principles of Operation, Form GA22-7000, IBM Corp., White Plains, N.Y.

IBM OS/VS—DOS/VS Assembler Language, Order No. GC33-4010, IBM, Corp., White Plains, N.Y.

14 BIT MANIPULATION

The IBM 360 and 370 computers are byte-oriented machines, in the sense that the smallest addressable unit is the byte. While in some machines it is possible to address individual bits, these systems are the exception rather than the rule.

In this chapter we shall find that it is possible to manipulate individual bits within byte or larger units. The principle instructions for this purpose are those that carry out the logical operations AND, OR, and exclusive OR. After a review of symbolic logic, in which these operations play a fundamental role, we shall investigate the machine instructions which carry out these operations.

The *shift* instructions move the contents of registers to the left or to the right. This permits the "packing" of data into compact forms for storage and analysis. The shift instructions also offer an efficient means for carrying out some arithmetic operations.

14.1. LOGIC AND COMPUTING

Logic is basically the study of methods of distinguishing between good and bad arguments or reasoning. Symbolic logic considers the relationships between variables which can have one of two values, True and False. The statements and proofs of symbolic logic are often based upon a computational system called Boolean algebra, which is a set of operations and relations and the rules for using them in determining the validity of a proposition in logic. In this section we shall review the logical operators, those of Boolean algebra, and some additional operators that are helpful in computing. The role of logic in computing will then be examined.

14.1.1. The Operations of Symbolic Logic

For our purposes, it is sufficient to consider four logical operators. These are the AND, inclusive OR, eXclusive OR (XOR), and NOT (complement) operations. The first three are binary operators in the sense that they are applied to two truth variables and they have a single truth value as a result. The NOT function is a unary operator, behaving much like the unary minus sign in arithmetic.

The AND Operator.   In English, the word *and* is used to connect two statements together into a single sentence. In logic, the AND operator works in much the same way, but we must be more rigorous in our interpretation of whether or not the resulting compound sentence is true. Suppose that a sentence has the form

[statement 1] and [statement 2]

and that statements 1 and 2 might both be true or that either or both of the statements might be false. Let us use the symbol A to represent the truth value (true or false) for statement 1 and let B have the same meaning for statement 2. The resulting "sentence" is then written

A AND B

We are interested in the truth value of this statement, given values of A and B. Logic follows common English usage for the word *and*. If statements 1 and 2 are both true, then the compound sentence

[statement1] and [statement 2]

is true. If either or both of the statements is false, the compound sentence is false.

Let statement 1 be the declaration

"a bit is a binary digit"

and let statement 2 be the claim that

"a cabbage is a vegetable"

Then the compound statement

[statement 1] and [statement 2]

is obviously true. On the other hand, if statement 1 is as above and statement 2 is the sentence

"a cabbage is a rock"

then the compound statement

[a bit is a binary digit] and [a cabbage is a rock]

is false.

Similarly, if A and B are logic variables, then the statement

A AND B

has the value True if and only if both A and B are true. We summarize this as follows.

A	B	A AND B
T	T	T
T	F	F
F	T	F
F	F	F

A more compact means of representing the effect of a logical operation is through the use of a *truth matrix*. Figure 14-1(a) shows a truth matrix for the AND operation. The top row shows the possible values for A, and the left column contains the values of B. We find the value of A AND B, under the column headed by the desired value of A in the row labeled with the desired value of B.

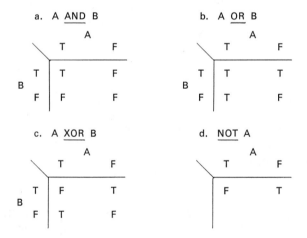

Fig. 14-1. Truth matrices for the logical operations AND, OR, XOR, and NOT.

The OR Operator.   The English language does not contain separate words for the two *or* operations, OR and XOR. Which *or* is really meant is a matter of emphasis. For example, a sentence of the form

(statement 1) or (statement 2) *or both*

represents the inclusive OR operation; the possibility that both statements are true is included. The OR operation applied to two logical variables has the value T if *either* or *both* of the variables is T:

A	B	A OR B
T	T	T
T	F	T
F	T	T
F	F	F

The only case in which A OR B is false is when both A and B are false.

The XOR Operator. The XOR operator *excludes* the possibility that both the variables upon which it operates are true. An English language sentence that has the effect of the XOR operation has the form

either (statement 1) or (statement 2) *but not both*

In other words, A XOR B is true when either A or B but not both A and B is true:

A	B	A XOR B
T	T	F
T	F	T
F	T	T
F	F	F

The NOT Operator. The NOT operator results in the logical complement of the single variable upon which it operates. Thus, if A is T, then NOT A is F; if A is F, then NOT A is T.

14.1.2. Logic in Computing

Symbolic logic uses the values true and false for the variables in logic statements. However, any two different values, such as *on* and *off*, or the binary digits 1 and 0 work equally well as the values for the variables; logic itself is independent of what meaning we assign to the truth values. Since the computer is a machine designed to deal with numbers, we usually think of the logic values in computer circuits and operations as having the values 1 and 0. Figure 14-2 shows the truth matrices using these values.

Modern digital computers are binary machines. From one point of view, they can do nothing more or less than apply the logic operators to binary numbers. From this point of view, the computer is a collection of switches, or *flip-flops*, each of which can be in one of two states T or F or 1 or 0. These

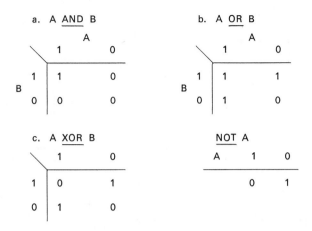

Fig. 14-2. Truth tables for the logical operations using the binary digits 1 and 0 for the values of the logical variables.

switches are wired to logic operators, or *gates*, which operate upon the inputs via operations such as those discussed above to produce values which are then used as inputs to other gates and flip-flops and so on. For example, we can write the sum S of two binary digits A and B as

$$S = (NOT\ A\ AND\ B)\ OR\ (A\ AND\ NOT\ B)$$

$$C = A\ AND\ B$$

where C is the carried digit. (The NOT operator is applied before any others in the expression above.) Figure 14-3 shows a logic diagram of a circuit to compute this sum.

All the arithmetic operations in the machine are carried out through circuits as described above. In fact, it is in principle possible to build a computer in which the only "arithmetic" instructions are logic and shift operations similar to those discussed in this chapter. Addition, subtraction, and all the other arithmetic operations could be programmed using sequences of logic and shift instructions.

In the 360 and 370 computers, the smallest units that can be used as operands are bytes. When we apply a logical operation to a computer unit of byte length or longer, the operation is carried out bit by bit using 1 bit at a time from each of the two operands. For example, if byte A contains binary

	0	1	2	3	4	5	6	7
A:	1	1	0	1	0	0	1	1

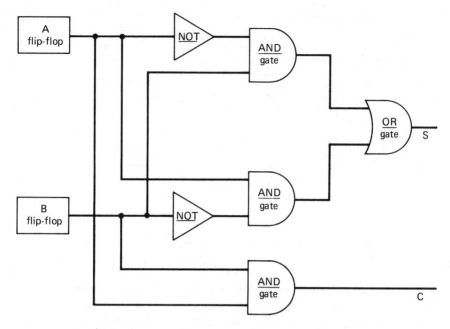

Fig. 14-3. A logic diagram for a circuit that computes the sum S and carry C of two binary digits A and B.

and byte B contains

	0	1	2	3	4	5	6	7
B:	1	0	0	1	1	0	1	0

the result of the computer operation A AND B is a byte containing

	0	1	2	3	4	5	6	7
Result:	1	0	0	1	0	0	1	0

What has happened can be written as follows,

	A	B	
bit 0	1	1	1 AND 1 = 1
bit 1	1	0	1 AND 0 = 0
bit 2	0	1	0 AND 1 = 0
bit 3	1	1	1 AND 1 = 1

and so on with the remaining 4 bits. Similarly, given A and B as above, A OR B is

0	1	2	3	4	5	6	7
1	1	0	1	1	0	1	1

A XOR B is

0	1	2	3	4	5	6	7
0	1	0	0	1	0	0	1

and NOT A is

0	1	2	3	4	5	6	7
0	0	1	0	1	1	0	0

While we have used 1 byte for the examples above, the same principle carries over to operands of longer length. In applying a logical operation to two full words, each bit of the result is the result of applying the operation to the corresponding bits from each operand.

In computing, we use the logical operations to set the contents of bits to desired values. The AND operation is used to set bits to 0, OR to set them to 1, and XOR to obtain their complement. We can use the following techniques, which are easily derived from the truth tables, to accomplish the following:

1. To set a given bit to 0, AND it with 0. (AND with 1 leaves the bit unchanged.)
2. To set a given bit to 1, OR it with 1. (OR with 0 leaves the bit unchanged.)
3. To set a given bit to the complement of its original contents, XOR it with 1. (XOR with 0 leaves the bit unchanged.)

Suppose that we wish to set bit 5 of a byte to 1, leaving the other 7 bits unchanged. We should calculate the logical OR of the desired byte with a byte containing

$$00000100_2$$

More than 1 bit can be changed at a time. For example, the logical AND of a given byte with a byte containing 10101010_2 sets the odd-numbered bits of the byte to 0, while the even-numbered bits remain as they were. Similarly, the XOR of a given byte with a byte containing 11110000_2 produces the complement of the first half of the byte and leaves the last 4 bits unchanged.

Notice that in a machine in which the AND, OR, and XOR operations are implemented, the NOT function is unnecessary. To compute the complement of a bit we compute the value of 1 XOR that bit.

Table 14-1   MNEMONICS FOR THE LOGICAL OPERATIONS

Operation \ Instruction Type	RX	RR	SI	SS
AND	N	NR	NI	NC
OR	O	OR	OI	OC
XOR	X	XR	XI	XC

14.2.   BIT MANIPULATION INSTRUCTIONS

The IBM 360 and 370 instruction repertoires include logical operations equivalent to the AND, OR, and XOR operations discussed above. The basic mnemonics for these, their RX forms, are N, O, and X, respectively. There are also RR, SI, and SS forms for each of these operations. Table 14-1 shows that we obtain the mnemonics for these alternative types by adding the letters R, I, and C to the end of the basic mnemonics. Thus, in all there are 12 logical instructions—four instruction types with each of three basic operations.

Examination of Table 14-2 shows that these instructions are written in the same way as the arithmetic and information move instructions we have covered. In all these instructions, the result is stored in the first operand location. The RX instructions use the specified register and a *full word* at the given memory address as operands. The result is left in the register named as the first operand. The RR forms apply the logical operation to the contents of the two registers and store the result in the first-named register.

The SI instructions use a byte from the memory as the first operand and an immediate byte from the instruction itself as the second. The result is stored in the memory at the first operand address. As is the case with MVC and CLC, in the SS logical instructions the length of the operand is specified in the L1 position of the first operand. The machine applies the operation byte by byte, using a pair of bytes from each operand. The logical operation is carried out bit by bit as discussed above for each pair of bytes. L1 may be from 1 to 256.

Tables 14-1 and 14-2 might look formidable, but if you know the instruc-

Table 14-2 LOGICAL INSTRUCTIONS

N	R1,D2(X2,B2)	aNd	$R1 \leftarrow (R1)$ AND $(D2 + (X2) + (B2))_F$
NR	R1,R2	aNd Register	$R1 \leftarrow (R1)$ AND $(R2)$
NI	D1(B1),I2	aNd Immediate	$D1 + (B1) \leftarrow (D1 + (B1))$ AND I2
NC	D1(L1,B1),D2(B2)	aNd Character	$D1 + (B1) \leftarrow (D1 + (B1))_{L1}$ AND $(D2 + (B2))_{L1}$
O	R1,D2(X2,B2)	Or	$R1 \leftarrow (R1)$ OR $(D2 + (X2) + (B2))_F$
OR	R1,R2	Or Register	$R1 \leftarrow (R1)$ OR $(R2)$
OI	D1(B1),I2	Or Immediate	$D1 + (B1) \leftarrow (D1 + (B1))$ OR I2
OC	D1(L1,B1),D2(B2)	Or Character	$D1 + (B1) \leftarrow (D1 + (B1))_{L1}$ OR $(D2 + (B2))_{L1}$
X	R1,D2(X2,B2)	eXclusive or	$R1 \leftarrow (R1)$ XOR $(D2 + (X2) + (B2))_F$
XR	R1,R2	eXclusive or Register	$R1 \leftarrow (R1)$ XOR $(R2)$
XI	D1(B1),I2	eXclusive or Immediate	$D1 + (B1) \leftarrow (D1 + (B1))$ XOR I2
XC	D1(L1,B1),D2(B2)	eXclusive or Character	$D1 + (B1) \leftarrow (D1 + (B1))_{L1}$ XOR $(D2 + (B2))_{L1}$

tion types and how to specify the operands with each type, you will have little trouble in using these instructions. For example, suppose that we have two 10-byte areas in the memory and we wish to calculate the logical OR of the contents of these areas. Since both operands are in the memory, we use the SS form of the Or instruction. The length we use is 10. If the two areas are called A and B, then the instruction

OC   A(10),B

leaves the result of the logical OR of these two areas stored in the 10-byte area starting at A. The answer replaces the original contents of the area starting at A. The 10 bytes starting at B are unchanged.

Now for some examples. Suppose that P and Q are both aligned on full-word boundaries and that they contain (in hexadecimal)

P: 0FCA0FF0CE6B

Q: A0F0A0F0A0F0

and suppose that the register contents are

(2) = AAAACCCC

(3) = 0F0F0F0F

The above are the register and memory contents before execution of each of the instructions discussed below.

The instruction

NR   2,3

results in

(2) = 0A0A0C0C

while

OR   3,2

produces

(3) = AFAFCFCF

The instruction

XR   2,3

produces the complement of the odd-numbered nibbles of the contents register 2; leaving the rest unchanged:

(2) = A5A5C3C3

Notice that the AND operation in effect selects desired bits out of an area. We say that the AND operation "masks out" those bits in the result that are ANDed with 0. For example, suppose that we want to move the contents of every other nibble stored in the full word at P into register 3. Register 3 has the proper contents to do this. The result of

N   3,P

is

$$(3) = 0F0A0F00$$

as desired.

What about

XC   P+2(3),Q+1

This computes the logical XOR for each pair of bits starting with the first bits at P+2 and Q+1, storing the results starting at P+2. Thus, after execution of the instruction above we have

P: 0FCAFF503E6B

Let's look at this more carfully in binary. The 3 bytes starting at P+2 written in binary are

0000 1111 1111 0000 1100 1110

while the 3 bytes starting at Q+1 are

1111 0000 1010 0000 1111 0000

The XOR of each pair of bits is

1111 1111 0101 0000 0011 1110

This result is stored starting at P+2, the first operand address.

We use the immediate forms of these instructions to set specific bits within a byte. To set bits 3 through 5 of a byte stored at D to 1, leaving the other bits unchanged, we write

OI   D,B'00011100'

Similarly, suppose that we want to set the first 5 bits of a byte 16 bytes beyond an address contained in register 6 to 11000, without changing the remaining bits. We write

OI   16(6),B'11000000'

to set the first 2 bits to 1 and then

NI   16(6), B'11000111'

to set bits 2, 3, and 4 to 0.

We often test individual bits or groups of bits within a byte to see if they contain desired values. For example, a program might use logical operations to set a series of bits as used switches which determine the nature of the processing to be done. At various stages of the calculations, the program tests the switches to determine what is to be done next.

The Test under Mask (TM) instruction permits the examination of one or more bits within a byte in the memory. It is an SI instruction; the first operand is the S-type memory address of the byte to be tested. The immediate operand is a mask which determines which bits within that byte are to be tested.

| TM | D1(B1),I2 | Test under Mask | Test (D1 + (B1)) using I2 as mask; set CC accordingly |

Each bit in the mask that is 1 indicates that the corresponding bit of the byte at the address D2 + (B2) is to be tested. A 0 in a given mask bit means that the corresponding bit in the memory operand is to be ignored.

The TM instruction sets the condition code to indicate the result of the test as follows:

CC = 0: 1. All tested bits are 0, or
         2. Mask is 0.
CC = 1: Tested bits were "mixed"; some are 0 and some are 1.
CC = 2: Not used.
CC = 3: Tested bits are all 1.

Thus, after a TM instruction, a BZ instruction can be used to determine if all the tested bits are 0, A BO instruction (we might interpret BO as meaning Branch if Ones) inquires as to whether all the tested bits are 1. Finally, a BM (Branch if Mixed) instruction tests to see if some of the bits tested are 1 and others are 0.

Consider the instruction

TM   BYT1,B'00110000'

This instruction tests the contents of the byte at BYT1. The mask indicates that bits 2 and 3 of this byte are to be tested. Thus, if the contents of the byte at BYT1 are

11110001

the condition code is set to 3, since the tested bits are bits are both 1. If BYT1 contains

11010001

the resulting condition code is 1, indicating that the bits tested are neither all 1s nor all 0s. If BYT1 contains

11000001

the TM instruction sets the condition code to 0. Notice how the mask selects those bits that are to be tested. TM ignores the remaining bits.

14.3. THE SHIFT INSTRUCTIONS

In football, a "shift" is a movement of line players to one side or the other with respect to the players on the opposing team. In computing, a *shift* is the movement of data "sideways" with respect to the boundaries in which the data are stored. This motion is often similar to dividing or multiplying the data by a power of 2. For example, consider a byte containing 00100010_2. A shift of this byte one bit position, or binary place, to the left

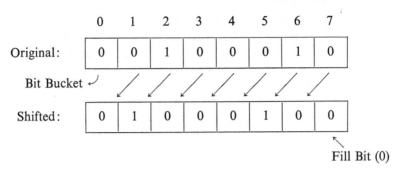

moves each bit of the byte 1 bit position to the left. A 0 *fill bit* is moved into the vacant position created at the right end of the byte. The original contents of bit 0 are shifted into the *bit bucket* and lost, doing their part to increase the entropy of the universe. Notice that the result is the same we would have obtained had we multiplied the contents of the byte by 2.

Similarly, the shifting of a byte containing 10101110_2 three places to the right proceeds as follows:

	0	1	2	3	4	5	6	7		
Original:	1	0	1	0	1	1	1	0		
Shifted:	0	0	0	1	0	1	0	1	1 1 0 ⟶ Bit Bucket

Fill Bits

Here the fill bits have been inserted into the left end of the number and the original contents of bits 5, 6, and 7 are destoryed. Notice that if we consider the contents of this byte as a *signed* binary integer, the shift is *not* the same as division, since the original contents are a negative number, while the result after the shift is positive.

In the 360 and 370 computers, there are two kinds of shifts, *logical* shifts and *arithmetic* shifts, which differ in the way the sign bit is treated. The arithmetic shifts answer the problem of what to do about the sign bit raised above. Arithmetic shifts give the proper results when used for arithmetic purposes. The logical shifts work as shown above in that no special significance is attached to the sign bit in their execution.

While the examples above dealt with data stored in 1 byte, we must emphasize the fact that in the IBM 360 and 370 computers *all shift instructions operate upon register contents.*

14.3.1.   Logical Shifts

The logical shifts are the simpler of the two kinds of shifts in that the fill bit is always 0 and the sign bit behaves like all the other bits. Because of this fact, the logical shifts are not normally used for arithmetic but instead for the packing of binary data into a more compact form for storage. The logical shift instructions have no effect on the condition code.

Let us begin with an example. Let register 5 contain (binary)

$$0010\ 1000\ 0111\ 0010\ 1001\ 1100\ 1111\ 0110$$

The instruction

$$\text{SLL} \qquad 5,6$$

a Shift Left Logical instruction, shifts the contents of register 5 to the left 6 bit positions with the result

$$(5) = 00011100101001110011111011100000000$$

The format of the shift instructions is a modification of the RS instruction format. The first operand designates a register as usual. This is the register or registers whose contents will be shifted. In the standard RS format, the second operand is a register. But in the shift instructions this operand is omitted. The last operand is written as a S-type address,

$$\text{D2(B2)}$$

but is not used as an address. Instead, the last 6 bits of the sum

$$\text{D2} + \text{(B2)}$$

indicate how many binary places the register's contents are to be shifted. We can shift the contents of a single register to the left or to the right the number of binary places given by this number.

SLL	R1,D2(B2)	Shift Left Logical	Shift (R1) left
			D2 + (B2) binary places
SRL	R1,D2(B2)	Shift Right Logical	Shift (R1) right
			D2 + (B2) binary places

The logical shift instructions are often used to pack binary data into more efficient forms for storage. For example, a series of 100 numbers stored in full words requires 3200 bits of storage. If we know that all the numbers are positive and less than 64, then we really need only 6 bits to store each number, or 600 bits for 100 such numbers. (Actually 640 bits are used if 5 numbers are stored per word.) Figure 14-4 shows a program segment that packs 5 such numbers stored in consecutive full words into register 7. The

```
        LA      7,0             R7 WILL HOLD RESULT
        LA      2,NMBRS         R2 CONTAINS ADDRESS OF NEXT WORD TO USE
        LA      4,4             INCREMENT FOR BXLE
        LA      5,NMBRS+16      ADDRESS OF LAST WORD
PACKER  SLL     7,6             PREPARE FOR NEXT NUMBER
        O       7,0(2)          OR IT INTO R7
        BXLE    2,4,PACKER      AND REPEAT IF NOT DONE
```

Fig. 14-4. Packing five 6-bit numbers stored in full words starting at NMBRS into register 7.

processing of each number involves shifting (7) to the left 6 places to make room for the number. An Or instruction inserts the number into the last 6 bits of register 7.

In unpacking packed data for use in their original form, it is convenient to be able to shift the contents of one register into another. To do this, we use the *double shift* instructions, Shift Left Double Logical and Shift Right Double Logical.

SLDL	R1,D2(B2)	Shift Left Double Logical	Shift (R1,R1+1) left D2 + (B2) binary places
SRDL	R1,D2(B2)	Shift Right Double Logical	Shift (R1,R1+1) right D2 + (B2) binary places

In these instructions R1 denotes the first of a pair of registers, R1 and R1+1, and must be an *even*-numbered register. The double shift instructions treat the register pair as a single 64-bit binary number and shift the entire number. In a left shift, bits shifted out of the left, or high-order, end of R1 are lost. Bits shifted out of the high-order end of R1+1 are shifted into the low-order end of R1. Fill bits are placed into the low-order end of R1+1.

R1   R1+1

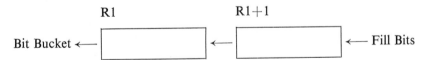

Bit Bucket ←— ⬚ ←— ⬚ ←— Fill Bits

Suppose that the contents of registers 4 and 5 are (binary)

$$(4) = 0011\ 0011\ 0011\ 0101\ 0110\ 0111\ 1000\ 1001$$
$$(5) = 1100\ 1011\ 1010\ 1001\ 1000\ 0111\ 0110\ 0101$$

The instruction

SLDL   4,7

shifts the contents of registers 4 and 5 to the left seven binary places. In so doing, the first 7 bits of register 4 go to the bit bucket, the first 7 bits of register 5 are shifted into the last 7-bit position of register 4, and seven 0 fill bits are inserted into the last 7 bits of register 5. The result is

$$(4) = 1001\ 1010\ 1011\ 0011\ 1100\ 0100\ \underbrace{1110\ 0101}$$
$$\text{from register 5}$$

$$(5) = 1101\ 0100\ 1100\ 0011\ 1011\ 0010\ \underbrace{1000\ 0000}$$
$$\text{fill bits}$$

The double right shift works in the same way. Bits shifted out of the low-order end of R1+1 go to the bit bucket. Bits shifted out of the low-order end of R1 go into the high-order end of R1+1. Fill bits are inserted into the high-order end of R1 as required.

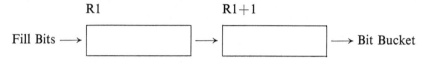

As we mentioned, the double shifts are useful in unpacking binary data. Suppose that we have a word BITDATA from which we want to extract bits 13–18 and store the result in a full word called bits. The instructions

```
L       11,BITDATA
SLDL    10,13
LA      10,0
SLDL    10,5
ST      10,BITS
```

accomplish the task.

Figure 14-5 shows a program segment that unpacks the contents of register 7 as created in Fig. 14-4 and stores the results back into the full words starting at NMBRS.

```
            SLL     7,2             FIRST TWO BITS AREN'T USED
            LA      2,NMBRS         START WITH FIRST WORD
            LA      4,4             INCREMENT FOR BXLE
            LA      5,NMBRS+16      FINAL VALUE FOR LOOP COUNTER
UNPACKER    LA      6,0             CLEAR R6 FOR NEXT NUMBER
            SLDL    6,6             SHIFT IT IN FROM R7
            ST      6,0(2)          STORE THE RESULT
            BXLE    2,4,UNPACKER    GO BACK FOR NEXT WORD
```

Fig. 14-5. Unpacking five 6-bit numbers in register 7, storing the results into consecutive full words starting at NMBRS.

14.3.2. Arithmetic Shifts

We hinted that the shift instructions can be used to multiply or divide register contents by powers of 2 but saw that a problem arises with the sign bit. For example, if we have

(9) = 0000 1000 0011 1101 0111 0010 0100 0010

then

SLL 9,3

produces

(9) = 0100 0001 1110 1011 1001 0010 0001 0000

which is $2^3 = 8$ times the original register contents. However, if we shift the original contents to the left four places, again using a *logical* shift, the result is

(9) = 1000 0011 1101 0111 0010 0100 0110 0000

which, if we follow the sign conventions, is a negative number which we obtained by "multiplying" a positive number by 16.

The *arithmetic shift* instructions help us around this problem. They differ from the logical shift instructions in that the sign bit is treated properly for arithmetic operations in the shift operation. The sign bit is not shifted. In a right shift, the fill bits shifted into bit position 1 (remember that the sign bit is bit 0) are copies of the sign bit. Thus, if the number is positive (the sign bit is 0), 0s are shifted into the high-order end of the number. If the number is negative (the sign bit is 1), 1s are shifted into bit position 1.

To illustrate the effect of a right shift, suppose that register 11 contains

(11) = 0001 0010 0011 0100 0101 0110 0111 1000

An arithmetic shift to the right three places, written

SRA 11,3

results in

fill bits
(11) = $\overbrace{0000}$ 0010 0100 0110 1000 1010 1100 1111

which is the original contents divided by 8, as expected.

On the other hand, if originally

(11) = 1100 1011 1010 1001 1000 0111 0110 0101

the same instruction produces

(11) = 1111 1001 0111 0101 001 0000 1110 1100
$\underbrace{\text{fill bits}}$

which is again the original contents divided by 8.

The sign bit is not shifted in arithmetic left shifts (multiplications). This means that the sign of the result will be the same as that of the original number. Fill bit 0s are shifted into the right end of the number as needed.

For example, if

(11) = 0000 0010 0100 0110 1000 1010 1100 1111

a left arithmetic shift three binary places

        SLA   11,3

produces

    (11) = 0001 0010 0011 0100 0101 0110 0111 1000

                                              fill bits

while if

    (11) = 1110 1011 1010 1001 1000 0111 0110 0101

the result of

        SLA   11,2

is

    (11) = 1010 1110 1010 0110 0001 1101 1001 0100

                                              fill bits

Notice that this result is the same we would have obtained using the logical shift

        SLL   11,2

The difference here is that if we were to shift one more place, given the same original contents of register 11,

        SLA   11,3

the result would have been a fixed-point overflow exception, while SLL 11,3 would have produced the result

    (11) = 0101 1101 0100 1100 0011 1011 0010 1000

                                              fill bits

which is not the correct arithmetic result.

In other words, execution of the arithmetic left shifts includes a check to see if an attempt is being made to change the sign of the shifted number. An attempt to shift a 0 to the left out of bit 1 when the sign bit is 1 or an attempt to shift a 1 to the left out of bit 1 when the sign bit is 0 results in a fixed-point overflow exception*, since either of these conditions means that the result is meaningless as an arithmetic multiplication by a factor of 2.

SRA	R1,D2(B2)	Shift Right Arithmetic	Shift (R1) right D2 + (B2) binary places
SLA	R1,D2(B2)	Shift Left Arithmetic	Shift (R1) left D2 + (B2) binary places

---

*The fixed-point overflow interruption can be disabled through the use of the set program mask instruction, if desired.

The arithmetic shifts set the condition code in the same way as do the binary addition and subtraction instructions. Thus, after execution of an arithmetic shift, the condition code is set as follows:

Condition Code Value	Meaning
0	Result = 0
1	Result < 0
2	Result > 0
3	Overflow (left shifts)

As an example of the use of the arithmetic shift instructions, the following instruction sequence multiplies (5) by 10:

LR	7,5	COPY (5) INTO REG. 7
SLA	5,1	MULTIPLY (5) BY 2
SLA	7,3	MULTIPLY THE NUMBER BY 8
AR	5,7	ADD THE TWO

As is the case with the logical shifts, double-length arithmetic shifts require an even-odd register pair as operands. The register pair is considered to contain a 64-bit binary number which is shifted the number of places indicated by $D2+(B2)$. The double arithmetic shifts set the condition code as detailed above, and a double left arithmetic shift can result in a fixed-point overflow exception.

SRDA	R1,D2(B2)	Shift Right Double Arithmetic	Shift (R1,R1+1) right D2 + (B2) binary places
(R1 *even*-numbered)			
SLDA	R1,D2(B2)	Shift Left Double Arithmetic	Shift (R1,R1+1) left D2 + (B2) binary places
(R1 *even*-numbered)			

In a right double arithmetic shift the 63 bits of registers R1 and R1+1 are shifted to the right as a single number. Bits shifted out of the right end of R1+1 are lost. Bits shifted out of the low-order end of R1 are shifted into the high-order end of R1+1. Fill bits are inserted into bit position 1 of R1; these bits are the same as the sign bit.

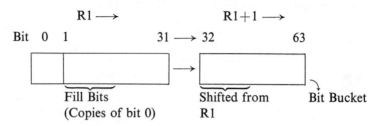

In a left double arithmetic shift, bits shifted out of bit 1 in R1 are lost. Bits shifted from the high-order end of R1+1 are shifted into the low-order end of R1. 0 fill bits are shifted into the low-order end of R1+1.

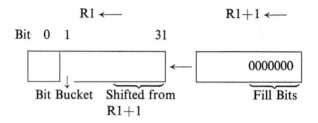

Suppose that

$$(4) = 1111\ 1110\ 1101\ 1100\ 1011\ 1010\ 1001\ 1000$$
$$(5) = 0111\ 0110\ 0101\ 0100\ 0011\ 0010\ 0001\ 0000$$

The instruction

SLDA   4,3

produces

$$(4) = 1111\ 0110\ 1110\ 0101\ 1101\ 0100\ 1100\ 0011$$
$$(5) = 1011\ 0010\ 0101\ 0001\ 1001\ 0000\ 1000\ 0000$$

while

SRDA   4,5

results in

$$(4) = 1111\ 1111\ 1111\ 0110\ 1110\ 0101\ 1101\ 0100$$
$$(5) = 1100\ 0011\ 1011\ 0010\ 1010\ 0001\ 1001\ 0000$$

CHAPTER SUMMARY

Table 14-2 shows the logical instructions. Table 14-3 summarizes the shift instructions.

Table 14-3 LOGICAL AND ARITHMETIC SHIFT INSTRUCTIONS

SLL	R1,D2(B2)	Shift Left Logical	Shift (R1) left D2 + (B2) binary places
SRL	R1,D2(B2)	Shift Right Logical	Shift (R1) right D2 + (B2) binary places
SLDL	R1,D2(B2)	Shift Left Double Logical	Shift (R1,R1+1) left D2 + (B2) binary places
SRDL	R1,D2(B2)	Shift Right Double Logical	Shift (R1,R1+1) right D2 + (B2) binary places
SLA	R1,D2(B2)	Shift Left Arithmetic	Shift (R1) left D2 + (B2) binary places
SRA	R1,D2(B2)	Shift Right Arithmetic	Shift (R1) right D2 + (B2) binary places
SLDA	R1,D2(B2)	Shift Left Double Arithmetic	Shift (R1,R1+1) left D2 + (B2) binary places
SRDA	R1,D2(B2)	Shift Right Double Arithmetic	Shift (R1,R1+1) right D2 + (B2) binary places

EXERCISES

1. Two additional operators of logical calculus are the *implication* operator, written A $\longrightarrow$ B, and the *equivalence* operator, written A $\longleftrightarrow$ B. Their truth tables are

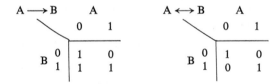

Express these operations in terms of the AND, OR, and XOR operations.

2. Because of its ability to carry out logical manipulations, the computer has proved to be a useful tool in proving theorems of logic. Write a program to prove or disprove the following statement of logic

(H $\longrightarrow$ I) AND (J $\longrightarrow$ K) AND [(I OR K) $\longrightarrow$ L] AND NOT
$$L \longrightarrow NOT (H OR J)$$

by determining whether or not the statement is true for all possible values of the variables.

3. A common use of packed binary data is in the analysis of questionnaire results. Suppose that the questionnaire answers are originally punched on data cards. A 0 in a given column means that question was answered *no*, while a 1 means that the corresponding question was answered *yes*. If the answers are stored as EBCDIC 0s and 1s, 8 bits per question are required for each respondent to the questionnaire. However, if the data are packed into binary form, only

1 bit per question is needed for each respondent. Write a program to analyze questionnaire data after first packing them. Assume that the first data card contains the number N of questions (you may assume that there are no more than 32 questions) and that the second card contains the number of respondents. The remaining M data cards contain the answers coded as described above. Your program should pack the data, 1 bit per answer, and then print order the number of yes answers there were for each question and the total number of yes answers.

4. Add a subroutine to your program of Exercise 3 that checks for correlations between answers. After producing the output as in Exercise 3, the main program should read pairs of numbers which indicate which questions are to be checked for correlation. For each pair of cards, the subroutine should print the number of times a yes answer was given for both questions by the same respondent.

5. Write a program to grade multiple-choice tests on which there are five possible answers for each question. The first data card shows the correct answers, chosen from letters A–E, the answer to question 1 in column 1 and so on. The remaining cards contain the student number in columns 1–10 and the answers the student gave in the remaining columns, the answer to question 1 in column 11 and so on. For each student, your program should print the student number and his percentage score on the test. Assume that there are no more than 70 questions. There may be a large number of students, and so you should pack all data as much as possible.

6. Modify your program of Exercise 5 so that after all the test results have been computed, it calculates the percentage of the students who answered each question correctly.

7. Write a program to read numbers from cards and print their binary equivalents.

8. Write a program to read numbers from cards and print their octal equivalents.

9. Write a program to read numbers from cards and print their hexadecimal equivalents.

10. Write a *single* instruction that stores 0s throughout a 256-byte memory area named ZEROES without using any other memory contents.

REFERENCES

IBM System/360 Disk and Tape Operating System Assembler Language, Form GC24-3414, IBM Corp., White Plains, N.Y.

IBM System/360 Operating System Assembler Language, Form GC28-6514 IBM Corp., White Plains, N.Y.

IBM System/360 Principles of Operation, Form GA22-6821, IBM Corp., White Plains, N.Y.

IBM System/370 Principles of Operation, Form GA22-7000, IBM Corp., White Plains, N.Y.

IBM OS/VS—DOS/VS Assembler Language, Order No. GC33-4010, IBM Corp., White Plains, N.Y.

SIEGEL, P., *Understanding Digital Computers*, John Wiley & Sons, Inc., New York, 1971.

15 DATA FORMS AND CONVERSION

Almost all data we deal with are, in their external form, character data, either on punched cards or on printed output. The internal form of character data is the EBCDIC code that we studied in Chapter 10. An internal form for numerical data representation is the binary system, which we have been using for arithmetic.

One question we must answer is how does one carry out the transformation of numerical data from their EBCDIC code form to binary for use in arithmetic and vice versa? We have depended on RWD and WWD to carry out this conversion. In this chapter we shall find out how to do it without these special aids.

In the process, we shall encounter two additional forms of numerical data representation. The *zoned decimal* format is an intermediate between EBCDIC and *packed decimal* format. In the next chapter we shall see how to do decimal arithmetic using packed decimal numbers as operands.

15.1. DATA REPRESENTATION

We usually present data and programs to the computer on punched cards. Let us examine the punched-card representation of computer information.

15.1.1. The Hollerith Code

The *Hollerith code* is the standard code for character representation on punched cards for IBM machines. An IBM data card contains room for 12 rows and 80 columns of hole punches. The rows are numbered 12, 11, 0, 1, 2, . . . , 9 starting from the top. Rows 12, 11, and 0 contain the *zone* punch, while rows 1 through 9 contain the *digit* punch.

328

The Hollerith codes for the letters consist of a zone punch and a digit punch. The letters A through I have zone punch 12 and digit punches 1 through 9, J through R have zone punch 11 and digit punches 1 through 9, and S through Z have zone punch 0 and digit punches 2 through 9. The numerical digits have no zone punch. The digit punch indicates which digit is desired. Notice that a 0 punch with no other holes punched represents the character 0 and is not considered to be a zone punch.

Reference manuals describe the Hollerith code for a given character by giving the numbers of the rows that contain holes. For example, the letter K has Hollerith code 11-2.

Since we shall soon be concerned primarily with numerical data forms, let us pick a number,

$$-137$$

say, and see how to represent it in the various formats. Its Hollerith code representation is the following hole punches,

11 = Hollerith code for "−" in column 1

1 = Hollerith code for " 1" in column 2

3 = Hollerith code for " 3" in column 3

7 = Hollerith code for " 7" in column 4

assuming that the number is punched starting in column 1.

15.1.2. The EBCDIC Code

Hopefully you have already noticed the similarity between the Hollerith code and EBCDIC. The translation from Hollerith to EBCDIC occurs when the card is read; the card reader transmits the resulting EBCDIC character codes to the computer I/O system.

Recall that in EBCDIC the first hexadecimal digit of each character code is a zone code. The Hollerith code zone punches are changed to the EBCDIC zone codes in the translation process. The binary equivalent of the row number of the Hollerith digit punch forms the last 4 bits of the EBCDIC code. The zones are related as follows:

Hollerith Zone Punch	EBCDIC Zone Code (Hexadecimal)
12	C
11	D
0	E
None	F

For example, the letter Q has Hollerith code 11-8. The EBCDIC code for Q is D8.

The above comments about translation hold only for the alphabetic and numeric characters. There is a system for translation from Hollerith to EBCDIC for the punctuation marks and special characters; look at the conversion table in Appendix C and see if you can discover the rules.

Returning to our previous example, we translate −137 from Hollerith to EBCDIC,

Hollerith	EBCDIC
11	60
1	F1
3	F3
7	F7

or 60F1F3F7.

15.1.3. Zoned Decimal Format

For the reminder of this chapter we shall concentrate on data formats for numerical data whose original form is that of decimal numbers. One of the differences between the internal machine data forms and those we are more accustomed to using is that, in the machine, the sign is part of the internal representation of the number. In a binary integer in the computer; for example, the sign bit is part of the number itself. On the other hand, we humans usually indicate the sign of a number by placing a symbol in front of the digits of which the number is composed. We say that a number is to be treated as positive by writing a + sign in front of it or by placing no sign symbol in front. The symbol − precedes a negative number.

Translation from the EBCDIC form of a number to its *zoned decimal* equivalent reflects this change in the treatment of the sign of a number. To obtain the zoned decimal form of an EBCDIC coded number, we place a code for the sign in the zone portion of the *last* character of the number, the *sign zone*, and replace the sign character code with the code for 0 (we shall see later that in conversion problems the latter step is not always necessary). The sign codes are

Code	Sign
C or F	+
D	−

In other words, if we find a C or F in the zone position of the last character of a zoned decimal number, we know that the number is positive. If this digit is D, the number is negative.

We saw that the EBCDIC equivalent of the number -137 is

60F1F3F7

Since this number is to be interpreted as negative, the sign code should be D. This goes into the zone digit, the first nibble of the last character of the number:

D
↓
60F1F3X7

to produce

60F1F3D7

To be strictly correct, we should also change the EBCDIC code for the $-$ sign, 60, to the code for 0, F0. Or we could simply delete the minus sign from the number to produce either

F0F1F3D7

or

F1F3D7

We shall see later that any of the last three forms given give the correct numerical result when converted to more compact data formats.

To give some further examples, the number

$+500$

has the zoned decimal form

F0F5F0C0

while the number

63

is represented in zoned decimal as

F6C3.

In both cases, the C in the zone portion of the last byte indicates a positive number.

15.1.4. Packed Decimal Format

It would be possible, in principle, to build a computer capable of doing arithmetic using zoned decimal or even EBCDIC coded numbers as operands. However, inspection of a number in one of these forms shows that almost half of the space they take up is occupied by the zones other than the sign zone, each of which contains an F and each of which has no effect upon the actual value of the number. The packed decimal format is nothing more than a more compact means of representing decimal numbers; to obtain the packed decimal form of a zoned decimal number we remove the meaningless F zones in the zoned decimal number. In the process, we move the contents of the sign zone to the low-order or right-hand end of the number. Figure 15-1 illustrates this conversion process.

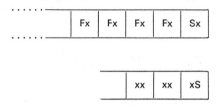

Fig. 15-1. Conversion from zoned decimal format to packed decimal. x represents any of the decimal digits. S is the sign code.

Thus, the packed decimal format requires at least one more digit than the number of digits in the original decimal number. If the original number has an even number of digits, a 0 goes in front of the number so that the number can be contained in an integral number of bytes.

We saw that the zoned decimal form of the number −137 is

F1F3D7

To obtain its packed decimal equivalent we move the sign code to last (or interchange the last two digits if you prefer to view it that way) to produce

F1F37D

and then remove the Fs,

137D

which is the final result. Similarly, the zoned decimal number

F5F0C0

has the packed decimal representation

500C

while the number

F6F3F2D3

is written

06323D

in packed decimal. In the last case we had to insert a leading 0.

You might recognize the packed decimal format as a modification of the BCD, Binary Coded Decimal, number representation scheme. In a BCD number, each group of 4 bits represents one decimal digit; the contents of a group of 4 bits is simply the 4-bit binary equivalent of the digit. For example, the decimal number 45 is written

$$0100\ 0101_2$$

or

$$45_{16}$$

in BCD. Notice that the BCD representation is *not* the binary equivalent of the number. To obtain the packed decimal format from the BCD format, we simply add a digit at the end which is a code for the sign of the number.

The packed decimal format is a more efficient means for representing numerical data in a binary machine than is the zoned decimal format. In packed decimal, each group of 4 bits represents one of the digits 0–9. But in a binary number a group of 4 bits represents a number between 0 and 15. We conclude that the packed decimal format, while more efficient in storage use than zoned decimal, is still less efficient than the binary representation of numerical data.

Nevertheless, as we shall see in the next chapter, the packed decimal format is often a convenient means of representing data for numerical computations. Most IBM 360 and 370 computers contain the instructions necessary to do arithmetic, comparison, and information move operations using packed decimal numbers as operands.

15.1.5. Binary

Perhaps the most important means of numerical data representation is in binary, either in integer or in floating-point form (See Chapter 19). Our example number −137 has the binary full-word equivalent

$$FFFFFF77$$

All the transformations mentioned above, EBCDIC to zoned decimal, zoned decimal to packed decimal, packed decimal to binary, are reversible. That is, given a number in any of the above forms it is possible to derive any of its other forms. For example, a full word containing

$$00000063_{16}$$

has the value

$$099C$$

in packed decimal,

$$F0F9C9$$

in zoned decimal, and

$$F0F9F9$$

as an EBCDIC character string. You should practice converting numbers back and forth among these forms until you are familiar with the process.

15.2. THE DATA CONVERSION PROBLEM

By now you probably have an idea as to what the data conversion problem is. We have been using RWD to read decimal numbers from data cards. The result of execution of RWD is the full-word binary equivalent of a data number. The RWD macro actually causes a subroutine to convert the original EBCDIC coded form of the number to zoned decimal, packed decimal, and finally to binary. WWD carries out the opposite process and eventually causes the resulting EBCDIC characters to be printed on the line printer. After you finish this chapter, you should forget about RWD and WWD because we shall find out how to do what they do.

Figure 15-2 summarizes the conversion process. The boxes show the data forms. Above the upper set of arrows are summaries of what must be

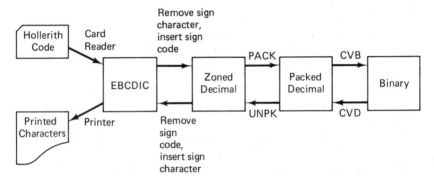

Fig. 15-2. Steps in conversion between the various data forms under consideration.

done to carry out the conversion going from left to right. We show summaries of the conversions going the opposite way below the lower set of arrows.

Suppose that we have the problem of converting a number on a data card to binary. The following steps are needed:

A1. The card reader translates the Hollerith card code to EBCDIC characters. Eventually, these EBCDIC characters are stored in the memory.

A2. Examine the number for a sign character, assuming that normal conventions are to be followed in designating whether the number is positive or negative. Usually, this means a test for a $+$ or $-$ sign or no sign in front of the number. Remove the sign character if present and insert the proper sign code into the number, producing the zoned decimal number.

A3. The PACK instruction converts the zoned decimal number to packed decimal. The number is now available for use as an operand in decimal arithmetic.

A4. The ConVert to Binary (CVB) instruction converts the packed decimal form of the number to a binary full word. The number can now be used as an operand in fixed-point binary arithmetic.

Let us now suppose that we have a binary integer we wish to have printed. The necessary steps are

B1. The ConVert to Decimal instruction converts the binary number to its packed decimal equivalent.

B2. The UNPacK instruction converts the packed decimal number into zoned decimal.

B3. Examine the sign zone and place the proper algebraic sign in front of the number. Move an F_{16} into the sign code position to complete the conversion to EBCDIC.

B4. Send the EBCDIC form of the number to the printer as part of a line to be printed. The printer translates the EBCDIC character codes to printed characters.

The translation from Hollerith code to EBCDIC by the card reader and from EBCDIC to printed characters by the line printer, steps A1 and B4, is automatic. Let us now consider the steps of concern to the programmer in the order A2, A3, A4, B1, B2, B3, which is their logical order in the input/output process.

15.2.1. EBCDIC to Zoned Decimal

As indicated above, this is the transformation in which we insert the algebraic sign of the number into the number itself. This means that we must first determine what the algebraic sign is and then move the proper sign code into the sign zone. For simplicity, let us first assume that the number consists of five characters: a sign character, $+$ or $-$, and four digit characters. That is, the number is of the form

$$\pm dddd$$

where the d's represent character codes for the digits 0–9. Suppose that we have such a number stored at EBCDICNO. Figure 15-3 shows the instructions that accomplish the sign test and sign code adjustment. The last instruction changes the sign character to a character 0.

Let us trace through the execution of these instructions with an example. Suppose that we have 60F1F2F3F4, the character codes for -1234, stored at EBCDICNO. Instructions 1 and 2 determine that the number is negative. Instruction 5 computes the AND of the last byte of the number with DF_{16}.

```
1.           CLI    EBCDICNO,C'+'   IS THE NUMBER POSITIVE
2.           BNE    MINUS             IF NOT, MUST BE NEGATIVE
3.           NI     EBCDICNO+4,X'CF'  PUT IN POSITIVE SIGN CODE
4.           B      SIGNFIX         GO TO REMOVE SIGN CHARACTER
5. MINUS     NI     EBCDICNO+4,X'DF'   PUT IN SIGN CODE FOR NEG. NO.
6. SIGNFIX   MVI    EBCDICNO,C'0'   COVER UP THE SIGN CHARACTER
```

Fig. 15-3. Converting a 5-digit EBCDIC number at EBCDICNO to zoned decimal.

The last byte contains $F4_{16}$, and so the result is $D4_{16}$. At this stage we have

$$60F1F2F3D4$$

stored at EBCDICNO. Finally, instruction 6 replaces the sign character 60_{16} with $F0_{16}$, to produce

$$F0F1F2F3D4$$

as the proper zoned decimal form of the original number.

The format used in the preceding example is much more restrictive than is necessary. To illustrate the EBCDIC-zoned decimal conversion process with a more relaxed input format, suppose that we require simply that the number consist of 10 characters. There may be a leading $+$ or $-$ sign. If there is no sign, the number is to be considered positive. All blanks are to be treated as zeros. The tenth character must be a digit. (FORTRAN fans will recognize the format described as a modification I10 format.) In this format, the following character strings are examples of valid inputs:

Byte number: 123456789A

$$+987654321$$
$$-2$$
$$0$$
$$+530$$
$$-48671$$

Figure 15-4 shows a program segment to convert such a number from EBCDIC to zoned decimal, assuming that the number is stored at EBNO. The primary difference between this example and the preceding one is that we now have to search for the sign character, whereas in the preceding example we know that the sign character is the first byte of the number. What we do is to start at the beginning of the number and search for the first nonblank character. Assuming that the data is supplied properly, as in Fig. 15-4, this character must contain the character $+$, $-$, or one of the digits 0–9. If this character is $+$ or $-$, we insert the proper sign code and replace the $+$ or $-$ with 0. If the first nonblank character is a digit, the number is positive, and the sign code should be so adjusted.

In Fig. 15-4, the first three instructions initialize registers 2, 4, and 5 for a search for the first nonblank character of the number at EBNO. A branch

```
          LA      2,EBNC          ACCRESS OF FIRST BYTE OF EBCDIC NUMBER
          LA      4,1             INCREMENT FOR LOOP TEST AND INDEX
          LA      5,EBNO+9        ACCRESS OF LAST BYTE OF EBCDIC NUMBER
BLNKTST   CLI     0(2),C' '       IS THIS CHARACTER BLANK
          BNE     FCUND           IF NOT, GO FIND OUT WHAT IT IS
          BXLE    2,4,BLNKTST     IF IT IS, LOOK AT NEXT CHARACTER
          B       ERRCR           IF WE GET HERE, CARD WAS ALL BLANKS
FOUND     CLI     0(2),C'-'       R2 CONTAINS ACCR. OF FIRST NONBLANK CHAR.
          BNE     PLUSTEST        IF NCT MINUS, GO CHECK FOR +
          NI      EBNC+9,X'DF'    PUT IN SIGN CCDE FOR MINUS
          MVI     0(2),C'0'       WIPE OUT SIGN CHARACTER
          B       DONE            AND THAT'S ALL
PLUSTEST  CLI     0(2),C'+'       IS IT A PLUS SIGN   IF NOT, ASSUME IT IS
          BNE     PLUSCCDE        IF NCT, ASSUME IT IS A DIGIT
          MVI     0(2),C'0'       IF SO, REMOVE + SIGN AND
PLUSCODE  NI      EBNO+9,X'CF'    INSERT POS. SIGN CODE
DONE      . . . . .
```

Fig. 15-4. Conversion of a 10-digit EBCDIC-coded number at EBNO to zoned decimal.

to FOUND occurs when the first one is found. Notice that register 2 contains its address at this point. The character is then tested and appropriate action taken, as in Fig. 15-3.

15.2.2. Zoned Decimal to Packed Decimal

The problem of converting a number from zoned decimal to packed decimal occurs whenever numeric input is to be used in arithmetic computations. The PACK instruction is specifically for that purpose.

PACK	D1(L1,B1),D2(L2,B2)	PACK zoned decimal to packed decimal	Convert $(D2 + (B2))_{L2}$ to packed decimal at $(D1 + (B1))_{L1}$

Since PACK is the first SS instruction we have encountered that requires two operand lengths, we digress a moment to consider the machine language form of such instructions. The basic format is that of the SS instruction:

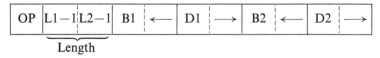

Length

In instructions with a single operand length, such as MVC, the length field, the second byte, contains the operand length less 1. In the SS instructions with separate lengths for the two operands, the second byte is split into two 4-bit areas, each of which contains one less than the actual length of the corresponding operand. For example, the operation code for the PACK instructions is F2. In the instruction

PACK   5(10,3),64(12,4)

the numbers 10 and 12 are the actual operand lengths as we write them in assembly language. The remainder of the operand field designates two S-type addresses in the usual base and displacement form. One less than each of the operand lengths goes into the machine language equivalent of the above instruction, which yields

F29B30054040

as the machine language version of the instruction. Since the largest number that can be specified in 4 bits is 15 and since one more than the machine language operand length will be the effective operand length, the longest either of the operands can be is 16 bytes.

The PACK instruction converts a *zoned decimal* number L2 bytes long stored starting at the second operand address to its *packed decimal* equivalent, which is then stored in the L1 bytes starting at the first operand address. In so doing, it carries out the transformation we discussed above. The two nibbles of the last byte of the second operand are interchanged and stored in the last byte of the first operand. Proceeding from right to left, the remaining zones of the second operand are removed. The digits that are left are packed two to a byte and stored into successive bytes in the first operand, leaving the second operand unchanged.

Let us start with a simple example. Suppose that we have the zoned decimal number

F2F3D6

stored at ZD. The instruction

PACK   PD(2),ZD(3)

packs the 3-byte zoned decimal number at ZD into a 2-byte packed decimal number at PD. The result at PD is 236D.

Notice that lengths are specified in bytes. In zoned decimal format, each byte represents one digit. In packed decimal format, an N-digit number requires $N+1$ half-bytes, one nibble for each digit and an extra nibble for the sign code. This means, among other things, that a packed decimal number with an even number of digits does not fit into an integral number of bytes unless, as is indeed the case, a leading zero is inserted into the packed decimal form of the number. To illustrate this fact, the instruction

PACK   A(3),B(4)

with

B: F1F2F6C3

produces

A: 01263C

A little though shows that the minimum number, M, of bytes required for a packed decimal number of N digits is

$$M = \left[\frac{N+1}{2} \right]$$

where

$$[x] = \text{smallest integer} \geq x$$

Thus, an 8-digit packed decimal number requires a minimum of

$$\left[\frac{9}{2} \right] = 5$$

bytes for storage, the same amount of storage as does a 9-digit number.

The length of the first operand does not have to be the minimum number of bytes required to contain the number. If we supply an area longer than necessary for the number, the PACK instruction automatically fills in the leading extra space with 0s. For example, if at D we have stored

D: F7F2F4D5

the instruction

PACK   F(6),D(4)

indicates that the 4-digit (byte) zoned decimal number at D is to be converted to a 6-byte packed decimal number at F. The result is

F: 00000007245D

In effect, seven leading zeros have been inserted at the left-hand end of the number. Notice that the result is always *right-justified*; the sign code, the last digit of the number, is always at the rightmost end of the first operand area. To do any further arithmetic with the packed decimal number, it must be in this form.

If the first operand area is not long enough to hold the entire result of the PACK instruction, the high-order digits that do not fit into the area are ignored. Given

G: F2F5F6F4F7F8C2

the instruction

PACK   H(2),G(7)

produces

H: 782C

in which the first four digits of the zoned decimal number at G have been ignored.

Finally, we point out that, while the PACK instruction was designed for its stated purpose, the second operand does not have to be a zoned decimal number. The PACK instruction removes the first nibble from each byte except the last and interchanges the nibbles of the last byte, regardless of what the contents of those bytes are. For example, if

$$Q: \quad 23E49C25$$

then

$$PACK \quad S(5),Q(4)$$

results in

$$0000034C52$$

This fact has applications in converting hexadecimal input to binary (see Exercise 7 at the end of this chapter). With the exception of the last byte of the number, the zones of the zoned decimal number have no effect upon the resulting packed decimal equivalent. Any leading bytes with 0s in their digit portions have no effect on the value of the packed decimal result if they are included in the second operand. In particular, the blank and minus sign both have 0 digit portions in their character codes. Consider the 6-byte representation of the number -100, which might be presented to us on a data card as

$$bb - 100$$

or, in EBCDIC,

$$404060F1F0F0$$

To prepare this area for conversion to packed decimal, all we really need to do is to change the sign code to D:

$$404060F1F0D0$$

If the above is stored at HDRED, then the instruction

$$PACK \quad PD(4),HDRED(6)$$

produces

$$PD: \quad 0000100D$$

In other words, the leading blanks and minus sign produced the proper digits (zeros) when packed. Observe that this is *not* the case with the $+$ sign, whose EBCDIC code is $4E_{16}$. The execution of

$$PACK \quad PD(4),HDRED(6)$$

with

$$HDRED: \quad 40404EF1F0C0$$

is

$$000E100C$$

which is *not* a valid packed decimal number, since all digits in a packed decimal number must be less than A_{16}.

15.2.3. Packed Decimal to Binary

We convert packed decimal numbers to their binary equivalents via the ConVert to Binary instruction (CVB).

CVB	R1,D2(X2,B2)	ConVert to Binary	R1 ← binary equivalent of $(D2 + (X2) + (B2))_D$

The CVB instruction is an RX instruction in which the second operand must be a *double word* aligned on a double-word boundary. The instruction assumes that the contents of this double word are a valid packed decimal number. Execution of the instruction places the full-word binary equivalent of the contents of the second operand double word into R1. (According to medieval alchemy, you can enter a circle of blood, but you cannot leave it if the circle is burning.)

The conversion occurs just as we might expect. Suppose that we have a double word PD containing

$$PD: \quad 000000000000010C$$

decimal 10. The instruction

$$CVB \quad 6,PD$$

produces

$$(6) = 0000000A$$

the full word binary equivalent of 10. If PD contains

$$PD: \quad 000000000000032D$$
$$decimal -32$$

the result of the same instruction is

$$(6) = FFFFFFD0$$

Two exceptions in particular need mentioning in connection with the CVB instruction. The result of the conversion must fit into the 32 bits of the register. If the number being converted is too large in magnitude (less than $-2,147,483,648$ or greater than $2,147,483,647$), the result is a fixed-point divide exception. If the contents of the double-word second operand are not a valid packed decimal number, a data exception results.

In the conversion process, it helps to anticipate the fact that a packed decimal number to be converted to binary must be stored in a double word. Therefore, if we wish to use the binary form of a number, we pack the number directly into a double word, using 8 for the length of the first operand. For example, a 3-byte zoned decimal number can be converted to binary and the result left in register 7 via the instructions

$$\text{PACK} \qquad \text{PD(8),ZD(3)}$$
$$\text{CVB} \qquad \text{7,PD}$$

where PD is a double word perhaps defined as

PD   DS   1D

15.2.4. Binary to Packed Decimal

We have traced the steps in converting numerical data from their original EBCDIC coded form to their binary full-word equivalent for use in integer arithmetic as discussed in Chapter 5. Let us now consider the reverse process: Given a full-word binary integer we shall describe the steps necessary in converting this number to its EBCDIC equivalent suitable for printing.

The first step is to convert the number from binary to its packed decimal equivalent. The ConVert to Decimal (CVD) instruction converts the contents of the first register operand to its packed decimal form and stores the result at the memory operand address.

CVD   R1,D2(X2,B2)   ConVert to Decimal   Decimal equivalent of (R1)
$$\longrightarrow \text{D2} + \text{(X2)} + \text{(B2)}_{\text{D}}$$

Like the CVB instruction, CVD requires that the memory operand address be that of a double word; the packed decimal form of the result, with as many leading zeros as necessary to ensure that the result is right-justified, is stored in this double word.

This means, for example, that the instruction

$$\text{CVD} \qquad \text{5,PD}$$

with

$$(5) = 00000340$$

produces

$$\text{PD:} \qquad 000000000000832C$$

provided that PD has been defined as a double word. (Of course, if PD is not aligned on a double-word boundary, the result is a specification exception.)

Similarly, if

$$(6) = \text{FFFFFF30}$$

and PACDECK is a double word, the result of the instruction

$$\text{CVD} \qquad \text{6,PACDECK}$$

is the negative number

$$\text{PACDECK:} \qquad 000000000000192D$$

We saw that the sign code F indicates a positive number. However, the machine always produces the strictly proper sign code C if it produces a positive decimal result. The result of the CVD instruction or any of the decimal arithmetic instructions has a C in the sign code position if the number is positive.

15.2.5. Packed Decimal to Zoned Decimal

What we need to do now, if we wish eventually to produce the EBCDIC representation of a number, is to "unpack" it. We must insert zone codes into the proper places within the number, and move the sign code into the first nibble of the last byte of the number. To do this, we use the UNPacK (UNPK) instruction, which is written in exactly the same way as the PACK instruction.

| UNPK | D1(L1,B1),D2(L2,B2) | UNPacK packed decimal to zoned decimal | Convert $(D2 + (B2))_{L2}$ to zoned decimal at $(D1 + (B1))_{L1}$ |

The L2 bytes stored starting at $D2 + (B2)$ are assumed to contain a right-justified packed decimal number. Its zoned decimal equivalent occupies the L1 bytes starting at $D1 + (B1)$ after execution of the instruction. The first step in the execution of UNPK is the interchanging of the two nibbles of the last byte of the second operand. The result is stored in the last byte of the first operand. The machine then proceeds from right to left, starting with the second-to-last byte of the second operand and converts each digit (nibble) to its character code equivalent by inserting the zone F in front of each digit. It goes on in this fashion, storing each byte as it is computed, until all L1 bytes of the first operand have been filled. The second operand is unchanged by UNPK. Let us suppose that we have a stop-action camera so that we can watch the execution of the UNPK instruction step by step. Let the memory contain the following,

$$PD: \quad 50134D$$
$$ZD: \quad 7777777777$$

and let us consider the execution of

$$UNPK \quad ZD(5),PD(3)$$

The first step is the interchange of the digits 4D of the number at PD, with the result

$$ZD: \quad 77777777D4$$

The machine then places an F before the digit 3 from PD and stores the result

$$ZD: \quad 777777F3D4$$

The next digit treated is the 1 from PD

$$ZD: \quad 7777F1F3D4$$

and the 0

$$ZD: \quad 77F0F1F3D4$$

and finally the 5

$$ZD: \quad F5F0F1F3D4$$

and we have the final result.

The minimum length required to hold the zoned decimal equivalent of an N-byte packed decimal number is $2N - 1$. Why? If we specify a length larger than the minimum, the UNPK instruction inserts a leading $F0_{16}$, the character code for 0, into each extra byte. If the length of the first operand is less than that required to contain the zoned decimal form of the number, the leftmost digits that do not fit are ignored. Thus, for example, given

$$PD: \quad 0123456C$$

the instruction

$$UNPK \quad ZD(10),PD(4)$$

produces

$$ZD: \quad F0F0F0F0F1F2F3F4F5C6$$

while

$$UNPK \quad ZD(3),PD(4)$$

results in

$$ZD: \quad F4F5C6$$

In preparing a line for printed output, we usually unpack numbers to be printed into their desired positions in the string of characters that will be output. Thus when using the UNPK instruction, we use as the length of the first operand the number of printed characters we wish the number to occupy in the line of output code. For example, if we wish to have a 6-byte packed decimal number at PD printed as a 12-character number starting in the fifteenth column of the output line stored at OUTPUT, we write, remembering to leave the first byte for carriage control,

$$UNPK \quad OUTPUT+15(12),PD(6)$$

Finally, although the UNPK instruction was designed specifically to convert packed decimal numbers to their zone decimal equivalents, the UNPK instruction does not test the second operand to see if it is indeed a packed decimal number. UNPK interchanges the nibbles of the last byte and inserts F zones into the remaining bytes, regardless of the nature of the second operand. For example, given

DAT: 1ABCDE53

the instruction

UNPK   DIS(7),DAT(4)

results in

DIS: F1FAFBFCF0FE35

15.2.6. Zoned Decimal to EBCDIC

The zoned decimal number resulting from execution of the UNPK instruction has the form

. . .FdFdFdFdSd

where the d's represent decimal digits and S is the sign code, either C_{16} or D_{16}. An example might be

ZD: F0F0F0F1F9D7

which represents the decimal number -197. If we send the number at ZD as is to the printer as part of an output line, the printed line will show

00019P

There are two problems here. First, the algebraic sign of the number is not printed. And the last digit, which should have been a 7, was printed as P instead. Both of these are to be expected, since we have not yet formed the EBCDIC equivalent of the number.

There are two necessary steps in the conversion from zoned decimal to EBCDIC:

1. Test the sign code and place the proper sign character in front of the number. Using the above example, the sign code D indicates a negative number, and so we place a minus sign in front. The EBCDIC codes for the string

$-0019P$

result.

2. Replace the sign code with an F zone code. The result in the example is

-00197

which is more like the desired result.

Figure 15-5 shows a set of instructions that converts a 10-byte zoned decimal number stored at ZONEDECI to its 10-byte EBCDIC equivalent. Here we have a use for some of our logic instructions. The TM instruction compares the sign code with D_{16}. If the result is not all 1, that is, if bits 0, 1,

```
         TM     ZONEDECI+9,B'11010000'   CHECK FOR MINUS SIGN CODE
         BNO    PLUS            IF NOT THERE, IS POSITIVE
         MVI    ZONEDECI,C'-'   INSERT MINUS SIGN CHARACTER IN FRONT
         B      SIGNFIX         AND GO TO COVER UP SIGN CODE
PLUS     MVI    ZONEDECI,C'+'   PUT IN PLUS SIGN CHARACTER
SIGNFIX  OI     ZONEDECI,X'F0'  OR OUT SIGN CODE
```

Fig. 15-5. Conversion of a 10-byte zoned decimal number at ZONEDECI to its EBCDIC equivalent.

and 3 of the last byte of ZONEDECI are not 1, the sign code must be C_{16} and a $+$ sign is moved into the first byte of the number; otherwise a $-$ is moved. The OI instruction at SIGNFIX "covers up" the sign zone with $1111_2 = F_{16}$.

The program segment shown in Fig. 15-5 produces output such as

$$+000013684$$

and

$$-000000001$$

which, while correct, leave something to be desired if one is interested in producing attractive-looking output. Figure 15-6 shows the program segment

```
         LA     2,ZONEDECI      ADDRESS OF FIRST BYTE
         LA     4,1             INCREMENT FOR BXLE
         LA     5,ZONEDECI+8    ADDRESS OF LAST CHARACTER TO TEST
ZEROTEST CLI    0(2),C'0'       IS THIS CHARACTER A 0
         BNE    DIGFOUND        IF NOT, IF FOUND FIRST NONZERO DIGIT
         MVI    0(2),C' '       REPLACE 0 WITH BLANK
         BXLE   2,4,ZEROTEST    GO LOOK AT NEXT CHARACTER
         B      ERROR           IF WE GET HERE, NUMBER WAS ALL BLANKS
DIGFOUND TM     ZONEDECI+9,B'11010000'   CHECK FOR NEG. NUMBER
         BNO    SIGNFIX         IF NOT, GO TO FIX SIGN CODE
         BCTR   2,0             BACK UP ONE CHARACTER
         MVI    0(2),C'-'       AND PUT IN MINUS SIGN
SIGNFIX  OI     ZONEDECI+9,X'F0'   FIX SIGN CODE TO MAKE PRINTED CHAR.
```

Fig. 15-6. Conversion of a 10-byte zoned decimal number at ZONEDECI to EBCDIC, removing leading zeros.

of Fig. 15-5 with the instructions necessary to replace the leading zeros with blanks and to place the sign immediately to the left of the first significant digit. Also, if the number is positive, no sign character is included. The results of this program segment, when printed, are of the form

$$13684$$

and

$$-1$$

The EDit and EDit and MarK instructions discussed in Chapter 20 offer more efficient means of accomplishing this same task.

15.3. RWD AND WWD REVISITED

Now you know all about what the RWD and WWD macros do. We have traced the steps in conversion from EBCDIC to binary as is done by RWD and the reverse process as is done by WWD. In fact, when we write RWD in a program, instructions which form the macro call a subroutine which does the complete conversion and returns the binary result. WWD calls a different portion of the same subroutine to convert a binary number to EBCDIC characters and cause a formatted output line containing the result to be printed. Do not use either of these macro instructions again. While the preceding material seems confusing at first, it becomes automatic with practice, provided you really understand the differences between the various data forms.

15.3.1. Input Conversions

To put the material of this chapter in proper perspective, let us consider some programming examples. Figure 15-7 shows a program segment that reads a card using RCD, so that the resulting card image is stored at CARDIN. We assume that the card contains a 12-digit right-justified decimal integer which may or may not have a leading algebraic sign. The number occupies columns 5–16 of the card. The program segment shown locates the

```
          RCD      CARDIN              READ CARD, STORING CHARACTERS AT CARDIN
          LA       4,CARDIN+4          ADDRESS OF FIRST CHARACTER OF NUMBER
          LA       8,1                 INCREMENT FOR BXLE
          LA       9,CARDIN+15         ADDR. OF LAST CHARACTER CODE IN NUMBER
FINDBLNK  CLI      0(4),C' '           CHECK FOR BLANK
          BNE      FOUND               FIRST NOT BLANK FOUND MEANS BRANCH
          BXLE     4,8,FINDBLNK        GO LOOK AT NEXT CHARACTER
          LA       7,0                 IF HERE, NUMBER IS ALL BLANKS
          B        DONE                PROGRAM SUPPLIES 0 IN TNIS CASE
FOUND     CLI      0(4),C'-'           CHECK CHAR. WITH ADDR. IN R4 FOR - SIGN
          BNE      PLSTST              GC CHECK FOR + IF NOT -
          OI       0(9),X'F0'          MAKE SURE SIGN CODE IS READY
          NI       0(9),X'DF'          AND INSERT MINUS CODE
          B        PACKIT              READY FOR PACKING
PLSTST    CLI      0(4),C'+'           IF FIRST CHAR. PLUS, MUST REMOVE IT
          BNE      PACKIT              IF NCT, READY FCR PACK
          MVI      0(4),X'F0'          CCVER UP + SIGN CHARACTER
PACKIT    PACK     PACDEC(8)CARDIN+4(12)   PACK THE NUMBER
          CVB      7,PACDEC            AND PUT ITS BINARY FORM IN R7
DONE      . . . .
                   .
                   .
                   .
CARDIN    DS       80C
PACDEC    DS       D
```

Fig. 15-7. A program segment that reads a data card and converts the decimal integer punched in columns 5 through 16 to its binary equivalent, placing the result in register 7.

first nonblank character number, if any; determines if it is a minus sign; and, if so, places a D into the sign code position of the number. If this character is a plus sign, a blank is stored in its position so that the result of the following PACK instruction has the proper value. All blanks are interpreted as zeros. Notice that we pack the number into a double word since we intend to convert the number to binary with the CVB instruction. Notice also that due account is taken of the possibility that all 12 characters of the number are blank, indicating a 0 result. The resulting binary integer is left in register 7. You should trace through the conversion steps in detail and play computer with data of your own design.

We are now in a position to choose our own data formats. In particular, we can place numerical data anywhere on the card we like and in any format. And we can put as many numbers as space will permit on one data card. Figure 15-8 shows a program segment that reads a card into an area called INPUT. The card contains eight 10-digit decimal integers of the form

```
          LA      2,0            R2 IS INDEX FOR STORING WORDS AT NMBRS
          LA      4,4            INCREMENT FOR R2 BY FULL WORDS
          LA      5,28           FINAL VALUE FOR INDEX, R2
          LA      6,INPUT        R6 CONTAINS ADDR. OF NUMBER TO CONVERT
          LR      3,6            KEEP A COPY IN R3
          LA      10,1           INCREMENT FOR R6
          RCD     INPUT          READ THE CARD
NEXTNUM   LA      11,10(6)       FINAL VALUE FOR R6 FOR THIS NUMBER
FINDBLNK  CLI     0(6),C' '      CHECK FOR BLANK CHARACTER
          BNE     FOUND          IF NOT, GOT TEST SIGNS
          BXLE    6,10,FINDBLNK  IF BLANK, GO LOOK AT NEXT CHAR.
          LA      7,0            IF,HERE, NUMBER IS ALL BLANKS
          B       STORE          0 IS RESULT, GO STORE IT
FOUND     CLI     0(6),C'-'      SEE IF FIRST NONBLANK IS MINUS SIGN
          BNE     PLSTST         IF NOT, GO SEE IF PLUS SIGN
          OI      0(11),X'F0'    OTHERWISE, PREPARE
          NI      0(11),X'DF'    TO PUT IN NEG. SIGN CODE
          B       PACKIT         AND GO PACK THE NUMBER
PLSTST    CLI     0(6),C'+'      CHECK FOR PLUS SIGN
          BNE     PACKIT         IF NOT, ASSUME IT IS DIGIT, PACK NUMBER
          MVI     0(6),X'F0'     COVER UP PLUS SIGN
PACKIT    PACK    PACDEC,0(12,3) CONVERT 12-BYTE Z.D. NO. TO 8-BYTE P. D.
          CVB     7,PACDEC       AND CONVERT THE RESULT TO BINARY
STORE     ST      7,NMBRS(2)     STORE RESULT IN TABLE OF BINARY NUMBERS
          LA      3,10(3)        R3 POINTS TO NEXT NUMBER
          LR      6,3            SO DOES R6 NOW
          BXLE    2,4,NEXTNUM    GO BACK FOR NEXT NUMBER
                  •
                  •
                  •
NMBRS     DS      8F
PACDEC    DS      D
INPUT     DS      80C
```

Fig. 15-8. A program segment that reads a card which contains eight 10-digit decimal numbers, converts each number to binary, and stores the results in consecutive full words.

discribed in the preceding paragraph. The program segment shown converts each number in turn to binary and stores the results in consecutive full words starting at NMBRS.

Notice the similarity between Figs. 15-8 and 15-7.

Finally, let us consider what we have called *free-format* input as RWD accepts. A number to be input can be anywhere on the card and may consist of up to nine digits and may have a preceding sign. No intermediate blanks or other nondigits may be within the number. In this case, we must find out where the number is on the card and where it stops. The number begins with the first nonblank character. It ends at the last digit before the next blank after the beginning of the number.

Thinking ahead a little bit, suppose that we determine the addresses of the first and last digits of the number by searching through the card image. After changing the number to zoned decimal, we have to pack it. But what are we to use as the length of the second operand? Logically, we should use one more than the difference between the addresses of the last and first bytes of the numbers for the length. We must be able to execute a PACK instruction in which the length of the second operand is not specified until execution time.

The best way to vary the number in the length field of an instruction at execution time is through the use of the EXecute instruction. The EXecute instruction causes the execution of a single instruction that is out of the normal instruction sequence.

EX	R1,D2(X2,B2)	EXecute	Execute instruction at D2 + (X2) + (B2)

After execution of the out-of-sequence *subject* instruction the next instruction after the EX instruction is executed, unless the subject instruction is a branch. In the execution of EX, the last 8 bits of (R1) are ORed with bits 8–15 of the subject instruction. The result of the OR is not stored in the memory but is used as if it were actually in that portion of the instruction. In SS instructions, bits 8–15 are the length field. In effect, the logical OR of the length field of the subject instruction and the last 8 bits of the register operand is the length field that is used when the subject instruction is executed.

The subject instruction of an EX instruction can be any instruction except another EX instruction. Thus, the EX instruction permits modification of immediate operands in SI instruction, conditions in branch instructions, the registers that are used as operands in RR instructions, and so on. You have probably already encountered problems in which it would be helpful to be able to move a variable number of bytes without using a loop. EX lets you do exactly that.

Figure 15-9 illustrates the use of the EX instruction to solve the problem at hand. The first loop, starting at FSTFND, locates the first nonblank

```
            LA      2,CARDIN        ADDRESS CF FIRST BYTE OF INPUT AREA
            LA      4,1             INCREMENT FCR R2
            LA      5,CARDIN+79     ADDRESS OF LAST BYTE CF INPUT AREA
            RCD     CARDIN          READ THE CARC
FSTFND      CLI     0(2),C' '       ARE LCOKING FOR THE FIRST NONBLANK CHAR.
            BNE     LSTFND          IF FCUND, MUST GO FINC LAST NONBLANK CHAR.
            BXLE    2,4,FSTFND      GO LOOK AT NEXT CHARACTER
LSTFND      LA      6,1(2)          LCOK AT NEXT CHARACTER
LOOK        CLI     0(6),C' '       IS IT BLANK
            BE      ENDFOUND        YES. GO CHECK SIGN
            BXLE    6,4,LCCK        NO, LOOK AT NEXT CHARACTER
ENDFOUND    BCTR    6,0             R6 NCW CONTAINS ACCR. OF LAST NONBLANK CH.
            CLI     0(2),C'-'       IS FIRST CHARACTER MINUS
            BNE     PLSTST          NC, GO SEE IF PLUS
            NI      0(6),X'DF'      YES, PUT IN MINUS SIGN CODE
            B       PACKIT          AND GO PACK IT
PLSTST      CLI     0(2),C'+'       FIRST CHARACTER PLUS
            BNE     PACKIT          IF NOT, ASSUME IT IS A DIGIT, GO PACK IT
            LA      2,1(2)          SKIP THE SIGN CHARACTER
PACKIT      SR      6,2             R6 NOW CONTAINS 1 LESS THAN LENGTH OF NC.
            EX      6,PACKER        EXECUTE PACK INST. USING LENGTH IN R6
            CVB     7,PACDEC        AND CCNVERT IT TO BINARY
                    •
                    •
                    •
PACKER      PACK    PACDEC(8),0(0,2)
PACDEC      DS      D
CARDIN      DS      80C
```

Fig. 15-9. Converting a free-format decimal number from a data card to binary.

character; its address is in register 2 when the loop is left. The next loop, starting at LSTFND, locates the next blank; its address is in register 6 upon exit from the loop. The instruction at ENDFOUND subtracts 1 from this address to leave the address of the last digit of the number in register 6. After testing for an algebraic sign and taking the appropriate action, we subtract (2) from (6). The number left in register 6 is one less than the number of digits in the number input. This is what should be used as the length of the second operand in the machine language form of the PACK instruction.

The PACK instruction at PACKER has the machine language form

$$F270C3002000$$

assuming that register 12 is the implied base register and that 300 is the displacement of PACDEC. Since the first operand is a double word, we write 8 as the length of the first operand in the PACK instruction and one less than 8 is placed into the machine language instruction. When we use either 0 or 1 as the length of an operand, the assembler uses 0 as its length, whence the length field 70 in the PACK instruction.

Suppose that the number to be packed is 10_{10} bytes long as determined by the first two loops in Fig. 15-9. After the SR instruction, register 6 contains

$$(6) = 00000009$$

The instruction

EX   6,PACKER

computes the logical OR of the length field of the PACK instruction, 70_{16}, and the last 8 bits of register 6, 09_{16}, with the result 79_{16}. PACK uses this value as if it were actually present in the instruction at PACKER. In other words, the effect is the same as if we had written the instruction

PACK   PACDEC(8),0(10,2)

in place of the EX instruction. The length field of the PACK instruction at PACKER is left the same as it was before execution of the EX instruction. Thus, if the next time the program segment of Fig. 15-9 is executed the number from the card is 5 bytes long, the EX instruction will have the same effect as if we had written

PACK   PACDEC(8),0(5,2)

in place of the EX instruction.

This concludes temporarily our discussion of input data conversion. We shall see in Chapter 20 that the TRanslate and TRanslate and Test instructions can be helpful in these problems. Of course, if the input data are to be used in decimal arithmetic as discussed in the next chapter, the final conversion to binary is unnecessary.

15.3.2. Output Conversions

The problem here is, given a binary integer in a register, print its decimal equivalent. We must transform the number through the binary, packed decimal, zoned decimal, and EBCDIC forms to prepare it for output.

As an example, suppose that we have computed an average of a series of numbers and left the result in register 8. We want to print this result in the form

AVERAGE $= \pm$ddddddddd

where the d's represent decimal digits. We leave the problem of removing the leading zeros for an exercise.

Figure 15-10 shows a program segment to accomplish this task. The output line being produced is called OUTPT. For convenience we have split this area up into segments with appropriate names. The CVD instruction converts the number in register 8 to decimal in the double word PACDEC. The UNPK instruction creates its nine-digit zoned decimal equivalent at NMBR. We then examine the sign code of the NMBR, which is at NMBR+ 8; move the proper sign character to SIGN; and change the sign code to F. The resulting EBCDIC coded number is then sent to the printer as part of the character string OUTPT.

```
           CVD      8,PACDEC        CONVERT (8) TC PACKED DECIMAL
           UNPK     NMBR(9),PACDEC(8)    CONVERT P. D. TO ZONED DEC.
           TM       NMBR+8,X'D0'    CHECK FOR SIGN CODE D
           BNO      PLUS            IF NCT, MUST BE POSITIVE
           MVI      SIGN,C'-'       MOVE IN MINUS SIGN
           B        SGNCDFIX        AND GO REPLACE THE SIGN CODE
PLUS       MVI      SIGN,C'+'       INSERT PLUS SIGN
SGNCDFIX   OI       NMBR+8,X'F0'    FIX UP LAST DIGIT
           PRT      CUTPT           AND PRINT THE RESULT
                    .
                    .
                    .
PACDEC     DS       D
OUTPT      DC       C' '            CARRIAGE CCNTROL CHARACTER
           DC       C'AVERAGE='
SIGN       DC       C' '
NMBR       DC       CL9' '          SPACE FOR EBCDIC NUMBER
           DC       CL114' '        REMAINDER OF OUTPUT AREA IS BLANK
```

Fig. 15-10. Printing the contents of register 8 as a decimal number.

CHAPTER SUMMARY

Commonly encountered forms of numerical data are

1. Hollerith punched card code
2. EBCDIC
3. Zoned decimal
4. Packed decimal
5. Binary

In processing numerical input data, it is necessary to convert the data from EBCDIC to packed decimal or binary. In processing numerical data for output, one must convert the data from binary or packed decimal (depending on its original form) to EBCDIC.

Table 15-1 shows some useful instructions for data conversion.

Table 15-1 DATA CONVERSION INSTRUCTIONS

PACK	D1(L1,B1),D2(L2,B2)	PACK	Convert $(D2 + (B2))_{L2}$ to packed decimal at $(D1 + (B1))_{L1}$
UNPK	D1(L1,B1),D2(L2,B2)	UNPacK	Convert $(D2 + (D2))_{L2}$ to zoned decimal at $(D1 + (B1))_{L1}$
CVB	R1,D2(X2,B2)	ConVert to Binary	$R1 \leftarrow$ binary equivalent of $(D2 + (X2) + (B2))_D$
CVD	R1,D2(X2,B2)	ConVert to Decimal	Packed decimal equivalent of $(R1) \rightarrow D2 + (X2) + (B2)$
EX	R1,D2(X2,B2)	EXecute	Execute instruction at $D2 + (X2) + (B2)$

EXERCISES

1. Write the instructions necessary to convert a 10-byte zoned decimal number stored starting at ZD to a 6-byte packed decimal number stored starting at PD *without* using the PACK instruction.

2. Write the instructions necessary to convert a packed decimal number stored in double word PD to its full-word binary equivalent. Do *not* use the CVB instruction. The answer should be left in register 7.

3. Write the instructions necessary to convert the contents of register 5 to packed decimal, storing the result in a double word PD. Do not *use* the CVD instruction.

4. Write the instructions necessary to convert a 7-byte packed decimal number stored starting at PACDEC to a 13-digit zoned decimal number stored starting at ZONDEC. Do *not* use the UNPK instruction.

5. Write a subroutine to print the decimal equivalents of the contents of 50 consecutive full words stored starting at LIST. Your subroutine should print 10 right-justified numbers per line, each of which occupies 12 spaces. Leading zeros should be removed.

6. Test your subroutine of Exercise 5 above.

7. Write a subroutine that reads decimal numbers and prints their eight-digit hexadecimal equivalents.

REFERENCES

IBM System/360 Disk and Tape Operating System Assembler Language, Form GC24-3414, IBM Corp., White Plains, N.Y.

IBM System/360 Operating System Assembler Language, Form GC28-6514, IBM Corp., White Plains, N.Y.

IBM System/360 Principles of Operation, Form GA22-6821, IBM Corp., White Plains, N.Y.

IBM System/370 Principles of Operation, Form GA22-7000, IBM Corp., White Plains, N.Y.

IBM OS/VS—DOS/VS Assembler Language, Form GC33-4010, IBM, Corp., White Plains, N.Y.

16 DECIMAL ARITHMETIC

We have seen that an intermediate form between the EBCDIC code and binary representations of numerical data is the *packed decimal* format. Most IBM 360 and 370 systems include a hardware option which permits arithmetic calculations using packed decimal numbers as operands. A third mode of arithmetic calculations, the *floating-point* mode, will be discussed in Chapter 19.

We use decimal arithmetic primarily in business and accounting applications in which the numerical calculations are a minor portion of the total computing job. For example, in updating an inventory file, most of the computing work is the location, input, and output of the control records and the records to be added, changed, or deleted. In such applications, the arithmetic involved is trivial in comparison with these other file management tasks.

In this chapter we shall present a preliminary discussion of the nature and uses of decimal arithmetic. We shall then discuss the decimal arithmetic, comparison, and information move instructions and shall conclude with a programming example.

16.1. DECIMAL ARITHMETIC—GENERAL CONSIDERATIONS

Before we delve into the specific instructions for use with decimal operands, let us first see what we mean by decimal arithmetic.

16.1.1. The Nature of Decimal Arithmetic

We have been writing packed decimal numbers by showing their hexadecimal form as they would look stored in the memory. For example,

137D

means the binary number

$$0001\ 0011\ 0111\ 1101$$

In decimal arithmetic, each of the hexadecimal digits in a number, with the exception of the sign code, behaves as if it were in fact a decimal digit. The machine uses the same algorithms of arithmetic—borrowing, carrying, and so on—that we use with pencil and paper. Using decimal arithmetic we compute the sum

$$\begin{array}{r} 137D \\ +200C \quad \text{(decimal)} \\ \hline 063C \end{array}$$

or

$$200 + (-137) = 63.$$

But if we add these two numbers using binary arithmetic, the result is

$$\begin{array}{r} 137D \quad \text{(binary)} \\ +200C \\ \hline 3389 \end{array}$$

which, in terms of a decimal result, is essentially meaningless. When we write packed decimal numbers in hexadecimal, the results of decimal arithmetic operations look just like they would if we were using pencil and paper to do the calculations. The data in the machine are still in the form of binary 0s and 1s. The decimal arithmetic instructions treat this binary data as if each group of 4 bits, except the last, is a decimal digit.

16.1.2. Use of Decimal Arithmetic

You may be wondering why we need to do decimal integer arithmetic if the computer already has the capability of doing binary integer arithmetic. Many computers do not offer decimal arithmetic capability. But there are circumstances in which decimal arithmetic is more efficient or convenient to use.

Let us first consider the possible magnitudes of the numbers that serve as operands with the two modes of arithmetic. The largest unit convenient for use as operands in binary integer arithmetic is the 32-bit full word. A number must be between $-2,147,483,648$ and $2,147,483,647$ to be stored in a full word. For many applications, such as in loop counting and indexing, this range is certainly sufficient. On the other hand, we shall see that it is in principle possible to have decimal operands with 31 decimal digits; the maximum magnitude for a decimal operand is $10^{31} - 1$, a string of 31 nines. In accounting problems in which dollar figures on the order of 10 million or more must be kept accurate to the penny, binary arithmetic will not do the job without special routines for multiple-precision integer arithmetic and conversions.

The decimal arithmetic instructions allow both operands to be of variable length, in contrast to the half-word and full-word restrictions in binary arithmetic. This means that it is possible, using decimal arithmetic, to change the number of places occupied by a number while doing the arithmetic. Such capability is unnecessary in loop control and counting applications but is often useful in business data-processing applications.

We have indicated that the binary system offers the most compact means for storing numerical data. But the smallest unit that is convenient for use in binary arithmetic is the half-word. Since decimal operands can be as short as 1 byte in length, in some cases the use of decimal operands can result in a saving of space, even though some space is wasted in the packed decimal representation.

The primary advantage that binary arithmetic has over decimal arithmetic is speed. On a typical computer, the decimal addition instruction, Add Packed, requires about six and one-half times as much time for execution as does the binary Add Register instruction.* The fact that AP is 6 bytes long in comparison with the 2-byte AR instruction makes this time difference even larger on some IBM models. We should point out, however, that a significant amount of time is required to convert a decimal number to binary and vice versa (about 12 AR times). Thus, if the numbers are obtained from input or are to be converted to character codes for output, we must consider the additional conversion time implied in binary arithmetic. Also, the decimal arithmetic instructions are all SS or memory-to-memory instructions. This means that to add two decimal numbers stored in the memory, only one instruction is required. On the other hand, a load, add, and store sequence of instructions must be used in order to compute the sum of two binary integers from the memory and store the result.

Table 16-1   COMPARISON OF BINARY AND DECIMAL INTEGER ARITHMETIC

	Binary	Decimal
Maximum operand magnitudes	About 9 decimal digits	31 decimal digits
Operand lengths	Fixed, half-word or full word	Variable, 1 to 16 bytes
Operand locations	Register to register, register to storage	Storage to storage
Instruction execution speed	Fast	About 6 times slower
Conversion time (binary to decimal)	Necessary in some cases, time-consuming	Unnecessary
Memory space 1. General	More efficient	
2. Small numbers		More efficient

*IBM 360/Model 65 Functional Characteristics, IBM SRL GA22-6884, IBM, Inc.

Thus, there are several factors, summarized in Table 16-1, that must be considered in deciding whether to use decimal or binary arithmetic for a given application. Binary arithmetic is significantly faster, but may require some "hidden" conversion time. Binary arithmetic is most appropriate for use in what we might call *program* arithmetic—those calculations such as loop counting and indexing, which require no data conversions but which occur often enough to make the use of fast arithmetic attractive. For *data* arithmetic in which the actual arithmetic is not the dominant part of the calculations and in which conversions to and from binary are unnecessarily time-consuming, decimal arithmetic is more appropriate.

16.1.3. Decimal Constants

The assembler interprets the letter P to mean Packed decimal in the specification of numerical constants. For example, the statement

THIRTEEN DC P'13'

instructs the assembler to create a decimal 13 stored starting at THIRTEEN. In response to this statement, the assembler stores

013C

starting at THIRTEEN.

If no length is specified in a decimal constant, the assembler reserves the smallest space necessary to hold the number, inserting a leading zero if necessary, as above, the ensure that the result has byte boundaries. The result is always right-justified. If we do specify a length, as in

ONE DC PL4'1'

the length value is the number of *bytes*, not digits, that will be reserved. Thus, the statement above produces

ONE: 0000001C

If the specified length is insufficient to contain the entire number given, the assembler ignores as many leading digits as necessary in order to fit the number into the requested space.

TOOMUCH DC PL2'−583679'

results in

TOOMUCH: 679D

Packed decimal constants can be used as literal operands in decimal instructions. For example, the instruction

AP COUNT(5),=P'1'

adds a decimal 1 to the 5-byte decimal number at COUNT.

16.2. ARITHMETIC AND COMPARISON INSTRUCTIONS

We shall now turn to arithmetic and comparison with decimal operands. All the decimal arithmetic and comparison instructions are SS instructions with two length fields, each of which specifies the length, in bytes, of the corresponding operand. To obtain the mnemonics for the operation, all we need to do is add a P to the mnemonic for the corresponding RX operation:

Operation	Binary Mnemonic	Decimal Mnemonic
Add	A	AP
Subtract	S	SP
Multiply	M	MP
Divide	D	DP
Compare	C	CP

As is the case with all instructions in which two operand lengths are given, the maximum operand length for either of the operands of decimal arithmetic instruction is 16 bytes. Since each byte except the last contains two digits, the maximum number of decimal digits allowable in an operand is 31.

Let us now look into these instructions in more detail.

16.2.1. Add Packed and Subtract Packed

The Add Packed and Subtract Packed instructions compute the sum and difference, respectively, of the L1-byte decimal integer starting at $D1 + (B1)$ and the L2-byte decimal integer starting at $D2 + (B2)$.

AP	D1(L1,B1),D2(L2,B2)	Add Packed	$D1 + (B1) \longleftarrow (D1 + (B1))_{L1} + (D2 + (B2))_{L2}$
SP	D1(L1,B1),D2(L2,B2)	Subtract Packed	$D1 + (B1) \longleftarrow (D1 + (B1))_{L1} - (D2 + (B2))_{L2}$

The result is stored right-justified in the L1 bytes starting at the first operand address. The decimal arithmetic instructions have no effect on the second operand contents unless the two operand areas overlap.

The instruction

$$\text{AP} \qquad \text{NUM1(3),NUM2(2)}$$

adds the 2-byte decimal number at NUM2 to the 3-byte number at NUM1. If we have

$$\begin{array}{ll} \text{NUM1:} & \text{75632C} \\ \text{NUM2:} & \text{493C} \end{array}$$

execution of the above instruction produces

NUM1:   76125C

Given the same original numbers at NUM1 and NUM2, execution of

SP   NUM1(3),NUM2(2)

yields

NUM1:   75139C

Similarly, given the original contents

AT: 00368D
BAT: 336C

execution of

AP   AT+1(2),BAT+1(1)

gives

AT: 00362D

while

SP   BAT(2),AT(3)

results in

BAT: 704C

If either of the two operands contains an invalid digit or does not have a proper sign code, a data exception (0C7) results. This is a very common error in programming with decimal arithmetic. When you have such an error, make sure that you have written the correct operand lengths in the offending instruction, for if the length of an operand is incorrect, chances are that the effective operand has an invalid sign code. If the lengths prove to be correct, look in the memory dump to see if what *should* be stored at the operand locations is actually there. Remember that improperly supplied data or the wrong operand lengths in the PACK instruction can also produce improper decimal numbers. These show up as errors long after the original data input and conversion.

If the result of an AP or SP instruction does not fit into the space provided for the first operation, a decimal overflow exception (0CA) occurs. Thus, if we have

AP   NINE(1),=P'1'

with

NINE: 9C

the result, 10C, does not fit into 1 byte. Notice that this does not mean that the first operand must be long enough to hold all possible results of the instruction. In effect, the machine calculates the result and then tries to store it. If it fits, all is well, regardless of the length of the first operand.

Thus, given

$$N1: \quad 958C$$
$$N2: \quad 0000042C$$

the instruction

$$AP \qquad N1(2),N2(4)$$

produces a data exception, while

$$SP \qquad N1(2),N2(4)$$

does not.

Both AP and SP set the condition code like other arithmetic instructions:

Condition Code	Meaning
0	Result $= 0$
1	Result < 0
2	Result > 0
3	Overflow

16.2.2. Multiply Packed and Divide Packed

The Multiply Packed instruction computes the product of the operands, leaving the result stored in the first operand area.

MP D1(L1,B1),D2(L2,B2)	Multiply Packed	$D1 + (B1) \longleftarrow (D1 + (B1))_{L1}$ $\times (D2 + (B2))_{L2}$

In preparing to use the MP instruction, we must ensure that the first operand area is long enough to contain the entire product. In fact, the machine demands that we provide enough space in the first operand so that the product will include at least one leading zero digit. If we fail to do this, a specification exception occurs.

To clarify this rule let us agree to call the first operand the *multiplicand* and the second operand the *multiplier*. The number of significant digits in the product is at most the sum of the numbers of significant digits in the multicand and multiplier, excluding sign digits. Suppose that the first operand has significant digits

$$38D$$

and the second

$$430C$$

The product

17340D

has five significant digits, but, in view of the requirement that the product include at least one leading zero, this must be extended to

017340D

The multiplicand has two significant digits, and the multiplier has three. The rule indicates that, before using the MP instruction, we must insert four leading zeros into the multiplicand; we must have

000038D

stored at the first operand to ensure that the product will fit into this space with room for a leading zero. To summarize, *the multiplicand must contain at least one leading zero for every digit* including the sign code *of the multiplier.*

The example above is further complicated by the fact that if we supply the minimum number of leading zeros that satisfies the rule, the result may not be an integral number of bytes, as in the case above. Thus, we really must have

0000038D

at the first operand location to compute the product of

38D

and

430C

The rule for multiplicand lengths as stated above is the most rigorous statement possible but may be difficult to carry out in practice, since we may not know how many significant digits there are in either of the operands. Therefore, a less rigorous but more practical statement of the requirement is the following: *Include at least one leading byte of zeros in the multiplicand for every byte in the multiplier.*

Returning to our example, the second operand, the multiplier, is 2 bytes long. We must insert 2 bytes of zeros; the result is the same as that obtained by the more complex rule stated above. If the multiplier is 5 bytes long, then we must insert 5 bytes of leading zeros and so on.

There is also an upper limit on the length of the multiplier; it can contain no more than 15 digits. Notice also that the multiplicand must be longer than the multiplier.

The considerations above mean that there is usually some preparation necessary before the MP instruction can be used. Suppose that we want to compute the product of a 5-byte number stored at NUM1 and a 6-byte number stored at NUM2. We shall not always be able to store the product at NUM1, since that area will not always be long enough to contain the entire product. We must find some way to insert 6 bytes of zeros in front of the number stored at NUM1. The easiest way to do this is to move the contents of the 5 bytes starting at NUM1 to an area already containing 6 bytes of zeros. (The ZAP instruction discussed in Section 16.3.1 is useful in such problems.) Thus, we could compute the desired product using the following statements:

```
           MVC        TEMP+6(5),NUM1
           MP         TEMP(11),NUM2
TEMP       DC         11X'00'
```

Supposing that

$$NUM1: \quad 103800010C$$
$$NUM2: \quad 60402000001D$$

the result at TEMP1 is

$$TEMP1: \quad 0062653282041238000010D$$

The Divide Packed instruction divides the decimal number (the divisor) stored in the second operand area into the decimal number (the dividend) stored starting at the first operand address. The resulting quotient and remainder are stored in the first operand area.

DP	D1(L1,B1),D2(L2,B2)	Divide Packed	Compute $(D1 + (B1))_{L1}$ $\div (D2 + (B2))_{L2}$:
			$(D1 + (B1))_{L1-L2}$
			⟵ quotient
			$(D1 + (B1) + L1 - L2)_{L2}$
			⟵ remainder

The question we must address is how the results are stored. Notice that the remainder in division can be no longer than the divisor. For example, if the divisor is 608C, the remainder cannot be larger than 607C. If the divisor is L2 bytes long, the remainder can occupy no more than L2 bytes. The DP instruction stores the remainder in the last L2 bytes of the first operand area. The quotient is stored in the first $L1 - L2$ bytes of the first operand area.

As in binary integer arithmetic, we can symbolize the division problem as done by the machine with the formula

$$dividend = quotient \times divisor + remainder$$

The remainder has the same sign as the dividend. The quotient is positive if the dividend and divisor have the same sign; otherwise the quotient is negative.

We now have enough information to consider an example. If we have

DIVDND: 05703C
DIVISR: 608C

and we divide the first number by the second, the quotient is

9C

and the remainder is

231C

The length of the divisor is 2, while that of the dividend is 3. The remainder is stored in the last $L2=2$ bytes of the 3-byte area starting at DIVDND, and the quotient is stored in the first $L1-L2=1$ byte of that area. Thus, given the operands above, the instruction

DP   DIVDND(3),DIVISR(2)

produces

DIVDND: 9C231C

Similarly, if the operands are

DIVDND: 000307685D
DIVSR: 00763C

the result of

DP   DIVDND(5),DIVSR(3)

is

DIVDND: 403D00196C

Notice that, given the same data,

DP   DIVDND(5),DIVSR+1(2)

yields

DIVDND: 00403D196C

If the divisor is small in comparison with the dividend, there may not be enough space to store the quotient. For example, if we have

P: 37605C
Q: 608C

the quotient is

61C

The instruction

DP   P(3),Q(2)

indicates that 1 byte is to be used for storage of the quotient, which requires more than 1 byte. When the quotient does not fit into the space provided, a decimal divide exception occurs. This problem can usually be avoided by providing a larger first operand area.

MP and DP do not change the condition code.

16.2.3. The CP Instruction

The decimal comparison instruction, Compare Packed, computes the difference between two decimal numbers, each of which has its own associated length, and sets the condition code to indicate whether the result is zero, negative, or positive. Memory contents are left unchanged in the process.

CP D1(L1,B1),D2(L2,B2)	Compare Packed	Set CC to indicate value of $(D1 + (B1))_{L1} - (D2 + (B2))_{L2}$

The resulting condition code values are

Condition Code	Meaning
0	First operand = second operand
1	First operand < second operand
2	First operand > second operand
3	Cannot occur

When the two operands are not of the same length, enough leading zeros are used with the shorter operand in order to make an arithmetic comparison valid. For example, if we write

$$CP \qquad N1(3),N5(1)$$

with

$$
\begin{aligned}
N1: &\quad 05683C \\
N5: &\quad 9C
\end{aligned}
$$

the effective operands are

$$05683C$$

and

$$00009C$$

respectively. The machine "pretends" that the leading zeros are there in making the comparison. In this example, the condition code is set to 2, indicating that the first operand is greater than the second, or, equivalently, that we would obtain a positive result if we subtracted the second operand from the first.

Given

$$N1: \quad 00005C$$
$$N5: \quad 9C$$

the same instruction sets the condition code to 1, as does

CP   M3(2),M7(5)

with

$$M3: \quad 400D$$
$$M7: \quad 000000500D$$

CP also checks for valid operands and produces a data exception if either operand is not a proper packed decimal number.

16.3. ZAP: MOVING DECIMAL DATA

In the preceding section we described the decimal arithmetic and comparison instructions. We shall now turn to some instructions that are useful in moving decimal numbers. Of course, the MVC instruction can be used to move *any* memory contents, decimal numbers included, from one area of the memory to another. We are concerned here with more specialized movements that lengthen or shorten numbers or produce the equivalent of a decimal shift of the data.

16.3.1. Zero and Add Packed

One problem we encountered in connection with the Multiply Packed instruction was that of extending a decimal number by inserting leading zeros in front of it. We accomplished this by moving the number to an area which had previously been set to zero. The Zero and Add Packed instruction can do this in one step and is often useful in other situations as well.

ZAP D1(L1,B1),D2(L2,B2)	Zero and Add Packed	$D1 + (B1) \leftarrow 0_{L1};$ $D1 + (B1) \leftarrow (D1 + (B1))_{L1}$ $+ (D2 + (B2))_{L2}$

The ZAP instruction proceeds in two steps. First, it stores a decimal zero L1 bytes long in the first operand area. The prior contents of this area do not have to be a decimal number since they play no part in the arithmetic. Then the second operand is added as a decimal number to the now-cleared first operand area. We can pretend that this step is the same as an AP instruction with a zero first operand.

ZAP sets the condition code just as does AP. A decimal overflow exception occurs when the first operand area is too short to contain all the significant digits of the second operand.

Suppose that we wish to move a 5-byte decimal number stored at B to a 7-byte area starting at C, inserting 2 byes of leading zeros in the process. The instruction

$$\text{ZAP} \qquad \text{C(7),B(5)}$$

does this and sets the condition code depending on the value of B. Supposing that B contains

$$678901234D$$

the result at C is

$$\text{C:} \qquad 0000678901234D$$

regardless of the previous contents of the 7 bytes starting at C. On the other hand,

$$\text{ZAP} \qquad \text{C(3),B(5)}$$

results in a decimal overflow, since the first four digits of B will not fit into the area provided.

Returning to our example of the use of MP in Section 16.2.2, we wish to multiply a 5-byte number at NUM1 by a 6-byte number at NUM2. In preparation for the MP instruction, we need to provide enough leading zeros in the first operand area so that the product fits, regardless of the contents of NUM1 and NUM2. We use the ZAP instruction to move NUM1 to a temporary storage area and insert the leading zeros:

$$\text{ZAP} \qquad \text{TEMP1(11),NU(5)}$$

If NUM1 contains

$$\text{NUM1:} \qquad 103800010C$$

then the ZAP instruction above produces

$$\text{TEMP1:} \qquad 0000000000000103800010C$$

regardless of the original contents of TEMP1. The condition code is set to 2. The MP is then written the same as before:

$$\text{MP} \qquad \text{TEMP1(11),NUM2(6)}$$

When the operands of the ZAP instruction overlap, the result is the same as if the instruction operated on a byte-by-byte basis going from right to left. I think this tidbit of information is useless.

16.3.2. MVZ, MVN, and MVO

The IBM 360 computers have no decimal shift instructions as such. However, the byte movement and logic instructions can often be used to produce the desired result. For example, the instruction

$$\text{MVC} \qquad \text{NUM}-2(5),\text{NUM}$$

has the effect of shifting a decimal number to the left 2 bytes, or four decimal places. The result is not yet the answer we get if we multiply the number by 10,000. But if we follow this with the instruction

$$\text{NC} \qquad \text{NUM}+2(3),=\text{X}'\text{F0000F}'$$

we succeed in putting the zeros into position to produce the desired product. Thus, if starting at NUM−2 the memory contents are originally

$$\text{NUM}-2: \qquad \text{FECB038602795C}$$

the two instructions above yield

$$0386027950000C$$

Thus, an MVC and an NC instruction can be used to multiply a number by an even power of 10 or shift a number an integral number of bytes to the left. But what do we do if we want to multiply by an odd power of 10, which involves shifting an odd number of 4-bit units? And how do we divide decimal numbers by shifting?

The 360 series of computers provides no simple answer to these questions. The MVZ, MVN, and MVO instructions can be used in such problems, but it is usually more efficient and easier in programming to use the MP and DP instructions for shifting decimal data in these machines. However, the MVZ, MVN, and MVO instructions are useful in other programming applications, as we shall see.

In the IBM 370 computers, the decimal arithmetic option includes the instruction Shift and Round Packed, which is a true decimal shift instruction. Since all 370 computers also have the MVZ, MVN, and MVO instructions in their repertoires, we shall describe these instructions first and then consider the IBM 370 SRP instruction.

MVZ	D1(L,B1),D2(B2)	MoVe Zones	Zone(D1 + B1)) ←— zone(D2 + (B2))$_L$
MVN	D1(L,B1),D2(B2)	MoVe Numeric	Numeric(D1 + (B1)) ←— numeric(D2 + (B2))$_L$
MVO	D1(L,B1),D2(L2,B2)	MoVe with Offset	See text

The MVZ instruction moves the zone portion, the first 4 bits of each operand byte, from the second operand to the corresponding position in first operand. The other nibbles, the numeric portions of the bytes of the first operand, and the entire second operand are left unchanged in the process, unless the operand areas overlap.

The MVN instruction moves each digit nibble, the low-order 4 bits of each byte, of the second operand to the corresponding position in the first operand area. MVN does not change the zone nibbles of the first operand or the second operand contents.

Suppose that we have

P1 : 12345678

P2 : ABCDEABC

The instruction

MVZ   P1(4),P2

produces

P2 : ABCDEABC

↓ ↓ ↓ ↓

P1 : A2 C4 E6 B8

The first nibble of each byte of P2 moves to the first nibble of each byte of P1. Similarly,

MVN   P1(4),P2

moves the second nibble of each byte of P2 to the second nibble of the corresponding byte of the area P1:

P2 : ABCDEABC

↓ ↓ ↓ ↓

P1 : 1 B3 D5 A7 C

As with the MVC instruction, when the operands overlap, the process appears to be carried out byte by byte, starting with the first or leftmost bytes of the operands and proceeding to the right. Thus,

MVZ   P1+1(3),P1

copies the zone of the first byte of P1 through the *remaining* bytes, yielding

P1 : 12141618

while

MVN   P2(2),P2+2

shifts the numeric portions of the last 2 bytes of P2 2 bytes to the left to give

P1 : EBBDEABC

The MVN instruction is handy in moving the sign code of a decimal number from place to place. For example, we can divide a decimal number by an even power of 10 simply by moving the sign code to the left. Thus, if we have

NUM: 3456789C

then moving the sign code C 2 bytes to the left to produce

NUM: 345C789C

has the affect of dividing the original number by 10,000. The instruction that does this is

MVN   NUM+1(1),NUM+3

Notice that the result is not quite the same as we would have obtained through the use of the DP instruction; the remainder is not correct. To use the result in further arithmetic operations, we use 2 as the length of NUM.

The MVZ instruction is useful in data conversion problems. One of the steps in conversion from EBCDIC to zoned decimal is the insertion of the proper sign code into the number. If the sign code is at INPT+3, using the methods of the preceding chapter, we write

OI   INPT+3,X'F0'
NI   INPT+3,X'DF'

to put in a sign code indicating a negative 4-byte zoned decimal number at INPT. The same task can be accomplished through the use of the instruction

MVZ   INPT+3(1),MZONE

with

MZONE   DC   X'DO'

defined in the data storage section of the program.

We have a similar problem in converting back from zoned decimal to EBCDIC in that we must move an F zone into the sign zone position in the number in order to convert the last byte into the character code for the last digit of the number. Given a 6-byte zoned decimal number at OUTPT, the instruction

MVZ   OUTPT+5(1),=X'F0'

does the trick.

The MVO instruction is useful in shifting decimal data an odd number of decimal places. In its execution the second nibble of each second operand byte is stored in the first nibble of the corresponding byte of the first operand. The first nibble of each second operand byte is stored in the second nibble of the preceding byte of the first operand. Leading zeros are inserted into the first operand if necessary to fill the area. If the second operand does not fit into the first operand area, those digits which do not fit are ignored.

The operand bytes are processed right to left. In effect, the MVO instruction behaves like the MVC instruction, except that the move occurs "slant-wise" (see Fig. 16-1), or with offset, and the additional features of inserting leading zeros or ignoring overflow do not occur with MVC.

Figure 16-1 illustrates the effect of the MVO instruction in general and in an example. Some further examples might help to make clear the func-

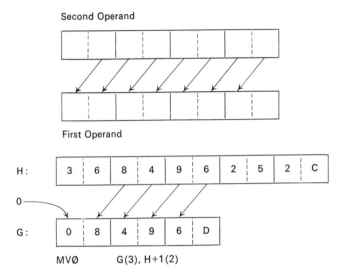

Fig. 16-1. The MVO instruction. The solid vertical lines represent byte boundaries; the dashed lines separate the nibbles with the bytes. In the example shown, G contained FFFFFD before execution.

tion of the MVO instruction. Suppose that we have

NUMS: 123456789C
ANS: AAAAAAAA

The following instructions produce the results indicated:

MVO	ANS(2),NUMS(1)
ANS:	012AAAAA
MVO	ANS(3),NUMS(1)
ANS:	00012AAA
MVO	ANS(3),NUMS(2)
ANS:	01234AAA
MVO	ANS(2),NUMS(4)
ANS:	89CAAAAA

As a further example, suppose that we have a 4-byte decimal number at Q,

Q: 6742198C

and that we wish to multiply this number by 1000, i.e., shift the number to the left three places. Let us further suppose that we want the resulting product to occupy 8 bytes at PROD, which originally contains

PROD: FFFFFFFFFFFFFFFF

We begin by moving Q with offset so that there are 2 bytes (room for three digits and sign) left over at the end of PROD. In other words, we want the

8 in Q to occupy the fifth nibble from the right of PROD. We might as well put in the leading zeros while we are at it, and so we write

MVO   PROD(7),Q(4)

After execution of this instruction, we have

PROD: 000006742198CFFF

Now we move the sign code of Q to the proper position in PROD,

MVN   PROD+(1),Q+3

which yields

PROD: 000006742198CFFC

and finally we AND in the trailing zeros,

NC   PROD+6(2),=X'000F'

to produce

PROD   000006742198000C

the desired result.

16.3.3. Shift and Round Packed

A single instruction implemented in the 370 series, but not to be found in the 360 machines, makes academic much of the preceding discussion about shifting decimal numbers in the 370 machines. The S̲hift and R̲ound P̲acked instruction can shift a decimal number any number of places to the right or left, inserting the necessary leading or trailing zeros in the process, and, in a right shift, the instruction rounds off the last digit of the result according to rules specified by the programmer.

SRP	D1(L1,B1),D2(B2),I3	Shift and	Shift $(D1 + (B1))_{L1}$
(370 *only*)		R̲ound P̲acked	to the left
			$(D2 + (B2))$ decimal
			places, using
			I3 as rounding factor

SRP is a special SS instruction. The first byte of the memory operand is at address $D1 + (B1)$ and L1 determines the length, in bytes, of this single operand. The last 6 bits, bits 26–31, of the *number* $D2 + (B2)$ determines the number of decimal places the memory operand is to be shifted; as in the binary shift instructions, this number is interpreted as a 6-bit 2's complement integer. If it is *positive*, the memory operand is shifted to the *left*, the number of places determined by the value of the number in these 6 bits. If bits 26–31 of $D2 + (B2)$ form a *negative* number, the memory operand is shifted to the *right* the number of places given by the magnitude of the number. Thus, if bits 26–31 of D2 + (B2) contain 000101_2, the memory operand is shifted to the left five decimal places, while if these 6 bits contain 111100_2, the computer shifts the memory operand to the right four decimal places.

The third operand, I3, is called a *rounding factor* and, in assembly language, is a decimal digit. To see how the rounding process works, let us take a closer look at how we go about rounding numbers off. Suppose that we decide to round numbers to the nearest integer. The number 12.7 rounds off to 13, 1.4 rounded off is 1, and 6.5 rounded off is 7. Our rule is that if the fraction is less than .5, we choose the next lower integer. Otherwise we pick the next highest one.

A more formal way of stating this rule is

$$R(x) = \{x + .5\}$$

where $R(x)$ is x rounded off to the nearest integer and the

$$\{y\} = \text{integer part of } y$$

The above holds for positive numbers x. If x is negative,

$$R(x) = \{x - .5\}$$

.5 is the rounding factor for rounding numbers off to the nearest integer. Other rounding factors of common use are 0, which results in *rounding down* or truncation and 1, which results in *rounding up* to the next higher digit.

A right shift of a decimal number corresponds to division by a power of 10. Thus, if we shift 1278 to the right two places, we obtain 12.78, which we can round off to the nearest integer by using a rounding factor of .5:

$$R\left(\frac{1278}{100}\right) = R(12.78) = \{12.78 + .5\} = 13$$

In the SRP instruction, I3 is 10 times the rounding factor as we have defined it above. In the execution of SRP when a right shift is involved, I3 is added to the last digit shifted out of the right end of the number. The carry digit from this addition is then added to the shifted result. Thus, if an SRP with I3 = 5 shifts the number

$$01278C$$

to the right two places, the result is computed as follows:

$$01278C \xrightarrow{\text{shift}} 00012C \qquad 7 = \text{last digit shifted out}$$
$$+1 \qquad\qquad +5 = \text{rounding factor}$$
$$\text{result} = \overline{00013C} \qquad\quad 2$$
$$\text{carry digit}$$

A similar process using

$$01213C$$

as the memory operand proceeds as follows:

$$01213C \xrightarrow{\text{shift}} 00012C \quad 1 = \text{last digit shifted out}$$
$$+0 \qquad +5 = \text{rounding factor}$$
$$\text{result} = \overline{00012C} \qquad 6$$
$$\text{carry digit}$$

The SRP instruction has the standard SS instruction format with the exception that the rounding factor, I3, occupies the position normally filled by the second operand length, L2.

FO	L1−1	I3	B1	←—	D1	—→	B2	←—	D2	—→

For example, the instruction

$$F072C2004002$$

shifts the 8-byte (did you forget to add one to L1−1?) decimal number starting at $200_{16} + (12)$, using 2 as a rounding factor. The number of places the memory operand is to be shifted and the direction of the shift is found in the last 6 bits of sum $2 + (4)$.

SRP checks the memory operand to be sure it is valid packed decimal number. If the number is not valid, a data exception occurs. A decimal overflow exception arises when an attempt is made to shift significant digits out of the left end of the number. This instruction sets the condition code in the same way as do the AP and SP instructions.

Use of SRP is simple. We put the number of places we wish to shift the memory operand in a register and use this register as the base register, B2, in the second operand designation. We normally use either 0 or 5 as a rounding factor; 0 rounds down, while 5 rounds to the nearest integer. All that is left to do is to specify the first operand.

Suppose that we have a 6-byte number at SNO and want to multiply it by 1000, that is, shift SNO to the left three places.

Using register 7 to contain the number of places to shift, we write

```
LA      7,3
SRP     SNO(6),0(7),5
```

Notice that, since we are considering a left shift, it does not matter what we give as a rounding factor. If SNO originally contains

$$\text{SNO}: \qquad 00000368427D$$

the result is

SNO: 00368427000D

The SRP instruction automatically inserts the trailing or leading zeros where necessary.

We assume here that SNO is long enough to contain the resulting product. If it is not, we can ZAP SNO into a longer area and proceed as above:

```
ZAP        TEMP(8),SNO(6)
LA         7,3
SRP        TEMP(8),0(7),5
```

Now let us suppose that we have a 5-byte number a BALL and wish to divide it by $10,000 = 10^4$, rounding the result to the nearest integer. Since we want a right shift, we must load the count register with -4.

```
LH         7,=H'−4'
SRP        BALL(5),0(7),5
```

These instructions produce the following results:

Before	After	Condition Code
BALL: 010358723B	000001036D	1
000000100C	000000000C	0
000056607C	000000006C	2

16.4. A PAYROLL PROGRAM

As an example of the use of decimal arithmetic in a practical example, we present in Fig. 16-2 a flow chart for a simple payroll calculation program. The input to the program is the employee's number and name, the number of hours he worked in the week, and the hourly rate at which he is paid. The input data are on one card per employee in the format

```
cols  1–9  :  employee number
cols 11–40:  employee name
cols 42–47:  hours worked
cols 49–52:  hourly wages
```

We assume that the hours worked and hourly wages are correct to two decimal places. In each number there must be a decimal place with two digits following it and it must be right-justified. Thus, inputs for the hours worked are up to six characters long and of the form *ddd.dd*. The hourly wages appear as *dd.dd* (we assume that nobody makes more than $100 per hour). No dollar

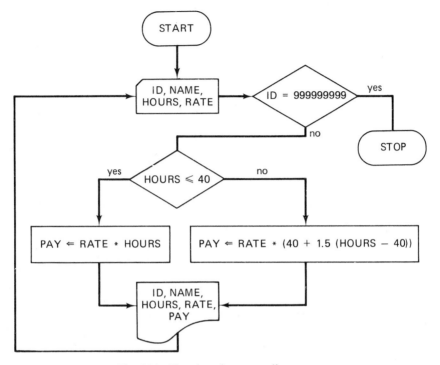

Fig. 16-2. Flowchart for a payroll program.

signs are used in the program. The program caculates each employee's weekly pay, proceeding until a trailer card containing 999999999 in the employee number field is encountered. We assume a 40-hour week and pay at time and a half for overtime.

The program shows how arithmetic with decimal fractions can be done using computer integer arithmetic. The program treats all money values as if they were in pennies. After reading the input data and making a copy of them for output, the program shifts each of the pair of last two digits in the input numbers to the left one place, so that the result is the original numbers as pennies or hundredths of hours worked. The data are then packed, and the calculations shown in Fig. 16-3 follow. Notice that to multiply a number by 1.5, we actually multiply it by 150 and then divide the result by 100 by moving the sign code to the left 1 byte. After unpacking the answer, the program inserts a decimal point, removes the leading blanks, prints the result, and starts the process over again.

You might notice that the preparation of decimal data for output is rather tedious. The EDit and EDit and MarK instructions discussed in Chaper 20 are very helpful in such problems. There is no reason you should-not learn to use these instruction now if you wish.

```
PAYROLL   START  0
          PRINT  NOGEN
          INITIAL
          PRT    HEADING        PRINT LABELS AT TOP OF PAGE
NEXTPAY   RCD    ID             READ CARD IMAGE INTO 80 BYTES STARTING ID
          CLC    ID(5),=9C'9'        CHECK FOR LAST CARD
          BE     DONE
          MVC    IDETC(80),ID   MAKE COPY AT IDETC
          MVC    HOURS+3(2),HOURS+4    COVER UP DECIMAL PLACE IN HOURS
          PACK   HRS(4),HOURS(5)   PACK HOURS WORKED
          MVC    RATE+2(2),RATE+3   COVER UP DECIMAL PLACE IN PAYRATE
          PACK   RT(4),RATE(4)  PACK THE PAYRATE
          CP     HRS(4),=P'4000'  SEE IF HE WORKED MORE THAN 40 HOURS
          BP     OVERTIME       IF SO TAKE THIS INTO ACCOUNT AT OVERTIME
          ZAP    PAY(9),HRS(4)  PREPARE TO MULTIPLY HOURS WORKED BY RATE
          MP     PAY(9),RT(4)   DO THE MULTIPLICATION
          B      OUTPUT         AND GO OUTPUT THE RESULT
OVERTIME  ZAP    PAY(10),HRS(4)  MOVE HOURS WORKED TO AREA FOR MULT.
          SP     PAY(10),=P'4000'  COMPUTE OVERTIME HOURS
          MP     PAY(10),=P'150'  TIMES TIME AND A HALF
          MVN    PAY+8(1),PAY+9  DIVIDE BY 100
          AP     PAY(9),=P'4000'  ADD THE 40 HOURS BACK IN
          MP     PAY(9),RT(4)   MULTIPLY BY THE HOURLY RATE
OUTPUT    UNPK   PAYOUT(10),PAY(8)  RESULT IN PAY, IGNORE LAST DIGIT
          MVZ    PAYOUT+9(1),=X'F0'  CORRECT SIGN CODE
          MVC    PAYOUT(7),PAYOUT+1  MAKE ROOM FOR DECIMAL PLACE
          MVI    PAYOUT+7,C'.'  MOVE DECIMAL POINT IN
          LA     2,PAYOUT       REMOVE LEADING 0'S
NDIG      CLI    0(2),C'0'      CHECK FOR 0
          BNE    PRINT          HAVE FOUND FIRST NONZERO DIGIT IF BRANCH
          MVI    0(2),C' '      REPLACE 0 WITH BLANK
          LA     2,1(2)         INCREMENT ADDRESS REGISTER
          B      NDIG           LOOK AT NEXT CHARACTER
PRINT     PRT    OUTLINE
          B      NEXTPAY        GO READ NEXT DATA CARD
DONE      EOJ
HRS       DS     4C
PAY       DS     10C
RT        DS     4C
ID        DS     10C
NAME      DS     31C
HOURS     DS     7C
RATE      DS     32C
HEADING   DC     CL13' 1EMPLOYEE NO. '
          DC     CL10' '
          DC     CL4'NAME'
          DC     CL16' '
          DC     CL6'HOURS'
          DC     CL8'RATE'
          DC     CL66'PAY'
OUTLINE   DC     C' '
IDETC     DS     53C
PAYOUT    DS     10C
          DC     69C' '
          END    PAYROLL
```

Fig. 16-3

CHAPTER SUMMARY

The decimal arithmetic and information move instructions are shown in Table 16-2.

Table 16-2 DECIMAL ARITHMETIC AND MOVE INSTRUCTIONS

AP	D1(L1,B1),D2(L2,B2)	Add Packed	$D1 + (B1) \leftarrow (D1 + (B1))_{L1} + (D2 + (B2))_{L2}$
SP	D1(L1,B1),D2(L2,B2)	Subtract Packed	$D1 + (B1) \leftarrow (D1 + (B1))_{L1} - (D2 + (B2))_{L2}$
MP	D1(L1,B1),D2(L2,B2)	Multiply Packed	$D1 + (B1) \leftarrow (D1 + (B1))_{L1} \times (D2 + (B2))_{L2}$
DP	D1(L1,B1),D2(L2,B2)	Divide Packed	Compute $(D1 + (B1))_{L1} \div (D2 + (B2))_{L2}$ $(D1 + (B1))_{L1-L2} \leftarrow$ quotient $(D2 + (B2)) + L1 - L2)_{L2} \leftarrow$ remainder
CP	D1(L1,B1),D2(L2,B2)	Compare Packed	Set CC to indicate value of $(D1 + (B1))_{L1} - (D2 + (B2))_{L2}$
ZAP	D1(L1,B1),D2(L2,B2)	Zero and Add Packed	$D1 + (B1) \leftarrow 0_{L1}; D1 + (B1) \leftarrow (D1 + (B1))_{L1} + (D2 + (B2))_{L2}$
MVZ	D1(L,B1),D2(B2)	MoVe Zone	$Zone(D1 + (B1)) \leftarrow zone(D2 + (B2))_L$
MVN	D1(L,B1),D2(B2)	MoVe Numeric	$Numeric(D1 + (B1)) \leftarrow numeric(D2 + (B2))_L$
MVO	D1(L,B1),D2(B2)	MoVe with Offset	See text, p. 369

EXERCISES

1. Write a program to compute weighted grade point averages using decimal arithmetic. The input data for each student should consist of a nine-digit student number followed by scores on each of three quizzes, a homework total, and a final exam in the format *ddd.dd* with one space between each number. The final average should be weighted as follows:

> 20% for each quiz
> 15% for homework
> 25% for final exam

Print the student number, all five scores, and the average for each student and the class average of all five scores. Your output should be in tabular form with appropriate labels.

2. A mortage ammortization table shows, for each monthly payment, the amount of the payment, the amount of the payment that is interest, the amount that is applied to paying of the principle, and the remaining balance. Write a program to compute and print mortgage ammortization tables. The input data are the original principle, PRINC; the amount of the monthly payment, MOPAY; and the annual interest rate, ANNINT. The calculations proceed as follows:
(a) Calculate the monthly interest rate,

$$MOINT = ANNINT/12.$$

(b) Compute the amount of interest paid this month $= INT = MOINT \times PRINC.$
(c) If $PRINC \le MOPAY$, this is the final payment: $PAY = PRINC = MOPAY$. Print these values and INT calculated in step (b) and stop.
(d) Otherwise, compute the payment on the principle, $PPAY = MOPAY - INT$ and the new principle $PRINC \rightarrow PRINC - MOPAY$. Print the results and go to step (b).

As an example, your output might look like this for the first few lines:

BEGINNING BALANCE = 5000.00, INTEREST RATE = 6.00

PAYMENT NO.	AMOUNT PAID	INTEREST	PAID ON BALANCE	NEW BALANCE
1	500.00	250.00	250.00	4750.00
2	500.00	237.50	262.50	4512.50
3	500.00	225.62	274.38	4238.12
		.		
		.		
		.		

3. Write a program to help MAW BELL calculate monthly telephone bills. Input data are in the format

> Cols. 1–10: Account number
> Col. 12: Type of account code:
> > B: Business
> > R: Residential
> Col. 14: Code for type of phone:
> > A: Basic black
> > B: Colored desk
> > C: Princess
> > D: Trimline
> > E: Pushbutton
> Col. 16: Number of extensions

The monthly service charge is computed as follows:

Type	Charge
A	$5.50
B	6.00
C	6.50
D	7.00
E	7.50

Extensions cost one-half of the monthly rate for the first extension and $1.50 for each additional extension. Businesses receive a 2.5% discount. Federal excise tax for all customers is 10%.

4. Write a program to manage the inventory system described in Exercises 3 and 4 in Chapter 10. Implement the following additional control characters in your program:

> S: Sold, subtract number starting in column 15 from number in stock
> A: Add, add number in column 15 to number in stock

Have your program print an appropriate message when the number in stock becomes less than the reorder number. When an E (End) control character is encountered, your program should list the updated inventory records and then compute and print the total value of all items in stock.

5. Exercise 12 in Chapter 10 describes a program to produce student grade reports. In addition to the data supplied for that program, assume that column 27 contains an integer which indicates the number of hours of credit the student received for taking the course. Using the values $A=4$, $B=3$, $C=2$, $D=1$, $F=0$, have your program calculate the semester grade average for each student.

REFERENCES

IBM System/360 Disk and Tape Operating System Assembler Language, Form GC24-3414, IBM Corp., White Plains, N.Y.

IBM System/360 Operating System Assembler Language, Form GC28-6514, IBM Corp., White Plains, N.Y.

IBM System/360 Principles of Operation, Form GA22-6821, IBM Corp., White Plains, N.Y.

IBM System/370 Principles of Operation, Form GA22-7000, IBM Corp., White Plains, N.Y.

IBM OS/VS—DOS/VS Assembler Language, Order No. GC33-4010, IBM Corp., White Plains, N.Y.

17 INPUT/OUTPUT PROGRAMMING

"You can compute all you like, but if you can't I/O it don't mean a thing."
John Voigt, 1971

One of the functions of the operating system is to provide for control of input/output devices and to manage the large amounts of data that go into and out of the computer system. Until now, we have depended on special macros, such as RCD and PLN, to do input/output for us. These macros link to a subroutine which uses operating system macros to carry out the desired I/O operations. Part of this chapter is devoted to a discussion of these *system data management macros* for DOS and OS systems.

We shall also investigate input/output at a more primitive level than that offered by the system input/output macros. In so doing, we shall see how the processor supervises input/output operations and directs the operation of the actual devices.

Before considering some of the more specialized aspects of input/output programming, we shall investigate some general principles of data storage.

17.1. DATA STRUCTURES

A *file* is a collection of related information in a form suitable for storage and processing by a computer system. A file consists of a number of *logical records*. We often leave out the qualifier "logical" when speaking of the records in a file. Each record contains the data for an individual entity. In an inventory file, a (logical) record is the data pertinent to a single part. In the registrar's student grade file, a record contains such information as the student's number, name, classification, and grades in courses he has taken. In a bank checking account file, a record might contain the customer's number, name, address, and current balance and a description of all the deposits and withdrawals the customer has made since the last monthly reporting time. In the income tax files maintained by the Internal Revenue Service, a record describes a year's income tax return from a taxpayer. Much of today's computing is dedicated to the construction and maintenance of files.

A large portion of the operating system is devoted to assisting users in processing data. But the operating system also has many other kinds of information to deal with, such as machine language programs, libraries of programs, jobs input, and output from jobs. A *data set* is a major unit of information that the operating system deals with. A data set is a collection of data stored in a prescribed arrangement, together with control information necessary to enable the system to access the data in the data set. The operating system offers several possible structures, or *data set organizations*, for data sets.

We use the operating system data management facilities to maintain our own data files. The structure we wish to use for our data determines the data set organization we use. We shall describe the data set organizations shortly, but let us first look more closely at the relationship between logical records and input/output operations.

17.1.1. Blocks and Records

As we said, a file consists of one or more *logical records*. The characters that form a printed line are a record, as are the data from a punched card. A logical record or simply a *record* in an assembly language source program is one source statement, which is 80 bytes long. A student record in the registrar's file might occupy 500 bytes. In general, the purpose for which the file is designed determines the lengths and contents of the individual records within the file.

A *physical record*, or *block*, is the amount of information transmitted by an I/O device in a single operation. In the case of a card reader or punch, since a punched card represents 80 bytes of information, a block is 80 bytes for these devices. A block for the line printer is commonly 132 bytes, the length of a printed line. On these and other devices in which the length of a block is fixed by the hardware, we cannot vary the number of (logical) records in a block; there is exactly one record per block. We call such devices *unit record devices*. On other devices, such as magnetic tapes and disks, the length of a block is not predetermined by the device or the storage medium. The programmer chooses the lengths of a block on such devices. Physical records are not necessarily of the same length as logical records. The *record format* of a data set is the relationship between the records and blocks in the data set. If a physical record is the same as a logical record, we say that the records are *unblocked*. If there is more than one record per block, the data set has a *blocked* record format. If more than one block is required to contain a record, the data set is said to have a *spanned* record format.

It is also possible to have blocks of different lengths in a single data set. If so, the block size is said to be *variable*. The lengths of the blocks in such a data set are stored in the blocks. If all blocks in a data set have the same length, the block size is *fixed*.

Various combinations of block-length descriptions and record formats can be used. Figure 17-1 illustrates some of the possible combinations. The data set depicted in Fig. 17-1(a) might be from a punched card file. Each block is 80 bytes long and contains exactly one record. In Fig. 17-1(b) we have a data set in which there are three 100-byte records stored in each 300-byte block. An I/O operation processing this data set transfers 300 bytes. The program, whether an operating system program or one written by the user, splits the block up into its component records for processing. In Fig. 17-1(c) we show a data set which contains spanned records of fixed length. Two I/O transfers are required for each record. Figure 17-1(d) shows how we can have different numbers of variable-length records in variable-length blocks. It is again up to a program to separate out the logical records from each physical record.

17.1.2. Data Set Organization

Having described the possible choices for designing the components—blocks and records—of a data set, we shall now turn to the overall structure of the data set. The *organization* of a data set is a description of the order in which its blocks are placed and how each block is related to the entire data set. The choice of data set organization depends on several factors, including the nature of the device on which the data are stored, the order in which records will be retrieved, and the purpose for which the data set is designed.

Sequential Organization. With some I/O equipment, such as magnetic tape units and unit record devices, we have no choice about the data set organization; the records must be processed in the order in which they are stored. A card reader reads cards one at a time in the order in which they are stacked in the machine. A line printer prints one line at a time in the order in which the records are sent to the printer. A magnetic tape unit writes blocks in the order in which they are transmitted to the unit. Subsequent input from a tape file produces the blocks in the same order as that in which they were written.

On the other hand, using magnetic disks and other *direct access* devices, it is possible to store and retrieve blocks from anywhere on the device through the use of the address of the record. In other words, we can process the records in any desired order, provided we know or can find out the addresses

a. Fixed length, unblocked.

Record length = 80 bytes
Block length = 80 bytes

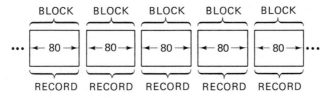

b. Fixed length, blocked.

Record length = 100 bytes
Block length = 300 bytes

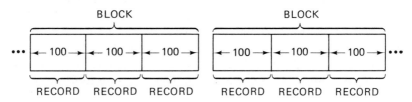

c. Fixed length, spanned.

Record length = 400 bytes
Block length = 200 bytes

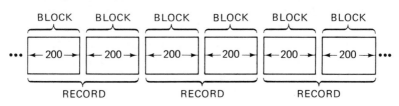

d. Variable length, blocked.

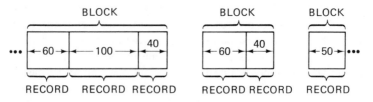

Fig. 17-1. Record formats.

at which they are or will be stored. But in most applications the physical order of the records is the same as the order in which we wish to use them. We rarely wish to process the records that constitute the source language statements in a program in any order besides that in which they are written. The same is true of a machine language object module or load module.

A file in which the records are processed in the same sequence as that in which they are stored is called a *sequential* file. In creating a sequential file or adding records to it, the records are written in the same order as that in which they are sent to the I/O device. Input from a sequential file is received in the same order as that in which the records are stored. Processing records in the order in which they are stored is called *serial* or *sequential* processing.

We store sequential files in data sets with sequential organization. Figure 17-2 illustrates the structure of a sequential data set. There is an end-of-file

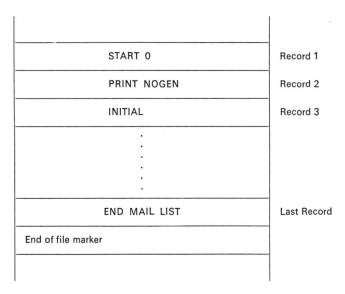

Fig. 17-2. A sequential file.

marker after the last block in the data. If we add a block to the data set, the new block replaces the end-of-file marker and a new end-of-file marker is written after the added block. When we input the blocks from the data set, we obtain them in the same order as that in which they are stored until the end-of-file marker is reached.

Partitioned Organization.   We have mentioned several libraries the system maintains for the user: the system macro library, the library of catalogued procedures, and libraries of systems programs are examples. Each *member* of such a library is itself a sequential data set. For example an OS system library of catalogued procedures contains members ASMFCLG, FORTGCLG, and COBUCG, among others.

We often need to retrieve a member of a library by its *member name.* When we use the macro INITIAL, the assembler asks the system to supply it the member named INITIAL from the macro library. A data set composed of one or more members, each of which is locatable by its name, is called a *partitioned data set.*

Partitioned data sets must be stored on a direct access device, so that, given the address of the beginning of a member, the device can retrieve the desired member. To facilitate finding a desired member, the system creates and maintains a *directory.* Each directory entry contains the name of a member of the data set and the (disk) address of the first block of that member. Figure 17-3 illustrates the structure of a partitioned data set. When asked to find a given member, the system searches through the directory until it finds the name of the desired member. It then uses the address associated with that member name to locate the sequential data set that is the member itself.

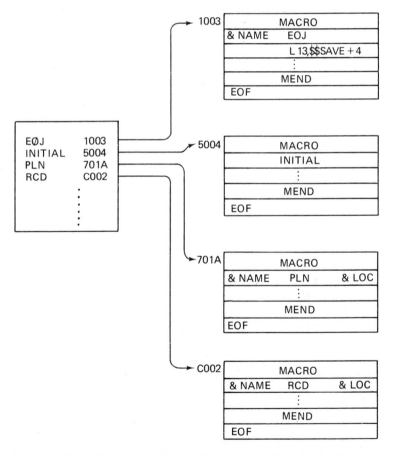

Fig. 17-3. The structure of a partitioned data set that contains the special macros for this text. The EØF record is the End-Of-File marker. Each member is itself a sequential file.

The Operating System provides the user with the subroutines necessary to create and maintain his own partitioned data sets. OS also uses partitioned data sets to maintain its own libraries. DOS maintains its libraries using similar techniques but does not include support for users to create and process their own partitioned data sets.

Indexed Sequential Organization. In many applications, it is convenient to process a file both sequentially, in the order in which the records are stored, and at random, reading, adding, or updating individual records without regard to their position within the file. In an inventory management system, we might keep a record for each kind of part in stock. We identify a part by its part number, which we use as a key. We keep the file sorted so that the keys of successive records are in numerical order. At the end of each week, we produce a report on the current inventory by listing the records sequentially. Since the records are ordered according to part number, the output will also be ordered by part number, making it easier to find given entries.

During the week, however, the company adds some parts to its stock by manufacturing or buying new items and removes items from stock by selling them. When the number in stock of a given part changes, we must make a change in its record in the inventory file. To do this we must first locate the desired record. We could perform a serial search of the file, starting at the beginning, until we find the record with the part number we are looking for. But in a file containing many thousands of records, such a search every time we want to update a single record is just too expensive and time-consuming. What we need is a data set organization in which it is possible to process the records in order and also to access individual records according to their keys.

The *indexed sequential data set organization* makes both these processing techniques possible. In creating an indexed sequential data set, we first sort the records in the file according to a key. We would use the part number for the key in the inventory example. We then output the records sequentially. The system writes the records sequentially on the direct access device. While doing so, the system creates one or more indexes. If we later process the file sequentially, we receive the records in the same order as that in which they were written. If we ask the system for a record with a given key, the system uses the indexes it created to speed up the search for the desired record.

Figure 17-4 illustrates an indexed sequential file with a single index. The file itself is split into subfiles, each of which has an entry in the index. The index entry for a subfile contains the key of the *last* record in the subfile and the address of the *first* record in the subfile. When asked to find a record with a given key, the system first searches through the index until it finds the

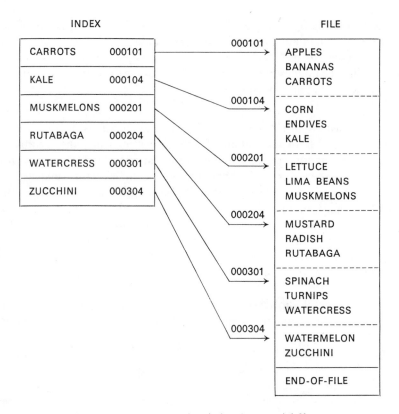

Fig. 17-4. Structure of an indexed sequential file.

first key higher than (or equal to) the one desired. The system then searches through the subfile until the record is found.

The system can add new records into their proper positions and delete old records from an indexed sequential data set. Thus, the indexed sequential organization provides a powerful means of maintaining sorted files so that we can process the records either in the order written or in random order.

Direct Organization.   If the choice of the addresses at which records are stored is left to the user, we say that the data set has *direct* organization. In normal use, the key of each record contains the information needed to calculate the address of the record or to determine a neighborhood in which the record is located. Direct organization offers the fastest means of retrieving records at random, but at the expense of increased responsibility for the programmer in creating and maintaining the file. We use the direct organization when we wish to create a file with a structure different from those supplied automatically by the operating system.

17.1.3. Access Methods

In Section 17.4 we shall outline the machine hardware input/output system and describe the requirements for direct control of input/output devices. But we rarely need to program at such a fundamental level. Instead, we rely upon sets of systems programs called *access methods* to control the actual transfer of data between memory and I/O devices and to create and maintain data sets in whatever organization we choose. An input/output command using an access method is a request issued to systems programs called the *I/O supervisor*. The I/O supervisor and its subroutines manage the entire I/O operation. This means that if we use an access method, we need not worry about the details of the input/output operations; the access method does the job.

Each operating system offers several access methods from which to choose. The decision as to which access method to use depends on the local operating system, the organization of the data set to be processed, and the buffer technique desired.

Buffers. A *buffer* is an area in memory used to receive the data transferred into memory from an input device or to contain the data to be sent from the memory to an output device. In a typical operation, we include a buffer address along with our request for input. The I/O supervisor responds by filling the buffer with a block from the device. On output, our program fills a buffer with the data to be output. When the data are to be transmitted, the program passes the address of the buffer to the system, which outputs the data from the buffer as requested.

Figure 17-5(a) illustrates the course of events that occur when a user program periodically requests input into a single buffer. The user program issues an input request. Since, presumably, his program cannot proceed further until it has received the requested data, the supervisor suspends execution of the program until the input request has been fulfilled.

Input/output operations, even with the fastest devices, require relatively large amounts of time during which the machine could be executing many thousands of instructions. Thus, the use of a single buffer slows down the execution of the program considerably. This is not to say that it is impossible to do input/output while the CPU is executing other instructions. As we shall see in Section 17.4, the 360 and 370 computers permit simultaneous CPU instruction processing and input/output operations. We say that input/output operations *overlap* the execution of instructions.

To take advantage of the overlap capability, we use more than one buffer, as is illustrated in Fig. 17-5(b). Assuming that the records in the file are processed sequentially, the supervisor knows that the next record to be input will be the next record in the file. Thus, the system can anticipate a future

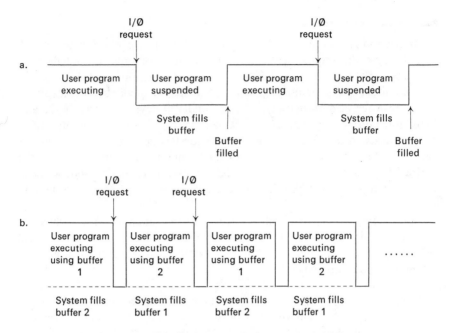

Fig. 17-5. (a) Basic buffering suspends the execution of the program until the buffer can be filled. (b) Use of more than one buffer allows concurrent program execution and I/Ø data transfer.

request for input by filling a buffer before the request is actually made. In effect, if the user program is not *I/O bound* (using buffers faster than the system can fill or empty them), the use of multiple buffers permits the user program to proceed with a minimum delay for input/output operations. Use of more than one buffer also improves efficiency in output data transfers.

If we process records in a file in random order, the system cannot antici- pate what the next I/O request will be, and we ordinarily use a single buffer.

Each operating system includes several access methods. How much concern the programmer must have about I/O buffers depends on the access method being used. Some access methods manage buffers automatically. Others require the programmer to take complete control of buffer manage- ment. In still others, the user chooses whether to manage the buffers himself or to leave that problem to the system.

DOS Access Methods.   The access methods available in the Disk Operat- ing System provide for semiautomatic buffering. The user supplies one or two buffer areas in the data storage part of his program. If he uses two buffer areas, the system provides anticipatory I/O in the processing of sequential files. The user may choose to have the system block records for output or deblock them upon input, if the records are in blocked format. DOS systems

Table 17-1 SOME OS ACCESS METHODS

Name	Acronym	Use
Queued Sequential Access Method	QSAM	Sequential files, queued access technique
Basic Sequential Access Method	BSAM	Sequential files, basic access technique
Queued Indexed Sequential Access Method	QISAM	Creation and sequential processing of indexed sequential files
Basic Indexed Sequential Access Method	BISAM	Random processing of indexed sequential files
Basic Partitioned Access Method	BPAM	Creation and processing of partitioned data sets
Basic Direct Access Method	BDAM	Processing files with direct organization
Telecommunications Access Method	TCAM	Communications with remote terminals

support sequential, indexed sequential, and direct organizations. The primary DOS access methods are

Sequential Access Method (SAM)
Indexed Sequential Access Method (ISAM)
Direct Access Method (DAM)

OS Access Methods.   The Operating System includes two types of access method, Basic and Queued. In the *queued* access methods buffering is completely automatic. The system supplies the buffer areas and provides for automatic deblocking of blocked records. Used only for processing sequential and indexed sequential files, the queued access methods provide for maximum program efficiency with a minimal amount of user effort.

The basic access methods are more primitive but more flexible than the queued access methods. The user has more responsibilities in buffer management and may be required to unblock his own records. The basic methods are used primarily in nonsequential file manipulations. Table 17-1 lists some of the more important OS access methods.

We have barely scratched the surface in the survey of data structures and I/O facilities presented above. But we have said enough now to discuss the use of the access methods in input/output programming. From here on we shall limit our discussion to how to use the DOS Sequential Access Method and the OS Queued Sequential Access Method. While the principles involved are the same for OS as in DOS, the details are different. Concentrate on learning how to use the input/output facilities at your local system, DOS in Section 17.2 or OS in Section 17.3, and then skim over the other section to observe the similar approaches in the two systems.

17.2. DOS INPUT/OUTPUT MACROS

There are three basic components involved in input/output processing:

1. The user program, which requests specific operations upon data sets and specifies details regarding the data set organization, buffer technique, record formats, and others.

2. The operating system input/output support programs and access methods, which serve as an interface between the user's program and the physical input/output devices.

3. The data as it appears on the physical device.

Before the user program is executed, these components are independent in that the operating system cannot predict the input/output processing the program will request. Nor does the system know which data sets the user program will require or anything about their organization. Therefore, the user program must issue the requests for input/output operations, supply the operating system with a description of the data set, and tell the system how to relate the program's requests for use of a specific data set to the operating system and to the data set itself.

In using DOS input/output facilities, there are three types of input/output macros that must be included in the user program. The *file description* macros all have the form <u>DTF</u>xx. DTF stands for <u>Define The File</u>. xx represents two letters which further delineate the type of file. The DTF macros produce a table of parameters the operating system needs to process the file. The OPEN and CLOSE macros initiate and terminate the processing of a given file. OPEN gives the information supplied by the DTF macro to the operating system and prepares the device for I/O operations. CLOSE indicates that the file will no longer be used by the program. We make actual requests for data transfer via the GET (input) and PUT (output) or READ (input) and WRITE (output) macro instructions. Which of these pairs of macro instructions we use depends on the data set organization and how the data are processed.

Table 17-2 DTF MACROS

Name	Use
DTFCD	CarD input files
DTFPR	PRinted output files
DTFMT	Magnetic Tape files
DTFSD	Sequential files stored on Direct access devices
DTFDA	Files with Direct organization
DTFIS	Indexed Sequential files

In the following we shall focus our attention upon the DOS Sequential Access Method input/output facilities. Use of other access methods differs in detail from the use of SAM, but the fundamentals are the same. When you have mastered the following material, you will be able to use the manuals when you need to use other access methods.

17.2.1 The Define The File Macros

The DTF macros produce tables of constants. When the file is OPENed, the operating system examines the constants to find out how the data set is organized, what the record format is, and how to do the buffering when the program requests input/output operations. The DTF macros are written

filename   DTFxx   operands

A program must include one DTF statement for each file used by the program. The *filename* field contains a name valid in assembly language. The program uses this name in an I/O request to specify which file to use. The operands specify the processing details. The letters we use in place of xx determine the data set organization and indicate the type of I/O device that will be used in processing the file. Table 17-2 shows some of the standard DTF macro names and the kinds of processing the macros are designed for. Since these macros establish tables of constants for use by the operating system, we usually place the DTF macros in the data and constant storage area of the program—somewhere between the last program instruction and the END statement.

All the assembly language operands we have been using are *positional* operands. The meaning of a positional operand depends on where the operand appears in the operand list. For example, in the instruction

ST   A,B

the symbol A is understood to represent a register number because it appears first in the operand field. The symbol B must be equivalent to a memory address because it appears as the second operand of this RX instruction.

The operands of the DTF macros and many other system macros are what we call *key-word* operands. We specify a key-word operand by writing

Keyword=value

where "keyword" is a symbol that the macro expects to find as an operand and "value" is a number or symbol whose value we wish to assign to that symbol. For example,

IOAREA1=INPTA

as an operand of a DTF macro assigns the value INPTA to the key-word operand IOAREA1.

A series of key-word operands may be written in any order; their meanings are independent of their position in the operand field. The two statements

CARDFILE   DTFCD   DEVADDR=SYSIPT,IOAREA1=INPTA

and

CARDFILE   DTFCD   IOAREA1=INPTA,DEVADDR=SYSIPT

are equivalent. As with all assembly language operands, we use commas to separate individual key-word operands in a series, and there can be no spaces within the operands field.

Recall that the DTF macro supplies to the operating system information concerning the program's input/output operations. To tell the system which device to use in processing the file, we use the *required* DEVice ADDRess operand,

DEVADDR=SYSxxx

The DOS system permits us to use *symbolic unit names* of the form SYSxxx to refer to I/O devices. We can designate a specific physical I/O device to be associated with a symbolic unit name using an ASSGN JCL statement. The value of the DEVADDR operand is the symbolic unit name of the device that is used to process the file described in the DTF macro. Thus, if we wish to process a card file read on the system input card reader (symbolic unit name SYSIPT), we write

DEVADDR=SYSIPT

Similarly, if we have a file stored on a disk with symbolic unit name SYSDSK, we write

DEVADDR=SYSDSK

All input/output operations require at least one memory buffer area. Input operations move the data into the buffer from the device. Output operations transfer the contents of the buffer to the device. The IOAREAx operands tell the system where to find the buffer(s) to use. Since we must have at least one buffer, a *required* DTF operand is the

IOAREA1=address

operand. Here the value "address" is usually the symbolic name of a memory area. Since input/output operations transmit a block of data at a time, the address given should be the address of a memory area that is long enough to contain one block. For punched-card input a block is 80 bytes. Thus, we might write a DTF macro for a card file as

CARDFILE   DTFCD   DEVADDR=SYSIPT,IOAREA1=CARDBUF

with the area CARDBUF defined by a statement such as

CARDBUF   DS   20F

Similarly, for a magnetic tape file written with blocks 400 bytes long we could write

TAPEINPT   DTFMT   DEVADDR=SYSTPE,IOAREA1=INPLACE

with INPLACE defined by

INPLACE   DS   CL400

We mentioned the fact that input/output processing is more efficient if we use more than one buffer area. DOS allows the designation of a second buffer area through the use of the IOAREA2 operand. A DTF macro which includes the operands

...IOAREA1=BUFFER1,IOAREA2=BUFFER2, ...

causes the use of two buffer areas and BUFFER1 and BUFFER2 when input/output requests are issued. We must reserve the memory space for both buffers. The system then has a better chance to overlap input/output operations with instruction execution.

In processing unblocked records (1 record = 1 block) with more than one buffer area or when using blocked records (more than one record per block) we must be able to determine where the record currently being processed is stored. After execution of the GET macro, we need to know where the system has stored the record just input. We must be able to specify the memory address of a record before we PUT the record for output.

There are two ways to determine the address of a record. The first is to supply the address of the record when we execute the input/output macro. For example, if we want a record input to be stored at RECIN, we write

GET   CARDFILE,RECIN

where CARDFILE is the file name for the card input file. When we supply the record address to the system as above, we indicate our intention to do this by including the operand

WORKA=YES

in the DTF for that file. In the example above, the DTF statement might be written

CARDFILE   DTFCD   DEVADDR=SYSIPT,IOAREA1=BUFFER1,

IOAREA2=BUFFER2,WORKA=YES

An alternative is to use a register to contain the address of a record. We indicate our intention to do so by writing

IOREG=n

as an operand in the DTF macro. n is the number of one of the general-purpose registers. The DTF macro

CARDFILE   DTFCD   DEVADDR=SYSIPT,IOAREA1=BUFFER1,

IOAREA2=BUFFER2,IOREG=5

says that after a GET is executed, the address of the record will be in register 5. On output, we place the address of the record to be output in the register named with the IOREG operand.

The IOREG and WORKA operands are mutually exclusive. We can ask the system to give us an address in a register or tell the system what the address is, but we cannot do both.

The three DTF statements named CARDFILE above are sufficient for input from a punched-card file, although the last two are more efficient for the reasons stated. Another useful operand for input files is the End Of File ADDRess operand, EOFADDR. If, for example, we include the operand

EOFADDR=NOMORE

as an operand in a DTF macro for an input file, the system branches to the statement named NOMORE in the program when an attempt is made to read the end-of-file marker. This eliminates the need for trailer cards or counters to determine when the last record in the file has been input.

Use of the DTFCD macro implies that the record format is unblocked and that the records are 80 bytes long. To process files with other record formats and block lengths, we use alternative forms of the DTF macro. To process a magnetic tape file we use the DTFMT macro. Because the record format on a magnetic tape depends on how the file was written, we must supply this information in the DTF macro. To do this we use the RECord FORMat, BLocK SIZE, and RECord SIZE operands. Table 17-3 summarizes the RECFORM operands, their meanings, and other operands required when we use them.

Table 17-3   RECFORM OPERAND

Value	Meaning	Other Operands Required
RECFORM = FIXUNB	Records are of fixed length and are unblocked	BLKSIZE
FIXBLK	Records are of fixed length and are blocked	BLKSIZE, RECSIZE
VARUNB	Records are of variable length and are unblocked	BLKSIZE = length of longest block
VARBLK	Records are of variable length and are blocked	BLKSIZE = length of longest block RECSIZE = length of longest record

To use the BLKSIZE and RECSIZE operands, we simply supply the desired lengths, in numbers of bytes, for their values. For example,

$$BLKSIZE = 5000$$

means that the blocks are 5000 bytes long, while

$$RECSIZE = 200$$

means each record consists of 200 bytes.

As an example, the DTF statement

TAPE   DTFMT   DEVADDR=SYSTPE,IOAREA1=IN1,

                      IOAREA2=IN2,WORKA=YES,

                      RECFORM=FIXBLK,BLKSIZE=720,

                      RECSIZE=120,EOFADDR=DONE

defines an input tape file named TAPE whose symbolic unit name is SYSTPE. Two buffers named IN1 and IN2 are to be used, and a record address will be submitted when the GET macro is executed. The records are of fixed length and are blocked. Each block contains six 120-byte records. The instruction at DONE is to be executed when an end-of-file is encountered.

We specify the type of processing—input, output, or both—using the TYPEFLE operand. The default value is

TYPEFLE=INPUT

Since we did not use a TYPEFILE operand in any of the DTF examples above, all those DTFs are for input. For an output file we write

TYPEFLE=OUTPUT

while if a file is used for both input and output, we use

TYPEFLE=INOUT

A DTF statement for the program that created the tape file in the preceding example might be written

```
TAPEOUT    DTFMT    DEVADDR=SYSTPE,IOAREA1=OUT1,
                    IOAREA2=OUT2,IOREG=6,
                    RECFORM=FIXBLK,BLKSIZE=720,
                    RECSIZE=120,TYPEFLE=OUTPUT
```

Here we indicate that the record address will be in register 6 when a PUT macro is executed. Notice that the EOFADDR operand is meaningless for an output file.

We conclude our discussion of the DTF macro with a description of DTFs for printed files. All the principles we have discussed above apply here also. The only addition we must make is an operand which determines how the carriage control is to be done. The ConTroL CHaRacter operand can have one of two values.

CTLCHR=ASA

means use the American Standards Association carriage control characters we discussed in Chapter 10 (blank means single space, 1 means top of page, etc.). If we wish to use IBM's carriage control method, we write

CTLCHR=YES

With IBM carriage control, we do not include an extra character at the beginning of each output line. If no other action is specified, each line is one space below the preceding one. The CNTRL macro is used to skip lines, go to the top of the page, and so on. If we use the CNTRL macro, we must include the operand

CONTROL=YES

in the DTF.

Most programmers find the ASA carriage control system convenient. A DTF macro for a printer file is

```
PRTFILE     DTFPR   DEVADDR=SYSLST,IOAREA1=LINE1,
                    IOAREA2=LINE2,WORKA=YES,
                    TYPEFLE=OUTPUT,CTLCHR=ASA
```

Here we have used the fact that the default value for RECFORM is FIXUNB and that the DTFPR macro "knows" how long each printed line is in a given system.

We have barely scratched the surface in our discussion of the DTF macro. Table 17-7 at the end of this chapter summarizes the features we have covered. Since you will be concerned primarily with card reader input and line printer output files, we show standard DTF macros and buffer space allocation statements for such files in Figs. 17-6 and 17-7, respectively.

```
CARDFILE  DTFCD  DEVADDR=SYSIPT,IOAREA1=CARD1,IOAREA2=CARD2,     X
                 WORKA=YES,EOFADDR=NOCARDS
             •
             •
             •
CARD1     DS     CL80
CARD2     DS     CL80
```

Fig. 17-6. A DTF statement and buffers for a card input data set.

```
PRINTFILE   DTFPR   DEVADDR=SYSLST,IOAREA1=LINE1,IOAREA2=LINE2,     X
                    WORKA=YES,TYPEFLE=OUTPUT,CTLCHR=ASA
```

Fig. 17-7. A DTF macro instruction for a printed file.

17.2.2. GET AND PUT

The DTF macros provide information the system needs to process a file. We use the GET and PUT macros to request input and output, respectively.

The GET macro is written

```
            GET         filename, areaname
```

or just

```
            GET         filename
```

depending on the operands in the DTF macro whose name is "filename." If we specify WORKA=YES in the DTF for the file, we use the first form shown above. If we do not request a WORKArea, we use the second form.

GET calls a supervisor program which is responsible for processing input files. This program uses the IOAREA(s) for input buffer(s), filling them with blocks from the input device as necessary, and moving the records in turn from the buffers to the memory area given by "areaname" as requested if we have requested use of a WORKArea.

Suppose that we are using a card file for input and have the DTFCD and buffer areas CARD1 and CARD2 shown in Fig. 17-6 included in our program. To input a card from the file we could write

GET   CARDFILE,CARDIN

The system moves the 80-byte card image of the next card from the file to CARDIN. We must make sure to have an 80-byte storage area named CARDIN to contain this card image. Each time we execute the GET macro written above, the system moves the next card image to the area CARDIN.

If instead of WORKA=YES we use the IOREG option, we do not specify an "areaname" operand with GET. Suppose that we use IOREG=3 instead of WORKA=YES in Fig. 17-6. We then write the GET in the form

GET   CARDIN

In this case, the system returns the address of the next record in register 3. Notice that this is a more efficient procedure than the use of a work area, since the system does not have to move the record from the input buffer to the work area.

When we give only a single IOREA in the DTF or when we use two but include neither an IOREG or a WORKA operand in the DTF, the program is responsible for unblocking blocked records and determining which IOAREA contains the data most recently input.

The PUT macro is an output request. Again there are two ways to specify the operands, and the choice of which to use depends on the DTF operands. If we include WORKA=YES in an output DTF, we write

PUT   filename,areaname

When the instructions that form the macro expansion are executed, the system moves the data stored starting at "areaname" to an output buffer for the file whose name appears as "filename" in the DTF. For example, to print a line using the DTFPR shown in Fig. 17-7, we could write

PUT   PRNTFILE,LINEOUT

LINEOUT could be a 133-byte area in which we have stored EBCDIC character codes for output. If we use the IOREG operand instead of the WORKA option, we do not specify the address of the output record when we write the PUT macro. Instead, we pass the address of the output record to the system in the register named with the IOREG operand. Supposing that we had IOREG=7 in place of WORKA=YES in Fig. 17-7, the statements

LA   7,LINEOUT

PUT   PRNTFILE

have the same effect as the PUT written above.

A comparison with the special RCD and PLN macros might be helpful here. To input an 80-byte card image to an area called CARDIN we write

    RCD   CARDIN

The GET macro with its associated DTFCD macro described above has exactly the same effect. Similarly,

    PLN   LINEOUT

has the same effect as the PUT macros written above with its associated DTFPR macro.

17.2.3. OPEN AND CLOSE

Before any processing can be done using a file, we must use the OPEN macro to prepare the file for processing. We can OPEN one or more files at any time by writing

        OPEN   filenames

The operands are simply the names of the files to be opened. For example, we write

        OPEN   CARDFILE,PRNTFILE

to open the files whose DTFs appear in Figs. 17-6 and 17-7. Or we can open the files separately:

        OPEN   CARDFILE
          .
          .
          .
        OPEN   PRNTFILE

The OPEN macro causes the supervisor to take the following actions:

1. Examine the DTF for the file to determine how the file is to be processed.

2. Load the necessary input/output programs into memory if they are not already there.

3. Prepare the input/output device to be used for operation. This could include positioning a magnetic tape for input or output of the first block, positioning the reading heads of a disk, or starting the card reader, for example.

4. If the file is sequential and is used for input, the supervisor fills the buffers provided with the first blocks of the file. Subsequent GETs simply move the records to the work areas or place record addresses in registers and refill the buffers as they are emptied.

We must use the CLOSE macro to inform the system that we have finished processing a file. The operands of CLOSE are a list of file names, just as for OPEN. To close the files we have been using in our examples, we write

CLOSE   CARDFILE,PRNTFILE

or

CLOSE   CARDFILE

.
.
.

CLOSE   PRNTFILE

The CLOSE macro causes the system to terminate the processing of the files named. This makes the devices that were being used in operations with the files available for other use. In use with an output file, CLOSE empties those buffers that have not yet been output to the device and writes a block that marks the end of file. Failure to close an output file may cause loss of some of the data that were supposed to be output.

17.2.4. Summary

For input/output processing in DOS systems we do the following:

1. Include a DTF macro for each file that is to be processed.
2. Issue OPEN macros to prepare the files for use.
3. Use GETs and PUTs for input and output, respectively, of records in the files.
4. Use the CLOSE macro to terminate processing of each file.

```
CARDLIST  START  0
          PRINT  NOGEN
          BALR   12,0        ESTABLISH BASE REGISTER
          USING  *,12
          LA     13,SAVE     SAVE AREA ADDRESS IN REG. 13
          OPEN   CARDFILE,PRNTFILE    OPEN INPUT, OUTPUT FILES
NEXTCARD  GET    CARDFILE,CARDIN  INPUT CARD IMAGE TO AREA CARDIN
          PUT    PRNTFILE,LINEOUT    PRINT THE CARD IMAGE
          B      NEXTCARD
NOCARDS   CLOSE  CARDFILE,PRNTFILE    BRANCHES TO HERE WHEN NO MORE CARDS
          EOJ                 THAT'S ALL THERE IS
CARDFILE  DTFCD  DEVADDR=SYSIPT,IOAREA1=CARD1,IOAREA2=CARD2,WORKA=YES,    X
                 EOFADDR=NOCARDS
PRNTFILE  DTFPR  DEVADDR=SYSLST,IOAREA1=LINE1,IOAREA2=LINE2,WORKA=YES,    X
                 TYPEFLE=OUTPUT,CTLCHR=ASA
CARD1     DS     CL80        INPUT BUFFER 1
CARD2     DS     CL80        INPUT BUFFER 2
LINE1     DS     CL133       OUTPUT BUFFER 1
LINE2     DS     CL133       OUTPUT BUFFER 2
LINEOUT   DC     C' '        CARRIAGE CONTROL CHAR.
CARDIN    DS     CL80        CARD IS READ INTO HERE
          DC     CL52' '     BLANKS FOR REST OF OUTPUT LINE
          END    CARDLIST
```

Fig. 17-8. A program that uses the DØS input/output macros to read and list a deck of cards.

Figure 17-8 shows the program of Fig. 10-3. We have replaced the special macros RCD and PLN with the standard DOS input/output macros.

17.3. OS INPUT/OUTPUT MACROS

The access methods are operating system programs that process user requests for input/output operations. The user requests the services of the access methods by including the appropriate system input/output macros in his programs. Among the OS system macros most often used are DCB, GET and PUT, READ and WRITE, and OPEN and CLOSE.

A program must include one Data Control Block macro for each data set processed by the program. The DCB furnishes information that the system needs in order to satisfy user requests for input/output. To request the actual transfer of data, we use the GET (input) and PUT (output) for processing sequential files using the queued access technique. The READ and WRITE macros request data transfers using the basic access technique. OPEN and CLOSE initiate and terminate, respectively, input/output processing of the data sets specified indirectly as operands.

In this section we shall present a discussion of the use of the Queued Sequential Access Method. QSAM is designed for use in sequential processing of data sets using the queued access technique. Virtually all card input, printed output, magnetic tape processing, and sequential disk file processing is done with the assistance of QSAM. Familiarity with the use of the I/O macros and QSAM will enable you to program input/output operations with no special aids, such as RCD and PLN, and will serve as a starting point for further studies into the use of the other, more specialized access methods.

17.3.1. The Data Control Block

The input/output facilities of the operating system use three independent sources of information to determine what it is to do in input/output operations upon a data set. The user program contains the actual input/output requests and indicates which access method is to be used and other details concerning the way in which the data set is to be processed. The JCL Data Definition statement tells the system which data set is to be used, where the data set is to be found, and what its disposition is to be. Each data set stored on a magnetic tape or direct access device has a data set label or data set control block written with the data set. These include a description of the physical characteristics of the data set.

There is no connection between these information sources until the processing program is executed. One of the functions of the OPEN macro is to gather the necessary pieces from the program, job control language, and data set labels and data set control blocks and put these pieces into a central table of constants, the Data Control Block. In servicing input/output requests, the system refers to the DCB for the parameters it needs.

In writing a program, we provide the space for a Data Control Block by using the Data Control Block macro instruction. We use the operands of the DCB macro to specify details of how we want the corresponding data set to be processed. We must include one DCB for each data set the program uses. The assembler constructs a skeleton DCB and fills in coded forms of the parameters we give as operands. When the DCB is OPENed at execution time, the system obtains the remaining parameters from the DD statement for the data set and from the data set label or control block written with the data set.

We write a DCB macro as

dcbname   DCB   operands

We refer to the DCB by the name, any name valid in assembly language, shown as "dcbname." Since a DCB is a table of constants, we usually put all the DCBs in the data and constants storage area of a program.

All the operands of the DCB macro are *key-word* operands, which have the form

keyword=value

where "keyword" is the name of the operand, and "value" is the symbol or quantity we wish the assembler to assign to the key word. Key-word operands can be written in any order, which contrasts them against the more familiar *positional* operands. The meaning of a positional operand depends on its relative position in the operand list.

The operands we supply depend on the details of the processing that is to be done with the data set to which the DCB refers. But regardless of the application, we must always supply two vital pieces of information: We must choose the data set, which is done indirectly via the DDNAME operand, and we must pick an access method, which we do by including the DSORG and MACRF operands.

The value of the DDNAME operand is the name of a DD statement included in the JCL for the job stop in which the program is to be executed. For example, we have been using the DD statement

//GO.SYSIN   DD   *

to indicate that the input data for the program follow on punched cards. The name of the step is GO and the ddname is SYSIN. In the DCB for the card input data set in the program we would write

DDNAME=SYSIN

as one of the operands. Similarly, if we have a catalogued data set CATDAT that we wish to use, we could use the DD statement

//GO.DSKDATA   DD   DSNAME=CATDAT,DISP=SHR

In the program, one of the operands of the DCB for this data set is then

DDNAME=DSKDATA

Thus, we tell the system which data set is to be used with a given DCB through an indirect route. In the program we supply the name of a DD statement as an operand of the DCB. The DD statement with that name specifies which data set is to be used. The advantage here is that we can change the actual data sets programs process by simply changing DD statements. No modification of the program is necessary. For example, if we wish to process data set RATCAT instead of CATDAT, we use the DD statement

//GO.DSKDATA   DD   DSNAME=RATCAT,DISP=SHR

The DCB statement in the program still refers to the DD statement named DSKDATA, and so we have specified a different data set for processing without altering the program.

OS offers many different access methods. Recall that the access method depends on the data set organization and the access technique. Possible data set organizations are sequential, indexed sequential, partitioned, and direct. For sequential processing of sequential or indexed sequential files, we can select a queued access technique. Otherwise, we must use a basic access technique.

The Data Set ORGanization (DSORG) operand selects one of the four possible data set organizations offered by OS as shown in Table 17-4. For QSAM, we choose DSORG=PS to indicate that we wish to use a sequential file.

Table 17-4   DSORG OPERAND

Operand	Meaning
DSORG=PS	Physical Sequential organization
DSORG=IS	Indexed Sequential organization
DSORG=PO	Partitioned Organization
DSORG=DA	Direct Access organization

We indicate our choice of access technique and tell the system some details of how the processing is to be done by using the MACRo Form (MACRF) operand (Table 17-5). The MACRF value indicates which macros we shall use for input/output. GET and PUT are the input and output macros for the queued access technique. READ and WRITE are the input and output macros for the basic access technique. We simply write the first letter of the desired macro operation to designate our choice. For example,

MACRF=G

Table 17-5   MACRF OPERAND AND SOME POSSIBLE VALUES

	First Letter	I/O Macro To Be Used	Second Letter	Meaning
MACRF =	G	GET	M	Move mode
	P	Put	L	Locate mode
	R	READ		
	W	WRITE		

means that the GET macro is to be used, implying a queued access technique, while

$$MACRF=W$$

requests a basic access technique using the WRITE macro.

To show how the DSORG and MACRF operands select an access method, consider the case if we include the operands

$$DSORG=IS$$

$$MACRF=R$$

in a DCB. The DSORG operand indicates that the data set referred to through the DDNAME operand of the DCB is an indexed sequential file. The choice of R for the MACRF value means that the READ macro will be used in processing the data set, implying that a basic access technique is to be used for input from the file. The combination of the operands values means that the Basic Indexed Sequential Access Method (BISAM) has been chosen. Similarly,

$$DSORG=PS$$

and

$$MACRF=G$$

or

$$MACRF=P$$

show that a sequential file is to be used for input or output, respectively, using GET or PUT. Use of a queued access technique and a sequential file means that the Queued Sequential Access Method (QSAM) will be used.

We specify further processing options by including additional letters in the value of the MACRF operand. In particular, two common processing *modes* for use with GET and PUT are the Move mode and the Locate mode. To indicate which of these we want, we simply write M or L after the G or P in the MACRF value. For example,

$$MACRF=PL$$

means the the PUT macro will be used in the Locate mode, while

$$MACRF = GM$$

means that the GET macro will be used in the Move mode.

Use of the Move option asks the system to physically move input data from the system buffer to a memory area given as an operand of the GET macro or to move output data from an area specified as an operand of the PUT macro to a system output buffer. In other words, using the move mode, *we* tell the system where to place the input record contents or where the next record for output is stored.

In the Locate mode, the system simply tells us where the next record is, without moving any data. Use of GET in the Locate mode asks the system to put the memory address where the next record is stored into register 1. Similarly, a PUT macro in the locate mode asks the system to return in register 1 the address of the memory area from which the next record will be output. We shall return to the use of these two processing modes when we describe GET and PUT in more detail.

To summarize to this point, the three required DCB operands— DDNAME, DSORG, and MACRF—designate which data set and which access method are to be used. In addition, the MACRF operand's values indicate further processing options.

The three required operands discussed above must be supplemented in most applications by the inclusion of some DCB operands that furnish further details on the actual structure and processing of the data set. In particular, the RECord ForMat (RECFM) operand describes the record format of the data set to the system. Table 17-6 shows some RECFM values.

The BLocK SIZE (BLKSIZE) and Logical RECord Length (LRECL) operands declare the lengths, in bytes, of blocks and records, respectively. For unblocked data sets, the block size is the same as the record length, since each block is also a record. This means that we need give only the block size, as the operands

$$RECFM = F, BLKSIZE = 400$$

do. Here we have said that each block contains one 400-byte record. If the records are blocked (more than one record per block), then we must specify both the block size and the record length. For example, the operands

$$RECFM = FB, BLKSIZE = 720, LRECL = 120$$

in a DCB mean that the data set used consists of blocked records, each block of which contains six 120-byte records.

When the records and/or blocks are of variable length, we give the maximum anticipated block size and record length as the values of BLKSIZE and LRECL. To use a data set with variable-length records in which the

Table 17-6   RECFM OPERAND

	Value	Meaning	Other Operands Required
RECFM =	F	Records are of F̲ixed length and are unblocked	BLKSIZE
	FB	Records are of F̲ixed length and are B̲locked	BLKSIZE,LRECL
	V	Records are of V̲ariable length and are unblocked	BLKSIZE = maximum block length
	VB	Records are of V̲ariable length and are B̲locked	BLKSIZE = maximum block length LRECL = maximum record length
	U	U̲ndefined, to be determined in subsequent processing	

maximum record length is 200 bytes and the longest block contains 1000 bytes, include the operands

$$RECFM=VB,BLKSIZE=1000,LRECL=200$$

in the DCB for that data set.

We shall now turn to some full examples of DCB macros. We treat DCBs for card input, printed output, and a disk file in turn, all using QSAM.

Card Input.   We have been supplying card input in the main job stream in a data set with the ddname SYSIN. The JCL statement to indicate the beginning of the data is

$$//GO.SYSIN \quad DD \quad *$$

To refer to this data set, we set DDNAME=SYSIN in the DCB statement for the card input file. Since we want to use QSAM, we write

$$DSORG=PS$$

and

$$MACRF=GM$$

choosing for now to use the M̲ove mode with the GET macro. The cards form an unblocked data set in which all blocks are 80 bytes long. Thus, we include RECFM=F and BLKSIZE=80.

A handy operand for use in DCB for a sequential input file is the E̲nd O̲f D̲ata AD̲dress (EODAD) operand. The value of the EODAD operand is the name for an address to which we want the system to branch when there are no more records to be input from the file. If we wish to name the DCB for the card file CARDDCB, we write

CARDDCB   DCB   DDNAME=SYSIN,DSORG=PS,

MACRF=GM,RECFM=F,BLKSIZE=80,

EODAD=NOMORE

This DCB contains all the information necessary to process a card input data set and requests that the system branch to a statement labeled NOMORE when an attempt is made to input more records than are in the data set. This eliminates the need for a trailer record or a record counter to count the number of cards input.

Printed Output. Line printer records are also unblocked and of fixed length. If we wish, we can request that the American Standards Association carriage control convention (see Chapter 10) be used in place of the IBM convention. We do this by adding the letter A to the end of the letter(s) that form the RECFM operand's value. The block length for a printer depends on the number of columns the local printer outputs on a line. Assuming that this number is 132, we use a block size of 133, since the printer will use up the first character for carriage control. Putting all the pieces together, we have

PRNTFILE   DCB   DDNAME=SYSPRINT,DSORG=PS,

MACRF=PM,RECFM=FA,BLKSIZE=133

Here we have chosen PRNTFILE for the name of the DCB and have again chosen to use the Move mode with the PUT macro. The system will use the data set with the ddname SYSPRINT for output. We normally supply the DD statement

//GO.SYSPRINT   DD   SYSOUT=A

for this file, indicating that the output is to go to the standard system output device.

A Disk File. Suppose that we have an uncatalogued sequential file named DSKDATA stored on a 2314 disk unit with serial number LSU007. The records are of fixed length and are 100 bytes long, and there are eight records per block. We wish to use the file for input using the locate mode. A DD statement for this file might be written

//GO.DSKIN   DD   DSNAME=DSKDATA,DISP=SHR,

UNIT=2314,VOL=SER=LSU007

We could write the following for the corresponding DCB:

DSKFILE   DCB   DSORG=PS,EODAD=DONE,MACRF=GL,

                         DDNAME=DSKIN,RECFM=FB,

                         BLKSIZE=800,LRECL=100

This example emphasizes the fact that the DCB operands can be written in any order. When an end-of-file on the data set is encountered, program execution will resume at the statement labeled DONE.

17.3.2. GET and PUT

Input/output requests using the queued access technique and in particular QSAM take the form of GET and PUT macros. The GET macro results in the input of the next record from the data set to the program, while the PUT macro outputs a record from the program to the output data set. Thus, all the programmer needs to worry about is the processing of individual records; the system takes care of all the actual input/output operations, buffering, and management of record blocking and deblocking.

The GET macro using the Move mode has the form

               GET   dcbname,areaaddress

"dcbname" is the name of the DCB describing the data set from which the input is to come. "areaaddress" is usually the symbolic name of a memory area, at least long enough to contain one record, into which the system will move the input record. For example, using our DCB named CARDDCB for card input (page 409) we might write

               GET   CARDDCB,INCARD

with the memory area INCARD defined by

INCARD   DS   CL80

In response to execution of the GET macro above, the system moves the next record from an input buffer into the 80-byte area starting at CARDIN.

Output is just as simple using the move mode. We again give the DCB name and an area address as operands as in

               PUT   dcbname,areaadress

The system responds to execution of the statements that form the PUT macro by moving the record starting at "areaaddress" to an output buffer for subsequent transfer to an I/O device. For example, using the DCB named PRNTFILE on page 409 we could write

               PUT   PRNTFILE,LINEOUT

with LINEOUT given by

LINEOUT   DC   CL133' THIS LINE WILL BE PRINTED'

Using these DCBs and GET and PUT as shown in the examples above has exactly the same effect as using RCD and PLN. And all OS systems offer GET and PUT.

In many applications, the actual moving of a record from an input buffer to an area inside a user's program is unnecessary. We might not need any or all of the data from an input record. In such cases, where processing a record in place is attractive, use of the Locate mode improves program efficiency. GET in the Locate mode is written

$$\text{GET} \quad \text{dcbname}$$

Execution of the GET macro in this form asks the system to simply point out where the next record is stored. The system responds by returning the record address in register 1. Similarly, PUT using the Locate mode is written

$$\text{PUT} \quad \text{dcbname}$$

The system returns in register 1 the address of the next record in the output buffer. Data to be output can then be moved into this area.

17.3.3. OPEN and CLOSE

Before a data set can be used by a program, we must use the OPEN macro to prepare the program, operating system, and I/O device to process the data set. Two operands are required for each file to be opened: the name of the DCB for the file and an option that indicates what kind of processing is to be done. That is, the OPEN macro is written in its simplest form,

$$\text{OPEN} \quad \text{dcbname,option}$$

The most often-used options are

INPUT: The data set for input only. This is the default value.

OUTPUT: The data set is for output only.

UPDAT: The data set is to be UPDATed. An output request rewrites the record at the same position as that from which it was obtained in the preceding input request.

Thus, to open a printer file whose DCB is named PRNTFILE we write

$$\text{OPEN} \quad \text{PRNTFILE,OUTPUT}$$

while to open a card input file with dcbname CARDDCB we could program

$$\text{OPEN} \quad \text{CARDDCB,INPUT}$$

or, since INPUT is the default, we can omit the option

$$\text{OPEN} \quad \text{CARDDCB}$$

To open more than one file at once, we put a list of operand pairs inside parentheses. The two files above are opened using

> OPEN   (CARDDCB,INPUT,PRNTFILE,
>
> OUTPUT)

or

> OPEN   (CARDDCB,,PRNTFILE,OUTPUT)

In the second example, we have omitted the INPUT option, but we have indicated that an operand was omitted by keeping the commas that go with it.

OPEN does several things. First, the system examines the information from the DCB as supplied in the program, the DD statement for the data set, and the Data Set Control Block. If this information is consistent and in the proper form, the system prepares the Data Control Block for use. The system loads the access method subroutines into the memory if they are not already there, prepares them for execution and allocates the necessary I/O buffers. Finally, the device is prepared to transfer the data. In processing a sequential file for input, OPEN causes the input buffers to be filled with the first few blocks of the file. For an output sequential data set, the device is positioned ready to output the first block.

Once the file has been opened, we use the input/output macros GET, PUT, READ, WRITE, and so on as desired. When we are through using a file, we use the CLOSE macro to indicate that we have completed the processing with that file. Like OPEN, CLOSE requires two operands per file closed:

> CLOSE   dcbname,option

The CLOSE options are REREAD, which repositions the device to read the file; LEAVE, leaving the device where processing left off; and DISP to use the value of the DISP parameter from the DD statement. DISP is the default.

The operating system automatically closes all files not closed by the processing program. Nevertheless, it is a good idea to close all files as soon as possible, since CLOSE frees the memory space occupied by the access method and buffers for the data set. Failure to close an output file might result in incomplete or erroneous output in the advent of a subsequent program abend.

17.3.4. Programming Examples

To summarize the use of OS facilities for input/output we list the following requirements:

1. Include one DCB in the program for every data set to be used.
2. Use the OPEN macro to prepare for input or output from each data set.

3. Use GET and PUT (queued access technique) or READ and WRITE (basic access technique) for input and output operations.

4. Use the CLOSE macro to terminate processing of each data set used.

To use QSAM with sequential files, use the operands

$$DSORG=PS$$

and

$$MACRF=\text{one of GM, GL, PM, PL}$$

in the DCB and include also the RECFM, BLKSIZE, and LRECL operands, if necessary.

We shall conclude this section with two examples of the use of QSAM in input/output programs. The first example program, shown in Fig. 17-9, simply reads and lists a deck of data cards. Notice the order in which the I/O macros are used and the use of the EODAD operand in the input DCB CARDDCB to cause the system to branch to the statement ALLGONE when there are no more cards to be read. The DD statement for the card input data set is assumed to be

$$//GO.SYSIN \quad DD \quad *$$

```
LISTER     START 0
           PRINT NOGEN
           STM   14,12,12(13)  SAVE THE REGISTERS
           BALR  12,0      SET UP BASE REGISTER
           USING *,12
           ST    13,SAVE+4   SAVE (13)
           LA    13,SAVE   SAVE AREA ADDRESS IN REGISTER 13
*
*                OPEN CARDDCB FOR INPUT, PRNTDCB FOR OUTPUT
*
           OPEN  (CARDDCB,,PRNTDCB,OUTPUT)
READREC    GET   CARDDCB,CARDIMGE   INPUT A CARD IMAGE
           PUT   PRNTDCB,LINEOUT        PRINT IT
           B     READREC     GO BACK FOR NEXT RECORD
*
*                SYSTEM WILL BRANCH TO ALLGONE AT END-OF-FILE
*
ALLGONE    CLOSE (CARDDCB,,PRNTDCB)     CLOSE THE FILES USING DEFAULT OPTS
           L     13,SAVE+4 RETRIEVE (13)
           LM    14,12,12(13)   RESTORE THE REGISTERS
           BR    14         RETURN TO CALLER
SAVE       DS    18F
LINEOUT    DC    C' '     BLANK FOR CARRIAGE CONTROL
CARDIMGE   DS    CL80     CARDS READ INTO HERE
BLANKS     DC    CL52' '    REST OF LINE BLANK
CARDDCB    DCB   DDNAME=SYSIN,DSORG=PS,MACRF=GM,RECFM=F,BLKSIZE=80,
                 EODAD=ALLGONE
PRNTDCB    DCB   DDNAME=SYSPRINT,DSORG=PS,MACRF=PM,RECFM=FA,BLKSIZE=80
           END   LISTER
```

Fig. 17-9. A program that uses the ØS input/output macros to input and list a card data set.

although the program would work just as well reading from any input device provided that the record format and data set organization requested in the DCB are compatible with the input device characteristics and with the structure of the input data set.

Use of GET in the Move mode requires that the system move the input data from a buffer it maintains to an area designated by an operand of the GET macro. This movement of data is often unnecessarily inefficient, particularly when not all the records input are used by the program or when the program uses only selected portions of the records. A similar comment applies to the use of PUT in the Move mode. Evidently, since the program must construct record contents before they are output, some movement of data is necessary in output programming. But the use of the Move mode requests that the system move the data again after the record is created, this time from the area in which the record is constructed to a system output buffer.

Use of the Locate mode for input and output helps to minimize the unnecessary movement of data. GET in the Locate mode shows us where the system input buffer that contains the next record is. The program can then determine which, if any, portions of that record should be moved. Similarly, PUT in the Locate mode furnishes the address of the next output buffer. Given the location of the buffer, the program can construct the output record in place, knowing that the system has designated this area for output to the device as the next record for the output data set.

Figure 17-10 illustrates the use of the locate mode for input and output. The input to the program is a large file on magnetic tape, which contains the academic records of every student in the university. The program selects the records for students registered in the College of Chemistry and Physics and outputs selected portions of these records to a sequential disk file. The output file is to be used as a prototype data base for more sophisticated management of the registrar's files.

To be more precise, the input consists of blocked records, with five 1000-byte records per block. The ddname for this data set is MASTER. Bytes 30–34 of each record contain a 5-byte abbreviation for the college in which the student is registered. For the College of Chemistry and Physics, this field contains the EBCDIC string CANDP. The records in the registrar's master file contain more information than is needed for the application. Therefore, when a record for a student in the College of Chemistry and Physics is encountered, the program creates an output record that is 320 bytes long. The data in the output records consists of bytes 0–119 and 300–499 from the input record. These records are written in the fixed-length unblocked format to make sorting the file and access to individual records easier. The ddname of the output data set is CPFILE.

```
SELECTCP  START  0
          PRINT  NOGEN
          STM    14,12,12(13)     SAVE THE REGISTERS
          BALR   12,0       SET UP BASE REGISTER
          USING  *,12
          ST     13,SAVE+4    PRESERVE (13)
          LA     13,SAVE    SAVE AREA ADDRESS IN REG. 13
          OPEN   (MSTFILE,,OUTFILE,OUTPUT)
CHECKREC  GET    MSTFILE    GET RECORD FROM MASTER FILE, ADDR. IN REG. 1
          CLC    30(5,1),=C'CANDP'    SEE IF WE ARE TO KEEP IT
          BNE    CHECKREC    IF NOT, GO GET NEXT RECORD
          LR     2,1       SAVE INPUT RECORD ADDRESS IN REG. 2
          PUT    OUTFILE    LOCATE OUTPUT BUFFER
          MVC    0(120,1),0(2)    AND MOVE DATA TO IT
          MVC    120(200,1),299(2)   (ITS ADDR. IS IN REG. 1 AFTER PUT)
          B      CHECKREC    DONE WITH THIS RECORD, GO DO ANOTHER
DONE      CLOSE  MSTFILE    COME HERE ON EOF AND
          CLOSE  OUTFILE    CLOSE BOTH FILES
          L      13,SAVE+4    RECOVER (13)
          LM     14,12,12(13)     RESTORE REGISTER CONTENTS
          BR     14       RETURN
SAVE      DS     18F
MSTFILE   DCB    DDNAME=MASTER,DSORG=PS,MACRF=GL,RECFM=FB,BLKSIZE=5000,   X
                 LRECL=1000,EODAD=DONE
OUTFILE   DCB    DDNAME=OPFILE,DSORG=PS,MACRF=PL,RECFM=F,BLKSIZE=320
          END    SELECTCP
```

Fig. 17-10. A program that selects records from a tape file and outputs them to a disk file.

The program begins with the usual subroutine linkage statements and then opens both files. The GET macro obtains the memory address of an input record of which bytes 30–34 are checked to see if the record is to be output or ignored. Notice that before doing the PUT, we must save the input record address, since PUT returns the address of the next output buffer, again using register 1. Notice also that using the Locate mode, we construct the output record *after* issuing the output command, in contrast with the procedure using the Move mode.

We have presented a very brief survey of the use of the OS access methods. Unfortunately, space does not permit further exploration of the power and flexibility available to the programmer through these facilities. We must therefore refer you to the *supervisor and data management services* and *data management macros* manuals for further details and examples.

17.4. INPUT/OUTPUT HARDWARE

We have seen how to use the operating system facilities to assist with input/output programming. To explore more fully the structure of the IBM 360 and 370 computers, we shall now examine the hardware input/output section of the machines in greater detail.

17.4.1. The I/O Channels

A *channel* is a computer-within-the-computer whose sole purpose is to control the operation of input/output devices and the transfer of data between the devices and the system memory. Figure 17-11 is a block diagram that

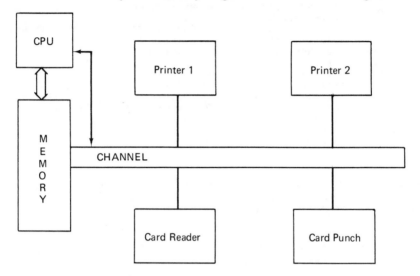

Fig. 17-11. The channel is intermediate between I/Ø devices and memory and controls information flow between them.

shows the position of a channel with respect to the computer memory, the CPU, and the I/O devices. In the sample configuration shown, the channel is the data path between the memory and two printers, a card reader and a card punch.

The channel "minicomputer" has its own machine language. Each instruction in this language is a Channel Command Word (CCW). A *channel program* is a series of CCWs stored in the main memory of the computer. The channel's control of input/output processing overlaps CPU execution of program instructions, thus leaving the CPU free to compute without worrying about what the channels are doing.

Perhaps the easiest way to see what the channel does is to see what can be done with channel command words. Figure 17-12 shows the structure of a single channel command word. A CCW is actually a double word, of which the first byte is the *operation code*. The possible operations include

Read: transfer data from device to memory
Write: transfer data from memory to device
Read backwards: appropriate for magnetic tapes which can be read backwards

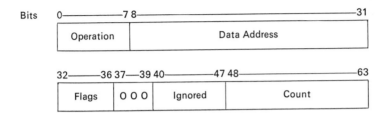

Bits

| Operation | Data Address |

0———————7 8—————————————————————31

| Flags | O O O | Ignored | Count |

32————36 37—39 40—————47 48—————————————63

Fig. 17-12. Channel Command Word structure. (In the 370 machines, bit 37 is also used as a flag.)

Control: an operation that does not transfer data, e.g., rewind a magnetic tape, position disk heads for input, move printer carriage to top of page

Sense: input information regarding status of a device

Transfer: causes the channel to branch to another CCW

Not all 8 bits are required to specify one of the operations above. The leftover bits are used as flags to signify options to be used with the operation. For example, a read command can be modified so that the channel does not transfer the data to the memory but instead compares the data from the device with some data stored in the memory, setting a flag to indicate the result of the comparison.

The *data address field* is 24 bits long and contains the memory address of the first byte of an I/O buffer. The channel uses this address to locate the data that are to be sent to the device in output operations. For input, this address determines where the data from the device are to be stored.

The *count field* is 16-bit binary number that says how many bytes are to be used in the current operation. For example, in a read operation, before the CCW is executed, the data address field contains the address of the first byte of the memory input buffer. The count field contains the number of bytes to be transmitted to the buffer. The channel transfers data 1 byte at a time from the device to the memory address in the data address field. After transferring each byte, the channel increments the data address field by 1 and decrements the count field. It continues this process until the count field contains 0, which means that all the data have been transferred.

The *flags field*, bits 32–36 (32–37 in the 370 machines), determines how the CCW is related to the rest of the channel program and to the CPU. The flag bits and their meanings are

Bit 32: Chain Data (CD). The channel transfers data in blocks. We usually think of the memory buffer for a single block as being one contiguous memory area. This is in fact not necessary. The channel can combine data from several sections of the memory into a single block for output or can break up a block read from a device, distributing the segments to separate memory areas.

When the CD bit is 1, the channel uses the data address and count fields from the next CCW in continuing the current operation.

Bit 33: Chain Command (CC). In normal operation (bit 33 = 0) the channel executes a channel command and then stops, awaiting further instructions and indicating the results by storing a Channel Status Word (see later) in the memory. If the Chain Command bit is 1, the channel executes the next CCW without stopping. Thus, if we have a string of CCWs to be executed, we would set the CC bit to 1 in all the CCWs except the last one. Barring error conditions, the channel continues executing CCWs in sequence until it has executed a CCW with bit 33 = 0.

Bit 34: Suppress Length Indication (SLI). When the number of bytes actually transferred to or from a device does not match the number of bytes requested in the count field of the CCW, an incorrect length condition results. This is usually an error condition and causes the channel to halt, displaying error indications in the channel status word. If bit 34 of the CCW is on, the system hardware proceeds as if nothing went wrong.

Bit 35: SKIP. The SKIP bit causes the channel to "pretend" to execute a read, backwards, or sense input operation, without transferring any data to the memory. The effect is that a block is skipped.

Bit 36: Program Controlled Interruption (PCI). If the PCI flag is 1, the channel interrupts the processor when it starts to execute the CCW.

Bit 37: Indirect Data Address (IDA). In the 360 computers bits 37–39 must all be 0. In the 370 computers, if bit 37 of a CCW is 1, the data address field of the CCW contains the address of a word, which in turn contains the address of the first byte of the data buffer.

17.4.2. Channel Programs

At the most fundamental level, input/output programming is the preparation of channel programs and control and monitoring of their execution. Let us consider the problem of locating a record with a given key in a data set stored on a magnetic disk unit. To do so we would prepare a channel program that contains CCWs to do the following:

CCW1: A Control command that moves the reading heads of the disk to a position so that the first block of the data set can be read.

CCW2: A read command with modifiers set so that no data are transferred from the disk to the memory. Instead, the channel compares the key of the record on the disk with the desired key, which is stored in the memory at the address given in the data address field of CCW2. If the comparison shows that the keys are identical, CCW3 is skipped.

CCW3: A transfer in channel to CCW2.

CCW4: A read command that reads the data from the block that was found.

CCW5: Another CCW with the PCI bit set to interrupt the processor, informing it that the input/output operation is done.

The example above shows how complex channel programs including conditional branches and loops can be written. Once a channel program has been stored in the memory, we use the Start Input Output instruction to begin its execution.

SIO	D1(B1)	Start IO	Start a channel program using device given as last 16 bits of D1 + (B1)

SIO is a special SI instruction. In the machine language for the instruction, the second byte must be 0. The effective operand, D1 + (B1), indicates the channel and device number, the hardware address of the device with which the channel is to communicate in executing the channel program.

The channel determines where the channel program is by referring to a fixed location in the memory, at which a Channel Address Word is stored. The first nibble of the CAW contains the protection key to be used in checking all addresses to or from which data are to be transferred in the execution of the channel program. The last 24 bits of the CAW contain the address of the first CCW of the channel program.

In response to an SIO instruction, the channel attempts to execute the CCW whose address is in the channel address word. There are some conditions which will not allow the channel to execute the channel program. Therefore, the SIO instruction sets the condition code to indicate whether or not the channel was able to begin. The CC values and their meanings are shown in Table 17-7.

After issuing an SIO instruction, the program should test the condition code to see if the channel could start. A condition code of 0 means that all is well and that the channel will execute the channel program. The CPU meanwhile is free to execute program instructions and will later be interrupted when the channel program finishes or an error condition occurs.

Condition code 1 means that an error was encountered in trying to start the first CCW execution. The Channel Status Word (CSW) is a double word at a fixed memory location. Its structure is shown in Fig. 17-13. The *key field* contains the protection key assigned to the user whose program requested execution of the channel program. The *command address field*

Table 17-7 CONDITION CODES RETURNED UPON EXECUTION OF SIO

Condition Code	Means
0	Everything is OK; the channel is proceeding with execution of the channel program
1	An error condition exists; the channel has stored a channel status word to indicate the nature of the error
2	The channel is busy servicing another device
3	The channel is not operational

Bits   0——3————7 8————————————————————————31

Key	0 0 0 0	Command Address

32———————————————47 48————————————63

	Status	Count

Fig. 17-13. Channel Status Word format.

contains the address of the CCW that was being executed when the error occurred. Bits 32–47 are *status bits* which can be tested to determine the source of the error, and bits 48–63 contain the *count field* from the CCW that failed. When an error occurs, the program can check the CSW to find out what happened.

If the channel is busy, we usually retry the SIO later in the hope that the channel is free then.

There are only four input/output instructions in the 360 computers, of which SIO is one. The other three are Test I/O, Halt I/O, and Test CHannel.

TIO D1(B1)	Test I/O	Test I/O channel and device given by D1 + (B1)
HIO D1(B1)	Halt I/O	Stop I/O operation on channel and device given by D1 + (B1)
TCH D1(B1)	Test CHannel	Test channel given by D1 + (B1)

The Test I/O instruction determines the status of an individual device and sets the condition code to indicate whether the device is available, is busy, or there is an error condition. In the last event, the channel stores a CSW to indicate the nature of the error. Halt I/O terminates an input/output operation being executed by the device and channel addressed. Test CHannel determines the status of a channel, setting the condition code and storing a CSW if necessary.

The 370 computers offer these four instructions and, in addition, the instructions Halt DeVice (HDV), CLeaR I/O (CLRIO), Start I/O Fast release (SIOF), and STore Channel ID (STIDC). Details on these instructions can be found in the manual *IBM System/370 Principles of Operation.*

All input/output instructions are privileged, which means they can be executed only when the processor is in the supervisor state. Since our programs usually run in the problem state, we cannot use these instructions directly.

We have seen that one way to have input/output done is through the use of access methods supplied by the operating system. The access method programs call supervisor programs which control the execution of channel programs for us. If we wish to write our own channel programs and have them executed, we can do so with the aid of the EXecute Channel Program macro-instruction. Our program creates a channel program. We pass the address of the first CCW to the operating system as an operand of the EXCP macro. EXCP causes a supervisor program to be executed, which can execute the necessary privileged instructions to start and monitor the channel program.

CHAPTER SUMMARY

Included in the operating system are *access methods*, programs that do input/output for the problem programmer. Requests for input/output services are in the form of *data management macros*. The programmer must make decisions regarding the data set *organization*, *record format*, *access method*, and *files* to be processed. He relays his choices to the system through the use of the DTFxx macro in DOS systems (Table 17-8) or the DCB macro (Table 17-9) in OS systems. Actual requests for input/output processing take the form of GET, PUT, READ, and WRITE macros. The OPEN and CLOSE macros initiate and terminate the use of a file.

The I/O *channels* control device operations and supervise the flow of data to and from the devices. The channels receive their commands from *channel programs*, which are series of *Channel Command Words*.

EXERCISES

Use the macros appropriate for the operating system at your local installation in solving the following problems:

1. Write a program to copy a deck of cards onto magnetic tape. The tape blocks are to be 400 bytes long. Each block is to contain five card images.

2. Write a subroutine $$RCD to be called by the RCD macro. The single argument is the address of an 80-byte memory area. Your subroutine should input a card

Table 17-8   DTFxx MACRO

Format: filename   DTFxx   operands

Operand	Meaning
DEVADDR=SYSxxx	Required; SYSxxx is the symbolic unit name for the device that transmits the data
IOAREA1=address	Required; *address* is the address of buffer area
IOAREA2=address	*address* is the address of a second buffer area; optional
WORKA=YES	The program will provide the address of a record as an operand of the GET or PUT macro
IOREG=n	The system will supply the address of a record in register n
EOFADDR=address	Causes branch to *address* if no more records in input file
RECFORM = FIXUNB	Records are unblocked and fixed in length
FIXBLK	Records are blocked and fixed in length
VARUNB	Records are unblocked and of variable length
VARBLK	Records are blocked and of variable length
TYPEFLE = INPUT / OUTPUT / INOUT	INPUT is the default
CTLCHR = ASA	ASA carriage control
YES	IBM carriage control
BLKSIZE=n	Blocks consist of at most n bytes
RECSIZE=m	Records consist of at most m bytes

Common DTFxx macros:

DTFCD	CarD input
DTFPR	PRinter output
DTFMT	Magnetic Tape
DTFSD	Sequential file on Direct access device
DTFDA	Direct Access file
DTFIS	Indexed Sequential file

image and store it at the argument address. (*Hint*: To use a register to pass a record address to the system, enclose the register number in parentheses.

GET   INDCB,(5)

moves the record to the area whose address is in register 5.)

3. Write a program to read a card file and list only those records that have a 3 in the tenth byte.

4. Write a single subroutine, $$IO, which is called by and has the same effect as the RWD, WWD, RCD, and PLN macros. (Be sure to use the modular approach.)

Table 17-9 SOME OPERANDS OF THE DATA CONTROL BLOCK MACRO†

Format: dcbname   DCB   operands

Operands			Meaning
DDNAME = ddname			Required; *ddname* is the name of the DD statement that designates which data set is to be used
DSORG =	PS PO IS DA	Sequential Partitioned Indexed Sequential Direct Access	Required; specifies the data set organization
MACRF =	GM GL PM PL		Required; G means Get, P means Put, M means Move, L means Locate; selects access technique, mode
RECFM =	F FB V VB U	Fixed length, unblocked Fixed length, Blocked Variable length, unblocked Variable length, Blocked Undefined	Describes RECord ForMat; append A for ASA carriage control for printed files
BLKSIZE = n			BLocKSIZE: n bytes per block
LRECL = m			Logical RECord Length; m bytes per record
EODAD = address			End Of Data ADdress causes branch to *address* when end-of-file is reached

†This is by no means an exhaustive list.

REFERENCES

DOS Data Management Concepts, Form GC24-3414, IBM Corp., White Plains, N.Y.

DOS/VS Supervisor and Input/Output Macros, Form GC33-5373, IBM Corp., White Plains, N.Y.

FLORES, I., *Data Structure and Management*, Prentice-Hall, Inc., Englewood Cliffs, N.J., 1970.

FLORES, I., *Job Control Language and File Definition*, Prentice-Hall, Inc., Englewood Cliffs, N.J., 1971.

IBM Operating System Data Management Macro Instructions, Form GC26-3794, IBM Corp., White Plains, N.Y.

IBM Operating System Data Management Services Guide, Form GC26-3746, IBM Corp., White Plains, N.Y.

IBM Operating System Supervisor Service and Macro Instructions, Form GN27-1419, IBM Corp., White Plains, N.Y.

IBM System/360 Disk and Tape Operating System Assembler Language, Form GC24-3414, IBM Corp., White Plains, N.Y.

IBM System/360 DOS Supervisor and Input/Output Macros, Form GC24-5037, IBM Corp., White Plains, N.Y.

IBM System/360 Operating System Assembler Language, Form GC28-6514, IBM Corp., White Plains, N.Y.

IBM OS/VS—DOS/VS Assembler Language, Form GC33-4010, IBM Corp., White Plains, N.Y.

OS/VS Data Management Macro Instructions, Form GC26-3793, IBM Corp., White Plains, N.Y.

OS/VS Data Management Services, Form GC26-3783, IBM Corp., White Plains, N.Y.

OS/VS Supervisor Services and Macro Instructions, Form GC28-0683, IBM Corp., White Plains, N.Y.

18 MACRO PROGRAMMING AND CONTROL OF THE ASSEMBLER

The assembler is itself a program whose primary chore is to translate assembly language statements into their machine language equivalents. But we can in fact ask much more of the assembler. We have described the use of some of the more common pseudooperations, such as EQU and PRINT, and we have used macro-instructions throughout the preceding material.

In this chapter we shall see that there is an entire language, designed specially for processing programs, that we can use to control the operation of the assembler. This language makes it possible for us to define our own macro-instructions, among other things. The advantages that accrue through the use of macros are evident. We request the insertion of a number of program instructions and data into our program by writing a single statement. Take a look at an expansion of the DCB macro, and see if you would like to write one of those for every DCB in a program.

Macro definition is but one of the advanced capabilities the assembler offers. In principle, through the use of macro definitions and control statements, we could have the assembler "compute" an entire assembly language program.

18.1. MACROS

We usually think of a programming variable, in FORTRAN, for example, as being a name for a memory location whose value (contents) is computed when the program is executed. Similarly, the symbols we use in an assembly language to name instructions and data storage areas represent addresses the machine program uses at *execution time*.

The assembler also recognizes *variable symbols*, symbols whose values are assigned or computed when the *assembler* is executed. There are two kinds of variable symbols. *Symbolic parameters* are variable symbols whose values are assigned when the assembler processes a statement whose operation mnemonic is a macro name. *SET symbols* are variable symbols whose values we assign through the use of the SETx pseudooperation. We use SET symbols for conditional assembly and the control of assembler loops, as we shall see later.

All variable symbol names begin with an ampersand (&). There can be from one to seven characters after the ampersand, the first of which must be a letter. Thus, &A, &A1, and &ALLIGTR are valid variable symbol names, while &1A and &TOOOLONG are not. When we really want to use an ampersand as a character, we write two in a row, as in

RAINING   DC   C'CATS && DOGS'

This DC statement produces the EBCDIC codes for the character string CATS & DOGS.

We shall now turn to the problem of using symbolic parameters in the definition and use of macro-instructions.

A macro *definition* is a series of assembler control statements and machine instructions that tells the assembler the name of the macro, how the operands will be given, and how to generate the instructions in the macro *expansion*, the machine instructions and assembler directives that result from the use of the macro in a program. The use of a macro in a program is often called a *macro-instruction*. Using this more restricted notion of a macro-instruction, we have three basic considerations with regard to macros: the macro definition, which determines the statements that form the macro; the macro-instruction, a specific *use* of a macro; and the macro expansion, the series of instructions obtained from the macro definition when the macro is used in a program.

We must define all macros to be used in a program prior to the beginning of the program. To do this, we can supply the macro definitions with the program as part of the card input to the assembler. Or we can store the macro definitions in a macro library, as is done with the system macros and the macros written for use with this text.

A macro *definition* consists of four parts in the following order:

1. A MACRO statement which tells the assembler that the following statements are part of a macro definition.
2. A *prototype* statement, which tells the assembler the name of the macro and describes how we shall supply the operands when the macro is used.
3. The *model* statements, a series of assembler control and machine instruction statements which dictate how the assembler is to compute the expansion of the macro.

4. A MEND (Macro END) statement which denotes the end of the macro definition.

The MACRO statement is simple; we simply write MACRO in the operation field, with blank label and operand fields. The MEND statement can have no operands or comments. Its name field can be left blank, or we can use a sequence symbol here, as described in Section 18.3.

The prototype statement is an outline of the macro that shows how the macro-instruction in the program will be written. The prototype has the form

    label   name   operands   comments

The *name* field, written in the operation field of the statement, contains the name of the macro as it will be used by the program and can be any valid assembly language name, as in GET, RWD, and MYMAC1. The *label* field can be blank or can contain a label, usually a symbolic parameter, which functions as a statement label when the macro is expanded. In the operands field, we write a list of the operands, separated by commas, as they will appear when the macro is used. Here we can use symbolic names and constants as operands, but more often the operands are symbolic parameters.

In macro definition and expansion, symbolic parameters come into the forefront. When we use a variable symbol in a macro prototype statement, that tells the assembler to wait until the macro is used in the program to assign a value to that variable. The value is the operand we write in the macro-instruction. The model statements dictate how that value is to be used. For example, if the symbolic parameter &VAR appears as the third operand of the macro prototype and the symbol XQW appears as the third operand in the macro-instruction in the program, the assembler replaces the characters &VAR with the characters XQW everywhere they appear in the model section of the macro definition. This means that the specification of the value of a symbolic parameter is in effect delayed until the macro in which it appears as a label or operand is actually used.

Let us try some examples to illustrate the use of symbolic parameters. Recall that the RWD macro calls a subroutine, $$IO, which inputs a card image, converts the number punched on the card to binary, and returns the value so obtained in register 1. The RWD macro then moves that value to the register or full word specified as the operand in the macro-instruction. Let us assume for now that the operand will always be a register. When we write the macro definition, we do not know which register the programmer will use as the RWD operand. Therefore, we use a symbolic parameter for the operand in the prototype statement. Later, when the programmer selects a register, he indicates his choice by writing the register number in the operand field of RWD. Figure 18-1 shows a macro definition for RWD.

The single operand in the prototype statement is the variable symbol

```
MACRO
RWD        &LOC        PROTOTYPE
L          15,=V($$IO)    LOAD SUBROUTINE ADDRESS
BALR       14,15
LTR        &LOC,1      LOAD RESULT INTO DESIRED REGISTER,SETTING CC
MEND
```

Fig. 18-1. A definition of the RWD macro, assuming that a register is the operand.

&LOC. In using RWD, the programmer might write

RWD   5

The assembler knows from the prototype statement

RWD   &LOC

in the macro-definition that it will find a single operand when RWD is used. In this case the operand is 5. When it expands the macro, the assembler plugs in 5 wherever it encounters the variable symbol &LOC. Thus, RWD 5 causes the expansion

L   15,=V($$IO)
BALR   14,15
LTR   5,1

to be inserted into the program in place of the macro-instruction.

Notice that nothing from the prototype statement itself appears in the macro expansion. This is in general the case; the prototype is simply an outline of the way in which the macro-instruction is to be written.

This fact has immediate significance if we wish to label statements within a macro expansion. The macro definition for RWD in Fig. 18-1 has no provision for use such as in a loop like

NEXTCARD   RWD   7
                       .
                       .
                       .

B   NEXTCARD

If the above macro definition were used, the resulting expansion

L   15,=V($$IO)
BALR   14,15
LTR   7,1

does not include the label NEXTCARD.

To modify the RWD definition to permit the use of labels we rewrite it as shown in Fig. 18-2. It looks as if we have defined the symbol &LAB twice in this definition. But this is not the case, since the prototype does not appear in the macro expansion. If we now use the definition in Fig. 18-2 with

```
        MACRO
&LAB    RWD      &LOC
&LAB    L        15,=V($$IO)
        BALR     14,15
        LTR      &LCC,1
        MEND
```

Fig. 18-2. An RWD macro definition that permits the use of a label on the macro call statement.

the macro-instruction

NEXTCARD   RWD   7

the assembler inserts the symbol NEXTCARD and the number 7 wherever the symbolic parameters &LAB and &LOC, respectively, appear in the model statements. The expansion is therefore

```
NEXTCARD    L        15,=V($$IO)
            BALR     14,15
            LTR      7,1
```

as desired.

As another example, we show in Fig. 18-3 the definition of a macro BEGIN, which saves the registers, establishes a base register whose number is given as an operand, saves (13), and loads register 13 with the address of a save area, also provided as an operand.

```
MACRO
BEGIN &ADDR,&REG
STM    14,12,12(13)   SAVE THE REGISTERS
USING  *,&REG         BASE POSITION NEXT INSTRUCTION
ST     13,&ADDR+4     PRESERVE OLD SAVE AREA ADDRESS
LA     13,&ADDR       SAVE AREA ADDRESS IN R13
MEND
```

Fig. 18-3. Definition of a macro BEGIN.

The assembler allows *concatenation* of symbolic parameter values onto the beginning or end of character strings in the model statements. To add the characters that are the value of a symbolic parameter onto the end of another series of characters, we write the name of the symbolic parameter immediately after the characters to which it is to be appended. If the symbolic parameter &LET has the value BAGE, then writing

GAR&LET

produces the character string

GARBAGE

when the macro is expanded. To append a symbolic parameter onto the beginning of a string we must place a period after the name of the symbolic parameter. If we write

&LETGAR

the assembler thinks we are using a new variable symbol with name &LETGAR. Thus, we write

&LET.GAR

which yields

BAGEGAR

when the macro is expanded.

We often use this capability when we need to change operation mnemonics to reflect the kind of operands desired. Figure 18-4 shows a definition

```
          MACRO
ELABEL  COMPARE   EA,EB,ETYPE,EECADD,ENEQACC
ELABEL  CETYFE    EA,EB
        BE        EECACC
        B         ENECADD
        MENC
```

Fig. 18-4. A COMPARE macro definition.

of a macro COMPARE, which compares two quantities and branches to one location if the result is equal or to another if the result is not equal. The operands are the two quantities to be compared, the type of the operands, and the two addresses to which to branch.

Here &TYPE is concatenated with the $\overline{\text{C}}$ mnemonic for the comparison. If we want to compare half-words, we specify H as the type operand. Writing

LOOP   COMPARE   3,HW,H,EQUAL,NOTEQUAL

leads to the expansion

LOOP   CH   3,HW
            BE   EQUAL
            B   NOTEQUAL

What happens if we wish to omit an operand, as when we want to use our COMPARE macro upon full words? To omit an operand, we simply leave it out, being sure to leave the commas in the proper places to remind the assembler that an operand should have been there. The macro-instruction

NEXT   COMPARE   6,FULWD,,EQ,NEQ

produces the expansion

NEXT   C   6,FULWD
            BE   EQ
            B   NEQ

So far, we have been using *positional* operands; the assembler assigns values to the symbolic parameters according to their order in the operands field of the prototype statement. An alternative kind of operand is the *key-word* operand. Key-word operands may be specified in any order in the use of a macro, but they must follow all the positional operands. The form of a key-word operand in the prototype statement is

varsym=default

where "varsym" is a symbolic parameter and "default" is the value the assembler will use if we do not specify a value in a macro-instruction.

Figure 18-5 shows the COMPARE macro rewritten so that &TYPE is a key-word operand. We have set the default of the type operand as blank so

```
           MACRO
&LABEL   COMPARE  &A,&B,&EQADD,&NEQADD,&TYPE=
&LABEL   C&TYPE   &A,&B
         BE       &EQADD
         B        &NEQADD
         MEND
```

Fig. 18-5. The COMPARE macro definition in which &TYPE is a keyword operand.

that if we do not specify a value for &TYPE the assembler will generate the C instruction to compare full words. To specify a value for a key-word operand, we write the name of the symbolic parameter, omitting the & in front, followed by an equals sign and then the desired value. Thus, if we want to use COMPARE as defined in Fig. 18-5 with type E (floating-point) operands, we write

FP   COMPARE   2,FPNO,FPEQ,FPNEQ,TYPE=E

This produces a macro expansion in which the CE instruction is used for the comparison.

18.2.   ATTRIBUTES AND SET SYMBOLS

In preparation for the following section on conditional assembly, we shall now take up two further aspects in the use of the assembler.

18.2.1.   Attributes

All symbols have *attributes*, or descriptive parameters, associated with them. Some examples are the *type* of a symbol (address, instruction, constant, for example), its *length* in bytes, and the *number* of characters in its name. We can refer to an attribute only in an expression that appears as the operand of a SETx operation or in a conditional assembly statement.

To use an attribute of a variable symbol, we write a letter followed by an apostrophe followed by the name of the symbol. Which letter we write first depends on which attribute we desire. To obtain the Type attribute of a variable symbol &SYM, we write T'&SYM.

The value of the Type attribute is single character constant. Table 18-1 is a list of some of the most often encountered types.

Table 18-1 SOME TYPES OF VARIABLE SYMBOLS

'A'	A-Type address constant
'B'	Binary constant
'C'	Character constant
'E'	Floating-point constant (single precision)
'F'	Full-word integer
'H'	Half-word integer
'I'	Machine instruction
'N'	Self-defining term (a number or an immediate operand, for example)
'O'	Omitted operand
'P'	Packed decimal constant
'V'	V-Type address constant
'X'	Hexadecimal constant

The Length attribute of a variable symbol &SYM is written L'&SYM.

An attribute refers specifically to the value assigned to a symbolic parameter in a macro-instruction. Suppose that we have defined a macro named CALC whose prototype statement is

&LABL   CALC   &A,&B,&C,&D,&E

and have written the macro-instruction

COMPUTE   CALC   3,LETTS,,AGAIN,NUM

where the symbols LETTS, AGAIN, and NUM are defined by the program statements

LETTS   DC   CL43'ERROR NUMBER 38'
AGAIN   B   OVER
NUM   DS   10F

Some of the attributes of the variables are

Attribute	Value
T'&D	'I'
T'&E	'F'
L'&E	40
T'&C	'O'
T'&A	'N'
L'&B	43
T'&B	'C'

18.2.2. SET Symbols

We present to the assembler names of symbolic parameters in the macro prototype statement, and we assign values to these parameters in a macro-instruction. The other kind of assembler variable is the SET symbol, whose value we assign through the use of a SETx statement (we shall worry about what the "x" is shortly). The SETx declarations permit arithmetic, logical, and character operations upon variable symbols. Values of SET symbols can be used to modify machine instructions and other statements of a program. We shall see later that conditional assembly statements provide for testing of the results of such calculations, so that conditional branching and loops by the assembler can be controlled.

Before a SET symbol can be used, it must be declared to be a SET symbol, so that the assembler will not confuse it with symbolic parameters. This is achieved through the use of a LCLx or a GBLx statement. GloBaL SET symbols have meaning through out the entire program in which they are defined and must be defined before any other symbols in the entire input to the assembler. Since LoCaL symbols are specific to particular macros, two local symbols with the same name declared in different macro definitions are really different symbols. Figure 18-6 illustrates the structure of input to the assembler in which the global symbols &P and &Q are declared and a macro

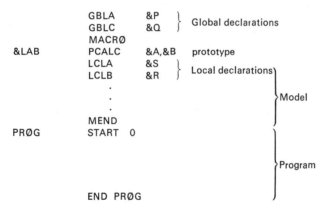

Fig. 18-6. The GBL and LCL statements in their proper positions in a macro definition and program.

PCALC is defined, which makes use of local symbols &R and &S. Notice that the format of a GBLx statement is

GBLx varsym

while the LCLx statement has the format

LCLx varsym

where "varsym" is a variable symbol.

Local or global variables may be of one of three types: Arithmetic, Binary, or Character. These are called SETA, SETB, and SETC symbols, respectively, because they are, respectively, the commands we use to assign values to SET variables. The type indicated in the LCLx or GBLx declaration must match the type of the SET symbols—LCLA or GBLA for SETA symbols, LCLB or GBLB for SETB symbols, and so on.

SETA symbols are used for arithmetic operations upon assembler variables. Internally they are integers which if used as an operand in a machine instruction take the form of a decimal number. The format of a SETA statement is

varsym   SETA   expression

This statement assigns the value of the expression that appears as the operand to the variable symbol whose name is in the name field. For example, if &B is a SETA symbol with value 100, then

&A   SETA   &B*10−20

assigns the value 980 to the SETA symbol &A (which must have been declared previously to be a SETA symbol via a LCLA or GBLA statement). The expression may contain variable symbols, constants, and the operators +, −, *, and /. We can also include variable attributes, such as the length attribute, which have numerical values. IF &C is a symbolic parameter and &CLEN is a SETA symbol, then the statement

&CLEN   SETA   L'&C−10

assigns a value 10 less than the length of the value of &C to the SETA symbol &CLEN. If later in the macro model we have the instruction

MVC   &B.(&CLEN),&C

the assembler will insert this value into the length field of the MVC instruction.

SETB symbols can have only one of two values, 0 or 1. Their values are assigned by statements of the form

symbol   SETB   expression

where here "expression" is a logical expression as we shall describe in Section 18.3. If the expression is true, the symbol acquires the value 1, and if false, 0.

A statement that assigns a value to a SETC symbol has the form

symbol   SETC   expression

Here the expression is a character string which may be formed by concatenation of several strings. Each string is enclosed in apostrophes, except when inherently of the character form, as is the case with the type attribute. For example, if &CHARS is a SETC symbol, then

&CHARS   SETC   T'&IN.'AB'.&GST

assigns the string

IABCD

to &CHARS if the type of &IN is 'I' and &GST is a SETC variable with value CD.

A SETA variable behaves as if it is the character representation of a decimal number when used as part of a machine instruction operand or in the expression of a SETC statement. Conversely, a SETC symbol must be the characters for a series of decimal digits if it is to be used in the expression of a SETA statement.

As we shall soon see, we use local SET symbols primarily within macros. Global SET symbols are used when we want to use a symbolic name for a parameter throughout an entire program. For example, the subroutine $$IO is written so that it works properly regardless of whether the local printer prints 120 or 132 characters per line. The line length is specified when $$IO is assembled.

To do this, we declare a global symbol &CHRPLN which represents the number of characters per line. The first statement of the program is

> GBLA   &CHRPLN

A SETA statement then assigns a value to &CHRPLN

&CHRPLN   SETA   133

Throughout the program, whenever we need to use the number of characters per line as a parameter, we use the SET symbol &CHRPLN as in

LINEOUT   DC   CL&CHRPLN' '

and

> MVC   LINEOUT+1(&CHRPLN−1),LINEOUT.

&CHRPLN is used in this way five or six times in the program. Now, to change to a 120-character-per-line printer, all we have to do is change the SETA statement to read

&CHRPLN   SETA   121

This is much easier and less likely to produce errors than trying to change a number everywhere it appears in a program.

18.3. CONDITIONAL ASSEMBLY

By conditional assembly we mean the ability to have the assembler respond in different ways to different conditions when the program is assembled. We have seen that the assembler recognizes two kinds of variables: symbolic parameters, whose values are assigned through the macro prototype and specific instances of the macro-instruction, and SET symbols, which receive their values when their names appear in name fields of SETx statements. We have also found that the assembler can determine variable attributes which depend on the values assigned to symbolic parameters. In a sense, we have established some of the prerequisites for treating the assembler as if it were a plain ordinary program. We have *data*, the assembly language program with values assigned to variables through the use of symbolic parameters. We have means of "computing" quantities by concatenation and the use of SET statements. We still need some means of controlling the operation of the assembler depending on the data supplied and the results of preceding calculations.

The assembler branch instructions are the unconditional branch, AGO (meaning Assembler GO) and the conditional branch, AIF (Assembler IF). We must distinguish between these *assembler* branches and the *machine* branch instructions BC and BCR. The latter cause the CPU to change the program counter contents during execution of a program, so that the sequence of machine execution of instructions is different from the order in which the instructions are stored. This allows us to skip over some instructions or to reexecute the instructions in a loop. On the other hand, assembler branches cause the assembler to consider the *symbolic* statements in the source program in a different order from that in which they are supplied. Thus, an assembler branch can cause some statements in the source program to be ignored, or, in the case of an assembler loop, some statements will be assembled more than once.

This difference between assembler and machine branches is even clearer when we note that the assembler demands that the statement to which an assembler branch refers be a *sequence symbol*, rather than an ordinary statement label. The first character in a sequence symbol is a period (.). There can be from one to seven characters following the period, the first of which must be a letter. Thus, .N, N135,. and .ABDDQ are all valid sequence symbols. A sequence symbol is nothing more than a label that the assembler uses to decide which source statement to process next. Unlike ordinary labels, which are really symbolic names for memory addresses, there is no physical counterpart to a sequence symbol. In fact, the assembler removes all sequence symbols from the program before translating it to machine language.

The unconditional AGO statement is written

Blank or sequence symbol   AGO   seqsym

where "seqsym" is a sequence symbol. AGO causes the assembler to resume processing the program with the statement whose sequence symbol appears as AGO's operand. For example, if we have

```
                .
                .
                .
                L        3,&CAT
                AGO      .SKIP
.STORE          ST       3,&DOG
.SKIP           A        3,&MOUSE
                .
                .
                .
```

the assembler will process the Load instruction and will then skip over the STore instruction. If &CAT has the value CT(5) and &MOUSE has the value MT, the code resulting from the statements above is

```
        .
        .
        .

L           3,CT(5)
A           3,MT
        .
        .
        .
```

Notice that the assembler removes the sequence symbol from the Add instruction.

The conditional assembler branch, AIF, has the format

Blank or seqsym   AIF   (logical expression)seqsym

As is the case with all assembler control statements, we can label AIF only with a sequence symbol.

The logical expression is a statement is a special format that can have only one of two values, true or false (1 or 0 in binary). If the expression has the value true (1), the assembler processes next the statement whose sequence symbol appears in the operand field. If the expression is false (0), the assembler proceeds with the statement after the AIF. In its simplest form a logical expression is written

op1   relation   op2

Here op1 and op2 are assembler variables, attributes, or constants. The relation is chosen from the following:

EQ: EQual
NE: Not Equal
GT: Greater Than
LT: Less Than
GE: Greater than or Equal
LE: Less than or Equal

(You FORTRAN programmers will recognize these as the relational operators for logical IF statements. But notice that there are no periods written with them.) The logical expression is true if the relationship

op1   relation   op2

is true. Thus, the expression

$$6 \quad GT \quad 4$$

is true, while the expression

$$T'\&OP \quad EQ \quad \text{'O'}$$

is false if the symbolic parameter &OP has been assigned a value in a macro-instruction (is not omitted).

As an example of the use of AIF, we offer the statement

.GO   AIF   (&CHAR EQ 'PUNT').QUIT

Here we have assumed that &CHAR is either a SETC variable or a symbolic parameter. In the latter case the characters that &CHAR represents are used in the comparison. The AIF above compares the character value of CHARS with the character string PUNT. If the two strings are identical, the assembler proceeds to analyze the program statements starting at .QUIT. If the comparison shows that the strings are not the same, the assembler goes on as if this AIF statement were not there.

We use AIF for conditional control of the assembler. One common use is to test operand types to see what kind of machine instruction should be put into the program. For example, in the RWD macro definition of Figs. 18-1 and 18-2 we have placed the restriction that the operand be a register number. If we wish to be able to use either memory addresses or register numbers as operands, we must have the assembler test the operand given in the macro-instruction and insert either an LR (for a register operand) or ST instruction (for a memory operand) after the subroutine call. Figure 18-7 shows how this

```
            MACRO
ELAB        RWD     ELOC
ELAB        L       15,=V($$IO)   SUBROUTINE ADDRESS TO R15
            BALR    14,15         CALL SUBROUTINE $$IO
            AIF     (THELOC NE 'N').SYMADD   IS OPERAND NUMERIC
            LTR     ELOC,1        MOVE RESULT TO REGISTER OPERAND
            AGO     .DONE         GO TO MEND
.SYMADD     LTR     1,1           SET CONDITION CODE
            ST      1,ELOC        AND STORE RESULT
.DONE       MEND
```

Fig. 18-7. The RWD macro using conditional assembly statements to permit either register or memory operands.

can be done. The AIF statement tests the type attribute of the symbolic parameter &LOC. If &LOC is not a self-defining term (as is a register number), we assume that it is a memory address and have the assembler include the statements starting at .SYMADD in the macro expansion. If &LOC is indeed a number, the assembler puts the LTR statement into the expansion. The AGO statement then routes the assembler to .DONE, ending the macro expansion.

Using the definition in Fig. 18-7, the macro-instruction

```
BNECH        RWD        ABL(6)
```

produces the expansion

```
BNECH        L          15,=V($$IO)
             BALR       14,15
             LTR        1,1
             ST         1,ABL(6)
```

while

```
HCENB        RWD        7
```

yields

```
HCENB        L          15,=V($$IO)
             BALR       14,15
             LTR        7,1
```

Some further features offered by the assembler help to make conditional assembly easier and more flexible. One of these is the ANOP (Assembler NO OPeration) directive, which does nothing except to provide a place for a sequence symbol. We often run into situations where we would like to put a sequence symbol on a machine instruction but that instruction already has a label. Figure 18-8 shows our COMPARE macro rewritten to make possible the comparing of characters as well as numerical data. In comparing character

```
              MACRO
&LABEL  COMPARE   &A,&B,&EQADD,&NEQADD,&TYPE=,&LEN=
        AIF       ('&TYPE' EQ 'LC').CHARS
&LABEL  CGTYPE    &A,&B
        AGO       .BRANCH
.CHARS  ANOP
&LABEL  CLC       &A.(&LEN),&B
        AGO       .BRANCH
.BRANCH BE        &EQADD
        B         &NEQADD
        MEND
```

Fig. 18-8. Use of ANØP.

data, we must provide for a length to put in the CLC instruction. Therefore, if the operand &TYPE has value LC, we obtain the length to be used from the key-word operand &LEN. The problem is that the AIF statement can branch only to a sequence symbol. We would like to have that sequence symbol appear in the name field of the CLC statement, but that space is already occupied by the statement label &LABEL. Therefore, we have the assemble branch to the ANOP statement with label .CHARS, and then the CLC statement, with label, is assembled.

As an example, if we write

```
HERE         COMPARE    5,BAT,EQULS,NEQULS,TYPE=H
```

we obtain the expansion

```
HERE        CH      5,BAT
            BE      EQULS
            B       NEQULS
```

while

```
THERE       COMPARE    WDS,MWDS,E,N,TYPE=LC,LEN=55
```

produces

```
THERE       CLC     WDS(55),MWDS
            BE      E
            B       N
```

The macros we have written so far are not very clever in that there is no provision for error in their use. For example, with RWD, we should check to see if the operand has been omitted, and, if it is a register, we want to make sure that none of the "special" registers 0, 1, 13, 14, or 15 is used.

To do this, we first note that logical expressions as discussed above can be compunded by using the logical connectives AND and OR. For example, the logical expression in the statement

```
AIF         (T'&LEN EQ 'O' AND
            '&TYPE' EQ 'LC').GHRN
```

has the value true only if both the key-word operand &LEN is omitted and the characters LC were supplied as the &TYPE operand. In this event, control proceeds to the statement with sequence symbol .CHRN.

The assembler allows us to print messages with the assembler output through the use of the MNOTE (Macro NOTE) directive. Written

```
MNOTE       severity code,'message'
```

the assembler prints this line where it appears in the macro expansion. The severity code is a number we can assign to indicate how serious the error is that prompted us to print an MNOTE about it. A severity code of 0 is the lowest and has no effect on subsequent processing. The largest severity code possible is 255. The assembler passes the severity code to the system when the assembly is complete. The operating system checks the code to determine whether or not to continue on to the next step. A severity code of 0 means that there were no important errors; 4 means that while errors were detected, they were probably not bad enough to keep the program from running; 8 or higher usually stops the job. Thus, the MNOTE statement

```
MNOTE       12,'***ERROR***MISSING OPERAND'
```

is printed with the macro expansion. The severity code 12 indicates that the error is so severe that further processing of the program will be a waste of computer time. It is wise to make MNOTEs as visible as possible. Otherwise they do not stand out well in the midst of all the other assembler output and are often overlooked. Include lots of asterisks and flashing lights to capture the programmer's attention.

In Fig. 18-9, we show our RWD macro definition again. This time the

```
         MACRC
ELAB     RWD        ELCC
         LCLA       EREC
         AIF        (T'ELCC NE '0').OPOK      IS OPERAND OMITTED
         MNOTE      12,'***ERROR*** NO OPERAND GIVEN'
         MEXIT
.CPCK    AIF        (T'ELOC NE 'N').REGOK
EREG     SETA       ELOC
         AIF        (EREG GE 2 OR EREG LE 12).REGOK
         AIF        (EREG GE 0 OR EREG _E 15).REGWAR
         MNCTE      12,'***ERROR*** NO SUCH REGISTER'
         MEXIT
.REGWAR  MNOTE      4,'***WARNING*** DANGEROUS USE OF REGISTER OPERAND'
.REGOK   ANCF
ELAE     L          15,=V($$IO)
         BALR       14,15
         AIF        (T'ELCC NE 'N').SYMACO
         LTR        ELOC,1
         MEXIT
.SYMACO  LTR        1,1
         ST         1,ELOC
         MEND
```

Fig. 18-9. Definition of RWD with checking for an invalid operand.

definition checks for errors such as failure to specify an operand or giving register numbers that are too large or too small. Notice the use of the SETA symbol &REG for arithmetic comparisons with numbers in the conditional assembly statements. In addition, we have used the MEXIT (Macro EXIT) assembler directive. MEXIT tells the assembler to discontinue the expansion of the macro in which it appears. It is different from MEND in that it can appear anywhere within a macro definition, while MEND must be last in a definition and signifies the end of the macro definition.

Figure 18-10 shows the BEGIN macro written so that if the user does not specify a save area address, the macro supplies one for him.

```
         MACRO
         BEGIN  EADDR=$$S,EREG=12
         STM    14,12,12(13)    SAVE THE REGISTERS
         BALR   EREG,0          LOAD BASE ADDRESS
         USING  *,12            BASE POSITION HERE
         ST     13,EADDR+4      KEEP SAVE AREA ADDRESS
         LA     13,EADDR        SAVE AREA ADDRESS IN 13
         AIF    (T'EADDR NE '0').DONE    SAVE AREA AN OPERAND
         B      $$OUT           IF NOT, BRANCH AROUND SAVE AREA DEFINED HERE
$$S      DS     18F             SAVE AREA
$$OUT    EQU    *               NEXT INSTRUCTION AFTER SAVE AREA
.DONE    MEND
```

Fig. 18-10. Another definition of the BEGIN macro. This one provides a register save area if the user does not designate his own.

As a final example of the use of the conditional assembly facilities, we shall illustrate the use of an assembler loop to create a table of powers of 2. The table consists of a series of full words, the number of which is given as the macro operand. Upon expansion of the macro the first word will contain 2, the second 4, the third 8, and so on. In the macro definition of TABTWO shown in Fig. 18-11 we have used the SETA symbols &CTR and &POWER

```
         MACRO
&LAB     TWOTAB   &NUM
         LCLA     &CTR
         LCLA     &POWER
         LCLA     &DLAB
         AIF      (T'&NUM NE N).CFERR
&CTR     SETA     &NUM
         AIF      (&CTR LE 0).OFERR
&POWER   SETA     2
&DLAB    SETC     '&LAB'
.NEXTP   ANOP
&DLAB    DS       F'&POWER'
&CTR     SETA     &CTR-1
         AIF      (&CTR LE 0).DONE
&DLAB    SETC     '        '
&POWER   SETA     &POWER*2
         AGO      .NEXTP
         MEXIT
.OFERR   MNOTE    12,'MISSING NON-NUMERIC, OR NON-POSITIVE OPERAND'
.DONE    MEND
```

Fig. 18-11. A macro that generates tables of powers of two.

as a loop counter and as the current power of 2, respectively. Furthermore, we have used a SETC symbol &DLAB to avoid the problem of multiple definitions of symbols. The first time through the loop, &DLAB has the value of the statement label &LAB. Thereafter, &DLAB is a string of blanks, so that the value of &LAB appears only once in the program as a label. An expansion of TABTWO resulting from

TWOS   TWOTAB   5

is

```
TWOS          DS        F'2'
              DS        F'4'
              DS        F'6'
              DS        F'8'
              DS        F'16'
```

A problem arises when we wish to label macro model statements. For example, suppose that a macro uses register 5 for temporary storage, but we want to preserve the contents of register 5 during execution of the instruction in the macro expansion. An outline of a macro that does this might appear as

```
          MACRO
      prototype
          ST        5,SAV5
          .
          .
          .
          L         5,SAV5
          B         *+4
SAV5      DS        F
          MEND
```

The technique above is fine, so long as we use this macro only once in a program. But as soon as we use it two or more times, SAV5 appears as a symbol defined more than once, which is an error.

The assembler provides a special *system variable symbol* named &SYSNDX to help us avoid this problem. &SYSNDX is like a SETA symbol in that it has a numeric value. It starts at the value 0001 and is incremented by 1 every time a macro-instruction appears in a program. When concatenated onto a name, &SYSNDX appears to be four decimal digits.

If we want to label statements, we should add &SYSNDX to the end of the labels. The macro definition above then becomes

```
             MACRO
         prototype
             ST          5,SAV5&SYSNDX
             .
             .
             .
             L           5,SAV5&SYSNDX
             B           *+4
SAV5&SYSNDX  DS F
             MEND
```

If this macro is the only one used in a program, SAV5&SYSNDX will have the value SAV50001 the first time the macro is used, SAV50002 the second time, and so on.

CHAPTER SUMMARY

The construction and use of *macros* involves three steps:

1. *Macro definition:* The following form a macro definition:
   a. MACRO statement.
   b. *Prototype:* operands supplied as *symbolic parameters.*

c. Model statements: determine statements, operands, and parameters that will appear in the macro expansion.

d. MEND statement.

2. *Macro-instruction:* Request for use of the macro in a program; values are supplied for symbolic parameters.

3. *Macro expansion:* The assembler inserts the statements from the macro definition into the assembly language program.

SET symbols and *variable attributes* provide for computations by the assembler in conditional assembly. The AGO and AIF assembler directives control the order in which program or macro model statements are assembled.

EXERCISES

1. Write a WWD macro which permits either register or full-word memory operands. Your macro should check for valid register operands and output appropriate error messages.

2. Write the definition for a macro that simulates the 370 Insert Characters under Mask instruction described in Chapter 20, Section 20.3.

3. Write a MOVE macro whose operands are a source memory address, a destination memory address, the number of bytes to be moved, and a key-word operand that gives the memory address of the first of four full words which can be used to save register contents. If this operand is omitted, your macro should provide the necessary space. You might find helpful the use of the system variable symbol &SYSNDX. Use MVCL (Chapter 20) if you have access to a 370 machine. Otherwise, use MVC. There should be no loops in the macro expansion.

4. Rewrite the RWD macro definition in Fig. 18-8 so that (1) is not lost when an RWD is used. Be careful to avoid multiple definition of symbols.

5. Write a definition for a macro CONVRT that converts an EBCDIC coded decimal number to binary. The operands should be the address of the EBCDIC number, the number of bytes in the number, and a register into which the result should be placed. The macro should supply its own double word for use with the CVB instruction. If the register operand is omitted, leave the result in register 1.

6. Write a macro SEARCH that locates a record in a linked list created by the program of Fig. 10-11.

7. We can supply variable numbers of macro operands through the use of an operand *sublist*. If in a macro prototype we have

&LAB   CALL   &A,&B,&C

and in a macro instruction we write

LOCO   CALL   H1,(QZ,LS,P),(Z5,H2)

then the symbolic parameter &A has the value H2, &B has the sublist (QZ,LS,P) as its value, and &C has the value (Z5,H2) when the sublist is expanded. To refer to the second operand of sublist &B we write &B(2). In this case, &B(2) = LS. We can also use a SET symbol to index a sublist, as in &B(&INDX). If &INDX = 1, then &B(&INDX) = QZ. The $\underline{N}$umber attribute determines the number of operands in a sublist. In the above we have

$$N'\&A = 1$$
$$N'\&B = 3$$
$$N'\&C = 2$$

Write a general-purpose subroutine CALL macro. The operands should be the name of the subroutine and a sublist of the subroutine arguments. Your macro should establish a storage area for the argument address table, store the proper values in this table, and link to the subroutine following normal system conventions.

8. Write a general-purpose ADD macro whose arguments are a location at which to place the computed sum, a sublist indicating which quantities are to be added, and an operand to determine the type of the arithmetic to be used.

9. Write a macro DIV to carry out binary integer division, leaving the quotient and remainder in specified registers and preserving the contents of all other registers.

REFERENCES

IBM System/360 Disk and Tape Operating System Assembler Language, Form GC24-3414, IBM Corp., White Plains, N.Y.

IBM System/360 Operating System Assembler Language, Form GC28-6514, IBM Corp., White Plains, N.Y.

IBM OS/VS—DOS/VS Assembler Language, Form GC33-4010, IBM Corp., White Plains, N.Y.

19 FLOATING-POINT ARITHMETIC

Decimal and integer arithmetic are fine for many computing applications in which a high degree of accuracy is required and in which the numbers used in the calculations are neither "too small" nor "too large" for convenient representation as integers. But in some cases, particularly scientific calculations, we are willing to sacrifice some accuracy in return for the ability to deal with numbers whose magnitudes fall outside the ranges allowable in integer arithmetic. For example, Avogadro's number is a constant often used in physical chemistry. Its value, approximately 6.023×10^{23} (6023 followed by 20 zeros), is the number of particles in a mole of a substance. The charge on an electron is 1.60210×10^{-19} (.160210 preceded by 18 zeros) coulomb. The charge on a mole of electrons would be the product of these two numbers.

Representation of such numbers as integers is at best impractical. Another difficulty is that if we do use integers in calculations with these numbers, the task of keeping track of where the decimal place belongs can be formidable.

Thus, we tend to use the *floating-point* mode of number representation and arithmetic in scientific calculations. While in practice we program our problems in a higher-level language such as FORTRAN or BASIC, the computational statements in these languages are eventually translated to machine language for execution. The machine language produced uses the machine floating-point instructions for the calculations. A knowledge of how numbers are represented and processed in floating-point calculations helps considerably in using higher-level languages.

Furthermore, situations arise in which we write assembly language programs to process floating point data. The subroutines that higher-level languages use to convert numbers from character representation to internal

446

floating-point and vice versa are assembly language programs, as are many of the subroutines, such as SIN and ABS, that compute special functions for FORTRAN or BASIC programs. A good scientific programmer has assembly language available for use when he needs to write his own subroutines, either to compute functions not available as part of a higher-level language or to make often-executed subroutines more efficient in their use of time and memory space.

19.1. FLOATING-POINT NUMBERS

The easiest way to see how the machine does floating-point calculations is by analogy with the way we do arithmetic using *scientific notation* to represent the numbers involved. In scientific notation, a quantity is written as a number times a power of 10. 3.564×10^5 is the number 356,400, for example. In the IBM machines, floating-point numbers have a similar structure, but the base of the number system is 16, instead of 10. A floating-point number in the hexadecimal system has the form

$$\text{fraction} \times 16^n$$

We require that the magnitude of the *fraction* be less than 1. The number n is called the *exponent* (other authors call the fraction portion of a floating-point number the *mantissa*).

The requirement that the fraction be less than 1 means that the (hexa) decimal point must precede all significant digits in the fraction. For example, the number $.C3A \times 16^2$ is really $C3.A_{16}$, while $.10E \times 16^{-3}$ is $.00010E_{16}$. The usual algorithms for decimal computations using scientific notation carry over directly to the equivalent hexadecimal-based system. To add two numbers we shift one of them, changing its exponent until the two exponents match, and then add the fractions. In multiplication, we add the exponents and multiply the fractions. Check the arithmetic in these examples:

$$.1C2 \times 16^3 - .8E \times 16^2 = .1C2 \times 16^3 - .08E \times 16^3 = .134 \times 16^3$$

$$(.3A \times 16^3) \times (.42 \times 16^2) = .EF4 \times 16^5$$

Pencil-and-paper conversion from decimal floating point to hexadecimal floating point is tedious but possible. For example, we have

$$.C1_{16} \times 16^3 = (12 \times 16^{-1} + 1 \times 16)^{-2} \times 16^3$$
$$= 12 \times 16^2 + 1 \times 16 = 3088_{10}$$

Let us now see how the IBM computers handle floating-point numbers.

19.1.1. Internal Representation

We have three quantities to represent in a floating-point number: the algebraic *sign*, the *exponent*, and the *fraction*. In all floating-point numbers, the first bit (bit 0) indicates the sign of the entire number, 0 for a positive number, 1 for a negative number. The next 7 bits contain the *characteristic*, which is the internal form of the exponent. The remaining space contains the fraction.

Bit   0 1   7 8

S	Characteristic	Fraction

The Sign.   The only difference between a floating-point number and its negative is in the sign bit. Note that this is different from binary integer arithmetic, in which the negative of a number is its 2's complement. To obtain the negative of a floating-point number we simply change the sign bit to the opposite value from the one which it had. The fraction portion of a floating-point number contains the absolute value of the fraction. The negative of the number C380315E is simply 4380315E.

The Characteristic.   Since the characteristic is a 7-bit number, it can have values between 00 and $7F_{16}$, or 0 through 127_{10}. But if these 7 bits were to represent the actual exponent of a number, we could use only numbers with positive exponents. The way we get around this problem is to follow this rule: *The 7-bit number stored in the characteristic portion of a floating-point number is 64_{10} more than the actual exponent of the number.* This usage is called the *excess-64* notation. The smallest characteristic is 0000000_2. This is 64 more than the actual exponent, which must therefore be -64. The largest possible characteristic is 127_{10}, which is equivalent to the exponent $127 - 64 = 63_{10}$. Thus, internal floating-point numbers range in magnitude between 16^{-64} and 16^{+63}, or roughly 5.4×10^{-79} to 7.2×10^{75}.

Given an exponent in the proper range, to find the equivalent characteristic we convert the exponent to binary and then add $64_{10} = 1000000_2$ to the result, using 7-bit 2's complement arithmetic. For example, if the exponent is 13_{10}, the characteristic is

$$13_{10} + 1000000_2 = 0001101_2 + 1000000_2 = 1001101_2 = 4D_{16}$$

Similarly, if the exponent is -5, the characteristic is

$$-5_{10} + 1000000_2 = 1111011_2 + 1000000_2 = 0111011_2 = 3B_{16}$$

Notice that positive exponents have a 1 in the first bit of the characteristic, while negative exponents have a 0 there. This might confuse *us* occasionally, but the *machine* knows what it's doing!

The Fraction.   The standard floating-point instruction set of the IBM 360 and 370 computers provides for the processing of floating-point numbers of either of two lengths. *Single-precision* (short) floating-point numbers are

32-bit full words. The sign and characteristic occupy the first 8 bits, leaving room for a 24-bit fraction. *Double-precision* floating-point numbers (for some reason called *long* floating-point numbers in the manuals) are double words consisting of a sign-characteristic byte followed by a 56-bit fraction.

In Chapter 2 we saw that many fractions cannot be represented exactly as binary numbers. The example we chose was the binary equivalent of the decimal number .1:

$$.1_{10} = .00011001100110011 \ldots_2$$
$$= .19999999 \ldots_{16}$$

Such numbers are repeating fractions when written in binary and thus require an infinite number of bits for exact representation in a machine. We must accept a *truncation error* when we use such numbers in a finite machine.

But the more bits we can use to represent a number, the closer we can approximate its actual value. A question that often arises is: How accurate is a binary approximation to decimal fraction? To determine this, we consider the relative change in the binary number that occurs when we change its least significant bit. If the number occupies N bits, then the fractional change in the number is 2^{-N}. Changing the last bit of a 4-bit number changes its value by $2^{-4} = 1/16$. We can find the decimal equivalent of this change by solving for x in the equation

$$10^{-x} = 2^{-N}$$

To determine x, we take the base 10 logarithm of each side, and change the signs

$$-x \log 10 = -N \log_{10} 2$$
$$x = N \log_{10} 2$$

or, roughly

$$x = .3N$$

Now returning to the IBM floating-point representations for a 24-bit fraction,

$$x = .3 \times 24 = 7.2$$

Using 24 bits we can represent numbers to within $10^{-7.2}$ of their actual value if they require more than 24 bits for exact representation as binary fractions. In other words, single-precision arithmetic offers a little better than 7-place accuracy. A similar calculation shows that double-precision arithmetic can produce results accurate to about 18 decimal places. These are estimates of the best accuracy possible. When we consider floating-point arithmetic in more detail, we shall see that *roundoff* errors can be so large as to make arithmetic results completely meaningless.

The IBM 360 Model 85 and the IBM 370 processors offer an *extended-precision* option which provides "double-double-precision" accuracy. An extended-precision number occupies four consecutive full words. The first double word has the same format as a double-precision number. Its sign and characteristic, however, apply to the entire four-word number. The machine ignores the sign and characteristic portion of the second double word when an extended-precision number is an operand. This means that we have $128 - 16 = 112$ bits for the fraction in an extended-precision number. This is equivalent to an accuracy of about 36 decimal places.

Figure 19-1 shows the formats of the three kinds of floating-point numbers. Given the internal representation of a floating-point number, what is

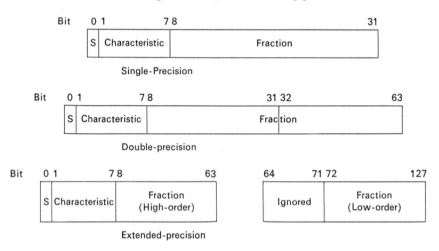

Fig. 19-1. Single-, double- (long), and extended-precision floating-point representations. S stands for the *sign* bit.

that number? To determine the answer, we split the number up into its three pieces. Consider the single-precision number

$$4300C000$$

Since bit 0 is 0, the number is positive. The characterstic, $43_{16} = 67_{10}$ is 64 more than the actual exponent, and so the exponent must be 3. The fraction is $.00C000_{16}$. Thus, the number is equivalent to

$$.00C000 \times 16^3$$

or

$$.C00000 \times 16^1 = 12_{10}$$

Similarly, the number

$$A56C429B$$

is negative, since bit 0 is 1. The characteristic is $25_{16} = 37_{10}$, and so the exponent is -27_{10}. Thus, A56C429B is equivalent to

$$-.6C429B \times 16^{-27}$$

The same technique applies to double- and extended-precision numbers. The only difference is that their fractions are longer.

Normalization.   A floating-point number is said to be *normalized* if the first *hexadecimal* digit of its fraction is not zero. In principle, a normalized number is the most accurate representation of a given number, since it contains the largest possible number of digits in its fraction. Consider the single-precision normalized representation of the number .2. This is

$$40333333$$

and is accurate to a little more than seven decimal places. An unnormalized equivalent is

$$43000333$$

While we still have a 24-bit fraction, we are really using only 3 hexadecimal digits = 12 bits for the number. Thus, the above representation has an equivalent decimal accuracy of less than four places. The same considerations apply to double- and extended-precision numbers. Use of unnormalized floating-point operands tends to decrease the overall accuracy of the calculations.

To normalize an unnormalized number we simply shift the fraction to the left one hexadecimal digit at a time, until the first hexadecimal digit is nonzero. Each time we shift the fraction, we subtract 1 from the characteristic. The normalized equivalent of the double-precision number

$$C5000638 \quad 4C8096E5$$

is

$$C26384C8 \quad 096E5000$$

The characteristic of the normalized number is three lower since we had to do three shifts to make the first hexadecimal digit nonzero. We have shifted 0s into the low-order end of the number in the normalization process. In arithmetic operations, this is not quite exactly what happens, as we shall see shortly.

19.1.2. Floating-Point Operands

All the floating-point instructions are of the RX or RR type. In the RX instructions, the memory operand must be full-word-aligned in single-precision operations. All extended-precision instructions are of the RR type.

The register operands are special-purpose *floating-point registers*. These registers (FP registers for short) are completely separate from and must not be confused with the general-purpose registers (GP registers). There are eight of these, numbered 0 through 7. But only the even-numbered floating-point registers can be specified as operands in single- and double-precision operations, and only registers 0 and 4 can be used as extended-precision operands. If we violate these rules, we get a specification exception.

Each floating-point register is one word long. The even-numbered registers are designed to hold a sign-characteristic byte and a 24-bit fraction. The odd-numbered registers contain 32-bit fractions. This means that an even-odd register pair holds one double-precision floating-point number. Single-precision operations do not affect the contents of odd-numbered registers. In extended-precision operations, registers 0–3 and 4–7 are assumed to contain extended-precision numbers.

The register operand in RX instructions or the first register operand in RR instructions functions as an accumulator, just as in binary integer arithmetic.

19.1.3. Arithmetic

The machine does floating-point calculations in much the same way as we do them with pencil and paper. The primary difference is that the computer has a fixed number of digits available for number representation. The techniques we describe here apply to all three levels of precision.

The first step in addition and subtraction operations is called *prenormalization*. The machine examines the characteristics of the operands. If they are the same, the fractions are added or their difference computed, depending on the signs of the operands and whether addition or subtraction was requested. If the characteristics of the two operands are different, the computer adjusts the number with the smaller characteristic to match its characteristic with that of the other operand. To do this, the machine shifts the fraction of the operand with the smaller characteristic to the right one hexadecimal digit at a time, incrementing its characteristic by 1 for each shift. The digit shifted out of the right end of the number is placed in a special location called the *guard digit*. This process, right shift followed by increment of the characteristic, is continued until the characteristics match. Once this is completed, the processor adds or subtracts the fractions as required.

In addition and subtraction, we can request that the result be left unnormalized, or we can have the computer normalize the sum or difference. Normalization of the result is called *postnormalization*. The extra guard digit is shifted into the right-hand end of the fraction in the post-normalization process. This gives us a little bit more accuracy than the use of only 6, 14, or 28 digits in single-, double-, and extended-precision operations would offer.

For example, let us compute the sum of the single-precision floating-point numbers

$$3B6386E2 \quad \boxed{0}$$

$$+ \ BB5C43A1 \quad \boxed{0}$$

The characteristics are both $3B_{16}$, and so no prenormalization is necessary. Before prenormalization both guard digits (enclosed in squares) contain 0, and since no fractions are shifted, they contain 0 when the addition begins. The second number is negative, and so we subtract the second fraction from the first. If we ask that the result be left unnormalized, the result is

3B074341 | 0 |

The normalized sum is

3A743410 | 0 |

The sum

438 1CA38
+ 46B2 2 C21

requires prenormalization, since the exponents are not the same. The first number has the smaller exponent, and so the machine shifts its fraction right three places and adds 3 to its exponent:

4600081C | A |

46B22C21 | 0 |

The sum is

46B2343D | A |

which is already normalized, and so no postnormalization is necessary. Check these calculations.

In multiplying two floating-point numbers, the machine prenormalizes the operands. The characteristic of the product is the sum of the characteristics of the operands minus 40_{16}. The fractions are multiplied and the product normalized, if necessary.

Let us compute the product

4 5300000
× 4C042A31

The second operand is not normalized, and so we shift its fraction to the left, subtracting 1 from its characteristic. To compute the characteristic of the product

45300000
× 4B42A310

we calculate

$$45 + 4B - 40 = 50$$

The product of the fractions is

$$300000 \times 42A310 = 0C7E93000000$$

which is stored as a six-digit fraction with guard digit

500C7E93 | 0 |

Postnormalization gives the product

4FC7E930

In this example the fraction product produced a zero guard digit. Had this not been the case, the guard digit would have furnished an extra digit of accuracy. Notice that we lost this extra digit because one of the operands was unnormalized.

Division of two floating-point numbers begins with prenormalization. The characteristic of the divisor is subtracted from that of the dividend and 40_{16} added to the result:

quotient characteristic = dividend characteristic − divisor characteristic + 40_{16}

The resulting fraction never needs postnormalization, but it is possible that it may need shifting to the right one digit.

Let us divide $.3 \times 16^2$ by $.9 \times 16^3$ using floating-point arithmetic. The problem is

$$42300000$$
$$\div 43900000$$

The characteristic of the quotient is

$$42 - 43 + 40 = 82 - 43 = 3F$$

representing an exponent of -1. A pencil-and-paper long division shows that the fraction is .55555555..., the hexadecimal equivalent of 1/3. Thus, the quotient is

3F555555

19.1.4. Floating-Point Constants

The assembler recognizes constants of type E, D, and L as single-, double-, and extended-precision floating-point constants, respectively. We write the value of the constant as a decimal number. The statements

SING	DC	E'.003'
DOUB	DC	D'.003'
LONG	DC	L'.003'

define floating-point constants with the value .003 in each of the three possible lengths. E-type constants are automatically aligned on full-word boundaries; D- and L-type constants are aligned on double-word boundaries.

If we wish, we can include a power of 10 in the definition of a floating-point constant. To do this, we write an E followed by the decimal exponent we desire. For example, the constant

AVOG   DC   D'6.023E23'

defines a double-precision floating-point constant with decimal equivalent 6.023×10^{23}, while

NANO   DC   E'1.E−9'

defines a constant with value 10^{-9}.

An alternative way to assign a decimal exponent is to write it before the value of the constant.

AVOG   DC   DE23'6.023'

and

NANO   DC   EE−9'1.'

define the same constants, respectively, as do the preceding examples. When we write the exponent outside the apostrophes, that exponent applies to all numbers within the apostrophes. The statement

THOU   DC   EE+4'1.,2.,3.'

establishes three single-precision constants, stored starting at THOU, with values 10,000, 20,000, and 30,000.

Literal floating-point operands are written the same way. For example, the statement

DE   4,=EE−9'1.'

divides the contents of floating-point register 4 by one-billionth.

19.2. FLOATING-POINT INSTRUCTIONS

We now know how floating-point arithmetic works. Here we shall present the floating-point instructions with some comments on their use in programming.

The floating-point mnemonics follow a logical naming pattern. We have the same basic operations,

Operation	Mnemonic
Load	L
STore	ST
Add	A
Subtract	S
Multiply	M
Divide	D
Compare	C
Load Positive	LP
Load Negative	LN
Load Complement	LC

and a new operation, Halve (H), which divides a floating-point number by 2. After any of the above, we write a letter which designates the precision of the operand and whether or not postnormalization is to be done. We write E for single-precision, D for Double-precision, and X for eXtended-precision. If a single-precision result of an addition or subtraction is to be left Unnormalized, we write U instead of E. W, a mediocre pun for Double-Unnormalized, indicates a double-precision unnormalized sum or difference. Finally, we write an R if we wish to use the Register-to-Register form of an instruction. For example, LPER means load a single-precision FP register with the absolute value of the contents of an FP register. AW computes the unnormalized sum of two double-precision numbers, one of which is in an FP register pair, and the other in the memory.

In the following we shall present the floating-point instructions, starting with those included in the standard floating-point instruction set. Since the extended-precision instructions are optional, we shall treat them separately. After a discussion of the error indications that can occur in floating-point calculations, we shall conclude this section with a programming example.

19.2.1. Single- and Double-Precision Instructions

Load and STore Instructions. There are four load instructions, which differ in the precision of the operands and in the location of the second operand.

LE	FPR1,D2(X2,B2)	Load single precision	FPR1 $\longleftarrow$ (D2 + (X2) + (B2))
LD	FPR1,D2(X2,B2)	Load Double-precision	FPR1$_D$ $\longleftarrow$ (D2 + (X2) + (B2))$_D$
LER	FPR1,FPR2	Load single-precision Register	FPR1 $\longleftarrow$ (FPR2)
LDR	FPR1,FPR2	Load Double-precision Register	FPR1$_D$ $\longleftarrow$ (FPR2)$_D$

In the descriptive notation for floating-point instructions, FPR stands for Floating-Point Register. The integer that follows indicates whether the register is the first or the second operand. Remember that *all* register operands in *all* floating-point instructions must be even-numbered registers and that double-precision numbers are stored in even-odd register pairs. We indicate the lengths of the operands by writing no subscript for single-precision, subscript D for double-precision, and subscript X for extended-precision. (D2 + (X2) + (B2))$_D$ means the contents of the double word stored in the memory starting at address D2 + (X2) + (B2). (FPR2)$_X$ means the contents of the four FP registers FPR2, FPR2+1, FPR2+2, and FPR2+3 treated as the second extended-precision operand.

A single-precision operation has no effect on the contents of the other register of the pair. Thus, the instruction

> LER   4,6

moves the contents of FP register 6 into FP register 4 and leaves the contents of FP register 5 unchanged.

> LD   0,DNUM(7)

moves the double word stored at DNUM indexed by general-purpose register 7 into FP registers 0 and 1. If the instruction

> LE   0,SINGNUM

follows the LD instruction above, the word at SINGNUM replaces the contents of floating-point register 0, leaving floating-point register 1 unchanged.

The two STore instructions

STE FPR1,D2(X2,B2)	STore single-precision	(FPR1) $\longrightarrow$ D2 + (X2) + (B2)
STD FPR1,D2(X2,B2)	STore Double-precision	(FPR1)$_D$ $\longrightarrow$ D2 + (X2) + (B2)

differ only in the precision of the number stored. STE stores a single-precision number and STD stores a double-precision number. The Load and STore instructions have no effect on the condition code.

Just as in binary integer arithmetic, there is a series of floating-point Load instructions that test and modify the numbers being moved. These are all register-to-register instructions, and the LTs set the condition code depending on the number moved.

LTER	FPR1,FPR2	Load and Test single-precision	FPR1 $\longleftarrow$ (FPR2), set CC
LTDR	FPR1,FPR2	Load and Test Double-precision	FPR1$_D$ $\longleftarrow$ (FPR2)$_D$, set CC
LCER	FPR1,FPR2	Load Complement single-precision	FPR1 $\longleftarrow$ $-$(FPR2)$_D$
LCDR	FPR1,FPR2	Load Complement Double-precision	FPR1$_D$ $\longleftarrow$ $-$(FPR2)$_D$
LNER	FPR1,FPR2	Load Negative single-precision	FPR1 $\longleftarrow$ $-|$(FPR2)$|$
LNDR	FPR1,FPR2	Load Negative Double-precision	FPR1$_D$ $\longleftarrow$ $-|$(FPR2)$_D|$
LPER	FPR1,FPR2	Load Positive single-precision	FPR1 $\longleftarrow$ $|$(FPR2)$|$
LPDR	FPR1,FPR2	Load Positive Double-precision	FPR1$_D$ $\longleftarrow$ $|$(FPR2)$_D|$

The condition-code values and meanings resulting from these instructions are the same as for other arithmetic modes:

Condition Code	Meaning
0	Result = 0
1	Result < 0
2	Result > 0
3	Cannot happen

LTER and LTDR set the condition code depending on the value of the number moved. To determine the sign of the number in floating-point register 6 we write

LTER   6,6

Ensuing conditional branch instructions can then test the condition code setting.

The Load Complement, Load Negative, and Load Positive instructions simply change the sign bit of the number moved. LCER and LCDR complement the sign bit, LNER and LNDR set it to 1, and LPER and LPDR set it to 0.

Addition and Subtraction.   For addition and subtraction we have eight possible instructions. Which to use depends on the precision of the operands, whether the second operand is in the memory or in a register, and whether or not we require the result to be normalized. Table 19-1 summarizes the floating-point addition and subtraction instructions. In all these operations, FPR1 behaves as an accumulator register in that it contains one of the initial operands and receives the final result.

The addition and subtraction instructions set the condition code as usual:

Condition Code	Meaning
0	Result = 0
1	Result < 0
2	Result > 0
3	Cannot happen

We shall discuss the floating-point equivalent of overflow later.

Multiplication, Division, and the Halve Instructions.   The single-precision multiply instructions change the second word of an even-odd register pair. They produce a double-precision product from two single-precision numbers. The result is always normalized.

Table 19-1 SINGLE- AND DOUBLE-PRECISION FLOATING-POINT ADDITION AND SUBTRACTION INSTRUCTIONS

1. Addition, normalized result

AE	FPR1,D2(X2,B2)	Add single-precision	$FPR1 \leftarrow (FPR1) + (D2 + (X2) + (B2))$
AER	FPR1,FPR2	Add single-precision Register	$FPR1 \leftarrow (FPR1) + (FPR2)$
AD	FPR1,D2(X2,B2)	Add Double-precision	$FPR1_D \leftarrow (FPR1)_D + (D2 + (X2) + (B2))_D$
ADR	FPR1,FPR2	Add Double-precision Register	$FPR1_D \leftarrow (FPR1)_D + (FPR2)_D$

2. Subtraction, normalized result

SE	FPR1,D2(X2,B2)	Subtract, single-precision	$FPR1 \leftarrow (FPR1) - (D2 + (X2) + (B2))$
SER	FPR1,FPR2	Subtract single-precision Register	$FPR1 \leftarrow (FPR1) - (FPR2)$
SD	FPR1,D2(X2,B2)	Subtract Double-precision	$FPR1_D \leftarrow (FPR1)_D - (D2 + (X2) + (B2))_D$
SDR	FPR1,FPR2	Subtract Double-precision Register	$FPR1_D \leftarrow (FPR1)_D - (FPR2)_D$

3. Addition, unnormalized result

AU	FPR1,D2(X2,B2)	Add single-precision Unnormalized	$FPR1 \leftarrow (FPR1) + (D2 + (X2) + (B2))$
AUR	FPR1,FPR2	Add single-precision Unnormalized Register	$FPR1 \leftarrow (FPR1) + (FPR2)$
AW	FPR1,D2(X2,B2)	Add Double-precision Unnormalized	$FPR1_D \leftarrow (FPR1)_D + (D2 + (X2) + (B2))_D$
AWR	FPR1,FPR2	Add Double-precision Unnormalized, Register	$FPR1_D \leftarrow (FPR1)_D + (FPR2)_D$

4. Subtraction, unnormalized result

SU	FPR1,D2(X2,B2)	Subtract single-precision Unnormalized	$FPR1 \leftarrow (FPR1) - (D2 + (X2) + (B2))$
SUR	FPR1,FPR2	Subtract single-precision Unnormalized, Register	$FPR1 \leftarrow (FPR1) - (FPR2)$
SW	FPR1,D2(X2,B2)	Subtract Double-precision Unnormalized	$FPR1_D \leftarrow (FPR1)_D - (D2 + (X2) + (B2))_D$
SWR	FPR1,FPR2	Subtract Double-precision Unnormalized, Register	$FPR1_D \leftarrow (FPR1)_D - (FPR2)_D$

ME	FPR1,D2(X2,B2)	Multiply single-precision	$FPR1_D \longleftarrow (FPR1) \times (D2 + (R2) + (B2))$
MER	FPR1,FPR2	Multiply single-precision Register	$FPR1_D \longleftarrow (FPR1) \times (FPR2)$
MD	FPR1,D2(X2,B2)	Multiply Double-precision	$FPR1_D \longleftarrow (FPR1)_D \times (D2 + (X2) + (B2))_D$
MDR	FPR1,FPR2	Multiply Double-precision Register	$FPR1_D \longleftarrow (FPR1)_D \times (FPR2)_D$

The double-precision instructions MD and MDR produce double-precision products from double-precision operands.

The divide instructions work as we have detailed earlier. Again we have the choice of single- or double-precision and register or memory second operands.

DE	FPR1,D2(X2,B2)	Divide single-precision	$FPR1 \longleftarrow (FPR1) \div (D2 + (X2) + (B2))$
DER	FPR1,FPR2	Divide single-precision Register	$FPR1 \longleftarrow (FPR1) \div (FPR2)$
DD	FPR1,D2(X2,B2)	Divide Double-precision	$FPR1_D \longleftarrow (FPR1)_D \div (D2 + (X2) + (B2))_D$
DDR	FPR1,FPR2	Divide Double-precision Register	$FPR1_D \longleftarrow (FPR1)_D \div (FPR2)_D$

The Halve instructions shift the fraction of a number 1 bit position to the right and normalize the result if necessary. The effect is to divide the number by 2.

| HER | FPR1,FPR2 | Halve single-precision Register | $FPR1 \longleftarrow (FPR2)_F/2$ |
| HDR | FPR1,FPR2 | Halve Double-precision Register | $FPR1,FPR1+1 \longleftarrow (FPR2)_D/2$ |

Both the halve instructions are RR instructions which divide the contents of the second register by 2 and place the result in the first register.

The Multiply, Divide, and Halve instructions do not change the condition code.

Comparison. Again we have the same four choices regarding the operands.

CE	FPR1,D2(X2,B2)	Compare single-precision	Compute (FPR1) $-$ (D2 $+$ (X2) $+$ (B2)), set CC
CER	FPR1,FPR2	Compare single-precision Register	Compute (FPR1) $-$ (FPR2), set CC
CD	FPR1,D2(X2,B2)	Compare Double-precision	Compute $(FPR1)_D$ $-$ (D2 $+$ (X2) $+$ (B2))$_D$, set CC
CDR	FPR2	Compare Double-precision Register	Compute $(FPR1)_D$ $-$ $(FPR2)_D$, set CC

The floating-point comparison instructions compute the difference between the first and second operands and set the condition code depending on the result:

Condition Code	Meaning
0	Operand 1 $=$ operand 2
1	Operand 1 $<$ operand 2
2	Operand 1 $>$ operand 2

19.2.2. Extended-Precision Instructions

We shall now describe the optional extended-precision floating-point instructions. Since they work only on those machines that include the option, check to see if your system supports extended-precision before using the instructions.

All the extended-precision instructions are of the RR type, and remember that an extended-precision operand must be either FP register 0 or 4. The extended addition and subtraction instructions are simple.

AXR	FPR1,FPR2	Add eXtended-precision Register	$FPR1_X \longleftarrow (FPR1)_X + (FPR2)_X$
SXR	FPR1,FRP2	Subtract eXtended-precision Register	$FPR1_X \longleftarrow (FPR1)_X - (FPR2)_X$

In both these instructions, the calculations are done as described above for single- and double-precision computations, except that the operands are the two indicated groups of four registers. Each group is considered to be an extended-precision number. The operands are prenormalized if necessary. The 28-digit fractions are then added and the result is postnormalized.

As we have seen, an extended-precision operand looks like two double-precision operands considered as a single number. When an extended-precision number is used as an operand, the machine ignores the characteristic and sign of its second double word. But in the extended-precision result, the characteristic and sign of the second double word appear to have the correct values. The sign of the second double word is the same as that of the first. The exponent of the second double word is 14 less than that of the first, reflecting the fact that the fraction of the second double word really starts 14 hexadecimal places after the (hexa) decimal point of the number. Thus, an extended-precision result is really the equivalent of a number such as

$$\underbrace{.\text{high-order fraction}}_{\substack{14 \text{ hexadecimal} \\ \text{digits}}} \times 16^n + \underbrace{.\text{low-order fraction}}_{\substack{14 \text{ more hexadecimal} \\ \text{digits}}} \times 16^{n-14}$$

We offer one example here, and without hesitation claim the longest arithmetic example in print. One operand, in registers 0–3, is

$$\underbrace{4918042C}_{\text{reg. 0}} \quad \underbrace{C46890D7}_{\text{reg. 1}} \quad \underbrace{FBCAA286}_{\text{reg. 2}} \quad \underbrace{2983E275}_{\text{reg. 3}}$$

The other operand, in registers 4–7, is

$$\underbrace{C8936C71}_{\text{reg. 4}} \quad \underbrace{22222222}_{\text{reg. 5}} \quad \underbrace{77333333}_{\text{reg. 7}} \quad \underbrace{55555555}_{\text{reg. 7}}$$

The instruction executed is

$$\text{AXR} \qquad 0,4$$

The first step is prenormalization, using the characteristics in the first bytes of the operands. The number starting in FP register 4 has the smaller exponent, and so we shift it to the right one digit and add 1 to the exponent. Notice that the "characteristic" bytes in registers 2 and 6 play no part in the arithmetic until the final result is produced. Prenormalization produces

FP regs 0–3: 49180427 C46890D7 FBCAA286 2983E275 | 0 |

FP regs 4–7: C90936C7 1222222 2 772 3 3 333 35555555 | 5 |

To compute the sum, we notice that the second operand is negative, and so we subtract the second fraction from the first, obtaining a positive result:

FP regs 0–3: 490ECD65 B2466EB5 FBA76F52 F42E8C1F | B |

In the postnormalization step, the number in registers 0–3 is normalized, shifting the guard digit into the right end, and the characteristic in the second double word (byte 0 of FP register 2) is adjusted as described above. The machine also returns the number in registers 4–7 to its original value. Thus, the final result is

FP regs 0–3: 48ECD65B   2466EB5A   7B76F52F   42E8C1FB
FP regs 4–7: C893 6C71   2222 2222   77333333   5555555 5

You might want to check the arithmetic, but the important thing here is to see how the calculations are done.

Three extended-precision multiply instructions come with the extended-precision floating-point option.

MXR	FPR1,FPR2	Multiply eXtended-precision Register	$FPR1_X \longleftarrow (FPR1)_X \times (FPR2)_X$
MXD	FPR1,D2(X2,B2)	Multiply eXtended-Double	$FPR1_X \longleftarrow (FPR1)_D \times (D2 + (B2) + (X2))_D$
MXDR	FPR1,FPR2	Multiply eXtended-Double Register	$FPR1_X \longleftarrow (FPR1)_D \times (FPR2)_D$

MXR computes the extended-precision product of two extended-precision numbers. With the exception of the treatment of the sign-characteristic byte of the second double word of the product as described above, the technique is identical with the single- and double-precision multiply instructions.

The MXD and MXDR instructions produce extended-precision results from two double-precision operands. This is the most common way of producing extended-precision numbers for use in later calculations. Notice that the instruction

$$\text{MXD} \qquad 4,=D'1.0'$$

in effect changes a double-precision number in FP registers 4 and 5 to an extended-precision number in FP registers 4–7. This does not increase the accuracy of the number, but it does prepare the number for use in other extended-precision operations.

The converse problem is to convert extended-precision numbers to double-precision or double-precision numbers to single-precision. The load and store instructions we have already covered can be used to do this, but with the loss of a little bit of accuracy. For example, if we have created a double-precision number in FP registers 2 and 3, then the instruction

$$\text{LER} \qquad 4,2$$

moves only the first word of the double-precision number to register 4. In the worst case, registers 2 and 3 contain something like

FP regs 2–3:   40803AC0   F683721C

The number moved to FP register 4 is 40803AC0. Rounded off, the number would be 40803AC1. In other words, the standard load and store instructions truncate the last half of the number if we move portions of numbers that are smaller than that offered by the full precision of the numbers.

To help remedy this problem, the extended-precision option includes two special Load Rounded instructions:

LRER FPR1,FPR2 Load Rounded single- precision Register $FPR1_F \leftarrow (FPR2)_D$ (rounded)

LRDR FPR1,FPR2 Load Rounded Double- precision Register $FPR1_D \leftarrow (FPR2)_X$ (rounded)

LRER and LRDR extract the high-order portion of a double- and extended-precision operand, respectively, and move the result, rounded off to the nearest digit, to FPR1. LRER moves the first word of a double-precision number to the first named register. LRDR moves the first double word of an extended-precision number to the FPR1, FPR1+1 register pair.

Before the machine moves the data, it checks the first fraction digit that is not moved. If this digit is 8 or more, the processor adds 1 to the last digit of the portion of the number moved. In the example above, the digit checked is F, the first digit of the number in FP register 3. Since this digit is greater than 8, the machine adds 1 to the fraction moved. Thus,

$$\text{LRER} \quad 4,2$$

moves the number 40803AC1 to FP register 4.

19.2.3. Errors and Exceptions

Roundoff Errors. We have already mentioned one source of error in floating-point calculations: the truncation of fractions that cannot be represented precisely in the number of bits provided. Another kind of error that is usually more serious and difficult to deal with is a *roundoff* error.

Roundoff errors are also due to the use of finite numbers of digits to represent numbers. It is not necessary to look to computing to find examples of roundoff problems. Suppose that we measure the voltage produced by two different batteries, each measurement accurate to three significant figures, but that we estimate a fourth figure. We then calculate the difference between the voltages. A typical result might be

$$
\begin{array}{r}
1.273 \\
- 1.271 \\
\hline
0.002
\end{array}
$$

Since we measured both voltages to almost four significant figures, we might (erroneously!) think that this difference is also accurate to four places. But in fact, we are not even sure of the first significant digit, 2, in the difference. We really have an accuracy of less than one place.

The equivalent problem in floating-point calculations occurs most frequently when we compute the difference between two numbers which are almost the same. Single-precision arithmetic offers six-hexadecimal-digit accuracy. In the subtraction problem

$$4068C10E$$
$$- 4068C108$$

the unnormalized result is

$$40000006$$

or, after normalization,

$$3B600000$$

We have lost all but one significant digit of the difference. In other words, ensuing calculations which depend on this difference can be accurate to at most one hexadecimal digit.

In most applications, the problem is not this severe and can be handled by using higher-precision arithmetic. There is one more point we should make, though, and this is that two different sequences of arithmetic calculations that, with pencil and paper, yield the same result often produce slightly different answers in floating-point arithmetic. For example,

$$.2^2 - .04 = 0$$

exactly. But let us now compare $.2^2$ and $.04$ as the computer would do it $.2$ in single-precision is 40333333. .04 is the repeating fraction

$$.0A3D70A3070A3D7. . .$$

or, stored as a normalized single-precision number,

$$3FA3D70A$$

But when we multiply .2 by .2 using single-precision, we get the double-precision product

$$3FA3D706 \quad F5C29000$$

The two results differ in the sixth hexadecimal place.

This kind of roundoff error, on the order of 10^{-6}, is often unimportant in practice. But the programmer must be aware that it happens, especially in program logic. A comparison instruction based upon the results above will show that $.2^2$ is *not* 04. The moral is that we must be careful when testing floating-point numbers for equality. Two floating-point numbers are "equal" when the absolute value of their difference is less than some "small" number. In comparing two floating-point numbers, A and B, for equality, we should ask not "Does $A = B$?," but instead "Is $|A - B| < .00001$?"

Significance Exception.   The computer assumes that the result of an addition or subtraction which has no significant digits is an error. What it really means is that the two operands were so close together in value that their difference is beyond the accuracy of the machine. A significance exception (completion code 0CE) occurs when, in computing a sum or difference, all digits including the guard digit of the result are zero.

Exponent Underflow and Overflow Exceptions.   The smallest possible characteristic is 00 and represents the exponent -64_{10}. When an arithmetic result arises that would require a smaller exponent, an exponent *underflow* exception occurs. The machine recognizes this condition during the post-normalization after an arithmetic operation. One good way to get an exponent underflow is accidentally to multiply a small floating-point number by an integer. The sum of the characteristics, less 64, is then less than zero.

Similarly, an exponent *overflow* exception occurs when we produce an arithmetic result that requires an exponent larger than $+63_{10}$. Division by an integer almost always produces this condition.

A floating-point divide exception arises when we attempt to divide by a number whose fraction is 0.

The SPM Instruction.   In Chapter 11 we introduced the *program mask* section of the PSW. The 4 bits in the program mask enable program exception interruptions due to the following conditions:

Bit	Condition
36	Fixed-point overflow
37	Fixed-point divide
38	Floating-point exponent underflow
39	Floating-point significance

In some applications, we wish to change the program mask, enabling and/or disabling interruptions selectively. In others, the problem is to set the condition code to a prescribed value.

Both of these tasks can be accomplished via the Set Program Mask instruction:

SPM	R1	Set Program Mask	CC, program mask $\longleftarrow (R1)_{2\text{-}7}$

The SPM instruction has a single GP register operand. It loads the condition code from bits 2 and 3 of the specified register and the program mask from bits 4–7. Thus, if register 3 contains

DA309684

the instruction

SPM   3

sets the condition code to 1, enables fixed-point overflow and floating-point exponent underflow exceptions, and disables fixed-point divide and floating-point significance exceptions.

19.2.4. An Example: Padé Approximants

We are often called upon to write subroutines that calculate values of functions, such as trigonometric functions, special functions, and functions that arise in research, whose values have not been tabulated. Among the methods of computing function values are interpolation from tables, Taylor series expansions, rational fraction approximations, and expansion in terms of Tchebyshev polynomials. The last has become a very popular technique because of the high degree of accuracy that is achieved with relatively little computational effort. However, the use of Tchebyshev polynomials is a bit more complex than we need to be in order to illustrate the typical use of floating-point arithmetic.

A rational fraction approximation represents a function, which presumably requires an infinite number of terms in its Taylor series expansion for exact representation, as the ratio of two polynomials of finite degree, as in

$$f(x) = \frac{p(x)}{q(x)}$$

Here $p(x)$ and $q(x)$ are polynomials of degree n and d, respectively:

$$p(x) = a_0 + a_1 x + a_2 x^2 + \cdots + a_n x^n$$
$$q(x) = b_0 + b_1 x + b_2 x^2 + \cdots + b_d x^d$$

The accuracy of a rational fraction approximation to a function depends on the degrees, d and n, of the polynominals $p(x)$ and $q(x)$ and on how the coefficients $a_0, \ldots, a_n$ and $b_0, \ldots, b_d$ are calculated.

One way to calculate the coefficients is to ensure that the quotient that arises from long division of the polynomials matches the Taylor series expansion for the first $d + n + 1$ terms. The resulting rational fraction is called a *Padé approximant*. It often happens in research that all we know about a function is the first few terms in its Taylor series expansion about a single point. Using the known terms we can calculate the coefficients in the Padé approximant, which generally is more accurate than the truncated Taylor series expansion and also gives us some qualitative information about the asymptotic behavior of the function and the nature of its singularities.

The numbers d and n determine the *order* of the Padé approximant; if the degree of the denominator polynomial is 5 and that of the numerator is 3, we say we have a (5, 3) Padé approximant. The general notation is that for given d and n, we have a (d, n) Padé approximant.

For example, let us consider the exponential function. Its Taylor series expansion about $x = 0$ is

$$e^x = 1 + x + \frac{x^2}{2!} + \frac{x^3}{3!} + \frac{x^4}{4!} + \frac{x^5}{5!} + \frac{x^6}{6!} + \cdots$$

We derive the (2, 2) Padé approximant for e^x by solving the equation

$$1 + x + \frac{x^2}{2} + \frac{x^3}{6} + \frac{x^4}{24} = \frac{1 + a_1 x + a_2 x^2}{b_0 + b_1 x + b_2 x^2}$$

for a_1, a_2, b_0, b_1, and b_2. We leave it to you to fill in the details. The result is

$$e^x \approx \frac{1 + x/2 + x^2/12}{1 - x/2 + x^2/12}$$

The increased accuracy obtainable with a Padé approximant can be illustrated by comparing the approximation we get by using the five-term Taylor series expansion

$$e^x \approx 1 + x + \frac{x^2}{2} + \frac{x^3}{6} + \frac{x^4}{24}$$

with the result of carrying out the long division in the Padé approximant, which yields

$$e^x \approx 1 + x + \frac{x^2}{2} + \frac{x^3}{6} + \frac{x^4}{24} + \frac{x^5}{144} + 0x^6 + \frac{x^7}{1728} + \cdots$$

In comparison with the infinite Taylor series, the five-term series leaves out all terms starting at $x^5/120$. The Padé approximant approximates this term by $x^5/144$ and includes some higher-order terms.

If you haven't kept up with the mathematics above, don't worry. The example program we shall now offer provides approximate values of e^x using the formula

$$e^x = \frac{1 + x/2 + x^2/12}{1 - x/2 + x^2/12}$$

The program is a subroutine which assumes that x is between 0 and 1. We can use this subroutine to help in calculating e^x for other values of x as described in Exercise 15 at the end of this chapter.

Linkage to floating-point subroutines is almost the same as for other argument types, the only differences being

1. General-purpose register 1 contains the address of a list of addresses on entry to the subroutine, even if there is only one input parameter.

2. A single- or double-precision result is returned to the programs in floating-point register 0 or FP registers 0 and 1, respectively, if the subroutine produces a single number as a result. Subroutines that follow these conventions are callable by FORTRAN programs and can call subroutines written in FORTRAN, provided the FORTRAN programs are compiled by any of

the standard IBM FORTRAN compilers. There is no convention regarding the saving of floating-point register contents by subroutines.

The program first computes the numerator in FP register 0 and the denominator in register 4. It then divides the denominator into the numerator and returns to the calling routine.

Notice how the polynomials in the numerator and denominator are calculated. The brute force method of evaluating polynomials requires the calculation of each term separately. For a term of the form $a_k x^k$, k multiplications are necessary: $k - 1$ to raise x to the power k and one more to multiply by a_k. To evaluate a polynomial of high degree, N, we must do approximately $N^2/2$ multiplications and N additions.

```
*              SUBROUTINE THAT CALCULATES (2,2) PADE APPROXIMANT
*              VALUES FOR THE EXPONENTIAL FUNCTION
*
EXPPAD   START 0
         STM   14,12,12(13)       SAVE THE REGISTERS
         BALR  12,0         ESTABLISH BASE REGISTER
         USING *,12
         ST    13,SAVE+4 SAVE REGISTER 13
         LA    13,SAVE    THIS PROGRAM'S SAVE AREA
         L     3,0(1)     ARGUMENT ADDRESS IN GPR 3
         LE    6,0(3)     ARGUMENT X IN FP REG 6
*
*              COMPUTE NUMERATOR POLYNOMIAL
*
         LE    0,A2       COEFFICIENT OF SQUARED TERM
         MER   0,6        TIMES X
         AE    0,A1       ADD FIRST ORDER COEFFICIENT
         MER   0,6        TIMES X
         AE    0,A0       ADD CONSTANT, NUMERATOR COMPLETE
*
*              COMPUTE DENOMINATOR POLYNOMIAL
*
         LE    4,B2       COEFF. OF SQUARED TERM IN FP REG 4
         MER   4,6        TIMES X
         AE    4,B1       ADD COEFFICIENT OF LINEAR TERM
         MER   4,6        MULTIPLY BY X
         AE    4,B0       ADD CONSTANT TERM
         DER   0,4        COMPUTE QUOTIENT AND RETURN
         L     13,SAVE+4 RESTORE REG 13
         LM    14,12,12(13)   AND OTHER REGS.
         BR    14         BRANCH BACK TO CALLING ROUTINE
SAVE     DS    18F        SAVE AREA
*                         COEFFICIENTS . . .
A0       DC    E'1.0'
A1       DC    E'.5'
A2       DC    E'.08333333'
B0       DC    E'1.0'
B1       DC    E'-.5'
B2       DC    E'.08333333'
         END
```

Fig. 19-2. A subroutine that returns the (2, 2) Padé approximant value for the function e^x.

A better way to evaluate polynomials is to first rewrite them in *nested* form. For example, the polynomial

$$8 + 3x - 4x^2 + 20x^3$$

written as a nested polynomial is

$$8 + x(3 + x(-4 + 20x))$$

The latter form requires three multiplications and three additions for evaluation, a significant improvement over the six multiplications and three additions necessary with the unnested form. In general, evaluation of a polynomial in nested form requires N multiplications and N additions.

In the example program, Fig. 19-2, we have evaluated the numerator and denominator as if they had been written

$$1 + x\left(\frac{1}{2} + \frac{x}{12}\right)$$

and

$$1 + x\left(-\frac{1}{2} + \frac{x}{12}\right)$$

respectively.

Table 19-2 compares the accuracy obtained with several different computational techniques. e^x is computed at $x = .5$ and $x = 1$. The row labeled FORTRAN is the value returned from the standard FORTRAN subroutine EXP. In all cases the Padé approximant values are more accurate than the Taylor series expansions using the same number of terms as used in calculating the Padé coefficients.

Table 19-2   COMPARISON OF RESULTS OF VARIOUS COMPUTATIONAL TECHNIQUES

	Values of e^x	
	$x = .5$	$x = 1$
Exact	1.6487213	2.7182818
FORTRAN	1.6487217	2.7182817
(2, 2) Padé (Fig. 19-2)	1.6486473	2.7142849
Four-term Taylor series	1.6484375	2.7083332
(3, 3) Padé	1.6487213	2.7183097
Six-term Taylor series	1.6487196	2.7180555

19.3. DATA CONVERSIONS

The aspect of floating-point calculations remaining to be covered is the conversion of data from character to floating-point representation on input and vice versa on output. In so doing we shall take full advantage of the instructions, such as PACK and CVB, that the system offers for other conversion processes.

In all floating-point conversion problems, we treat the whole number portion and fraction of the number to be converted in separate steps. We anticipate writing programs that convert numbers such as -198.263 punched on data cards to their internal floating-point representation in any of the three available precisions. The whole number part, $-198.$, is treated separately from the fractional part, $.263$. For the reverse process, we must again treat the two parts separately, so that we can determine the location of the decimal place correctly.

19.3.1. Character to Floating Point

We are concerned here with the final steps in the conversion process. In other words, let us assume that a program analyzes the character data input and passes to a subroutine the full-word binary equivalents of the whole number and fractional parts of a number read from a data card. Our job is to write a subroutine that takes these integers and forms a floating-point number from them.

Our subroutine must make some assumptions regarding the format in which the numbers were input. Let us suppose that at most seven digits appear after the decimal point in input numbers. The program that converts the whole number and fraction part to binary and calls our subroutine always treats the fractional part as if it is a seven-digit decimal number to be converted to binary. Suppose that the number input is

$$55.1$$

The numbers it passes to the subroutine are

$$00000037_{16} \qquad (=55_{10})$$

and

$$000F3240_{16} \qquad (=1000000_{10})$$

Our subroutine expects to find these numbers passed as arguments in the conventional way, the whole number portion first.

We assume that the sign of the whole number part is the sign desired for the floating-part equivalent of the number. Therefore, the conversion routine first checks the sign of the first integer argument and inserts the appropriate bit value into what will eventually be the sign bit of the floating-point number. In the process, we take the absolute value of the whole number argument. We assume that the fractional part, the second argument, is a positive integer.

Now, what does the subroutine do about the whole number part? What we must do is take a binary full-word integer and represent it as a floating-point number. One way to do this is to put the integer, right-justified, into a floating-point fraction and adjust the exponent so that the result has the appropriate whole number value. In single-precision, our example number looks like

$$46000037$$

We have an effective exponent of $46_{16} - 40_{16} = 6$. Therefore, the number above represents the number

$$.000037_{16} \times 16^6 = 37_{16} \times 16^0 = 55_{10}$$

as desired. For better accuracy in conversions, it is best to represent the integer as a double word, as in

$$4E000000 \quad 00000037$$

This also has the value

$$.000000 \quad 00000037_{16} \times 16^{14} = 55_{10}$$

The next step is to normalize this number, which is best accomplished by adding a *true zero* to it. A true zero has a zero exponent (characteristic = 40_{16}) and a zero fraction. Supposing that the number above is in FP registers 4 and 5, the instruction

$$AD \qquad 4,=D'0.0'$$

produces the normalized result

$$FP \text{ regs } 4 \text{ and } 5: \quad 42370000 \quad 00000000$$

Figure 19-3 shows the segment of the conversion subroutine that converts the whole number part to decimal. Later, when we look at the whole program in Fig. 19-5, we shall see that preceding instructions have placed the whole number part into register 7 and the fractional part into register 8.

The calculations are basically as described above. We place the absolute value of the number in register 5 and isolate its sign with the aNd instruction. We then load a constant, SKELETON, into register 4 and Or in the sign bit.

```
       .
       .
       LPR    5,7         ABS. VALUE OF INTEGER PART IN REG. 5
       N      7,SIGNMASK  SIGN BIT IN REG. 7
       L      4,SKELETON  HIGH ORDER HALF IN REG. 4
       OR     4,7         SIGN BIT INSERTED
       STM    4,5,FPNUM   BOTH HALVES AT FPUM SO CAN PUT IN FP REGS.
       LD     4,FPNUM     UNNCRMALIZED NUMBER IN FP REGS. 4 AND 5
       AD     4,=D'0.0'   NORMALIZE INTEGER PART
       .
       .
FPNUM     DS   D
SKELETON  DS   X'4E000000'
SIGNMASK  DS   X'80000000'
```

Fig. 19-3. A program segment that converts an integer in GP register 7 to its floating-point equivalent, leaving the result in FP register 4.

Unfortunately, there are no instructions to move numbers from general-purpose registers to floating-point registers and vice versa. Thus, we store the contents of GP registers 4 and 5 into a double word FPNUM and then load FP registers 4 and 5 with the number. The AD instruction normalizes the number as shown above.

The procedure for the fractional part is much the same, except that we must divide the fraction by 10^7, since we were given the fraction as an integer. Figure 19-4 shows this section of the program. The Or instruction produces

```
           .
           .
           .
           O       7,SKELETCN   INSERT SIGN,CHARACTERISTIC
           STM     7,8,FPNUM  MOVE OO MEMORY
           LD      0,FPNUM    NOW IN FP REGS. 0-1
           CD      0,=D'1.0E7'    CIVIDE BY SCALE FACTOR
           .
           .
FPNUM      DS      D
SKELETON   DC      X'4E000000'
```

Fig. 19-4. Conversion of a 7-digit fraction to its floating-point equivalent. This segment is designed to follow the segment of Fig. 20-4.

```
BINFP      START  0
           STM    14,12,12(13)     STORE THE REGISTERS
           EALR   12,0       ESTABLISH BASE REGISTER
           USING  *,12
           ST     13,SAVE+4  SAVE (13)
           LA     13,SAVE    SAVE AREA ADDR. IN R13
           L      3,0(1)     PARAMETER LIST ADDRESS IN REG. 3
           L      7,0(3)     INTEGER PART IN REG. 7
           L      8,4(3)     FRACTION PART IN REG. 8
           LPR    5,7        ABS. VALUE OF INTEGER PART IN REG. 5
           N      7,SIGNMASK  SIGN BIT IN REG. 7
           L      4,SKELETON  HIGH ORDER HALF IN REG. 4
           OR     4,7         SIGN BIT INSERTED
           STM    4,5,FPNUM  BOTH HALVES AT FPUM SO CAN PUT IN FP REGS.
           LD     4,FPNUM    UNNORMALIZED NUMBER IN FP REGS. 4 AND 5
           AD     4,=D'0.0'     NORMALIZE INTEGER PART
           O      7,SKELETCN  INSERT SIGN,CHARACTERISTIC
           STM    7,8,FPNUM  MOVE TO MEMORY
           LD     0,FPNUM    NOW IN FP REGS. 0-1
           CD     0,=D'1.0E7'    CIVIDE BY SCALE FACTOR
           ADR    0,4        ADD WHOLE NUMBER PART AND
           L      13,SAVE+4       RETURN
           LM     14,12,12(13)
           BR     14
SAVE       DS     18F
FPNUM      DS     D
SKELETCN   DC     X'4E0CC000'
SIGNMASK   DC     X'80000000'
           END
```

Fig. 19-5. A subroutine that converts binary integers representing the whole number and fractional part of a number to floating-point.

the unnormalized fraction $\times$ 10^7 in GP registers 7 and 8 with the proper sign. Division by 10^7 leaves the fraction in FP registers 0 and 1.

The complete subroutine appears in Fig. 19-5. The first portion locates the arguments and places them in registers 7 and 8. After converting two pieces of the number, the program adds them together, leaving the result in FP register 0 for return to the calling program.

19.3.2. Floating Point to Character

Given a single-precision floating-point number, our chore is just the converse of that discussed above; we must separate out the whole number and fraction parts of the number and express them as binary integers. The two integers can then be converted to decimal, unpacked, and printed, separated by a decimal place. Let us consider the structure of a subroutine whose input argument is a floating-point number and whose output is two full-word binary integers representing the whole number and fractional parts of the floating-point number. The sign of the result will be that of the first output argument word.

We again point out that a whole number in double-precision floating-point representation has the characteristic $4E_{16}$. Using our example number again, decimal 55.1, we want to perform operations upon its floating-point equivalent

$$42371999$$

to extract the integer part stored as

$$4E000000 \quad 00000037$$

The second word of this double word is the desired integer portion.

```
        .
        .
        LD      4,=D'0.0'  CLEAR OUT LOW-ORDER PART OF REGS. 4-5
        LE      6,0(3)     FP. NUMBER IN FP REG. 6
        LPER    4,6        ABSOLUTE VALUE IN FP. REG. 4
        AW      4,DZERO    SHIFT OUT THE FRACTION
        STD     4,FPNUM    MOVE TO MEMORY
        L       5,FPNUM+4  INTEGER PART TO GP REG. 5
        TM      0(3),B'10000000'  CHECK SIGN OF ORIGINAL NUMBER
        BNO     POS
        LCR     5,5        COMPLEMENT IF NEGATIVE
POS     . . .
        .
        .
FPNUM   DS      D
DZERO   DC      X'4E00000000000000'
        .
        .
```

Fig. 19-6. A program segment that extracts the integer part of a floating-point number whose address is in register 3. The result is left in register 5.

Figure 19-6 shows how this can be done. The LD instruction puts a 0 in FP register 5. Anticipating further use of the number to be converted, we load it into FP register 6 for safekeeping. Since the subroutine is to work for both positive and negative numbers, we place the absolute value of the number into register 4. The AW instruction shifts the fraction digits out of the right-hand end of register 5 in the prenormalization step. Adding 0 does not change the number, and no post-normalization is done. We calculate

$$\text{FP regs 4 and 5:} \quad \begin{array}{l} 42371999 \quad 00000000 \\ + \ 4E000000 \quad 00000000 \end{array}$$

Prenormalization gives

$$\text{FP regs 4 and 5:} \quad \begin{array}{l} 4E000000 \quad 00000037 \\ + \ 4E000000 \quad 00000000 \\ \hline 4E000000 \quad 00000037 \end{array}$$

This sum is what we want. We then move the contents of FP register 5 to GP register 5 and complement this number if the floating-point number is negative.

Once we have isolated the integer portion of the number, determining its fractional part is easy. We simply subtract the integer part from the original number. In our example, this amounts to computing

$$55.1 - 55.0 = .1$$

If the output routine is to print seven digits after the decimal place, we multiply the fraction by 10^7 and use the same trick with an AW instruction to produce the integer equivalent of the fraction in the low-order part of a double-precision register. Figure 19-7 shows how this is done.

```
            •
            •
POS    •  •  •
            •
            •
        AD      4,=D'0.0'   NORMALIZE INTEGER PART
        LD      2,=D'0.0'   CLEAR FP REG. 3
        LPER    2,6         ABS VALUE OF INPUT ARGUMENT IN FP REG.2
        SDR     2,4         SUBTRACT INTEGER PART, LEAVING FRACTION
        MD      2,=D'1.0E7' SCALE IT UP
        AW      2,DZERO     AND SHIFT OFF REMAINING DIGITS
        STD     2,FPNUM     MOVE IT TO MEMORY SO WE CAN PUT IT INTO
        L       6,FPNUM+4   GP REGISTER 6
            •
            •
FPNUM   DS      D
DZERO   DC      X'4E00000000000000'
            •
            •
```

Fig. 19-7. A segment to follow Fig. 19-6. The fractional part of a floating-point number is extracted and placed in register 6.

```
FPBIN     START   0
          STM     14,12,12(13)    SAVE THE REGISTERS
          BALR    12,0            ESTABLISH BASE REGISTER
          USING   *,12
          ST      13,SAVE+4
          LA      13,SAVE
          L       3,0(1)          ADDRESS OF FIRST ARGUMENT IN REGISTER 3
          LD      4,=D'0.0'       CLEAR OUT LOW-ORDER PART OF REGS. 4-5
          LE      6,0(3)          FP. NUMBER IN FP REG. 6
          LPER    4,6             ABSOLUTE VALUE IN FP. REG. 4
          AW      4,DZERO         SHIFT OUT THE FRACTION
          STD     4,FPNUM         MOVE TO MEMORY
          L       5,FPNUM+4       INTEGER PART TO GP REG. 5
          TM      0(3),B'10000000'   CHECK SIGN OF ORIGINAL NUMBER
          BNO     POS
          LCR     5,5             COMPLEMENT IF NEGATIVE
POS       L       4,4(1)          ADDRESS OF SECOND ARGUMENT IN GP REG. 4
          ST      5,0(4)          STORE INTEGER PART
          AD      4,=D'0.0'       NORMALIZE INTEGER PART
          LD      2,=D'0.0'       CLEAR FP REG. 2
          LPER    2,6             ABS VALUE OF INPUT ARGUMENT IN FP REG.2
          SDR     2,4             SUBTRACT INTEGER PART, LEAVING FRACTION
          MD      2,=D'1.0E7'     SCALE IT UP
          AW      2,DZERO         AND SHIFT OFF REMAINING DIGITS
          STD     2,FPNUM         MOVE IT TO MEMORY SO WE CAN PUT IT INTO
          L       6,FPNUM+4       GP REGISTER 6
          L       4,8(1)          ADDRESS OF THIRD ARGUMENT IN REGISTER 4
          ST      6,0(4)          STORE FRACTION
          L       13,SAVE+4       RETURN
          LM      14,12,12(13)
          BR      14
SAVE      DS      18F
FPNUM     DS      D
DZERO     DC      X'4E00000000000000'
          END
```

Fig. 19-8. A subroutine that extracts the whole number and fractional part of a floating-point number and returns them as full word binary integers.

A complete subroutine to do the conversions as described above appears in Fig. 19-8.

CHAPTER SUMMARY

Floating-point calculations provide for manipulation of numbers larger than those offered by integer modes of arithmetic and automatically adjust the position of the decimal place in arithmetic operations. In the IBM computers, a floating-point number consists of a *sign bit;* a 7-bit *characteristic,* which is 64_{10} more than the exponent; and a 24-, 56-, or 112-bit *fraction,* depending on whether the number is *single*-precision, *double-precision,* or *extended-precision* (see Fig. 19-1).

Table 19-3 shows the floating-point instructions offered with the standard

Table 19-3 SINGLE- AND DOUBLE-PRECISION FLOATING-POINT INSTRUCTIONS

1. Load instructions:

LE	FPR1,D2(X2,B2)	Load single-precision	$FPR1 \leftarrow (D2 + (X2) + (B2))$
LD	FPR1,D2(X2,B2)	Load Double-precision	$FPR1_D \leftarrow (D2 + (X2) + (B2))_D$
LER	FPR1,FPR2	Load single-precision Register	$FPR1 \leftarrow (FPR2)$
LDR	FPR1,FPR2	Load Double-precision Register	$FPR1_D \leftarrow (FPR2)_D$
LTER	FPR1,FPR2	Load and Test Register, single-precision	$FPR1 \leftarrow (FPR2)$, set CC
LTDR	FPR1,FPR2	Load and Test Register, Double-precision	$FPR1_D \leftarrow (FPR2)_D$, set CC
LCER	FPR1,FPR2	Load and Complement Register, single-precision	$FPR1 \leftarrow -(FPR2)$
LCDR	FPR1,FPR2	Load and Complement Register, Double-precision	$FPR1_D \leftarrow -(FPR2)_D$
LNER	FPR1,FPR2	Load Negative Register, single-precision	$FPR1 \leftarrow -|(FPR2)|$
LNDR	FPR1,FPR2	Load Negative Register Double-precision	$FPR1_D \leftarrow -|(FPR2)_D|$
LPER	FPR1,FPR2	Load Positive Register, single-precision	$FPR1 \leftarrow |(FPR2)|$
LPDR	FPR1,FPR2	Load Positive Register, Double-precision	$FPR1_D \leftarrow |(FPR2)_D|$

2. Store instructions:

STE	FPR1,D2(X2,B2)	STore single-precision	$FPR1 \rightarrow D2 + (X2) + (B2)$
STD	FPR1,D2(X2,B2)	STore Double-precision	$FPR1_D \rightarrow D2 + (X2) + (B2)$

3. Addition instructions, normalized result:

AE	FPR1,D2(X2,B2)	Add single-precision	$FPR1 \leftarrow (FPR1) + (D2 + (X2) + (B2))$
AD	FPR1,D2(X2,B2)	Add Double-precision	$FPR1_D \leftarrow (FPR1)_D + (D2 + (X2) + (B2))_D$
AER	FPR1,FPR2	Add single-precision Register	$FPR1 \leftarrow (FPR1) + (FPR2)$
ADR	FPR1,FPR2	Add Double-precision Register	$FPR1_D \leftarrow (FPR1)_D + (FPR2)_D$

4. Subtraction instructions, normalized result:

SE	FPR1,D2(X2,B2)	Subtract single-precision	$FPR1 \leftarrow (FPR1) - (D2 + (X2) + (B2))$
SD	FPR1,D2(X2,B2)	Subtract Double-precision	$FPR1_D \leftarrow (FPR1)_D - (D2 + (X2) + (B2))_D$
SER	FPR1,FPR2	Subtract single-precision Register	$FPR1 \leftarrow (FPR1) - (FPR2)$
SDR	FPR1,FPR2	Subtract Double-precision Register	$FPR1_D \leftarrow (FPR1)_D - (FPR2)_D$

Table 19-3 (CONT.)

---

5. Addition instructions, unnormalized result:

AU	FPR1,D2(X2,B2)	Add single-precision, Unnormalized	FPR1 ⟵ (FPR1) + (D2 + (X2) + (B2))
AW	FPR1,D2(X2,B2)	Add Double-precision, Unnormalized	FPR1$_D$ ⟵ (FPR1)$_D$ + (D2 + (X2) + (B2))$_D$
AUR	FPR1,FPR2	Add single-precision, Unnormalized, Register	FPR1 ⟵ (FPR1) + (FPR2)
AWR	FPR1,FPR2	Add Double-precision, Unnormalized, Register	FPR1$_D$ ⟵ (FPR1)$_D$ + (FPR2)$_D$

6. Subtraction instructions, unnormalized result:

SU	FPR1,D2(X2,B2)	Subtract single-precision, Unnormalized	FPR1 ⟵ (FPR1) − (D2 + (X2) + (B2))
SW	FPR1,D2(X2,B2)	Subtract Double-precision, Unnormalized	FPR1$_D$ ⟵(FPR1)$_D$ − (D2 + (X2) + (B2))$_D$
SUR	FPR1,FPR2	Subtract single-precision, Unnormalized, Register	FPR1 ⟵ (FPR1) − (FPR2)
SWR	FPR1,FPR2	Subtract Double-precision, Unnormalized, Register	FPR1$_D$ ⟵ (FPR1)$_D$ − (FPR2)$_D$

7. Multiplication instructions:

ME	FPR1,D2(X2,D2)	Multiply single-precision	FPR1$_D$ ⟵ (FPR1) × (D2 + (X2) + (D2))
MD	FPR1,D2(X2,B2)	Multiply Double-precision	FPR1$_D$ ⟵ (FPR1)$_D$ × (D2 + (X2) + (B2))$_D$
MER	FPR1,FPR2	Multiply single-precision Register	FPR1$_D$ ⟵ (FPR1) × (FPR2)
MDR	FPR1,FPR2	Multiply Double-precision Register	FPR1$_D$ ⟵ (FPR1)$_D$ × (FPR2)$_D$

Table 19-3 (CONT.)

8. *Division instructions:*

DE	FPR1,D2(X2,B2)	Divide single-precision	$FPR1 \leftarrow (FPR1) \div (D2 + (X2) + (B2))$
DD	FPR1,D2(X2,B2)	Divide Double-precision	$FPR1_D \leftarrow (FPR1)_D \div (D2 + (X2) + (B2))_D$
DER	FPR1,FPR2	Divide single-precision Register	$FPR1 \leftarrow (FPR1) \div (FPR2)$
DDR	FPR1,FPR2	Divide Double-precision Register	$(FPR1)_D \leftarrow (FPR1)_D \div (FPR2)_D$

9. *Halve instructions:*

HER	FPR1,FPR2	Halve single-precision Register	$FPR1 \leftarrow (FPR1)/2$
HDR	FPR1,FPR2	Halve Double-precision Register	$(FPR1)_D \leftarrow (FPR2)_D/2$

10. *Comparison instructions:*

CE	FPR1,D2(X2,B2)	Compare single-precision	Compute $(FPR1) - (D2 + (X2) + (B2))$, set CC
CD	FPR1,D2(X2,D2)	Compare Double-precision	Compute $(FPR1)_D - (D2 + (X2) + (B2))_D$, set CC
CER	FPR1,FPR2	Compare single-precision Register	Compute $(FPR1) - (FPR2)$, set CC
CDR	FPR1,FPR2	Compare Double-precision Register	Compute $(FPR1)_D - (FPR2)_D$, set CC

Table 19-4 EXTENDED-PRECISION INSTRUCTION SET

1. *Addition and Subtraction instructions:*

AXR	FPR1,FPR2	Add eXtended-precision Register	$FPR1_x \leftarrow (FPR1)_x + (FPR2)_x$
SXR	FPR1,FPR2	Subtract eXtended-precision Register	$FPR1_x \leftarrow (FPR1)_x - (FPR2)_x$
MXR	FPR1,FPR2	Multiply eXtended-precision Register	$FPR1_x \leftarrow (FPR1)_x \times (FPR2)_x$
MXD	FPR1,D2(X2,B2)	Multiply eXtended Double-precision	$FPR1_x \leftarrow (FPR1)_D \times (D2 + (X2) + (B2))_D$
MXDR	FPR1,FPR2	Multiply eXtended Double-precision Register	$FPR1_x \leftarrow (FPR1)_D \times (FPR2)_D$

2. *Load Rounded instructions:*

LRER	FPR1,FPR2	Load Rounded single-precision Register	$FPR1 \leftarrow (FPR2)_D$ (rounded)
LRDR	FPR1,FPR2	Load Rounded Double-precision Register	$FPR1_D \leftarrow (FPR2)_x$ (rounded)

option. Increased accuracy can often be obtained using the *extended-precision* instructions shown in Table 19-4.

Conversion problems involve treating the whole number and fractional parts separately, as is illustrated in Figs. 19-5 and 19-8.

EXERCISES

1. W, X, Y, and Z contain single-precision floating-point numbers. Write the instructions necessary to compute the following:

   (a) $X^2 - 2XY + Y^2$.

   (b) $\dfrac{X + Y}{W + Z}$

   (c) $W + YX + ZX^2$.

2. Do Exercise 1 above assuming that W, X, Y, and Z are double-precision numbers.

3. Do Exercises 1(a) and 1(c) above, assuming that W, X, Y, and Z are extended-precision numbers.

4. You may be wondering why we failed to discuss division of extended-precision floating-point numbers. We did not forget this topic; it's just that there is no extended-precision divide instruction. We could make a start at providing for extended-precision division by writing a subroutine or macro that divides an extended-precision number by a double-precision number. But we cannot simply divide the high- and low-order parts of the extended-precision number by a double-precision number and get the correct result every time because
   (a) Division might produce a left shift of the high-order quotient, which loses a digit from the right-hand end of the high-order quotient.
   (b) Postnormalization of the result might insert 0s into the right-hand end of the high-order part.
   (c) Postnormalization might produce improper exponents.
   None of these difficulties is insurmountable. Try writing a subroutine to divide an extended-precision number by a double-precision number.

5. Once the subroutine in Exercise 4 has been written, we might think of using it to help divide extended-precision numbers by extended-precision numbers. If we let x be the extended-precision dividend and h and l the high- and low-order parts of the divisor, respectively, we can use the following trick to provide for extended-precision division:

$$\frac{x}{h + l} = \frac{x}{h[1 + (l/h)]} = \frac{x}{h}\left(1 - \frac{l}{h} + \frac{l^2}{h^2} - \frac{l^3}{h^3} + \cdots\right)$$

Note that h and l have the forms

$$h = s.a \times 16^n$$
$$l = r.b \times 16^{n-14}$$

where a and b are the 14-digit high- and low-order fractions and n is the exponent of the high-order part. Write a subroutine to divide extended-precision numbers using the equation above and your solution to Exercise 4.

6. Write a subroutine to call the conversion subroutine of Fig. 19-5. Assume that the data numbers start in column 1 of the card and that the decimal place is in column 8.

7. Write a subroutine to call the conversion subroutine of Fig. 19-8 and print the floating-point result in the format

dddddddd.dddddd

8. Modify your program for Exercise 6 to provide for the E format, wherein numbers on data cards are punched in what amounts to scientific notation. For example, the data numbers

1.087E16

and

3.83E-2

represent the numbers

$$1.087 \times 10^{16}$$

and

.0383

respectively. (*Hint*: Use conditional assembly to create a table of powers of 10. Call the subroutine of Fig. 19-5 to compute the fraction and characteristic and then multiply the result by the appropriate power of 10.)

9. Write a subroutine PEVAL to evaluate polynomials of the form

$$A_o + A_1 X + A_2 X^2 + \cdots + A_n X^n$$

The arguments are X, n, and a series of consecutive full words containing the coefficients $A_0, \ldots, A_n$.

10. Write a program to compute e^x using the Taylor series expansion

$$e^x = 1 + x + \frac{x^2}{2!} + \frac{x^3}{3!} + \frac{x^4}{4!} + \frac{x^5}{5!} + \cdots$$

$n!$ (n factorial) is the product of the integers

$$n \times (n-1) \times (n-2) \times \cdots \times 2 \times 1$$

11. Write a subroutine to calculate the square root of a number N using the Newton-Raphson iteration technique. The nth estimate x_n of the square root of N is calculated from the preceding estimate x_{n-1} using the equation

$$x_n = \frac{1}{2}\left(x_{n-1} + \frac{N}{x_{n-1}}\right)$$

Given an initial guess x_0, this process is continued until $|x_n - x_{n-1}|/x_n$ is less than some small error limit.

12. Use your result of Exercise 11 to write a program to solve quadratic equations.

13. Write a macro CX to compare two extended-precision numbers.

14. The BAL or BALR instruction and the SPM instruction can be used to save the condition-code setting during execution of a subroutine or macro. We did not mention it before, but BAL and BALR load the condition code and program mask contents into bits 2–7 of the first register operand. The instruction

BALR   14,15

saves these values in the first byte of register 14. How should a subroutine return be written so as to return with the same condition-code contents as when the subroutine was entered?

15. The Padé approximant routine of Fig. 19-2 is most accurate for small values of the argument x. In particular, let us assume that x will always be between 0 and 1. Write a program that uses the subroutine of Fig. 19-2 in calculating e^x for other values of x, assuming that $-10 \leq x \leq 10$. To do this, take advantage of the fact that

$$e^{-x} = \frac{1}{e^x}$$

and that

$$e^{a+b} = e^a e^b$$

Set up a table of e to integer powers and let a be the integer part and b the fractional part of x, $|x| = a.b$. Since b is less than 1, the program of Fig. 19-2 suffices to calculate e^b. Look up e^a in the table, compute the product $e^a e^b$, and invert the result if x is negative.

REFERENCES

IBM System/360 Disk and Tape Operating System Assembler Language, Form GC24-3414, IBM Corp., White Plains, N.Y.

IBM System/360 Operating System Assembler Language, Form GC28-6514, IBM Corp., White Plains, N.Y.

IBM System/360 Principles of Operation, Form GA22-6821, IBM Corp., White Plains, N.Y.

IBM System/370 Principles of Operation, Form GA22-7000, IBM Corp., White Plains, N.Y.

IBM OS/VS—DOS/VS Assembler Language, Form GC33-4010, IBM Corp., White Plains, N.Y.

20 FANCY INSTRUCTIONS

In this, the final chapter, we shall put the icing on the cake by describing some powerful special-purpose instructions that make life easier for the programmer and help get the most out of the computing machines.

The 370 computers offer extended character manipulation facilities not available in the 360 series. Among the extra instructions are Insert Characters under Mask, STore Characters under Mask, and Compare Logical under Mask. These permit increased use of the registers in character and byte manipulation.

The machine language format of the MVC and CLC instructions limits their operands to 256 bytes. This rather severe restriction means that we must write a series of instructions, a loop, a macro, or a subroutine to move or compare the contents of large memory areas. The 370 machines offer two instructions—MoVe Character Long and Compare Logical Character Long—which provide for operand lengths up to the theoretical maximum possible storage size, 16,777,216 bytes.

The TRanslate and TRanslate and Test instructions make translation of long strings of characters from one code to another a simple matter. All 360 and 370 machines offer these instructions, without which translation would be a time-consuming process.

Finally, we saw in Chapter 15 that we must do a lot of bothersome busywork to translate a packed decimal number to its EBCDIC character code equivalent. The EDit and EDit and MarK instructions reduce this chore to a matter of two or three instructions.

484

20.1. EXTENDED CHARACTER MANIPULATION IN THE 370 COMPUTERS

The instructions discussed in this section are to be found only in 370 computers. Usually if we try to use them in a 360 machine, either the assembler does not recognize their mnemonics or we get an operation exception. Some 360 operating systems include *simulator* subroutines, which carry out the operations as if the program were actually run on a 370 machines. The use of these simulators is beyond the scope of this text; the manual *IBM System/360 Systems Programmer's Guide* illustrates how this can be done.

20.1.1. ICM, STCM, and CLM

One disadvantage of the 360 instruction set is that the registers are almost useless in moving and comparing byte data. The best we can do is use the IC and STC instructions to load and store 1 byte at a time. Comparison of a selected byte in a register with a byte in the memory requires a significant amount of preparation, including zeroing out the high-order register contents and loading both characters to be compared into registers. Only then can we use the CR or CLR instructions to see if the 2 bytes are the same. Alternatively, we can store the byte from the register into the memory and use a CLC instruction with length 1. Both approaches are tedious and inefficient.

The Insert Characters under Mask (ICM), STore Characters under Mask (STCM), and Compare Logical under Mask (CLM) instructions make such tasks a lot easier, since, using them, we can load, store, and compare from 1 to 4 selected bytes using the registers.

ICM	R1,M3,D2(B2)	Insert Characters under Mask	R1 ⟵ (D2 + (B2)) according to M3
STCM	R1,M3,D2(B2)	STore Characters under Mask	(R1) ⟶ D2 + (B2) according to M3
CLM	R1,M3,D2(B2)	Compare Logical under Mask	Compute (R1) − (D2 + (B2)) according to M3, set CC

The format of these instructions is a modification of the RS format. The usual RS format, in STM, for example, requires specification of two register and one memory operands. In the three instructions above, we write a 4-bit *mask*, M3, in place of the second register operand, R3, in the RS format.

The mask determines which bytes of the register operand are used in the operation. Each bit of the mask identifies a corresponding byte of

R1—bit 0 for byte 0 (the first byte of R1), bit 1 for byte 1, and so on. If a given mask bit is 1, the corresponding byte of R1 participates in the operation. A mask of 6 (=B'0110') means that bytes 1 and 2, the second and third bytes, of the register operand are loaded from the memory, stored into the memory, or compared with the memory operand, depending on the operation. Bytes whose corresponding mask bits are 0 do not participate in the operation.

The machine treats the memory operand as if it were a series of contiguous bytes of length equal to the number of 1 bits in the mask. The memory operand length is 3, given any of the masks 1110, 1101, 1011, or 0111. The first 3 bytes starting at D2 + (B2) are the memory operand, regardless of which of these masks is used.

To illustrate, let us consider ICM in more detail. Suppose that we have

$$\text{CHARS:}\quad \text{C301E300C1B5}$$

stored in the memory and

$$(5) = \text{FFFEFDFC}$$

before execution of each of the examples presented below. The instruction

$$\text{ICM}\qquad 5,\text{B}'1101',\text{CHARS}$$

loads three consecutive bytes starting at CHARS into bytes 0, 1, and 3 of register 5. Since the mask bit for byte 2 is 0, byte 2 remains unchanged. The result is

$$(5) = \text{C301FDE3}$$

Unlike the other instructions that load registers from memory, ICM sets the condition code depending on the data moved. If all bits moved are 0 or if the mask is 0, the condition code is set to 0. If the *first bit* moved is 1, indicating a negative algebraic sign, the machine sets CC to 1. If the data moved are not zero, but the first bit moved is zero, CC is set to 2, which shows that a positive number was moved.

CC Value	Meaning
0	0 moved, or M3 = 0
1	First bit moved = 1
2	First bit moved = 0, data moved $\neq$ 0

Since the first byte moved by the ICM above is $C3_{16}$, CC = 1 after the instruction is executed.

Notice that

$$\text{ICM}\qquad 5,1,\text{CHARS}+3$$

has the same effect as the instruction

$$\text{IC}\qquad 5,\text{CHARS}+3$$

except that the former sets CC = 0, while the latter leaves it unchanged. The result is (5) = FFFEFD00. Also,

ICM   5,B'1111',CHARS+1

loads all of register 5 with the 4 bytes starting at CHARS+1, producing

$$(5) = 01E300C1$$

and setting the condition code to 2. With the exception of the condition code change this looks as if we had written

L   5,CHARS+1

But, as is true of all character manipulation instructions, there are *no boundary rules* associated with ICM, STCM, and CLM. ICM allows us to load a full word into a register from anywhere in the memory.

As an example of the use of ICM, consider the problem of setting the condition code and program mask segments of the PSW to selected values. Ordinarily, this requires the reservation of a full word in the memory, only the first 8 bits of which are used. We load this word into a register and use the SPM instruction, as in

L   7,MASKWD

SPM   7

.

.

.

DS   0F   FULL WORD ALIGNMENT

MASKWD   DC   X'03000000'

Use of ICM saves memory space and preserves the lower 3 bytes of the register used:

ICM   7,8,MASKBYTE

SPM   7

MASKBYTE   DC   X'03'

STCM stores the bytes selected by the mask bits into consecutive byte locations in the memory, starting at D2 + (B2). It has no effect upon the condition code. Suppose that we have

$$(8) = FFFEFDFC$$

and at DATA we have stored

DATA: 00010203040506

Then

STCM   8,B'1010',DATA

stores the contents of bytes 0 and 2 of register 8 at DATA and DATA $+$ 1, with the result

DATA: FFFD0203040506

STCM   8,1,DATA$+$2

is exactly the same as

STC   8,DATA$+$2

And we can store a full word without worrying about boundary rules by using mask $15_{10} = B'1111'$.

STCM   8,15,DATA$+$1

produces

DATA: 00FFFEFDFC0506

Compare Logical under Mask compares the selected bytes from the register operand with consecutive bytes of the memory operand. The resulting condition codes are

CC Value	Meaning
0	Operands equal
1	Operand 1 $<$ operand 2
2	Operand 1 $>$ operand 2

As in other character comparison instructions, unsigned arithmetic is used in the comparison.

Given

$$(2) = 40CDC1E3$$

and memory contents

COMP: 40C0D1A30002

the instruction

CLM   2,B'1000',COMP

compares the first byte of register 2 with the byte at COMP, setting CC to 0. But

CLM   2,B'1100',COMP

sets CC to 2 since bytes 0 and 2 of register 2 contain $40C1_{16}$, which is greater than $20C0_{16}$ stored starting at COMP.

20.1.2. MoVe Character Long

MVCL moves large quantities of data from one memory area to another and provides for automatic filling in of leftover space with any desired character as well. Both MVCL and CLCL, discussed shortly hereafter, are RR instructions which use four registers to describe the memory operands.

MVCL	R1,R2	MoVe Character Long	See Table 20-1

R1 and R2 must be even-numbered registers. The contents of the registers R1, R1+1, R2, and R2+1 have the following meanings:

$$(R1)_{8-31} = \text{Destination Address} = DA$$

$$(R2)_{8-31} = \text{Source Address} = SA$$

$$(R1+1)_{8-31} = \text{Destination Length} = DL$$

$$(R2+1)_{8-31} = \text{Source Length} = SL$$

$$(R2+1)_{0-7} = \text{Padding Character} = P$$

We shall use the abbreviations in the list above in the discussion of the MVCL instruction. Whenever we say SL, for example, we mean the contents of bits 8–31 of register R2+1.

Basically, MVCL moves the data starting at address SA to the memory area starting at DA. DL and SL determine the number of bytes to be moved and whether or not the padding character, P, is to be used to fill in space in the destination area into which data are not moved. The source length need not be the same as the destination length. In fact, we have three different cases to consider, depending on whether the source length is equal to, less than, or greater than the destination length. Since the length operands are 24 bits long, the largest a length can be is 16,777,215.

$SL = DL$. When the source and destination lengths are the same, MVCL works much like the MVC instruction, except that there is no limit to the number of bytes to be moved. The machine moves SL bytes starting at address SA to the SL-byte-long area starting at DA. But, unlike MVC, MVCL changes register contents and sets the condition code. After the data have been moved, the register contents are as follows:

$$(R1)_{8-31} = SA + SL = \text{address of next byte after source area}$$

$$(R1+1)_{8-31} = 0$$

$$(R2)_{8-31} = DA + DL = \text{address of next byte after destination area}$$

$$(R2+1)_{8-31} = 0$$

In other words, while moving the data, the machine counts the contents of the length registers down and the address registers up by 1 each time it moves a byte. The final result is that the length registers contain 0, indicating that all bytes of both areas have been used, and that the address registers point to the next byte after the respective memory areas. MVCL sets the condition code to 0 if $SL = DL$.

Suppose that we want to move 2000_{16} bytes from an area starting at address 35000 to an area starting at address 40000. We load the registers as follows:

$$(4) = 00040000 = DA$$
$$(5) = 00002000 = DL$$
$$(8) = 00035000 = SA$$
$$(9) = 00002000 = SL$$

$$\text{MVCL} \quad 4,8$$

moves the data as requested and produces

$$(4) = 00042000 = DA + DL$$
$$(5) = 00000000$$
$$(6) = 00037000 = SA + SL$$
$$(7) = 00000000$$

and

$$CC = 0$$

$DL > SL$. When the source length is less than the destination length, the implication is that we have fewer actual bytes to be moved than are provided in the destination area. When this occurs, the system moves SL bytes from the source area to the destination area and stores the padding character P throughout the remainder of the destination area. A special case of this operation occurs when $SL = 0$; the machine stores P throughout the DL bytes starting at DA.

The final register contents are

$$(R1)_{8-31} = DA + DL$$
$$(R1+1)_{8-31} = 0$$
$$(R2)_{8-31} = SA + SL$$
$$(R2+1)_{8-31} = 0$$

The condition code is set to 2, indicating that originally, $(R1+1) > (R2+1)_{8-31}$.

Figure 20-1 illustrates the use of MVCL in formatting a line for printed output. The LA instructions load the registers with source and destination addresses and lengths. The LCM inserts the padding character into bits 0–7 of register 11. After the MVCL we have

$$(6)_{8-31} = A(LINE) + 132_{10}$$
$$(7)_{8-31} = 00000000$$
$$(10) = A(MESS) + 10_{10}$$
$$(11) = 00000000$$

```
      LA      6,LINE      CESTINATION ADDRESS IN REGISTER 6
      LA      7,132       DESTINATION LENGTH IN REGISTER 7
      LA      10,MESS     SOURCE ADDRESS IN REGISTER 10
      LA      11,10       SOURCE LENGTH IN REGISTER 11
      ICM     11,8,BLANKPAD    PADDING CHAR. IN BYTE 0 OF REG. 11
      MVCL    6,10        DO THE MOVE
              •
              •
              •
MESS      CS      10C
LINE      DS      132C
BLANKPAD  DC      X'40'
```

Fig. 20-1. Moving 10 bytes stored starting at MESS to the first 10 bytes of the area starting at LINE and padding the rest of the area with blanks.

and

$$CC = 2$$

DL < SL. Here there is not enough space in the destination area to contain all the data in the source area. The machine moves DL bytes starting as SA to the area starting at DA. It leaves the register contents so that the next MVCL instruction will start from where the one executed left off. In other words, the SL register is decreased and the SA register increased by DL, the number of bytes moved. After execution,

$$(R1)_{8-31} = DA + DL$$

$$(R1+1)_{8-31} = 0$$

$$(R2)_{8-31} = SA + DL$$

$$(R2+1)_{8-31} = SL - DL$$

and

$$CC = 1$$

This feature is handy when we have a large segment of data to be split up into smaller pieces and supplied to a program one segment at a time, as the operating system does in furnishing individual records from input data blocks. For example, suppose that a data block is 4000 bytes long and that a program requests the data 1000 bytes at a time. The system inputs the block and loads its address and the number 1000 into the source address and destination length registers, respectively. The calling program supplies a destination address in a register. The original source length is 4000. The first request for data by the calling program moves 1000 bytes to the destination address. The final source address and source length are saved and will be used in the next record transfer. Figure 20-2 illustrates the structure of a subroutine that does this.

In summary, MVCL moves arbitrary amounts of data from one memory area to another. In so doing, it adjusts the register operand contents to indicate how many bytes were moved and the next addresses that would

First call or calls requiring new data blocks enter here
.
.
.
GET data block, first byte at DBLOCK
.
.
.

```
                      LA      6,DBLOCK
                      LA      7,4000
                      B       MOVE
Subsequent requests cause execution starting here
                      LM      6,7,RSAVE
MØVE                  LR      2,1          AREA ADDRESS IN REG 2
                      LA      3,1000       DESTINATION LENGTH
                      MVCL    2,6
                      BZ      SETFLAG      Is this the last record?
                      STM     6,7,RSAVE    Keep source length and address
                                           for next time
Return
SETFLAG                       Here the program stores an indicator that says the next request
                              will require input of a new block
                              Return
RSAVE                 DS      2F
DBLOCK                DS      1000F
```

Fig. 20-2. Outline of a subroutine that splits up and moves consecutive 1000-byte segments of a data block to a calling program.

have been used had one more byte been moved. Table 20-1 shows the effect
of the MVCL instruction.

We must exercise some judgment in deciding whether to use MVCL
or MVC in a given application. The MVCL instruction does eliminate a
lot of time-consuming program logic and instruction fetches in moving large
amounts of data. But this is at the expense of the time required to load four
registers with the necessary parameters. There is an additional hidden cost
here, because we must be sure that the registers used are indeed available,
which may require saving and restoring their contents before using them
with the MVCL instruction. You may have thought that the example of Fig.
20-1 is not so efficient as would be the use of a couple of MVCs and an
MVI to accomplish the same task. That is absolutely correct; we chose that
example so that we could emphasize this point here.

20.1.3. Compare Logical Character Long

The operands for CLCL are written in the same way as for MVCL and
have basically the same meaning.

CLCL   R1,R2   Compare Logical Character Long   See Table 20-2

Table 20-1 SUMMARY OF THE MVCL INSTRUCTION

Instruction: MVCL   R1,R2

   R1, R2 *even*-numbered

Original register contents:

$(R1)_{8-31}$ $\quad$ = Destination area Address = DA

$(R1+1)_{8-31}$ = Destination area Length = DL

$(R2)_{8-31}$ $\quad$ = Source area Address = SA

$(R2+1)_{8-31}$ = Source area Length = SL

$(R2+1)_{0-7}$ $\quad$ = Padding character = P

Final register contents:

$(R1)_{8-31}$ $\quad$ = DA + DL

$(R1+1)_{8-31}$ = 0

$(R2)_{8-31}$ $\quad$ = SA + smaller of DL, SL

$(R2+1)_{8-31}$ = larger of SL − DL, 0

Condition Code:

CC Value	Meaning
0	DL = SL
1	DL < SL
2	DL > SL
3	Source and destination areas overlap; no data moved

Data moved:

DL = SL: $\quad$ SL bytes from DA to SA

DL < SL: $\quad$ DL bytes from DA to SA

DL > SL: $\quad$ SL bytes from DA to SA; remainder of destination area filled with P

$$(R1)_{8-31} = \text{First operand Address} = FA$$

$$(R1+1)_{8-31} = \text{First operand Length} = FL$$

$$(R2)_{8-31} = \text{Second operand Address} = SA$$

$$(R2+1)_{8-31} = \text{Second operand Length} = SL$$

$$(R2+1)_{0-7} = \text{Padding character} = P$$

The contents of the two memory areas are compared, byte by byte, until either the end of the areas is reached, indicating that the two areas have the same contents, or two unequal bytes are found. The condition code is set to indicate the result of the comparison.

CC Value	Meaning
0	Operand 1 = operand 2
1	Operand 1 < operand 2
2	Operand 1 > operand 2

If the operand lengths in registers R1+1 and R2+1 are not the same, the machine "pretends" that the shorter operand is filled in with the padding character.

If the operands are the same, the register contents after execution of CLCL are

$$(R1)_{8-31} = FA + FL$$

$$(R1+1)_{8-31} = 0$$

$$(R2)_{8-31} = SA + SL$$

$$(R2+1)_{8-31} = 0$$

and

$$CC = 0$$

If the operands are not the same, let us suppose that the first M bytes of the areas matched. The register contents are then

$$(R1)_{8-31} = FA + M$$

$$(R1+1)_{8-31} = \text{larger of } 0, FL - M$$

$$(R2)_{8-31} = SA + M$$

$$(R2+1)_{8-31} = \text{larger of } 0, SL - M$$

The condition code is set to 1 or 2 if the first operand was less than or greater than the second, respecively.

In other words, if the two areas compared do not have the same contents, CLCL stops at the first pair of bytes that are not equal and sets CC to show which of those 2 bytes is the larger. The address registers contain the addresses of the bytes that did not match, while the length registers show how many bytes remain to be compared.

In illustrating the use of CLCL, we shall use examples in which the memory areas are much shorter than those used in practice, but the same principles apply regardless of the operand lengths. Suppose that we have the memory contents

```
OP1:    404040C3C1E3404040404040
OP2:    404040C3C1D9404040404040
```

To compare the two areas in their entirety, we write

```
LA      6,OP1
LA      7,12
LA      10,OP2
LR      11,7
CLCL    6,10
```

The contents of OP1 are greater than those of OP2, and the sixth byte is the first that differs. Therefore, we observe the following after execution of the CLCL:

$$(6) = A(OP1) + 5$$
$$(7) = 00000007$$
$$(10) = A(OP2) + 5$$
$$(11) = 00000007$$

and

$$CC = 2$$

Now suppose that we have the following sequence of instructions:

```
LA      6,OP1
LA      7,4
LA      10,OP2
LA      11,12
ICM     11,8,=X'40'
CLCL    6,10
```

Since the first operand length is less than the second, the CLCL proceeds as if OP1 contained

OP1:   404040C14040404040404040

Table 20-2 SUMMARY OF THE CLCL INSTRUCTION

Instruction: CLCL   R1,R2
    R1,R2 even-numbered
Original register contents:

$(R1)_{8-31}$ = First operand Address = FA
$(R1+1)_{8-31}$ = First operand Length = FL
$(R2)_{8-31}$ = Second operand Address = SA
$(R2+1)_{8-31}$ = Second operand Length = SL
$(R2+1)_{0-7}$ = Padding character = P

Find register contents if first M bytes equal:

$(R1)_{8-31}$ = FA + M
$(R1+1)_{8-31}$ = larger of 0, FL − M
$(R2)_{8-31}$ = SA + M
$(R2+1)_{8-31}$ = larger of 0, SL − M

Condition Code:

CC Value	Meaning
0	First operand = Second operand
1	First operand < Second operand
2	First operand > Second operand

instead of what is written above. The machine pretends that the padding character occupies the remaining area. The result is

$$(6) = A(OP1) + 4$$
$$(7) = 00000000$$
$$(10) = A(OP2) + 4$$
$$(11) = 40000008$$

and

$$CC = 1$$

The first mismatch is in the fifth byte of the areas. 40 is less than C1, and so the condition code is set to 1.

20.2.   THE TRANSLATE INSTRUCTIONS

A common problem is the translation of a string of character codes from one code to another. In telecommunications, most teletype-like remote computer terminals transmit and receive data in the ASCII character code. However, most programs that process character data in IBM machines assume that the characters are in the EBCDIC code. Thus, in communicating with teletype terminals, we must translate EBCDIC character codes to their ASCII equivalents, and vice versa. (The operating system does this for us if we use a telecommunications access method, but let's see how it's done.) Similar problems arise in number conversion, coding, and translation of binary data to forms suitable for punched output. Other problems frequently encountered are the rearrangement of data and the need to search byte strings for characters that have special meanings. The TRanslate and the TRanslate and Test instructions were designed with just such problems in mind.

20.2.1.   TRanslate

The first operand of the TRanslate instruction is the address of a memory area whose contents are to be translated byte by byte according to a *translate table* (sometimes called a *function table*), whose address is the second operand. The single length field specifies the number of bytes to be translated.

TR	D1(L1,B1),D2(B2)	TRanslate	Translate $(D1 + (B1))_{L1}$ using table at $D2 + (B2)$

The machine assumes that the translate table is 256 bytes long, 1 byte for each possible 8-bit number. Each byte of the area to be translated, the *argument* area, is used as an index into the translate table. The byte stored at the indexed location in the translate table replaces the byte from the argument area. For example, if the first 4 bytes of the translate table contain

TRTAB:
Byte 0:   C6
Byte 1:   C7
Byte 2:   C8
Byte 3:   C9   (and 252 more bytes)

and the argument area contains

03010200

then the translated result is

C9C7C8C6

Let us watch how this works in slow motion. The first argument byte contains 03, which is used as an index into the translate table. The byte at TRTAB+03 contains C9. This number is stored at the first byte of the argument, producing

C9010200

The second argument byte contains 01, indicating that byte 01 of TRTAB is to replace the argument byte containing 01. This process proceeds from left to right, until all the argument bytes have been translated.

Perhaps, in staring at a dump, you have wondered how all those hexadecimal numbers were converted to their EBCDIC equivalents. Let us consider the problem of converting a number stored in a full word in the memory to its character-code equivalent so that it might be printed as part of a dump. Figure 20-3 shows a program segment that does this, assuming that the word to be converted is stored at NUM.

```
        UNPK   HEX(9),NUM(5)   INSERT 'F' ZONES INTO NUMBER
        TR     HEX(8),TRTAB-X'F0'   TRANSLATE FA-FF TO C1-C6
               .
               .
               .
NUM     CS     F
HEX     CS     CL9
TRTAB   DC     X'F0F1F2F3F4F5F6F7F8F9C1C2C3C4C5C6'
```

Fig. 20-3. Conversion of the contents of a full word, NUM, to EBCDIC character codes for its hexadecimal digits.

The first step is to unpack the number. But we must be careful here, because UNPK interchanges the nibbles of the last byte, which changes the number. We avoid this problem by unpacking one extra byte. We ignore this byte, the ninth byte at HEX, from now on.

Supposing that we have

NUM: 6AC3408050

we now have

HEX: F6FAFCF3F4F0F8F005

Notice that those digits that should be printed as 0–9 are already in the proper EBCDIC form for printing. But the digits A–F have been converted to the meaningless character codes FA–FF. What we must do is carry out the following translation,

$$FA \longrightarrow C1$$
$$FB \longrightarrow C2$$
$$FC \longrightarrow C3$$
$$FD \longrightarrow C4$$
$$FE \longrightarrow C5$$
$$FF \longrightarrow C6$$
$$FF \longrightarrow C6$$

leaving F0–F9 unchanged. While there are many ways to do this translation, the easiest and most efficient is to use TR. Since the only numbers we shall translate are F0 through FF, we need store only the last 16 bytes of the translate table. We fool the machine into thinking it really has a 256-byte translate table by telling it that the table starts X'F0' bytes before the area we reserved for it. We could just as well have defined the translate table via

TRTAB   DC   C'0123456789ABCDEF'

Each argument byte acts as an index into the translate table. In effect, then, the machine uses the argument to select bytes from a table and stores them in the order determined by the positions of the argument bytes. We can take advantage of this fact in problems requiring the rearrangement of data. We store, in the argument area, a series of bytes containing indexes of bytes from the translate table. Here, however, the translate table is actually the data we wish to rearrange.

Suppose that we have a table of employee numbers and social security numbers. Each entry in the table is 14 bytes long. The first 5 bytes contain the EBCDIC coded employee number, and the last 9 are the social security number of that employee. An entry in this table might contain the 14-byte character string

Emp. No.   SS no.
10365   297463792

What we want to do is print this table, but with the social security number first and the employee number second, separated by two blanks. In addition, we want to insert hyphens after the third and fifth digits of the social security number. The entry above would be printed as

297-46-3792   10365

It is evident that we must do the following rearrangement:

Input Byte	Goes to	Output Byte Number
5		0
6		1
7		2
Hyphen		3
8		4
9		5
Hyphen		6
A		7
B		8
C		9
D		A
Space		B
Space		C
0		D
1		E
2		F
3		10
4		11

The input bytes are the 14-byte table entry and two extra bytes containing the character code for blank and for hyphen. It might be defined by

```
TABENTRY   DS      CL14
BLANK      DC      C' '
HYPHEN     DC      C'—'
```

We move the employee number-SS number into TABENTRY and use these 16 bytes for the "translate table." The argument area is simply the indexes of the characters of the translate table we wish to move into the argument string. We could define the argument as follows:

```
ARG        DC      X'0506070F08090F0A0B0C0C0E0E0001020304'
```

Supposing that we want the rearranged data to be stored starting at OUT-LINE, the instructions

```
           MVC     OUTLINE(18),ARG
           TR      ARG(18),TABENTRY
```

accomplish the rearrangement. Play computer with the TR instruction above to see how it works. Notice that using TR· in this way destroys the argument. This is why we must MVC the argument into the output area.

As a final example, we shall illustrate the use of TR in a simple encoding problem. A *Caesar cypher* is a (not very good) way of translating a character message into coded form. To obtain the Caesar cypher of a message we "add" a *key letter* to each letter of the message. Supposing, for example, that the key letter is C, the Caesar cypher of the message

MEET ME AT THE CASBAH. I HAVE SMUGGLED SOME TOOTHPASTE.

is

OGGV OG CV VJG ECUDCJ. K JCXG UOWIINGF UQOG VQQVJRCUVG.

Do you see how this is done? We assign a digit to each letter, $A = 0$, $B = 1$, $C = 2, \ldots, Z = 25$. To each message of the text to be encoded (the *cypher* text), we add the digit that corresponds to the key letter, modulo 26. $M + C = 12 + 2 = 14 = O$, $E + C = 4 + 2 = 6 = G$, and so on. We can make the message a little harder to decipher if we make each "word" in the coded text five letters long and remove all punctuation. Our message above would then look like this:

OGGVO GCVVJ GECUD CJKJC XGUOW IINGF UQOGV QQVJR CUVG

Figure 20-4 shows a program segment that uses TR to produce the Caesar cypher of a message. Thirty bytes of a message to be encoded, with all blanks and punctuation removed, are stored at MESS. The first TR translates each letter into its digit equivalent. We assume that the key digit is in register 3. The second TR translates the digit codes back to letters. The contents of register 3 is used to modify the starting address of the digit-to-letter translate table CAESAR. The encoded message is then split into five-character "words" by the final translate instruction.

```
           TR      MESS(30),LETDIG   TRANSLATE LETTERS TO INTEGERS
           LA      4,CAESAR(3)    REG. 4 GETS ADD. OF CAESAR + KEY DIGIT
           TR      MESS(30),0(4)   TRANSLATE TO CAESAR CYPHER
           MVC     OUTPUT(36),RERRANGE    MOVE ARGUMENT FOR THE
           TR      OUTPUT(36),BLANK    TRANSLATE TO INSERT BLANKS
                   .
                   .
                   .
BLANK      DC      C' '
MESS       DS      CL30
OUTPUT     DS      CL36
LETDIG     EQU     *-X'C1'
           DC      X'000102030405060708'
           ORG     LETDIG+X'D1'
           DC      X'090A0B0C0D0E0F1011'
           ORG     LETDIG+X'E2'
           DC      X'12131415161718191'
CAESAR     DC      C'ABCDEFGHIJKLMNOPQRSTUVWXYZ '
           DC      C'ABCDEFGHIJKLMNOPQRSTUVWXYZ'
RERRANGE   DC      X'0102030405000607080900ACCOBOCODOEOFC0'
           DC      X'101112131400151617181900 1A 1B 1C 1D 1E 00'
```

Fig. 20-4. A program segment that translates a 30-byte message at MESS to a Caesar cypher, leaving the result at ØUTPUT.

Notice how we have used the ORG pseudooperation to assist in the construction of the letter-to-digit translate table LETDIG. ORG sets the location counter to the value in the operand field. The statement

$$\text{ORG} \qquad \text{LETDIG}+X'D1'$$

sets the location counter $D1_{16}$ bytes beyond its value at LETDIG. The first byte in the following DC statement is stored at $\text{LETDIG} + D1_{16}$.

20.2.2 TRanslate and Test

We use TRT to search byte strings for bytes with preselected contents. Such problems occur frequently in character data processing. We might wish to locate the decimal place in a floating-point number punched on a data card, determine the locations of blanks in textual data, or test numerical data to see that all the characters are legal digits.

Use of TRT is much like that of TR.

TRT   D1(L1,B1),D2(B2)   TRanslate and Test   Search $(D1 + (B1))_{L1}$
for characters
indicated in
$(D2 + (B2))_{256}$

We again have an argument memory area and a translate table. Unlike TR, however, TRanslate and Test makes no changes in any memory contents. Instead, it locates characters within the argument string according to the information given in the translate table.

Specifically, TRT proceeds from left to right in the argument string, looking up each byte in the translate table, using the argument bytes as indexes. When and if an argument byte is encountered whose corresponding entry in the translate table is not zero, TRT loads the address of that byte into register 1, the byte itself into bits 24–31 of register 2, and sets the condition code:

CC Value	Meaning
0	All argument bytes tested had corresponding translate table bytes equal to 0.
1	An argument byte (not the last byte in the area) was encountered that has a nonzero translate table entry.
2	The last byte in the argument area was the first encountered with a nonzero translate table entry.

Thus, to use TRT we set up a 256-byte translate table. Each byte we wish to search for has a nonzero entry; all other bytes in the table contain 0. For example, suppose that we have a data field 10 bytes long that should contain either blanks or codes for the digits 0–9. We wish to use TRT to determine whether or not any illegal characters are in this field. The translate table should therefore contain 0s in bytes 40_{16} and F0–F9 and nonzero values everywhere else. Such a table can be constructed as follows:

```
DIGTEST    DC       256X'FF'
           ORG      DIGTEST+X'40'
           DC       X'00'
           ORG      DIGTEST+X'F0'
           DC       10X'00'
           ORG
```

An ORG statement with no operands sets the location counter to its highest preceding value, in this case DIGTEST+256.

Let us suppose that originally we have

$$(1) = 00000000$$

$$(2) = FFFFFFFF$$

and that the number to be tested is stored at NUM, which corresponds to address 2000. Then the instruction

TRT   NUM(10),DIGTEST

produces the results shown below for the character strings shown at NUM:

10 Characters Starting at NUM	CC	(1)	(2)
4893602718	0	Unchanged	Unchanged
489.602718	1	00002003	FFFFFF4B
489 602718	0	Unchanged	Unchanged
489360A718	1	00002006	FFFFFFC1
489360271D	2	00002009	FFFFFFC4

20.3. THE EDIT INSTRUCTIONS

Remember, from Chapter 15, how messy the problem of converting packed decimal numbers to their EBCDIC equivalents is? The <u>ED</u>it and the <u>ED</u>it and <u>Ma</u>r<u>K</u> instructions transfer this chore from the programmer to the computer.

20.3.1. EDit

EDit is basically a glorified UNPK instruction.

ED	D1(L1,B1),D2(B2)	<u>ED</u>it	Convert (D2 + (B2)) to EBCDIC at D1 + (B1) using pattern at D1 + (B1)

To use it, we first store a *pattern* in the area that is to receive the EBCDIC coded number. The pattern consists of a string of bytes containing some special code numbers and other characters. The codes determine the course of execution of EDit. There are three of them:

Code	Name
20	Digit selector
21	Significance starter
22	Field separator

The first character of the pattern is called the *fill character*. The fill character replaces leading zeros produced by unpacking the second operand.

EDit proceeds from the left-hand end of the second operand, unpacking each 4-bit digit as it is encountered by inserting F_{16} in front of it. The machine contains a special switch, called the *significance indicator*. When EDit starts, the significance indicator is *off* and it remains off until either (1) a nonzero digit is encountered in the second operand or (2) a significance starter code is reached in the pattern. As long as the signifiance indicator is off, zero digits from the second operand are replaced by the fill character. When it is *on*, each digit is unpacked and stored, even if it is zero. Thus, one thing EDit does is to replace leading zeros with the fill character, which we usually want to be a blank.

The pattern is of the same length as the eventual EBCDIC character string. We give this length in the L1 field of the instruction. In the simplest case, we want to unpack the number, replacing leading zeros with blanks. If the packed number is 3 bytes long, we need space for five digits. We use the pattern

PATTRN: 4020202020

Notice that the digit selectors are essentially place holders for characters that will be stored in their place. Suppose that the number to be unpacked is stored at PACDEC. We then write the EDit instruction

ED   PATTRN(5),PACDEC

If PACDEC originally contains 00036C, then the EDit instruction yields

PATTRN: 404040F3F6

the character code representation of bbb36. Notice that EDit does not interchange the nibbles of the last byte. In this example, EDit replaces the F0s produced by unpacking the three leading zeros at PACDEC with blanks, since the significance indicator is off. The fourth digit, 3, turns the significance indicator on so that F3 is stored into the fourth byte of PATTRN. The last byte F6 is also stored.

Any ordinary characters after the fill character in the pattern are left alone and appear in the final EBCDIC result, if the significance indicator is on when the character is reached. Suppose that we again want to print five-digit numbers, but that we want to insert a decimal place before the last two digits. To accomplish this, we simply put the character code for ".," $4B_{16}$, in the proper place in the pattern. We use

PATTRN: 4020204B2020

Now if we have 05349D at PACDEC, the instruction

ED   PATTRN(6),PACDEC

produces

PATTRN: 40F5F34BF4F9

equivalent to the string

b53.49

as desired.

We run into trouble, though, when we EDit a number such as 00002C using the above pattern. Since the significance indicator is off until the last digit is unpacked, only the 2 is produced as a character code. The result is

PATTRN: 4040404040F2

This is where the significance starter code comes in handy. The code 21 turns the significance indicator on, regardless of the digit being unpacked. The remaining characters will be treated as usual when the significance indicator is on. Thus, if we use the pattern

PATTRN: 4020214B2020

the decimal place and the last two digits are always printed. If 00002C is at PACDEC, EDit with this pattern produces

4040404BF0F2

or

bbb.02

Use of the pattern

4021204B2020

instead yields

4040F04BF0F2

or

bbb0.00

The field separator code, 22, turns the significance indicator off. It is always replaced by the fill character. Using the field separator, we can EDit a long number into several separate shorter fields.

How do we know what to do about the sign of the number? EDit sets the condition code as follows:

CC Value	Meaning
0	Number unpacked was 0
1	Number unpacked was less than 0
2	Number unpacked was greater than 0

If we use a field separator, the condition code is set according to the last field unpacked.

One final comment to make is that EDit destroys the pattern. We usually keep a copy of it and move it to the area where the unpacking is to be done. To produce a six-character number at OUTNUM using the pattern and data above, we write

```
        MVC     OUTNUM(6),PATTRN
        ED      OUTNUM(6),PACDEC
          .
          .
          .

PATTRN          DC      X'4021204B2020'
```

20.3.2. EDit and MarK

EDit and MarK is virtually the same as the EDit instruction. The only difference is that EDMK presents in register 1 the address of the byte that turned on the significance indicator. This is useful in situations in which we want to print a character immediately before the first significant digit of a number.

EDMK D1(L1,B1),D2(L2) EDit	Convert (D2 + (B2)) to EBCDIC
and	at D1 + (B1) using pattern at
MarK	D1 + (B1)

Suppose that we are writing a program to print paychecks. We wish to print the amount of each check in the format

$$xx,xxx.xx$$

There can be up to five significant digits before the decimal place, but, regardless of how many there are, we want to print a dollar sign before the first significant digit. We use the pattern

PATT: 40206B2021204B2020

Supposing that the EBCDIC string is to be stored at PAY and that the packed number is at PAYPAC, the instructions

MVC	PAY(10),PATT
EDMK	PAY(10),PAYPAC
BCTR	1,0
MVI	0(1),C'$'

accomplish our task.

Table 20-3   INSTRUCTIONS DISCUSSED IN CHAPTER 20

ICM	R1,M3,D2(B2)	Insert Characters under Mask†	R1 ← (D2 + (B2)) according to M3
STCM	R1,M3,D2(B2)	STore Characters under Mask†	(R1) → D2 + (B2) according to M3
CLM	R1,M3,D2(B2)	Compare Logical under Mask†	Compute (R1) − (D2 + (B2)) according to M3, set CC
MVCL	R1,R2	MoVe Character Long†	See Table 20-1
CLCL	R1,R2	Compare Logical Character Long†	See Table 20-2
TR	D1(L1,B1),D2(B2)	TRanslate	Translate (D1 + (B1))$_{L1}$ using table at D2 + (B2)
TRT	D1(L1,B1),D2(B2)	TRanslate and Test	Search (D1 + (B1))$_{L1}$ for characters indicated in (D2 + (B2))$_{256}$
ED	D1(L1,B1),D2(B2)	EDit	Convert (D2 + (B2)) to EBCDIC at D1 + (B1) using pattern at D1 + (B1)
EDMK	D1(L1,B1),D2(B2)	EDit and MarK	Convert (D2 + (B2)) to EBCDIC at D1 + (B1) using pattern at D1 + (B1)

†Available only in System 370 models.

CHAPTER SUMMARY

The extended character manipulation instructions in the 370 computers provide increased power and flexibility in character data processing.

The TRanslate uses a *translate table* to determine how to modify the contents of an *argument* area. TRanslate and Test locates desired characters in a character string.

EDit and EDit and MarK simplify conversion of numeric data from packed decimal to EBCIDIC coded format.

Table 20-3 summarizes these instructions.

EXERCISES

1. Rewrite the program segment of Fig. 15-10 using EDMK to do as much work as possible.

2. Write a program that uses TRT to analyze textual data (an example is the statement of this problem) by word length. The input is a paragraph; the output is a table showing how many words with lengths of one, two, three, . . . letters are in the paragraph. Also to be computed is the mean and variance of the word lengths. (*Hint*: the EX instruction might prove useful in both Exercises 2 and 3.)

3. Write a program to translate textual data to pig Latin (igpay atinLay). Use TRT to isolate words and TR with rearrangement to translate words into pig Latin. The pig Latin required here is its simplest form: To translate a word, move the first letter to last and add *ay* to the end, regardless of what the first letter is.

4. Write a program to decode a Caesar coded message. The coders of the original message inserted the word PIZZAZZ into the message somewhere before coding it. To decode the message, try all possible key letters. After decoding with a given key letter, use TRT to locate Ps and then check to see if the word PIZZAZZ is there. Once PIZZAZZ is found, we know we have decoded the message. Assume that the "words" in the coded message are each five letters long and are separated by one blank.

5. A useful feature of ED and EDMK is their treatment of the sign digit of a packed decimal operand. A positive number (sign code C) leaves the significance indicator on, while a negative number turns it off, provided that the operand length is such that the instruction checks the sign code. If debits to an account are negative numbers, then a credit is a positive number, which, in listing the account transactions, we indicate by printing CR after the amount of the transaction. Write a subroutine that simply lists account transactions and prints the remaining balance owed. The subroutine argument is the address of a series of 3-byte packed decimal numbers. A transaction amount 0 indicates the end of the list. Given the argument

03654D06849C000098D00000D

your program should print the following:

$36.54
$68.49CR
$ .98
BALANCE = $30.97CR

6. Write a subroutine to print a monthly checking account statement. The argument for the subroutine is the address of an area which contains the following data:

> Bytes 0–49: name
> Bytes 50–58: EBCDIC coded account number
> Bytes 59–63: packed decimal date

Bytes 64–67: starting balance, packed decimal
Bytes 68– : transaction fields in the format
    Bytes 0–3: date of transaction (packed)
    Bytes 4–7: amount of transaction (packed)

After byte 67 comes a series of transaction fields, each of which is 8 bytes long. A data field that contains 0 signals the end of the transaction data. All dates are to be printed in the format xx/xx/xx. For example, a date field that contains 0061473C should be printed as 6/14/73 (use ED to do this). A positive transaction amount is a deposit. A negative amount is a withdrawal. For a single account, your output should look something like this:

CUSTOMER   JOE KOLLAGE   DATE 6/22/70
NUMBER   682379312

DATE	WITHDRAWALS	DEPOSITS	BALANCE
			$100.00
5/20/70	42.60		57.40
5/23/70	57.38		.02
5/24/70		200.00	200.02
6/20/70	210.00		−9.98
6/22/70	3.00*		−12.98

*YOUR ACCOUNT HAS BEEN CHARGED 3.00
FOR BEING OVERDRAWN BY 12.98

7. Write a subroutine that formats the output for a paycheck-printing program to be run on a 370 computer. The calling routine passes your program the address of a 399-byte area to hold the output from the subroutine and the address of an area containing the following:

    Bytes 0–39: name
    Bytes 40–44: date in packed decimal
    Bytes 45–49: amount of check in packed decimal

The output area must first be cleared to blanks, and then the following fields are to be filled:

Bytes 100–107: date in the format xx/xx/xx; use EDit to unpack the date; for example, the input date field 0062173C is converted to 6/21/73
Bytes 150–189: name
Bytes 200–209: amount of check in format $xx,xxx.xx
Bytes 290–369: verbal description of amount of check, e.g., ONE HUNDRED FORTY-FIVE and 33/100 DOLLARS

REFERENCES

IBM System/360 Disk and Tape Operating System Assembler Language, Form GC24-3414, IBM Corp., White Plains, N.Y.

IBM System/360 Operating System Assembler Language, Form GC28-6514, IBM Corp., White Plains, N.Y.

IBM System/360 Principles of Operation, Form GA22-6821, IBM Corp., White Plains, N.Y.

IBM System/370 Principles of Operation, Form GA22-7000, IBM Corp., White Plains, N.Y.

IBM OS/VS—DOS/VS Assembler Language, Order No. GC33-4010, IBM Corp., White Plains, N.Y.

A FLOW CHARTS

A flow chart is a pictorial description of an algorithm, in which the program logic—the order and nature of the computational steps in a program—is displayed. Boxes of various shapes indicate computational steps. Arrows going from box to box describe the order in which the computations and computer operations are done.

The most fundamental component of a flow chart is the *assignment* box, which represents a step in which some arithmetic or logical calculations are done and the results are stored in the memory. The assignment box is a rectangle, and inside it is a statement of one or more calculations. Its general form is

$$\boxed{\text{var} \longleftarrow \text{expression}}$$

var is the name of a memory location, and *expression* is usually an algebraic expression whose computed value is stored at *var*. The backward arrow represents the store operation. Thus, a box like the above means "Calculate the value of the expression on the right-hand side of the arrow and store the result at the location whose name or address is on the left-hand side of the arrow." As an example we might have

$$\boxed{x \longleftarrow y^2 - 2}$$

which means calculate the square of the number stored at y, subtract 2, and store the result at x. It is impossible to calculate the value of the expression unless values have been assigned to all variables appearing in it. In the example above, we cannot evaluate $y^2 - 2$ unless a number has been stored previously at y. We might have something like

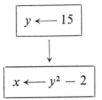

or we can put both statements in one box:

When there is more than one statement in a box, the calculations are done in the order written, top to bottom.

The first box in a flow chart is a *start* box to help the reader find out where to begin in tracing through the flow chart. We write a start box as a circle with START inside:

Similarly, a *stop* box signifies the end of the flow chart:

We represent input from punched cards via a box shaped like a punched card. Inside the box we write the names of the locations into which the data are read. The symbol

means "Read three numbers from cards, storing the first at x, the second at y, and the third at z." The box for printed output is supposed to look like a piece of computer paper with the bottom torn off unevenly. A list of names of locations whose contents are to be printed appears inside the box.

means "Print the contents of locations a, b, and c."

We connect the boxes in a flow chart with arrows. To read a flow chart, we simply follow the arrows, pretending that the computations inside the boxes are done as we pass through them. Figure A-1 is a flow chart of a program that reads two numbers, called S and T; computes their sum, SUM, and difference, DIF; and prints the four numbers S, T, SUM, and DIF.

Conventions differ in the way to describe a decision or conditional transfer in flow charts. In this text, a *decision box* is drawn as a diamond, with a statement inside whose validity is to be tested. Coming out of the box are two arrows. Which arrow to follow depends on whether the statement inside the box is true or false. For example, we might have this as part of a flow chart:

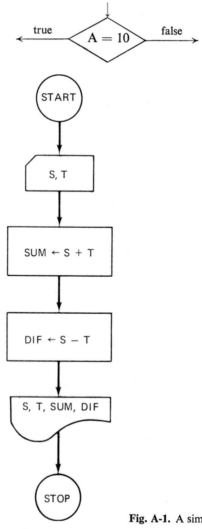

Fig. A-1. A simple flowchart.

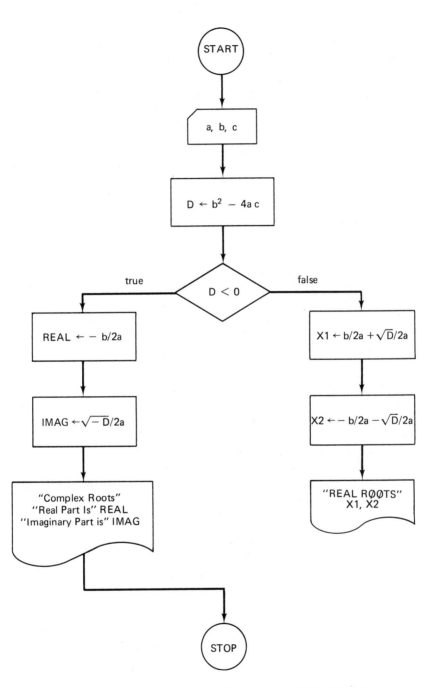

Fig. A-2. Flowchart for a program that solves quadratic equations.

This box is symbolic for a test of the current contents of a location called A. When we reach the box, if the number stored there is 10, we follow the arrow labeled *true*. Otherwise we go the route labeled *false*. Other authors might write a rectangle with pointed edges

b

$$\xleftarrow{\text{yes}} \left\langle A = 10? \right\rangle \xrightarrow{\text{no}}$$

or a sausage

$$\xrightarrow{=} \left(A = 10 \right) \xrightarrow{\neq}$$

to represent the same flow chart symbol. We choose the diamond because it is easier to draw freehand.

To illustrate the drawing of flow charts, we offer in Fig. A-2 a flow chart for a program that solves quadratic equations. The program reads from data cards the coefficients a, b, and c in the equation

$$ax^2 + bx + c = 0$$

We assume that a and c are not zero. The solution is of course

$$x = \frac{-b}{2a} \pm \frac{\sqrt{b^2 - 4ac}}{2a}$$

The decision box tests the value of the discriminant $D = b^2 - 4ac$. If D is positive, we have real roots, called X1 and X2, in the flow chart. These are computed and printed with a label. (Flow chart notation for printed labels is to enclose the characters to be printed in quotation marks.) If D is negative, we compute the real and imaginary parts, REAL and IMAG, and print them with labels. Trace through the flow chart of Fig. A-2 and convince yourself that if the data cards read have the numbers 1, 2, and 5 punched on them, the output will be

COMPLEX ROOTS
REAL PART IS   1
IMAGINARY PART IS   2

while if the input coefficients are 1, 1, and −6, the output is

REAL ROOTS
2   −3

B GLOSSARY

abend   abnormal ending of a program

absolute addressing   an addressing technique in which the actual operand address is in the machine language operand field

access method   a set of systems programs that control transfer of data in I/O operations and maintain data sets according to specific data set organizations

accumulator   a register in which results of arithmetic and logical calculations are left

algorithm   a method for solving a problem

argument   information passed to or from a subroutine

arithmetic unit   the basic computer component which carries out arithmetic and logical operations

assembler   a program that translates assembly language instructions to machine language

attribute   a parameter that describes a symbol; e.g., the length of the area requested in the statement that defines the symbol

base (of number system)   see *radix*

base address   the memory address of the base position of a program when it is stored in the memory

base position   a position in a program relative to which operand addresses are calculated

base register   a register designated to contain a base address

binary coded decimal (BCD)   a representation for decimal numbers in which each 4 bits contain the binary equivalent of a decimal digit

bit   binary digit

block   see *physical record*

branch   an instruction that alters the normal order of execution of program instructions

buffer   a memory area used for storage of data transferred in an I/O operation

bug   an error in a program, data, or a computer system

byte   a unit of information storage; 8 bits in the IBM 360 and 370 computers

call   cause execution of a subroutine

CCW   see *channel command word*

central processing unit   the control and arithmetic units considered as a single component

channel   a computer component that controls input/output operations

channel command word   an instruction in a channel program

compiler   a program that translates a compiler language into machine language

completion code   a number a program passes to the operating system to indicate whether or not the program ran successfully

condition code   an indicator that describes computational results for testing by conditional branch instructions

conditional branch   a transfer of control that occurs if a test criterion is met

control unit   the portion of the computer electronics responsible for supervision and control of the other parts of the computer system

CPU   see *central processing unit*

data set   the major unit of storage for the operating system

data set organization   structure of a data set; describes the relationship between and the order of storage of the blocks in the data set

debug   to find and fix bugs

displacement   the address of a quantity relative to the base position

double word   an information unit 64 bits long

dump   a printout of memory and register contents

EBCDIC   Extended Binary Coded Decimal Interchange Code; an 8-bit code used in character representation in the IBM 360 and 370 and other computers *effective address*   the final operand address used when storage is accessed

entry point   a location in a program to which control is passed when the program is executed

exception   an error condition detectable by the computer system

explicit address   an assembly language operand field containing the numerical value of the displacement and the number of the base register

external symbol   a symbol defined in a different program from that which is using the symbol

fetch   the computer operation that retrieves information from the memory

field   a portion of a machine or assembly language instruction or a portion of a data record

file   a collection of related data

fixed-point arithmetic   integer arithmetic

flip-flop   an electronic device or switch in which a binary digit is stored

floating-point arithmetic   system for doing arithmetic in which numbers are stored and manipulated as fractions and associated exponents

flow chart   a graphic description of an algorithm

full word   an information unit consisting of 32 binary digits

gate   an electronic device whose output is a logical function of its inputs

half-word   an information unit comprised of 16 bits

hardware   the electronic and mechanical portions of the computer system

Hollerith code   a binary code for data on punched cards

immediate operand   an operand whose actual numerical value is specified in a machine language instruction

implied address   a symbol which represents a base register-displacement pair

indexed addressing   an addressing technique in which the contents of a register modify an operand address

instruction register   a temporary storage location in the CPU; it contains the machine language instruction being executed

interruption   hardware-controlled suspension of program execution so that another program can be executed

job control language   a computer language that tells the operating system what computational steps and computer resources are needed in a job

key   a unique number that identifies a record

key-word operand   an operand whose meaning is independent of its position in the operand list

link editor   a program that combines machine language programs and their subroutines into a single package, or load module

linked list   a data storage structure in which each record contains a pointer which indicates where the next record is located

literal   an operand specified by value; the assembler causes the value to be stored in the memory and places its address in the machine language instructions that use it

load address   the address at which the first byte of a program is stored

load module   a collection of object modules linked together, ready for loading into the memory and execution

location counter   a software counter that contains the address of an instruction or datum in a program relative to the address of the first byte of the program

logical complement   see *1's complement*

logical record   a user-defined record in a file

loop   a series of instructions executed repetitively

macro   a series of assembly language statements inserted into a program as a result of the use of the macro name as an operand

macro definition   assembly language and control statements that form a macro

macro expansion   the assembly language statements that a macro-instruction produces

macro-instruction   use of a macro in an assembly language program

macro prototype   a statement which tells the assembler the name of a macro and how the macro operands will be given in a macro-instruction

magnitude   the absolute value of a number

mantissa   the fraction portion of a floating-point number

mask   a binary number which designates test conditions

memory   a portion of a computer in which programs and data can be stored

mnemonic   in computing, a symbolic substitute for a machine language operation code

modulus   the absolute value of a number

multiprogramming   permitting more than one user at a time to have access to the computer resources

nibble   4 bits, one-half of a byte

normalize   in floating-point arithmetic, a number is normalized if the first digit of its fraction is not zero

object code   the machine language form of a program

object module   the machine language form of a program

1's complement   a number obtained from a binary number by replacing all 1s with 0s and vice versa

operand   information upon which an instruction operates

operating system   a collection of programs that manage the computer system resources and assist in processing users' requests for program preparation, execution, and data management

operation code   that portion of a machine language instruction that determines what the control unit is to do

overflow   a situation in which a computed result does not fit into the space provided for it

packed decimal   a code for decimal numbers in which the decimal digits are in BCD code and a code for the algebraic sign of the number is appended to the end of the number

padding characters   extra characters, usually blanks, used to fill unused space in space reserved for a character string

PC   see *program counter*

physical record   the amount of information transferred in an input/output operation

pointer   a field in a record that indicates where the next record is to be found

positional operand   an operand whose position in a statement determines its meaning and use

program   a series of computer instructions that direct the control unit

program counter   a register that indicates the location of the instruction being executed; in the IBM 360 and 370 computers it contains the memory address of the next instruction to be executed

program exception   hardware-diagnosed error in the use of a machine instruction

program status word   a double word that contains the program counter and other information that determines the state of the executing program

prototype   see *macro prototype*

pseudooperation   an assembler control statement

PSW   see *program status word*

radix   the number which is raised to powers in the series representation of a number in a positional number system

record   a unit of information in a file; usually consists of all the information relevant to a single item; e.g., a record in an inventory file contains the data for a given part

record format   the relationship between the logical records and the physical records in a data set

register   a temporary information storage location

relative address   the address of a quantity relative to another address

relocatable   a program quantity or symbol that can be addressed as an operand regardless of where the program is stored in the memory

return   pass control from a subroutine to the calling program

roundoff error   error in results in floating-point arithmetic operations due to the use of operands of finite length

save (registers)   preserve register contents during execution of a subroutine

shift   movement of a number sideways relative to the boundaries within which the number is stored

sign bit   a bit that indicates whether a binary number is positive or negative

software   the programs, data, and documentation in a computer system

source code   a program in a symbolic computer language

store   the computer operation which places information into the memory

S-type address   an address that consists of a base register-displacement pair

subroutine   a program whose execution can be requested by another program

symbol   a name for a computer quantity

symbol table   a table the assembler constructs and uses to locate symbols in a program

truncation error   an error in computer representation of fractions because they must be stored in a finite number of bits

2's complement   a way of representing negative binary integers; 2's complement = 1's complement + 1

unconditional branch   a transfer of control that occurs regardless of the results of preceding calculations *underflow*   an error in floating-point arithmetic in which the exponent required for the result is smaller than the smallest exponent the machine can provide

variable symbol   a symbol the assembler recognizes as a variable whose value is to be obtained from the assembly language source program

X-type address   an address designated by a displacement, a base register, and an index register

zoned decimal   an 8-bit code for decimal numbers in which a code for the algebraic sign of the number is stored in the zone digit of the code for the last digit of the number

zone digit   the first nibble of an EBCDIC coded character

C NUMERICAL TABLES

1. POWERS OF 2

2^n	n
1	0
2	1
4	2
8	3
16	4
32	5
64	6
128	7
256	8
512	9
1,024	10
2,048	11
4,096	12
8,192	13
16,384	14
32,768	15
65,536	16
131,072	17
262,144	18
524,288	19
1,048,576	20
2,097,152	21
4,194,304	22
8,388,608	23
16,777,216	24
33,554,432	25
67,108,864	26
134,217,728	27

1. POWERS OF 2, (*continued*)

2^n	n
268,435,456	28
536,870,912	29
1,073,741,824	30
2,147,483,648	31
4,294,967,296	32

2. POWERS OF 16

16^n	n
1	0
16	1
256	2
4,096	3
65,536	4
1,048,576	5
16,777,216	6
268,435,456	7
4,294,967,296	8
68,719,476,236	9
1,099,511,627,776	10
17,592,186,044,416	11
281,474,976,710,656	12
4,503,599,627,370,496	13
72,057,594,037,927,936	14
1,152,921,504,606,846,976	15
18,446,744,073,709,551,616	16

3. INSTRUCTION FORMATS

RR	OP	R1	R2						
RX	OP	R1	X2	B2	← D2 →				
RS	OP	R1	R3	B2	← D2 →				
SI	OP	I1		B2	← D2 →				
SS	OP	L		B1	← D1 →	B2	← D2 →		

4. HEXADECIMAL-DECIMAL CONVERSION

Value \ Digit	6	5	4	3	2	1
0	0	0	0	0	0	0
1	1,048,576	65,536	4,096	256	16	1
2	2,097,152	131,072	8,192	512	32	2
3	3,145,728	196,068	12,288	768	48	3
4	4,194,304	262,144	16,384	1024	64	4
5	5,242,880	327,680	20,480	1280	80	5
6	6,291,456	393,216	24,576	1536	96	6
7	7,340,032	458,752	28,672	1792	112	7
8	8,388,608	524,288	32,768	2048	128	8
9	9,437,184	589,824	36,864	2304	144	9
A	10,485,760	655,360	40,960	2560	160	10
B	11,534,336	720,896	45,056	2816	176	11
C	12,582,912	786,432	49,152	3072	192	12
D	13,631,488	851,968	53,248	3328	208	13
E	14,680,064	917,504	57,344	3584	224	14
F	15,728,640	983,040	61,440	3840	240	15

Use:

1. Hexadecimal to decimal:
   a. Number digits from right to left.
   b. For each hexadecimal digit, locate the corresponding decimal number in the table in the row for that hexadecimal value and column for its digit number.
   c. Compute the sum of the decimal numbers found.
   d. Example: Convert A23FC to decimal:

Digit	Value	Decimal from Table
5	A	655,360
4	2	8,192
3	3	768
2	F	240
1	C	12
	Sum =	664,572

2. Decimal to hexadecimal:
   a. Locate in the table the next number smaller than or equal to the (remaining) decimal number.
   b. Record the corresponding value as the next hexadecimal digit in the number.

c. Subtract the number found from the (remaining) decimal number.
d. Go to step 1 if the remaining decimal number is not zero.
e. Example: Convert 1,738,402 to hexadecimal:

Step	Result
a	1,048,576
b	1
c	1,738,402 − 1,048,576 = 689,826
a	655,360
b	A
c	689,826 − 655,360 = 34,466
a	32,768
b	8
c	34,466 − 32,768 = 1698
a	1536
b	6
c	1698 − 1536 = 162
a	160
b	A
c	162 − 160 = 2
a	2
b	2
c	2 − 2 = 0
Result:	1A86A2

5. CHARACTER AND OPERATION CODES

Hexadecimal	Decimal	Binary	EBCDIC	Hollerith	Mnemonic
00	0	00000000	NUL	12-0-1-8-9	
01	1	00000001	SOH	12-1-9	
02	2	00000010	STX	12-2-9	
03	3	00000011	ETX	12-3-9	
04	4	00000100	PF	12-4-9	SPM
05	5	00000101	HT	12-5-9	BALR
06	6	00000110	LC	12-6-9	BCTR
07	7	00000111	DEL	12-7-9	BCR
08	8	00001000		12-8-9	SSK
09	9	00001001		12-1-8-9	ISK
0A	10	00001010	SMM	12-2-8-9	SVC
0B	11	00001011	VT	12-3-8-9	
0C	12	00001100	FF	12-4-8-9	
0D	13	00001101	CR	12-5-8-9	
0E	14	00001110	SO	12-6-8-9	MVCL
0F	15	00001111	SI	12-7-8-9	CLCL
10	16	00010000	DLE	12-11-1-8-9	LPR
11	17	00010001	DC1	11-1-9	LNR

5. CHARACTER AND OPERATION CODES, (*continued*)

Hexadecimal	Decimal	Binary	EBCDIC	Hollerith	Mnemonic
12	18	00010010	DC2	11-2-9	LTR
13	19	00010011	TM	11-3-9	LCR
14	20	00010100	RES	11-4-9	NR
15	21	00010101	NL	11-5-9	CLR
16	22	00010110	BS	11-6-9	OR
17	23	00010111	IL	11-7-9	XR
18	24	00011000	CAN	11-8-9	LR
19	25	00011001	EM	11-1-8-9	CR
1A	26	00011010	CC	11-2-8-9	AR
1B	27	00011011	CU1	11-3-8-9	SR
1C	28	00011100	IFS	11-4-8-9	MR
1D	29	00011101	IGS	11-5-8-9	DR
1E	30	00011110	IRS	11-6-8-9	ALR
1F	31	00011111	IUS	11-7-8-9	SLR
20	32	00100000	DS	11-0-1-8-9	LPDR
21	33	00100001	SOS	0-1-9	LNDR
22	34	00100010	FS	0-2-9	LTDR
23	35	00100011		0-3-9	LCDR
24	36	00100100	BYP	0-4-9	HDR
25	37	00100101	LF	0-5-9	LRDR
26	38	00100110	ETB	0-6-9	MXR
27	39	00100111	ESC	0-7-9	MXDR
28	40	00101000		0-8-9	LDR
29	41	00101001		0-1-8-9	CDR
2A	42	00101010	SM	0-2-8-9	ADR
2B	43	00101011	CU2	0-3-8-9	SDR
2C	44	00101100		0-4-8-9	MDR
2D	45	00101101	ENQ	0-5-8-9	DDR
2E	46	00101110	ACK	0-6-8-9	AWR
2F	47	00101111	BEL	0-7-8-9	SWR
30	48	00110000		12-11-0-1-8-9	LPER
31	49	00110001		1-9	LNER
32	50	00110010	SYN	2-9	LTER
33	51	00110011		3-9	LCER
34	52	00110100	PN	4-9	HER
35	53	00110101	RS	5-9	LRER
36	54	00110110	UC	6-9	AXR
37	55	00110111	EOT	7-9	SXR
38	56	00111000		8-9	LER
39	57	00111001		1-8-9	CER
3A	58	00111010		2-8-9	AER
3B	59	00111011	CU3	3-8-9	SER
3C	60	00111100	DC4	4-8-9	MER
3D	61	00111101	NAK	5-8-9	DER
3E	62	00111110		6-8-9	AUR
3F	63	00111111	SUB	7-8-9	SUR
40	64	01000000	SP	No punch	STH

5. CHARACTER AND OPERATION CODES, (*continued*)

Hexadecimal	Decimal	Binary	EBCDIC	Hollerith	Mnemonic
41	65	01000001		12-0-1-9	LA
42	66	01000010		12-0-2-9	STC
43	67	01000011		12-0-3-9	IC
44	68	01000100		12-0-4-9	EX
45	69	01000101		12-0-5-9	BAL
46	70	01000110		12-0-6-9	BCT
47	71	01000111		12-0-7-9	BC
48	72	01001000		12-0-8-9	LH
49	73	01001001		12-1-8	CH
4A	74	01001010	¢	12-2-8	AH
4B	75	01001011	.	12-3-8	SH
4C	76	01001100	<	12-4-8	MH
4D	77	01001101	(	12-5-8	
4E	78	01001110	+	12-6-8	CVD
4F	79	01001111	|	12-7-8	CVB
50	80	01010000	&	12	ST
51	81	01010001		12-11-1-9	
52	82	01010010		12-11-2-9	
53	83	01010011		12-11-3-9	
54	84	01010100		12-11-4-9	N
55	85	01010101		12-11-5-9	CL
56	86	01010110		12-11-6-9	O
57	87	01010111		12-11-7-9	X
58	88	01011000		12-11-8-9	L
59	89	01011001		11-1-8	C
5A	90	01011010	!	11-2-8	A
5B	91	01011011	$	11-3-8	S
5C	92	01011100	*	11-4-8	M
5D	93	01011101	)	11-5-8	D
5E	94	01011110	;	11-6-8	AL
5F	95	01011111	¬	11-7-8	SL
60	96	01100000	−	11	STD
61	97	01100001	/	0-1	
62	98	01100010		11-0-2-9	
63	99	01100011		11-0-3-9	
64	100	01100100		11-0-4-9	
65	101	01100101		11-0-5-9	
66	102	01100110		11-0-6-9	
67	103	01100111		11-0-7-9	MXD
68	104	01101000		11-0-8-9	LD
69	105	01101001		0-1-8	CD
6A	106	01101010	¦	12-11	AD
6B	107	01101011	,	0-3-8	SD
6C	108	01101100	%	0-4-8	MD
6D	109	01101101		0-5-8	DD
6E	110	01101110	≥	0-6-8	AW
6F	111	01101111	?	0-7-8	SW

5. CHARACTER AND OPERATION CODES, (*continued*)

Hexadecimal	Decimal	Binary	EBCDIC	Hollerith	Mnemonic
70	112	01110000		12-11-0	STE
71	113	01110001		12-11-0-1-9	
72	114	01110010		12-11-0-2-9	
73	115	01110011		12-11-0-3-9	
74	116	01110100		12-11-0-4-9	
75	117	01110101		12-11-0-5-9	
76	118	01110110		12-11-0-6-9	
77	119	01110111		12-11-0-7-9	
78	120	01111000		12-11-0-8-9	LE
79	121	01111001	\	1-8	CE
7A	122	01111010	:	2-8	AE
7B	123	01111011	#	3-8	SE
7C	124	01111100	@	4-8	ME
7D	125	01111101	'	5-8	DE
7E	126	01111110	=	6-8	AU
7F	127	01111111	''	7-8	SU
80	128	10000000		12-0-1-8	SSM
81	129	10000001	a	12-0-1	
82	130	10000010	b	12-0-2	LPSW
83	131	10000011	c	12-0-3	
84	132	10000100	d	12-0-4	WRD
85	133	10000101	e	12-0-5	RRD
86	134	10000110	f	12-0-6	BXH
87	135	10000111	g	12-0-7	BXLE
88	136	10001000	h	12-0-8	SRL
89	137	10001001	i	12-0-9	SLL
8A	138	10001010		12-0-2-8	SRA
8B	139	10001011		12-0-3-8	SLA
8C	140	10001100		12-0-4-8	SRDL
8D	141	10001101		12-0-5-8	SLDL
8E	142	10001110		12-0-6-8	SRDA
8F	143	10001111		12-0-7-8	SLDA
90	144	10010000		12-11-1-8	STM
91	145	10010001	j	12-11-1	TM
92	146	10010010	k	12-11-2	MVI
93	147	10010011	l	12-11-3	TS
94	148	10010100	m	12-11-4	NI
95	149	10010101	n	12-11-5	CLI
96	150	10010110	o	12-11-6	OI
97	151	10010111	p	12-11-7	XI
98	152	10011000	q	12-11-8	LM
99	153	10011001	r	12-11-9	
9A	154	10011010		12-11-2-8	
9B	155	10011011		12-11-3-8	
9C	156	10011100		12-11-4-8	SIO
9D	157	10011101		12-11-5-8	TIO
9E	158	10011110		12-11-6-8	HIO
9F	159	10011111		12-11-7-8	TCH

5. CHARACTER AND OPERATION CODES, (*continued*)

Hexadecimal	Decimal	Binary	EBCDIC	Hollerith	Mnemonic
A0	160	10100000		11-0-1-8	
A1	161	10100001	~	11-0-1	
A2	162	10100010	s	11-0-2	
A3	163	10100011	t	11-0-3	
A4	164	10100100	u	11-0-4	
A5	165	10100101	v	11-0-5	
A6	166	10100110	w	11-0-6	
A7	167	10100111	x	11-0-7	
A8	168	10101000	y	11-0-8	
A9	169	10101001	z	11-0-9	
AA	170	10101010		11-0-2-8	
AB	171	10101011		11-0-3-8	
AC	172	10101100		11-0-4-8	
AD	173	10101101		11-0-5-8	
AE	174	10101110		11-0-6-8	
AF	175	10101111		11-0-7-8	
B0	176	10110000		12-11-0-1-8	
B1	177	10110001		12-11-0-1	
B2	178	10110010		12-11-0-2	
B3	179	10110011		12-11-0-3	
B4	180	10110100		12-11-0-4	
B5	181	10110101		12-11-0-5	
B6	182	10110110		12-11-0-6	
B7	183	10110111		12-11-0-7	
B8	184	10111000		12-11-0-8	
B9	185	10111001		12-11-0-9	
BA	186	10111010		12-11-0-2-8	
BB	187	10111011		12-11-0-3-8	
BC	188	10111100		12-11-0-4-8	
BD	189	10111101		12-11-0-5-8	CLM
BE	190	10111110		12-11-0-6-8	STCM
BF	191	10111111		12-11-0-7-8	ICM
C0	192	11000000	{	12-0	
C1	193	11000001	A	12-1	
C2	194	11000010	B	12-2	
C3	195	11000011	C	12-3	
C4	196	11000100	D	12-4	
C5	197	11000101	E	12-5	
C6	198	11000110	F	12-6	
C7	199	11000111	G	12-7	
C8	200	11001000	H	12-8	
C9	201	11001001	I	12-9	
CA	202	11001010		12-0-2-8-9	
CB	203	11001011		12-0-3-8-9	
CC	204	11001100	⌐	12-0-4-8-9	
CD	205	11001101		12-0-5-8-9	
CE	206	11001110	⊔	12-0-6-8-9	
CF	207	11001111		12-0-7-8-9	

5. CHARACTER AND OPERATION CODES, (*continued*)

Hexadecimal	Decimal	Binary	EBCDIC	Hollerith	Mnemonic
D0	208	11010000	}	11-0	
D1	209	11010001	J	11-1	MVN
D2	210	11010010	K	11-2	MVC
D3	211	11010011	L	11-3	MVZ
D4	212	11010100	M	11-4	NC
D5	213	11010101	N	11-5	CLC
D6	214	11010110	O	11-6	OC
D7	215	11010111	P	11-7	XC
D8	216	11011000	Q	11-8	
D9	217	11011001	R	11-9	
DA	218	11011010		12-11-2-8-9	
DB	219	11011011		12-11-3-8-9	
DC	220	11011100		12-11-4-8-9	TR
DD	221	11011101		12-11-5-8-9	TRT
DE	222	11011110		12-11-6-8-9	ED
DF	223	11011111		12-11-7-8-9	EDMK
E0	224	11100000	\	0-2-8	
E1	225	11100001		11-0-1-9	
E2	226	11100010	S	0-2	
E3	227	11100011	T	0-3	
E4	228	11100100	U	0-4	
E5	229	11100101	V	0-5	
E6	230	11100110	W	0-6	
E7	231	11100111	X	0-7	
E8	232	11101000	Y	0-8	
E9	233	11101001	Z	0-9	
EA	234	11101010		11-0-2-8-9	
EB	235	11101011		11-0-3-8-9	
EC	236	11101100	⊣	11-0-4-8-9	
ED	237	11101101		11-0-5-8-9	
EE	238	11101110		11-0-6-8-9	
EF	239	11101111		11-0-7-8-9	
F0	240	11110000	0	0	SRP
F1	241	11110001	1	1	MVO
F2	242	11110010	2	2	PACK
F3	243	11110011	3	3	UNPK
F4	244	11110100	4	4	
F5	245	11110101	5	5	
F6	246	11110110	6	6	
F7	247	11110111	7	7	
F8	248	11111000	8	8	ZAP
F9	249	11111001	9	9	CP
FA	250	11111010	|	12-11-0-2-8-9	AP
FB	251	11111011		12-11-0-3-8-9	SP
FC	252	11111100		12-11-0-4-8-9	MP
FD	253	11111101		12-11-0-5-8-9	DP
FE	254	11111110		12-11-0-6-8-9	
FF	255	11111111		12-11-0-7-8-9	

D TABLE OF INSTRUCTIONS

Abbreviations:

Bi	base register for ith operand
CC	condition code
Di	displacement of ith operand
FPRi	ith floating-point register operand
L	length of single-length SS operands
Li	length of ith operand
PC	program counter
Ri	ith general-purpose register operand
Xi	index register for ith operand

Subscripts:

D	double word
F	full word
H	half-word
L	number of bytes (length) of operands
Li	number of bytes (length) of ith operand
X	extended operand

Instructions		Function	Description	Operation Code	Type	Condition Code Set	Remarks
A	R1,D2(X2,B2)	Add	$R1 \leftarrow (R1) + (D2 + (X2) + (B2))_F$	5A	RX	X	
AD	FPR1,D2(X2,B2)	Add Double-precision	$FPR1_D \leftarrow (FPR1)_D + (D2 + (X2) + (B2))_D$	6A	RX	X	
ADR	FPR1,FPR2	Add Double-precision Register	$FPR1_D \leftarrow (FPR1)_D + (FPR2)_D$	2A	RR	X	
AE	FPR1,D2(X2,B2)	Add single-precision	$FPR1 \leftarrow (FPR1) + (D2 + (X2) + (B2))$	7A	RX	X	
AER	FPR1,FPR2	Add single-precision Register	$FPR1 \leftarrow (FPR1) + (FPR2)$	3A	RR	X	
AH	R1,D2(X2,B2)	Add Half-word	$R1 \leftarrow (R1) + (D2 + (X2) + (B2))_H$	4A	RX	X	
AP	D1(L1,B1),D2(L2,B2)	Add Packed	$D1 + (B1) \leftarrow (D1 + (B1))_{L1} + (D2 + (B2))_{L2}$	FA	SS	X	
AR	R1,R2	Add Register	$R1 \leftarrow (R1) + (R2)$	1A	RR	X	
AU	FPR1,D2(X2,B2)	Add single-precision, Unnormalized	$FPR1 \leftarrow (FPR1) + (D2 + (X2) + (B2))$	7E	RX	X	
AUR	FPR1,FPR2	Add single-precision, Unnormalized, Register	$FPR1 \leftarrow (FPR1) + (FPR2)$	3E	RR	X	
AWR	FPR1,FPR2	Add Double-precision, Unnormalized, Register	$FPR1_D \leftarrow (FPR1)_D + (FPR2)_D$	2E	RR	X	
AW	FPR1,D2(X2,B2)	Add Double-precision, Unnormalized	$FPR1_D \leftarrow (FPR1)_D + (D2 + (X2) + (B2))_D$	6E	RX	X	
AXR	FPR1,FPR2	Add eXtended-precision Register	$FPR1_X \leftarrow (FPR1)_X + (FPR2)_X$	36	RR	X	370
BAL	R1,D2(X2,B2)	Branch And Link	$R1 \leftarrow (PC);$ $PC \leftarrow D2 + (X2) + (B2)$	45	RX		
BALR	R1,R2	Branch And Link Register	$R1 \leftarrow (PC);$ $PC \leftarrow (R2)$	05	RR		
BC	M1,D2(X2,B2)	Branch on Condition	$PC \leftarrow D2 + (X2) + (B2)$ if CC is as specified by M1	47	RX		
BCR	M1,R2	Branch on Condition to Register	$PC \leftarrow (R2)$ if CC is as specified by M1	07	RR		
BCT	R1,D2(X2,B2)	Branch on CounT	$R1 \leftarrow (R1) - 1;$ $PC \leftarrow D2 + (X2) + (B2)$ if $(R1) \neq 0$	46	RX		
BCTR	R1,R2	Branch CounT to Register	$R1 \leftarrow (R1) - 1;$ $(R2) \rightarrow PC$ if $(R1) \neq 0$	06	RR		
BXH	R1,R3,D2(B2)	Branch on indeX High	$R1 \leftarrow (R1) + (R3);$ $D2 + (B2) \rightarrow PC$ if $(R1) > (R3 + 1)$	86	RS		
BXLE	R1,R3,D2(B2)	Branch on indeX Low or Equal	$R1 \leftarrow (R3) + (R1);$ $D2 + (B2) \rightarrow PC$ if $(R1) \leq (R3+1)$	87	RS		

Instructions	Function	Description	Operation Code	Type	Condition Code Set	Remarks
C	R1,D2(X2,B2)	Compare	Set CC according to value of (R1) − (D2 + (X2) + (B2))$_F$	59	RX	X	
CD	FPR1,D2(X2,B2)	Compare Double-precision	Compute (FPR1)$_D$ − (D2 + (X2) + (B2))$_D$, set CC	69	RX	X	
CDR	FPR1,FPR2	Compare Double-precision Register	Compute (FPR1)$_D$ − (FPR2)$_D$, set CC	29	RR	X	
CE	FPR1,D2(X2,B2)	Compare single-precision	Compute (FPR1) − (D2 + (X2) + (B2)) set CC	79	RX	X	
CER	FPR1,FPR2	Compare single-precision Register	Compute (FPR1) − (FPR2), set CC	39	RR	X	
CH	R1,D2(X2,B2)	Compare Half-word	Set CC according to value of (R1) − (D2 + (X2) + (B2))$_H$	49	RX	X	
CLC	D1(L1,B1),D2(B2)	Compare Logical Character	Compare (D1 + (B1))$_{L1}$ with (D2 + (B2))$_{L1}$ and set CC	D5	SS	X	
CLCL	R1,R2	Compare Logical Character Long	See Table 20-2	0F	RR	X	370 only
CLI	D1(B1),I2	Compare Logical Immediate	Compare (D1 + (B1))$_C$ with I2 and set CC	95	SI	X	
CLM	R1,M3,D2(B2)	Compare Logical under Mask	Compare (R1) − (D2 + (B2)) according to M3, set CC	BD	RS	X	370 only
CP	D1(L1,B1),D2(L2,B2)	Compare Packed	Set CC to indicate value of (D1 + (B1))$_{L1}$ − (D2 + (B2))$_{L2}$	F9	SS	X	
CVB	R1,D2(X2,B2)	ConVert to Binary	R1 ← binary equivalent of (D2 + (X2) + (B2))$_D$	4F	RX		
CVD	R1,D2(X2,B2)	ConVert to Decimal	Decimal equivalent of (R1) → D2 + (X2) + (B2)$_D$	4E	RX		
D	R1,D2(X2,B2)	Divide	(R1,R1+1) ÷ (D2 + (X2) + (B1)): R1 ← remainder R1 + 1 ← quotient	5D	RX		R1 even-numbered
DD	FPR1,D2(X2,B2)	Divide Double-precision	FPR1$_D$ ← (FPR1)$_D$ ÷ (D2 + (X2) + (B2))$_D$	6D	RX		
DDR	FPR1,FPR2	Divide Double-precision Register	FPR1$_D$ ← (FPR1)$_D$ ÷ (FPR2)$_D$	2D	RR		
DE	FPR1,D2(X2,B2)	Divide single-precision	FPR1 ← (FPR1) ÷ (D2 + (X2) + (B2))	7D	RX		
DER	FPR1,FPR2	Divide single-precision Register	FPR1 ← (FPR1) ÷ (FPR2)	3D	RR		

Instructions		Function	Description	Operation Code	Type	Condition Code Set	Remarks
DP	D1(L1,B1),D2(L2,B2)	Divide Packed	Compute $(D1 + (B1))_{L1} \div (D2 + (B2))_{L2}$: $(D1 + (B1))_{L1-L2} \leftarrow$ quotient $(D1 + (B1))_{L2} \leftarrow$ remainder	FD	SS		R1 even-numbered
DR	R1,R2	Divide Register	$(R1,R1+1) \div (R2)$: $R1 \leftarrow$ remainder $R1+1 \leftarrow$ quotient	1D	RR		
ED	D1(L1,B1)D2(B2)	EDit	Convert $(D2 + (B2))$ to EBCDIC at $D1 + (B1)$ using pattern at $D1 + (B1)$	DE	SS	X	
EDMK	D1(L1,B1),D2(L2)	EDit and MarK	Convert $(D2 + (B2))$ to EBCDIC at $D1 + (B1)$ using pattern at $D1 + (B1)$	DF	SS	X	
EX	R1,D2(X2,B2)	EXecute	Execute instruction at $D2 + (X2) + (B2)$	44	RX		
HDR	FPR1,FPR2	Halve Double-precision Register	$FPR1,FPR1+1 \leftarrow (FPR2)_D/2$	24	RR		
HER	FPR1,FPR2	Halve single-precision Register	$FPR1 \leftarrow (FPR2)_F/2$	34	RR		
HIO	D1(B1)	Halt I/O	Stop I/O operation on channel and device given by $D1 + (B1)$	9E	SI	X	Privileged
IC	R1,D2(X2,B2)	Insert Character	$R1_{24-31} \leftarrow (D2 + (X2) + (B2))_C$	43	RX		
ICM	R1,M3,D2(B2)	Insert characters under Mask	$R1 \leftarrow (D2 + (B2))$ according to M3	BF	RS	X	370 only
L	R1,D2(X2,B2)	Load	$R1 \leftarrow (D2 + (X2) + (B2))_F,$	58	RX		
LA	R1,D2(X2,B2)	Load Address	$R1 \leftarrow D2 + (X2) + (B2)$	41	RX		
LCDR	FPR1,FPR2	Load Complement Double-precision	$FPR1_D \leftarrow -(FPR2)_D$	23	RR	X	
LCER	FPR1,FPR2	Load Complement single-precision	$FPR1 \leftarrow -(FPR2)$	33	RR	X	
LCR	R1,R2	Load Complement Register	$R1 \leftarrow -(R2)$	13	RR	X	
LD	FPR1,D2(X2,B2)	Load Double-precision	$FPR1_D \leftarrow (D2 + (X2) + (B2))_D$	68	RX		
LDR	FPR1,FPR2	Load Double-precision Register	$FPR1_D \leftarrow (FPR2)_D$	28	RR		
LE	FPR1,D2(X2,B2)	Load single-precision	$FPR1 \leftarrow (D2 + (X2) + (B2))$	78	RX		
LER	FPR1,FPR2	Load single-precision Register	$FPR1 \leftarrow (FPR2)$	38	RR		
LH	R1,D2(X2,B2)	Load Half-word	$R1 \leftarrow (D2 + (X2) + (B2))_H$	48	RX		

Instructions	Function	Description	Operation Code	Type	Condition Code Set	Remarks
LM	Load Multiple	Load registers R1 through R3 from consecutive full words starting at D2 + (B2)	98	RS		
LNDR	Load Negative Double-precision Register	$FPR1_D \leftarrow -|(FPR2)_D|$	21	RR	X	
LNER	Load Negative single-precision Register	$FPR1 \leftarrow -|(FPR2)|$	31	RR	X	
LNR	Load Negative Register	$R1 \leftarrow -|(R2)|$	11	RR	X	
LPDR	Load Positive Double-precision Register	$FPR1_D \leftarrow |(FPR2)_D|$	20	RR	X	
LPER	Load Positive single-precision Register	$FPR1 \leftarrow |(FPR2)|$	30	RR	X	
LPR	Load Positive Register	$R1 \leftarrow |(R2)|$	10	RR	X	
LR	Load Register	$R1 \leftarrow (R2)$	18	RR		
LRDR	Load Rounded Double-precision Register	$FPR1_D \leftarrow (FPR2)_X$ (rounded)	25	RR		370
LRER	Load Rounded single-precision Register	$FPR1_F \leftarrow (FPR2)_D$ (rounded)	35	RR		370
LTDR	Load and Test Double-precision Register	$FPR1_D \leftarrow (FPR2)_D$, set CC	22	RR	X	
LTER	Load and Test single-precision Register	$FPR \leftarrow (FPR2)$, set CC	32	RR	X	
LTR	Load Test Register	$R1 \leftarrow (R2)$, set CC	12	RR	X	
M	Multiply	$R1,R1+1 \leftarrow (R1+1) \times (D2 + (X2) + (B2))_F$	5C	RX		R1 even-numbered
MD	Multiply Double-precision	$FPR1_D \leftarrow (FPR1)_D \times (D2 + (X2) + (B2))_D$	6C	RX		
MDR	Multiply Double-precision Register	$FPR1_D \leftarrow (FPR1)_D \times (FPR2)_D$	2C	RR		
ME	Multiply single-precision	$FPR1_D \leftarrow (FPR1) \times (D2 + (R2) + (B2))$	7C	RX		
MER	Multiply single-precision Register	$FPR1_D \leftarrow (FPR1) \times (FPR2)$	3C	RR		
MH	Multiply Half-word	$R1 \leftarrow (R1) \times (D2 + (X2) + (B2))_H$	4C	RX		
MP	Multiply Packed	$D1 + (B1) \leftarrow (D1 + (B1))_{L1} \times (D2 + (B2))_{L2}$	FC	SS		
MR	Multiply Register	$R1,R1+1 \leftarrow (R1+1) \times (R2)$	1C	RR		R1 even-numbered

Instructions	Function	Description	Operation Code	Type	Condition Code Set	Remarks
MVC	D1(L1,B1),D2(B2)	MoVe Character	D1 + (B1) ← (D2 + (B2))L1	D2	SS		
MVCL	R1,R2	MoVe Character Long	See Table 20-1	OE	RR	X	370 only
MVI	D1(B1),I2	MoVe Immediate	D2 + (B1) ← I2	92	SI		
MVO	D1(L1,B1),D2(L2,B2)	MoVe with Offset	See text page 370	F1	SS		
MVN	D1(L,B1),D2(B2)	MoVe Numeric	Numeric (D1 + (B1)) ← numeric (D2 + (B2))L	D1	SS		
MVZ	D1(L,B1),D2(B2)	MoVe Zones	Zone (D1 + (B1)) ← Zone (D2 + (B2))L	D3	SS		
MXD	FPR1,D2(X2,B2)	Multiply eXtended Double	FPR1x ← (FPR1)D × (D2 + (B2) + (X2))D	67	RX		370
MXDR	FPR1,FPR2	Multiply eXtended Double Register	FPR1x ← (FPR1)D × (FPR2)D	27	RR		370
MXR	FPR1,FPR2	Multiply eXtended-precision Register	FPR1x ← (FPR1)x × (FPR2)x	26	RR		370
N	R1,D2(X2,B2)	aNd	R1 ← (R1) AND (D2 + (X2) + (B2))F	54	RX	X	
NC	D1(L1,B1),D2(B2)	aNd Character	D1 + (B1) ← (D1 + (B1))L1 AND (D2 + (B2))L1	D4	SS	X	
NI	D1(B1),I2	aNd Immediate	D1 + (B1) ← (D1 + (B1)) AND I2	94	SI	X	
NR	R1,R2	aNd Register	R1 ← (R1) AND (R2)	14	RR	X	
O	R1,D2(X2,B2)	Or	R1 ← (R1) OR (D2 + (X2) + (B2))F	56	RX	X	
OC	D1(L1,B1),D2(B2)	Or Character	D1 + (B1) ← (D1 + (B1))L1 OR (D2 + (B2))L1	06	SS	X	
OI	D1(B1),I2	Or Immediate	D1 + (B1) ← (D1 + (B1)) OR I2	96	SI	X	
OR	R1,R2	Or Register	R1 ← (R1) OR (R2)	16	RR	X	
PACK	D1(L1,B1),D2(L2,B2)	PACK zoned decimal to packed decimal	Convert (D2 + (B2))L2 to packed decimal at (D1 + (B1))L1	F2	SS	X	
S	R1,D2(X2,B2)	Subtract	R1 ← (R1) − (D2 + (X2) + (B2))F	5B	RX	X	
SD	FPR1,D2(X2,B2)	Subtract Double-precision	FPR1D ← (FPR1)D − (D2 + (X2) + (B2))D	6B	RX	X	
SDR	FPR1,FPR2	Subtract Double-precision Register	FPR1D ← (FPR1)D − (FPR2)D	2B	RR	X	
SE	FPR1,D2(X2,B2)	Subtract single-precision	FPR1 ← (FPR1) − (D2 + (X2) + (B2))	7B	RX	X	
SER	FPR1,FPR2	Subtract single-precision Register	FPR1 ← (FPR1) − (FPR2)	3B	RR	X	
SH	R1,D2(X2,B2)	Subtract Half-word	R1 ← (R1) − (D2 + (X2) + (B2))H	4B	RX	X	
SIO	D1(B1)	Start IO	Start a channel program using device given as last 16 bits of D1 + (B1)	9C	SI	X	Privileged
SLA	R1,D2(B2)	Shift Left Arithmetic	Shift (R1) left D2 + (B2) binary places	8B	RS	X	
SLDA	R1,D2(B2)	Shift Left Double Arithmetic	Shift (R1,R1+1) left D2 + (B2) binary places	8F	RS	X	R1 even-numbered

Instructions	Function	Description	Operation Code	Type	Condition Code Set	Remarks
SLDL	R1,D2(B2)	Shift Left Double Logical	Shift (R1,R1+1) left D2 + (B2) binary places	8D	RS		R1 even-numbered
SLL	R1,D2(B2)	Shift Left Logical	Shift (R1) left D2 + (B2) binary places	89	RS	X	
SP	D1(L1,B1),D2(L2,B2)	Subtract Packed	D1 + (B1) ← (D1 + (B1))$_{L1}$ − (D2 + (B2))$_{L2}$	FB	SS	X	
SPM	R1	Set Program Mask	CC, program mask ← (R1)$_{2-7}$	04	RR	X	
SR	R1,R2	Subtract Register	R1 ← (R1) − (R2)	1B	RR	X	
SRA	R1,D2(B2)	Shift Right Arithmetic	Shift (R1) right D2 + (B2) binary places	8A	RS	X	
SRDA	R1,D2(B2)	Shift Right Double Arithmetic	Shift (R1,R1+1) right D2 + (B2) binary places	8E	RS	X	R1 even-numbered
SRDL	R1,D2(B2)	Shift Right Double Logical	Shift (R1,R1+1) right D2 + (B2) binary places	8C	RS		R1 even-numbered
SRL	R1,D2(B2)	Shift Right Logical	Shift (R1) right D2 + (B2) binary places	88	RS		
SRP	D1(L1,B1),D2(B2),I3	Shift and Round Packed	Shift (D1 + (B1))$_{L1}$ to the left (D2 + (B2)) decimal places, using I3 as rounding factor	F0	RS	X	370 only
ST	R1,D2(X2,B2)	STore	(R1)$_F$ → D2 + (X2) + (B2)	50	RX		
STC	R1,D2(X2,B2)	STore Character	(R1)$_{24-31}$ → D2 + (X2) + (B2)	42	RX		
STCM	R1,M3,D2(B2)	STore Characters under Mask	(R1) → D2 + (B2) according to M3	BE	RS		370 only
STD	FPR1,D2(X2,B2)	STore Double-precision	(FPR1)$_D$ → D2 + (X2) + (B2)	60	RX		
STE	FPR1,D2(X2,B2)	STore single-precision	(FPR1) → D2 + (X2) + (B2)	70	RX		
STH	R1,D2(X2,B2)	Store Half-word	(R1)$_H$ → D2 + (X2) + (B2)	40	RX		
STM	R1,R3,D2(B2)	STore Multiple	Store (R1) through (R2) into consecutive full words starting at D2 + (B2)	90	RS		
SU	FPR1,D2(X2,B2)	Subtract single-precision, Unnormalized	FPR1 ← (FPR1) − (D2 + (X2) + (B2))	7F	RX	X	
SUR	FPR1,FPR2	Subtract single-precision, Unnormalized, Register	FPR1 ← (FPR1) − (FPR2)	3F	RR	X	
SW	FPR1,D2(X2,B2)	Subtract Double-precision, Unnormalized	FPR1$_D$ ← (FPR1)$_D$ − (D2 + (X2) + (B2))$_D$	6F	RX	X	
SWR	FPR1,FPR2	Subtract Double-precision, Unnormalized, Register	FPR1$_D$ ← (FPR1)$_D$ − (FPR2)$_D$	2F	RR	X	
SXR	FPR1,FPR2	Subtract eXtended-precision Register	FPR1$_X$ ← (FPR1)$_X$ − (FPR2)$_X$	37	RR	X	370
TCH	D1(B1)	Test CHannel	Test channel given by D1 + (B1)	9F	SI	X	Privileged
TIO	D1(B1)	Test I/O	Test I/O channel and device given by D1 + (B1)	9D	SI	X	Privileged

Instructions	Function	Description	Operation Code	Type	Condition Code Set	Remarks
TM	D1(B1),I2	Test under Mask	Test $(D1 + (B1))$ using I2 as mask; set CC accordingly	91	SI	X	
TR	D1(L1,B1),D2(B2)	TRanslate	Translate $(D1 + (B1))_{L1}$ using table at $D2 + (B2)$	DC	SS	
TRT	D1(L1,B1),D2(B2)	TRanslate and Test	Search $(D1 + (B1))_{L1}$ for characters indicated in $(D2 + (B2))_{256}$	DD	SS	X
UNPK	D1(L1,B1),D2(L2,B2)	UNPacK packed decimal to zoned decimal	Convert $(D2 + (B2))_{L2}$ to zoned decimal at $(D1 + (B1))_{L1}$	F3	SS	
X	R1,D2(X2,B2)	eXclusive or	$R1 \leftarrow (R1)\ \text{XOR}\ (D2 + (X2) + (B2))_F$	57	RX	X
XC	D1(L1,B1),D2(B2)	eXclusive or Character	$D1 + (B1) \leftarrow (D1 + (B1))_{L1}\ \text{XOR}\ (D2 + (B2))_{L1}$	D7	SS	X
XI	D1(B1),I2	eXclusive or Immediate	$D1 + (B1) \leftarrow (D1 + (B1))\ \text{XOR}\ I2$	97	SI	X
XR	R1,R2	eXclusive or Register	$R1 \leftarrow (R1)\ \text{XOR}\ (R2)$	17	RR	X
ZAP	D1(L1,B1),D2(L2,B2)	Zero and Add Packed	$D1 + (B1) \leftarrow 0_{L1};$ $D1 + (B1) \leftarrow (D1 + (B1))_{L1} + (D2 + (B2))_{L2}$	F8	SS	X

INDEX